CW00613377

Yamah FZR600, 750 & 1000 Owners Workshop Manual

by Alan Ahlstrand and John H Haynes
Member of the Guild of Motoring Writers

Models covered:

US: Yamaha FZR600/600R. 599cc. 1989 through 1994
Yamaha FZR750R. 750cc. 1987 and 1988
Yamaha FZR1000. 989cc. 1987 and 1988
Yamaha FZR1000. 1002cc. 1989 through 1993

UK: Yamaha FZR 600. 599cc. 1989 through 1993
Yamaha FZR750R (OW01). 749cc.
   1989 through 1992
Yamaha FZR1000. 989cc. 1987 through 1988
Yamaha FZR1000 EXUP. 1002cc.
   1989 through 1993

(1X1-2056)

ABCDE
FGHIJ
KLMNO
PQRS

Haynes Publishing
Sparkford Nr Yeovil
Somerset BA22 7JJ England

Haynes North America, Inc
861 Lawrence Drive
Newbury Park
California 91320 USA

Acknowledgements

Our thanks to Mitsui Machinery Sales (UK) Ltd for permission to reproduce certain illustrations used in this manual. We would also like to thank NGK Spark Plugs (UK) Ltd for supplying the color spark plug condition photos and the Avon Rubber Company for supplying information on tire fitting. Special thanks to Grand Prix Kawasaki/Yamaha, Santa Clara, California, for providing the motorcycle used in these photographs; to Pete Sirett, service manager, for arranging the facilities and fitting the mechanical work into his shop's busy schedule; and to Chris Campbell, service technician, for doing the mechanical work and providing valuable technical information.

© **Haynes North America, Inc.   1994**

With permission from J.H. Haynes & Co. Ltd.

A book in the Haynes Owners Workshop Manual Series

Printed in the U.S.A.

All rights reserved. No part of this book may be reproduced or transmitted in any form or by any means, electronic or mechanical, including photocopying, recording or by any information storage or retrieval system, without permission in writing from the copyright holder.

ISBN 1 56392 056 5

Library of Congress Catalog Card Number 94-76571

British Library Cataloguing in Publication Data
A catalogue record for this book is available from the British Library

We take great pride in the accuracy of information given in this manual, but motorcycle manufacturers make alterations and design changes during the production run of a particular motorcycle of which they do not inform us. No liability can be accepted by the authors or publishers for loss, damage or injury caused by any errors in, or omissions from, the information given.

Contents

Yamaha FZR600

Yamaha FZR1000

About this manual

Its purpose

The purpose of this manual is to help you get the best value from your motorcycle. It can do so in several ways. It can help you decide what work must be done, even if you choose to have it done by a dealer service department or a repair shop; it provides information and procedures for routine maintenance and servicing; and it offers diagnostic and repair procedures to follow when trouble occurs.

We hope you use the manual to tackle the work yourself. For many simpler jobs, doing it yourself may be quicker than arranging an appointment to get the vehicle into a shop and making the trips to leave it and pick it up. More importantly, a lot of money can be saved by avoiding the expense the shop must pass on to you to cover its labor and overhead costs. An added benefit is the sense of satisfaction and accomplishment that you feel after doing the job yourself.

Using the manual

The manual is divided into Chapters. Each Chapter is divided into numbered Sections, which are headed in bold type between horizontal lines. Each Section consists of consecutively numbered paragraphs.

At the beginning of each numbered Section you will be referred to any illustrations which apply to the procedures in that Section. The reference numbers used in illustration captions pinpoint the pertinent Section and the Step within that Section. That is, illustration 3.2 means the illustration refers to Section 3 and Step (or paragraph) 2 within that Section.

Procedures, once described in the text, are not normally repeated. When it's necessary to refer to another Chapter, the reference will be given as Chapter and Section number. Cross references given without use of the word "Chapter" apply to Sections and/or paragraphs in the same Chapter. For example, "see Section 8" means in the same Chapter.

References to the left or right side of the vehicle assume you are sitting on the seat, facing forward.

Motorcycle manufacturers continually make changes to specifications and recommendations, and these, when notified, are incorporated into our manuals at the earliest opportunity.

Even though we have prepared this manual with extreme care, neither the publisher nor the author can accept responsibility for any errors in, or omissions from, the information given.

NOTE

A **Note** provides information necessary to properly complete a procedure or information which will make the procedure easier to understand.

CAUTION

A **Caution** provides a special procedure or special steps which must be taken while completing the procedure where the Caution is found. Not heeding a Caution can result in damage to the assembly being worked on.

WARNING

A **Warning** provides a special procedure or special steps which must be taken while completing the procedure where the Warning is found. Not heeding a Warning can result in personal injury.

Introduction to the Yamaha FZR

The Yamaha FZR series are highly successful and popular high-performance sport bikes.

The engine on all models is a liquid-cooled, inline four with double overhead camshafts. FZR600 models have four valves per cylinder; FZR750 and 1000 models have five (three intake and two exhaust).

Fuel is delivered to four Mikuni carburetors by an electric fuel pump. California models and some UK models use Yamaha's Exhaust Ultimate Powervalve (EXUP) device in the exhaust system. This valve varies exhaust backpressure for improved performance and reduced exhaust emissions.

The front suspension uses a pair of conventional or cartridge forks. Spring preload is adjustable on FZR750/1000 models.

The rear suspension uses the Yamaha Monocross design, which employs a shock absorber/spring unit mounted ahead of the swingarm. The suspension provides a progressive damping effect. Spring preload is adjustable.

The front brake uses dual discs and the rear brake uses a single disc.

Identification numbers

The frame serial number is stamped into the right side of the frame and printed on a label affixed to the frame. The engine number is stamped into the right upper side of the crankcase. Both of these numbers should be recorded and kept in a safe place so they can be furnished to law enforcement officials in the event of a theft.

The frame serial number, engine serial number and carburetor identification number should also be kept in a handy place (such as with your driver's license) so they are always available when purchasing or ordering parts for your machine.

The models covered by this manual are as follows:

FZR600/600R, 1989 through 1994*
FZR750R, 1987 and 1988 (US), 1989 through 1992 (UK)
FZR1000, 1987 through 1993

*Not including 1994 UK FZR600R models.

Identifying model years

The procedures in this manual identify the bikes by model year. To determine which model year a given machine is, look for the following identification codes in the engine and frame numbers. The initial frame/engine no. is given in parentheses for UK models.

Year	Code

FZR600 models

1989	3HH1 - US except California
	3HW1 - California
	3HE1 - UK (3HE-000101)
1990	3HH4 - US except California
	3HW2 - California
	3HE3 - UK (3HE-026101)
1991	3HH6 - US except California
	3UU2 - California
	3HE7 - UK (3HE-054101)
1992	3HH8 - US except California
	3UU3 - California
	3HE8 - UK (3HE-088101)
1993	3HHA - US except California
	—— - California
	3HEE - UK (3HE-106101)
1994	3HHC - US except California
	3UU5 - California

FZR750 models

1987	2NK - US
1988	3CS1 - US
1989	3SG1 - UK (3PK-001101)
1990	3SG2 - UK (3PK-003101)
1991/2	As 1989 model - UK

FZR1000 models

1987	2LH - US except California
	2LJ - California
	2RG - UK (2RG-000101)
1988	3DU1 - US except California
	3CA1 - California
	2RG - UK
1989	3LK1 - US except California
	3LK2 - California
	3LG1 - UK (3LG-000101)
1990	3LK4 - US except California
	3LK5 - California
	3LG2 - UK (3LG-004101)
1991	3LK7 - US except California
	3LK8 - California
	3LG3 - UK (3LG-009101)
1992	3LKA - US except California
	3LKB - California
	3LG4 - UK (LG6-012101)
1993	3LKD - US except California
	3LKE - California
	3LG5 - UK (LG5-017101)

The frame number is stamped in the right side of the frame and is also displayed on a decal

The engine number is stamped in the right side of the crankcase

Buying parts

Once you have found all the identification numbers, record them for reference when buying parts. Since the manufacturers change specifications, parts and vendors (companies that manufacture various components on the machine), providing the ID numbers is the only way to be reasonably sure that you are buying the correct parts.

Whenever possible, take the worn part to the dealer so direct comparison with the new component can be made. Along the trail from the manufacturer to the parts shelf, there are numerous places that the part can end up with the wrong number or be listed incorrectly.

The two places to purchase new parts for your motorcycle - the accessory store and the franchised dealer - differ in the type of parts they carry. While dealers can obtain virtually every part for your motorcycle, the accessory store is usually limited to normal high wear items such as shock absorbers, tune-up parts, various engine gaskets, cables, chains, brake parts, etc. Rarely will an accessory outlet have major suspension components, cylinders, transmission gears, or cases.

Used parts can be obtained for roughly half the price of new ones, but you can't always be sure of what you're getting. Once again, take your worn part to the wrecking yard (breaker) for direct comparison.

Whether buying new, used or rebuilt parts, the best course is to deal directly with someone who specializes in parts for your particular make.

General specifications

FZR600 models

Wheelbase	
1989	1420 mm (55.9 inches)
1991 on	1425 mm (56.1 inches)
Overall length	2095 mm (82.5 inches)
Overall width	700 mm (27.6 inches)
Overall height	
1989 and 1990	1160 mm (45.7 inches)
1991-on	1155 mm (45.5 inches)
Seat height	785 mm (30.9 inches)
Ground clearance (minimum)	135 mm (5.3 inches)
Weight (with oil and full fuel tank)	
1989 and 1990	
US except California	199 kg (439 lbs)
California	204 kg (450 lbs)
UK	201 kg (443 lbs)
1991-on	
US except California	201 kg (443 lbs)
California	206 kg (454 lbs)
UK	203 kg (448 lbs)

FZR750R models (US)

Wheelbase	1470 mm (57.9 inches)
Overall length	2125 mm (83.7 inches)
Overall width	730 mm (28.7 inches)
Overall height	1215 mm (47.8 inches)
Seat height	775 mm (30.5 inches)
Ground clearance (minimum)	140 mm (5.5 inches)
Weight (with oil and full fuel tank)	228 kg (503 lbs)

FZR750R models (UK)

Wheelbase	1445 mm (56.9 inches)
Overall length	2180 mm (85.8 inches)
Overall width	705 mm (27.8 inches)
Overall height	1160 mm (45.7 inches)
Seat height	775 mm (30.5 inches)
Ground clearance (minimum)	120 mm (4.7 inches)
Weight (with oil and full fuel tank)	210 kg (463 lbs)

FZR1000 models (US)

Wheelbase...	1470 mm (57.9 inches)
Overall length	
1987 and 1988...	2205 mm (86.8 inches)
1989 and 1990...	2200 mm (86.8 inches)
1991-on..	2110 mm (83.1 inches)
Overall width	
1987 through 1990...	730 mm (28.7 inches)
1991-on..	745 mm (29.3 inches)
Overall height	
1987 and 1988...	1215 mm (47.8 inches)
1989 and 1990...	1160 mm (45.7 inches)
1991-on..	1170 mm (46.1 inches)
Seat height	
1987 and 1988...	775 mm (30.5 inches)
1989 and 1990...	765 mm (30.1 inches)
1991-on..	775 mm (30.5 inches)
Ground clearance (minimum)	
1987 and 1988...	140 mm (5.5 inches)
1989-on..	135 mm (5.3 inches)
Weight (with oil and full fuel tank)	
1987 and 1988	
US except California..	229 kg (505 lbs)
California...	230 kg (507 lbs)
1989 and 1990	
Except California..	235 kg (518 lbs)
California...	236 kg (520 lbs)

FZR1000 models (UK)

Wheelbase	
1987 and 1988, 1991-on	1470 mm (57.9 inches)
1989 and 1990...	1460 mm (57.5 inches)
Overall length	
1987 and 1988, 1991-on	2205 mm (86.8 inches)
1989 and 1990...	2200 mm (86.8 inches)
Overall width	
1987 through 1990...	730 mm (28.7 inches)
1991-on..	745 mm (29.3 inches)
Overall height	
1987 and 1988...	1215 mm (47.8 inches)
1989 and 1990...	1160 mm (45.7 inches)
1991-on..	1170 mm (46.1 inches)
Seat height	
1987 and 1988...	775 mm (30.5 inches)
1989 and 1990...	765 mm (30.1 inches)
1991-on..	775 mm (30.5 inches)
Ground clearance (minimum)	
1987 and 1988...	140 mm (5.5 inches)
1989-on..	135 mm (5.3 inches)
Weight (with oil and full fuel tank)	
1987 and 1988...	229 kg (505 lbs)
1989 and 1990...	235 kg (518 lbs)
1991-on..	Not specified

Maintenance techniques, tools and working facilities

Basic maintenance techniques

There are a number of techniques involved in maintenance and repair that will be referred to throughout this manual. Application of these techniques will enable the amateur mechanic to be more efficient, better organized and capable of performing the various tasks properly, which will ensure that the repair job is thorough and complete.

Fastening systems

Fasteners, basically, are nuts, bolts and screws used to hold two or more parts together. There are a few things to keep in mind when working with fasteners. Almost all of them use a locking device of some type (either a lock washer, locknut, locking tab or thread adhesive). All threaded fasteners should be clean, straight, have undamaged threads and undamaged corners on the hex head where the wrench fits. Develop the habit of replacing all damaged nuts and bolts with new ones.

Rusted nuts and bolts should be treated with a penetrating oil to ease removal and prevent breakage. Some mechanics use turpentine in a spout type oil can, which works quite well. After applying the rust penetrant, let it -work" for a few minutes before trying to loosen the nut or bolt. Badly rusted fasteners may have to be chiseled off or removed with a special nut breaker, available at tool stores.

If a bolt or stud breaks off in an assembly, it can be drilled out and removed with a special tool called an E-Z out (or screw extractor). Most dealer service departments and motorcycle repair shops can perform this task, as well as others (such as the repair of threaded holes that have been stripped out).

Flat washers and lock washers, when removed from an assembly, should always be replaced exactly as removed. Replace any damaged washers with new ones. Always use a flat washer between a lock washer and any soft metal surface (such as aluminum), thin sheet metal or plastic. Special locknuts can only be used once or twice before they lose their locking ability and must be replaced.

Tightening sequences and procedures

When threaded fasteners are tightened, they are often tightened to a specific torque value (torque is basically a twisting force). Overtightening the fastener can weaken it and cause it to break, while under-tightening can cause it to eventually come loose. Each bolt, depending on the material it's made of, the diameter of its shank and the material it is threaded into, has a specific torque value, which is noted in the Specifications. Be sure to follow the torque recommendations closely.

Fasteners laid out in a pattern (i.e. cylinder head bolts, engine case bolts, etc.) must be loosened or tightened in a sequence to avoid warping the component. Initially, the bolts/nuts should go on finger tight only. Next, they should be tightened one full turn each, in a criss-cross or diagonal pattern. After each one has been tightened one full turn, return to the first one tightened and tighten them all one half turn, following the same pattern. Finally, tighten each of them one quarter turn at a time until each fastener has been tightened to the proper torque. To loosen and remove the fasteners the procedure would be reversed.

Disassembly sequence

Component disassembly should be done with care and purpose to help ensure that the parts go back together properly during reassembly. Always keep track of the sequence in which parts are removed. Take note of special characteristics or marks on parts that can be installed more than one way (such as a grooved thrust washer on a shaft). It's a good idea to lay the disassembled parts out on a clean surface in the order that they were removed. It may also be helpful to make sketches or take instant photos of components before removal.

When removing fasteners from a component, keep track of their locations. Sometimes threading a bolt back in a part, or putting the washers and nut back on a stud, can prevent mixups later. If nuts and bolts can't be returned to their original locations, they should be kept in a compartmented box or a series of small boxes. A cupcake or muffin tin is ideal for this purpose, since each cavity can hold the bolts and nuts from a particular area (i.e. engine case bolts, valve cover bolts, engine mount bolts, etc.). A pan of this type is especially helpful when working on assemblies with very small parts (such as the carburetors and the valve train). The cavities can be marked with paint or tape to identify the contents.

Whenever wiring looms, harnesses or connectors are separated, it's a good idea to identify the two halves with numbered pieces of masking tape so they can be easily reconnected.

Gasket sealing surfaces

Throughout any motorcycle, gaskets are used to seal the mating surfaces between components and keep lubricants, fluids, vacuum or pressure contained in an assembly.

Many times these gaskets are coated with a liquid or paste type gasket sealing compound before assembly. Age, heat and pressure can sometimes cause the two parts to stick together so tightly that they are very difficult to separate. In most cases, the part can be loosened by striking it with a soft-faced hammer near the mating surfaces. A regular hammer can be used if a block of wood is placed between the hammer and the part. Do not hammer on cast parts or parts that could be easily damaged. With any particularly stubborn part, always recheck to make sure that every fastener has been removed.

Avoid using a screwdriver or bar to pry apart components, as they can easily mar the gasket sealing surfaces of the parts (which must remain smooth). If prying is absolutely necessary, use a piece of wood, but keep in mind that extra clean-up will be necessary if the wood splinters.

After the parts are separated, the old gasket must be carefully scraped off and the gasket surfaces cleaned. Stubborn gasket material can be soaked with a gasket remover (available in aerosol cans) to soften it so it can be easily scraped off. A scraper can be fashioned from a piece of copper tubing by flattening and sharpening one end. Copper is recommended because it is usually softer than the surfaces to be scraped, which reduces the chance of gouging the part. Some gaskets can be removed with a wire brush, but regardless of the method used, the mating surfaces must be left clean and smooth. If for some reason the gasket surface is gouged, then a gasket sealer thick enough to fill scratches will have to be used during reassembly of the components. For most applications, a non-drying (or semi-drying) gasket sealer is best.

Hose removal tips

Hose removal precautions closely parallel gasket removal precautions. Avoid scratching or gouging the surface that the hose mates against or the connection may leak. Because of various chemical reactions, the rubber in hoses can bond itself to the metal spigot that the hose fits over. To remove a hose, first loosen the hose clamps that secure it to the spigot. Then, with slip joint pliers, grab the hose at the clamp and rotate it around the spigot. Work it back and forth until it is completely free, then pull it off (silicone or other lubricants will ease removal if they can be applied between the hose and the outside of the spigot). Apply the same lubricant to the inside of the hose and the outside of the spigot to simplify installation.

If a hose clamp is broken or damaged, do not reuse it. Also, do not reuse hoses that are cracked, split or torn.

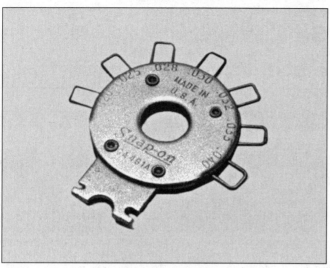

Spark plug gap adjusting tool

Feeler gauge set

Control cable pressure luber

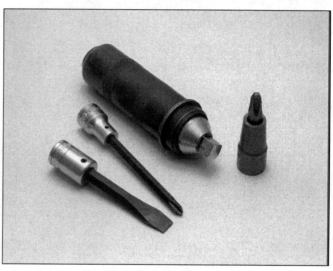

Hand impact screwdriver and bits

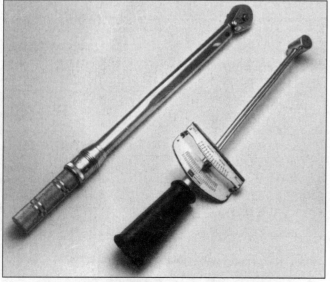

Torque wrenches (left - click type; right - beam type)

Tools

A selection of good tools is a basic requirement for anyone who plans to maintain and repair a motorcycle. For the owner who has few tools, if any, the initial investment might seem high, but when compared to the spiraling costs of routine maintenance and repair, it is a wise one.

To help the owner decide which tools are needed to perform the tasks detailed in this manual, the following tool lists are offered: Maintenance and minor repair, Repair and overhaul and Special. The newcomer to practical mechanics should start off with the Maintenance and minor repair tool kit, which is adequate for the simpler jobs. Then, as confidence and experience grow, the owner can tackle more difficult tasks, buying additional tools as they are needed. Eventually the basic kit will be built into the Repair and overhaul tool set. Over a period of time, the experienced do-it-yourselfer will assemble a tool set complete enough for most repair and overhaul procedures and will add tools from the Special category when it is felt that the expense is justified by the frequency of use.

Maintenance and minor repair tool kit

The tools in this list should be considered the minimum required for performance of routine maintenance, servicing and minor repair work. We recommend the purchase of combination wrenches (box end and open end combined in one wrench); while more expensive than

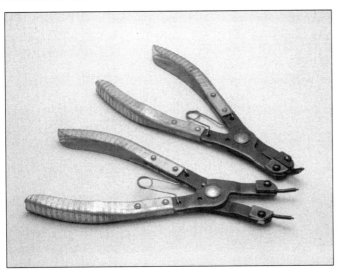

Snap-ring pliers (top - external; bottom - internal)

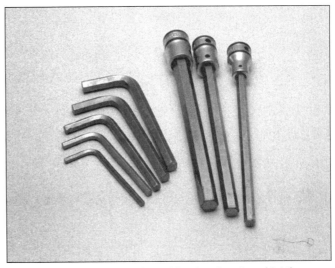

Allen wrenches (left) and Allen head sockets (right)

Valve spring compressor

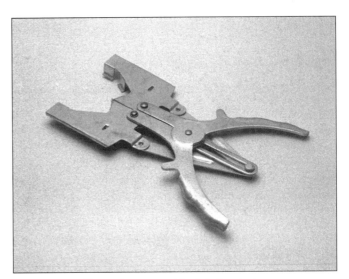

Piston ring removal/installation tool

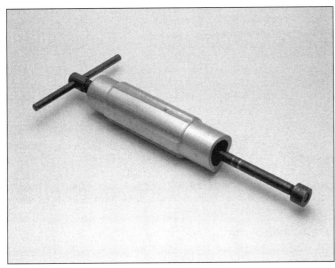

Piston pin puller

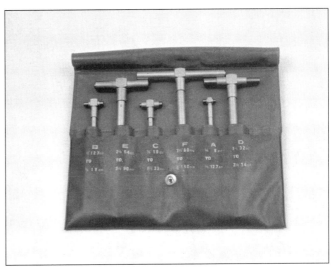

Telescoping gauges

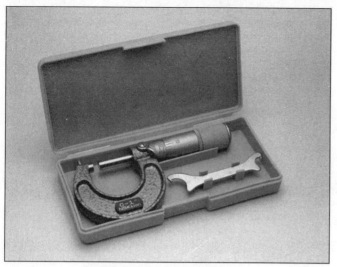

0-to1-inch micrometer

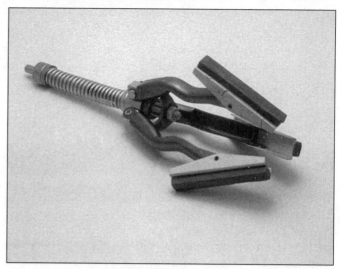

Cylinder surfacing hone

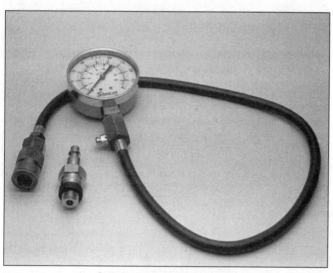

Cylinder compression gauge

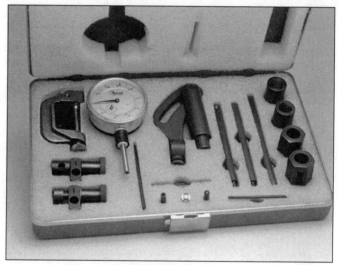

Dial indicator set

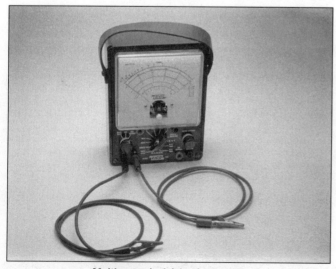

Multimeter (volt/ohm/ammeter)

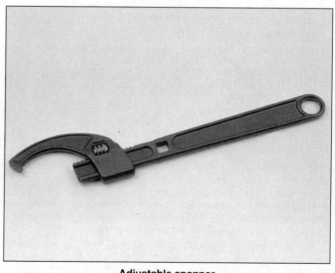

Adjustable spanner

open-ended ones, they offer the advantages of both types of wrench.

Combination wrench set (6 mm to 22 mm)
Adjustable wrench - 8 in
Spark plug socket (with rubber insert)
Spark plug gap adjusting tool
Feeler gauge set
Standard screwdriver (5/16 in x 6 in)
Phillips screwdriver (No. 2 x 6 in)
Allen (hex) wrench set (4 mm to 12 mm)
Combination (slip-joint) pliers - 6 in
Hacksaw and assortment of blades
Tire pressure gauge
Control cable pressure luber
Grease gun
Oil can
Fine emery cloth
Wire brush
Hand impact screwdriver and bits
Funnel (medium size)
Safety goggles
Drain pan
Work light with extension cord

Repair and overhaul tool set

These tools are essential for anyone who plans to perform major repairs and are intended to supplement those in the Maintenance and minor repair tool kit. Included is a comprehensive set of sockets which, though expensive, are invaluable because of their versatility (especially when various extensions and drives are available). We recommend the 3/8 inch drive over the 1/2 inch drive for general motorcycle maintenance and repair (ideally, the mechanic would have a 3/8 inch drive set and a 1/2 inch drive set).

Socket set(s)
Reversible ratchet
Extension - 6 in
Universal joint
Torque wrench (same size drive as sockets)
Ball pein hammer - 8 oz
Soft-faced hammer (plastic/rubber)
Standard screwdriver (1/4 in x 6 in)
Standard screwdriver (stubby - 5/16 in)
Phillips screwdriver (No. 3 x 8 in)
Phillips screwdriver (stubby - No. 2)
Pliers - locking
Pliers - lineman's
Pliers - needle nose
Pliers - snap-ring (internal and external)
Cold chisel - 1/2 in
Scriber
Scraper (made from flattened copper tubing)
Center punch
Pin punches (1/16, 1/8, 3/16 in)
Steel rule/straightedge - 12 in
Pin-type spanner wrench
A selection of files
Wire brush (large)

Note: Another tool which is often useful is an electric drill with a chuck capacity of 3/8 inch (and a set of good quality drill bits).

Special tools

The tools in this list include those which are not used regularly, are expensive to buy, or which need to be used in accordance with their manufacturer's instructions. Unless these tools will be used frequently, it is not very economical to purchase many of them. A consideration would be to split the cost and use between yourself and a friend or friends (i.e. members of a motorcycle club).

This list primarily contains tools and instruments widely available to the public, as well as some special tools produced by the vehicle manufacturer for distribution to dealer service departments. As a result, references to the manufacturer's special tools are occasionally included in the text of this manual. Generally, an alternative method of doing the job without the special tool is offered. However, sometimes there is no alternative to their use. Where this is the case, and the tool can't be purchased or borrowed, the work should be turned over to the dealer service department or a motorcycle repair shop.

Valve spring compressor
Piston ring removal and installation tool
Piston pin puller
Telescoping gauges
Micrometer(s) and/or dial/Vernier calipers
Cylinder surfacing hone
Cylinder compression gauge
Dial indicator set
Multimeter
Adjustable spanner
Manometer or vacuum gauge set
Small air compressor with blow gun and tire chuck

Buying tools

For the do-it-yourselfer who is just starting to get involved in motorcycle maintenance and repair, there are a number of options available when purchasing tools. If maintenance and minor repair is the extent of the work to be done, the purchase of individual tools is satisfactory. If, on the other hand, extensive work is planned, it would be a good idea to purchase a modest tool set from one of the large retail chain stores. A set can usually be bought at a substantial savings over the individual tool prices (and they often come with a tool box). As additional tools are needed, add-on sets, individual tools and a larger tool box can be purchased to expand the tool selection. Building a tool set gradually allows the cost of the tools to be spread over a longer period of time and gives the mechanic the freedom to choose only those tools that will actually be used.

Tool stores and motorcycle dealers will often be the only source of some of the special tools that are needed, but regardless of where tools are bought, try to avoid cheap ones (especially when buying screwdrivers and sockets) because they won't last very long. There are plenty of tools around at reasonable prices, but always aim to purchase items which meet the relevant national safety standards. The expense involved in replacing cheap tools will eventually be greater than the initial cost of quality tools.

It is obviously not possible to cover the subject of tools fully here. For those who wish to learn more about tools and their use, there is a book entitled *Motorcycle Workshop Practice Manual* (Book no. 1454) available from the publishers of this manual. It also provides an introduction to basic workshop practice which will be of interest to a home mechanic working on any type of motorcycle.

Care and maintenance of tools

Good tools are expensive, so it makes sense to treat them with respect. Keep them clean and in usable condition and store them properly when not in use. Always wipe off any dirt, grease or metal chips before putting them away. Never leave tools lying around in the work area.

Some tools, such as screwdrivers, pliers, wrenches and sockets, can be hung on a panel mounted on the garage or workshop wall, while others should be kept in a tool box or tray. Measuring instruments, gauges, meters, etc. must be carefully stored where they can't be damaged by weather or impact from other tools.

When tools are used with care and stored properly, they will last a very long time. Even with the best of care, tools will wear out if used frequently. When a tool is damaged or worn out, replace it; subsequent jobs will be safer and more enjoyable if you do.

Working facilities

Not to be overlooked when discussing tools is the workshop. If anything more than routine maintenance is to be carried out, some sort of suitable work area is essential.

It is understood, and appreciated, that many home mechanics do not have a good workshop or garage available and end up removing an engine or doing major repairs outside (it is recommended, however, that the overhaul or repair be completed under the cover of a roof).

A clean, flat workbench or table of comfortable working height is an absolute necessity. The workbench should be equipped with a vise that has a jaw opening of at least four inches.

As mentioned previously, some clean, dry storage space is also required for tools, as well as the lubricants, fluids, cleaning solvents, etc. which soon become necessary.

Sometimes waste oil and fluids, drained from the engine or cooling system during normal maintenance or repairs, present a disposal problem. To avoid pouring them on the ground or into a sewage system, simply pour the used fluids into large containers, seal them with

caps and take them to an authorized disposal site or service station. Plastic jugs (such as old antifreeze containers) are ideal for this purpose.

Always keep a supply of old newspapers and clean rags available. Old towels are excellent for mopping up spills. Many mechanics use rolls of paper towels for most work because they are readily available and disposable. To help keep the area under the motorcycle clean, a large cardboard box can be cut open and flattened to protect the garage or shop floor.

Whenever working over a painted surface (such as the fuel tank) cover it with an old blanket or bedspread to protect the finish.

Safety first

Professional mechanics are trained in safe working procedures. However enthusiastic you may be about getting on with the job at hand, take the time to ensure that your safety is not put at risk. A moment's lack of attention can result in an accident, as can failure to observe simple precautions.

There will always be new ways of having accidents, and the following is not a comprehensive list of all dangers; it is intended rather to make you aware of the risks and to encourage a safe approach to all work you carry out on your bike.

Essential DOs and DON'Ts

DON'T start the engine without first ascertaining that the transmission is in neutral.

DON'T suddenly remove the filler cap from a hot cooling system - cover it with a cloth and release the pressure gradually first, or you may get scalded by escaping coolant.

DON'T attempt to drain oil until you are sure it has cooled sufficiently to avoid scalding you.

DON'T grasp any part of the engine or exhaust system without first ascertaining that it is cool enough not to burn you.

DON'T allow brake fluid or antifreeze to contact the machine's paint work or plastic components.

DON'T siphon toxic liquids such as fuel, hydraulic fluid or antifreeze by mouth, or allow them to remain on your skin.

DON'T inhale dust - it may be injurious to health (see *Asbestos* heading).

DON'T allow any spilled oil or grease to remain on the floor - wipe it up right away, before someone slips on it.

DON'T use ill fitting wrenches or other tools which may slip and cause injury.

DON'T attempt to lift a heavy component which may be beyond your capability - get assistance.

DON'T rush to finish a job or take unverified short cuts.

DON'T allow children or animals in or around an unattended vehicle.

DON'T inflate a tire to a pressure above the recommended maximum. Apart from over stressing the carcase and wheel rim, in extreme cases the tire may blow off forcibly.

DO ensure that the machine is supported securely at all times. This is especially important when the machine is blocked up to aid wheel or fork removal.

DO take care when attempting to loosen a stubborn nut or bolt. It is generally better to pull on a wrench, rather than push, so that if you slip, you fall away from the machine rather than onto it.

DO wear eye protection when using power tools such as drill, sander, bench grinder etc.

DO use a barrier cream on your hands prior to undertaking dirty jobs - it will protect your skin from infection as well as making the dirt easier to remove afterwards; but make sure your hands aren't left slippery. Note that long-term contact with used engine oil can be a health hazard.

DO keep loose clothing (cuffs, ties etc. and long hair) well out of the way of moving mechanical parts.

DO remove rings, wristwatch etc., before working on the vehicle- especially the electrical system.

DO keep your work area tidy - it is only too easy to fall over articles left lying around.

DO exercise caution when compressing springs for removal or installation. Ensure that the tension is applied and released in a controlled manner, using suitable tools which preclude the possibility of the spring escaping violently.

DO ensure that any lifting tackle used has a safe working load rating adequate for the job.

DO get someone to check periodically that all is well, when working alone on the vehicle.

DO carry out work in a logical sequence and check that everything is correctly assembled and tightened afterwards.

DO remember that your vehicle's safety affects that of yourself and others. If in doubt on any point, get professional advice.

IF, in spite of following these precautions, you are unfortunate enough to injure yourself, seek medical attention as soon as possible.

Asbestos

Certain friction, insulating, sealing and other products - such as brake pads, clutch linings, gaskets, etc. - contain asbestos. *Extreme care must be taken to avoid inhalation of dust from such products since it is hazardous to health*. If in doubt, assume that they *do* contain asbestos.

Fire

Remember at all times that gasoline (petrol) is highly flammable. Never smoke or have any kind of naked flame around, when working on the vehicle. But the risk does not end there - a spark caused by an electrical short-circuit, by two metal surfaces contacting each other, by careless use of tools, or even by static electricity built up in your body under certain conditions, can ignite gasoline (petrol) vapor, which in a confined space is highly explosive. Never use gasoline (petrol) as a cleaning solvent. Use an approved safety solvent.

Always disconnect the battery ground (earth) terminal before working on any part of the fuel or electrical system, and never risk spilling fuel on to a hot engine or exhaust.

It is recommended that a fire extinguisher of a type suitable for fuel and electrical fires is kept handy in the garage or workplace at all times. Never try to extinguish a fuel or electrical fire with water.

Fumes

Certain fumes are highly toxic and can quickly cause unconsciousness and even death if inhaled to any extent. Gasoline (petrol) vapor comes into this category, as do the vapors from certain solvents such as trichloroethylene. Any draining or pouring of such volatile fluids should be done in a well ventilated area.

When using cleaning fluids and solvents, read the instructions carefully. Never use materials from unmarked containers - they may give off poisonous vapors.

Never run the engine of a motor vehicle in an enclosed space such as a garage. Exhaust fumes contain carbon monoxide which is extremely poisonous; if you need to run the engine, always do so in the open air or at least have the rear of the vehicle outside the workplace.

The battery

Never cause a spark, or allow a naked light near the vehicle's battery. It will normally be giving off a certain amount of hydrogen gas, which is highly explosive.

Always disconnect the battery ground (earth) terminal before working on the fuel or electrical systems (except where noted).

If possible, loosen the filler plugs or cover when charging the battery from an external source. Do not charge at an excessive rate or the battery may burst.

Take care when topping up, cleaning or carrying the battery. The acid electrolyte, even when diluted, is very corrosive and should not be allowed to contact the eyes or skin. Always wear rubber gloves and goggles or a face shield. If you ever need to prepare electrolyte yourself, always add the acid slowly to the water; never add the water to the acid.

Electricity

When using an electric power tool, inspection light etc., always ensure that the appliance is correctly connected to its plug and that, where necessary, it is properly grounded (earthed). Do not use such appliances in damp conditions and, again, beware of creating a spark or applying excessive heat in the vicinity of fuel or fuel vapor. Also ensure that the appliances meet national safety standards.

A severe electric shock can result from touching certain parts of the electrical system, such as the spark plug wires (HT leads), when the engine is running or being cranked, particularly if components are damp or the insulation is defective. Where an electronic ignition system is used, the secondary (HT) voltage is much higher and could prove fatal.

Motorcycle chemicals and lubricants

A number of chemicals and lubricants are available for use in motorcycle maintenance and repair. They include a wide variety of products ranging from cleaning solvents and degreasers to lubricants and protective sprays for rubber, plastic and vinyl.

Contact point/spark plug cleaner is a solvent used to clean oily film and dirt from points, grime from electrical connectors and oil deposits from spark plugs. It is oil free and leaves no residue. It can also be used to remove gum and varnish from carburetor jets and other orifices.

Carburetor cleaner is similar to contact point/spark plug cleaner but it usually has a stronger solvent and may leave a slight oily reside. It is not recommended for cleaning electrical components or connections.

Brake system cleaner is used to remove grease or brake fluid from brake system components (where clean surfaces are absolutely necessary and petroleum-based solvents cannot be used); it also leaves no residue.

Silicone-based lubricants are used to protect rubber parts such as hoses and grommets, and are used as lubricants for hinges and locks.

Multi-purpose grease is an all purpose lubricant used wherever grease is more practical than a liquid lubricant such as oil. Some multi-purpose grease is colored white and specially formulated to be more resistant to water than ordinary grease.

Gear oil (sometimes called gear lube) is a specially designed oil used in transmissions and final drive units, a s well as other areas where high friction, high temperature lubrication is required. It is available in a number of viscosities (weights) for various applications.

Motor oil, of course, is the lubricant specially formulated for use in the engine. It normally contains a wide variety of additives to prevent corrosion and reduce foaming and wear. Motor oil comes in various weights (viscosity ratings) of from 5 to 80. The recommended weight of the oil depends on the seasonal temperature and the demands on the engine. Light oil is used in cold climates and under light load conditions; heavy oil is used in hot climates and where high loads are encountered. Multi-viscosity oils are designed to have characteristics of both light and heavy oils and are available in a number of weights from 5W-20 to 20W-50.

Gas (petrol) additives perform several functions, depending on their chemical makeup. They usually contain solvents that help dissolve gum and varnish that build up on carburetor and intake parts. They also serve to break down carbon deposits that form on the inside surfaces of the combustion chambers. Some additives contain upper cylinder lubricants for valves and piston rings.

Brake fluid is a specially formulated hydraulic fluid that can withstand the heat and pressure encountered in brake systems. Care must be taken that this fluid does not come in contact with painted surfaces or plastics. An opened container should always be resealed to prevent contamination by water or dirt.

Chain lubricants are formulated especially for use on motorcycle final drive chains. A good chain lube should adhere well and have good penetrating qualities to be effective as a lubricant inside the chain and on the side plates, pins and rollers. Most chain lubes are either the foaming type or quick drying type and are usually marketed as sprays.

Degreasers are heavy duty solvents used to remove grease and grime that may accumulate on engine and frame components. They can be sprayed or brushed on and, depending on the type, are rinsed with either water or solvent.

Solvents are used alone or in combination with degreasers to clean parts and assemblies during repair and overhaul. The home mechanic should use only solvents that are non-flammable and that do not produce irritating fumes.

Gasket sealing compounds may be used in conjunction with gaskets, to improve their sealing capabilities, or alone, to seal metal-to-metal joints. Many gasket sealers can withstand extreme heat, some are impervious to gasoline and lubricants, while others are capable of filling and sealing large cavities. Depending on the intended use, gasket sealers either dry hard or stay relatively soft and pliable. They are usually applied by hand, with a brush, or are sprayed on the gasket sealing surfaces.

Thread cement is an adhesive locking compound that prevents threaded fasteners from loosening because of vibration. It is available in a variety of types for different applications.

Moisture dispersants are usually sprays that can be used to dry out electrical components such as the fuse block and wiring connectors. Some types can also be used as treatment for rubber and as a lubricant for hinges, cables and locks.

Waxes and polishes are used to help protect painted and plated surfaces from the weather. Different types of paint may require the use of different types of wax polish. Some polishes utilize a chemical or abrasive cleaner to help remove the top layer of oxidized (dull) paint on older vehicles. In recent years, many non-wax polishes (that contain a wide variety of chemicals such as polymers and silicones) have been introduced. These non-wax polishes are usually easier to apply and last longer than conventional waxes and polishes.

Troubleshooting

Contents

Engine doesn't start or is difficult to start

1   Starter motor does not rotate

1   Engine kill switch Off.
2   Fuse blown. Check fuse block (Chapter 10).
3   Battery voltage low. Check and recharge battery (Chapter 10).
4   Starter motor defective. Make sure the wiring to the starter is secure. Make sure the starter relay clicks when the start button is pushed. If the relay clicks, then the fault is in the wiring or motor.
5   Starter relay faulty. Check it according to the procedure in Chapter 10.
6   Starter button not contacting. The contacts could be wet, corroded or dirty. Disassemble and clean the switch (Chapter 10).
7   Wiring open or shorted. Check all wiring connections and harnesses to make sure that they are dry, tight and not corroded. Also check for broken or frayed wires that can cause a short to ground (see wiring diagram, Chapter 10).
8   Ignition switch defective. Check the switch according to the procedure in Chapter 10. Replace the switch with a new one if it is defective.
9   Engine kill switch defective. Check for wet, dirty or corroded contacts. Clean or replace the switch as necessary (Chapter 10).
10   Faulty starter lockout circuit. Check the wiring and the switch itself according to the procedures in Chapter 10.

2   Starter motor rotates but engine does not turn over

1   Starter motor clutch defective. Inspect and repair or replace (Chapter 2 or Chapter 3).
2   Damaged idler or starter gears. Inspect and replace the damaged parts (Chapter 2 or Chapter 3).

3   Starter works but engine won't turn over (seized)

Seized engine caused by one or more internally damaged components. Failure due to wear, abuse or lack of lubrication. Damage can include seized valves, valve lifters, camshaft, pistons, crankshaft, connecting rod bearings, or transmission gears or bearings. Refer to Chapter 2 or Chapter 3 for engine disassembly.

4   No fuel flow

1   No fuel in tank.
2   Fuel tap in off position.
3   Tank cap air vent obstructed. Usually caused by dirt or water. Remove it and clean the cap vent hole.
4   Inline fuel filter clogged. Replace the filter (Chapter 1).
6   Electric fuel pump not working. Test it according to the procedures in Chapter 5.
7   Fuel line clogged. Pull the fuel line loose and carefully blow through it.
8   Inlet needle valve clogged. For all of the valves to be clogged, either a very bad batch of fuel with an unusual additive has been used, or some other foreign material has entered the tank. Many times after a machine has been stored for many months without running, the fuel turns to a varnish-like liquid and forms deposits on the inlet needle valves and jets. The carburetors should be removed and overhauled if draining the float bowls doesn't solve the problem.

5   Engine flooded

1   Float level too high. Check and adjust as described in Chapter 5
2   Inlet needle valve worn or stuck open. A piece of dirt, rust or other debris can cause the inlet needle to seat improperly, causing excess

fuel to be admitted to the float bowl. In this case, the float chamber should be cleaned and the needle and seat inspected. If the needle and seat are worn, then the leaking will persist and the parts should be replaced with new ones (Chapter 5).
3   Starting technique incorrect. Under normal circumstances (i.e., if all the carburetor functions are sound) the machine should start with little or no throttle. When the engine is cold, the choke should be operated and the engine started without opening the throttle. When the engine is at operating temperature, only a very slight amount of throttle should be necessary. If the engine is flooded, turn the fuel tap off and hold the throttle open while cranking the engine. This will allow additional air to reach the cylinders. Remember to turn the fuel tap back on after the engine starts.

6   No spark or weak spark

1   Ignition switch Off.
2   Engine kill switch turned to the Off position.
3   Battery voltage low. Check and recharge battery as necessary (Chapter 10).
4   Spark plug dirty, defective or worn out. Locate reason for fouled plug(s) using spark plug condition chart and follow the plug maintenance procedures in Chapter 1.
5   Spark plug cap or secondary (HT) wiring faulty. Check condition. Replace either or both components if cracks or deterioration are evident (Chapter 6).
6   Spark plug cap not making good contact. Make sure that the plug cap fits snugly over the plug end.
7   Igniter defective. Check the unit, referring to Chapter 6 for details.
8   Signal generator defective. Check the unit, referring to Chapter 6 for details.
9   Ignition coil(s) defective. Check the coils, referring to Chapter 6.
10   Ignition or kill switch shorted. This is usually caused by water, corrosion, damage or excessive wear. The switches can be disassembled and cleaned with electrical contact cleaner. If cleaning does not help, replace the switches (Chapter 10).
11   Wiring shorted or broken between:
   a)   Ignition switch and engine kill switch (or blown fuse)
   b)   Igniter and engine kill switch
   c)   Igniter and ignition coil
   d)   Ignition coil and plug
   e)   Igniter and signal generator
     Make sure that all wiring connections are clean, dry and tight. Look for chafed and broken wires (Chapters 6 and 10).

7   Compression low

1   Spark plug loose. Remove the plug and inspect the threads. Reinstall and tighten to the specified torque (Chapter 1).
2   Cylinder head not sufficiently tightened down. If the cylinder head is suspected of being loose, then there's a chance that the gasket or head is damaged if the problem has persisted for any length of time. The head nuts should be tightened to the proper torque in the correct sequence (Chapter 2 or Chapter 3).
3   Improper valve clearance. This means that the valve is not closing completely and compression pressure is leaking past the valve. Check and adjust the valve clearances (Chapter 1).
4   Cylinder and/or piston worn. Excessive wear will cause compression pressure to leak past the rings. This is usually accompanied by worn rings as well. A top end overhaul is necessary (Chapter 2 or Chapter 3).
5   Piston rings worn, weak, broken, or sticking. Broken or sticking piston rings usually indicate a lubrication or carburetion problem that causes excess carbon deposits or seizures to form on the pistons and rings. Top end overhaul is necessary (Chapter 2 or Chapter 3).
6   Piston ring-to-groove clearance excessive. This is caused by excessive wear of the piston ring lands. Piston replacement is necessary (Chapter 2 or Chapter 3).

7   Cylinder head gasket damaged. If the head is allowed to become loose, or if excessive carbon build-up on the piston crown and combustion chamber causes extremely high compression, the head gasket may leak. Retorquing the head is not always sufficient to restore the seal, so gasket replacement is necessary (Chapter 2 or Chapter 3).

8   Cylinder head warped. This is caused by overheating or improperly tightened head nuts. Machine shop resurfacing or head replacement is necessary (Chapter 2 or Chapter 3).

9   Valve spring broken or weak. Caused by component failure or wear; the spring(s) must be replaced (Chapter 2 or Chapter 3).

10 Valve not seating properly. This is caused by a bent valve (from over-revving or improper valve adjustment), burned valve or seat (improper carburetion) or an accumulation of carbon deposits on the seat (from carburetion or lubrication problems). The valves must be cleaned and/or replaced and the seats serviced if possible (Chapter 2 or Chapter 3).

8   Stalls after starting

1   Improper choke action. Make sure the choke rod is getting a full stroke and staying in the out position.
2   Ignition malfunction. See Chapter 6.
3   Carburetor malfunction. See Chapter 5.
4   Fuel contaminated. The fuel can be contaminated with either dirt or water, or can change chemically if the machine is allowed to sit for several months or more. Drain the tank and float bowls (Chapter 5).
5   Intake air leak. Check for loose carburetor-to-intake manifold connections, loose or missing vacuum gauge access port cap or hose, or loose carburetor top (Chapter 5).
6   Engine idle speed incorrect. Turn throttle stop screw until the engine idles at the specified rpm (Chapter 1).

9   Rough idle

1   Ignition malfunction. See Chapter 6.
2   Idle speed incorrect. See Chapter 1.
3   Carburetors not synchronized. Adjust carburetors with vacuum gauge or manometer set as described in Chapter 1.
4   Carburetor malfunction. See Chapter 5.
5   Fuel contaminated. The fuel can be contaminated with either dirt or water, or can change chemically if the machine is allowed to sit for several months or more. Drain the tank and float bowls (Chapter 5).
6   Intake air leak. Check for loose carburetor-to-intake manifold connections, loose or missing vacuum gauge access port cap or hose, or loose carburetor top (Chapter 5).
7   Air cleaner clogged. Service or replace air filter element (Chapter 1).

Poor running at low speed

10   Spark weak

1   Battery voltage low. Check and recharge battery (Chapter 10).
2   Spark plug fouled, defective or worn out. Refer to Chapter 1 for spark plug maintenance.
3   Spark plug cap or high tension wiring defective. Refer to Chapters 1 and 6 for details on the ignition system.
4   Spark plug cap not making contact.
5   Incorrect spark plug. Wrong type, heat range or cap configuration. Check and install correct plugs listed in Chapter 1. A cold plug or one with a recessed firing electrode will not operate at low speeds without fouling.
6   Igniter defective. See Chapter 6.
7   Signal generator defective. See Chapter 6.
8   Ignition coil(s) defective. See Chapter 6.

11   Fuel/air mixture incorrect

1   Pilot screw(s) out of adjustment (Chapters 1 and 5).
2   Pilot jet or air passage clogged. Remove and overhaul the carburetors (Chapter 5).
3   Air bleed holes clogged. Remove carburetor and blow out all passages (Chapter 5).
4   Air cleaner clogged, poorly sealed or missing.
5   Air cleaner-to-carburetor boot poorly sealed. Look for cracks, holes or loose clamps and replace or repair defective parts.
6   Fuel level too high or too low. Adjust the floats (Chapter 5).
7   Fuel tank air vent obstructed. Make sure that the air vent passage in the filler cap is open.
8   Carburetor intake manifolds loose. Check for cracks, breaks, tears or loose clamps or bolts. Repair or replace the rubber boots.

12   Compression low

1   Spark plug loose. Remove the plug and inspect the threads. Reinstall and tighten to the specified torque (Chapter 1).
2   Cylinder head not sufficiently tightened down. If the cylinder head is suspected of being loose, then there's a chance that the gasket and head are damaged if the problem has persisted for any length of time. The head nuts should be tightened to the proper torque in the correct sequence (Chapter 2 or Chapter 3).
3   Improper valve clearance. This means that the valve is not closing completely and compression pressure is leaking past the valve. Check and adjust the valve clearances (Chapter 1).
4   Cylinder and/or piston worn. Excessive wear will cause compression pressure to leak past the rings. This is usually accompanied by worn rings as well. A top end overhaul is necessary (Chapter 2 or Chapter 3).
5   Piston rings worn, weak, broken, or sticking. Broken or sticking piston rings usually indicate a lubrication or carburetion problem that causes excess carbon deposits or seizures to form on the pistons and rings. Top end overhaul is necessary (Chapter 2 or Chapter 3).
6   Piston ring-to-groove clearance excessive. This is caused by excessive wear of the piston ring lands. Piston replacement is necessary (Chapter 2 or Chapter 3).
7   Cylinder head gasket damaged. If the head is allowed to become loose, or if excessive carbon build-up on the piston crown and combustion chamber causes extremely high compression, the head gasket may leak. Retorquing the head is not always sufficient to restore the seal, so gasket replacement is necessary (Chapter 2 or Chapter 3).
8   Cylinder head warped. This is caused by overheating or improperly tightened head nuts. Machine shop resurfacing or head replacement is necessary (Chapter 2 or Chapter 3).
9   Valve spring broken or weak. Caused by component failure or wear; the spring(s) must be replaced (Chapter 2 or Chapter 3).
10 Valve not seating properly. This is caused by a bent valve (from over-revving or improper valve adjustment), burned valve or seat (improper carburetion) or an accumulation of carbon deposits on the seat (from carburetion, lubrication problems). The valves must be cleaned and/or replaced and the seats serviced if possible (Chapter 2 or Chapter 3).

13   Poor acceleration

1   Carburetors leaking or dirty. Overhaul the carburetors (Chapter 5).
2   Timing not advancing. The signal generator or the igniter may be defective. If so, they must be replaced with new ones, as they can't be repaired.
3   Carburetors not synchronized. Adjust them with a vacuum gauge set or manometer (Chapter 1).

4   Engine oil viscosity too high. Using a heavier oil than that recommended in Chapter 1 can damage the oil pump or lubrication system and cause drag on the engine.

5   Brakes dragging. Usually caused by debris which has entered the brake piston sealing boot, or from a warped disc or bent axle. Repair as necessary (Chapter 8).

Poor running or no power at high speed

14   Firing incorrect

1   Air filter restricted. Clean or replace filter (Chapter 1).

2   Spark plug fouled, defective or worn out. See Chapter 1 for spark plug maintenance.

3   Spark plug cap or secondary (HT) wiring defective. See Chapters 1 and 6 for details of the ignition system.

4   Spark plug cap not in good contact. See Chapter 6.

5   Incorrect spark plug. Wrong type, heat range or cap configuration. Check and install correct plugs listed in Chapter 1. A cold plug or one with a recessed firing electrode will not operate at low speeds without fouling.

6   Igniter defective. See Chapter 6.

7   Ignition coil(s) defective. See Chapter 6.

15   Fuel/air mixture incorrect

1   Main jet clogged. Dirt, water or other contaminants can clog the main jets. Replace the fuel filter and clean the float bowl area, and the jets and carburetor orifices (Chapter 5).

2   Main jet wrong size. The standard jetting is for sea level atmospheric pressure and oxygen content.

3   Throttle shaft-to-carburetor body clearance excessive. Refer to Chapter 5 for inspection and part replacement procedures.

4   Air bleed holes clogged. Remove and overhaul carburetors (Chapter 5).

5   Air filter clogged, poorly sealed, or missing.

6   Air filter-to-carburetor boot poorly sealed. Look for cracks, holes or loose clamps, and replace or repair defective parts.

7   Fuel level too high or too low. Adjust the float(s) (Chapter 5).

8   Fuel tank air vent obstructed. Make sure the air vent passage in the filler cap is open.

9   Carburetor intake manifolds loose. Check for cracks, breaks, tears or loose clamps or bolts. Repair or replace the rubber boots (Chapter 5).

10   Fuel tap clogged. Remove the tap and clean it (Chapter 5).

11   Fuel line clogged. Pull the fuel line loose and carefully blow through it.

12   Fuel Filter clogged. Replace it.

16   Compression low

1   Spark plug loose. Remove the plug and inspect the threads. Reinstall and tighten to the specified torque (Chapter 1).

2   Cylinder head not sufficiently tightened down. If the cylinder head is suspected of being loose, then there's a chance that the gasket and head are damaged if the problem has persisted for any length of time. The head nuts should be tightened to the proper torque in the correct sequence (Chapter 2 or Chapter 3).

3   Improper valve clearance. This means that the valve is not closing completely and compression pressure is leaking past the valve. Check and adjust the valve clearances (Chapter 1).

4   Cylinder and/or piston worn. Excessive wear will cause compression pressure to leak past the rings. This is usually accompanied by worn rings as well. A top end overhaul is necessary (Chapter 2 or Chapter 3).

5   Piston rings worn, weak, broken, or sticking. Broken or sticking piston rings usually indicate a lubrication or carburetion problem that causes excess carbon deposits or seizures to form on the pistons and rings. Top end overhaul is necessary (Chapter 2 or Chapter 3).

6   Piston ring-to-groove clearance excessive. This is caused by excessive wear of the piston ring lands. Piston replacement is necessary (Chapter 2 or Chapter 3).

7   Cylinder head gasket damaged. If the head is allowed to become loose, or if excessive carbon build-up on the piston crown and combustion chamber causes extremely high compression, the head gasket may leak. Retorquing the head is not always sufficient to restore the seal, so gasket replacement is necessary (Chapter 2 or Chapter 3).

8   Cylinder head warped. This is caused by overheating or improperly tightened head nuts. Machine shop resurfacing or head replacement is necessary (Chapter 2 or Chapter 3).

9   Valve spring broken or weak. Caused by component failure or wear; the spring(s) must be replaced (Chapter 2 or Chapter 3).

10   Valve not seating properly. This is caused by a bent valve (from over-revving or improper valve adjustment), burned valve or seat (improper carburetion) or an accumulation of carbon deposits on the seat (from carburetion or lubrication problems). The valves must be cleaned and/or replaced and the seats serviced if possible (Chapter 2 or Chapter 3).

17   Knocking or pinging

1   Carbon build-up in combustion chamber. Use of a fuel additive that will dissolve the adhesive bonding the carbon particles to the crown and chamber is the easiest way to remove the build-up. Otherwise, the cylinder head will have to be removed and decarbonized (Chapter 2 or Chapter 3).

2   Incorrect or poor quality fuel. Old or improper grades of fuel can cause detonation. This causes the piston to rattle, thus the knocking or pinging sound. Drain old fuel and always use the recommended fuel grade.

3   Spark plug heat range incorrect. Uncontrolled detonation indicates the plug heat range is too hot. The plug in effect becomes a glow plug, raising cylinder temperatures. Install the proper heat range plug (Chapter 1).

4   Improper air/fuel mixture. This will cause the cylinder to run hot, which leads to detonation. Clogged jets or an air leak can cause this imbalance. See Chapter 5.

18   Miscellaneous causes

1   Throttle valve doesn't open fully. Adjust the cable slack (Chapter 1).

2   Clutch slipping. May be caused by a cable that is improperly adjusted (FZR600 and UK F2R750 models) or loose or worn clutch components. Refer to Chapter 1 for cable adjustment and Chapter 2 or Chapter 3 for clutch component replacement.

3   Timing not advancing.

4   Engine oil viscosity too high. Using a heavier oil than the one recommended in Chapter 1 can damage the oil pump or lubrication system and cause drag on the engine.

5   Brakes dragging. Usually caused by debris which has entered the brake piston sealing boot, or from a warped disc or bent axle. Repair as necessary.

Overheating

19   Engine overheats

1   Coolant level low. Check coolant level as described in Chapter 1. If coolant level is low, the engine will overheat.

2   Leak in cooling system. Check cooling system hoses and radiator

for leaks and other damage. Repair or replace parts as necessary (Chapter 4).

3 Thermostat stuck closed. Check and replace as described in Chapter 5.

4 Faulty radiator cap. Remove the cap and have it pressure checked.

5 Coolant passages clogged. Drain and flush the entire system, then refill with new coolant.

6 Water pump defective. Remove the pump and check the components.

7 Clogged radiator fins. Clean them by blowing compressed air through the fins from the back side.

8 Engine oil level low. Check and add oil (Chapter 1).

9 Wrong type of oil. If you're not sure what type of oil is in the engine, drain it and fill with the correct type (Chapter 1).

10 Air leak at carburetor intake boots. Check and tighten or replace as necessary (Chapter 5).

11 Float level low. Check and adjust if necessary (Chapter 5).

12 Worn oil pump or clogged oil passages. Check oil pressure (Chapter 2 or Chapter 3). Replace pump or clean passages as necessary.

13 Clogged oil cooler or lines (if equipped). Remove and check for foreign material (see Chapter 2 or Chapter 3).

14 Carbon build-up in combustion chambers. Use of a fuel additive that will dissolve the adhesive bonding the carbon particles to the piston crowns and chambers is the easiest way to remove the build-up. Otherwise, the cylinder head will have to be removed and decarbonized (Chapter 2 or Chapter 3).

20 Firing incorrect

1 Spark plug fouled, defective or worn out. See Chapter 1 for spark plug maintenance.

2 Incorrect spark plug (see Chapter 1).

3 Faulty ignition coil(s) (Chapter 6).

21 Fuel/air mixture incorrect

1 Main jet clogged. Dirt, water and other contaminants can clog the main jets. Clean the fuel tap filter, the float bowl area and the jets and carburetor orifices (Chapter 5).

2 Main jet wrong size. The standard jetting is for sea level atmospheric pressure and oxygen content.

3 Air filter poorly sealed or missing.

4 Air filter-to-carburetor boot poorly sealed. Look for cracks, holes or loose clamps and replace or repair.

5 Fuel level too low. Adjust the float(s) (Chapter 5).

6 Fuel tank air vent obstructed. Make sure that the air vent passage in the filler cap is open.

7 Carburetor intake manifolds loose. Check for cracks, breaks, tears or loose clamps or bolts. Repair or replace the rubber boots (Chapter 5).

22 Compression too high

1 Carbon build-up in combustion chamber. Use of a fuel additive that will dissolve the adhesive bonding the carbon particles to the piston crown and chamber is the easiest way to remove the build-up. Otherwise, the cylinder head will have to be removed and decarbonized (Chapter 2 or Chapter 3).

2 Improperly machined head surface or installation of incorrect gasket during engine assembly.

23 Engine load excessive

1 Clutch slipping. Can be caused by damaged, loose or worn clutch components. Refer to Chapter 2 or Chapter 3 for overhaul procedures.

2 Engine oil level too high. The addition of too much oil will cause pressurization of the crankcase and inefficient engine operation. Check Specifications and drain to proper level (Chapter 1).

3 Engine oil viscosity too high. Using a heavier oil than the one recommended in Chapter 1 can damage the oil pump or lubrication system as well as cause drag on the engine.

4 Brakes dragging. Usually caused by debris which has entered the brake piston sealing boot, or from a warped disc or bent axle. Repair as necessary.

24 Lubrication inadequate

1 Engine oil level too low. Friction caused by intermittent lack of lubrication or from oil that is overworked can cause overheating. The oil provides a definite cooling function in the engine. Check the oil level (Chapter 1).

2 Poor quality engine oil or incorrect viscosity or type. Oil is rated not only according to viscosity but also according to type. Some oils are not rated high enough for use in this engine. Check the Specifications section and change to the correct oil (Chapter 1).

3 Camshaft or journals worn. Excessive wear causing drop in oil pressure. Replace cam and/or cylinder head. Abnormal wear could be caused by oil starvation at high rpm from low oil level or improper weight or type of oil (Chapter 1).

4 Crankshaft and/or bearings worn. Same problems as paragraph 3. Check and replace crankshaft and/or bearings (Chapter 2 or Chapter 3).

25 Miscellaneous causes

Modification to exhaust system. Most aftermarket exhaust systems cause the engine to run leaner, which make them run hotter. When installing an accessory exhaust system, always rejet the carburetors.

Clutch problems

26 Clutch slipping

2 Friction plates worn or warped. Overhaul the clutch assembly (Chapter 2 or Chapter 3).

2 Steel plates worn or warped (Chapter 2 or Chapter 3).

3 Clutch springs broken or weak. Old or heat-damaged springs (from slipping clutch) should be replaced with new ones (Chapter 2 or Chapter 3).

4 Worn or warped clutch plates. Replace (Chapter 2 or Chapter 3).

5 Clutch release mechanism defective. Replace any defective parts (Chapter 2 or Chapter 3).

6 Clutch boss or housing unevenly worn. This causes improper engagement of the plates. Replace the damaged or worn parts (Chapter 2 or Chapter 3).

27 Clutch not disengaging completely

1 Clutch lever play excessive (see Chapter 1). Clutch cable improperly adjusted or hydraulic components worn. Adjust cable (Chapter 1) or repair hydraulic components (Chapter 3).

2 Clutch plates warped or damaged. This will cause clutch drag, which in turn will cause the machine to creep. Overhaul the clutch assembly (Chapter 2 or Chapter 3).

3 Clutch spring tension uneven. Usually caused by a sagged or broken spring. Check and replace the springs (Chapter 2 or Chapter 3).

4 Engine oil deteriorated. Old, thin, worn out oil will not provide proper lubrication for the plates, causing the clutch to drag. Replace the oil and filter (Chapter 1).

5 Engine oil viscosity too high. Using a heavier oil than recommended in Chapter 1 can cause the plates to stick together, putting a drag on the engine. Change to the correct weight oil (Chapter 1).

6 Clutch housing seized on shaft. Lack of lubrication, severe wear or damage can cause the housing to seize on the shaft. Overhaul of the clutch, and perhaps transmission, may be necessary to repair the damage (Chapter 2 or Chapter 3).

7 Clutch release mechanism defective. Worn or damaged release mechanism parts can stick and fail to apply force to the pressure plate. Overhaul the release mechanism (Chapter 2 or Chapter 3).

8 Loose clutch hub nut. Causes housing and boss misalignment putting a drag on the engine. Engagement adjustment continually varies. Overhaul the clutch assembly (Chapter 2 or Chapter 3).

Gear shifting problems

28 Doesn't go into gear or lever doesn't return

1 Clutch not disengaging. See Section 26.

2 Shift fork(s) bent or seized. Often caused by dropping the machine or from lack of lubrication. Overhaul the transmission (Chapter 2 or Chapter 3).

3 Gear(s) stuck on shaft. Most often caused by a lack of lubrication or excessive wear in transmission bearings and bushings. Overhaul the transmission (Chapter 2 or Chapter 3).

4 Shift cam binding. Caused by lubrication failure or excessive wear. Replace the cam and bearing (Chapter 2 or Chapter 3).

5 Shift lever return spring weak or broken (Chapter 2 or Chapter 3).

6 Shift lever broken. Splines stripped out of lever or shaft, caused by allowing the lever to get loose or from dropping the machine. Replace necessary parts (Chapter 2 or Chapter 3).

7 Shift mechanism pawl broken or worn. Full engagement and rotary movement of shift drum results. Replace shaft assembly (Chapter 2 or Chapter 3).

8 Pawl spring broken. Allows pawl to float, causing sporadic shift operation. Replace spring (Chapter 2 or Chapter 3).

29 Jumps out of gear

1 Shift fork(s) worn. Overhaul the transmission (Chapter 2 or Chapter 3).

2 Gear groove(s) worn. Overhaul the transmission (Chapter 2 or Chapter 3).

3 Gear dogs or dog slots worn or damaged. The gears should be inspected and replaced. No attempt should be made to service the worn parts.

30 Overshifts

1 Pawl spring weak or broken (Chapter 2 or Chapter 3).

2 Shift drum stopper lever not functioning (Chapter 2 or Chapter 3).

3 Overshift limiter broken or distorted (Chapter 2 or Chapter 3).

Abnormal engine noise

31 Knocking or pinging

1 Carbon build-up in combustion chamber. Use of a fuel additive

that will dissolve the adhesive bonding the carbon particles to the piston crown and chamber is the easiest way to remove the build-up. Otherwise, the cylinder head will have to be removed and decarbonized (Chapter 2 or Chapter 3).

2 Incorrect or poor quality fuel. Old or improper fuel can cause detonation. This causes the pistons to rattle, thus the knocking or pinging sound. Drain the old fuel and always use the recommended grade fuel (Chapter 5).

3 Spark plug heat range incorrect. Uncontrolled detonation indicates that the plug heat range is too hot. The plug in effect becomes a glow plug, raising cylinder temperatures. Install the proper heat range plug (Chapter 1).

4 Improper air/fuel mixture. This will cause the cylinders to run hot and lead to detonation. Clogged jets or an air leak can cause this imbalance. See Chapter 5.

32 Piston slap or rattling

1 Cylinder-to-piston clearance excessive. Caused by improper assembly. Inspect and overhaul top end parts (Chapter 2 or Chapter 3).

2 Connecting rod bent. Caused by over-revving, trying to start a badly flooded engine or from ingesting a foreign object into the combustion chamber. Replace the damaged parts (Chapter 2 or Chapter 3).

3 Piston pin or piston pin bore worn or seized from wear or lack of lubrication. Replace damaged parts (Chapter 2 or Chapter 3).

4 Piston ring(s) worn, broken or sticking. Overhaul the top end (Chapter 2 or Chapter 3).

5 Piston seizure damage. Usually from lack of lubrication or overheating. Replace the pistons and bore the cylinders, as necessary (Chapter 2 or Chapter 3).

6 Connecting rod upper or lower end clearance excessive. Caused by excessive wear or lack of lubrication. Replace worn parts.

33 Valve noise

1 Incorrect valve clearances. Adjust the clearances by referring to Chapter 1.

2 Valve spring broken or weak. Check and replace weak valve springs (Chapter 2 or Chapter 3).

3 Camshaft or cylinder head worn or damaged. Lack of lubrication at high rpm is usually the cause of damage. Insufficient oil or failure to change the oil at the recommended intervals are the chief causes. Since there are no replaceable bearings in the head, the head itself will have to be replaced if there is excessive wear or damage (Chapter 2 or Chapter 3).

34 Other noise

1 Cylinder head gasket leaking.

2 Exhaust pipe leaking at cylinder head connection. Caused by improper fit of pipe(s) or loose exhaust flange. All exhaust fasteners should be tightened evenly and carefully. Failure to do this will lead to a leak.

3 Crankshaft runout excessive. Caused by a bent crankshaft (from over-revving) or damage from an upper cylinder component failure. Can also be attributed to dropping the machine on either of the crankshaft ends.

4 Engine mounting bolts loose. Tighten all engine mount bolts to the specified torque (Chapter 2 or Chapter 3).

5 Crankshaft bearings worn (Chapter 2 or Chapter 3).

6 Camshaft chain tensioner defective. Replace according to the procedure in Chapter 2 or Chapter 3.

7 Camshaft chain, sprockets or guides worn (Chapter 2 or Chapter 3).

Abnormal driveline noise

35 Clutch noise

1   Clutch housing/friction plate clearance excessive (Chapter 2 or Chapter 3).
2   Loose or damaged clutch pressure plate and/or bolts (Chapter 2 or Chapter 3).

36 Transmission noise

1   Bearings worn. Also includes the possibility that the shafts are worn. Overhaul the transmission (Chapter 2 or Chapter 3).
2   Gears worn or chipped (Chapter 2 or Chapter 3).
3   Metal chips jammed in gear teeth. Probably pieces from a broken clutch, gear or shift mechanism that were picked up by the gears. This will cause early bearing failure (Chapter 2 or Chapter 3).
4   Engine oil level too low. Causes a howl from transmission. Also affects engine power and clutch operation (Chapter 1).

37 Final drive noise

1   Chain not adjusted properly (Chapter 1).
2   Engine sprocket or rear sprocket loose. Tighten fasteners (Chapter 7).
3   Sprocket(s) worn. Replace sprocket(s). (Chapter 7).
4   Rear sprocket warped. Replace (Chapter 7).
5   Wheel coupling worn. Replace coupling (Chapter 7).

Abnormal frame and suspension noise

38 Front end noise

1   Low fluid level or improper viscosity oil in forks. This can sound like spurting and is usually accompanied by irregular fork action (Chapter 7).
2   Spring weak or broken. Makes a clicking or scraping sound. Fork oil, when drained, will have a lot of metal particles in it (Chapter 7).
3   Steering head bearings loose or damaged. Clicks when braking. Check and adjust or replace as necessary (Chapter 7).
4   Fork clamps loose. Make sure all fork clamp pinch bolts are tight (Chapter 7).
5   Fork tube bent. Good possibility if machine has been dropped. Replace tube with a new one (Chapter 7).
6   Front axle or axle clamp bolt loose. Tighten them to the specified torque (Chapter 8).

39 Shock absorber noise

1   Fluid level incorrect. Indicates a leak caused by defective seal. Shock will be covered with oil. Replace shock (Chapter 7).
2   Defective shock absorber with internal damage. This is in the body of the shock and can't be remedied. The shock must be replaced with a new one (Chapter 7).
3   Bent or damaged shock body. Replace the shock with a new one (Chapter 7).

40 Brake noise

1   Squeal caused by pad shim not installed or positioned correctly (Chapter 8).
2   Squeal caused by dust on brake pads. Usually found in combina-

tion with glazed pads. Clean using brake cleaning solvent (Chapter 8).
3   Contamination of brake pads. Oil, brake fluid or dirt causing brake to chatter or squeal. Clean or replace pads (Chapter 8).
4   Pads glazed. Caused by excessive heat from prolonged use or from contamination. Do not use sandpaper, emery cloth, carborundum cloth or any other abrasive to roughen the pad surfaces as abrasives will stay in the pad material and damage the disc. A very fine flat file can be used, but pad replacement is suggested as a cure (Chapter 8).
5   Disc warped. Can cause a chattering, clicking or intermittent squeal. Usually accompanied by a pulsating lever and uneven braking. Replace the disc (Chapter 8).
6   Loose or worn wheel bearings. Check and replace as needed (Chapter 8).

Oil level indicator light comes on

41 Engine lubrication system

1   Yamaha FZR models use an oil level light rather than an oil pressure light.
2   Engine oil level low. Inspect for leak or other problem causing low oil level and add recommended oil (Chapters 1, 2 and 3).

42 Electrical system

1   Oil level switch defective. Check the switch according to the procedure in Chapter 10. Replace it if it's defective.
2   Oil level indicator light circuit defective. Check for pinched, shorted, disconnected or damaged wiring (Chapter 1).

Excessive exhaust smoke

43 White smoke

1   Piston oil ring worn. The ring may be broken or damaged, causing oil from the crankcase to be pulled past the piston into the combustion chamber. Replace the rings with new ones (Chapter 2 or Chapter 3).
2   Cylinders worn, cracked, or scored. Caused by overheating or oil starvation. If worn or scored, the cylinders will have to be rebored and new pistons installed. If cracked, the cylinder block will have to be replaced (see Chapter 2 or Chapter 3).
3   Valve oil seal damaged or worn. Replace oil seals with new ones (Chapter 2 or Chapter 3).
4   Valve guide worn. Perform a complete valve job (Chapter 2 or Chapter 3).
5   Engine oil level too high, which causes the oil to be forced past the rings. Drain oil to the proper level (Chapter 1).
6   Head gasket broken between oil return and cylinder. Causes oil to be pulled into the combustion chamber. Replace the head gasket and check the head for warpage (Chapter 2 or Chapter 3).
7   Abnormal crankcase pressurization, which forces oil past the rings. Clogged breather or hoses usually the cause (Chapter 2 or Chapter 3).

44 Black smoke

1   Air filter clogged. Clean or replace the element (Chapter 1).
2   Main jet too large or loose. Compare the jet size to the Specifications (Chapter 5).
3   Choke stuck, causing fuel to be pulled through choke circuit (Chapter 5).
4   Fuel level too high. Check and adjust the float level as necessary

(Chapter 5).

5   Inlet needle held off needle seat. Clean the float bowls and fuel line and replace the needles and seats if necessary (Chapter 5).

45   Brown smoke

1   Main jet too small or clogged. Lean condition caused by wrong size main jet or by a restricted orifice. Clean float bowl and jets and compare jet size to Specifications (Chapter 5).

2   Fuel flow insufficient. Fuel inlet needle valve stuck closed due to chemical reaction with old fuel. Float level incorrect. Restricted fuel line. Clean line and float bowl and adjust floats if necessary.

3   Carburetor intake manifolds loose (Chapter 5).

4   Air filter poorly sealed or not installed (Chapter 1).

Poor handling or stability

46   Handlebar hard to turn

1   Steering stem locknut too tight (Chapter 7).

2   Bearings damaged. Roughness can be felt as the bars are turned from side-to-side. Replace bearings and races (Chapter 7).

3   Races dented or worn. Denting results from wear in only one position (e.g., straight ahead), from a collision or hitting a pothole or from dropping the machine. Replace races and bearings (Chapter 7).

4   Steering stem lubrication inadequate. Causes are grease getting hard from age or being washed out by high pressure car washes. Disassemble steering head and repack bearings (Chapter 7).

5   Steering stem bent. Caused by a collision, hitting a pothole or by dropping the machine. Replace damaged part. Don't try to straighten the steering stem (Chapter 7).

6   Front tire air pressure too low (Chapter 1).

47   Handlebar shakes or vibrates excessively

1   Tires worn or out of balance (Chapter 8).

2   Swingarm bearings worn. Replace worn bearings by referring to Chapter 7.

3   Rim(s) warped or damaged. Inspect wheels for runout (Chapter 8).

4   Wheel bearings worn. Worn front or rear wheel bearings can cause poor tracking. Worn front bearings will cause wobble (Chapter 8).

5   Handlebar clamp bolts loose (Chapter 7).

6   Steering stem or fork clamps loose. Tighten them to the specified torque (Chapter 7).

7   Engine mount bolts loose. Will cause excessive vibration with increased engine rpm (Chapter 2 or Chapter 3).

48   Handlebar pulls to one side

1   Frame bent. Definitely suspect this if the machine has been dropped. May or may not be accompanied by cracking near the bend. Replace the frame (Chapter 7).

2   Wheel out of alignment. Caused by improper location of axle spacers or from bent steering stem or frame (Chapter 7).

3   Swingarm bent or twisted. Caused by age (metal fatigue) or impact damage. Replace the arm (Chapter 7).

4   Steering stem bent. Caused by impact damage or by dropping the motorcycle. Replace the steering stem (Chapter 7).

5   Fork leg bent. Disassemble the forks and replace the damaged parts (Chapter 8).

6   Fork oil level uneven. Check and add or drain as necessary (Chapter 7).

49   Poor shock absorbing qualities

1   Too hard:
  a) Fork oil level excessive (Chapter 7).
  b) Fork oil viscosity
too high. Use a lighter oil (see the Specifications in Chapter 1).
  c) Fork tube bent. Causes a harsh, sticking feeling (Chapter 7).
  d) Shock shaft or body bent or damaged (Chapter 7).
  e) Fork internal damage (Chapter 7).
  f) Shock internal damage.
  g) Tire pressure too high (Chapter 1).

2   Too soft:
  a) Fork or shock oil insufficient and/or leaking (Chapter 7).
  b) Fork oil level too low (Chapter 7).
  c) Fork oil viscosity too light (Chapter 7).
  d) Fork springs weak or broken (Chapter 7).

Braking problems

50   Brakes are spongy, don't hold

1   Air in brake line. Caused by inattention to master cylinder fluid level or by leakage. Locate problem and bleed brakes (Chapter 8).

2   Pad or disc worn (Chapters 1 and 8).

3   Brake fluid leak. See paragraph 1.

4   Contaminated pads. Caused by contamination with oil, grease, brake fluid, etc. Clean or replace pads. Clean disc thoroughly with brake cleaner (Chapter 8).

5   Brake fluid deteriorated. Fluid is old or contaminated. Drain system, replenish with new fluid and bleed the system (Chapter 8).

6   Master cylinder internal parts worn or damaged causing fluid to bypass (Chapter 8).

7   Master cylinder bore scratched by foreign material or broken spring. Repair or replace master cylinder (Chapter 8).

8   Disc warped. Replace disc (Chapter 8).

51   Brake lever or pedal pulsates

1   Disc warped. Replace disc (Chapter 8).

2   Axle bent. Replace axle (Chapter 8).

3   Brake caliper bolts loose (Chapter 8).

4   Brake caliper shafts damaged or sticking, causing caliper to bind. Lube the shafts or replace them if they are corroded or bent (Chapter 8).

5   Wheel warped or otherwise damaged (Chapter 8).

6   Wheel bearings damaged or worn (Chapter 8).

52   Brakes drag

1   Master cylinder piston seized. Caused by wear or damage to piston or cylinder bore (Chapter 8).

2   Lever balky or stuck. Check pivot and lubricate (Chapter 8).

3   Brake caliper binds. Caused by inadequate lubrication or damage to caliper shafts (Chapter 8).

4   Brake caliper piston seized in bore. Caused by wear or ingestion of dirt past deteriorated seal (Chapter 8).

5   Brake pad damaged. Pad material separated from backing plate. Usually caused by faulty manufacturing process or from contact with chemicals. Replace pads (Chapter 8).

6   Pads improperly installed (Chapter 8).

7   Front brake lever or rear brake pedal freeplay insufficient (Chapter 1).

Electrical problems

53 Battery dead or weak

1   Battery faulty. Caused by sulfated plates which are shorted through sedimentation or low electrolyte level. Also, broken battery terminal making only occasional contact (Chapter 10).
2   Battery cables making poor contact (Chapter 10).
3   Load excessive. Caused by addition of high wattage lights or other electrical accessories.
4   Ignition switch defective. Switch either grounds internally or fails to shut off system. Replace the switch (Chapter 10).
5   Regulator/rectifier defective (Chapter 10).

6   Stator coil open or shorted (Chapter 10).
7   Wiring faulty. Wiring grounded or connections loose in ignition, charging or lighting circuits (Chapter 10).

54 Battery overcharged

1   Regulator/rectifier defective. Overcharging is noticed when battery gets excessively warm or boils over (Chapter 10).
2   Battery defective. Replace battery with a new one (Chapter 10).
3   Battery amperage too low, wrong type or size. Install manufacturer's specified amp-hour battery to handle charging load (Chapter 10).

Notes

Chapter 1 Tune-up and routine maintenance

Contents

Specifications

FZR600

Engine

Spark plugs	
Type	NGK CR9E or CR8E, ND U27ESR-N or U24ESR-N
Gap	0.7 to 0.8 mm (0.028 to 0.032 inch)
Valve clearances (COLD engine)	
Intake	0.11 to 0.20 mm (0.004 to 0.008 inch)
Exhaust	0.21 to 0.30 mm (0.008 to 0.012 inch)
Engine idle speed	
Except California	1150 to 1250 rpm
California	1250 to 1350 rpm
Cylinder compression pressure (at sea level)	
Standard	11.02 Bars (160 psi)
Maximum	11.29 Bars (164 psi)
Minimum	9.99 Bars (145 psi)
Carburetor synchronization	
Vacuum at idle speed	155 to 165 mm Hg (6.1 to 6.5 inch Hg)
Maximum vacuum difference between cylinders	10 mm Hg (0.39 inch Hg)
Cylinder numbering (from left side to right side of bike)	1-2-3-4

Miscellaneous

Brake pad material minimum thickness	05 mm (0.02 inch) - see text
Brake pedal position	44 mm (1.7 inch) below the top of the footpeg
Freeplay adjustments	
Throttle grip	3 to 7 mm (0.12 to 0.28 inch)
Clutch lever	2 to 3 mm (0.08 to 0.12 inch)
Front brake lever	2 to 5 mm (0.08 to 0.20 inch)
Drive chain	
Slack	20 to 30 mm (0.8 to 1.2 inch)
10-link length	150.1 mm (5.91 inch)
Battery electrolyte specific gravity	1.280 at 20-degrees C (68 degrees F)
Minimum tire tread depth*	1 mm (0.04 inch)
Tire pressures (cold)	
Front	
Up to 90 kg (198 lbs)	2.27 Bars (33 psi)
Above 90 kg (198 lbs) or high speed riding	2.48 Bars (36 psi)
Rear	
Up to 90 kg (198 lbs)	2.48 Bars (36 psi)
Above 90 kg (198 lbs or high speed riding)	2.89 Bars (42 psi)

Torque specifications

Oil drain plug	43 Nm (31 ft-lbs)
Oil filter bolt - cartridge type	15 Nm (11 ft-lbs)
Oil filter - spin-on type	17 Nm (12.5 ft-lbs)

1

FZR600 (continued)

Torque specifications

Coolant drain plug in water pump	7 Nm (5.1 ft-lbs)
Coolant drain plug in coolant tube	10 Nm (7.2 ft-lbs)
Coolant drain plugs in cylinder block	7 Nm (5.1 ft-lbs)
Spark plugs	12.5 Nm (9 ft-lbs)
Steering head bearing lower ring nut	
Initial torque	52 Nm (37 ft-lbs)
Final torque	3 Nm (2.2 ft-lbs)
Valve cover bolts	See Chapter 2

Recommended lubricants and fluids

Engine/transmission oil	
Type	API grade SE or SF
Viscosity	
Consistently below 15 degrees C (60 degrees F)	SAE 10W30
Consistently above 5 degrees C (40 degrees F)	SAE 20W40
Capacity (without oil cooler)	
With filter change	2.5 liters (2.6 US qt, 4.4 Imperial pt)
Oil change only	2.2 liters (2.3 US qt, 3.8 Imperial pt)
Coolant type	50/50 mixture of water and ethylene glycol antifreeze containing corrosion inhibitors for aluminum engines
Brake fluid	DOT 4 (DOT 3 may be used in the rear, but not the front, if DOT 4 is unavailable)
Fork oil	
Type	SAE 10W - fork oil
Amount	435cc (14.7 US fl oz, 15.3 Imperial fl oz)
Oil level (fully compressed with spring removed)	101 mm (3.98 inch)

Miscellaneous

Drive chain	SAE 30 to 50W engine oil
Wheel bearings	Medium weight, lithium-based multi-purpose grease
Swingarm pivot bearings	Medium weight, lithium-based multi-purpose grease
Cables and lever pivots	Chain and cable lubricant or 10W30 motor oil
Sidestand/centerstand pivots	Medium-weight, lithium-based multi-purpose grease
Brake pedal/shift lever pivots	Chain and cable lubricant or 10W30 motor oil
Throttle grip	Multi-purpose grease or dry film lubricant

In the UK, tread depth must be at least 1 mm over 3/4 of the tread breadth all the way around the tire, with no bald patches.

FZR750/1000

Engine

Spark plugs

Type	
US	NGK DP8EA-9, ND X24EP-U9
UK	NGK DR8ES-L, ND X24ESR-U
Gap	
US	0.8 to 0.9 mm (0.031 to 0.035 inch)
UK	0.6 to 0.7 mm (0.024 to 0.028 inch)
Valve clearances (COLD engine)	
Intake	0.11 to 0.20 mm (0.004 to 0.008 inch)
Exhaust	0.21 to 0.30 mm (0.008 to 0.012 inch)
Engine idle speed	950 to 1050 rpm
Cylinder compression pressure (at sea level)	
1987 and 1988 models	
Standard	11.02 Bars (160 psi)
Maximum	11.29 Bars (164 psi)
Minimum	9.99 Bars (145 psi)
Maximum variation	0.96 Bar (14 psi)
1989-on models	
Standard	13.71 Bars (199 psi)
Maximum	14.47 Bars (210 psi)
Minimum	13.37 Bars (194 psi)
Maximum variation	0.96 Bar (14 psi)
Carburetor synchronization	
Vacuum at idle speed	195 to 205 mm Hg (7.67 to 8.07 inch Hg)
Maximum vacuum difference between cylinders	10 mm Hg (0.39 inch Hg)
Cylinder numbering (from left side to right side of bike)	1-2-3-4

Miscellaneous

Brake pad material minimum thickness
    1989-on (UK) FZR750
        Front.. 1.0 mm (0.04 inch)
        Rear .... 0.5 mm (0.02 inch)
    1987-1988 FZR750 and all FZR1000 .... 1.0 mm (0.04 inch) - see text
Brake pedal position
    FZR750 and 1987/1988 FZR1000........................... 50 mm (1.97 inch) below top of footpeg
    1989-on FZR1000 .... 60 mm (2.36 inch) below top of footpeg
Freeplay adjustments
    Throttle grip.. 3 to 7 mm (0.12 to 0.28 inch)
    Front brake lever .... 2 to 5 mm (0.08 to 0.20 inch)
    Clutch lever (UK FZR750).. 2 to 3 mm (0.08 to 0.12 inch)
Drive chain
    Slack .... 15 to 20 mm (0.6 to 0.8 inch)
    10-link length.. 150.1 mm (5.91 inch)
Battery electrolyte specific gravity .... 1.280 at 20-degrees C (68-degrees F)
Minimum tire tread depth* .... 1 mm (0.04 inch)
Tire pressures (cold)
    Front (all loads and conditions) .... 2.48 Bars (36 psi)
    Rear
        Up to 90 kg (198 lbs)... 2.48 Bars (36 psi)
        Above 90 kg (198 lbs) or high speed riding .... 2.89 Bars (42 psi)

Torque specifications

Oil drain plug .... 43 Nm (31 ft-lbs)
Oil filter bolt - cartridge type.. 15 Nm (11 ft-lbs)
Oil filter - spin-on type.. 17 Nm (12.5 ft-lbs)
Coolant drain plugs in water pump and cylinder
    1987 and 1988 FZR750/1000 .... 8 Nm (5.8 ft-lbs)
    1989-on FZR750/1000 .... 10 Nm (7.2 ft-lbs)
Spark plugs... 17.5 Nm (12.5 ft-lbs)
Steering head bearing lower ring nut
    All except 1989-on UK FZR750
        Initial torque .... 52 Nm (37 ft-lbs)
        Final torque .... 3 Nm (2.2 ft-lbs)
    1989-on UK FZR750
        Initial torque .... 48 Nm (35 ft-lbs)
        Final torque .... 16 Nm (11 ft-lbs)
Valve cover bolts .... See Chapter 3

Recommended lubricants and fluids

Engine/transmission oil
    Type .... API grade SE or SF
    Viscosity
        Consistently below 15 degrees C (60 degrees F)................. SAE 10W30
        Consistently above 5 degrees C (40 degrees F)................. SAE 20W40
    Capacity (without oil cooler)
        All except 1989-on UK FZR750
            With filter change.. 3.0 liters (3.2 US qt, 5.2 Imperial pt)
            Oil change only.. 2.7 liters (2.9 US qt, 4.8 Imperial pt)
        1989-on UK FZR750
            With filter change.. 3.2 liters (3.4 US qt, 5.6 Imperial pt)
            Oil change only.. 2.8 liters (2.6 US qt, 4.6 Imperial pt)
Brake fluid DOT 4 .... (DOT 3 may be used in the rear, but not the front,
                                 if DOT 4 is unavailable)

Fork oil
    Type
        1987 through 1990 (except UK FZR750)........................... SAE 10W - fork oil
        UK FZR750 and 1991-on FZR1000 .... SAE 5W - fork oil
        1991-on.. SAE 5W - fork oil
    Amount
        1987 and 1988 FZR750 .... 434cc (14.7 US fl oz, 15.3 Imperial fl oz)
        1989-on (UK) FZR750 .... 437cc (14.8 US fl oz, 15.4 Imperial fl oz)
        1987 and 1988 FZR1000 .... 425 cc (14.4 US fl oz, 15.0 Imperial fl oz)
        1989 and 1990 FZR1000 .... 535cc (18.1 US fl oz, 18.9 Imperial fl oz)
        1991-on.. 462cc (15.6 US fl oz, 16.3 Imperial fl oz)
    Oil level (fully compressed with spring removed)
        1987 and 1988 FZR750 .... 138 mm (5.43 inches)
        1989-on (UK) FZR750 .... 131 mm (5.16 inches)
        1987 and 1988 FZR1000 .... 143 mm (5.64 inches)

1

FZR750/1000 (continued)

Oil level (fully compressed with spring removed)
  1989 and 1990 FZR1000 .... 116 mm (4.57 inches)
  1991-on FZR1000 .... 124 mm (4.88 inch)

Miscellaneous

Drive chain.. SAE 30 to 50W engine oil
Wheel bearings... Medium weight, lithium-based multi-purpose grease
Swingarm pivot bearings .... Medium weight, lithium-based multi-purpose grease
Cables and lever pivots .... Chain and cable lubricant or 10W30 motor oil
Sidestand/centerstand pivots.. Medium-weight, lithium-based multi-purpose grease
Brake pedal/shift lever pivots .... Chain and cable lubricant or 10W30 motor oil
Throttle grip .... Multi-purpose grease or dry film lubricant
In the UK, tread depth must be at least 1 mm over 3/4 of the tread breadth all the way around the tire, with no bald patches.

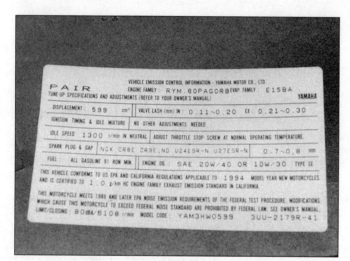

1.3a Maintenance information printed on decals includes tune-up data . . .

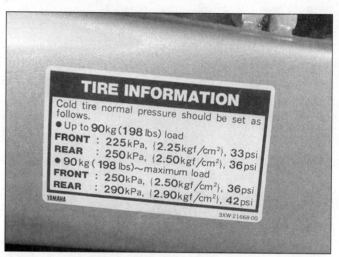

1.3b . . . tire pressure specifications (1994 FZR600 shown) . . .

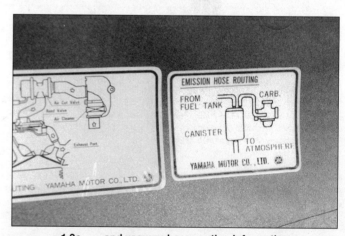

1.3c . . . and vacuum hose routing information

1   Introduction to tune-up and routine maintenance

Refer to illustrations 1.3a, 1.3b and 1.3c

This Chapter covers in detail the checks and procedures necessary for the tune-up and routine maintenance of your motorcycle. Section 1 includes the routine maintenance schedule, which is designed to keep the machine in proper running condition and prevent possible problems. The remaining Sections contain detailed procedures for carrying out the items listed on the maintenance schedule, as well as additional maintenance information designed to increase reliability.

Since routine maintenance plays such an important role in the safe and efficient operation of your motorcycle, it is presented here as a comprehensive check list. For the rider who does all his own maintenance, these lists outline the procedures and checks that should be done on a routine basis.

Maintenance information is printed on labels attached to the motorcycle (**see illustrations**). If the information on the labels differs from that included here, use the information on the label.

Deciding where to start or plug into the routine maintenance schedule depends on several factors. If you have a motorcycle whose warranty has recently expired, and if it has been maintained according to the warranty standards, you may want to pick up routine maintenance as it coincides with the next mileage or calendar interval. If you have owned the machine for some time but have never performed any maintenance on it, then you may want to start at the nearest interval and include some additional procedures to ensure that nothing important is overlooked. If you have just had a major engine overhaul, then you may want to start the maintenance routine from the beginning. If you have a used machine and have no knowledge of its history or maintenance record, you may desire to combine all the checks into

one large service initially and then settle into the maintenance schedule prescribed.

The Sections which outline the inspection and maintenance procedures are written as step-by-step comprehensive guides to the performance of the work. They explain in detail each of the routine inspections and maintenance procedures on the check list. References to additional information in applicable Chapters is also included and should not be overlooked.

Before beginning any maintenance or repair, the machine should be cleaned thoroughly, especially around the oil filter, spark plugs, cylinder head covers, side covers, carburetors, etc. Cleaning will help ensure that dirt does not contaminate the engine and will allow you to detect wear and damage that could otherwise easily go unnoticed.

2 Yamaha FZR
Routine maintenance intervals

Note: *The pre-ride inspection outlined in the owner's manual covers checks and maintenance that should be carried out on a daily basis. It's condensed and included here to remind you of its importance. Always perform the pre-ride inspection at every maintenance interval (in addition to the procedures listed). The intervals listed below are the shortest intervals recommended by the manufacturer for each particular operation during the model years covered in this manual. Your owner's manual may have different intervals for your model.*

Daily or before riding

Check the engine oil level
Check the coolant level
Check the fuel level and inspect for leaks
Check the operation of both brakes - also check the fluid level and look for leakage
Check the tires for damage, the presence of foreign objects and correct air pressure
Check the throttle for smooth operation and correct freeplay
Check the operation of the clutch - make sure the freeplay is correct (cable clutch models), check the fluid level and look for leakage (hydraulic clutch models)
Make sure the steering operates smoothly, without looseness and without binding
Check for proper operation of the headlight, taillight, brake light, turn signals, indicator lights, speedometer and horn
Make sure the sidestand returns to its fully up position and stays there under spring pressure
Make sure the engine kill switch works properly

After the initial 600 miles/1000 km

Perform all of the daily checks plus:
Check/adjust the carburetor synchronization
Check/adjust the drive chain slack
Change the engine oil and oil filter
Check the battery electrolyte level
Check the tightness of all fasteners
Check the steering
Check/adjust clutch freeplay (cable clutch)
Check the clutch fluid level (hydraulic clutch)
Check the brake fluid level
Check/adjust the brake pedal position
Check the operation of the brake light
Check the operation of the sidestand switch
Lubricate the clutch cable (if equipped), throttle cables and speedometer cable

Every 300 miles/500 km

Check/adjust the drive chain slack
Lubricate the drive chain

Every 4000 miles/6000 km or 6 months

Change the engine oil
Clean the air filter element and replace it if necessary
Inspect the cooling system hoses

Clean and gap the spark plugs
Check/adjust throttle cable free play
Check/adjust the idle speed
Check/adjust the carburetor synchronization
Check the brake fluid level
Check the brake discs and pads
Check/adjust the brake pedal position
Check the operation of the brake light
Lubricate the clutch and front brake lever pivots
Lubricate the shift/brake pedal pivots and the sidestand pivots
Check the steering for looseness or binding
Check the front forks for proper operation and fluid leaks
Check the tires, wheels and wheel bearings
Check the battery electrolyte level and specific gravity; inspect the breather tube
Check the exhaust system for leaks and check the tightness of the fasteners
Check the cleanliness of the fuel system and the condition of the fuel lines and vacuum hoses
Inspect the crankcase ventilation system
Check the operation of the sidestand switch
Lubricate the clutch cable (if equipped), throttle cables and speedometer cable

Every 8,000 miles/12,000 km or 12 months

All of the items above plus:
Change the engine oil and oil filter
Replace the spark plugs
Check rear suspension operation and swingarm play

Every 18,000 miles/30,000 km

Replace the fuel filter
Every 16,000 miles/24,000 km or two years
Adjust the valve clearances (FZR600)
Change the brake fluid
Clean and repack the steering head bearings
Lubricate the swingarm bearings and rear suspension pivot points

Every 26,000 miles/42,000 km

Adjust the valve clearances (FZR750/1000)

Every 60,000 miles/1000,000 km

Replace the alternator brushes (FZR750/1000)

Every two years

Change the coolant
Replace the brake/clutch master cylinder seals and caliper/release cylinder seals
Every four years
Replace the brake hoses

3.3 Check oil level at the inspection window with the motorcycle held straight up; it should be between the Minimum and Maximum marks (fairing removed for clarity)

3.4a The oil filler cap is located on the right side of the engine above the clutch cover; this is an FZR600 . . .

3.4b . . . and this is an FZR1000; the outboard cap (arrow) is the oil filler

3.7a With the master cylinder in a level position, check fluid level in the inspection window (arrow) - this is the front brake master cylinder; the clutch master cylinder, mounted on the left handlebar, has a similar inspection window

3.7b The fluid level in the rear brake master cylinder can be checked by looking through the plastic reservoir - fluid must be above the Lower mark (arrow)

---

3   Fluid levels - check

Engine oil

Refer to illustrations 3.3, 3.4a and 3.4b

1   Run the engine and allow it to reach normal operating temperature. **Caution:** *Do not run the engine in an enclosed space such as a garage or shop.*

2   Stop the engine and allow the machine to sit undisturbed for about five minutes.

3   Hold the motorcycle level. With the engine off, check the oil level in the window located at the lower part of the right crankcase cover. The oil level should be between the Maximum and Minimum level marks next to the window **(see illustration)**.

4   If the level is below the Minimum mark, remove the oil filler cap from the right side of the crankcase **(see illustrations)** and add enough oil of the recommended grade and type to bring the level up to the Maximum mark. Do not overfill.

Brake and clutch fluid

Refer to illustrations 3.7a, 3.7b, 3.9a and 3.9b

5   In order to ensure proper operation of the hydraulic disc brakes

(and the hydraulic clutch if equipped), the fluid level in the master cylinder reservoir(s) must be properly maintained.

6   Remove the right side cover for access to the rear brake reservoir (see Chapter 9). With the motorcycle held level, turn the handlebars until the top of the master cylinder is as level as possible.

7   Look closely at the inspection window in the master cylinder reservoir (front brakes and clutch) or at the level mark on the reservoir (rear brake). Make sure that the fluid level is above the Lower mark on the reservoir **(see illustrations)**.

8   If the level is low, the fluid must be replenished. Before removing the master cylinder cap, cover the fuel tank to protect it from brake fluid spills (which will damage the paint) and remove all dust and dirt from the area around the cap.

9   To top up front brake or clutch fluid, remove the screws **(see illustration)** and lift off the cap and rubber diaphragm. To top up rear brake fluid, unscrew the cap from the reservoir **(see illustration)**. **Note:** *Do not operate the brakes or clutch with the cap removed.*

10   Add new, clean brake fluid of the recommended type until the level is above the inspection window. Do not mix different brands of brake fluid in the reservoir, as they may not be compatible.

11   On front brakes and clutch, replace the rubber diaphragm and the cover. Tighten the screws evenly, but do not overtighten them. On rear brakes, screw the cap onto the reservoir.

3.9a To add fluid to the front brake or clutch reservoir, remove the master cylinder cover screws (arrows) and lift off the cover and diaphragm

3.9b To add fluid to the rear master cylinder, unscrew the reservoir cap (arrow)

3.16a Coolant should be between the Low and Full marks in the reservoir (FZR600 shown)

3.16b To add coolant, remove the reservoir cap

4.4a Detach the negative cable (left arrow) from the battery first, then detach the positive cable (right arrow); the plastic cap protects the positive terminal from accidental contact with metal

12   Wipe any spilled fluid off the reservoir body and reposition and tighten the brake lever and master cylinder assembly if it was moved.

13   If the brake fluid level was low, inspect the brake system for leaks.

Coolant

Refer to illustrations 3.16a and 3.16b

14   The engine must be cold for the results to be accurate, so always perform this check before starting the engine for the first time each day. The reservoir is located on the right side of the motorcycle below the seat.

15   If you're working on an FZR600, remove the seat (see Chapter 9). The level marks are on the inboard side of the reservoir. The marks on FZR/750/1000 models are visible without removing the seat, but you'll need to remove it if it's necessary to add coolant.

16   The coolant level is satisfactory if it is between the Low and Full marks on the reservoir **(see illustration)**. If the level is at or below the Low mark, remove the reservoir cap and add the recommended coolant mixture (see this Chapter's Specifications) until the Full level is reached **(see illustration)**. If the coolant level seems to be consistently low, check the entire cooling system for leaks.

4   Battery electrolyte level/specific gravity - check

Refer to illustrations 4.4a, 4.4b, 4.5, 4.7, 4.11a, 4.11b, 4.11c and 4.11d
Caution: *Be extremely careful when handling or working around the battery. The electrolyte is very caustic and an explosive gas (hydrogen) is given off when the battery is charging.* **Note:** *The first Steps describe battery removal. If the electrolyte level is known to be sufficient it won't be necessary to remove the battery.*

1   This procedure applies to batteries that have removable filler caps, which can be removed to add water to the battery. The sealed maintenance-free batteries used on some models can't be topped up.

2   Remove the seat (see Chapter 9).

3   If necessary for access to remove the battery, remove the side covers (see Chapter 9).

4   Remove the screws securing the battery cables to the battery terminals (remove the negative cable first, positive cable last) **(see illustration)**. Remove the battery retaining strap and pull the battery straight up to remove it **(see illustration)**. The electrolyte level will now be visible through the translucent battery case - it should be between the Upper and Lower level marks.

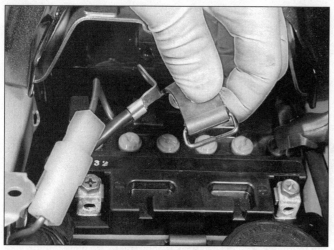

4.4b Unhook the retaining strap and lift out the battery

4.5 Remove the filler caps with a screwdriver

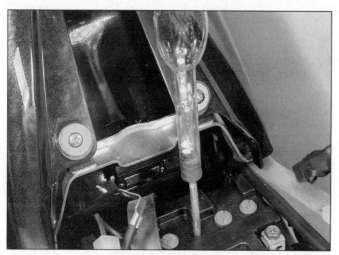

4.7 Check the specific gravity with a hydrometer

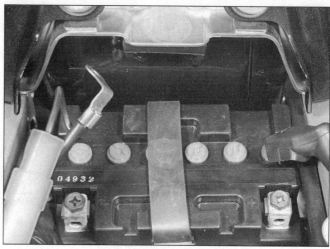

4.11a Pull the retaining strap over the battery and hook its end

5   If the electrolyte is low, remove the cell caps and fill each cell to the upper level mark with distilled water **(see illustration)**. Do not use tap water (except in an emergency), and do not overfill. The cell holes are quite small, so it may help to use a plastic squeeze bottle with a small spout to add the water. If the level is within the marks on the case, additional water is not necessary.

6   Next, check the specific gravity of the electrolyte in each cell with a small hydrometer made especially for motorcycle batteries. These are available from most dealer parts departments or motorcycle accessory stores.

7   Remove the caps, draw some electrolyte from the first cell into the hydrometer **(see illustration)** and note the specific gravity. Compare the reading to the Specifications listed in this Chapter. **Note:** *Add 0.004 points to the reading for every 10-degrees F above 20-degrees C (68-degrees F) - subtract 0.004 points from the reading for every 10-degrees below 20-degrees C (68-degrees F). Return the electrolyte to the appropriate cell and repeat the check for the remaining cells. When the check is complete, rinse the hydrometer thoroughly with clean water.*

8   If the specific gravity of the electrolyte in each cell is as specified, the battery is in good condition and is apparently being charged by the machine's charging system.

9   If the specific gravity is low, the battery is not fully charged. This may be due to corroded battery terminals, a dirty battery case, a mal-functioning charging system, or loose or corroded wiring connections. On the other hand, it may be that the battery is worn out, especially if the machine is old, or that infrequent use of the motorcycle prevents normal charging from taking place.

10   Be sure to correct any problems and charge the battery if necessary. Refer to Chapter 10 for additional battery maintenance and charging procedures.

11   Install the battery cell caps, tightening them securely. Secure the battery with the strap **(see illustration)**. Reconnect the cables to the battery, attaching the positive cable first and the negative cable last. Make sure to install the insulating boot over the positive terminal. Install the side cover (if removed) and the seat. Be very careful not to pinch or otherwise restrict the battery vent tube **(see illustrations)**, as the battery may build up enough internal pressure during normal charging system operation to explode.

---

5   Brake pads - wear check

Refer to illustrations 5.2a, 5.2b and 5.4

1   The front and rear brake pads should be checked at the recommended intervals and replaced with new ones when worn beyond the limit listed in this Chapter's Specifications.

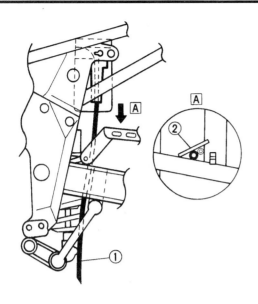

4.11b Be sure the battery vent tube is routed correctly, with no kinking or obstruction; this is an FZR600 vent tube . . .

| 1 | Vent tube | 2 | Hose guide on swingarm |

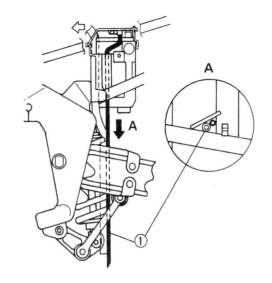

4.11c . . . this is an early FZR750/1000 vent tube . . .

1   Vent tube

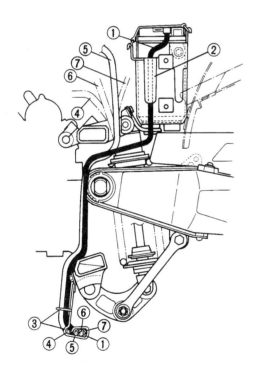

4.11d . . . and this is a 1989 and later FZR1000 vent tube

1	Vent tube	5	Fuel tank vent hose
2	Tube holder	6	Air filter housing vent hose
3	Tube guide	7	Coolant reservoir tank
4	Carburetor overflow hose		breather hose

2   To check the front brake pads, remove the pad covers **(see illustration)**. Reach up and operate the brake lever while you look at the back of each caliper. On all except UK FZR750 models, if the pad wear indicator is close to the disc **(see illustration)**, the pads are worn excessively and must be replaced with new ones (see Chapter 8). On UK FZR750 models, replace the pads if the friction material is worn to the minimum.

5.2a Lift off the front pad cover to expose the pads . . .

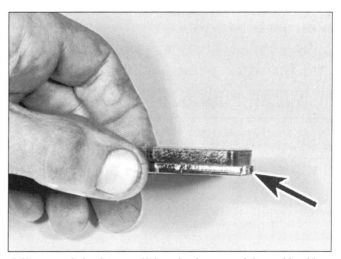

5.2b . . . and check to see if the raised corner of the pad backing metal (arrow) is close to the disc; if it is, the pad is worn and the full set of pads must be replaced (pad removed for clarity)

5.4 Lift off the rear pad cover to inspect the rear pads

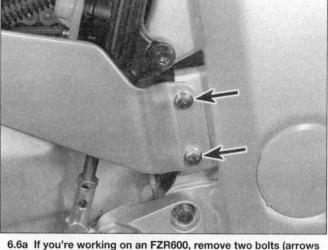

6.6a If you're working on an FZR600, remove two bolts (arrows and take off the protective cover

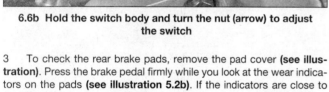

6.6b Hold the switch body and turn the nut (arrow) to adjust the switch

7.2 To adjust the front brake lever freeplay, loosen the locknut (arrow) and turn the screw; be sure to tighten the locknut after adjustment

3   To check the rear brake pads, remove the pad cover **(see illustration)**. Press the brake pedal firmly while you look at the wear indicators on the pads **(see illustration 5.2b)**. If the indicators are close to the disc, replace the pads (see Chapter 8).
4   If the pads are in good condition, reinstall the covers. The words "Uncover for pad service" stamped in the front pad covers may be upside down when the cover is installed. This doesn't mean the cover is upside down.

---

6   Brake system - general check

Refer to illustrations 6.6a and 6.6b
1   A routine general check of the brakes will ensure that any problems are discovered and remedied before the rider's safety is jeopardized.
2   Check the brake lever and pedal for loose connections, excessive play, bends, and other damage. Replace any damaged parts with new ones (see Chapter 8).
3   Make sure all brake fasteners are tight. Check the brake pads for wear (see Section 5) and make sure the fluid level in the reservoirs is correct (see Section 3). Look for leaks at the hose connections and check for cracks in the hoses. If the lever or pedal is spongy, bleed the brakes as described in Chapter 8.
4   Make sure the brake light operates when the brake lever is depressed.

5   Make sure the brake light is activated just before the rear brake takes effect.
6   If adjustment is necessary, remove the aluminum protective cover **(see illustration)**. Hold the switch and turn the adjusting nut on the switch body **(see illustration)** until the brake light is activated when required. If the switch doesn't operate the brake lights, check it as described in Chapter 10.
7   The front brake light switch is not adjustable. If it fails to operate properly, replace it with a new one (see Chapter 10).

---

7   Brake lever play and pedal position - check and adjustment

Front brakes

Refer to illustration 7.2
1   The front brake lever on models without a span adjuster must have the amount of freeplay listed in this Chapter's Specifications to prevent brake drag.
2   Operate the lever and check freeplay at the ball end of the lever. If it's not correct, loosen the adjuster locknut, turn the adjuster to bring freeplay within the Specifications and tighten the locknut **(see illustration)**.

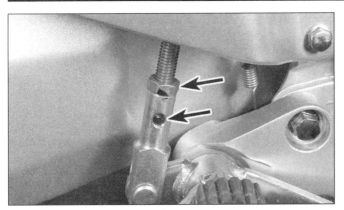

7.4 To adjust the brake pedal height, loosen the locknut (upper arrow) and turn the adjusting bolt; the end of the adjusting bolt must be visible in the hole (lower arrow) after adjustment

8.4 Use an accurate gauge to check the air pressure in the tires

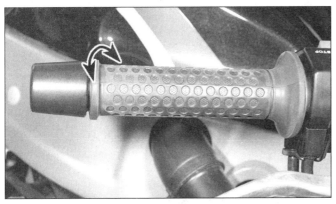

9.2 Twist the throttle grip lightly and check freeplay

9.6 The throttle cable adjusters are located at the right handlebar

Rear brakes

Refer to illustration 7.4

3   The rear brake pedal should be positioned below the top of the footpeg the distance listed in this Chapter's Specifications.

4   To adjust the position of the pedal, loosen the locknut on the adjuster, turn the adjuster to set the pedal position and tighten the locknut **(see illustration)**.

5   If necessary, adjust the brake light switch (see Section 6).

8   Tires/wheels - general check

Refer to illustration 8.4

1   Routine tire and wheel checks should be made with the realization that your safety depends to a great extent on their condition.

2   Check the tires carefully for cuts, tears, embedded nails or other sharp objects and excessive wear. Operation of the motorcycle with excessively worn tires is extremely hazardous, as traction and handling are directly affected. Measure the tread depth at the center of the tire and replace worn tires with new ones when the tread depth is less than specified.

3   Repair or replace punctured tires as soon as damage is noted. Do not try to patch a torn tire, as wheel balance and tire reliability may be impaired.

4   Check the tire pressures when the tires are cold and keep them properly inflated **(see illustration)**. Proper air pressure will increase tire life and provide maximum stability and ride comfort. Keep in mind that low tire pressures may cause the tire to slip on the rim or come off, while high tire pressures will cause abnormal tread wear and unsafe handling.

5   The cast wheels used on this machine are virtually maintenance free, but they should be kept clean and checked periodically for cracks

and other damage. Never attempt to repair damaged cast wheels; they must be replaced with new ones.

6   Check the valve stem locknuts to make sure they are tight. Also, make sure the valve stem cap is in place and tight. If it is missing, install a new one made of metal or hard plastic.

9   Throttle operation/grip freeplay - check and adjustment

Throttle check

Refer to illustration 9.2

1   Make sure the throttle grip rotates easily from fully closed to fully open with the front wheel turned at various angles. The grip should return automatically from fully open to fully closed when released. If the throttle sticks, check the throttle cables for cracks or kinks in the housings. Also, make sure the inner cables are clean and well-lubricated.

2   Check for a small amount of freeplay at the grip and compare the freeplay to the value listed in this Chapter's Specifications **(see illustration)**. If adjustment is necessary, adjust idle speed first (see Section 18).

Throttle cable adjustment

Refer to illustrations 9.6 and 9.8

Note: *Some models use two throttle cables - an accelerator cable and a decelerator cable.*

3   Initial freeplay adjustments are made at the carburetor end of the cable.

4   Remove the seat and side covers (see Chapter 9).

5   Remove the fuel tank cover (FZR600), fuel tank (all others) and air filter case. (see Chapter 5).

6   Make sure the locknuts at the handlebar throttle cable adjusters are tight **(see illustration)**.

7   On early UK models with adjusters at the carburetor ends of both

9.8 Initial adjustments are made at the carburetor throttle cable adjuster(s)

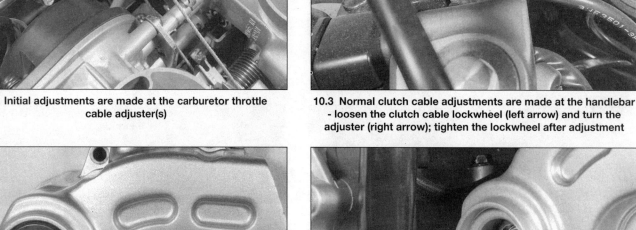

10.3 Normal clutch cable adjustments are made at the handlebar - loosen the clutch cable lockwheel (left arrow) and turn the adjuster (right arrow); tighten the lockwheel after adjustment

10.4a Initial FZR600 clutch cable adjustments are made at the engine; pry off the cover . . .

10.4b . . . loosen the locknut and turn the screw in until it bottoms lightly, then back it out 1/4 turn and tighten the locknut

cables, loosen the locknuts on the decelerator cable (the one that closes the throttle). Turn the adjuster to eliminate throttle grip freeplay, then tighten the locknuts.

8   Loosen the cable locknuts at the carburetor (the accelerator cable locknut on early UK models) **(see illustration)**. Turn the adjuster nuts to change freeplay, then tighten the locknuts.

9   To make fine adjustments, loosen the locknut on the handlebar cable adjuster **(see illustration 9.6)**. Turn the adjuster until the desired freeplay is obtained, then retighten the lockwheel.

10   Make sure the throttle grip is in the fully closed position.

11   Make sure the throttle linkage lever contacts the idle adjusting screw when the throttle grip is in the closed throttle position. **Warning:** *Turn the handlebars all the way through their travel with the engine idling. Idle speed should not change. If it does, the cables may be routed incorrectly. Correct this condition before riding the bike.*

---

10   Clutch - check and adjustment

Cable clutch

Refer to illustrations 10.3, 10.4a and 10.4b

1   Correct clutch freeplay is necessary to ensure proper clutch operation and reasonable clutch service life. Freeplay normally changes because of cable stretch and clutch wear, so it should be checked and adjusted periodically.

2   Clutch cable freeplay is checked at the lever on the handlebar.

Slowly pull in on the lever until resistance is felt, then note how big the gap is between the lever but end and its pivot bracket. Compare this distance with the value listed in this Chapter's Specifications. Too little freeplay might result in the clutch not engaging completely. If there is too much freeplay, the clutch might not release fully.

3   Normal freeplay adjustments are made at the clutch lever by loosening the lockwheel and turning the adjuster until the desired freeplay is obtained **(see illustration)**. Always retighten the lockwheel once the adjustment is complete.

4   If freeplay can't be adjusted at the handlebar, check the initial adjustment at the engine. On FZR600 models, remove the adjuster cover from the engine sprocket cover **(see illustration)**. Loosen the locknut on the adjuster, turn the screw in until it bottoms lightly and back it out 1/4 turn **(see illustration)**. Retighten the locknut. On UK FZR750 models, loosen the locknut at the engine end of the cable, turn the adjuster as needed and tighten the locknut.

5   Recheck freeplay at the clutch lever and make further adjustments (if necessary) with the adjuster at the lever. If freeplay still can't be adjusted within the Specifications, the cable may be stretched or the clutch may be worn. Refer to Chapter 2 or Chapter 3 for inspection and repair procedures.

Hydraulic clutch

Refer to illustration 10.7

6   The hydraulic clutch release mechanism eliminates the need for freeplay adjustment. No means of manual adjustment is provided.

7   Check the fluid level (see Section 3). Check for fluid leaks around

10.7 Follow the hydraulic line from the master cylinder to the release cylinder and check for fluid leaks at the fitting (arrow)

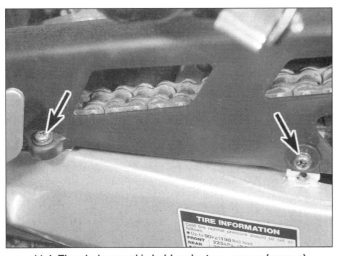

11.4 The chain guard is held on by two screws (arrows)

11.3 Push up on the lower run of the chain and measure how far it deflects - if it's not within the specified limits, adjust the slack in the chain

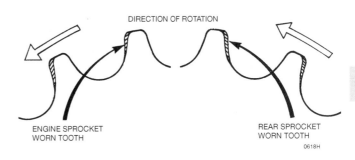

11.5 Check the sprockets in the areas indicated to see if they are worn excessively

the master cylinder, at the fluid line connections and at the release cylinder on the left side of the engine **(see illustration)**. If leaks are found, refer to Chapter 3 for repair procedures.

8   Start the bike, release the clutch and ride off, noting the position of the clutch lever when the clutch begins to engage. If it's too close to the handlebar, there may be air in the clutch fluid (the air compresses, rather than transmitting lever force to the release mechanism). Refer to Chapter 3 and bleed the system.

---

11   Drive chain and sprockets - check, adjustment and lubrication

Check

Refer to illustrations 11.3, 11.4 and 11.5

1   A neglected drive chain won't last long and can quickly damage the sprockets. Routine chain adjustment and lubrication isn't difficult and will ensure maximum chain and sprocket life.

2   To check the chain, support the bike securely so it can't be knocked over and shift the transmission into Neutral. Make sure the ignition switch is off.

3   Push up on the bottom run of the chain and measure the slack midway between the two sprockets **(see illustration)**, then compare your measurements to the value listed in this Chapter's Specifications.

As wear occurs, the chain will actually stretch, which means adjustment usually involves removing some slack from the chain. In some cases where lubrication has been neglected, corrosion and galling may cause the links to bind and kink, which effectively shortens the chain's length. If the chain is tight between the sprockets, rusty or kinked, it's time to replace it with a new one. **Note**: *Repeat the chain slack measurement along the length of the chain - ideally, every inch or so. If you find a tight area, mark it with felt pen or paint and repeat the measurement after the bike has been ridden. If the chain's still tight in the same area, it may be damaged or worn. Because a tight or kinked chain can damage the transmission output shaft bearing, it's a good idea to replace it.*

4   Remove the chain guard **(see illustration)**. Check the entire length of the chain for damaged rollers, loose links and pins. Hang a 20-lb (9 kg) weight on the bottom run of the chain and measure the length of 10 links along the top run. Rotate the wheel and repeat this check at several places on the chain, since it may wear unevenly. Compare your measurements with the maximum 10-link length listed in this Chapter's Specifications. If any of your measurements exceed the maximum, replace the chain. **Note**: *Never install a new chain on old sprockets, and never use the old chain if you install new sprockets - replace the chain and sprockets as a set.*

5   Remove the engine sprocket cover (see Chapter 7). Check the teeth on the engine sprocket and the rear sprocket for wear **(see illustration)**.

11.7a On FZR600 models, remove the cotter pin (lower arrow); the marks (upper arrows) are used to adjust the chain evenly

11.7b Loosen the axle nut with a socket or box wrench (ring spanner)

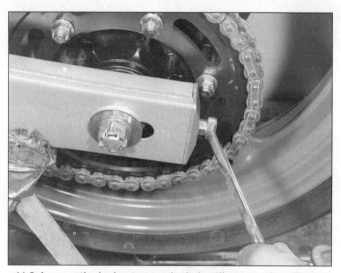

11.8 Loosen the locknut on each chain adjuster so the adjuster can be turned

11.10 This is the correct way to bend the axle nut cotter pin - always use a new cotter pin whenever the old one is removed

1   Cotter pin

Adjustment

6   Rotate the rear wheel until the chain is positioned with the least amount of slack present.

FZR600 and early FZR750/1000 models

Refer to illustrations 11.7a, 11.7b, 11.8 and 11.10

7   Remove the cotter pin from the axle nut and loosen the nut **(see illustrations)**.

8   Loosen and back-off the locknuts on the adjuster bolts **(see illustration)**.

9   Turn the axle adjusting nut on both sides of the swingarm until the proper chain tension is obtained (get the adjuster on the chain side close, then set the adjuster on the opposite side). Be sure to turn the adjusting nuts evenly to keep the rear wheel in alignment. If the adjusting nuts reach the end of their travel, the chain is excessively worn and should be replaced with a new one (see Chapter 7).

10   When the chain has the correct amount of slack, make sure the marks on the adjusters correspond to the same relative marks on each side of the swingarm **(see illustration 11.7a)**. Tighten the axle nut to the torque listed in the Chapter 6 Specifications, then install a new cotter pin and bend it properly **(see illustration)**. If necessary, turn the nut an additional amount to line up the cotter pin hole with the castellations in the nut - don't loosen the nut to do this.

11.11a On UK FZR750 and all later FZR1000 models, pull out the cotter pin (arrow) . . .

Later FZR750/1000 models

Refer to illustrations 11.11a, 11.11b, 11.12 and 11.14

11   Remove the cotter pin from the axle nut and loosen the nut **(see illustrations)**.

12   Loosen and back-off the locknuts on the adjuster bolts, then back-off the bolts **(see illustration)**.

13   Turn the axle adjusting bolts on both sides of the swingarm until the proper chain tension is obtained (get the adjuster on the chain side

11.11b . . . and loosen the axle nut with a socket or box wrench (ring spanner)

11.12 Loosen the locknut (arrow), then turn the adjusting bolt to change position of the chain adjuster

11.14 The marks on the swingarm behind the adjuster on each side of the bike (arrow) are used to adjust the chain evenly

12.4a Remove the oil pan drain plug (this is an FZR600) . . .

close, then set the adjuster on the opposite side). Be sure to turn the adjusting bolts evenly to keep the rear wheel in alignment. If the adjusting bolts reach the end of their travel, the chain is excessively worn and should be replaced with a new one (see Chapter 7).

14   When the chain has the correct amount of slack, make sure the marks on the adjusters correspond to the same relative marks on each side of the swingarm **(see illustration)**. Tighten the axle nut to the torque listed in the Chapter 8 Specifications, then install a new cotter pin and bend it properly **(see illustration 11.10)**. If necessary, turn the nut an additional amount to line up the cotter pin hole with the castellations in the nut - don't loosen the nut to do this.

All models

15   Tighten the chain adjuster locknuts securely.

Lubrication

Note: *If the chain is extremely dirty, it should be removed and cleaned before it's lubricated* (see Chapter 7).

16   The best time to lubricate the chain is after the motorcycle has been ridden. When the chain is warm, the lubricant will penetrate the joints between the side plates more easily. **Note**: *If the chain is dirty, remove and clean it (see Chapter 7). Yamaha specifies SAE 30 to SAE 50 engine oil only; do not use chain lube, which may contain solvents that could damage the O-rings. Apply the oil to the area where the side plates overlap - not the middle of the rollers. Apply the oil to the top of*

the lower chain run, so centrifugal force will work the oil into the chain when the bike is moving. After applying the lubricant, let it soak in a few minutes before wiping off any excess.

---

12   Engine oil/filter - change

Refer to illustrations 12.4a, 12.4b and 12.4c

1   Consistent routine oil and filter changes are the single most important maintenance procedure you can perform on a motorcycle. The oil not only lubricates the internal parts of the engine, transmission and clutch, but it also acts as a coolant, a cleaner, a sealant, and a protectant. Because of these demands, the oil takes a terrific amount of abuse and should be replaced often with new oil of the recommended grade and type. Saving a little money on the difference in cost between a good oil and a cheap oil won't pay off if the engine is damaged.

2   Before changing the oil and filter, warm up the engine so the oil will drain easily. Be careful when draining the oil, as the exhaust pipes, the engine, and the oil itself can cause severe burns.

3   Remove the oil filler cap to vent the crankcase and act as a reminder that there is no oil in the engine. Remove fairing panels as necessary for access (see Chapter 9). On FZR600 models with a cartridge filter, remove the exhaust pipes (see Chapter 5).

4   Support the motorcycle securely over a clean drain pan. Remove

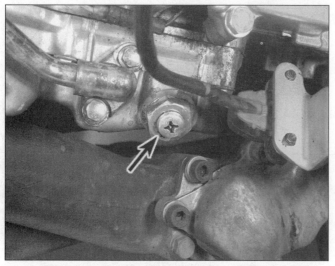

12.4b . . . and this is an FZR1000 (arrow) - FZR750 similar

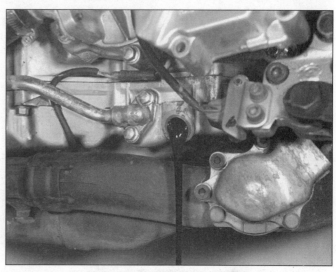

12.4c Let the oil drain completely

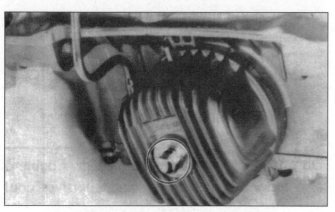

12.5 Remove the oil filter cover bolt (circled) . . .

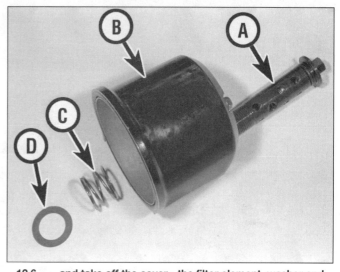

12.6 . . . and take off the cover - the filter element, washer and spring are inside

| A | Filter bolt | C | Spring |
| B | Cover | D | Washer |

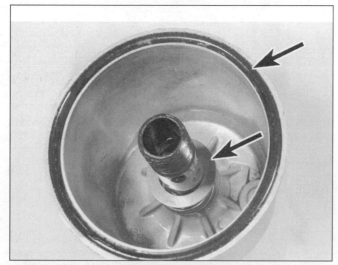

12.7 Remove the O-ring (upper arrow) from its groove - the washer (lower arrow) tends to stick to the old filter, so be sure not to throw it away accidentally

the drain plug from the engine **(see illustrations)** and allow the oil to drain into the pan **(see illustration)**. Discard the sealing washer on the drain plug; it should be replaced whenever the plug is removed.

Cartridge filter models

Refer to illustrations 12.5, 12.6, 12.7 and 12.11

5   Remove the oil filter bolt and take off the filter cover **(see illustration)**.

6   Remove the filter element, washer and spring from the cover **(see illustration)**.

7   Remove the O-ring from its groove in the cover **(see illustration)**.

8   Clean the filter cover and housing with solvent or clean rags. Make sure the holes in the filter bolt are clear. Wipe any remaining oil off the filter sealing area of the crankcase.

9   Clean the components and check them for damage - especially, be sure to check the spring for distortion. If any damage is found, replace the damaged part(s).

10   Check the condition of the drain plug threads and the sealing washer.

11   Install a new O-ring in the cover groove and make sure it's positioned securely **(see illustration 12.7)**. Install the spring, washer and filter element in the cover. Install the cover on the engine with the adjusting tab in the slot **(see illustration)** and tighten the bolt to the torque listed in this Chapter's Specifications.

12.11 Position the tab on the filter cover in the slot (arrow)

12.12a This tool is used to remove spin-on oil filters . . .

12.12b . . . you'll need an extension to reach between the exhaust pipes

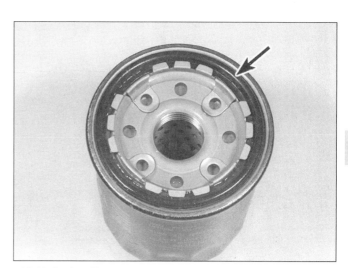

12.13 Apply a film of clean engine oil to the filter gasket (arrow)

Spin-on filter models

Refer to illustrations 12.12a, 12.12b and 12.13

12   Unscrew the filter element with a ratchet and filter wrench (Yamaha tool no. J-37140A/part no. 90890-04126 or equivalent) **(see illustrations)**. Let the oil drain from the filter adapter.

13   Apply a film of oil to the gasket on the new filter **(see illustration)**. Thread the filter onto the adapter and tighten it to the torque listed in this Chapter's Specifications.

All models

14   Slip a new sealing washer over the oil drain plug, then install and tighten it to the torque listed in this Chapter's Specifications. Avoid overtightening, as damage to the engine case will result.

15   Before refilling the engine, check the old oil carefully. If the oil was drained into a clean pan, small pieces of metal or other material can be easily detected. If the oil is very metallic colored, then the engine is experiencing wear from break-in (new engine) or from insufficient lubrication. If there are flakes or chips of metal in the oil, then something is drastically wrong internally and the engine will have to be disassembled for inspection and repair.

16   If there are pieces of fiber-like material in the oil, the clutch is experiencing excessive wear and should be checked.

17   If the inspection of the oil turns up nothing unusual, refill the crankcase to the proper level with the recommended oil and install the filler cap. Start the engine and let it run. If your working on an

FZR750/1000, slightly loosen (DO NOT remove) the oil gallery bolt at the upper corner of the cylinder head, just below and behind the half-circle cutout in the rear cam tower. Oil should seep out within one minute; if not, shut the engine off immediately so it won't seize. Shut it off, wait a few minutes, then check the oil level. If necessary, add more oil to bring the level up to the Maximum mark. Check around the drain plug and filter housing for leaks.

18   The old oil drained from the engine cannot be reused in its present state and should be disposed of. Check with your local refuse disposal company, disposal facility or environmental agency to see whether they will accept the used oil for recycling. Don't pour used oil into drains or onto the ground. After the oil has cooled, it can be drained into a suitable container (capped plastic jugs, topped bottles, milk cartons, etc.) for transport to one of these disposal sites.

13   Air filter element - servicing

Refer to illustrations 13.5a, 13.5b, 13.5c and 13.5d

1   Remove the seat.

2   If you're working on an FZR600, remove the top cover (see Chapter 9).

3   If you're working on a 1987 or 1988 model, remove the side covers (see Chapter 9) and fuel tank (see Chapter 5).

4   If you're working on a 1989 or later FZR750/1000, remove the fuel tank (see Chapter 5).

13.5a Remove the four cover screws (arrows) on FZR600 and UK 750 models . . .

13.5b . . . or the single screw (US750 and all 1000 models)

13.5c . . . and lift out the element; this is an FZR600
(UK 750 similar) . . .

13.5d . . . and this is an FZR1000 (US750 similar

5   Remove the cover screw(s) and lift off the housing cover **(see il-lustrations)**. Inspect the cover O-ring and replace it if it's damaged or deteriorated.
6   Lift out the filter and tap the element on a hard surface to shake out any dirt. If compressed air is available, use it to clean the element by blowing from the outside in. If the element is extremely dirty or torn, replace it with a new one.
7   Reinstall the filter by reversing the removal procedure. Make sure the element is seated properly in the filter housing before installing the cover.
8   Install all components removed for access.

---

14   Cylinder compression - check

Refer to illustrations 14.8 and 14.9
1   Among other things, poor engine performance may be caused by leaking valves, incorrect valve clearances, a leaking head gasket, or worn pistons, rings and/or cylinder walls. A cylinder compression check will help pinpoint these conditions and can also indicate the presence of excessive carbon deposits in the cylinder heads.
2   The only tools required are a compression gauge and a spark plug wrench. Depending on the outcome of the initial test, a squirt-type oil can may also be needed.
3   Start the engine and allow it to reach normal operating

temperature.
4   Support the bike securely so it can't be knocked over during this procedure.
5   Remove fairing panels as necessary for access to the spark plug holes (see Chapter 9).
6   Remove the spark plugs (see Section 15, if necessary). Work carefully - don't strip the spark plug hole threads and don't burn your hands.
7   Disable the ignition by unplugging the primary wires from the coils (see Chapter 6). Be sure to mark the locations of the wires before de-taching them.
8   Install the compression gauge in one of the spark plug holes **(see illustration)**.
9   Hold or block the throttle wide open **(see illustration)**.
10   Crank the engine over a minimum of four or five revolutions (or until the gauge reading stops increasing) and observe the initial move-ment of the compression gauge needle as well as the final total gauge reading. Repeat the procedure for the other cylinders and compare the results to the value listed in this Chapter's Specifications.
11   If the compression in all four cylinders built up quickly and evenly to the specified amount, you can assume the engine upper end is in reasonably good mechanical condition. Worn or sticking piston rings and worn cylinders will produce very little initial movement of the gauge needle, but compression will tend to build up gradually as the engine spins over. Valve and valve seat leakage, or head gasket leak-age, is indicated by low initial compression which does not tend to

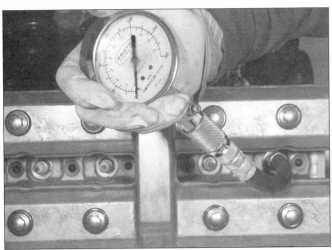

14.8 A compression gauge with a threaded fitting for the spark plug hole is preferred over the type that requires hand pressure to maintain the seal

14.9 Twist the throttle wide open while you crank the engine

15.3a Rotate the spark plug caps back and forth to loosen them, then pull them off the plugs and check them for brittleness and cracking

15.3b Use an extension and a deep socket (preferably one with a rubber insert to prevent damage to the plug) to remove the spark plugs

build up.

12   To further confirm your findings, add a small amount of engine oil to each cylinder by inserting the nozzle of a squirt-type oil can through the spark plug holes. The oil will tend to seal the piston rings if they are leaking. Repeat the test for the other cylinders.

13   If the compression increases significantly after the addition of the oil, the piston rings and/or cylinders are definitely worn. If the compression does not increase, the pressure is leaking past the valves or the head gasket. Leakage past the valves may be due to insufficient valve clearances, burned, warped or cracked valves or valve seats or valves that are hanging up in the guides.

14   If compression readings are considerably higher than specified, the combustion chambers are probably coated with excessive carbon deposits. It is possible (but not very likely) for carbon deposits to raise the compression enough to compensate for the effects of leakage past rings or valves. Remove the cylinder head and carefully decarbonize the combustion chambers (see Chapter 2 or 3).

15 Spark plugs - replacement

Refer to illustrations 15.3a, 15.3b, 15.7a and 15.7b

1   Make sure your spark plug socket is the correct size before at-

tempting to remove the plugs.

2   Remove fairing components as necessary for access to the plugs (see Chapter 9).

3   Disconnect the spark plug caps from the spark plugs **(see illustration)**. If available, use compressed air to blow any accumulated debris from around the spark plugs. Remove the plugs **(see illustration)**.

4   Inspect the electrodes for wear. Both the center and side electrodes should have square edges and the side electrode should be of uniform thickness. Look for excessive deposits and evidence of a cracked or chipped insulator around the center electrode. Compare your spark plugs to the color spark plug reading chart. Check the threads, the washer and the ceramic insulator body for cracks and other damage.

5   If the electrodes are not excessively worn, and if the deposits can be easily removed with a wire brush, the plugs can be regapped and reused (if no cracks or chips are visible in the insulator). If in doubt concerning the condition of the plugs, replace them with new ones, as the expense is minimal.

6   Cleaning spark plugs by sandblasting is permitted, provided you clean the plugs with a high flash-point solvent afterwards.

7   Before installing new plugs, make sure they are the correct type and heat range. Check the gap between the electrodes, as they are not preset. For best results, use a wire-type gauge rather than a flat gauge

15.7a Spark plug manufacturers recommend using a wire type gauge when checking the gap - if the wire doesn't slide between the electrodes with a slight drag, adjustment is required

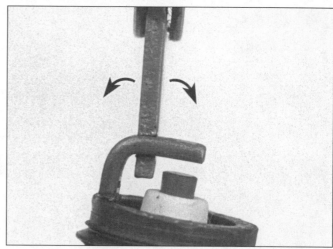

15.7b To change the gap, bend the side electrode only, as indicated by the arrows, and be very careful not to crack or chip the ceramic insulator surrounding the center electrode

16.2a Lubricate the front footpegs and the brake pedal at their pivot points . . .

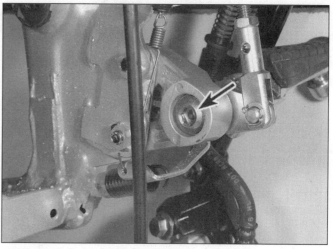

16.2b . . . to lubricate the brake pedal, remove the retaining bolt (arrow)

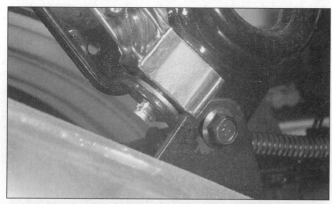

16.2c Lubricate the rear footpegs at their pivot points1

to check the gap **(see illustration)**. If the gap must be adjusted, bend the side electrode only and be very careful not to chip or crack the insulator nose **(see illustration)**. Make sure the washer is in place before installing each plug.

8   Since the cylinder head is made of aluminum, which is soft and easily damaged, thread the plugs into the heads by hand. Since the

plugs are recessed, slip a short length of hose over the end of the plug to use as a tool to thread it into place. The hose will grip the plug well enough to turn it, but will start to slip if the plug begins to cross-thread in the hole - this will prevent damaged threads and the accompanying repair costs.

9   Once the plugs are finger-tight, the job can be finished with a socket. If a torque wrench is available, tighten the spark plugs to the torque listed in this Chapter's Specifications. If you do not have a torque wrench, tighten the plugs finger-tight (until the washers bottom on the cylinder head) then use a wrench to tighten them an additional 1/4 turn. Regardless of the method used, do not over-tighten them.

10   Reconnect the spark plug caps and reinstall all removed components.

---

16   Lubrication - general

Refer to illustrations 16.2a through 16.2e and 16.3

1   Since the controls, cables and various other components of a motorcycle are exposed to the elements, they should be lubricated periodically to ensure safe and trouble-free operation.

2   The footpegs, clutch and brake lever, brake pedal, shift lever and sidestand pivots should be lubricated frequently **(see illustrations)**. In

Spark plug maintenance: Checking plug gap with feeler gauges

Altering the plug gap. Note use of correct tool

Spark plug conditions: A brown, tan or grey firing end is indicative of correct engine running conditions and the selection of the appropriate heat rating plug

White deposits have accumulated from excessive amounts of oil in the combustion chamber or through the use of low quality oil. Remove deposits or a hot spot may form

Black sooty deposits indicate an over-rich fuel/air mixture, or a malfunctioning ignition system. If no improvement is obtained, try one grade hotter plug

Wet, oily carbon deposits form an electrical leakage path along the insulator nose, resulting in a misfire. The cause may be a badly worn engine or a malfunctioning ignition system

A blistered white insulator or melted electrode indicates over-advanced ignition timing or a malfunctioning cooling system. If correction does not prove effective, try a colder grade plug

A worn spark plug not only wastes fuel but also overloads the whole ignition system because the increased gap requires higher voltage to initiate the spark. This condition can also affect air pollution

16.2d Lubricate the front brake lever at its pivot point, then lubricate the clutch lever in the same way

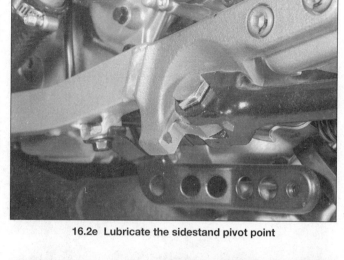

16.2e Lubricate the sidestand pivot point

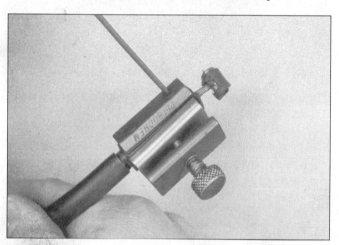

16.3 Lubricating a cable with a pressure lube adapter (make sure the tool seats around the inner cable)

17.9a The line next to the T mark on the alternator rotor must be exactly aligned with the crankcase seam (arrows) . . .

order for the lubricant to be applied where it will do the most good, the component should be disassembled. However, if chain and cable lubricant is being used, it can be applied to the pivot joint gaps and will usually work its way into the areas where friction occurs. If motor oil or light grease is being used, apply it sparingly as it may attract dirt (which could cause the controls to bind or wear at an accelerated rate). **Note**: *One of the best lubricants for the control lever pivots is a dry-film lubricant (available from many sources by different names).*

3   To lubricate the throttle and choke cables, disconnect the cable(s) at the lower end, then lubricate the cable with a pressure lube adapter **(see illustration)**. See Chapter 3 for the choke cable removal procedure. **Note**: *Yamaha recommends that the throttle twist grip be disassembled and lubricated whenever the throttle cables are lubricated. Refer to the handlebars section of Chapter 7.*

4   The speedometer cable should be removed from its housing and lubricated with motor oil or cable lubricant.

5   Refer to Chapter 7 for the swingarm needle bearing and rear suspension linkage lubrication procedures.

---

17   Valve clearances - check and adjustment

1   The engine must be completely cool for this maintenance procedure, so let the machine sit overnight before beginning.

2   Disconnect the cable from the negative terminal of the battery.

3   Refer to Chapter 9 and remove the seat. Remove fairing panels as necessary for access.

4   Remove the air filter housing (see Chapter 5).

5   If you're working on an FZR600, remove the top covers, unbolt the fuel tank, lift it up enough to provide access and support it in that position. If you're working on an FZR750/1000, remove the fuel tank.

6   Remove the radiator (see Chapter 4).

7   Remove the oil cooler (if equipped) and the valve cover (see Chapter 2 or Chapter 3).

FZR600 models

Refer to illustrations 17.9a, 17.9b, 17.9c, 17.11, 17.21a, 17.21b, 17.21c, 17.21d, 17.23a and 17.23b

8   Remove the alternator cover from the left side of the engine (see Chapter 10).

9   Position the number 1 piston (on the left side of the engine) at Top Dead Center (TDC) on the compression stroke. Do this by turning the crankshaft, with a socket placed on the alternator rotor bolt, until the line next to the T mark on the rotor is aligned with the crankcase seam and the punch marks on the camshafts align with the marks on the cam bearing caps **(see illustrations)**. Now, check the position of the no. 1 cylinder cam lobes - they should be pointing away from each other **(see illustration)**. Piston number 1 is now at TDC compression. **Note**: *Turn the engine in the normal direction of rotation (counterclockwise (anti-clockwise), viewed from the signal generator end).*

10   With the engine in this position, all of the valves for cylinder no. 1 can be checked.

11   Start with the no. 1 intake valve clearance. Insert a feeler gauge of the thickness listed in this Chapter's Specifications between each cam lobe and its lifter **(see illustration)**. Pull the feeler gauge out slowly -

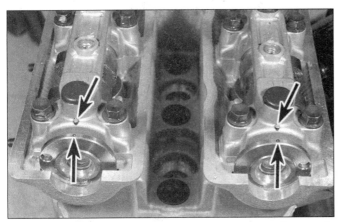

17.9b . . . and the punch marks on the camshafts must be exactly aligned with the cast marks on the bearing caps (arrows); if the crankcase seam and rotor mark are lined up but the camshaft marks aren't, turn the crankshaft exactly one full turn

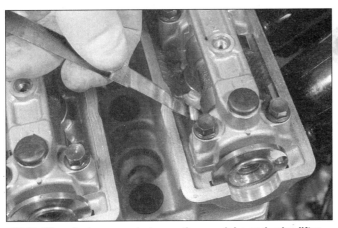

17.11 Slip a feeler gauge between the cam lobe and valve lifter - it should pull out with a very light drag

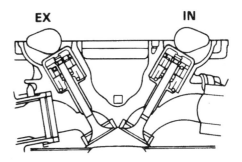

17.9c Make sure the cam lobes for no. 1 cylinder point away from each other as shown - if the cam lobes aren't in this position, no. 4 cylinder is at TDC on the compression stroke; turn the crankshaft exactly one full turn to bring no. 1 cylinder to TDC

17.21a Pull the lifter out with a magnet (use a suction cup if it's stuck) . . .

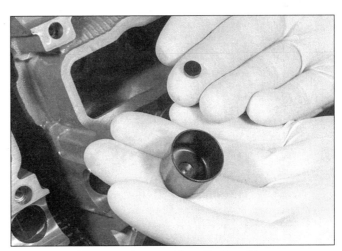

17.21b . . . and remove the adjusting shim . . .

you should feel a slight drag. If there's no drag, the clearance is too loose. If there's a heavy drag, the clearance is too tight.

12   If the clearance is incorrect, write down the actual measured clearance. You'll need this information later to select a new valve adjusting shim.

13   Now measure the no. 1 exhaust valves, following the same procedure you used for the intake valves. Make sure to use a feeler gauge of the specified thickness and write down the actual clearances of any valves that aren't within the Specifications.

14   Rotate the crankshaft exactly one-half turn to place piston no. 2 at TDC compression. The cam lobes for no. 2 cylinder should now point away from each other (see illustration 17.9c).

15   Measure the clearances of all four valves on cylinder no. 2 and write down any that aren't within the Specifications.

16   Turn the engine exactly one-half turn again to place cylinder no. 4 at TDC. The alternator rotor mark will align with the crankcase seam (see illustration 17.9a) and the no. 4 cam lobes will be pointing away from each other (see illustration 17.9c). The punch marks on the camshafts will be straight down, so they won't be visible. Measure the valve clearances for all four valves on no. 4 cylinder and write them down.

17   Turn the engine exactly one-half turn again to place cylinder no. 3 at TDC (its cam lobes facing away from each other) and measure its valve clearances.

18   If any of the clearances need to be adjusted, go to Step 19. If all the clearances were within the Specifications, no adjustment is necessary; reinstall all removed components and be sure to refill the cooling system.

19   Remove the camshafts (see Chapter 2). **Caution:** *Follow the procedure in Chapter 2 carefully to prevent breaking a cam bearing cap. If a cap breaks, it may be necessary to replace the entire cylinder head. Be sure to wire the cam chain up so it doesn't fall down off the crankshaft sprocket. Also, pack clean shop rags into the timing chain cavity so the valve lifters don't fall into the crankcase when they're removed.*

20   Make a holder to keep the lifters in order so they can be returned to their original bores.

21   Remove the lifter for each valve to be adjusted with a magnet (see illustrations).

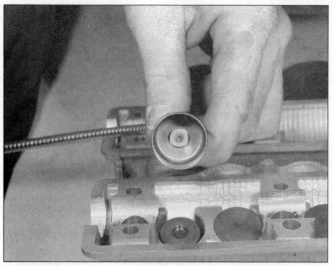

17.21c ... the shim may be held on the underside of the lifter by the magnet ...

17.21d ... there's a thickness mark on the top of each valve shim (be sure to place the marked side of the shim upward during installation)

INTAKE

B MEASURED CLEARANCE	A INSTALLED PAD NUMBER																								
	120	125	130	135	140	145	150	155	160	165	170	175	180	185	190	195	200	205	210	215	220	225	230	235	240
0.00~0.02				120	125	130	135	140	145	150	155	160	165	170	175	180	185	190	195	200	205	210	215	220	225
0.03~0.07			120	125	130	135	140	145	150	155	160	165	170	175	180	185	190	195	200	205	210	215	220	225	230
0.08~0.10		120	125	130	135	140	145	150	155	160	165	170	175	180	185	190	195	200	205	210	215	220	225	230	235
0.11~0.20	RECOMMENDED CLEARANCE																								
0.21~0.22	125	130	135	140	145	150	155	160	165	170	175	180	185	190	195	200	205	210	215	220	225	230	235	240	
0.23~0.27	130	135	140	145	150	155	160	165	170	175	180	185	190	195	200	205	210	215	220	225	230	235	240		
0.28~0.32	135	140	145	150	155	160	165	170	175	180	185	190	195	200	205	210	215	220	225	230	235	240			
0.33~0.37	140	145	150	155	160	165	170	175	180	185	190	195	200	205	210	215	220	225	230	235	240				
0.38~0.42	145	150	155	160	165	170	175	180	185	190	195	200	205	210	215	220	225	230	235	240					
0.43~0.47	150	155	160	165	170	175	180	185	190	195	200	205	210	215	220	225	230	235	240						
0.48~0.52	155	160	165	170	175	180	185	190	195	200	205	210	215	220	225	230	235	240							
0.53~0.57	160	165	170	175	180	185	190	195	200	205	210	215	220	225	230	235	240								
0.58~0.62	165	170	175	180	185	190	195	200	205	210	215	220	225	230	235	240									
0.63~0.67	170	175	180	185	190	195	200	205	210	215	220	225	230	235	240										
0.68~0.72	175	180	185	190	195	200	205	210	215	220	225	230	235	240											
0.73~0.77	180	185	190	195	200	205	210	215	220	225	230	235	240												
0.78~0.82	185	190	195	200	205	210	215	220	225	230	235	240													
0.83~0.87	190	195	200	205	210	215	220	225	230	235	240														
0.88~0.92	195	200	205	210	215	220	225	230	235	240															
0.93~0.97	200	205	210	215	220	225	230	235	240																
0.98~1.02	205	210	215	220	225	230	235	240																	
1.03~1.07	210	215	220	225	230	235	240																		
1.08~1.12	215	220	225	230	235	240																			
1.13~1.17	220	225	230	235	240																				
1.18~1.22	225	230	235	240																					
1.23~1.27	230	235	240																						
1.28~1.32	235	240																							
1.33~1.37	240																								

EXAMPLE:

VALVE CLEARANCE (cold):

0.11 ~ 0.20 mm (0.004 ~ 0.008 in)

Installed is 148 (Rounded off number is 150)

Measured clearance is 0.24 mm (0.009 in)

Replace 148 pad with 160 pad

17.23a Intake valve shim selection chart

22   Determine the thickness of the shim you removed. It should be marked on the top of the shim (see illustration 17.21d). The number indicates the shim thickness in hundredths of a millimeter. For example, the shim marked 170 in illustration 17.21d is 1.70 mm thick. The ideal way to judge shim thickness is to measure it with a micrometer. **Note**: *If the number on the shim does not end in 0 or 5, round it off to the nearest zero or 5. For example, if the number on the shim is 179,* *round it off to 180. If it's 234, round it off to 235.*

23   If the measured clearance was too large, you need a thicker shim. If the clearance was too small, you need a thinner shim. Calculate the thickness of the replacement shim by referring to the accompanying charts (see illustrations).

24   Install the new shims and recheck the clearance. If they're within the Specifications, the valves are properly adjusted.

EXHAUST

B MEASURED CLEARANCE	A INSTALLED PAD NUMBER																								
	120	125	130	135	140	145	150	155	160	165	170	175	180	185	190	195	200	205	210	215	220	225	230	235	240
0.00~0.02						120	125	130	135	140	145	150	155	160	165	170	175	180	185	190	195	200	205	210	215
0.03~0.07					120	125	130	135	140	145	150	155	160	165	170	175	180	185	190	195	200	205	210	215	220
0.08~0.12				120	125	130	135	140	145	150	155	160	165	170	175	180	185	190	195	200	205	210	215	220	225
0.13~0.17			120	125	130	135	140	145	150	155	160	165	170	175	180	185	190	195	200	205	210	215	220	225	230
0.18~0.20		120	125	130	135	140	145	150	155	160	165	170	175	180	185	190	195	200	205	210	215	220	225	230	235
0.21~0.30	RECOMMENDED CLEARANCE																								
0.31~0.32	125	130	135	140	145	150	155	160	165	170	175	180	185	190	195	200	205	210	215	220	225	230	235	240	
0.33~0.37	130	135	140	145	150	155	160	165	170	175	180	185	190	195	200	205	210	215	220	225	230	235	240		
0.38~0.42	135	140	145	150	155	160	165	170	175	180	185	190	195	200	205	210	215	220	225	230	235	240			
0.43~0.47	140	145	150	155	160	165	170	175	180	185	190	195	200	205	210	215	220	225	230	235	240				
0.48~0.52	145	150	155	160	165	170	175	180	185	190	195	200	205	210	215	220	225	230	235	240					
0.53~0.57	150	155	160	165	170	175	180	185	190	195	200	205	210	215	220	225	230	235	240						
0.58~0.62	155	160	165	170	175	180	185	190	195	200	205	210	215	220	225	230	235	240							
0.63~0.67	160	165	170	175	180	185	190	195	200	205	210	215	220	225	230	235	240								
0.68~0.72	165	170	175	180	185	190	195	200	205	210	215	220	225	230	235	240									
0.73~0.77	170	175	180	185	190	195	200	205	210	215	220	225	230	235	240										
0.78~0.82	175	180	185	190	195	200	205	210	215	220	225	230	235	240											
0.83~0.87	180	185	190	195	200	205	210	215	220	225	230	235	240												
0.88~0.92	185	190	195	200	205	210	215	220	225	230	235	240													
0.93~0.97	190	195	200	205	210	215	220	225	230	235	240														
0.98~1.02	195	200	205	210	215	220	225	230	235	240															
1.03~1.07	200	205	210	215	220	225	230	235	240																
1.08~1.12	205	210	215	220	225	230	235	240																	
1.13~1.17	210	215	220	225	230	235	240																		
1.18~1.22	215	220	225	230	235	240																			
1.23~1.27	220	225	230	235	240																				
1.28~1.32	225	230	235	240																					
1.33~1.37	230	235	240																						
1.38~1.42	235	240																							
1.43~1.47	240																								

EXAMPLE:

VALVE CLEARANCE (cold):
0.21 ~ 0.30 mm (0.008 ~ 0.012 in)
Installed is 175
Measured clearance is 0.35 mm (0.014 in)
Replace 175 pad with 185 pad

17.23b Exhaust valve shim selection chart

17.25a Remove the cover from the timing window . . .

17.25b . . . remove the screws that secure the left crankshaft end cover . . .

17.25c . . . and lift the cover off

FZR750/1000 models

Refer to illustrations 17.25a, 17.25b, 17.25c, 17.26, 17.27a, 17.27b, 17.29a and 17.29b

25   Remove the timing window cover and crankshaft end cover from the left side of the engine **(see illustrations)**.

26   Install a timing rotor and dowel on the end of the crankshaft **(see illustration)**. This special tool consists of three parts:
   a) Timing rotor (part no. 33M-81673-10)
   b) Dowel pin (part no. 93604-08071)
   c) 8 mm bolt (part no. 91316-08030)
The timing rotor isn't used to indicate crankshaft position; it's simply a means of turning the engine by hand.

27   Position the number 1 piston (on the left side of the engine) at Top Dead Center (TDC) on the compression stroke. Do this by turning the crankshaft, with a wrench placed on the timing rotor flats, until the pointer inside the timing window is aligned with the line next to the T mark on the crankshaft web and the cam lobes for no. 1 cylinder point

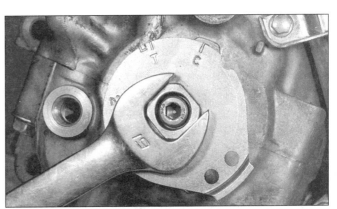

17.26 This special Yamaha tool provides a way to turn the engine in its normal direction of rotation; place a wrench on the square section (DO NOT use the timing marks on the timing plate)

17.27a This pointer inside the timing window (arrow) must be aligned with the line next to the T mark on the crankshaft web . . .

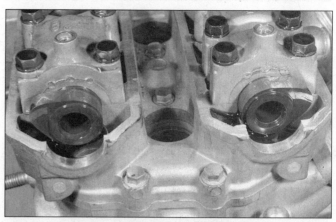

17.27b . . . and the cam lobes for no. 1 cylinder must be pointing away from each other like this; if the cam lobes are in a different position, turn the crankshaft one full turn

17.29a You'll need tapered feeler gauges like this one to fit between the bolt bosses on the cam bearing caps

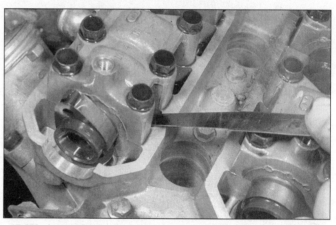

17.29b Insert the feeler gauge blade between the camshaft and lifter to measure the clearance

away from each other **(see illustrations)**. Piston number 1 is now at TDC compression. **Note**: *Turn the engine in the normal direction of rotation (counterclockwise (anti-clockwise), viewed from the left end).*

28   With the engine in this position, all of the valves for cylinder no. 1 can be checked.

29   Start with the no. 1 intake valve clearance. Insert a tapered feeler gauge of the thickness listed in this Chapter's Specifications between each cam lobe and its lifter **(see illustrations)**. Pull the feeler gauge out slowly - you should feel a slight drag. If there's no drag, the clearance is too loose. If there's a heavy drag, the clearance is too tight.

30   If the clearance is incorrect, write down the actual measured clearance. You'll need this information later to select a new valve adjusting shim.

31   Now measure the no. 1 exhaust valves, following the same procedure you used for the intake valves. Make sure to use a feeler gauge of the specified thickness and write down the actual clearances of any valves that aren't within the Specifications.

32   Rotate the crankshaft exactly one-half turn to place piston no. 2 at TDC compression. The cam lobes for no. 2 cylinder should now point away from each other **(see illustration 17.9c)**.

33   Measure the clearances of all five valves on cylinder no. 2 and write down any that aren't within the Specifications.

34   Turn the engine exactly one-half turn again to place cylinder no. 4 at TDC. The T mark line will align with the timing window pointer **(see illustration 17.27a)** and the no. 4 cam lobes will be pointing away from each other **(see illustration 17.9c)**. Measure the valve clearances for all five valves on no. 4 cylinder and write them down.

35   Turn the engine exactly one-half turn again to place cylinder no. 3 at TDC (its cam lobes facing away from each other) and measure its valve clearances.

36   If any of the clearances need to be adjusted, go to Step 37. If all the clearances were within the Specifications, no adjustment is necessary; reinstall all removed components and be sure to refill the cooling system.

37   Remove the camshafts (see Chapter 3). **Caution**: *Follow the procedure in Chapter 3 carefully to prevent breaking a cam bearing cap. If a cap breaks, it may be necessary to replace the entire cylinder head. Be sure to wire the cam chain up so it doesn't fall down off the crankshaft sprocket. Also, pack clean shop rags into the timing chain cavity so the valve lifters don't fall into the crankcase when they're removed.*

38   Make a holder to keep the lifters in order so they can be returned to their original bores.

39   Remove the lifter for each valve to be adjusted with a magnet **(see illustrations 17.21a, 17.21b, 17.21c and 17.21d)**.

40   Determine the thickness of the shim you removed. It should be marked on the top of the shim **(see illustration 17.21d)**. The number indicates the shim thickness in hundredths of a millimeter. For example, the shim marked 170 in illustration 17.21d is 1.70 mm thick. The ideal way to judge shim thickness is to measure it with a micrometer. **Note**: *If the number on the shim does not end in 0 or 5, round it off to the nearest zero or 5. For example, if the number on the shim is 179, round it off to 180. If it's 234, round it off to 235.*

41   If the measured clearance was too large, you need a thicker shim. If the clearance was too small, you need a thinner shim. Calculate the thickness of the replacement shim by referring to the accompanying charts **(see illustrations 17.23a and 17.23b)**.

42   Install the new shims and recheck the clearance. If they're within the Specifications, the valves are properly adjusted. Reinstall all removed components and refill the cooling system.

18.3a Turn the throttle stop screw (arrow) in or out until the correct idle speed is obtained (this is an FZR600) . . .

18.3b . . . and this is an FZR1000 (FZR750 similar) (arrow)

18   Idle speed - check and adjustment

Refer to illustrations 18.3a and 18.3b

1   The idle speed should be checked and adjusted before and after the carburetors are synchronized and when it is obviously too high or too low. Before adjusting the idle speed, make sure the valve clearances and spark plug gaps are correct. Also, turn the handlebars back-and-forth and see if the idle speed changes as this is done. If it does, the accelerator cable may not be routed correctly, or it may be worn out. This is a dangerous condition that can cause loss of control of the bike. Be sure to correct this problem before proceeding.

2   The engine should be at normal operating temperature, which is usually reached after 10 to 15 minutes of stop and go riding. Support the motorcycle securely and make sure the transmission is in Neutral.

3   Turn the throttle stop screw **(see illustrations)**, until the idle speed listed in this Chapter's Specifications is obtained.

4   Snap the throttle open and shut a few times, then recheck the idle speed. If necessary, repeat the adjustment procedure.

5   If a smooth, steady idle can't be achieved, the fuel/air mixture may be incorrect. Refer to Chapter 5 for additional carburetor information.

19   Carburetor synchronization - check and adjustment

Refer to illustrations 19.9a, 19.9b, 19.12, 19.13 and 19.14

Warning: *Gasoline (petrol) is extremely flammable, so take extra precautions when you work on any part of the fuel system. Don't smoke or allow open flames or bare light bulbs near the work area, and don't work in a garage where a natural gas-type appliance (such as a water heater or clothes dryer) is present. If you spill any fuel on your skin, rinse it off immediately with soap and water. When you perform any kind of work on the fuel system, wear safety glasses and have a class B type fire extinguisher on hand.*

1   Carburetor synchronization is simply the process of adjusting the carburetors so they pass the same amount of fuel/air mixture to each cylinder. This is done by measuring the vacuum produced in each cylinder. Carburetors that are out of synchronization will result in decreased fuel mileage, increased engine temperature, less than ideal throttle response and higher vibration levels.

2   To properly synchronize the carburetors, you will need some sort of vacuum gauge setup, preferably with a gauge for each cylinder, or a mercury manometer, which is a calibrated tube arrangement that utilizes columns of mercury to indicate engine vacuum. You'll also need an auxiliary fuel tank, since the bike's fuel tank must be removed for access to the vacuum fittings and synchronizing screws.

3   A manometer can be purchased from a motorcycle dealer or ac-

cessory shop and should have the necessary rubber hoses supplied with it for hooking into the vacuum hose fittings on the carburetors.

4   A vacuum gauge setup can also be purchased from a dealer or fabricated from commonly available hardware and automotive vacuum gauges.

5   The manometer is the more reliable and accurate instrument, and for that reason is preferred over the vacuum gauge setup; however, since the mercury used in the manometer is a liquid, and extremely toxic, extra precautions must be taken during use and storage of the instrument.

6   Because of the nature of the synchronization procedure and the need for special instruments, most owners leave the task to a dealer service department or a reputable motorcycle repair shop.

7   Remove the side covers, seat and fuel tank (see Chapters 9 and 5).

8   Start the engine and let it run until it reaches normal operating temperature, then shut it off.

9   Remove the screws from the vacuum ports on the carburetors and install vacuum fittings **(see illustration)**, then hook up the vacuum gauge set or the manometer according to the manufacturer's instructions **(see illustration)**. Make sure there are no leaks in the setup, as false readings will result.

10   Start the engine and make sure the idle speed is correct. If it isn't, adjust it (see Section 18).

11   The vacuum readings for all of the cylinders should be the same, or at least within the tolerance listed in this Chapter's Specifications. If the vacuum readings vary, adjust as necessary.

19.9a Remove the vacuum hoses or screws and install fittings like this one . . .

19.9b . . . so a test gauge setup like this can be installed

19.12 Turn this screw (arrow) to synchronize carburetors no. 1 and 2 to each other (it's located between the two left-hand carburetors)

12   To perform the adjustment, synchronize the carburetors for no. 1 and no. 2 cylinders by turning the synchronizing screw, as needed, until the vacuum is identical or nearly identical for both cylinders **(see illustration)**. Snap the throttle open and shut 2 or 3 times, then recheck the adjustment and readjust as necessary.

13   Next synchronize the carburetors for no. 3 and no. 4 cylinders to each other by turning the synchronizing screw for those two carburetors **(see illustration)**. As with the no. 1 and no. 2 carburetors, snap the throttle open and shut 2 or 3 times, then recheck the adjustment and readjust as necessary.

14   Finally, turn the center synchronizing screw to synchronize the two pairs of carburetors to each other **(see illustration)**.

15   When the adjustment is complete, recheck the vacuum readings and idle speed, then stop the engine. Remove the vacuum gauge or manometer and install the screws or carburetor vacuum hoses.

20   Crankcase ventilation system - inspection

Inspect the hose that runs from the ventilation fitting on the top of the engine to the air filter case. Make sure it's securely attached. Replace the hose if it's cracked or deteriorated.

21   Exhaust system - check

1   Periodically check all of the exhaust system joints for leaks and

loose fasteners. The lower fairing(s) will have to be removed to do this properly (see Chapter 9). If tightening the clamp bolts fails to stop any leaks, replace the gaskets with new ones (a procedure which requires disassembly of the system - see Chapter 5).

2   The exhaust pipe flange nuts at the cylinder heads are especially prone to loosening, which could cause damage to the head. Check them frequently and keep them tight.

22   Steering head bearings - check, adjustment and repacking

1   This vehicle is equipped with tapered roller type steering head bearings which can become dented, rough or loose during normal use of the machine. In extreme cases, worn or loose steering head bearings can cause steering wobble that is potentially dangerous.

Check

Refer to illustration 22.4

2   To check the bearings, support the motorcycle securely and block the machine so the front wheel is in the air.

3   Point the wheel straight ahead and slowly move the handlebars from side-to-side. Dents or roughness in the bearing races will be felt and the bars will not move smoothly.

4   Next, grasp the wheel and try to move it forward and backward **(see illustration)**. Any looseness in the steering head bearings will be felt as front-to-rear movement of the fork legs. If play is felt in the bearings, adjust the steering head as follows:

19.13 Turn this screw (arrow) to synchronize carburetors no. 3 and 4 to each other (it's located between the two right-hand carburetors)

19.14 Turn this screw (arrow) to synchronize the two pairs of carburetors to each other (it's located in the center of the carburetor assembly)

22.4 Grasp the front wheel and try to pull it back and forth; if it moves, the steering head bearings are loose and in need of adjustment

22.5a Loosen the lower triple clamp bolt or bolts on each fork; this is an FZR600 . . .

22.5b . . . and this is an FZR1000

22.7 Remove the lockwasher from the ring nuts

Adjustment

Refer to illustrations 22.5a, 22.5b, 22.7, 22.8a and 22.8b

5 Loosen the lower triple clamp bolts **(see illustrations)**. This allows the necessary vertical movement of the steering stem in relation to the fork tubes.

6 Remove the handlebars and upper triple clamp (see Chapter 7).

7 Remove the lockwasher from the ring nuts **(see illustration)**.

8 Use a ring nut wrench (Yamaha tool no. YU-33975/part no. 90890-01430 or equivalent) to remove the upper ring nut and rubber washer **(see illustrations)**.

9 Carefully tighten the lower ring nut to the initial torque listed in this Chapter's Specifications, then loosen it all the way and retighten to the final torque listed in this Chapter's Specifications.

10 Turn the steering from lock to lock and check for binding. If there is any, remove the bearings for inspection (see Chapter 7).

11 If the steering operates properly, install the rubber washer and upper ring nut. Tighten the upper ring nut so its slots align with those of

22.8a Use a ring nut wrench like this one to loosen the upper ring nut . . .

22.8b . . . then unscrew the upper ring nut and remove the washer from beneath it (arrow)

24.6 Fuel filter details (FZR600 shown; others similar)

25.3 Check above and below the fork seals (arrows) for signs of oil leakage

the lower ring nut (don't allow the lower ring nut to turn). If necessary, use the ring nut wrench to keep the lower ring nut from turning while you tighten the upper ring nut.

12   Install the lockwasher with its tabs in the ring nut slots.

13   Recheck the steering head bearings for play as described above. If necessary, repeat the adjustment procedure. Reinstall all parts previously removed. Tighten the steering stem nut, triple clamp bolts and handlebar bolts to the torques listed in the Chapter 7 Specifications.

Lubrication

14   Periodic cleaning and repacking of the steering head bearings is recommended by the manufacturer. Refer to Chapter 7 for steering head bearing lubrication and replacement procedures.

23   Fasteners - check

1   Since vibration of the machine tends to loosen fasteners, all nuts, bolts, screws, etc. should be periodically checked for proper tightness.
2   Pay particular attention to the following:
   Spark plugs
   Engine oil drain plug
   Oil filter cover bolt and drain plug
   Gearshift lever
   Footpegs, sidestand and centerstand
   Engine mount bolts
   Exhaust system mounts
   Shock absorber mount bolts
   Rear suspension linkage bolts
   Front axle and clamp bolt
   Rear axle nut
3   If a torque wrench is available, use it along with the torque specifications at the beginning of this, or other, Chapters.

24   Fuel system - check and filter replacement

Warning: *Gasoline (petrol) is extremely flammable, so take extra precautions when you work on any part of the fuel system. Don't smoke or allow open flames or bare light bulbs near the work area, and don't work in a garage where a natural gas-type appliance (such as a water heater or clothes dryer) is present. If you spill any fuel on your skin, rinse it off immediately with soap and water. When you perform any kind of work on the fuel system, wear safety glasses and have a class B type fire extinguisher on hand.*

Check

1   Check the fuel tank, the tank breather hose, the fuel tap, the lines and the carburetors for leaks and evidence of damage.
2   If carburetor gaskets are leaking, the carburetors should be disassembled and rebuilt (see Chapter 5).
3   If the fuel tap is leaking, tightening the screws may help. If leakage persists, the tap should be disassembled and repaired or replaced with a new one.
4   If the fuel lines are cracked or otherwise deteriorated, replace them with new ones.

Filter replacement

Refer to illustration 24.6
5   Remove the fuel tank (see Chapter 5).
6   Disconnect the lines from the filter and remove it from its bracket **(see illustration)**.
7   Install a new filter and reconnect the lines.

25   Suspension - check

Refer to illustration 25.3
1   The suspension components must be maintained in top operating condition to ensure rider safety. Loose, worn or damaged suspension parts decrease the vehicle's stability and control.
2   While standing alongside the motorcycle, lock the front brake and push on the handlebars to compress the forks several times. See if they move up-and-down smoothly without binding. If binding is felt, the forks should be disassembled and inspected as described in Chapter 7.
3   Carefully inspect the area around the fork seals for any signs of fork oil leakage **(see illustration)**. If leakage is evident, the seals must be replaced as described in Chapter 7.
4   Check the tightness of all suspension nuts and bolts to be sure none have worked loose.
5   Inspect the rear shock for fluid leakage and tightness of the mounting nuts. If leakage is found, the shock should be replaced.
6   Support the bike securely so it can't be knocked over during this procedure. Grab the swingarm on each side, just ahead of the axle. Rock the swingarm from side to side - there should be no discernible movement at the rear. If there's a little movement or a slight clicking can be heard, make sure the pivot shaft nuts are tight. If the pivot nuts are tight but movement is still noticeable, the swingarm will have to be removed and the bearings replaced as described in Chapter 7.
7   Inspect the tightness of the rear suspension nuts and bolts.

26.7a Be sure to let all cooling system pressure escape before removing the pressure cap completely

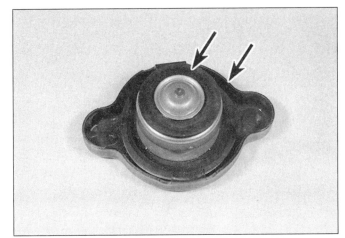

26.7b Inspect both cap gaskets (arrows)

26 Cooling system - inspection

Refer to illustrations 26.7a, 26.7b and 26.8
Warning: *The engine must be cool before beginning this procedure.*
Note: *Refer to Section 3 and check the coolant level before performing this check.*

1   The entire cooling system should be checked carefully at the recommended intervals. Look for evidence of leaks, check the condition of the coolant, check the radiator for clogged fins and damage and make sure the fan operates when required.

2   Remove fairing panels as necessary for access to the cooling system components (see Chapter 9).

3   Examine each of the rubber coolant hoses along its entire length. Look for cracks, abrasions and other damage. Squeeze each hose at various points. They should feel firm, yet pliable, and return to their original shape when released. If they are dried out or hard, replace them with new ones.

4   Check for evidence of leaks at each cooling system joint. Tighten the hose clamps careful to prevent future leaks. If coolant has been leaking from the joints of steel or aluminum coolant tubes, remove the tubes and replace the O-rings (see Chapter 4).

5   Check the radiator for evidence of leaks and other damage. Leaks in the radiator leave telltale scale deposits or coolant stains on the outside of the core below the leak. If leaks are noted, remove the radiator (see Chapter 4) and have it repaired by a radiator shop or replace it with a new one. **Caution**: *Do not use a liquid leak stopping compound to try to repair leaks.*

6   Check the radiator fins for mud, dirt and insects, which may impede the flow of air through the radiator. If the fins are dirty, force water or low pressure compressed air through the fins from the backside. If the fins are bent or distorted, straighten them carefully with a screwdriver.

7   Remove the pressure cap by turning it counterclockwise (anti-clockwise) until it reaches a stop. If you hear a hissing sound (indicating there is still pressure in the system), wait until it stops. Now, press down on the cap with the palm of your hand and continue turning the cap counterclockwise (anti-clockwise) until it can be removed **(see illustration)**. Check the condition of the coolant in the system. If it is rust colored or if accumulations of scale are visible, drain, flush and refill the system with new coolant. Check the cap gaskets for cracks and other damage **(see illustration)**. Have the cap tested by a dealer service department or replace it with a new one. Install the cap by turning it clockwise until it reaches the first stop, then push down on the cap and continue turning until it can turn no further.

8   Check the antifreeze content of the coolant with an antifreeze hydrometer **(see illustration)**. Sometimes coolant may look like it's In good condition, but might be too weak to offer adequate protection. If the hydrometer indicates a weak mixture, drain, flush and refill the

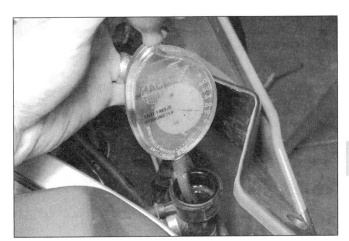

26.8 An antifreeze hydrometer is helpful in determining the condition of the coolant

cooling system (see Section 27).

9   Start the engine and let it reach normal operating temperature, then check for leaks again. As the coolant temperature increases, the fan should come on automatically and the temperature should begin to drop. If it doesn't, refer to Chapter 4 and check the fan and fan circuit carefully.

10   If the coolant level is consistently low, and no evidence of leaks can be found, have the entire system pressure checked by a Yamaha dealer service department, motorcycle repair shop or service station.

27 Cooling system - draining , flushing and refilling

Warning: *Allow the engine to cool completely before performing this maintenance operation. Also, don't allow antifreeze to come into contact with your skin or painted surfaces of the motorcycle. Rinse off spills immediately with plenty of water. Antifreeze is highly toxic if ingested. Never leave antifreeze lying around in an open container or in puddles on the floor; children and pets are attracted by its sweet smell and may drink it. Check with local authorities (councils) about disposing of used antifreeze. Many communities have collection centers which will see that antifreeze is disposed of safely. Antifreeze is also combustible, so don't store or use it near open flames.*

Draining

Refer to illustrations 27.2a, 27.2b, 27.2c and 27.2d

1   Place a large, clean drain pan under the left side of the engine.

27.2a Later models have a drain bolt on the water pump; this is an FZR600 . . .

27.2b . . . and this is an FZR750/1000

27.2c The coolant will shoot out of the drain hole, so position the pan accordingly

27.2d In addition to the lower drain bolt, there's a drain screw on each front corner or side of the cylinder block

2   Remove the drain bolt from the bottom of the coolant tube or water pump cover **(see illustrations)** and allow the coolant to drain into the pan. After removing the drain bolt, remove the pressure cap **(see illustration 26.7a)** to ensure that all of the coolant can drain. **Note:** *The coolant will rush out with considerable force as soon as the cap is removed, so position the drain pan accordingly* **(see illustration)**. Remove the drain plugs from the front of the cylinder block **(see illustration)**.

3   Drain the coolant reservoir. Refer to Chapter 4 for the reservoir removal procedure. Wash the reservoir out with water.

Flushing

4   Flush the system with clean tap water by inserting a garden hose in the radiator filler neck. Allow the water to run through the system until it is clear when it exits the drain bolt holes. If the radiator is extremely corroded, remove it (see Chapter 4) and have it cleaned at a radiator shop.

5   Check the drain bolt gaskets. Replace them with new ones if necessary.

6   Clean the holes, then install the drain bolts and tighten them to the torque listed in this Chapter's Specifications.

7   Fill the cooling system with clean water mixed with a flushing compound. Make sure the flushing compound is compatible with aluminum components, and follow the manufacturer's instructions carefully.

8   Start the engine and allow it to reach normal operating temperature. Let it run for about ten minutes.

9   Stop the engine. Let the machine cool for a while, then cover the pressure cap with a heavy rag and turn it counterclockwise (anti-clockwise) to the first stop, releasing any pressure that may be present in the system. Once the hissing stops, push down on the cap and remove it completely.

10   Drain the system once again.

11   Fill the system with clean water, then repeat Steps 8, 9 and 10.

Refilling

12   Fill the system with the proper coolant mixture (see this Chapter's Specifications). When the system is full (all the way up to the top of the radiator cap filler neck), start the engine. Watch the coolant and level as the engine runs, and add coolant when the level drops. When the coolant level stabilizes, shut the engine off.

13   Fill the system with coolant to the top of the filler neck.

14   Allow the engine to cool, then check the coolant level in the reservoir (see Section 3). If the coolant level is low, add the specified mixture until it reaches the Full mark in the reservoir.

15   Check the system for leaks.

16   Do not dispose of the old coolant by pouring it down a drain. Instead, pour it into a heavy plastic container, cap it tightly and take it to an authorized disposal site or a service station.

Chapter 2
FZR600 engine, clutch and transmission

Contents

Specifications

General

Bore	59 mm (2.323 inches)
Stroke	54.8 mm (2.158 inches)
Displacement	599 cc
Compression ratio	12 to 1

Camshafts

Intake camshaft
Lobe height
Standard	32.75 to 32.85 mm (1.2894 to 1.2933 inch)
Minimum	32.7 mm (1.287 inch)

Base circle
Standard	24.998 to 25.098 mm (0.9842 to 0.9881 inch)
Minimum	24.95 mm (0.982 inch)

Camshafts (continued)

Exhaust camshaft
    Lobe height
        Standard .... 32.55 to 32.65 mm (1.2815 to 1.2854 inch)
        Minimum .... 32.5 mm (1.280 inch)
    Base circle
        Standard .... 24.998 to 25.098 mm (0.9842 to 0.9881 inch)
        Minimum .... 24.95 mm (0.982 inch)
    Bearing oil clearance
        Standard .... 0.020 to 0.054 mm (0.0008 to 0.0021 inch)
        Maximum .... 0.08 mm (0.0031 inch)
    Journal diameter .... 22.967 to 22.980 mm (0.9042 to 0.9047 inch)
    Bearing bore .... 23.000 to 23.021 mm (0.9055 to 0.9063 inch)
    Camshaft runout limit .... 0.06 mm (0.0024 inch)

Cylinder head, valves and valve springs

Cylinder head warpage limit .... 0.05 mm (0.002 inch)
Valve stem bend limit .... 0.04 mm (0.0016 inch)
Valve head diameter
    Intake .... 23.9 to 24.1 mm (0.941 to 0.949 inch)
    Exhaust .... 20.9 to 21.1 mm (0.823 to 0.831 inch)
Valve margin thickness (minimum) .... 0.7 mm (0.0276 inch)
Valve stem diameter
    Standard
        Intake .... 4.475 to 4.490 mm (0.1762 to 0.1768 inch)
        Exhaust .... 4.460 to 4.475 mm (0.1756 to 0.1762 inch)
    Minimum
        Intake .... 4.45 mm (0.1752 inch)
        Exhaust .... 4.435 mm (0.1746 inch)
Valve head thickness (intake and exhaust)
    Standard .... 0.6 to 0.8 mm (0.236 to 0.0315 inch)
    Minimum .... 0.5 mm (0.020 inch)
Valve guide inside diameter (intake and exhaust)
    Standard .... 4.500 to 4.512 mm (0.1772 to 0.1776 inch)
    Maximum .... 4.542 mm (0.179 inch)
Stem-to-guide clearance limit
    Intake .... 0.08 mm (0.0031 inch)
    Intake .... 0.10 mm (0.0039 inch)
Valve seat width (intake and exhaust) .... 0.9 to 1.1 mm (0.0354 to 0.0433 inch)
Valve face width (intake and exhaust) .... 1.56 to 2.40 mm (0.061 to 0.095 inch)
Valve spring free length (intake and exhaust)
    Standard .... 43.15 mm (1.70 inch)
    Minimum .... 41.2 mm (1.62 inch)
Valve spring installed length
    (intake and exhaust) .... 37.5 mm (1.48 inch)
Compressed pressure at installed length .... 11.6 to 13.4 kg (25.9 to 29.6 lbs)
Valve spring bend limit .... 1.9 mm (0.075 inch)

Cylinder block

Bore diameter
    Standard .... 59.00 to 59.01 mm (2.3228 to 2.3232 inch)
    Maximum .... 59.15 mm (2.3288 inch)
    Bore measuring point .... 40 mm (1.57 inch) from top of cylinder
Taper and out-of-round limit .... Not specified

Pistons

Piston diameter
    Standard .... 58.940 to 58.955 mm (2.320 to 2.321 inch)
    First oversize .... 59.5 mm (2.343 inch)
    Second oversize .... 60.0 mm (2.362 inch)
Diameter measuring point .... 5.0 mm (0.197 inch) from bottom of skirt
Piston-to-cylinder clearance
    Standard .... 0.03 to 0.05 mm (0.0012 to 0.0020 inch)
    Maximum .... 0.10 mm (0.0039 inch)
Ring side clearance
    Top ring
        Standard .... 0.03 to 0.07 mm (0.0012 to 0.0028 inch)
        Maximum .... 0.10 mm (0.0039 inch)
    Second ring
        Standard .... 0.02 to 0.06 mm (0.0008 to 0.0024 inch)
        Maximum .... 0.10 mm (0.0039 inch)
    Oil ring .... Not specified

Ring thickness
    Top and second rings .... 0.8 mm (0.0315 inch)
    Oil ring (spacer and rails)... 1.5 mm (0.0591 inch)
Ring end gap
    Top and second rings .... 0.15 to 0.30 mm (0.0059 to 0.0118 inch)
    Oil ring .... 0.2 to 0.6 mm (0.0079 to 0.0236 inch)
Ring width
    Top and second rings .... 2.1 mm (0.0827 inch)
    Oil ring .... 2.2 mm (0.0866 inch)

Crankshaft, connecting rods and bearings

Main bearing oil clearance
    Standard... 0.025 to 0.043 mm (0.0010 to 0.0017 inch)
    Maximum.. 0.08 mm (0.003 inch)
Connecting rod side clearance
    Standard... 0.160 to 0.262 mm (0.0063 to 0.0103 inch)
    Maximum.. 0.5 mm (0.02 inch)
Connecting rod bearing oil clearance.. 0.043 to 0.066 mm (0.0017 to 0.0026 inch)
Crankshaft runout limit .... 0.03 mm (0.0012 inch)

Oil pump and relief valve

Inner to outer rotor clearance .... 0.03 to 0.09 mm (0.0012 to 0.0035 inch)
Outer rotor to housing clearance.. 0.03 to 0.08 mm (0.0012 to 0.0031 inch)
Bypass valve setting pressure.. 0.76 to 1.17 Bars (11 to 17 psi)
Relief valve opening pressure... 4.47 to 5.44 Bars (64 to 78 psi)

Clutch and transmission

Friction plate thickness
    Standard... 2.9 to 3.1 mm (0.1142 to 0.1220 inch)
    Minimum... 2.8 mm (0.11 inch)
Steel plate thickness .... 1.8 to 2.2 mm (0.072 to 0.085 inch)
Steel plate warpage limit .... 0.1 mm (0.004 inch)
Pushrod bend limit .... 0.5 mm (0.02 inch)
Spring length
    Standard... 33.5 mm (1.32 inch)
    Minimum... 32.6 mm (1.28 inch)
Driveshaft and mainshaft runout limit....................................... 0.08 mm (0.0031 inch)

Torque specifications

Cam chain guide (intake side) Allen bolts.................................. 10 Nm (7.2 ft-lbs) (1)
Cam chain sprocket bolts... 24 Nm (17 ft-lbs)
Cam chain tensioner mounting bolts.. 10 Nm (7.2 ft-lbs)
Cam chain tensioner cap bolt.. 10 Nm (7.2 ft-lbs)
Camshaft bearing cap bolts .... 10 Nm (7.2 ft-lbs)
Cylinder block coolant passage plug screws............................. 7 Nm (5.1 ft-lbs)
Cylinder head nuts.. 25 Nm (18 ft-lbs)
Clutch boss nut .... 70 ft-lbs (50 Nm) (2)
Clutch cover bolts .... 10 Nm (7.2 ft-lbs)
Clutch push lever screw .... 5 Nm (3.6 ft-lbs) (1)
Clutch pushrod adjuster locknut .... 16 Nm (11 ft-lbs)
Clutch pressure plate bolts .... 6 Nm (4.3 ft-lbs)
Connecting rod cap nuts .... 23 Nm (17 ft-lbs) (3)
Crankcase bolts
    M8 x 1.25 .... 24 Nm (17 ft-lbs) (4)
    M6 x 1.0 .... 12 Nm (8.7 ft-lbs) (4)
Crankcase studs to crankcase .... 13 Nm (9.4 ft-lbs) (4)
Engine mounting bolts
    Upper rear and lower front .... 55 Nm (40 ft-lbs)
    Lower rear .... 45 Nm (32 ft-lbs)
Frame downtube bolts
    Upper .... 60 Nm (43 ft-lbs) (1)
    Lower .... 33 Nm (24 ft-lbs) (1)
Oil baffle plate screws .... 7 Nm (5.1 ft-lbs)
Oil cooler banjo bolts.. 25 Nm (18 ft-lbs)
Oil cooler hose bolts... 32 Nm (23 ft-lbs)
Oil cooler mounting bolts .... 10 Nm (7.2 ft-lbs)
Oil pan mounting bolts .... 10 Nm (7.2 ft-lbs)
Oil passage plugs .... 37 Nm (27 ft-lbs)
Oil pickup bolts... 10 Nm (7.2 ft-lbs)
Oil pump housing screw .... 7 Nm (5.1 ft-lbs)
Oil pump mounting bolts .... 10 Nm (7.2 ft-lbs) (1)

2

Torque specifications (continued)

Shift cam retaining plate bolt.. 10 Nm (7.2 ft-lbs) (1)
Shift cam stopper lever bolt .... 10 Nm (7.2 ft-lbs) (1)
Starter clutch cover bolts .... 10 Nm (7.2 ft-lbs)
Starter clutch securing bolt .... 80 Nm (58 ft-lbs)
Valve cover bolts .... 10 Nm (7.2 ft-lbs)

1   Apply non-permanent thread locking agent to the threads.
2   Use a new lockwasher.
3   Apply molybdenum disulfide grease to the threads.
4   Apply engine oil to the threads.

1   General information

The engine/transmission unit is a liquid-cooled, in-line four. The valves are operated by double overhead camshafts which are chain driven off the crankshaft. The engine/transmission assembly is constructed from aluminum alloy. The crankcase is divided horizontally.

The crankcase incorporates a wet sump, pressure-fed lubrication system which uses a gear-driven oil pump, an oil filter, relief valve and an oil level switch. The starter clutch is mounted on the right side of the crankcase.

Power from the crankshaft is routed to the transmission via the clutch, which is of the coil spring, wet multi-plate type and is geardriven off the crankshaft. The transmission is a six-speed, constant-mesh unit.

2   Operations possible with the engine in the frame

The components and assemblies listed below can be removed without having to remove the engine from the frame. If, however, a number of areas require attention at the same time, removal of the engine is recommended.

Gear selector mechanism external components
Starter motor
Alternator
Clutch assembly
Oil pump
Oil pan and relief valve
Valve cover, camshafts and lifters
Cam chain tensioner
Cylinder head
Cylinder block and pistons
Starter clutch

3   Operations requiring engine removal

It is necessary to remove the engine/transmission assembly from the frame and separate the crankcase halves to gain access to the following components:
Crankshaft, connecting rods and bearings
Transmission shafts
Shift cam and forks
Camshaft chain and starter chain

4   Major engine repair - general note

1   It is not always easy to determine when or if an engine should be completely overhauled, as a number of factors must be considered.
2   High mileage is not necessarily an indication that an overhaul is needed, while low mileage, on the other hand, does not preclude the need for an overhaul. Frequency of servicing is probably the single most important consideration. An engine that has regular and frequent oil and filter changes, as well as other required maintenance, will most

likely give many miles of reliable service. Conversely, a neglected engine, or one which has not been broken in properly, may require an overhaul very early in its life.
3   Exhaust smoke and excessive oil consumption are both indications that piston rings and/or valve guides are in need of attention. Make sure oil leaks are not responsible before deciding that the rings and guides are bad. Refer to Chapter 1 and perform a cylinder compression check to determine for certain the nature and extent of the work required.
4   If the engine is making obvious knocking or rumbling noises, the connecting rod and/or main bearings are probably at fault.
5   Loss of power, rough running, excessive valve train noise and high fuel consumption rates may also point to the need for an overhaul, especially if they are all present at the same time. If a complete tune-up does not remedy the situation, major mechanical work is the only solution.
6   An engine overhaul generally involves restoring the internal parts to the specifications of a new engine. During an overhaul the piston rings are replaced and the cylinder walls are bored and/or honed. If a rebore is done, then new pistons are also required. The main and connecting rod bearings are generally replaced with new ones and, if necessary, the crankshaft is also replaced. Generally the valves are serviced as well, since they are usually in less than perfect condition at this point. While the engine is being overhauled, other components such as the carburetors and the starter motor can be rebuilt also. The end result should be a like-new engine that will give as many trouble free miles as the original.
7   Before beginning the engine overhaul, read through all of the related procedures to familiarize yourself with the scope and requirements of the job. Overhauling an engine is not all that difficult, but it is time consuming. Plan on the motorcycle being tied up for a minimum of two weeks. Check on the availability of parts and make sure that any necessary special tools, equipment and supplies are obtained in advance.
8   Most work can be done with typical shop hand tools, although a number of precision measuring tools are required for inspecting parts to determine if they must be replaced. Often a dealer service department or motorcycle repair shop will handle the inspection of parts and offer advice concerning reconditioning and replacement. As a general rule, time is the primary cost of an overhaul so it doesn't pay to install worn or substandard parts.
9   As a final note, to ensure maximum life and minimum trouble from a rebuilt engine, everything must be assembled with care in a spotlessly clean environment.

5   Engine - removal and installation

Note: *Engine removal and installation should be done with the aid of an assistant to avoid damage or injury that could occur if the engine is dropped. A hydraulic floor jack should be used to support and lower the engine if possible (they can be rented at low cost).*

Removal

Refer to illustrations 5.17a, 5.17b, 5.17c, 5.18a, 5.18b, 5.18c and 5.20
1   Support the bike securely so it can't be knocked over during this procedure.

5.17a Remove the hex bolts from the upper end of each downtube . . .

5.17b . . . and the Allen bolts from the lower end . . .

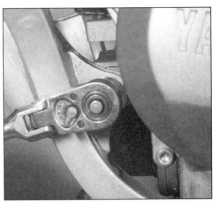

5.17c . . . and unbolt the down tubes from the engine

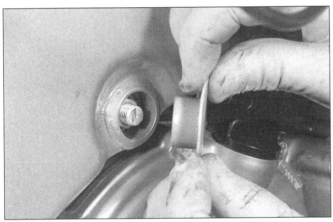

5.18a The nut for the upper engine mounting bolt is beneath a plastic cap

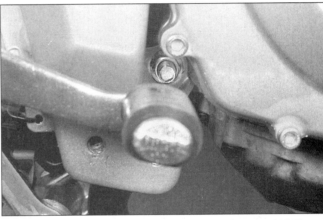

5.18b The nut for the lower mounting bolt is inboard of the brake pedal

2

2   Remove the fuel tank (see Chapter 5).
3   Remove the left, right and upper fairings and the seat (see Chapter 9).
4   Remove the air filter housing (see Chapter 5).
5   Drain the engine oil and coolant (see Chapter 1).
6   Remove the carburetors (see Chapter 5) and plug the intake openings with rags.
7   Remove the radiator and the coolant tubes on the intake side of the engine. Remove the radiator outlet tubes (see Chapter 4).
8   If you're working on a California model, disconnect the EXUP cables at the upper end (see Chapter 5). If you're working on an early UK model, remove the oil cooler (see Section 31).
9   Remove the exhaust system (see Chapter 5).
10   Disconnect the clutch cable (see Section 20).
11   Remove the engine sprocket cover and engine sprocket (see Chapter 7). It isn't necessary to remove the drive chain completely, but if the engine sprocket is difficult to remove, loosen the rear axle nut and chain adjusters, then push the rear wheel forward to create slack in the chain (see Chapter 1 for details).
12   Disconnect both battery cables from the battery. **Warning:** *Always disconnect the negative cable first and reconnect it last to prevent a battery explosion.*
13   Refer to Chapter 10 and disconnect the following electrical connectors:

a) alternator
b) neutral, oil level and sidestand switches
c) spark plug wires
d) starter motor
e) engine ground cable

14   Remove the cover and detach the choke lever assembly from the left side of the motorcycle (see Chapter 4).

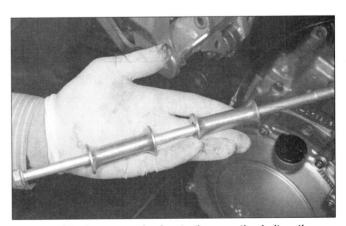

5.18c Slip the spacers back onto the mounting bolt so they won't be lost

15   Detach the shift lever adjusting rod from the engine (see Section 21).
16   Support the engine securely with a floor jack and a wood block.
17   Remove the bolts holding the downtubes to the frame **(see illustrations)**.
18   Remove the upper and lower engine mounting bolts and spacers **(see illustrations)**.
19   Make sure no wires or hoses are still attached to the engine assembly. **Warning:** *The engine is heavy and may cause injury if it falls. Be sure it's securely supported. Have an assistant help you steady the engine on the jack as you remove it.*

5.20 Use a jack to lower the engine and have an assistant help guide it out of the frame

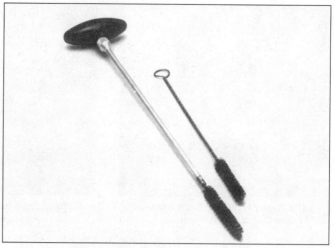

6.2a A selection of brushes is required for cleaning holes and passages in the engine components

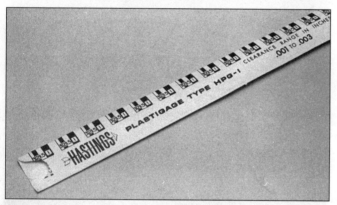

6.2b Type HPG-1 Plastigage is needed to check the crankshaft, connecting rod and camshaft oil clearances

20   Slowly and carefully lower the engine assembly to the floor, then guide it out from under the bike **(see illustration)**.

Installation

21   Installation is the reverse of removal. Note the following points:
  a) Don't tighten any of the engine mounting bolts until they all have been installed.
  b) Use new gaskets at all exhaust pipe connections.
  c) Tighten the engine mounting bolts and frame downtube bolts to the torques listed in this Chapter's Specifications.
  d) Adjust the drive chain, clutch cable and throttle cables following the procedures in Chapter 1 and Chapter 5.
  e) Be sure to refill the cooling system and engine oil before starting the engine.

---

6   Engine disassembly and reassembly - general information

Refer to illustrations 6.2a, 6.2b and 6.3

1   Before disassembling the engine, clean the exterior with a degreaser and rinse it with water. A clean engine will make the job easier and prevent the possibility of getting dirt into the internal areas of the engine.
2   In addition to the precision measuring tools mentioned earlier, you will need a torque wrench, a valve spring compressor, oil gallery brushes, a piston ring removal and installation tool, piston ring compressors and a clutch holder tool (which is described in Section 19). Some new, clean engine oil of the correct grade and type, some engine assembly lube (or moly-based grease), a tube of Yamaha Quick Gasket (part no. 11001-05-01) or equivalent, and a tube of RTV (silicone) sealant will also be required. Although it may not be considered a tool, some Plastigage (type HPG-1) should also be obtained to use for checking bearing oil clearances **(see illustrations)**.

6.3 An engine stand can be made from short lengths of 2 x 4 lumber and lag bolts or nails

3   An engine support stand made from short lengths of 2 x 4's bolted together will facilitate the disassembly and reassembly procedures **(see illustration)**. The perimeter of the mount should be just big enough to accommodate the engine oil pan. If you have an automotive-type engine
stand, an adapter plate can be made from a piece of plate, some angle iron and some nuts and bolts.
4   When disassembling the engine, keep "mated" parts together (including gears, cylinders, pistons, etc. that have been in contact with each other during engine operation). These "mated" parts must be reused or replaced as an assembly.
5   Engine/transmission disassembly should be done in the following general order with reference to the appropriate Sections.
  Remove the camshafts
  Remove the cylinder head
  Remove the cylinder block
  Remove the pistons
  Remove the starter clutch and idle gears
  Remove the clutch
  Remove the oil pan
  Remove the external shift mechanism
  Remove the alternator and starter (see Chapter 10)
  Separate the crankcase halves
  Remove the crankshaft and connecting rods
  Remove the transmission shafts/gears
  Remove the shift cam/forks
6   Reassembly is accomplished by reversing the general disassembly sequence.

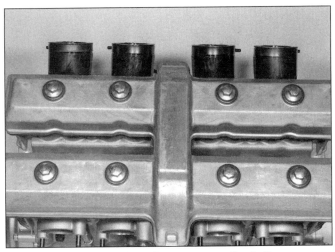

7.7 Remove the valve cover mounting bolts

7 Valve cover - removal and installation

Note: *The valve cover can be removed with the engine in the frame. If the engine has been removed, ignore the steps which don't apply.*

Removal

Refer to illustrations 7.7 and 7.8

1   Support the bike securely so it can't be knocked over during this procedure.
2   Remove the left and right fairings, fuel tank cover and seat (see Chapter 9).
3   Remove the radiator (see Chapter 4).
4   Remove the air cleaner housing, carburetors and exhaust system (see Chapter 5).
5   Remove the right frame downtube (see Section 5).
6   Remove the spark plugs (see Chapter 1).
7   Remove the valve cover bolts **(see illustration)**.
8   Lift the cover off the cylinder head **(see illustration)**. If it's stuck, don't attempt to pry it off - tap around the sides with a plastic hammer to dislodge it.

7.8 Valve cover and cylinder head - exploded view

   1   *Washer*
   2   *Rubber seals*
   3   *Valve cover gasket*
   4   *Spark plug*
   5   *Cylinder head nut*
   6   *Washer*
   7   *Valve guide*
   8   *Snap-ring*
   9   *Head gasket*
10   *Valve cover*
11   *Cylinder head*

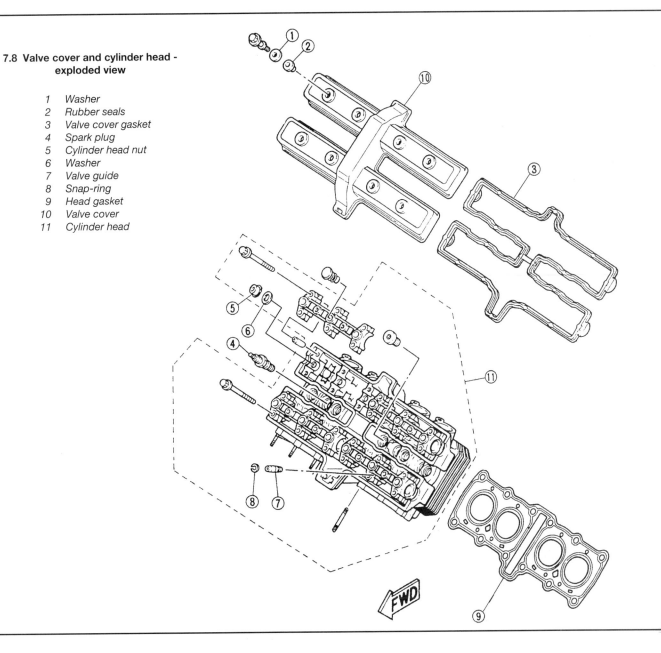

2

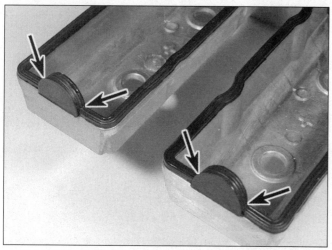

7.11 Make sure the cover fits securely into the groove on the head; apply silicone sealant to the corners of the gasket (arrows)

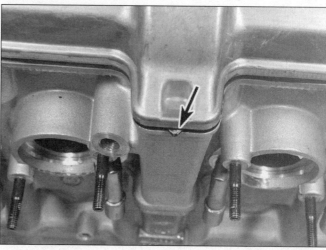

7.12 The gasket tab (arrow) should protrude when the valve cover is installed

7.13 Replace the rubber seals on the valve cover bolts if they're compressed or brittle

8.1 Loosen the tensioner cap bolt before unbolting the tensioner from the engine

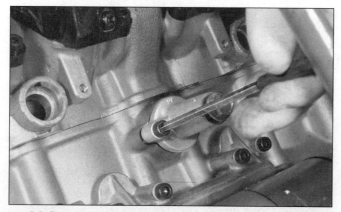

8.2 Remove the tensioner bolts and take the tensioner off

Installation
Refer to illustrations 7.11, 7.12 and 7.13

9   Peel the rubber gasket from the cover. If it's cracked, hardened, has soft spots or shows signs of general deterioration, replace it with a new one.
10   Clean the mating surfaces of the cylinder head and the valve cover with lacquer thinner, acetone or brake system cleaner. Apply a thin film of RTV sealant to the half-circle cutouts on each side of the head.

11   Install the gasket to the cover. Make sure it fits completely into the cover groove **(see illustration)**. Apply a small amount of silicone sealer to the corners of the half-circle portions of the gasket.
12   Position the cover on the cylinder head, making sure the gasket doesn't slip out of place. The tab on the gasket should protrude from the front (exhaust) side of the engine **(see illustration)**.
13   Check the rubber seals on the valve cover bolts, replacing them if necessary **(see illustration)**. Install the bolts with their seals and washers, tightening them evenly to the torque listed in this Chapter's Specifications.
14   The remainder of installation is the reverse of removal.

---

8   Camshaft chain tensioner - removal and installation

Removal
Refer to illustrations 8.1, 8.2 and 8.3

Caution: *Once you start to remove the tensioner bolts, you must remove the tensioner all the way and reset it before tightening the bolts. The tensioner extends and locks in place, so if you loosen the bolts partway and then retighten them, the tensioner or cam chain will be damaged.*

1   Loosen the tensioner cap bolt while the tensioner is still installed **(see illustration)**.
2   Remove the tensioner mounting bolts and take it off the engine **(see illustration)**.

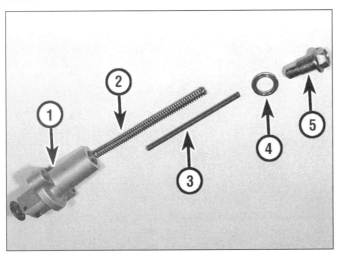

8.3 Tensioner components

1	*Tensioner body*	4	*Copper washer*
2	*Outer spring*	5	*Cap bolt*
3	*Inner spring*		

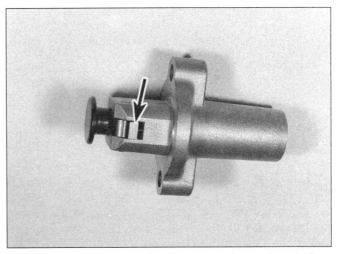

8.5 Release the latch (arrow) and compress the tensioner before installing it

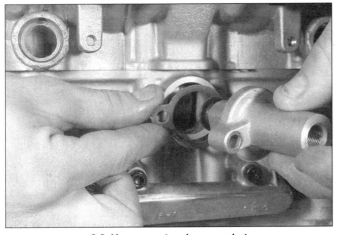

8.6 Use a new tensioner gasket

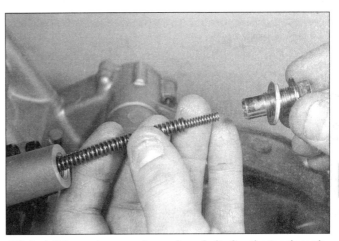

8.8 Install the springs, washer and cap bolt after the tensioner is installed on the engine

It's a good idea to replace this washer whenever the tensioner cap is removed.

5   Release the one-way cam on the chain tensioner and compress the rod **(see illustration)**.

6   Turn the tensioner so the one-way cam is downward and install the tensioner on the cylinder block, using a new gasket **(see illustration)**. The word Up cast in the tensioner housing should be upward.

7   Tighten the mounting bolts to the torque listed in this Chapter's Specifications.

8   Install the tensioner springs, cap and sealing washer **(see illustration)**. Tighten the cap to the torque listed in this Chapter's Specifications.

9   Camshafts and lifters - removal, inspection and installation

Note: *This procedure can be performed with the engine in the frame.*

Camshafts

Removal

Refer to illustrations 9.2, 9.4, 9.5a, 9.5b, 9.6 and 9.8

1   Remove the valve cover (see Section 7).

2   Turn the engine to position no. 1 cylinder at TDC compression (see Chapter 1 - Valve clearances - check and adjustment). When the engine is positioned correctly, the punch marks on the camshafts will align with the marks on the bearing caps **(see illustration)**.

9.2 The small punch mark on each camshaft should be aligned with the mark on the bearing cap (arrows)

3   Remove the tensioner cap bolt and sealing washer **(see illustration)**.

Installation

Refer to illustrations 8.5, 8.6 and 8.8

4   Check the sealing washer on the cap bolt for cracks or hardening.

9.4 Remove the bolts (arrows) and lift off the upper chain guide

9.5a Remove the bearing caps evenly

9.5b Note the location and position of the bearing cap identification marks

9.6 Remove the bearing cap dowels

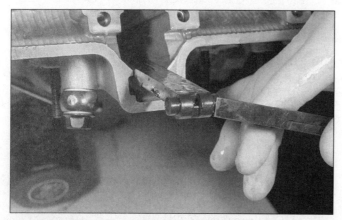

9.8 Lift the exhaust side chain guide out of the engine

3   Remove the camshaft chain tensioner (see Section 8).
4   Remove the upper cam chain guide (see illustration).
5   Unscrew the bearing cap bolts for the camshafts bearing caps, a little at a time, working from the outer to the inner bolts (see illustration). Caution: *If the bearing cap bolts aren't loosened evenly, the bearing caps may break. Because they're line-bored with the cylinder head, this may necessitate replacing the entire cylinder head.* Remove

the bolts and lift off the caps. Note that each bearing cap is labeled for position and direction. The small triangular mark on each cap points toward the clutch side of the engine (see illustration). *The letters E and I indicate exhaust and intake sides of the engine. The caps labeled E1 and I1 go on the alternator side of the engine; the caps labeled E2 and I2 go on the clutch side. If you can't see the marks, make your own.*
6   Remove the bolts and lift off the bearing caps and their dowel pins (see illustration).
7   Remove the camshafts. Keep the chain taut by wiring it to the engine so it can't fall down off the crankshaft. While the camshafts are out, don't allow the chain to go slack - the chain may fall off and bind between the crankshaft and case, which could damage these components. Also, cover the top of the cylinder head with a rag to prevent foreign objects from falling into the engine.
8   Lift the exhaust side (front) cam chain guide out of the engine (see illustration).

Inspection

Refer to illustrations 9.9, 9.10a, 9.10b, 9.11, 9.15a, 9.15b and 9.18
Note: *Before replacing camshafts or the cylinder head and bearing caps because of damage, check with local machine shops specializing in motorcycle engine work. In the case of the camshafts, it may be possible for cam lobes to be welded, reground and hardened, at a cost far lower than that of a new camshaft. If the bearing surfaces in the cylinder head are damaged, it may be possible for them to be bored out to accept bearing inserts. Due to the cost of a new cylinder head it is rec-*

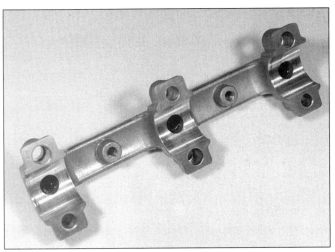

9.9 Inspect the bearing surfaces in the cylinder head and bearing caps

9.10a Check the lobes of the camshaft for wear - here's a good example of damage which will require replacement (or repair) of the camshaft

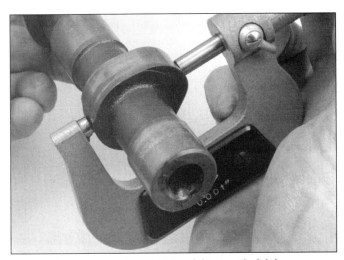

9.10b Measure the height of the camshaft lobes with a micrometer

9.11 The exhaust and intake camshafts are identified by cast marks

2

ommended that all options be explored before condemning it as trash!

9   Inspect the cam bearing surfaces of the head and the bearing caps (see illustration). Look for score marks, deep scratches and evidence of spalling (a pitted appearance).

10   Check the camshaft lobes for heat discoloration (blue appearance), score marks, chipped areas, flat spots and spalling (see illustration). Measure the height of each lobe with a micrometer (see illustration) and compare the results to the minimum lobe height listed in this Chapter's Specifications. If damage is noted or wear is excessive, the camshaft must be replaced.

11   Next, check the camshaft bearing oil clearances. Clean the camshafts, the bearing surfaces in the cylinder head and the bearing caps with a clean, lint-free cloth, then lay the cams in place in the cylinder head. Be sure the punch marks on the camshafts are upward (see illustration 9.2). Be sure to place the camshafts in the correct bearings; the exhaust and intake camshafts are identified by EX and IN marks (see illustration).

12   Cut twelve strips of Plastigage (type HPG-1) and lay one piece on each bearing journal, parallel with the camshaft centerline.

13   Make sure the bearing cap dowels are installed (see illustration 9.6). Install the bearing caps in their proper positions (see Step 5). Tighten the bolts in two steps to the torque listed in this Chapter's Specifications. Caution: Tighten the bearing caps evenly to specifications, starting with the inner bolts and working outward. While tighten-

9.15a Lay a strip of Plastigage (1) lengthwise along each journal

ing, DO NOT let the camshafts rotate!

14   Now unscrew the bolts, a little at a time, and carefully lift off the bearing caps. Be sure to start with the outer bolts and work inward.

15   To determine the oil clearance, compare the crushed Plastigage (at its widest point) on each journal to the scale printed on the Plastigage container (see illustration). Compare the results to this Chap-

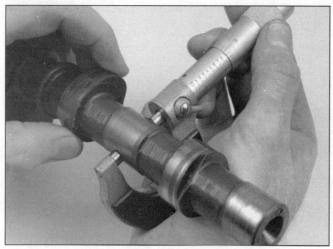

9.15b Measure the cam bearing journal diameter with
a micrometer

9.18 Check the pad on the upper chain guide for score marks
or damage

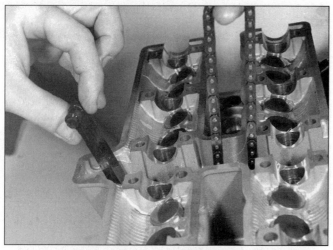

9.21 Lower the exhaust-side chain guide into the engine and
make sure it rests securely on the bottom of the crankcase

9.23 Lay the exhaust camshaft in the engine; because some of
the lobes will hold it up, the alignment mark will be slightly
counterclockwise (anti-clockwise) of the installed position

ter's Specifications. If the oil clearance is greater than specified, measure the diameter of the cam bearing journal with a micrometer **(see illustration)**. If the journal diameter is less than the specified limit, replace the camshaft with a new one and recheck the clearance. If the
clearance is still too great, replace the cylinder head and bearing caps
with new parts (see the Note that precedes Step 9).
16   Except in cases of oil starvation, the camshaft chain wears very
little. If the chain has stretched excessively, which makes it difficult to
maintain proper tension, replace it with a new one (see Section 27).
17   Check the sprockets for wear, cracks and other damage, replacing them if necessary. If the sprockets are worn, the chain is also worn,
and also the sprocket on the crankshaft (which can only be remedied
by replacing the crankshaft). If wear this severe is apparent, the entire
engine should be disassembled for inspection.
18   Check the chain guides for wear or damage **(see illustration)**. If it
is worn or damaged, the chain may be worn out or improperly adjusted. Replacement of the chain requires removal of the cylinder head
and cylinder block.

Installation

Refer to illustrations 9.21, 9.23 and 9.25
19   Make sure the crankshaft is still at no. 1 TDC (refer to Chapter 1 -
Valve clearances - check and adjustment).
20   Bolt the camshaft sprockets to the camshafts (if removed) and
tighten the bolts to the torque listed in this Chapter's Specifications.

21   Install the exhaust side chain guide (if removed) **(see illustration)**.
22   Make sure the bearing surfaces in the cylinder head and the bearing caps are clean, then apply a light coat of engine assembly lube or
moly-based grease to each of them.
23   Apply a coat of moly-based grease to the lobes of the exhaust
camshaft. Make sure the camshaft bearing journals are clean, then slip
the exhaust camshaft through the chain and lay it in the cylinder head
(the camshaft won't fit all the way down into the bearing saddles and
locating slot because some of the lobes will be pointed downward).
Make sure the small punch mark on the camshaft is very slightly counterclockwise (anti-clockwise) from its installed position (straight up)
(see illustration). Engage the chain with the sprocket so there is no
slack in the exhaust side of the chain.
24   Carefully set the bearing caps in place with the small arrowhead
cast in the top of each cap pointing toward the right (clutch) end of the
engine. Make sure the caps are in their proper positions (see Step 5)
and install the bolts. Tighten them in two stages to the torque listed in
this Chapter's Specifications, working from the inner bolts outward. As
the bearing caps are tightened, the camshaft should settle down into
its bearing saddles, the locating flange on the left end of the camshaft
should settle into its groove and the exhaust camshaft alignment mark
should move into the straight-up position. If the alignment mark isn't
positioned correctly, disengage the chain from the camshaft and turn
the camshaft to align the mark.

9.25 Lay the intake camshaft in the engine

25   Place the intake camshaft in its bearing saddles with its alignment mark just counterclockwise (anti-clockwise) from the straight-up position **(see illustration)**. Drape the chain over the intake camshaft sprocket so there is no slack in the upper run of the chain (between the two sprockets).

26   Insert a finger or wooden dowel in the cam chain tensioner hole and push against the chain to remove the slack in the upper run of the chain. Make sure the crankshaft mark is still in the no. 1 TDC position and both camshaft marks are in the straight-up positions.

27   If the crankshaft and camshaft alignment marks are not in the correct positions, lift the chain off the sprocket, turn the cam to obtain correct alignment and re-engage the chain with the sprocket.

28   Once all timing marks - those on the camshafts and alternator rotor - are aligned correctly, install the cam chain tensioner as described in Section 8. **Caution:** *If the marks are not aligned exactly as described, the valve timing will be incorrect and the valves may contact the pistons, causing extensive damage to the engine. Be sure to recheck all timing marks to make sure they haven't shifted.*

29   Pour clean engine oil over the cam chain and along the camshafts. Use enough that it flows down onto the sprockets and the valve area.

30   Install the upper cam chain guide **(see illustration 9.4)**.

31   Turn the engine with a wrench on the crankshaft turning bolt. If you feel a sudden increase in resistance, stop turning. The valves may be hitting the pistons due to incorrect assembly. Find the problem and fix it before turning the engine any further, or serious damage may occur. Once again, check the alignment of the camshaft punch marks

with the marks on the bearing caps and the mark on the alternator rotor with the crankcase seam.

32   The remainder of installation is the reverse of removal.

Valve lifters
Removal

33   Remove the camshafts following the procedure given above. Be sure to keep tension on the camshaft chain.

34   Make a holder with a separate section for each lifter and its valve adjusting shim (a pair of egg cartons will work). Label the sections according to cylinder number (1, 2, 3 or 4), valve number (starting from the left end of the engine) and whether the lifter belongs with an intake or exhaust valve. The lifters form a wear pattern with their bores and must be returned to their original locations if reused.

35   Pull the lifter out of the bore with a magnet together with its valve adjusting shim (see Chapter 1). If the lifters are stuck, spray the area around them with carburetor cleaner and let it soak in. Place the lifters in order in their holder.

Inspection

36   Check the lifters and their bores for wear, scuff marks, scratches or other damage. Yamaha doesn't provide specifications or wear tolerances for the lifters or their bores. If wear or damage is found, replace the lifters and cylinder head as a set.

Installation

37   Coat the lifters and their bores with clean engine oil.

38   Installation is the reverse of the removal steps. Be sure to reinstall a valve adjusting shim between the each valve and its lifter.

10   Cylinder head - removal and installation

Caution: *The engine must be completely cool before beginning this procedure, or the cylinder head may become warped.*
Note: *This procedure can be performed with the engine in the frame. If the engine has been removed, ignore the steps which don't apply.*

Removal

Refer to illustrations 10.6a, 10.6b, 10.6c, 10.7a, 10.7b, 10.7c, 10.8, and 10.10

1   Support the bike securely so it can't be knocked over during this procedure.

2   Remove the carburetors and exhaust system (see Chapter 5).

3   Remove the valve cover (see Section 7).

4   Remove the cam chain tensioner (see Section 8).

5   Remove the camshafts (see Section 9).

6   Unbolt the oil line from the cylinder head, cylinder block and crankcase **(see illustrations)**.

10.6a Remove the oil line banjo bolt from the cylinder head . . .

10.6b . . . unbolt the bracket from the cylinder block . . .

10.6c . . . and remove the banjo bolt from the crankcase

10.7a Cylinder head **TIGHTENING** sequence

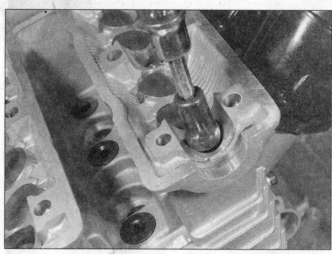

10.7b Remove the cylinder head nuts with an Allen bolt bit . . .

10.7c . . . and lift out the washers (you may need a magnet)

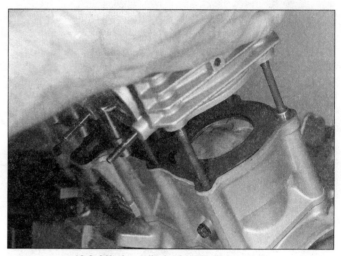

10.8 Lift the cylinder head off the studs

10.10 Find the dowels (arrows) if they aren't in position

8   Pull the cylinder head off the cylinder block studs, together with the lifters **(see illustration)**. If the head is stuck, tap upward with a rubber mallet to jar it loose, or use two wooden dowels inserted into the intake or exhaust ports to rock the head back and forth slightly (its movement will be limited by the studs). Don't attempt to pry the head off by inserting a screwdriver between the head and the cylinder block - you'll damage the sealing surfaces.

9   Lift the head gasket off the cylinder block. Stuff a clean rag into the cam chain tunnel to prevent the entry of debris.

10   Remove the dowel pins **(see illustration)**.

11   Check the cylinder head gasket and the mating surfaces on the cylinder head and block for leakage, which could indicate warpage. Refer to Section 12 and check the flatness of the cylinder head.

12   Clean all traces of old gasket material from the cylinder head and block. Be careful not to let any of the gasket material fall into the crankcase, the cylinder bores or the coolant passages.

Installation

Refer to illustrations 10.14, 10.16a and 10.16b

13   Install the dowels on the cylinder head studs **(see illustration 10.10)**.

14   Lay the new gasket in place on the cylinder block. Make sure the UP cutout on the gasket is upright and toward the rear of the engine (if the word UP reads backwards, the gasket is upside down) **(see illustration)**. Never reuse the old gasket and don't use any type of gasket sealant.

7   Loosen the cylinder head nuts, 1/2 turn at a time, in the reverse of the tightening sequence **(see illustration 7.8 and the accompanying illustration)**. Once all of the nuts are loose, remove the nuts and washers **(see illustrations)**.

10.14 The UP cutout in the head gasket should be upright

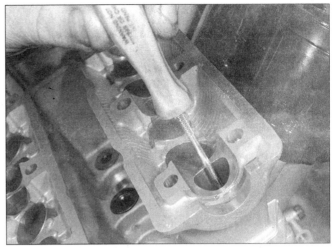

10.16a Seat the cylinder head washers in their bores with a small screwdriver

10.16b Tighten the cylinder head nuts in sequence, in two stages

15   Carefully lower the cylinder head over the studs. It's helpful to have an assistant support the camshaft chain with a piece of wire so it doesn't fall and become kinked or detached from the crankshaft. When the head is resting against the cylinder block, wire the cam chain to another component to keep tension on it.
16   Install the head washers and nuts. Push the washers down with a small screwdriver to make sure they've seated completely (see illustration). Starting with the inner nuts and working outward (see illustration 10.7a), tighten the nuts to approximately half of the torque listed in this Chapter's Specifications (see illustration).
17   Using the same sequence, tighten the nuts to the full torque listed in this Chapter's Specifications.
18   Install the camshafts, timing chain tensioner and valve cover (see Sections 9, 8 and 7).
19   Change the engine oil (see Chapter 1).
20   The remainder of installation is the reverse of the removal steps.

11   Valves/valve seats/valve guides - servicing

1   Because of the complex nature of this job and the special tools and equipment required, servicing of the valves, the valve seats and the valve guides (commonly known as a valve job) is best left to a professional.
2   The home mechanic can, however, remove and disassemble the head, do the initial cleaning and inspection, then reassemble and deliver the head to a dealer service department or properly equipped mo-

torcycle repair shop for the actual valve servicing. Refer to Section 12 for those procedures.
3   The dealer service department will remove the valves and springs, recondition or replace the valves and valve seats, replace the valve guides, check and replace the valve springs, spring retainers and keepers/collets (as necessary), replace the valve seals with new ones and reassemble the valve components.
4   After the valve job has been performed, the head will be in like-new condition. When the head is returned, be sure to clean it again very thoroughly before installation on the engine to remove any metal particles or abrasive grit that may still be present from the valve service operations. Use compressed air, if available, to blow out all the holes and passages.

12   Cylinder head and valves - disassembly, inspection and reassembly

1   As mentioned in the previous Section, valve servicing and valve guide replacement should be left to a dealer service department or motorcycle repair shop. However, disassembly, cleaning and inspection of the valves and related components can be done (if the necessary special tools are available) by the home mechanic. This way no expense is incurred if the inspection reveals that service work is not required at this time.
2   To properly disassemble the valve components without the risk of damaging them, a valve spring compressor is absolutely necessary. This special tool can usually be rented, but if it's not available, have a dealer service department or motorcycle repair shop handle the entire process of disassembly, inspection, service or repair (if required) and reassembly of the valves.

Disassembly
Refer to illustrations 12.7a, 12.7b and 12.7c
3   Remove the lifters and their shims if you haven't already done so (see Section 9). Store the components in such a way that they can be returned to their original locations without getting mixed up.
4   Before the valves are removed, scrape away any traces of gasket material from the head gasket sealing surface. Work slowly and do not nick or gouge the soft aluminum of the head. Gasket removing solvents, which work very well, are available at most motorcycle shops and auto parts stores.
5   Carefully scrape all carbon deposits out of the combustion chamber area. A hand held wire brush or a piece of fine emery cloth can be used once the majority of deposits have been scraped away. Do not use a wire brush mounted in a drill motor, or one with extremely stiff bristles, as the head material is soft and may be eroded away or scratched by the wire brush.

2

12.7a **Valves and camshafts - exploded view**

1   Intake camshaft
2   Sprocket
3   Valve lifter
4   Adjusting shim
5   Valve keepers (collets)
6   Valve spring retainer
7   Valve spring
8   Spring seat
9   Valve stem oil seal
10 Intake valve
11 Exhaust valve
12 Cam chain tensioner
13 Tensioner gasket
14 Intake side chain guide
15 Exhaust camshaft
16 Upper chain guide
17 Cam chain
18 Exhaust side chain guide

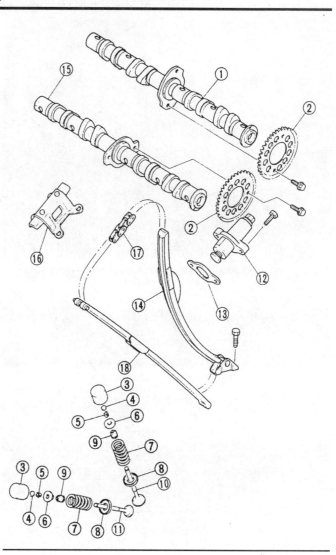

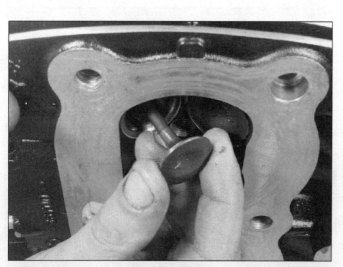

12.7b **Take the valve out of the combustion chamber, but don't force it if it's stuck . . .**

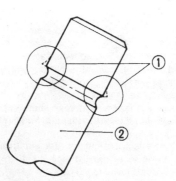

12.7c **. . . check the area around the keeper groove for burrs and remove any that you find**

valve assembly **(see illustration)**. Do not compress the springs any more than is absolutely necessary. Carefully release the valve spring compressor and remove the spring and the valve from the head **(see illustration)**. If the valve binds in the guide (won't pull through), push it back into the head and deburr the area around the keeper groove with a very fine file or whetstone **(see illustration)**.

8   Repeat the procedure for the remaining valves. Remember to keep the parts for each valve together so they can be reinstalled in the same location.

6   Before proceeding, arrange to label and store the valves along with their related components so they can be kept separate and reinstalled in the same valve guides they are removed from (labeled plastic bags work well for this).

7   Compress the valve spring on the first valve with a spring compressor, then remove the keepers and the spring retainer from the

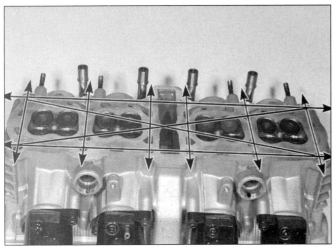

12.14 Measure the head along these lines with a feeler gauge and straightedge

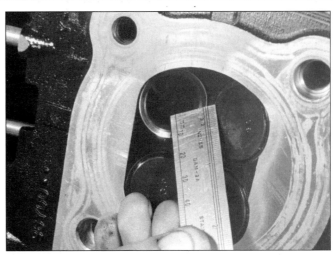

12.15 Measuring the valve seat width

12.16a Insert a small hole gauge into the valve guide and expand it so there's a slight drag when it's pulled out

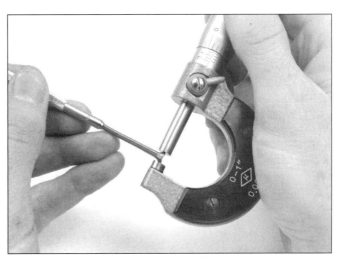

12.16b Measure the small hole gauge with a micrometer

2

9   Once the valves have been removed and labeled, pull off the valve stem seals with pliers and discard them (the old seals should never be reused), then remove the spring seats.

10   Next, clean the cylinder head with solvent and dry it thoroughly. Compressed air will speed the drying process and ensure that all holes and recessed areas are clean.

11   Clean all of the valve springs, keepers, retainers and spring seats with solvent and dry them thoroughly. Do the parts from one valve at a time so that no mixing of parts between valves occurs.

12   Scrape off any deposits that may have formed on the valve, then use a motorized wire brush to remove deposits from the valve heads and stems. Again, make sure the valves do not get mixed up.

Inspection

Refer to illustrations 12.14, 12.15, 12.16a, 12.16b, 12.17, 12.18a, 12.18b, 12.19a and 12.19b

13   Inspect the head very carefully for cracks and other damage. If cracks are found, a new head will be required. Check the cam bearing surfaces for wear and evidence of seizure. Check the camshafts and lifters for wear as well (see Section 9).

14   Using a precision straightedge and a feeler gauge, check the head gasket mating surface for warpage. Lay the straightedge length-wise, across the head and diagonally (corner-to-corner), intersecting the head bolt holes, and try to slip a feeler gauge under it, on either

side of each combustion chamber **(see illustration)**. The gauge should be the same thickness as the cylinder head warp limit listed in this Chapter's Specifications. If the feeler gauge can be inserted between the head and the straightedge, the head is warped and must either be machined or, if warpage is excessive, replaced with a new one. Minor surface imperfections can be cleaned up by sanding on a surface plate in a figure-eight pattern with 400 or 600 grit wet or dry sandpaper. Be sure to rotate the head every few strokes to avoid removing material unevenly.

15   Examine the valve seats in each of the combustion chambers. If they are pitted, cracked or burned, the head will require valve service that's beyond the scope of the home mechanic. Measure the valve seat width **(see illustration)** and compare it to this Chapter's Specifications. If it is not within the specified range, or if it varies around its circumference, valve service work is required.

16   Clean the valve guides to remove any carbon buildup, then measure the inside diameters of the guides (at both ends and the center of the guide) with a small hole gauge and a 0-to-1-inch micrometer **(see illustrations)**. Record the measurements for future reference. These measurements, along with the valve stem diameter measurements, will enable you to compute the valve stem-to-guide clearance. This clearance, when compared to the Specifications, will be one factor that will determine the extent of the valve service work required. The guides are measured at the ends and at the center to determine if they are worn in

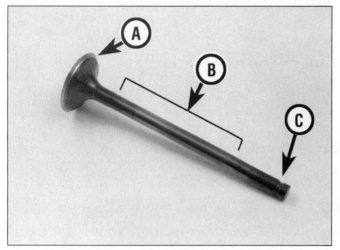

12.17 Check the valve face (A), stem (B) and keeper groove (C) for signs of wear and damage

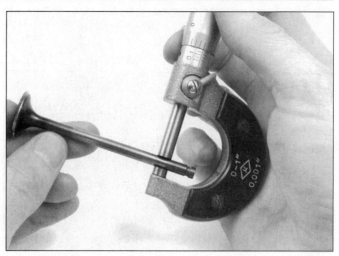

12.18a Measure the valve stem diameter with a micrometer

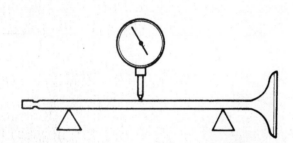

12.18b Check the valve stem for bends with V-blocks and a dial indicator

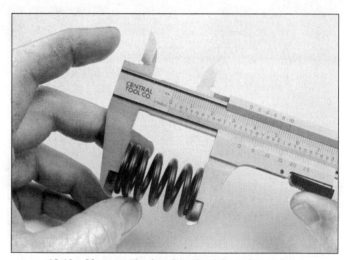

12.19a Measure the free length of the valve springs

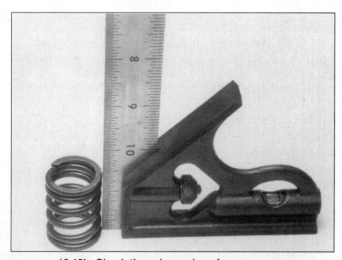

12.19b Check the valve springs for squareness

18   Measure the valve stem diameter (see illustration). By subtracting the stem diameter from the valve guide diameter, the valve stem-to-guide clearance is obtained. If the stem-to-guide clearance is greater than listed in this Chapter's Specifications, the guides and valves will have to be replaced with new ones. Also check the valve stem for bending. Set the valve in a V-block with a dial indicator touching the middle of the stem (see illustration). Rotate the valve and note the reading on the gauge. If the stem runout exceeds the value listed in this Chapter's Specifications, replace the valve.

19   Check the end of each valve spring for wear and pitting. Measure the free length (see illustration) and compare it to this Chapter's Specifications. Any springs that are shorter than specified have sagged and should not be reused. Stand the spring on a flat surface and check it for squareness (see illustration).

20   Check the spring retainers and keepers for obvious wear and cracks. Any questionable parts should not be reused, as extensive damage will occur in the event of failure during engine operation.

21   If the inspection indicates that no service work is required, the valve components can be reinstalled in the head.

Reassembly

Refer to illustrations 12.23, 12.24a, 12.24b, and 12.28

22   Before installing the valves in the head, they should be lapped to ensure a positive seal between the valves and seats. This procedure requires coarse and fine valve lapping compound (available at auto

a bell-mouth pattern (more wear at the ends). If they are, guide replacement is an absolute must.

17   Carefully inspect each valve face for cracks, pits and burned spots. Check the valve stem and the keeper groove area for cracks (see illustration). Rotate the valve and check for any obvious indication that it is bent. Check the end of the stem for pitting and excessive wear and make sure the margin is the specified width. The presence of any of the above conditions indicates the need for valve servicing.

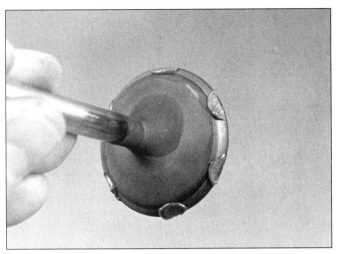

12.23 Apply the lapping compound very sparingly, in small dabs, to the valve face only

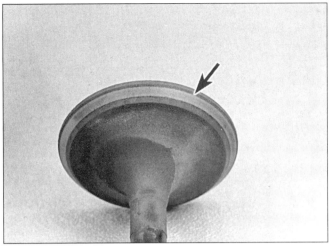

12.24a After lapping, the valve face should have a uniform, unbroken contact pattern (arrow) . . .

12.24b . . . and the seat should be the specified width (arrow) with a smooth unbroken appearance

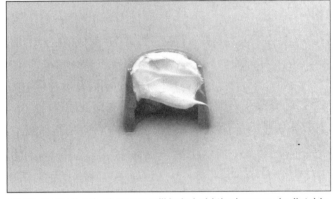

12.28 A small dab of grease will help hold the keepers (collets) in place on the valve spring while the spring is released

parts stores) and a valve lapping tool. If a lapping tool is not available, a piece of rubber or plastic hose can be slipped over the valve stem (after the valve has been installed in the guide) and used to turn the valve.

23 Apply a small amount of coarse lapping compound to the valve face **(see illustration)**, then slip the valve into the guide. **Note:** *Make sure the valve is installed in the correct guide and be careful not to get any lapping compound on the valve stem.*

24 Attach the lapping tool (or hose) to the valve and rotate the tool between the palms of your hands. Use a back-and-forth motion rather than a circular motion. Lift the valve off the seat and turn it at regular intervals to distribute the lapping compound properly. Continue the lapping procedure until the valve face and seat contact area is of uniform width and unbroken around the entire circumference of the valve face and seat **(see illustrations)**.

25 Carefully remove the valve from the guide and wipe off all traces of lapping compound. Use solvent to clean the valve and wipe the seat area thoroughly with a solvent soaked cloth.

26 Repeat the procedure with fine valve lapping compound, then repeat the entire procedure for the remaining valves.

27 Lay the spring seats in place in the cylinder head, then install new valve stem seals on each of the guides **(see illustration 12.7a)**. Use an appropriate size deep socket to push the seals into place until they are properly seated. Don't twist or cock them, or they will not seal properly against the valve stems. Also, don't remove them again or they will be damaged.

28 Coat the valve stems with assembly lube or moly-based grease, then install one of them into its guide. Next, install the springs and retainers, compress the springs and install the keepers. **Note:** *Install the springs with the tightly wound coils at the bottom (next to the spring seat). When compressing the springs with the valve spring compressor, depress them only as far as is absolutely necessary to slip the keepers into place. Apply a small amount of grease to the keepers* **(see illustration)** *to help hold them in place as the pressure is released from the springs. Make certain that the keepers are securely locked in their retaining grooves.*

29 Support the cylinder head on blocks so the valves can't contact the workbench top, then very gently tap each of the valve stems with a soft-faced hammer. This will help seat the keepers in their grooves.

30 Once all of the valves have been installed in the head, check for proper valve sealing by pouring a small amount of solvent into each of the valve ports. If the solvent leaks past the valve(s) into the combustion chamber area, disassemble the valve(s) and repeat the lapping procedure, then reinstall the valve(s) and repeat the check. Repeat the procedure until a satisfactory seal is obtained.

13 Cylinder block - removal, inspection and installation

Removal

Refer to illustrations 13.3a and 13.3b

1 Following the procedure given in Section 10, remove the cylinder head. Make sure the crankshaft is positioned at Top Dead Center (TDC) for cylinder no. 1.

13.3a Lift the cylinder block straight off the studs . . .

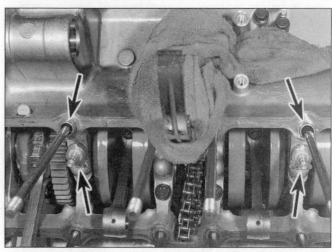

13.3b . . . and note the location of the dowels and oil jets (arrows)

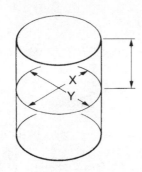

13.7 Measure across the bore in two directions, at the specified distance from the top of the bore

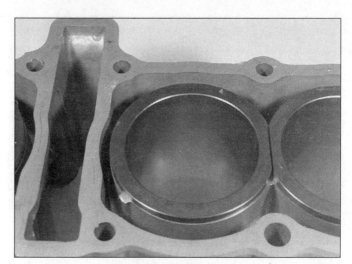

13.10 A bore in good condition will have an even crosshatched appearance, without vertical score marks

2   Remove the coolant tube from the right side of the cylinder block (see Chapter 4).

3   Lift the cylinder block straight up to remove it **(see illustration)**. If it's stuck, tap around its perimeter with a soft-faced hammer. Don't attempt to pry between the block and the crankcase, as you will ruin the sealing surfaces. As you lift, note the location of the dowel pins and oil jet nozzles **(see illustration)**. Be careful not to let these drop into the engine. Remove the O-ring from the base of each cylinder.

4   Stuff clean shop towels around the pistons and remove the gasket and all traces of old gasket material from the surfaces of the cylinder block, cylinder head and crankcase.

Inspection

Refer to illustrations 13.7, 13.10 and 13.12

5   Don't attempt to separate the liners from the cylinder block.

6   Check the cylinder walls carefully for scratches and score marks.

7   Using the appropriate precision measuring tools, check each cylinder's diameter. Measure parallel to the crankshaft axis and across the crankshaft axis, at the depth from the top of the cylinder listed in this Chapter's Specifications **(see illustration)**. Average the two measurements and compare the results to this Chapter's Specifications. If the cylinder walls are tapered, out-of-round, worn beyond the specified limits, or badly scuffed or scored, have them rebored and honed by a dealer service department or a motorcycle repair shop. If a rebore is done, oversize pistons and rings will be required as well.

8   As an alternative, if the precision measuring tools are not available, a dealer service department or motorcycle repair shop will make the measurements and offer advice concerning servicing of the cylinders.

9   If they are in reasonably good condition and not worn to the outside of the limits, and if the piston-to-cylinder clearances can be maintained properly (see Section 14), then the cylinders do not have to be rebored; honing is all that is necessary.

10   To perform the honing operation you will need the proper size flexible hone with fine stones, or a "bottle brush" type hone, plenty of light oil or honing oil, some shop towels and an electric drill motor. Hold the cylinder block in a vise (cushioned with soft jaws or wood blocks) when performing the honing operation. Mount the hone in the drill motor, compress the stones and slip the hone into the cylinder. Lubricate the cylinder thoroughly, turn on the drill and move the hone up and down in the cylinder at a pace which will produce a fine crosshatch pattern on the cylinder wall with the crosshatch lines intersecting at approximately a 60-degree angle **(see illustration)**. Be sure to use plenty of lubricant and do not take off any more material than is absolutely necessary to produce the desired effect. Do not withdraw the hone from the cylinder while it is running. Instead, shut off the drill and continue moving the hone up and down in the cylinder until it comes to a complete stop, then compress the stones and withdraw the hone. Wipe the oil out of the cylinder and repeat the procedure on the remaining cylinders. Remember, do not remove too much material from the cylinder wall. If you do not have the tools, or do not desire to perform the honing operation, a dealer service department or motorcycle repair shop will generally do it for a reasonable fee.

11   Next, the cylinders must be thoroughly washed with warm soapy water to remove all traces of the abrasive grit produced during the

13.12 Lift out the oil jets and install new O-rings, then insert the oil jets firmly into their passages

13.13 Lubricate the cylinder bores with clean engine oil

13.14a Be sure the spray nozzles on the oil jets point in the proper direction (arrows)

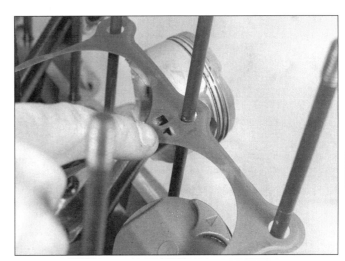

13.14b Make sure the UP mark on the cylinder base gasket is positioned correctly

2

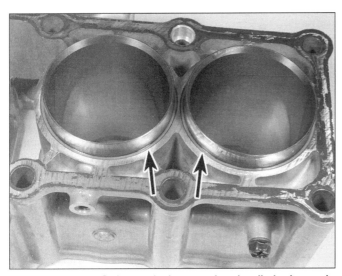

13.14c Install an O-ring on the bottom of each cylinder (arrows)

honing operation. Be sure to run a brush through the bolt holes and coolant passages and flush them with running water. After rinsing, dry the cylinders thoroughly and apply a coat of light, rust-preventative oil to all machined surfaces.

12   Lift the oil jets out of their passages, replace the O-rings and reinstall the jets (see illustration).

Installation

Refer to illustrations 13.13, 13.14a, 13.14b, 13.14c and 13.17

13   Lubricate the cylinder bores and pistons with plenty of clean engine oil (see illustration).

14   Install the dowel pins and oil jet nozzles (see illustration), then place a new cylinder base gasket on the crankcase (see illustration). Make sure the UP mark on the gasket is upright and toward the front of the engine (if the UP cutout reads backwards, the gasket is upside down). Install new O-rings on the base of each cylinder (see illustration).

15   Slowly rotate the crankshaft until two of the pistons are at the top of their travel and two are at the bottom.

16   Attach four piston ring compressors to the pistons and compress the piston rings. Large hose clamps can be used instead - just make sure they don't scratch the pistons, and don't tighten them too much.

13.17 If you're experienced and very careful, you can install the cylinders over the rings using only a screwdriver, but it's a good idea to use a ring compressor

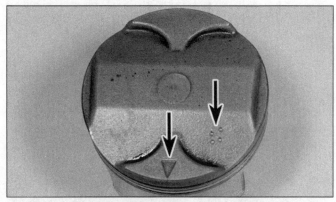

14.3a Mark the piston with its cylinder number (right arrow); the triangular mark (left arrow) points to the front (exhaust) side of the engine when the piston is installed

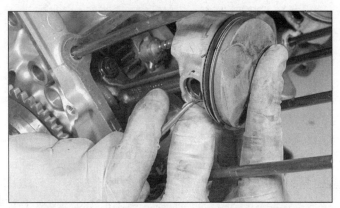

14.3b Wear eye protection and pry out the clip with a pointed tool

14.4a Pull out the piston pin and lift the piston off the connecting rod

18   Slide the cylinder block down over the remaining two pistons and guide the rings into the bores.
19   Remove the piston ring compressors or hose clamps, being careful not to scratch the pistons.
20   The remainder of installation is the reverse of removal.

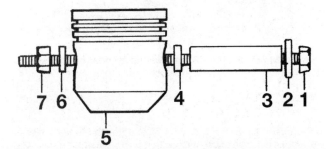

14.4b The piston pins should come out with hand pressure - if they don't, this removal tool can be fabricated with readily available parts

1	Bolt	4	Padding*	6	Washer**
2	Washer	5	Piston	7	Nut**
3	Pipe*				

*Large enough for piston pin to fit inside
**Small enough to fit through piston pin bore

17   Install the cylinder block over the pistons and carefully lower it down until the piston crowns fit into the cylinder liners (see illustration). While doing this, pull the camshaft chain up, using a hooked tool or a piece of coat hanger. Also keep an eye on the cam chain guide to make sure it doesn't wedge against the block. Push down on the cylinder block, making sure the pistons don't get cocked sideways, until the bottoms of the cylinder liners slide down past the piston rings. A wood or plastic hammer handle can be used to gently tap the block down, but don't use too much force or the pistons will be damaged.

14   Pistons - removal, inspection and installation

1   The pistons are attached to the connecting rods with piston pins that are a slip fit in the pistons and rods.
2   Before removing the pistons from the rods, stuff a clean shop towel into each crankcase hole, around the connecting rods. This will prevent the circlips from falling into the crankcase if they are inadvertently dropped.

Removal

Refer to illustrations 14.3a, 14.3b, 14.4a, 14.4b and 14.4c
3   Using a sharp scribe, scratch the number of each piston into its crown (or use a felt pen if the piston is clean enough). Each piston should also have a triangular mark pointing to the front of the engine (see illustration). If not, scribe an arrow into the piston crown before removal. Support the first piston, grasp the circlip with a pointed tool or needle-nose pliers and remove it from the groove (see illustration).
4   Push the piston pin out from the opposite end to free the piston from the rod (see illustration). You may have to deburr the area around the groove to enable the pin to slide out (use a triangular file for this procedure). If the pin won't come out, remove the remaining circlip. Fabricate a piston pin removal tool from threaded stock, nuts, washers and a piece of pipe (see illustration). Repeat the procedure for the other pistons (see illustration).

14.4c Cylinder block and piston - exploded view

1   Dowel
2   Sealing washer (replace if removed)
3   Cylinder block
4   O-ring
5   Base gasket
6   Coolant drain plugs
7   Piston pin clip (replace if removed)
8   Piston
9   Piston pin
10 Piston pin clip (replace if removed)
11 Piston rings

2

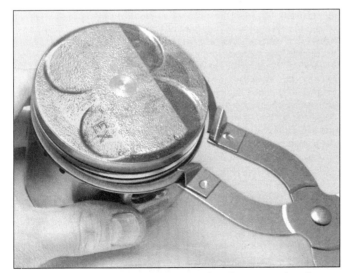

14.6 Remove the piston rings with a ring removal and installation tool

Inspection

Refer to illustrations 14.6, 14.11, 14.13, 14.14 and 14.15

5   Before the inspection process can be carried out, the pistons must be cleaned and the old piston rings removed.

6   Using a piston ring installation tool, carefully remove the rings from the pistons **(see illustration)**. Do not nick or gouge the pistons in the process.

7   Scrape all traces of carbon from the tops of the pistons. A hand-held wire brush or a piece of fine emery cloth can be used once most of the deposits have been scraped away. Do not, under any circumstances, use a wire brush mounted in a drill motor to remove deposits from the pistons; the piston material is soft and will be eroded away by the wire brush.

8   Use a piston ring groove cleaning tool to remove any carbon deposits from the ring grooves. If a tool is not available, a piece broken off the old ring will do the job. Be very careful to remove only the carbon deposits. Do not remove any metal and do not nick or gouge the sides of the ring grooves.

9   Once the deposits have been removed, clean the pistons with solvent and dry them thoroughly. Make sure the oil return holes below the oil ring grooves are clear.

10   If the pistons are not damaged or worn excessively and if the

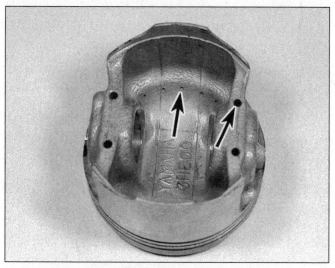

14.11 Check the piston pin bore and the piston skirt for wear, and make sure the internal holes are clear (arrows)

14.13 Measure the piston ring-to-groove clearance with a feeler gauge

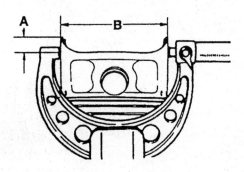

14.14 Measure the piston diameter with a micrometer

A   *Specified distance from bottom of piston*
B   *Piston diameter*

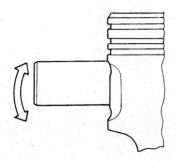

14.15 Slip the pin into the piston and try to wiggle it back-and-forth; if it's loose, replace the piston and pin

cylinders are not rebored, new pistons will not be necessary. Normal piston wear appears as even, vertical wear on the thrust surfaces of the piston and slight looseness of the top ring in its groove. New piston rings, on the other hand, should always be used when an engine is rebuilt.

11   Carefully inspect each piston for cracks around the skirt, at the pin bosses and at the ring lands **(see illustration)**.

12   Look for scoring and scuffing on the thrust faces of the skirt, holes in the piston crown and burned areas at the edge of the crown. If the skirt is scored or scuffed, the engine may have been suffering from overheating and/or abnormal combustion, which caused excessively high operating temperatures. The oil pump and cooling system should be checked thoroughly. A hole in the piston crown, an extreme to be sure, is an indication that abnormal combustion (pre-ignition) was occurring. Burned areas at the edge of the piston crown are usually evidence of spark knock (detonation). If any of the above problems exist, the causes must be corrected or the damage will occur again.

13   Measure the piston ring-to-groove clearance by laying a new piston ring in the ring groove and slipping a feeler gauge in beside it **(see illustration)**. Check the clearance at three or four locations around the groove. Be sure to use the correct ring for each groove; they are different. If the clearance is greater than specified, new pistons will have to be used when the engine is reassembled.

14   Check the piston-to-bore clearance by measuring the bore (see Section 13) and the piston diameter. Make sure that the pistons and cylinders are correctly matched. Measure the piston across the skirt on

the thrust faces at a 90-degree angle to the piston pin, at the distance from the bottom of the skirt listed in this Chapter's Specifications **(see illustration)**. Subtract the piston diameter from the bore diameter to obtain the clearance. If it is greater than specified, the cylinders will have to be rebored and new oversized pistons and rings installed. If the appropriate precision measuring tools are not available, the piston-to-cylinder clearances can be obtained, though not quite as accurately, using feeler gauge stock. Feeler gauge stock comes in 12-inch lengths and various thicknesses and is generally available at auto parts stores. To check the clearance, select a feeler gauge of the same thickness as the piston clearance listed in this Chapter's Specifications and slip it into the cylinder along with the appropriate piston. The cylinder should be upside down and the piston must be positioned exactly as it normally would be. Place the feeler gauge between the piston and cylinder on one of the thrust faces (90-degrees to the piston pin bore). The piston should slip through the cylinder (with the feeler gauge in place) with moderate pressure. If it falls through, or slides through easily, the clearance is excessive and a new piston will be required. If the piston binds at the lower end of the cylinder and is loose toward the top, the cylinder is tapered, and if tight spots are encountered as the feeler gauge is placed at different points around the cylinder, the cylinder is out-of-round. Repeat the procedure for the remaining pistons and cylinders. Be sure to have the cylinders and pistons checked by a dealer service department or a motorcycle repair shop to confirm your findings before purchasing new parts.

15   Apply clean engine oil to the pin, insert it into the piston and

14.17 Make sure the piston pin clips are securely seated in the grooves (arrow)

15.3a Square the ring in the bore by turning the piston upside down and tapping on the ring . . .

15.3b . . . then lift the piston out and check the ring end gap with a feeler gauge

15.5 If the end gap is too small, clamp a file in a vise and file the ring ends (from the outside in only) to enlarge the gap slightly

2

check for freeplay by rocking the pin back-and-forth **(see illustration)**. If the pin is loose, new pistons and pins must be installed.

16   Refer to Section 15 and install the rings on the pistons.

Installation

Refer to illustration 14.17

17   Install the pistons in their original locations with the arrows pointing to the front of the engine. Lubricate the pins and the rod bores with clean engine oil. Install new circlips in the grooves in the inner sides of the pistons (don't reuse the old circlips). Push the pins into position from the opposite side and install new circlips. Compress the circlips only enough for them to fit in the piston. Make sure the clips are properly seated in the grooves **(see illustration)**.

15   Piston rings - installation

Refer to illustrations 15.3a, 15.3b, 15.5, 15.9a, 15.9b, 15.11 and 15.15

1   Before installing the new piston rings, the ring end gaps must be checked.

2   Lay out the pistons and the new ring sets so the rings will be matched with the same piston and cylinder during the end gap mea-surement procedure and engine assembly.

3   Insert the top (No. 1) ring into the bottom of the first cylinder and square it up with the cylinder walls by pushing it in with the top of the piston **(see illustration)**. The ring should be about one inch above the bottom edge of the cylinder. To measure the end gap, slip a feeler gauge between the ends of the ring **(see illustration)** and compare the measurement to the Specifications.

4   If the gap is larger or smaller than specified, double check to make sure that you have the correct rings before proceeding.

5   If the gap is too small, it must be enlarged or the ring ends may come in contact with each other during engine operation, which can cause serious damage. The end gap can be increased by filing the ring ends very carefully with a fine file **(see illustration)**. When performing this operation, file only from the outside in.

6   Excess end gap is not critical unless it is greater than 1 mm (0.04 inch). Again, double check to make sure you have the correct rings for your engine.

7   Repeat the procedure for each ring that will be installed in the first cylinder and for each ring in the remaining cylinder. Remember to keep the rings, pistons and cylinders matched up.

8   Once the ring end gaps have been checked/corrected, the rings can be installed on the pistons.

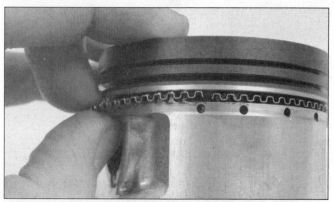

15.9a Installing the oil ring expander - make sure the ends don't overlap

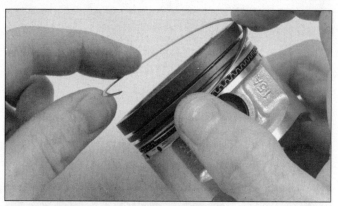

15.9b Installing an oil ring side rail - don't use a ring installation tool to do this

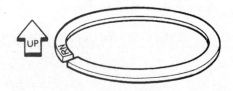

15.11 The second ring has an RN mark; the top ring has an R mark or no mark; make sure the marks on the rings face up when the rings are installed on the pistons

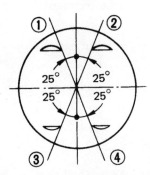

15.15 Arrange the ring gaps like this

1 Top compression ring	3 Oil ring upper rail
2 Oil ring lower rail	4 Second compression ring

make sure that the identification mark is facing up **(see illustration 15.11)**. Fit the ring into the middle groove on the piston. Do not expand the ring any more than is necessary to slide it into place.

13   Finally, install the top ring in the same manner. Make sure the identifying mark is facing up.

14   Repeat the procedure for the remaining pistons and rings. Be very careful not to confuse the top and second rings.

15   Once the rings have been properly installed, stagger the end gaps, including those of the oil ring side rails **(see illustration)**.

16.6a Remove the oil pan bolts (arrows) . . .

16 Oil pan and relief valve - removal, relief valve inspection and installation

Note: *The oil pan can be removed with the engine in the frame.*

Removal

Refer to illustrations 16.6a, 16.6b, 16.6c, 16.8, 16.9a, 16.9b and 16.11

1   Support the bike securely so it can't be knocked over during this procedure.

2   Remove the left and right fairings and the fairing stay (see Chapter 9).

3   Disconnect the wires for the oil level switch and neutral switch (see Chapter 10).

4   Remove the exhaust system (see Chapter 5).

5   Drain the engine oil and remove the oil filter (see Chapter 1). If you're working on a model equipped with a spin-on oil filter, remove the filter mounting base **(see illustrations 22.8a, 22.8b and 22.8c)**.

6   Remove the oil pan bolts and detach the pan from the crankcase **(see illustrations)**.

9   The oil control ring (lowest on the piston) is installed first. It is composed of three separate components. Slip the expander into the groove, then install the upper side rail **(see illustrations)**. Do not use a piston ring installation tool on the oil ring side rails as they may be damaged. Instead, place one end of the side rail into the groove between the spacer expander and the ring land. Hold it firmly in place and slide a finger around the piston while pushing the rail into the groove. Next, install the lower side rail in the same manner.

10   After the three oil ring components have been installed, check to make sure that both the upper and lower side rails can be turned smoothly in the ring groove.

11   Install the second (middle) ring next. It can be distinguished from the top ring by its RN mark (the top ring is marked R or not marked) **(see illustration)**. Do not mix the top and middle rings.

12   To avoid breaking the ring, use a piston ring installation tool and

16.6b . . . this bolt secures the harness clip for the oil level sender . . .

16.6c . . . and take the oil pan off

16.8 The arrow on the strainer cover points in the opposite direction from the Front arrow cast in the oil pickup

16.9a Remove the pickup mounting bolts (arrows) . . .

16.9b . . . and take the pickup off the engine

16.11 Pull the relief valve out of the case; it's a good idea to replace the O-ring whenever the relief valve is removed

7   Remove all traces of old gasket material from the mating surfaces of the oil pan and crankcase.
8   Remove the strainer from the oil pickup **(see illustration)**.

9   Unbolt the pickup from the crankcase and lift it off **(see illustrations)**.
10   Remove all traces of old gasket from the pickup and crankcase.
11   Remove the relief valve from the crankcase **(see illustration)**. It should pull out with light hand pressure. If it's stuck, rock it back and forth slightly.

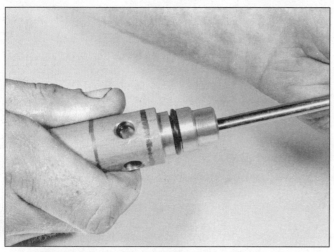

16.12 Push in on the relief valve plunger to make sure it moves freely

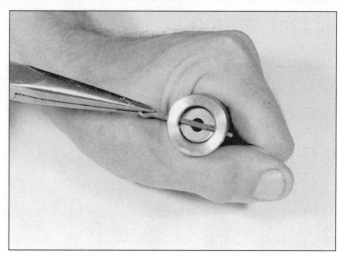

16.13 Straighten the ends of the cotter pin and pull it out

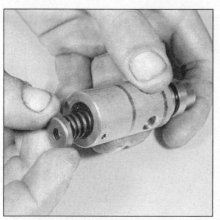

16.14a Remove the spring retainer . . .

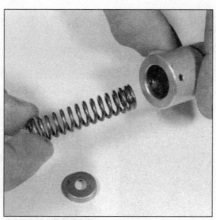

16.14b . . . the spring . . .

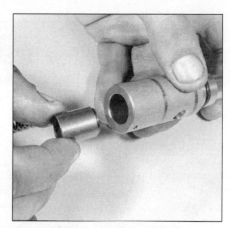

16.14c . . . and the plunger

16.16 Make sure the oil pan dowels are in position (arrows)

15   Check all parts for wear and damage. Clean the parts thoroughly, reassemble the valve and recheck its movement. If the valve still sticks, replace it. **Caution**: *If you reuse the relief valve, install a new cotter pin before reinstalling the relief valve in the engine.*

Installation

Refer to illustration 16.16

16   Install the oil pan dowels **(see illustration)**. Install the relief valve in the crankcase, using a new O-ring.
17   Install the oil pickup and tighten the bolts to the torque listed in this Chapter's Specifications. Install the strainer on the pickup with its arrow pointing away from the relief valve.
18   Position a new gasket on the oil pan. A thin film of RTV sealant can be used to hold the gasket in place. Install the oil pan and bolts, tightening the bolts to the torque listed in this Chapter's Specifications, using a criss-cross pattern.
19   The remainder of installation is the reverse of removal. Install a new filter and fill the crankcase with oil (see Chapter 1), then run the engine and check for leaks.

Relief valve inspection

Refer to illustrations 16.12, 16.13, 16.14a, 16.14b and 16.14c

12   Push the plunger into the relief valve and check for free movement **(see illustration)**. If the valve sticks, perform Steps 13 through 15 to disassemble and inspect it.
13   Straighten the cotter pin and pull it out **(see illustration)**.
14   Remove the spring retainer, spring and plunger **(see illustrations)**.

---

17   Oil pump - oil pressure check, removal, inspection and installation

---

Note: *The oil pump can be removed with the engine in the frame.*

Oil pressure check

Refer to illustration 17.2
Warning: *If the oil passage plug is removed when the engine is hot, hot*

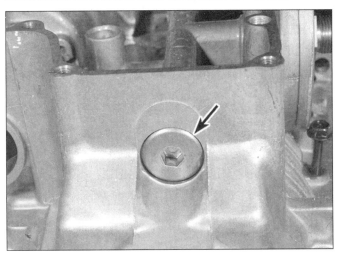

17.2 To check the oil pressure, remove the plug (arrow) and connect an oil pressure gauge using the proper adapter

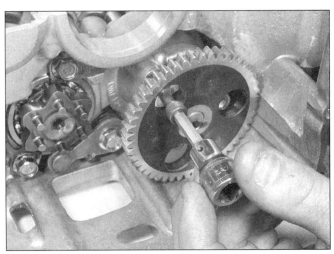

17.8a Insert an Allen bolt bit through the holes in the oil pump gear to remove the mounting bolts . . .

17.8b . . . then take off the pump

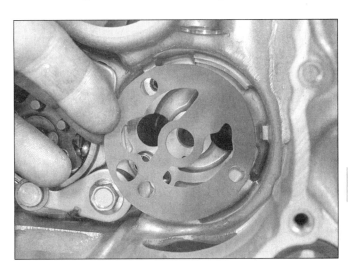

17.9a Remove the gasket . . .

17.9b . . . and the dowel

oil will drain out - wait until the engine is cold before beginning this check.

1 Remove the left and right fairings (see Chapter 9).
2 Remove the plug at the bottom of the crankcase on the right-hand side and install an oil pressure gauge **(see illustration)**.

3 Start the engine and watch the gauge while varying the engine rpm. The pressure should stay within the relief valve opening pressure listed in this Chapter's Specifications. If the pressure is too high, the relief valve is stuck closed. To check it, see Section 16.
4 If the pressure is lower than the standard, either the relief valve is stuck open, the oil pump is faulty, or there is other engine damage. Begin diagnosis by checking the relief valve (see Section 16), then the oil pump. If those items check out okay, chances are the bearing oil clearances are excessive and the engine needs to be overhauled.
5 If the pressure reading is in the desired range, allow the engine to warm up to normal operating temperature and check the pressure again, at the specified engine rpm. Compare your findings with this Chapter's Specifications.
6 If the pressure is significantly lower than specified, check the relief valve and the oil pump.

Removal
Refer to illustrations 17.8a, 17.8b, 17.9a and 17.9b

7 Remove the clutch (see Section 19).
8 Remove the oil pump mounting bolts and remove the pump **(see illustrations)**.
9 Remove the oil pump gasket and dowel **(see illustrations)**.

Inspection
Refer to illustrations 17.11, 17.12, 17.14a, 17.14b and 17.15

10 Wash the oil pump in solvent, then dry it off.

17.11 Remove the Phillips screw (you may need an impact driver) . . .

17.12 . . . and lift the housing and rotors off the pump shaft

17.14a Measure clearance between the inner rotor tip and the outer rotor (arrow) with a feeler gauge

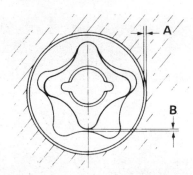

17.14b Measure clearance between the outer rotor and pump body with a feeler gauge (A) and rotor tips (B)

17.17a Align the arrow cast in the crankcase with the arrow cast in the pump body

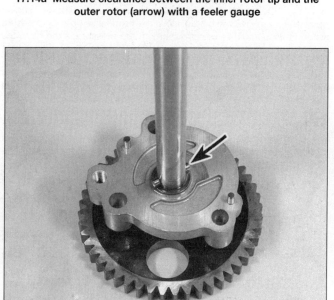

17.15 Make sure the pin (arrow) is centered in the pump shaft

11   Remove the pump housing screws (use an impact driver if they're tight) **(see illustration)**. Lift off the housing.
12   Lift off the rotors **(see illustration)**.
13   Check the pump body and rotors for scoring and wear. If any damage or uneven or excessive wear is evident, replace the pump (individual parts aren't available). If you are rebuilding the engine, it's a good idea to install a new oil pump.
14   Measure the clearance between the inner and outer rotor tips and between the outer rotor and housing **(see illustrations)**. Replace the pump if the clearance is excessive.
15   If the pump is good, reverse the disassembly steps to reassemble it. Make sure the pin is centered in the rotor shaft so it will align with the slot in the inner rotor **(see illustration)**.

17.17b Tighten the pump mounting bolts with an Allen bolt bit

18.2a Loosen the cover bolts (arrows) evenly in a criss-cross pattern . . .

18.2b . . . then take the cover off

18.3 Remove the gasket and dowels (arrows)

18.4a Remove the upper idle gear and its shaft . . .

Installation

Refer to illustrations 17.17a and 7.7b

16   Before installing the pump, prime it by pouring oil into it while turning the shaft by hand - this will ensure that it begins to pump oil quickly.

17   Installation is the reverse of removal, with the following additions:
  a) Align the arrow mark on the pump body with the cast mark on the crankcase **(see illustration)**.
  b) Use non-permanent thread locking agent on the pump mounting bolts and tighten the bolts to the torque listed in this Chapter's Specifications **(see illustration)**.

---

18   **Starter clutch - removal, inspection and installation**

Removal

Refer to illustrations 18.2a, 18.2b, 18.3, 18.4a, 18.4b, 18.4c, 18.5, 18.6 and 18.7

1   Remove the left and right fairings (see Chapter 9).

2   Loosen the starter clutch cover bolts in a criss-cross pattern, 1/4 turn at a time, until all are loose, then lift the cover off **(see illustrations)**.

3   Remove the cover gasket and dowels **(see illustration)**.

4   Remove the idle gears **(see illustrations)**.

18.4b ... then the starter drive gear ...

18.4c ... then the lower idle gear and its shaft

18.5 Remove the starter clutch securing bolt and washer

18.6 Remove the starter clutch with a three-legged puller

18.7 Remove the woodruff key and starter clutch gear

18.8 Check the starter clutch rollers (right arrow) and the friction surface of the gear (left arrow) for wear or damage

18.9 Place the gear in the starter clutch and try to rotate it; it should turn freely in one direction but not in the other direction

18.10 Check the idle gears and shafts for wear or damage

Inspection

Refer to illustrations 18.8, 18.9, 18.10, 18.11a and 18.11b

8   Check the rollers inside the starter clutch for wear and damage **(see illustration)**. If any undesirable conditions can be seen, replace the starter clutch. Check the friction surface on the starter clutch gear for scoring or other defects. Replace the gear if the friction surface isn't perfectly smooth.

9   Place the starter clutch gear in the starter clutch and try to rotate it separately from the starter clutch **(see illustration)**. It should turn easily counterclockwise (anti-clockwise), but lock up when you try to turn it clockwise. If not, replace the starter clutch.

10   Check the idle gears for chipped or worn teeth **(see illustration)**.

5   Remove the starter clutch securing bolt and washer **(see illustration)**.

6   Attach a three-legged puller (Yamaha tool no. YU-33270, part no. 90890-01362 or equivalent) to the starter clutch, then tighten the puller bolt to pull the starter clutch off **(see illustration)**.

7   Remove the woodruff key and starter clutch gear **(see illustration)**.

18.11a Have the ball bearing inside the cover replaced if it's worn or damaged

18.11b Also check the needle roller bearing inside the crankcase

18.12 Install the woodruff key in the shaft

18.14a Install the starter drive gear . . .

18.14b . . . the lower idle gear and shaft . . .

18.14c . . . and the upper idle gear and shaft

Check the shafts for wear. Replace them if any of these conditions are found.

11   Check the bearing inside the starter clutch cover and the idler gear bearing in the crankcase for wear, damage or looseness **(see illustrations)**. Have the bearings replaced by a Yamaha dealer or machine shop if their condition is in doubt.

Installation

Refer to illustrations 18.12, 18.14a, 18.14b and 18.14c

12   Install the woodruff key in its slot **(see illustration)**. Install the starter clutch gear on the shaft with its friction surface facing outward **(see illustration 18.7)**.

13   Install the starter clutch, washer and securing bolt **(see illustration 18.5)**. Tighten the center bolt to the torque listed in this Chapter's Specifications.

14   Install the starter drive gear and idle gears **(see illustrations)**.

15   Install the cover dowels and a new gasket **(see illustration 18.3)**.

16   Install the cover. Tighten its bolts in several stages, in a criss-cross pattern, to the torque listed in this Chapter's Specifications.

***

19   Clutch - removal, inspection and installation

Note: *The clutch can be removed with the engine in the frame.*

Removal

Refer to illustrations 19.3a, 19.3b, 19.3c, 19.3d, 19.4a, 19.4b, 19.4c, 19.5a, 19.5b, 19.6a, 19.6b, 19.7a, 19.7b, 19.7c, 19.8, 19.9, 19.10 and 19.11

1   Support the bike securely so it can't be knocked over during this procedure. Remove the right fairing (see Chapter 9).

2   Drain the engine oil (see Chapter 1).

19.3a Loosen the clutch cover bolts (arrows) 1/4 turn at a time in a criss-cross pattern . . .

19.3b . . . then take the cover off the engine . . .

19.3c . . . and remove the gasket

3   Loosen the clutch cover bolts 1/4 turn at a time in a criss-cross pattern, then remove the clutch cover **(see illustrations)**.
4   Loosen the pressure plate bolts evenly in a criss-cross pattern, then remove the bolts, springs and pressure plate **(see illustrations)**.
5   Remove the friction plates and steel plates **(see illustrations)**.
6   Remove the short pushrod and the steel ball that fits behind it **(see illustration)**. There's another, longer pushrod behind the steel ball

which can be removed for inspection with a magnet. If it won't come out easily, it can be removed from the other side of the engine if the engine sprocket cover is removed **(see illustration)**.
7   Bend back the lockwasher on the clutch boss nut **(see illustration)**. Remove the nut, using a special holding tool (Yamaha tool no. YM-91402, part no. 90890-04086 or equivalent) to prevent the clutch housing from turning **(see illustration)**. An alternative to this tool can

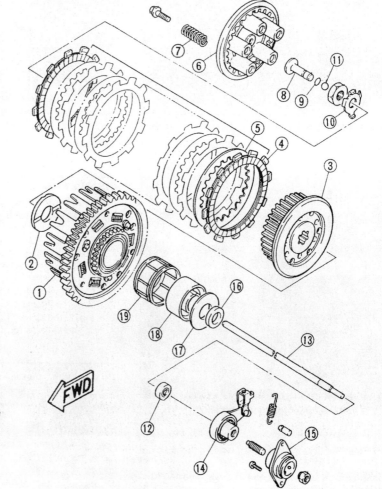

19.3d Clutch - exploded view

1   Clutch housing
2   Thrust washer
3   Clutch boss
4   Friction plate
5   Steel plate
6   Pressure plate
7   Pressure plate spring
8   Short pushrod
9   O-ring
10 Lockwasher
11 Steel ball
12 Oil seal
13 Long pushrod
14 Release mechanism
15 Release mechanism housing
16 Collar
17 Thrust washer
18 Spacer
19 Bearing

19.4a Loosen the pressure plate bolts
evenly with a Phillips screwdriver
or socket . . .

19.4b . . . then remove the bolts
and springs . . .

19.4c . . . and take off the pressure plate

19.5a Take off a friction plate . . .

19.5b . . . then a steel plate

19.6a Remove the short pushrod and
steel ball . . .

19.6b . . . then remove the long pushrod
from behind them - it can also be
removed from the other side of the
engine, as shown here, if the engine
sprocket cover is removed

19.7a Bend back the tab on
the lockwasher . . .

19.7b . . . hold the clutch from turning
with a tool like the one shown here and
remove the nut . . .

2

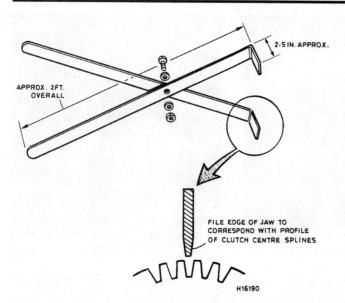

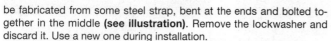

19.7c ... you can make your own holding tool out of steel strap

19.8 Remove the grooved washer

be fabricated from some steel strap, bent at the ends and bolted together in the middle **(see illustration)**. Remove the lockwasher and discard it. Use a new one during installation.

8   Remove the clutch boss and thrust washer **(see illustration)**.

9   Thread a pair of bolts into the spacer and pull it out **(see illustration)**.

10   Pull out the bearing and remove the clutch housing **(see illustration)**.

11   Remove the thrust washer and collar from behind the clutch housing **(see illustration)**.

Inspection

Refer to illustrations 19.12, 19.13, 19.14, 19.15, 19.17, 19.19 and 19.20

12   Examine the splines on both the inside and the outside of the clutch boss **(see illustration)**. If any wear is evident, replace the clutch boss with a new one.

13   Measure the free length of the clutch springs **(see illustration)**. Replace the springs as a set if any one of them is not within the values listed in this Chapter's Specifications.

14   If the lining material of the friction plates smells burnt or if it's glazed, new parts are required. If the metal clutch plates are scored or discolored, they must be replaced with new ones. Measure the thickness of each friction plate **(see illustration)** and compare the results to this Chapter's Specifications. Replace the friction plates as a set if any are near the wear limit.

15   Lay the metal plates, one at a time, on a perfectly flat surface (such as a piece of plate glass) and check for warpage by trying to slip a feeler gauge between the flat surface and the plate **(see illustration)**. The feeler gauge should be the same thickness as the warpage limit listed in this Chapter's Specifications. Do this at several places around the plate's circumference. If the feeler gauge can be slipped under the plate, it is warped and should be replaced with a new one.

16   Check the tabs on the friction plates for excessive wear and mushroomed edges. They can be cleaned up with a file if the deformation is not severe.

17   Check the edges of the slots in the clutch housing for indentations made by the friction plate tabs **(see illustration)**. If the indentations are deep they can prevent clutch release, so the housing should be replaced with a new one. If the indentations can be removed easily with a file, the life of the housing can be prolonged to an extent.

18   Check the pressure plate, thrust washers, spacer and collar for wear and damage. Replace any worn or damaged parts.

19   If you removed the long pushrod, make sure it isn't bent (roll it on a perfectly flat surface or use V-blocks and a dial indicator). Check both pushrods and the steel ball for wear or damage and replace them if defects are visible. Install a new O-ring on the short pushrod **(see illustration)**.

19.9 Thread a pair of bolts into the spacer and pull it out

19.10 Remove the bearing

19.11 Remove the large and small washers

19.12 Check the inner and outer splines of the clutch boss for wear

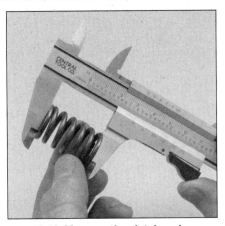

19.13 Measure the clutch spring free length

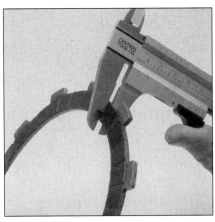

19.14 Measure the thickness of the friction plates

19.15 Check the metal plates for warpage

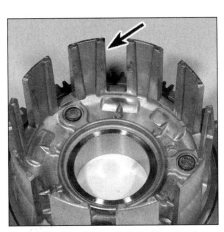

19.17 Check the slots in the clutch housing (arrow) for uneven wear

19.19 Check the pushrods and steel ball for wear or damage; install a new O-ring on the short pushrod

2

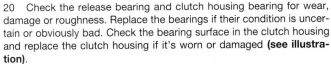

19.20 Check the springs in the clutch housing for breakage; check the gear teeth for wear or damage

19.24 Place a new lockwasher on the shaft and install the nut

20   Check the release bearing and clutch housing bearing for wear, damage or roughness. Replace the bearings if their condition is uncertain or obviously bad. Check the bearing surface in the clutch housing and replace the clutch housing if it's worn or damaged (see illustration).
21   Clean all traces of old gasket material from clutch cover and its mating surface on the crankcase.

Installation

Refer to illustrations 19.24, 19.26, 19.27a, 19.27b, 19.27c, 19.28, 19.29a, 19.29b, 19.30a, 19.30b and 19.30c
22   Install the collar, thrust washer and clutch housing.
23   Coat the clutch housing bearing with engine oil, then install the bearing and spacer (see illustration 19.3d).
24   Install the thrust washer, the clutch boss, a new lockwasher and the clutch boss nut (see illustration).

19.26 Bend the lockwasher against the nut

19.27a Install the long pushrod (narrow end first) . . .

19.27b . . . the steel ball . . .

19.27c . . . and the short pushrod

19.28 Install a friction plate . . .

19.29a . . . then a steel plate . . .

19.29b . . . the rounded edge of each steel plate faces in toward the engine; the sharp edge faces out

25   Tighten the clutch boss nut to the torque listed in this Chapter's Specifications, using the technique described in Step 7 to prevent the housing from turning.

26   Bend the lockwasher against one of the flats on the nut with pliers **(see illustration)**.

27   Coat the pushrods and steel ball with multi-purpose grease, then install the long pushrod, the ball and the short pushrod **(see illustrations)**.

28   Coat one of the friction plates with engine oil and install it in the clutch housing **(see illustration)**. Engage the tabs on the friction plate with the slots in the clutch housing.

29   Install a steel plate on top of the friction plate with its rounded side inward **(see illustrations)**. Continue to install alternate friction and steel plates (a friction plate is the last one installed).

30   The remainder of installation is the reverse of the removal steps, with the following additions:

a) Align the hole in the pressure plate with the triangular mark on the clutch boss **(see illustration)**. Tighten the pressure plate bolts in several stages in a criss-cross pattern to the torque listed in this Chapter's Specifications.

b) Make sure the clutch cover dowels are in position and install a new gasket **(see illustration)**.

c) Install the shouldered clutch cover bolts in the same holes as the dowels **(see illustration)**. Tighten the clutch cover bolts in several stages to the torque listed in this Chapter's Specifications.

31   Fill the crankcase with the recommended type and amount of engine oil (see Chapter 1).

20 Clutch cable - removal and installation

Refer to illustration 20.4

1   Loosen the clutch cable locknut and adjusting nut at the handlebar (see Chapter 1).

2   Loosen the pinch bolt on the shift arm, then slide the arm off the shaft (see Section 21).

3   Remove the bolts and remove the engine sprocket cover (see Chapter 7).

19.30a After installing the last friction plate, align the marks on pressure plate and clutch boss (arrow) . . .

19.30b . . . and install the pressure plate screws, dowels and gasket. . .

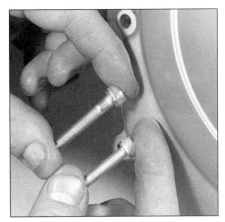

19.30c . . . install the cover with the shouldered bolts in the dowel holes

20.4 Disconnect the lower end of the cable from the release mechanism inside the engine sprocket cover

21.2 The marks on the shift shaft and shift arm must be aligned to ensure the correct shift arm position, or shifting problems will occur

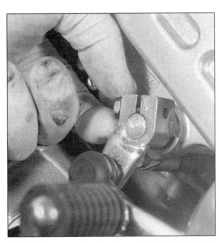

21.3 Remove the bolt and slide the shift arm off the shaft

21.4 Remove the bracket bolts (arrows) and take the bracket off together with the footpeg, shift pedal and linkage

4   Disconnect the lower end of the cable from the release mechanism and take the cable out (see illustration).
5   Installation is the reverse of the removal steps. Adjust the cable (see Chapter 1).

21   External shift mechanism - removal, inspection and installation

Shift linkage and pedal

Refer to illustrations 21.2, 21.3 and 21.4

1   Support the bike securely so it can't be knocked over during this procedure.
2   Look for a punch mark on the end of the shift shaft (see illustration). This should align with the mark in the arm. If you can't find it, make your own punch mark so the arm can be realigned correctly during installation.
3   Remove the lever pinch bolt (see illustration). Pull the lever off the shaft, together with the linkage rod.
4   Remove the shift pedal/footpeg bracket bolts and take the assembly off (see illustration). If necessary, remove the Allen bolt and separate the footpeg and shift pedal from the bracket.

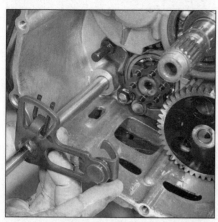

21.7 Pull the shift shaft out of the engine

21.9 Remove the stopper lever bolt, then remove the lever and spring

21.11 If the shift shaft springs and worn, distorted or broken, replace the shaft

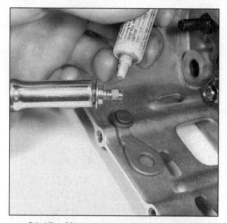

21.15a Use non-permanent thread locking agent on the threads of the stopper lever bolt . . .

21.15b . . . and install the lever, making sure its spring is correctly engaged

21.18 Slide the shift shaft into the engine and position the ends of the large spring on either side of the guide bar (arrows)

5   Installation is the reverse of removal. Adjust the linkage as needed with the nuts on the linkage shaft.

Shift mechanism removal
Refer to illustrations 21.7 and 21.9

6   Remove the shift pedal and linkage (Steps 1 through 4), clutch (see Chapter 19) and engine sprocket cover (see Chapter 7).
7   Slide the shift shaft out of the crankcase **(see illustration)**.
8   Remove the oil pump (see Section 17).
9   Remove the stopper lever, and return spring **(see illustration)**.

Shift mechanism inspection
Refer to illustration 21.11

10   Inspect the shift shaft guide bar **(see illustration 21.9)**. If it's worn or damaged, replace it. If it's loose, unscrew it, apply a non-permanent thread locking compound to the threads, reinstall the guide bar and tighten it securely.
11   Check the shift shaft for bends and damaged splines. If the shaft is bent, you can attempt to straighten it, but replace it if the splines are damaged. Inspect the pawls and springs on the shift shaft and replace the shaft if they're worn or damaged **(see illustration)**.
12   Check the condition of the stopper lever and spring. Replace the stopper lever if it's worn where it contacts the shift cam. Replace the spring if it's distorted.
13   Inspect the pins on the end of the shift cam. If they're worn or damaged, you'll have to disassemble the crankcase to replace the shift cam.
14   Check the condition of the seals in the crankcase and engine sprocket cover (see Chapter 7). If they've been leaking, replace them.

Installation
Refer to illustrations 21.15a, 21.15b and 21.18

15   Apply non-permanent thread locking agent to the threads of the stopper lever bolt **(see illustration)**, then install the stopper lever and return spring. Make sure the stopper lever engages the neutral detent in the shift cam **(see illustration)**. Tighten the bolt to the torque listed in this Chapter's Specifications.
16   Install the oil pump (see Section 17).
17   Apply high-temperature grease to the lip of the seal. Wrap the splines of the shift shaft with electrical tape, so the splines won't damage the seal as the shaft is installed.
18   Slide the shaft into the crankcase. Engage the pawls evenly with the pins on the shift cam and position the return spring over the guide bar **(see illustration)**. Adjust the pawls if they're not even.
19   The remainder of installation is the reverse of the removal steps.
20   Check the engine oil level and add some, if necessary (see Chapter 1).

22 Crankcase - disassembly and reassembly

1   To examine and repair or replace the crankshaft, primary chains, connecting rods, bearings, or transmission components, the crankcase must be split into two parts.

Disassembly
Refer to illustrations 22.5, 22.6a, 22.6b, 22.7a, 22.7b, 22.7c, 22.8a, 22.8b, 22.8c

2   Remove the clutch and starter clutch covers and the oil pan. Remove the cylinder head, cylinder block and pistons (see Sections 10,

LOWER

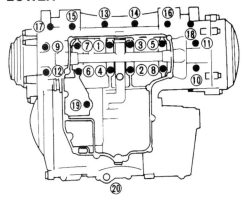

UPPER

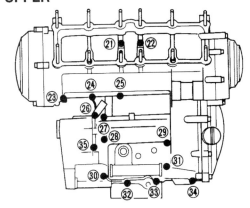

22.5 Crankcase bolt TIGHTENING sequence

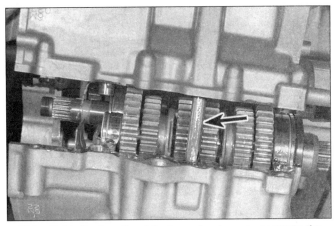

22.6a Guide the breather tube (arrow) out as you separate the crankcase halves

22.6b The breather assembly is secured by four screws (arrows)

13 and 14). Remove the clutch if you are separating the crankcase halves to disassemble the transmission main shaft or remove the internal shift linkage (see Section 19).

3   Remove the water pump (see Chapter 4).

4   Remove the engine sprocket and the oil seal retainer behind it (see Chapter 7). Remove the alternator cover.

5   Remove the upper crankcase bolts, then the lower crankcase bolts, starting with the highest-numbered bolt and working to the lowest (the reverse of the tightening sequence) **(see illustration)**.

6   Carefully separate the crankcase halves, guiding the breather tube out of its opening as you do so **(see illustration)**. If they won't come easily, make sure all fasteners have been removed. Don't pry against the crankcase mating surfaces or they will leak. Once the halves are separated, remove the breather assembly **(see illustration)**.

7   Look for the oil jet and the dowels **(see illustrations)**. If they're not in one of the crankcase halves, locate them.

22.7a Remove the oil jet (arrow) . . .

22.7b . . . its O-ring should be replaced whenever the crankcase is disassembled

22.7c Find the case dowels if they're not in their holes

22.8a Unscrew the filter mount . . .

22.8b . . . lift the mount and base off
the engine . . .

22.8c . . . and remove the O-ring

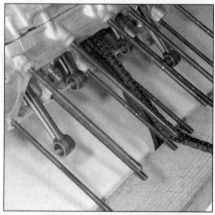

22.11 Rest the ends of the cylinder studs
on a board to angle the case correctly
for reassembly

22.14 Apply sealant to the mating surface

22.16a Guide the breather tube into
its opening

8   On models with a one-piece oil filter, remove the filter mount and
O-ring **(see illustrations)**.
9   Refer to Sections 23 through 30 for information on the internal
components of the crankcase.

Reassembly

*Refer to illustrations 22.11, 22.14, 22.16a, 22.16b, 22.16c, 22.17a,
22.17b, 22.17c, and 22.17d*

10   Make sure the crankshaft and transmission shafts are correctly
positioned in the upper crankcase half (see Sections 25 and 28).
11   Place the ends of the crankcase studs on a piece of 2-by-4 lumber or equivalent **(see illustration)**. This will prevent the connecting
rods from pushing against the workbench and forcing the crankshaft
out of its bearings.
12   Remove all traces of sealant from the crankcase mating surfaces.
Be careful not to let any fall into the case as this is done. Check to
make sure the oil jet (with a new O-ring) and the two dowel pins are in
place **(see illustrations 22.7a and 22.7b)**.
13   Pour some engine oil over the transmission gears, the crankshaft
main bearings and the shift cam. Don't get any oil on the crankcase
mating surfaces.
14   Apply a thin, even bead of Yamaha Bond or Quick Gasket sealant
(part no. ACC-11001-05-01) or equivalent to the crankcase mating surfaces **(see illustration)**. **Caution:** *Don't apply an excessive amount of
sealant. Don't let it contact the oil jet. Don't apply it within 2 to 3 mm
(0.8 to 1.2 inch) of the bearing inserts, as it will ooze out when the case
halves are assembled and may obstruct oil passages and prevent the
bearings from seating.*
15   Check the position of the shift cam, shift forks and transmission

22.16b The transmission and pushrod seals should be flush with
the crankcase surface

shafts - make sure they're in the neutral position (see Section 28).
Make sure the locating pins in the transmission bearings are positioned
correctly.
16   Carefully assemble the crankcase halves over the dowels. While
doing this, make sure the shift forks fit into their gear grooves. Guide
the breather tube into position in its hole **(see illustration)**. Make sure
the crankshaft end seal, transmission seal and clutch pushrod seal are
positioned correctly in the case **(see illustrations)**. The seals should fit
flush with the case surfaces when the case halves are assembled.
Caution: *The crankcase halves should fit together completely without
being forced. If they're slightly apart, DO NOT force them together by*

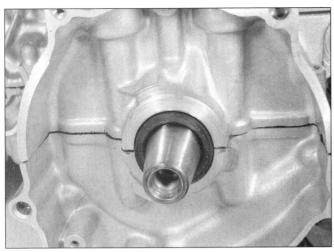

22.16c The crankshaft seal should be seated securely in
its groove

22.17a Crankcase bolts one through 12 have steel
washers (arrows) . . .

22.17b . . . bolts 23 and 26 secure wiring harness clips

22.17c . . . bolt 29 has a copper washer . . .

22.17d . . . and bolt 34 secures a ground wire

*tightening the crankcase bolts. The most likely reason they're apart is
that the transmission bearing pins aren't positioned correctly. If the
pins are forced against the crankcase halves, the cases will crack and
have to be replaced.*

17   Oil the threads and install the crankcase bolts in the correct holes
(see illustration 22.5). Bolts 1 through 12 have steel washers **(see illustration)**. Bolts 23 and 26 secure wiring harness clips **(see illustration)**. Bolt 29 has a copper washer **(see illustration)**. Bolt 34 secures a
ground wire **(see illustration)**.
18   Tighten the bolts in numerical order, referring to the numbers cast
in the crankcase. Tighten all bolts to the torque listed in this Chapter's
Specifications. **Note:** *There are different torque settings for the 8 mm
bolts and the 6 mm bolts.*
19   Turn the mainshaft and the transmission driveshaft to make sure
they turn freely. Also make sure the crankshaft turns freely.
20   Install the oil pan (see Section 16).
21   The remainder of assembly is the reverse of disassembly, with the
following additions:
  a) Once the external shift linkage is installed, shift the transmission
     through all the gear positions and back to Neutral.
  b) Be sure to refill the engine oil.

23 Crankcase components - inspection and servicing

Refer to illustrations 23.2a, 23.2b and 23.3
1   After the crankcases have been separated and the crankshaft,
shift cam and forks and transmission components removed, the

23.2a Make sure oil passages
are clear . . .

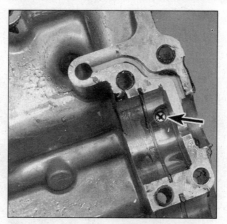

23.2b . . . including this small one in the
transmission bearing saddle (arrow)

23.3 Small burrs can be removed from
the gasket surfaces with a fine stone

crankcases should be cleaned thoroughly with new solvent and dried with compressed air.

2   Remove any oil passage plugs that haven't already been removed. All oil passages should be blown out with compressed air **(see illustrations)**.

3   All traces of old gasket sealant should be removed from the mating surfaces. Minor damage to the surfaces can be cleaned up with a fine sharpening stone or grindstone **(see illustration)**. **Caution:** *Be very careful not to nick or gouge the crankcase mating surfaces or leaks will result. Check both crankcase halves very carefully for cracks and other damage.*

4   Check the cam chain guides for wear (see Section 27). If they appear to be worn excessively, replace them.

5   If any damage is found that can't be repaired, replace the crankcase halves as a set.

24   Main and connecting rod bearings - general note

1   Even though main and connecting rod bearings are generally replaced with new ones during the engine overhaul, the old bearings should be retained for close examination as they may reveal valuable information about the condition of the engine.

2   Bearing failure occurs mainly because of lack of lubrication, the presence of dirt or other foreign particles, overloading the engine and/or corrosion. Regardless of the cause of bearing failure, it must be corrected before the engine is reassembled to prevent it from happening again.

3   When examining the bearings, remove the main bearings from the case halves and the rod bearings from the connecting rods and caps and lay them out on a clean surface in the same general position as their location on the crankshaft journals. This will enable you to match any noted bearing problems with the corresponding side of the crankshaft journal.

4   Dirt and other foreign particles get into the engine in a variety of ways. It may be left in the engine during assembly or it may pass through filters or breathers. It may get into the oil and from there into the bearings. Metal chips from machining operations and normal engine wear are often present. Abrasives are sometimes left in engine components after reconditioning operations such as cylinder honing, especially when parts are not thoroughly cleaned using the proper cleaning methods. Whatever the source, these foreign objects often end up imbedded in the soft bearing material and are easily recognized. Large particles will not imbed in the bearing and will score or gouge the bearing and journal. The best prevention for this cause of bearing failure is to clean all parts thoroughly and keep everything spotlessly clean during engine reassembly. Frequent and regular oil and filter changes are also recommended.

5   Lack of lubrication or lubrication breakdown has a number of in-

terrelated causes. Excessive heat (which thins the oil), overloading (which squeezes the oil from the bearing face) and oil leakage or throw off (from excessive bearing clearances, worn oil pump or high engine speeds) all contribute to lubrication breakdown. Blocked oil passages will also starve a bearing and destroy it. When lack of lubrication is the cause of bearing failure, the bearing material is wiped or extruded from the steel backing of the bearing. Temperatures may increase to the point where the steel backing and the journal turn blue from overheating.

6   Riding habits can have a definite effect on bearing life. Full throttle low speed operation, or lugging the engine, puts very high loads on bearings, which tend to squeeze out the oil film. These loads cause the bearings to flex, which produces fine cracks in the bearing face (fatigue failure). Eventually the bearing material will loosen in pieces and tear away from the steel backing. Short trip driving leads to corrosion of bearings, as insufficient engine heat is produced to drive off the condensed water and corrosive gases produced. These products collect in the engine oil, forming acid and sludge. As the oil is carried to the engine bearings, the acid attacks and corrodes the bearing material.

7   Incorrect bearing installation during engine assembly will lead to bearing failure as well. Tight fitting bearings which leave insufficient bearing oil clearances result in oil starvation. Dirt or foreign particles trapped behind a bearing insert result in high spots on the bearing which lead to failure.

8   To avoid bearing problems, clean all parts thoroughly before reassembly, double check all bearing clearance measurements and lubricate the new bearings with engine assembly lube or moly-based grease during installation.

25   Crankshaft and main bearings - removal, inspection, main bearing selection and installation

Crankshaft removal

Refer to illustrations 25.2 and 25.3

1   Before removing the crankshaft check the endplay, using a dial indicator mounted in-line with the crankshaft. Yamaha doesn't provide endplay specifications, but if the endplay is excessive (more than a few thousandths of an inch), consider replacing the case halves.

2   Lift the crankshaft out, together with the connecting rods and cam chain and set them on a clean surface **(see illustration)**. Remove the oil seal from one end of the crankshaft.

3   The main bearing inserts can be removed from their saddles by pushing their centers to the side, then lifting them out **(see illustration)**. Keep the bearing inserts in order. The main bearing oil clearance should be checked, however, before removing the inserts (see Step 8).

25.2 Lift the crankshaft out with the connecting rods and cam chain

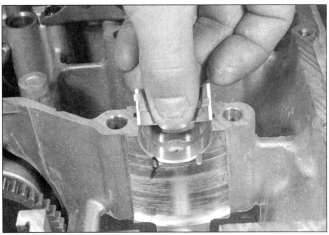

25.3 Push the center of the bearing sideways to tilt it out of its saddle

25.5 Inspect the journals, gear and chain sprocket (arrows) for wear, damage, pitted surfaces or chipped teeth

25.8 Lay a strip of Plastigage lengthwise on the journal

2

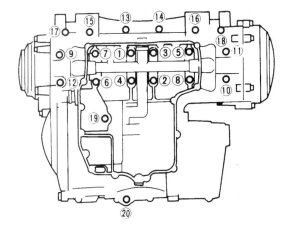

25.9 Tighten the lower crankcase bolts in this sequence to check bearing clearance

Inspection

Refer to illustration 25.5

4   If you haven't already done so, mark and remove the connecting rods from the crankshaft (see Section 26).

5   Clean the crankshaft with solvent, using a rifle-cleaning brush to scrub out the oil passages. If available, blow the crank dry with com-

pressed air. Check the main and connecting rod journals for uneven wear, scoring and pits **(see illustration)**. Rub a copper coin across the journal several times - if a journal picks up copper from the coin, it's too rough. Replace the crankshaft.

6   Check the primary gear and camshaft chain sprocket on the crankshaft for chipped teeth and other wear. If any undesirable conditions are found, replace the crankshaft. Check the chain as described in Section 27. Check the rest of the crankshaft for cracks and other damage. It should be magnafluxed to reveal hidden cracks - a dealer service department or motorcycle machine shop will handle the procedure.

7   Set the crankshaft on V-blocks and check the runout with a dial indicator touching each of the main journals, comparing your findings with this Chapter's Specifications. If the runout exceeds the limit, replace the crank.

Main bearing selection

Refer to illustrations 25.8, 25.9, 25.10, 25.13, 25.15a, 25.15b, 25.15c and 25.15d

8   To check the main bearing oil clearance, clean off the bearing inserts (and reinstall them, if they've been removed from the case) and lower the crankshaft into the upper half of the case. Cut four pieces of Plastigage (type HPG-1) and lay them on the crankshaft main journals, parallel with the journal axis **(see illustration)**.

9   Very carefully, guide the lower case half down onto the upper case half. Install the lower crankcase retaining bolts and tighten them, using the recommended sequence, to the torque listed in this Chapter's Specifications **(see illustration)**. **Caution:** *DO NOT tighten the bolts unless the case halves fit together completely. Don't rotate the crankshaft!*

10   Now, loosen the bolts in reverse sequence, remove them and carefully lift the lower case half off. Compare the width of the crushed

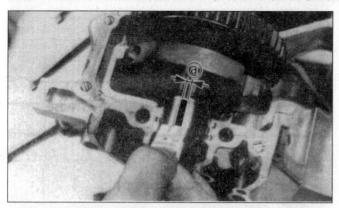

25.10 Measuring the width of the crushed Plastigage (be sure to use the correct scale - inch and metric are included)

A   Plastigage

25.15a These numbers on the crankshaft indicate journal thickness; reading from left to right, the first six numbers correspond with main bearing journals no. 1 through no. 6 - the next four numbers correspond with connecting rod journals no. 1 through no. 4

25.13 Measure the diameter of each crankshaft journal at several points to detect taper and out-of-round conditions

25.15b The numbers on the crankcase correspond with the crankshaft main journals no. 1 through no. 6 (the numbers are upside down when the crankcase is right side up)

1	No. 1 journal	4	No. 4 journal
2	No. 2 journal	5	No. 5 journal
3	No. 3 journal	6	No. 6 journal

BEARING COLOR CODE	
No. 1	Blue
No. 2	Black
No. 3	Brown
No. 4	Green
✴ No. 5	Yellow

✴ No. 5 applies only to the main journal bearing selection.

25.15c Calculate the bearing number by subtracting the crankshaft number from the crankcase number, then use the bearing number to select a color code

placement is required (provided they are in good shape). If the clearance is more than the standard range, replace the bearing inserts with new ones of the same thickness and check the oil clearance once again. Always replace all of the inserts at the same time.

12   The clearance should be within the range listed in this Chapter's Specifications.

13   If the clearance is greater than the service limit listed in this Chapter's Specifications, measure the diameter of the crankshaft journals with a micrometer or vernier caliper **(see illustration)**. Yamaha doesn't provide journal diameter or wear specifications, but by measuring the diameter at a number of points around each journal's circumference, you'll be able to determine whether or not the journal is out-of-round. Take the measurement at each end of the journal, near the crank throws, to determine if the journal is tapered.

14   If any crank journal is out-of-round or tapered or the bearing clearance is beyond the limit listed in this Chapter's Specifications with new bearings, replace the crankshaft.

15   Use the number marks on the crankshaft and on the case to determine the bearing sizes required. The first six numbers on the

Plastigage on each journal to the scale printed on the Plastigage envelope to obtain the main bearing oil clearance **(see illustration)**. Write down your findings, then remove all traces of Plastigage from the journals, using your fingernail or the edge of a credit card.

11   If the oil clearance falls into the specified range, no bearing re-

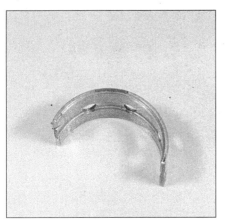

25.15d The color codes, painted on the sides of the bearings, identify bearing thickness

25.16a Make sure the oil holes are clear (arrow), then install the bearings in their saddles . . .

25.16b . . . engage the locating tab securely in its slot (arrow)

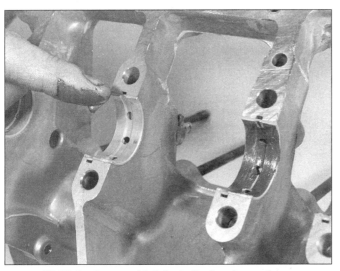

25.17 Apply assembly lube to the bearing surfaces

25.21 Make sure the crankshaft seal is seated securely in its groove

25.22 Lay the crankshaft in the bearing saddles

crankshaft are the main journal numbers, starting with the left journal **(see illustrations)**. These correspond with the numbers on the upper crankcase half **(see illustration)**. To determine the bearing number for each bearing, subtract the crankshaft number from the case number. For example, the crankshaft number for journal no. 1 is 1 and the case

number for journal no. 1 is 6. Subtracting 1 from 6 produces 5, which is the bearing number for journal no. 1. According to the accompanying chart, bearing no. 5 is color-coded yellow **(see illustration)**. The color codes are painted on the edges of the bearings **(see illustration)**.

Installation

Refer to illustrations 25.16a, 25.16b, 25.17, 25.21 and 25.22

16 Clean the bearing saddles in the case halves, then install the bearing inserts in their webs in the case **(see illustrations)**. When installing the bearings, use your hands only - don't tap them into place with a hammer.
17 Lubricate the bearing inserts with engine assembly lube or moly-based grease **(see illustration)**.
18 You can install the connecting rods on the crankshaft at this point (see Section 26).
19 Loop the camshaft chain over the crankshaft and engage it with its sprocket.
20 If the connecting rods are on the crankshaft, recheck side clearances (see Section 26).
21 Install the seal on the end of the crankshaft **(see illustration)**.
22 Carefully lower the crankshaft into place **(see illustration)**. If the connecting rods are on the crankshaft, guide them through their openings.
23 Assemble the case halves (see Section 22) and check to make sure the crankshaft and the transmission shafts turn freely.

26.1 Measure the clearance between the crankshaft and the big end of the connecting rod with a feeler gauge

26.3a Remove the connecting rod nuts (arrows) . . .

26.3b . . . and separate the rod from the cap

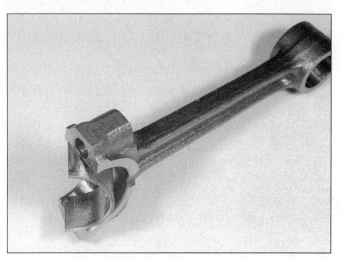

26.4 Push the center of the bearing insert sideways to tilt it out of its saddle

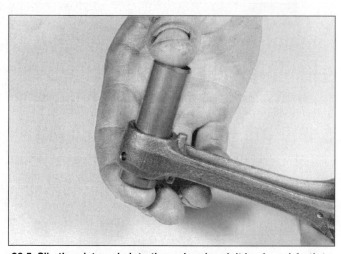

26.5 Slip the piston pin into the rod and rock it back-and-forth to check for looseness

26 Connecting rods and bearings - removal, inspection, bearing selection and installation

Removal

Refer to illustrations 26.1, 26.3a, 26.3b and 26.4

1   Before removing the connecting rods from the crankshaft, measure the side clearance of each rod with a feeler gauge **(see illustration)**. If the clearance on any rod is greater than that listed in this Chapter's Specifications, that rod will have to be replaced with a new one.

2   Using a center punch, mark the position of each rod and cap, relative to its position on the crankshaft (one through four, counting from the left side of the engine).

3   Unscrew the bearing cap nuts, separate the cap from the rod, then detach the rod from the crankshaft **(see illustrations)**. If the cap is stuck, tap on the ends of the rod bolts with a soft face hammer to free them.

4   Roll the bearing inserts sideways to separate them form the rods and caps **(see illustration)**. Keep them in order so they can be reinstalled in their original locations. Wash the parts in solvent and dry them with compressed air, if available.

Inspection

Refer to illustration 26.5

5   Check the connecting rods for cracks and other obvious damage. Lubricate the piston pin for each rod, install it in the proper rod and

check for play **(see illustration)**. If it wobbles, replace the connecting rod and/or the pin.

6   Refer to Section 25 and examine the connecting rod bearing inserts. If they are scored, badly scuffed or appear to have been seized, new bearings must be installed. Always replace the bearings in the connecting rods as a set. If they are badly damaged, check the corresponding crankshaft journal. Evidence of extreme heat, such as discoloration, indicates that lubrication failure has occurred. Be sure to thoroughly check the oil pump and pressure relief valves as well as all oil holes and passages before reassembling the engine.

7   Have the rods checked for twist and bending at a dealer service department or other motorcycle repair shop.

Connecting rod bearing selection

Refer to illustrations 26.18a and 26.18b

8   If the bearings and journals appear to be in good condition, check the oil clearances as follows:

9   Start with the rod for the number one cylinder. Wipe the bearing inserts and the connecting rod and cap clean, using a lint-free cloth.

10   Install the bearing inserts in the connecting rod and cap. Make sure the tab on the bearing engages with the notch in the rod or cap.

11   Wipe off the connecting rod journal with a lint-free cloth. Lay a strip of Plastigage (type HPG-1) across the top of the journal, parallel with the journal axis.

12   Position the connecting rod on the bottom of the journal, then install the rod cap and nuts. Tighten the nuts to the torque listed in this Chapter's Specifications, but don't allow the connecting rod to rotate at all.

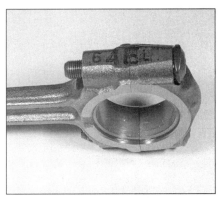

26.18a The halves of the letter stamped on the rod should match perfectly when the rod is assembled; if they don't, the cap is on the wrong rod

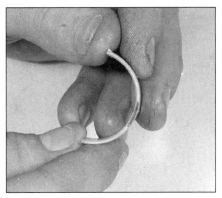

26.18b The color code is painted on the side of the bearing

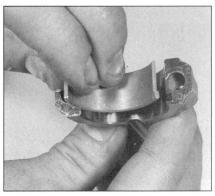

26.20a Be sure the tab fits in the notch

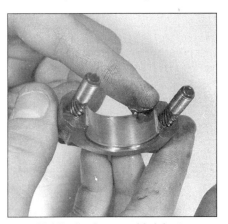

26.20b Apply assembly lube to the bearing

26.21 The Y mark on the rod faces the left side of the engine

26.22 Snug both nuts evenly, then tighten them to the correct torque in one continuous motion

13   Unscrew the nuts and remove the connecting rod and cap from the journal, being very careful not to disturb the Plastigage. Compare the width of the crushed Plastigage to the scale printed in the Plastigage envelope to determine the bearing oil clearance.

14   If the clearance is within the range listed in this Chapter's Specifications and the bearings are in perfect condition, they can be reused. If the clearance is beyond the standard range, replace the bearing inserts with new inserts that have the same color code, then check the oil clearance once again. Always replace all of the inserts at the same time.

15   The clearance should be within the range listed in this Chapter's Specifications.

16   If the clearance is greater than the maximum clearance listed in this Chapter's Specifications, measure the diameter of the connecting rod journal with a micrometer. As with the main bearing journals, Yamaha doesn't provide diameter or wear limit specifications, but by measuring the diameter at a number of points around the journal's circumference, you'll be able to determine whether or not the journal is out-of-round. Take the measurement at each end of the journal to determine if the journal is tapered.

17   If any journal is tapered or out-of-round or bearing clearance is beyond the maximum listed in this Chapter's Specifications, replace the crankshaft.

18   Each connecting rod has a 3 or 4 stamped on it in ink (see illustration). Subtract this number from the connecting rod journal number on the crankshaft to get a bearing number (see illustration 25.15a). For example, the number on the connecting rod shown in illustration 26.18a is 4. The corresponding number for that connecting rod's journal, stamped into the crankshaft, is 2. Subtracting 2 from 4 produces 2, which is the bearing number for that journal. According to the chart, bearing no. 2 is color-coded black. The color codes are painted

on the edges of the bearings (see illustration).

19   Repeat the bearing selection procedure for the remaining connecting rods.

Installation

Refer to illustrations 26.20a, 26.20b, 26.21 and 26.22

20   Wipe off the bearing inserts, connecting rods and caps. Install the inserts into the rods and caps, using your hands only, making sure the tabs on the inserts engage with the notches in the rods and caps (see illustrations). When all the inserts are installed, lubricate them with engine assembly lube or moly-based grease (see illustration). Don't get any lubricant on the mating surfaces of the rod or cap.

21   Assemble each connecting rod to its proper journal, referring to the previously applied cylinder numbers. Make sure the Y mark on the rod is toward the left side of the engine (see illustration). Also, the letter present at the rod/cap seam on one side of the connecting rod should fit together perfectly when the rod and cap are assembled (see illustration 26.18a). If it doesn't, the wrong cap is on the rod. Fix this problem before assembling the engine any further.

22   When you're sure the rods are positioned correctly, lubricate the threads of the rod bolts with molybdenum disulphide grease and tighten the nuts to the torque listed in this Chapter's Specifications (see illustration). Note: *Snug both nuts evenly, then tighten them to the specified torque in a continuous motion. If you must stop before the nuts are fully tightened, loosen them completely, then retighten them to the specified torque.*

23   Turn the rods on the crankshaft. If any of them feel tight, tap on the bottom of the connecting rod caps with a hammer - this should relieve stress and free them up. If it doesn't, recheck the bearing clearance.

27.6 The chain guide is secured to the crankcase by two Allen bolts (arrows)

28.3b . . . and the driveshaft

24   As a final step, recheck the connecting rod side clearances (see Step 1). If the clearances aren't correct, find out why before proceeding with engine assembly.

28.3a Note the positions of the bearing pins and retainer rings (arrows), then lift out the mainshaft . . .

28.5 Place new retainer rings in their grooves and push them down flush with the crankcase surface

---

27   Camshaft chain and guides - removal, inspection and installation

---

Warning: *Although the cam chain can be cut and reconnected, this should be done by a qualified Yamaha technician with the proper special tool. Chain separation while the engine is running may cause engine seizure, leading to loss of control of the motorcycle.*

Removal

Refer to illustration 27.6
1   Remove the engine (see Section 5).
2   Separate the crankcase halves (see Section 22).
3   Remove the crankshaft (see Section 25).
4   Remove the chain from the crankshaft.
5   The cam chain front guide can be lifted from the cylinder head once the camshafts have been removed **(see illustration 9.8)**.
6   The cam chain rear guide is held in position by two Allen bolts **(see illustration)**. Separate the crankcase halves (see Section 22), then remove the Allen bolts and lift out the guide.

Inspection

7   Check the chain for binding and obvious damage. If these conditions are visible, or if the chain appears to be stretched, replace it.
8   Check the guides for deep grooves, cracking and other obvious damage, replacing them if necessary.

Installation

9   Installation of these components is the reverse of the removal

procedure, with the following additions:
a) When installing the rear cam chain guide, apply a non-hardening thread locking compound to the threads of the bolts. Tighten the bolts to the torque listed in this Chapter's Specifications.
b) Apply engine oil to the faces of the guides and to the chain.

---

28   Transmission shafts - removal and installation

Refer to illustrations 28.3a and 28.3b

Removal

1   Remove the engine and clutch, then separate the case halves (see Sections 5, 19 and 22).
2   If you haven't already done so, remove the long clutch pushrod from the mainshaft (see Section 19).
3   Lift out the mainshaft, then the driveshaft **(see illustrations)**. If they are stuck, use a soft-face hammer and gently tap on the bearings on the ends of the shafts to free them. Lift out the half-circle retainer rings.
4   Refer to Section 29 for information pertaining to transmission shaft service and Section 30 for information pertaining to the shift cam and forks.

Installation

Refer to illustrations 28.5 and 28.7

5   Install new half-circle retaining rings in their grooves in the crankcase **(see illustration)**.
6   Carefully lower each shaft into place. The pins in the bearing outer

28.7 Make sure the transmission and clutch pushrod seals are in position

races must engage with the locating holes in the crankcase, and the grooves in the crankcase and the ball bearing outer races must engage with the retaining rings **(see illustration 28.3a)**. **Caution:** *If the pins are out of position and you try to force the crankcase halves together by tightening the bolts, the crankcase halves will crack and will have to be*

replaced.

7   The remainder of installation is the reverse of removal. Make sure the clutch pushrod seal and driveshaft end seal are in position **(see illustration)**.

8   Make sure the gears are in the neutral position. When they are, it will be possible to rotate the transmission shafts independently of each other. Align the shaft forks with the gear grooves.

---

29   Transmission shafts - disassembly, inspection and reassembly

---

Note: *When disassembling the transmission shafts, place the parts on a long rod or thread a wire through them to keep them in order and facing the proper direction.*

1   Remove the shafts from the case (see Section 28).

Mainshaft

Disassembly

Refer to illustrations 29.2a, 29.2b, 29.3a, 29.3b, 29.4, 29.5a and 29.5b

2   Slide the bearing off the mainshaft **(see illustrations)**.

2

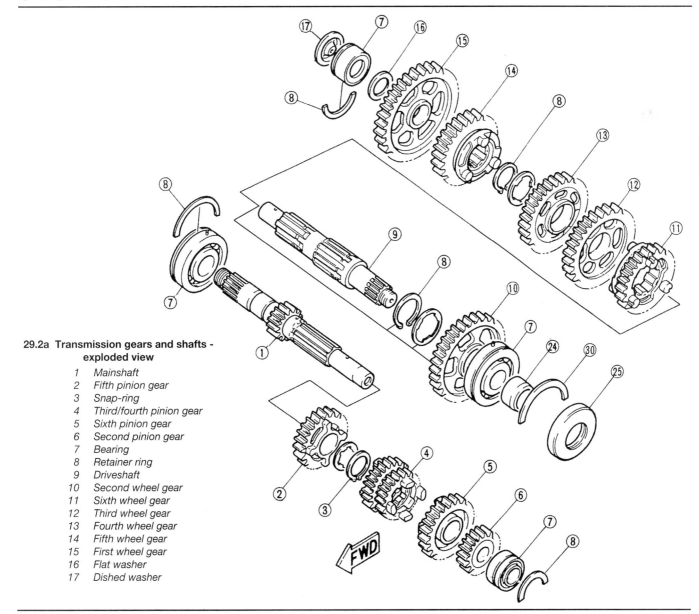

29.2a Transmission gears and shafts - exploded view

1   Mainshaft
2   Fifth pinion gear
3   Snap-ring
4   Third/fourth pinion gear
5   Sixth pinion gear
6   Second pinion gear
7   Bearing
8   Retainer ring
9   Driveshaft
10   Second wheel gear
11   Sixth wheel gear
12   Third wheel gear
13   Fourth wheel gear
14   Fifth wheel gear
15   First wheel gear
16   Flat washer
17   Dished washer

29.2b Slide the bearing off the shaft

29.3a Press the shaft out of the second and sixth pinion gears . . .

29.3b . . . slide second pinion gear off . . .

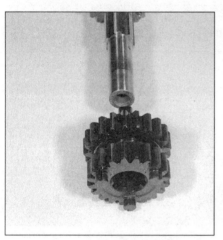

29.4 Slide off the third-fourth pinion gear

29.5a Remove the snap-ring and thrust washer (arrow) . . .

29.5b . . . and slide fifth pinion gear off

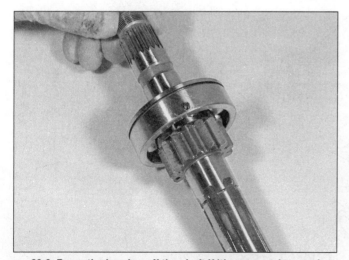

29.6 Press the bearing off the shaft if it's worn or damaged

3　Press second and sixth pinion gears loose from the shaft together, then remove them from the shaft (see illustrations).

4　Slide third-fourth pinion gear off the shaft (see illustration).

5　Remove the snap-ring and thrust washer, then slide fifth pinion gear off the shaft (see illustrations).

Inspection

Refer to illustration 29.6

6　Wash all of the components in clean solvent and dry them off. Rotate the ball bearing on the shaft, feeling for tightness, rough spots and excessive looseness and listening for noises (see illustration). If any of these conditions are found, replace the bearing with a press.

7　Check the ball bearing that was removed from the other end of the shaft and replace it if it has any of the conditions described in Step 6. The bearing should also be replaced if oil has been leaking from its seal.

8　Check the gear teeth for cracking and other obvious damage. Check the gear bushings and the surface in the inner diameter of each gear for scoring or heat discoloration. If the gear or bushing is damaged, replace it.

9　Inspect the dogs and the dog holes in the gears for excessive wear. Replace the paired gears as a set if necessary.

10　Place the shaft in V-blocks and check runout with a dial indicator. Replace the shaft if runout exceeds the value listed in this Chapter's Specifications.

Reassembly

Refer to illustrations 29.12a and 29.12b

11　During reassembly, always use new snap-rings. Lubricate the components with engine oil before assembling them.

29.12a Press sixth and second pinion gears onto the shaft

29.12b The assembled mainshaft should look like this

29.13a Take the dished washer off
the driveshaft . . .

29.13b . . . slide off the needle
roller bearing . . .

29.13c . . . remove the flat washer . . .

2

29.13d . . . slide off first wheel gear . . .

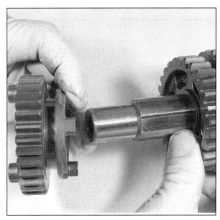

29.13e . . . slide off fifth wheel gear . . .

29.13f . . . remove the snap-ring . . .

12   Assembly is the reverse of the disassembly procedure with the
following additions:
  a) The sharp side of the snap-ring faces away from the thrust
     washer; the rounded side faces toward the thrust washer.
  b) Press sixth and second gears onto the mainshaft together **(see il-
     lustration)**.
  c) Check the positions of the gears on the assembled shaft to make
     sure they are correct **(see illustration)**.

Driveshaft

Disassembly

Refer to illustrations 29.13a through 29.13o

13   To disassemble the driveshaft, refer to the **accompanying illustrations**.

Inspection

14   Refer to Steps 6 through 10 above to inspect the driveshaft com-

29.13g . . . and the thrust washer . . .

29.13h . . . slide off fourth wheel gear . . .

29.13i . . . and third wheel gear . . .

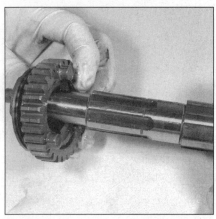

29.13j . . . and sixth wheel gear . . .

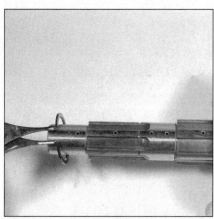

29.13k . . . remove another snap ring . . .

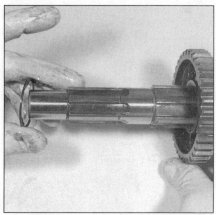

29.13l . . . and thrust washer . . .

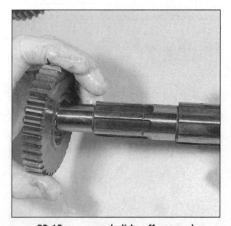

29.13m . . . and slide off second wheel gear . . .

29.13n . . . take the oil seal off the shaft . . .

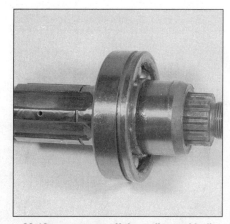

29.13o . . . press off the collar and ball bearing if they're worn or damaged

ponents. If the ball bearing and seal collar need to be replaced, remove them with a press; otherwise, they can be left on the shaft.

Reassembly

Refer to illustration 29.15

15   Assembly is the reverse of the disassembly procedure. Use new snap-rings and lubricate the components with engine oil before assembling them. Check the assembled shaft to make sure the gears are in the correct positions **(see illustration)**.

30   Shift cam and forks - removal, inspection and installation

Removal

Refer to illustrations 30.3, 30.4a, 30.4b and 30.5

1   Remove the engine, separate the crankcase halves and remove the transmission shafts (see Sections 5, 22 and 28).
2   Remove the external shift mechanism (see Section 21).
3   Remove the shift cam retainers **(see illustration)**.

29.15 The assembled driveshaft should look like this

30.3 Remove the stopper lever (if not already done), shift cam retainer bolts and the guide bar (arrows)...

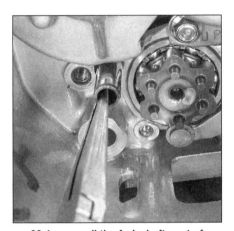

30.4a ... pull the fork shafts out of the case ...

30.4b ... and lift out the forks

30.5 Slide the shift cam out of the crankcase

2

30.6a Check the shift cam grooves for wear, especially at the tips (arrow)

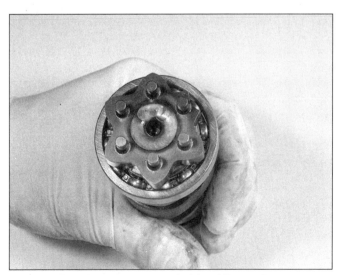

30.6b Check the pins at the end of the shift cam for wear ...

4   Support the shift forks and pull the guide bars out (see illustrations).
5   Pull the shift cam out of the case (see illustration).

Inspection

Refer to illustrations 30.6a, 30.6b, 30.6c, 30.6d and 30.7

6   Check the edges of the grooves in the shift cam for signs of excessive wear (see illustration). Check the pins on each end of the shift cam for wear and damage (see illustrations). If undesirable conditions are found, replace the shift cam.

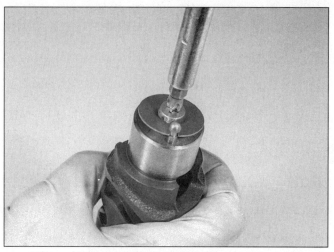

30.6c . . . if the neutral indicator pin is worn, remove the retainer screw . . .

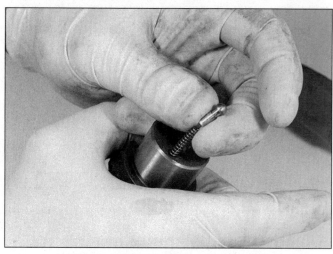

30.6d . . . and take out the pin and spring

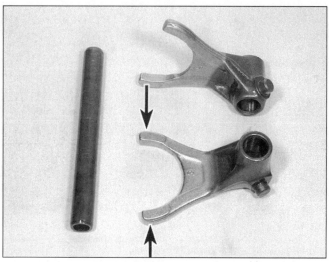

30.7 Check the shift forks for wear at the tips (arrows); check the guide bars for wear

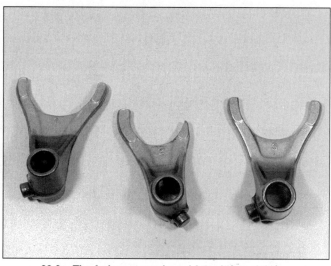

30.9a The forks are numbered from left to right . . .

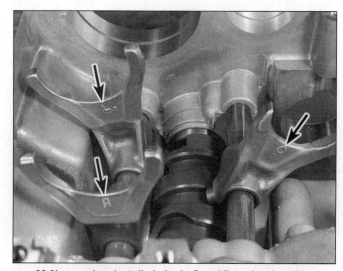

30.9b . . . when installed, the L, C and R marks should be positioned as shown (arrows)

7   Check the shift forks for distortion and wear, especially at the fork tips (see illustration). If they are discolored or severely worn they are probably bent. If damage or wear is evident, check the shift fork groove in the corresponding gear as well. Inspect the guide pins and the shaft bore for excessive wear and distortion and replace any defective parts with new ones.

8   Check the shift fork guide bars for evidence of wear, galling and other damage (see illustration 30.7). Make sure the shift forks move smoothly on the bar. If the bar is worn or bent, replace it with a new one.

Installation

Refer to illustrations 30.9a through 30.9f

9   Installation is the reverse of removal, noting the following points:
  a) Lubricate all parts with engine oil before installing them.
  b) Use the numbers on the forks to position them correctly. The forks are numbered from one to three, starting from the left side of the engine (see illustration). The numbers face the left side of the engine when the forks are installed. The letters L, C and R (left, center and right) also indicate fork position (see illustration).
  c) Engage the follower pin on each shift fork with the shift cam as you pass the guide bar through the fork. Position the shift cam and forks in the neutral position (see illustrations).

30.9c Engage the pins with the grooves in the shift cam and place the cam and forks in the neutral position . . .

30.9d . . . in neutral, the notch in the end of the shift cam (arrow) . . .

30.9e . . . will engage with the stopper lever (arrow)

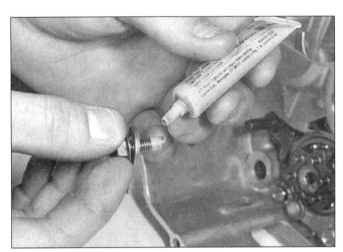

30.9f Apply a non-permanent thread locking agent to the shift cam retainer bolts and to the threads of the guide bar

2

d) Apply a non-permanent locking agent to the threads of the shift cam retainer bolts **(see illustration)** and tighten them to the torque listed in this Chapter's Specifications.

31 Oil cooler (early UK models) - removal and installation

Refer to illustration 31.2

1   Early UK models are equipped with an external oil cooler. The oil cooler on later models is mounted between the oil filter and crankcase (see Chapter 4).

2   To replace the oil lines, drain the engine oil and remove fairing panels as needed for access. Remove the oil line retaining bolts at the engine and banjo bolts at the cooler **(see illustration)**.

3   To replace the cooler, remove the oil line banjo bolts and cooler mounting bolts **(see illustration 31.2)**. Lift the cooler out.

4   Installation is the reverse of the removal steps. Use new sealing washers at the banjo fittings and new O-rings at the oil line fittings on the engine.

32 Initial start-up after overhaul

1   Make sure the engine oil level is correct and the cooling system is

full, then remove the spark plugs from the engine. Place the engine kill switch in the Off position and unplug the primary (low tension) wires from the coils.

2   Turn on the key switch and crank the engine over with the starter several times to build up oil pressure. Reinstall the spark plugs, connect the wires and turn the switch to On.

3   Make sure there is fuel in the tank, then turn the fuel tap to the On position and operate the choke.

4   Start the engine and allow it to run at a moderately fast idle until it reaches operating temperature.

5   Check carefully for oil leaks and make sure the transmission and controls, especially the brakes, function properly before road testing the machine. Refer to Section 33 for the recommended break-in procedure.

6   Upon completion of the road test, and after the engine has cooled down completely, recheck the valve clearances (see Chapter 1).

33 Recommended break-in procedure

1   Any rebuilt engine needs time to break-in, even if parts have been installed in their original locations. For this reason, treat the machine gently for the first few miles to make sure oil has circulated throughout the engine and any new parts installed have started to seat.

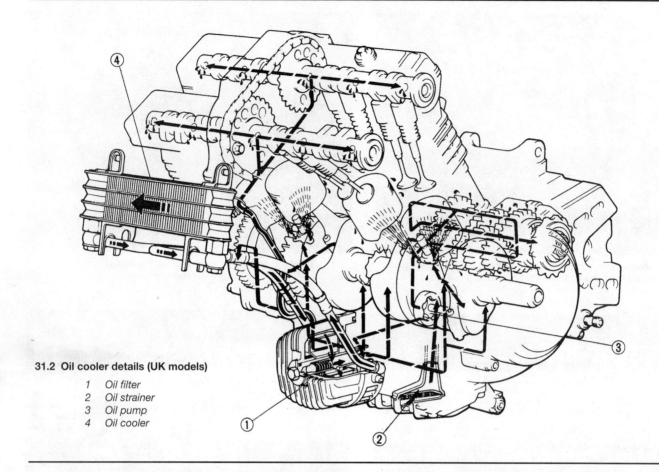

31.2 Oil cooler details (UK models)

1   Oil filter
2   Oil strainer
3   Oil pump
4   Oil cooler

2   Even greater care is necessary if the engine has been rebored or a new crankshaft has been installed. In the case of a rebore, the engine will have to be broken in as if the machine were new. This means greater use of the transmission and a restraining hand on the throttle until at least 500 miles (800 Km) have been covered. There's no point in keeping to any set speed limit - the main idea is to keep from lugging (labouring) the engine and to gradually increase performance until the 500 mile (800 Km) mark is reached. These recommendations can be lessened to an extent when only a new crankshaft is installed. Experience is the best guide, since it's easy to tell when an engine is running freely. The following recommendations, which Yamaha provides for new motorcycles, can be used as a guide:

   a)   0 to 90 miles (0 to 150 km): Keep engine speed below 5,000 rpm.

Turn off the engine after each hour of operation and let it cool for 5 to 10 minutes. Vary the engine speed and don't use full throttle.

   b)   90 to 300 miles (150 to 500 km): Don't run the engine for long periods above 6,500 rpm. Rev the engine freely through the gears, but don't use full throttle.

   c)   300 to 600 miles (500 to 1000 km): Don't use full throttle for prolonged periods and don't cruise at speeds above 8,000 rpm.

   d)   After 600 miles (1,000 km): Full throttle can be used. Don't exceed maximum recommended engine speed (redline).

3   If a lubrication failure is suspected, stop the engine immediately and try to find the cause. If an engine is run without oil, even for a short period of time, severe damage will occur.

Chapter 3
FZR750/1000 engine, clutch and transmission

Contents

3

Specifications

FZR750R

General

Bore x stroke	
1987 and 1988 (US)	68.0 mm x 51.6 mm (2.6772 inches x 2.0315 inches)
1989-on (UK)	72.0 x 46.0 mm (2.835 x 1.811 inches)
Displacement	
1987 and 1988 (US)	750 cc (45.8 cubic inches)
1989-on (UK)	749 cc (45.7 cubic inches)
Compression ratio	11.2 to 1

Camshafts

Intake camshaft lobe height (1987 and 1988 - US)	
Standard	32.55 to 32.65 mm (1.2815 to 1.2854 inch)
Minimum	32.45 mm (1.278 inch)
Intake camshaft lobe height (1989-on - UK)	
Standard	32.60 to 32.70 mm (1.2835 to 1.2874 inch)
Minimum	32.50 mm (1.280 inch)
Intake camshaft base circle	
Standard	24.95 to 25.05 mm (0.9823 to 0.9862 inch)
Minimum	24.85 mm (0.978 inch)
Exhaust camshaft lobe height (1987 and 1988 - US)	
Standard	32.4 to 32.5 mm (1.2756 to 1.2795 inch)
Minimum	32.3 mm (1.2717 inch)
Exhaust camshaft lobe height (1989-on - UK)	
Standard	33.0 to 33.1 mm (1.2992 to 1.3031 inch)
Minimum	32.9 mm (1.30 inch)
Exhaust camshaft base circle	
Standard	24.95 to 25.05 mm (0.9823 to 0.9862 inch)
Minimum	24.85 mm (0.978 inch)
Bearing oil clearance (cylinders 1 and 4)	0.020 to 0.054 mm (0.0008 to 0.0021 inch)
Bearing oil clearance (cylinders 2 and 3)	0.050 to 0.84 mm (0.0020 to 0.0033 inch)
Journal diameter	24.437 to 24.450 mm (0.9621 to 0.9626 inch)
Bearing bore (cylinders 1 and 4)	24.470 to 24.491 mm (0.9634 to 0.9642 inch)
Bearing bore (cylinders 2 and 3)	24.500 to 24.521 mm (0.9646 to 0.9654 inch)
Camshaft runout limit	0.03 mm (0.0012 inch)

Cylinder head, valves and valve springs

Cylinder head warpage limit	0.03 mm (0.0012 inch)
Valve stem bend limit	0.01 mm (0.0006 inch)
Valve head diameter (1987 and 1988 - US)	
Intake	20.9 to 21.1 mm (0.8228 to 0.8307 inch)
Exhaust	22.9 to 23.1 mm (0.9016 to 0.9094 inch)
Valve head diameter (1989-on - UK)	
Intake	22.9 to 23.1 mm (0.9016 to 0.9094 inch)
Exhaust	24.4 to 24.5 mm (0.9606 to 0.9685 inch)
Valve stem diameter (1987 and 1988 - US)	
Intake (standard)	4.975 to 4.990 mm (0.1959 to 0.1965 inch)
Intake (minimum)	4.945 mm (0.1947 inch)
Exhaust (standard)	4.960 to 4.975 mm (0.1953 to 0.1959 inch)
Exhaust (minimum)	4.930 mm (0.1941 inch)
Valve stem diameter (1989-on - UK)	
Intake (standard)	4.475 to 4.490 mm (0.1762 to 0.1766 inch)
Intake (minimum)	4.445 mm (0.175 inch)
Exhaust (standard)	4.460 to 4.475 mm (0.1756 to 0.1762 inch)
Exhaust (minimum)	4.430 mm (0.174 inch)
Valve head thickness limit (intake and exhaust)	0.6 to 0.8 mm (0.236 to 0.0315 inch)
Valve guide inside diameter (1987 and 1988 - US)	
Standard	5.000 to 5.012 mm (0.1969 to 0.1973 inch)
Maximum	5.05 mm (0.1988 inch)
Valve guide inside diameter (1989-on - UK)	
Standard	4.500 to 4.512 mm (0.1772 to 0.1776 inch)
Maximum	4.55 mm (0.179 inch)
Valve seat width (intake and exhaust)	0.9 to 1.1 mm (0.0354 to 0.0433 inch)
Valve face width	
1987 and 1988 (US) - intake and exhaust	1.98 to 2.55 mm (0.0780 to 0.1004 inch)
1989-on (UK) - intake	1.49 to 2.48 mm (0.0587 to 0.0976 inch)
1989-on (UK) - exhaust	1.76 to 2.76 mm (0.0693 to 0.1087 inch)
Valve spring free length (1987 and 1988 - US)	
Standard (intake and exhaust)	40.46 mm (1.593 inch)
Minimum (intake and exhaust)	39.96 mm (1.573 inch)
Valve spring free length (1989-on - UK)	
Intake	40.38 mm (1.59 inch)
Exhaust	44.40 mm (1.75 inch)
Valve spring installed length	
1987 and 1988 (US)	35.0 mm (1.378 inch)
1989-on (UK) - intake	38.5 mm (1.44 inch)
1989-on (UK) - exhaust	40.5 mm (1.59 inch)
Compressed pressure at installed length	
1987 and 1988 (US)	7.3 to 8.7 kg (16.1 to 19.2 lbs)
1989-on (UK) - intake	12.2 to 13.2 kg (26.9 to 29.1 lbs)
1989-on (UK) - exhaust	21 to 23 kg (46.3 to 50.7 lbs)

Valve spring bend limit (1987 and 1988)	1.7 mm (0.067 inch)
Valve spring bend limit (1989-on intake)	1.7 mm (0.067 inch)
Valve spring bend limit (1989-on exhaust)	1.9 mm (0.075 inch)

Cylinder block

Bore diameter (1987 and 1988 - US)..	68.000 to 68.005 mm (2.6772 to 2.6774 inches)
Bore diameter (1989-on - UK)	71.98 to 72.02 mm (2.834 to 2.835 inches)
Bore measuring point	40 mm (1.57 inch) from top of cylinder
Taper and out-of-round limit	0.05 mm (0.002 inch)

Pistons

Piston diameter (1987 and 1988 - US)	
Standard..	69.93 to 69.94 mm (2.674 to 2.675 inch)
First oversize	68.5 mm (2.697 inches)
Second oversize	69.0 mm (2.717 inches)
Diameter measuring point	3.0 mm (0.12 inch) from bottom of skirt
Piston diameter (1989-on - UK)....................................	71.90 to 71.94 mm (2.831 to 2.832 inches)
Diameter measuring point	3.5 mm (0.14 inch) from bottom of skirt
Piston-to-cylinder clearance (1987 and 1988 - US)	0.06 to 0.08 mm (0.0024 to 0.0031 inch)
Piston-to-cylinder clearance (1989-on - UK).............................	0.07 to 0.09 mm (0.0028 to 0.0035 inch)
Ring side clearance (1987 and 1988 - US)	
Top and second	0.03 to 0.07 mm (0.0012 to 0.0028 inch)
Oil ring	Not specified
Ring side clearance (1989-on - UK)	
Top	0.03 to 0.07 mm (0.0012 to 0.0028 inch)
Second and oil	Not specified
Ring thickness (1987 and 1988 - US)	
Top ring	0.8 mm (0.0315 inch)
Second ring	1.0 mm (0.0394 inch)
Oil ring spacer	2.0 mm (0.0787 inch)
Ring thickness (1989-on - UK)	
Top ring	1.0 mm (0.0394 inch)
Second ring	Not specified
Oil ring spacer	2.0 mm (0.0787 inch)
Ring end gap (1987 and 1988 - US)	
Top ring	0.15 to 0.30 mm (0.0059 to 0.0118 inch)
Second ring	0.20 to 0.35 mm (0.0079 to 0.0138 inch)
Oil ring	0.20 to 0.70 mm (0.0078 to 0.0276 inch)
Ring end gap (1989-on - UK)	
Top ring	0.15 to 0.30 mm (0.0059 to 0.0118 inch)
Second ring	Not specified
Oil ring	0.10 to 0.60 mm (0.0039 to 0.0236 inch)
Ring width (1987 and 1988 - US)	
Top ring	2.6 mm (0.1024 inch)
Second ring	2.8 mm (0.1102 inch)
Oil ring	2.2 mm (0.0866 inch)
Ring width (1989-on - UK)	
Top and oil rings..................................	2.8 mm (0.1102 inch)
Second ring	Not specified

Crankshaft, connecting rods and bearings

Main bearing oil clearance..	0.040 to 0.064 mm (0.0016 to 0.0025 inch)
Connecting rod side clearance.......................................	0.160 to 0.262 mm (0.0063 to 0.0103 inch)
Connecting rod bearing oil clearance..............................	0.032 to 0.056 mm (0.0013 to 0.0022 inch)
Crankshaft runout limit	0.03 mm (0.0012 inch)

Oil pump and relief valve

Inner to outer rotor clearance limit	0.02 mm (0.008 inch)
Outer rotor to housing clearance limit..........................	0.15 mm (0.006 inch)
Relief valve opening pressure..	3.82 to 4.60 Bars (55.5 to 66.8 psi)

Clutch and transmission

Friction plate thickness..	2.9 to 3.1 mm (0.1142 to 0.1220 inch)
Steel plate thickness	1.9 to 2.2 mm (0.075 to 0.085 inch)
Steel plate warpage limit	0.1 mm (0.004 inch)
Spring length (minimum)..	54.0 mm (2.126 inches)
Driveshaft and mainshaft runout limit	0.08 mm (0.0031 inch)
Mainshaft gearset assembled length (1989-on - UK)....................	116.6 mm (4.59 inches)

3

FZR1000

General

Bore x stroke	
1987 and 1988	75.0 mm x 56.0 mm (2.9528 x 2.2047 inches)
1989-on	75.5 mm (2.972 inches x 2.2047 inches)
Displacement (1987 and 1988).................................	989 cc (60.3 cubic inches)
Displacement (1989-on)	1002 cc (61.15 cubic inches)
Compression ratio (1987 and 1988)	11.2 to 1
Compression ratio (1989-on)	12.0 to 1

Camshafts

Intake camshaft lobe height (standard)	32.55 to 32.65 mm (1.2815 to 1.2854 inch)
Intake camshaft lobe height (minimum)......................	32.45 mm (1.278 inch)
Base circle (standard)	24.95 to 25.05 mm (0.9823 to 0.9862 inch)
Base circle (minimum)	24.85 mm (0.978 inch)
Exhaust camshaft lobe height	
1987 and 1988 (standard)	32.4 to 32.5 mm (1.2756 to 1.2795 inch)
1987 and 1988 (minimum)	32.3 mm (1.2717 inch)
1989-on (standard)	32.95 to 33.05 mm (1.2972 to 1.3012 inches)
1989-on (minimum)	32.85 mm (1.293 inch)
Base circle (standard)	24.95 to 25.05 mm (0.9823 to 0.9862 inch)
Base circle (minimum)	24.85 mm (0.978 inch)
Bearing oil clearance (cylinders 1 and 4)..................	0.020 to 0.054 mm (0.0008 to 0.0021 inch)
Bearing oil clearance (cylinders 2 and 3)..................	0.050 to 0.84 mm (0.0020 to 0.0033 inch)
Journal diameter..	24.437 to 24.450 mm (0.9621 to 0.9626 inch)
Bearing bore (cylinders 1 and 4)...............................	24.470 to 24.491 mm (0.9634 to 0.9642 inch)
Bearing bore (cylinders 2 and 3)...............................	24.500 to 24.521 mm (0.9646 to 0.9654 inch)
Camshaft runout limit	0.03 mm (0.0012 inch)

Cylinder head, valves and valve springs

Cylinder head warpage limit	0.03 mm (0.0012 inch)
Valve stem bend limit	0.01 mm (0.0006 inch)
Valve head diameter (intake)	23.4 to 23.6 mm (0.9213 to 0.9291 inch)
Valve head diameter (exhaust)	24.9 to 25.1 mm (0.9803 to 0.9882 inch)
Valve stem diameter (1987 and 1988)	
Intake (standard)	4.975 to 4.990 mm (0.1959 to 0.1965 inch)
Intake (minimum)	4.945 mm (0.1947 inch)
Exhaust (standard)	4.960 to 4.975 mm (0.1953 to 0.1959 inch)
Exhaust (minimum)	4.930 mm (0.1941 inch)
Valve stem diameter (1989-on)	
Intake (standard)	4.475 to 4.490 mm (0.1762 to 0.1768 inch)
Intake (minimum)	4.445 mm (0.175 inch)
Exhaust (standard)	4.460 to 4.475 mm (0.1756 to 0.1762 inch)
Exhaust (minimum)	4.43 mm (0.174 inch)
Valve head thickness limit (intake)	0.45 to 0.95 mm (0.0177 to 0374 inch)
Valve head thickness limit (exhaust)..........................	0.75 to 1.25 mm (0.0295 to 0.0492 inch)
Valve guide inside diameter (intake and exhaust)	
1987 and 1988 (standard)	5.000 to 5.012 mm (0.1969 to 0.1973 inch)
1987 and 1988 (maximum)...................................	5.05 mm (0.1988 inch)
1989-on (standard)	4.500 to 4.512 mm (0.1772 to 0.1776 inch)
1989-on (maximum)	4.55 mm (0.179 inch)
Valve seat width (intake and exhaust)	
Standard...	0.9 to 1.1 mm (0.0354 to 0.0433 inch)
Limit	1.8 mm (0.071 inch)
Valve face width (intake and exhaust)	1.63 to 2.90 mm (0.0642 to 0.1142 inch)
Valve spring free length (1987 and 1988)	
Intake	39.76 mm (1.565 inch)
Exhaust	39.96 mm (1.573 inch)
Valve spring free length (1989-on)	
Intake	40.73 mm (1.604 inch)
Exhaust	44.01 mm (1.733 inch)
Valve spring installed length (all)	35.0 mm (1.378 inch)
Compressed pressure at installed length	
1987 and 1988	7.3 to 8.7 kg (16.1 to 19.2 lbs)
1989-on	12.2 to 13.2 kg (26.9 to 29.1 lb)
Valve spring bend limit	1.7 mm (0.067 inch)

Cylinder block

Bore diameter (1987 and 1988)	75.000 to 75.005 mm (2.9528 to 2.9529 inches)
Bore diameter (1989-on)..	75.500 to 75.505 mm (2.9724 to 2.9726 inches)
Bore measuring point	40 mm (1.57 inch) from top of cylinder
Taper and out-of-round limit	0.05 mm (0.002 inch)

Pistons

Piston diameter (1987 and 1988)	
Standard	74.93 to 74.94 mm (2.949 to 2.950 inches)
Oversize	75.5 mm (2.97 inches)
Piston diameter (1989-on)	
Standard	75.425 to 75.440 mm (2.700 to 2.970 inches)
Oversize	76.0 mm (3.00 inches)
Diameter measuring point	3.0 mm (0.12 inch) from bottom of skirt
Piston-to-cylinder clearance	0.06 to 0.08 mm (0.0024 to 0.0031 inch)
Ring side clearance	
Top ring (standard)	0.03 to 0.07 mm (0.0012 to 0.0028 inch)
Top ring (maximum)	0.15 mm (0.0059 inch)
Second ring (standard)	0.02 to 0.06 mm (0.0008 to 0.0024 inch)
Second ring (maximum)	0.15 mm (0.0059 inch)
Oil ring	Not specified
Ring thickness	
Top ring	0.8 mm (0.0315 inch)
Second ring (1987 and 1988)	1.0 mm (0.0394 inch)
Second ring (1989-on)	0.8 mm (0.0315 inch)
Oil ring spacer (1987 and 1988)	2.0 mm (0.0787 inch)
Oil ring spacer (1989-on)	1.5 mm (0.0591 inch)
Ring end gap	
Top and second rings (standard)	0.3 to 0.5 mm (0.0118 to 0.0197 inch)
Top and second rings (maximum)	0.7 mm (0.0276 inch)
Oil ring	0.20 to 0.80 mm (0.0078 to 0.0315 inch)
Ring width	
Top and second rings (1987 and 1988)	3.1 mm (0.1220 inch)
Top and second rings (1989-on)	2.8 mm (0.1102 inch)
Oil ring	2.5 mm (0.0984 inch)

Crankshaft, connecting rods and bearings

Main bearing oil clearance	0.020 to 0.044 mm (0.0008 to 0.0017 inch)
Connecting rod side clearance	0.160 to 0.262 mm (0.0063 to 0.0103 inch)
Connecting rod bearing oil clearance	0.032 to 0.056 mm (0.0013 to 0.0022 inch)
Crankshaft runout limit	0.03 mm (0.0012 inch)
Connecting rod bolt stretch - see text (UK FZR750)	0.15 to 0.19 mm (0.0059 to 0.0075

Oil pump and relief valve

Inner to outer rotor clearance limit	0.2 mm (0.008 inch)
Outer rotor to housing clearance	0.15 mm (0.006 inch)
Relief valve opening pressure	3.82 to 4.60 Bars (55.5 to 66.8 psi)

Clutch and transmission

Friction plate thickness	2.9 to 3.1 mm (0.1142 to 0.1220 inch)
Steel plate thickness	2.8 mm (0.110 inch)
Steel plate warpage limit	0.1 mm (0.004 inch)
Spring length (minimum)	54.0 mm (2.126 inches)
Driveshaft and mainshaft runout limit	0.08 mm (0.0031 inch)

Torque specifications (all models)

Alternator driveshaft bearing retainer	10 Nm (7.2 ft-lbs)
Cam chain guide (intake side) Allen bolts	10 Nm (7.2 ft-lbs)
Cam chain sprocket bolts	24 Nm (17 ft-lbs)
Cam chain tensioner mounting bolts	10 Nm (7.2 ft-lbs)
Cam chain tensioner cap bolt	20 Nm (14 ft-lbs)
Camshaft bearing cap bolts	10 Nm (7.2 ft-lbs)
Clutch bleed valve	6 Nm (4.3 ft-lbs)
Clutch boss nut	70 ft-lbs (50 Nm) (1)
Clutch cover bolts	10 Nm (7.2 ft-lbs)
Clutch hydraulic line union bolts	25 Nm (18 ft-lbs)
Clutch master cylinder bolts	9 Nm (6.5 ft-lbs)
Clutch master cylinder cap screws	
1987 and 1988 FZR750	1 Nm (0.7 ft-lbs)
FZR1000	2 Nm (1.4 ft-lbs)
Clutch pressure plate bolts	8 Nm (5.8 ft-lbs)
Clutch release cylinder bolts	10 Nm (7.2 ft-lbs)
Connecting rod cap nuts (2)	
All except 1989-on (UK) FZR750	36 Nm (25 ft-lbs)
1989-on (UK) FZR750	
Initial torque	8 Nm (5.8 ft-lbs)
Final torque	42 Nm (30 ft-lbs) (6)

3

Crankcase bolts
    9 mm .... 32 Nm (23 ft-lbs) (3)
    8 mm .... 24 Nm (17 ft-lbs) (3)
    6 mm .... 12 Nm (8.7 ft-lbs) (3)
Crankcase studs to crankcase .... 10 Nm (7.2 ft-lbs) (3)
Crankshaft end cover screws .... 7 Nm (5.1 ft-lbs)
Cylinder head nuts
    1987 and 1988 FZR750 .... 25 Nm (18 ft-lbs) (3)
    1987 and 1988 FZR1000 .... 37 Nm (27 ft-lbs) (3)
    1989-on FZR750/1000 .... 41 Nm (30 ft-lbs) (3)
Engine mounting bolts
    1987 and 1988 (tighten in order listed)
        Lower rear bolt .... 42 Nm (30 ft-lbs)
        Upper rear bolt .... 55 Nm (40 ft-lbs)
        Upper front downtube bolts .... 63 Nm (46 ft-lbs)
        Lower front downtube bolts .... 63 Nm (46 ft-lbs)
        Forward lower downtube bolts .... 28 Nm (20 ft-lbs)
        Rearward lower downtube bolts .... 28 Nm (20 ft-lbs)
        Lower front engine bolt .... 55 Nm (40 ft-lbs)
        Frame slit pinch bolt .... 15 Nm (11 ft-lbs)
        Fairing stay bolts .... 15 Nm (11 ft-lbs)
    1989-on (UK) FZR750
        Front of engine stay to frame .... 55 Nm (40 ft-lbs)
        Rear of engine stay to frame .... 23 Nm (17 ft-lbs)
        Lower rear mounting bolt .... 47 Nm (34 ft-lbs)
        Pinch bolts .... 15 Nm (11 ft-lbs)
    1989-on FZR1000
        Lower rear mounting bolt .... 55 Nm (40 ft-lbs)
        Upper rear mounting bolt .... 60 Nm (43 ft-lbs)
        Frame to cylinder head bolts .... 60 Nm (43 ft-lbs)
        Frame to cylinder block bolts .... 33 Nm (24 ft-lbs)
        Rear pinch bolts .... 15 Nm (11 ft-lbs)
        Center and front pinch bolts .... 22 Nm (16 ft-lbs)
Neutral switch screws .... 4 Nm (2.9 ft-lbs) (4)
Oil baffle plate bolts .... 10 Nm (7.2 ft-lbs)
Oil cooler banjo bolts .... 25 Nm (18 ft-lbs)
Oil line (external) banjo bolts .... 21 Nm (15 ft-lbs)
Oil pan mounting bolts .... 10 Nm (7.2 ft-lbs)
Oil passage plugs .... Not specified
Oil pick-up bolts .... 10 Nm (7.2 ft-lbs)
Oil pump body screws .... 10 Nm (7.2 ft-lbs)
Oil pump mounting bolts .... 10 Nm (7.2 ft-lbs)
Shift cam retainer bolt .... 10 Nm (7.2 ft-lbs) (4)
Shift mechanism stopper lever bolts
    All except 1989-on (UK) FZR750 .... 10 Nm (7.2 ft-lbs) (4)
    1989-on (UK) FZR750 .... 22 Nm (16 ft-lbs)
Starter chain guide bolts .... 10 Nm (7.2 ft-lbs)
Starter clutch bolts .... 25 Nm (18 ft-lbs) (5)
Transmission bearing retainer screws .... 10 Nm (7.2 ft-lbs) (4)
Valve cover bolts .... 10 Nm (7.2 ft-lbs)

1   *Use a new lockwasher.*
2   *Apply molybdenum disulphide grease to the threads.*
3   *Apply engine oil to the threads.*
4   *Apply non-permanent thread locking agent to the threads.*
5   *Apply non-permanent thread locking agent to the threads and stake the bolts after installation.*
6   *Final tightness is determined by bolt stretch; see text.*

1 General information

The engine/transmission unit is a liquid-cooled, in-line four. The valves are operated by double overhead camshafts which are chain driven off the crankshaft. The engine/transmission assembly is constructed from aluminum alloy. The crankcase is divided horizontally.

The crankcase incorporates a wet sump, pressure-fed lubrication system which uses a gear-driven oil pump, an oil filter, relief valve and an oil level switch. Also contained in the crankcase is the starter motor clutch.

Power from the crankshaft is routed to the transmission via the clutch, which is of the coil spring, wet multi-plate type and is gear-driven off the crankshaft. The transmission is a five-speed (FZR1000) or six-speed (FZR750), constant-mesh unit.

2 Operations possible with the engine in the frame

The components and assemblies listed below can be removed without having to remove the engine from the frame. If, however, a number of areas require attention at the same time, removal of the engine is recommended.

Gear selector mechanism external components
Water pump
Starter motor
Alternator
Clutch assembly
Valve cover, camshafts and lifters
Cam chain tensioner
Cylinder head
Cylinder block and pistons
Oil pan and pump

3 Operations requiring engine removal

It is necessary to remove the engine/transmission assembly from the frame and separate the crankcase halves to gain access to the following components:

Crankshaft, connecting rods and bearings
Transmission shafts
Shift cam and forks
Camshaft chain and starter chain
Starter clutch

4 Major engine repair - general note

1   It is not always easy to determine when or if an engine should be completely overhauled, as a number of factors must be considered.
2   High mileage is not necessarily an indication that an overhaul is needed, while low mileage, on the other hand, does not preclude the need for an overhaul. Frequency of servicing is probably the single most important consideration. An engine that has regular and frequent oil and filter changes, as well as other required maintenance, will most likely give many miles of reliable service. Conversely, a neglected engine, or one which has not been broken in properly, may require an overhaul very early in its life.
3   Exhaust smoke and excessive oil consumption are both indications that piston rings and/or valve guides are in need of attention. Make sure oil leaks are not responsible before deciding that the rings and guides are bad. Refer to Chapter 1 and perform a cylinder compression check to determine for certain the nature and extent of the work required.
4   If the engine is making obvious knocking or rumbling noises, the connecting rod and/or main bearings are probably at fault.
5   Loss of power, rough running, excessive valve train noise and high fuel consumption rates may also point to the need for an overhaul, especially if they are all present at the same time. If a complete tune-up does not remedy the situation, major mechanical work is the only solution.

6   An engine overhaul generally involves restoring the internal parts to the specifications of a new engine. During an overhaul the piston rings are replaced and the cylinder walls are bored and/or honed. If a rebore is done, then new pistons are also required. The main and connecting rod bearings are generally replaced with new ones and, if necessary, the crankshaft is also replaced. Generally the valves are serviced as well, since they are usually in less than perfect condition at this point. While the engine is being overhauled, other components such as the carburetors and the starter motor can be rebuilt also. The end result should be a like-new engine that will give as many trouble free miles as the original.
7   Before beginning the engine overhaul, read through all of the related procedures to familiarize yourself with the scope and requirements of the job. Overhauling an engine is not all that difficult, but it is time consuming. Plan on the motorcycle being tied up for a minimum of two weeks. Check on the availability of parts and make sure that any necessary special tools, equipment and supplies are obtained in advance.
8   Most work can be done with typical shop hand tools, although a number of precision measuring tools are required for inspecting parts to determine if they must be replaced. Often a dealer service department or motorcycle repair shop will handle the inspection of parts and offer advice concerning reconditioning and replacement. As a general rule, time is the primary cost of an overhaul so it doesn't pay to install worn or substandard parts.
9   As a final note, to ensure maximum life and minimum trouble from a rebuilt engine, everything must be assembled with care in a spotlessly clean environment.

5 Engine - removal and installation

Note: *Engine removal and installation should be done with the aid of an assistant to avoid damage or injury that could occur if the engine is dropped. A hydraulic floor jack should be used to support and lower the engine if possible (they can be rented at low cost).*

Removal

Refer to illustration 5.19
1   Support the bike securely so it can't be knocked over during this procedure.
2   Remove the fuel tank (see Chapter 5).
3   Remove the left and right fairings, the front fairing (1989 and later FZR1000), the left and right side covers and the seat (see Chapter 9).
4   Disconnect the negative cable from the battery, then disconnect the positive cable (see Chapter 1). **Warning**: *Always disconnect the negative cable first and reconnect it last to prevent a battery explosion.*
5   Remove the air filter housing (see Chapter 5).
6   Disconnect the spark plug wires (see Chapter 1).
7   If you're working on a 1989 or later model, remove the air baffle plate together with the ignition coils (see Chapter 6).
8   Drain the engine oil and coolant (see Chapter 1).
9   Remove the carburetors (see Chapter 5) and plug the intake openings with rags.
10   Remove the radiator and the coolant tubes on the intake side of the engine. Remove the radiator outlet tubes (see Chapter 4).
11   Remove the oil cooler (see Section 32).
12   If you're working on an EXUP model, disconnect the EXUP cables at the upper end (see Chapter 5). On UK FZR750 models, remove the EXUP servo motor.
13   Remove the exhaust system (see Chapter 5).
14   Remove the external shift linkage from the shift shaft (see Section 21).
15   Disconnect the clutch cable or remove the release cylinder (see Section 20).
16   Remove the engine sprocket cover and engine sprocket (see Chapter 7). It isn't necessary to remove the drive chain completely, but if the engine sprocket is difficult to remove, loosen the rear axle nut and chain adjusters, then push the rear wheel forward to create slack in the chain (see Chapter 1 for details).

3

17   Refer to Chapter 10 and disconnect the following electrical connectors:
  A) alternator
  B) neutral switch
  C) oil level switch
  D) starter motor
  E) sidestand switch
  F) pickup coil
18   Disconnect the engine ground lead from the crankcase (refer to crankcase reassembly procedures in Section 22).
19   Support the engine securely with a floor jack and a wood block **(see illustration)**.

1987 and 1988 models

20   Remove the bolts holding the downtubes to the frame (see Chapter 7).
21   Remove the upper and lower engine mounting bolts and spacers.

1989 and later FZR1000 models

Refer to illustrations 5.22a, 5.22b, 5.22c, 5.22d, 5.23a, 5.23b, 5.23c and 5.23d

22   Loosen the spacer pinch bolts at the front and rear of the engine on each side, and at the back of the engine on top **(see illustrations)**.
23   Remove the nuts from the engine mounting bolts and remove the bolts **(see illustrations)**.

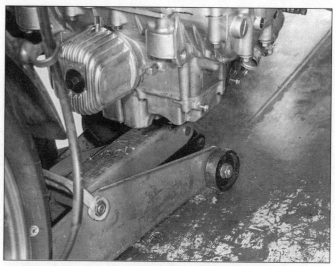

KL5.19   Place a jack under the oil pan (use a wooden block between the jack and oil pan to protect the pan and be sure not to place the jack against the oil level sensor)

5.22a   On each side of the bike, loosen the collar pinch bolt at the front mount but don't loosen the engine mounting bolt (arrow) yet . . .

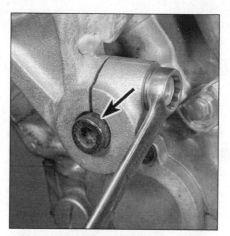

5.22b   . . . also loosen the pinch bolt at the rear engine mount on each side of the bike but don't loosen the engine mounting bolt (arrow) yet

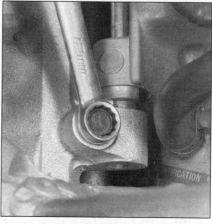

5.22c   Loosen the pinch bolt on the upper rear mounting bolt collar at the left . . .

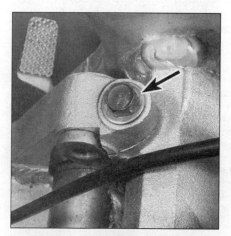

5.22d   . . . and at the right (arrow)

5.23a   Remove the outer nut and exhaust hanger bracket from the lower rear mounting bolt . . .

5.23b   . . . remove the inner nut . . .

5.23c . . . pull out the lower rear mounting bolt . . .

5.23d . . . and remove the upper rear mounting bolt

5.29 Have an assistant steady the engine while you lower the jack

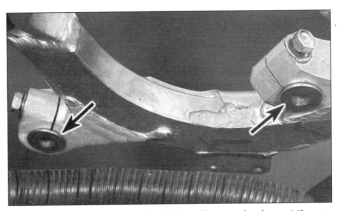

5.30a Be sure the mounting bolt collars are in place at the sides of the frame (arrows) . . .

1989 and later FZR750 models

24 Loosen the pinch bolts at the lower rear of the engine and the rear of the engine stay.

25 Loosen the bolts at the front of the engine stay.

26 Remove the lower rear mounting bolt, then the lower rear engine stay bolts.

27 Unbolt the front of the engine stay from the frame.

All models

Refer to illustration 5.29

28 Make sure no wires or hoses are still attached to the engine assembly. **Warning:** *The engine is heavy and may cause injury if it falls. Be sure it's securely supported. Have an assistant help you steady the*

5.30b . . . and where the upper rear mounting bolt passes through (arrow)

engine on the jack as you remove it.

29 Slowly and carefully lower the engine assembly to the floor, then guide it out from under the bike to the right **(see illustration)**.

Installation

Refer to illustrations 5.30a and 5.30b

30 Installation is the reverse of removal. Note the following points:
  a) Don't tighten any of the engine mounting bolts until they all have been installed.
  b) If you're working on a 1987 or 1988 model, tighten the mounting bolts in the order and to the torque listed in this Chapter's Specifications. Tighten the downtube bolts with the full weight of the engine resting on them.
  c) If you're working on a 1989 or later model, be sure the mounting bolt collars are in place **(see illustrations)**.
  d) Use new gaskets at all exhaust pipe connections.
  e) Tighten the engine mounting bolts and frame downtube bolts (if equipped) to the torques listed in this Chapter's Specifications.
  f) Adjust the drive chain and throttle cable(s)s following the procedures in Chapter 1.
  g) Be sure to refill the cooling system and engine oil before starting the engine.

---

6   Engine disassembly and reassembly - general information

Refer to illustrations 6.2a, 6.2b and 6.3

1   Before disassembling the engine, clean the exterior with a degreaser and rinse it with water. A clean engine will make the job easier and prevent the possibility of getting dirt into the internal areas of the engine.

2   In addition to the precision measuring tools mentioned earlier,

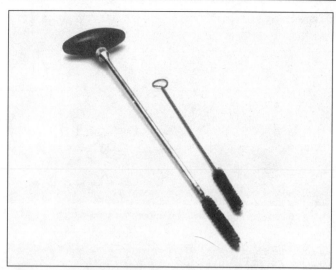

6.2a A selection of brushes is required for cleaning holes and passages in the engine components

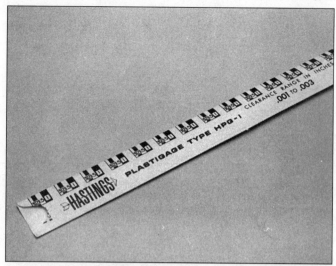

6.2b Type HPG-1 Plastigage is needed to check the crankshaft, connecting rod and camshaft oil clearances

6.3 An engine stand can be made from short lengths of 2 x 4 lumber and lag bolts or nails

7.8 Remove the valve cover bolts . . .

you will need a torque wrench, a valve spring compressor, oil gallery brushes, a piston ring removal and installation tool, piston ring compressors and a clutch holder tool (which is described in Section 19). Some new, clean engine oil of the correct grade and type, some engine assembly lube (or moly-based grease), a tube of Yamaha Quick Gasket (part no. ACC11001-05-01) or equivalent, and a tube of RTV (silicone) sealant will also be required. Although it may not be considered a tool, some Plastigage (type HPG-1) should also be obtained to use for checking bearing oil clearances (see illustrations).

3   An engine support stand made from short lengths of 2 x 4's bolted together will facilitate the disassembly and reassembly procedures (see illustration). The perimeter of the mount should be just big enough to accommodate the engine oil pan. If you have an automotive-type engine stand, an adapter plate can be made from a piece of plate, some angle iron and some nuts and bolts.

4   When disassembling the engine, keep "mated" parts together (including gears, cylinders, pistons, etc. that have been in contact with each other during engine operation). These "mated" parts must be reused or replaced as an assembly.

5   Engine/transmission disassembly should be done in the following general order with reference to the appropriate Sections.

Remove the camshafts
Remove the cylinder head
Remove the cylinder block
Remove the pistons
Remove the clutch
Remove the oil pan

7.9a . . . and lift the cover off the engine; note the dab of sealer in the corners of the half-circle portion of the gasket (arrows)

Remove the external shift mechanism
Remove the alternator and starter (see Chapter 10)
Separate the crankcase halves
Remove the crankshaft and connecting rods
Remove the transmission shafts/gears
Remove the shift cam/forks
Remove the starter clutch and idle gears

6   Reassembly is accomplished by reversing the general disassembly sequence.

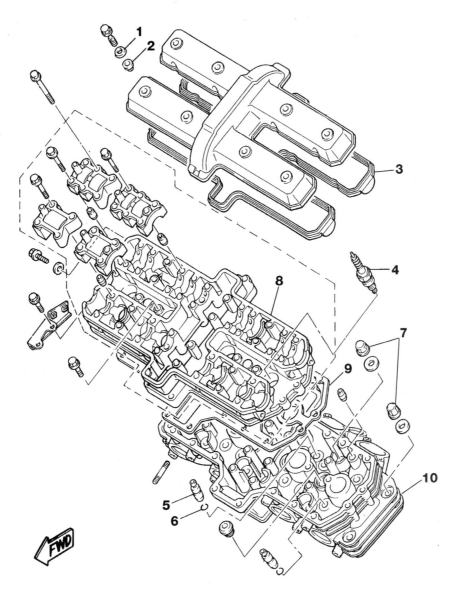

7.9b Valve cover and cylinder head - exploded view

1	Washer	6	Snap-ring
2	Rubber seals	7	Cylinder head end nuts and washers
3	Valve cover gasket	8	Cylinder head upper section (camshaft case)
4	Spark plug	9	Gasket
5	Valve guide	10	Cylinder head main section

7   Valve cover - removal and installation

Note: *The valve cover can be removed with the engine in the frame. If the engine has been removed, ignore the steps which don't apply.*

Removal

Refer to illustrations 7.8, 7.9a and 7.9b

1   Support the bike securely so it can't be knocked over during this procedure.

2   Remove the left and right fairings, front fairing (1989 and later models) and seat (see Chapter 9).

3   Remove the fuel tank (see Chapter 5).

4   Remove the radiator (see Chapter 4) and oil cooler (see Section 32).

5   Remove the air cleaner housing. If you're working on a 1989 or later model, remove the air baffle plate (see Chapter 5).

6   If you're working on a 1987 or 1988 model, remove the right frame downtube (see Section 5).

7   Remove the spark plugs (see Chapter 1).

8   Remove the valve cover bolts **(see illustration)**.

9   Lift the cover off the cylinder head **(see illustrations)**. If it's stuck, don't attempt to pry it off - tap around the sides with a plastic hammer to dislodge it.

Installation

Refer to illustrations 7.11, 7.13 and 7.14

10   Peel the rubber gasket from the cover. If it's cracked, hardened, has soft spots or shows signs of general deterioration, replace it with a new one.

7.11 Apply a thin film of sealer to the half-circle cutouts in the cylinder head

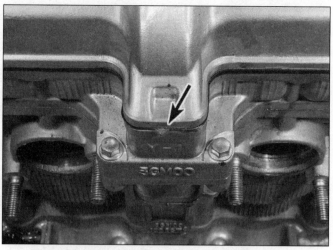

7.13 The tab at the front of the gasket (arrow) should protrude when the gasket is installed

7.14 Replace the rubber grommets on the valve cover bolts (arrow) if they're cracked or deteriorated

8.1 Loosen the tensioner cap bolt before unbolting the tensioner from the engine

11   Clean the mating surfaces of the cylinder head and the valve cover with lacquer thinner, acetone or brake system cleaner. Apply a thin film of RTV sealant to the half-circle cutouts on each side of the head **(see illustration)**.

12   Install the gasket to the cover. Make sure it fits completely into the cover groove. Apply a small amount of silicone sealer to the corners of the half-circle portions of the gasket **(see illustration 7.9a)**.

13   Position the cover on the cylinder head, making sure the gasket doesn't slip out of place. The tab on the gasket should protrude from the front (exhaust) side of the engine **(see illustration)**.

14   Check the rubber seals on the valve cover bolts, replacing them if necessary **(see illustration)**. Install the bolts with their seals and washers, tightening them evenly to the torque listed in this Chapter's Specifications.

15   The remainder of installation is the reverse of removal.

8   Camshaft chain tensioner - removal and installation

Removal

Refer to illustrations 8.1, 8.2 and 8.3

Caution: *Once you start to remove the tensioner bolts, you must remove the tensioner all the way and reset it before tightening the bolts. The*

tensioner extends and locks in place, so if you loosen the bolts partway and then retighten them, the tensioner or cam chain will be damaged.

1   Loosen the tensioner cap bolt while the tensioner is still installed **(see illustration)**.

2   Remove the tensioner mounting bolts and take it off the engine **(see illustration)**.

3   Remove the tensioner cap bolt and sealing washer **(see illustration)**.

Installation

Refer to illustrations 8.5, 8.6 and 8.8

4   Check the sealing washer on the cap bolt for cracks or hardening. It's a good idea to replace this washer whenever the tensioner cap is removed.

5   Release the one-way cam on the chain tensioner and compress the rod **(see illustration)**.

6   Turn the tensioner so the one-way cam is downward and install the tensioner on the cylinder block, using a new gasket **(see illustration)**. The word Up cast in the tensioner housing should be upward.

7   Tighten the mounting bolts to the torque listed in this Chapter's Specifications.

8   Install the tensioner springs, cap and sealing washer **(see illustration)**. Tighten the cap to the torque listed in this Chapter's Specifications.

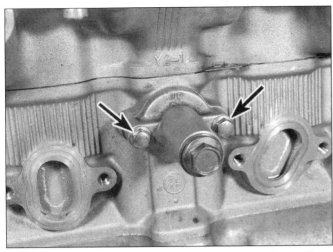

8.2 Remove the tensioner bolts and take the tensioner off

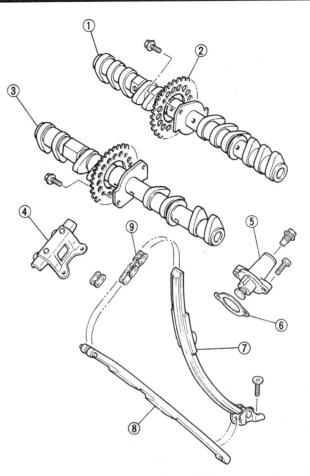

8.3 Camshafts, tensioner and cam chain components -
exploded view

1   Intake camshaft
2   Sprocket
3   Exhaust camshaft
4   Upper cam chain guide
5   Cam chain tensioner
6   Tensioner gasket
7   Intake side (rear) cam chain guide
8   Exhaust side (front) cam chain guide
9   Cam chain

8.5 Release the one-way cam (arrow) and compress the
tensioner before installing it

8.6 Install the tensioner body with a new gasket

8.8 Install the plunger, springs, washer and cap bolt after
the tensioner is installed on the engine

9   Camshafts and lifters - removal, inspection and installation

Note: *This procedure can be performed with the engine in the frame.*

Camshafts

Removal

Refer to illustrations 9.2, 9.4, 9.5a, 9.5b, 9.6 and 9.8

1   Remove the valve cover (see Section 7).
2   Turn the engine to position no. 1 cylinder at TDC compression (see Chapter 1 - Valve clearances - check and adjustment). When the engine is positioned correctly, the dots on the camshafts will align with the marks on the bearing caps **(see illustration)**.
3   Remove the camshaft chain tensioner (see Section 8).
4   Remove the upper cam chain guide **(see illustration)**.
5   Unscrew the cam bearing cap bolts, a little at a time, working from the outer to the inner bolts **(see illustration)**. **Caution**: *If the bearing cap bolts aren't loosened evenly, the bearing caps may break. Because they're line-bored with the cylinder head, this may necessitate replacing the entire cylinder head. Remove the bolts and lift off the caps. Note that each bearing cap is labeled EX for exhaust (front side of the engine) or IN for intake (rear side of the engine)* **(see illustration)**. *They're also numbered from 1 through 4, starting at the left side of the engine.*
6   Remove the bolts and lift off the bearing caps and their dowel pins **(see illustration)**.
7   Remove the camshafts. Keep the chain taut by wiring it to the engine so it can't fall down off the crankshaft. While the camshafts are

9.2 The small punch mark on each camshaft should be aligned with the mark on the bearing cap (arrows)

out, don't allow the chain to go slack - the chain may fall off and bind between the crankshaft and case, which could damage these components. Also, cover the top of the cylinder head with a rag to prevent foreign objects from falling into the engine.
8   Lift the exhaust side (front) cam chain guide out of the engine **(see illustration)**.

9.4 Remove the bolts (arrows) and lift off the upper chain guide

9.5a Remove the bearing caps evenly

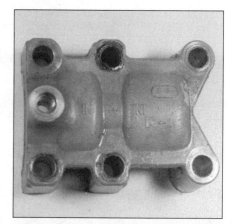

9.5b Note the location and position of the bearing cap identification marks

9.6 Remove the bearing cap dowels (arrows)

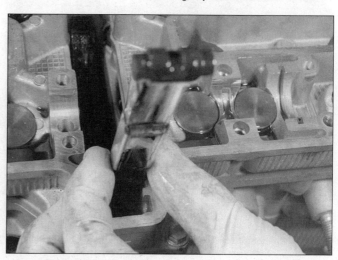

9.8 Lift the exhaust side chain guide out of the engine

9.9 Inspect the bearing surfaces in the cylinder head and bearing caps

9.10a Check the lobes of the camshaft for wear - here's a good example of damage which will require replacement (or repair) of the camshaft

9.10b Measure the height of the camshaft lobes with a micrometer

Inspection

Refer to illustrations 9.9, 9.10a, 9.10b, 9.11, 9.15a and 9.15b

Note: *Before replacing camshafts or the cylinder head and bearing caps because of damage, check with local machine shops specializing in motorcycle engine work. In the case of the camshafts, it may be possible for cam lobes to be welded, reground and hardened, at a cost far lower than that of a new camshaft. If the bearing surfaces in the cylinder head are damaged, it may be possible for them to be bored out to accept bearing inserts. Due to the cost of a new cylinder head it is recommended that all options be explored before condemning it as trash!*

9 Inspect the cam bearing surfaces of the head and the bearing caps **(see illustration)**. Look for score marks, deep scratches and evidence of spalling (a pitted appearance).

10 Check the camshaft lobes for heat discoloration (blue appearance), score marks, chipped areas, flat spots and spalling **(see illustration)**. Measure the height of each lobe with a micrometer **(see illustration)** and compare the results to the minimum lobe height listed in this Chapter's Specifications. If damage is noted or wear is excessive, the camshaft must be replaced.

11 Next, check the camshaft bearing oil clearances. Clean the camshafts, the bearing surfaces in the cylinder head and the bearing caps with a clean, lint-free cloth, then lay the cams in place in the cylinder head. Be sure the punch marks on the camshafts are upward **(see illustration 9.2)**. Be sure to place the camshafts in the correct bearings; the exhaust camshaft has a total of eight lobes and the intake camshafts has twelve lobes **(see illustration)**.

12 Cut one strip of Plastigage (type HPG-1) for each bearing journal and lay it the pieces on the journals, parallel with the camshaft centerline.

13 Make sure the bearing cap dowels are installed **(see illustration 9.6)**. Install the bearing caps in their proper positions (see Step 5). Tighten the bolts in two steps to the torque listed in this Chapter's Specifications. **Caution:** *Tighten the bearing caps evenly to*

9.11 The exhaust and intake camshafts are identified by the number of lobes; the intake camshaft has three lobes per cylinder and the exhaust camshaft has two lobes per cylinder

specifications, starting with the inner bolts and working outward. While tightening, DO NOT let the camshafts rotate!

14 Now unscrew the bolts, a little at a time, and carefully lift off the bearing caps. Be sure to start with the outer bolts and work inward.

15 To determine the oil clearance, compare the crushed Plastigage (at its widest point) on each journal to the scale printed on the Plastigage container **(see illustration)**. Compare the results to this Chapter's Specifications. If the oil clearance is greater than specified, measure the diameter of the cam bearing journal with a micrometer **(see illustration)**. If the journal diameter is less than the specified limit, replace the camshaft with a new one and recheck the clearance. If the

9.15a Compare the crushed Plastigage (1) to the scale

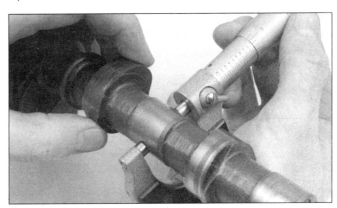

9.15b Measure the cam bearing journal diameter with a micrometer

3

9.21 Lower the front (exhaust side) chain guide into the engine and make sure it rests securely on the bottom of the crankcase

9.23 Lay the exhaust camshaft in the engine; because some of the lobes will hold it up, the alignment mark (arrow) will be slightly counterclockwise (anti-clockwise) of the installed position

9.24 Lay the intake camshaft in the engine

9.25a Install the exhaust camshaft bearing caps; the alignment mark on this cap (arrow) should be next to the punch mark on the camshaft

clearance is still too great, replace the cylinder head and bearing caps with new parts (see the Note that precedes Step 9).

16   Except in cases of oil starvation, the camshaft chain wears very little. If the chain has stretched excessively, which makes it difficult to maintain proper tension, replace it with a new one (see Section 27).

17   Check the sprockets for wear, cracks and other damage, replacing them if necessary. If the sprockets are worn, the chain is also worn, and also the sprocket on the crankshaft (which can only be remedied by replacing the crankshaft). If wear this severe is apparent, the entire engine should be disassembled for inspection.

18   Check the front guide and upper chain guide's rubber pad for wear or damage. If it is worn or damaged, the chain may be worn out or improperly adjusted. Refer to Section 27 for chain replacement.

Installation

Refer to illustrations 9.21, 9.23, 9.24, 9.25a, 9.25b, 9.25c and 9.30

19   Make sure the crankshaft is still at no. 1 TDC (refer to Chapter 1 - Valve clearances - check and adjustment).

20   Bolt the camshaft sprockets to the camshafts (if removed) and tighten the bolts to the torque listed in this Chapter's Specifications.

21   Install the exhaust side chain guide (if removed) **(see illustration)**.

22   Make sure the bearing surfaces in the cylinder head and the bearing caps are clean, then apply a light coat of engine assembly lube or moly-based grease to each of them.

23   Apply a coat of moly-based grease to the lobes of each camshaft.

Make sure the camshaft bearing journals are clean, then slip the exhaust camshaft through the chain and lay it in the cylinder head (the camshaft won't fit all the way down into the bearing saddles and locating slot because some of the lobes will be pointed downward). Make sure the small punch mark on the camshaft is very slightly forward from its installed position (straight up) **(see illustration)**. Engage the chain with the sprocket so there is no slack in the exhaust side of the chain.

24   Place the intake camshaft in its bearing saddles with its alignment mark just forward of the straight-up position **(see illustration)**. Drape the chain over the intake camshaft sprocket so there is no slack in the upper run of the chain (between the two sprockets).

25   Make sure the dowels are in position **(see illustration 9.6)**. Carefully set the bearing caps in place **(see illustrations)**. Make sure the caps are in their proper positions (see Step 5) and install all of the bolts except the four that secure the upper chain guide. Tighten them in two stages to the torque listed in this Chapter's Specifications, working from the inner bolts outward. As the bearing caps are tightened, the camshaft should settle down into its bearing saddles, the locating flange on the camshaft should settle into its groove and the exhaust camshaft alignment mark should move into the straight-up position. If the alignment mark isn't positioned correctly, disengage the chain from the camshaft and turn the camshaft to align the mark.

26   Insert a finger or wooden dowel in the cam chain tensioner hole and push against the chain to remove the slack in the upper run of the

9.25b Install the intake camshaft bearing caps - the alignment marks on both camshafts will be slightly out of position until the caps are bolted down

9.25c Install the cap bolts and tighten them evenly, working from the inner bolts outward

9.30 After the other cap bolts are tightened and the tensioner installed, install the upper chain guide

chain. Make sure the crankshaft mark is still in the no. 1 TDC position and both camshaft marks are in the straight-up positions.

27 If the crankshaft and camshaft alignment marks are not in the correct positions, lift the chain off the sprocket, turn the cam to obtain correct alignment and re-engage the chain with the sprocket.

28 Once all timing marks - those on the camshafts and crankshaft - are aligned correctly, install the cam chain tensioner (see Section 8). **Caution:** *If the marks are not aligned exactly as described, the valve timing will be incorrect and the valves may contact the pistons, causing extensive damage to the engine. Be sure to recheck all timing marks to make sure they haven't shifted.*

29 Pour clean engine oil over the cam chain and along the camshafts. Use enough that it flows down onto the sprockets and the valve area.

30 Install the upper cam chain guide **(see illustration)**.

31 Turn the engine with a wrench on the crankshaft turning bolt. If you feel a sudden increase in resistance, stop turning. The valves may be hitting the pistons due to incorrect assembly. Find the problem and fix it before turning the engine any further, or serious damage may occur. After two full turns, recheck the alignment of the camshaft punch marks with the marks on the bearing caps and the timing mark pointer with the line next to the T mark. If all marks are not in correct alignment, remove the cam bearing caps and reposition the camshaft(s) in the cam chain so the marks are correctly aligned.

32 The remainder of installation is the reverse of removal.

Valve lifters

Removal

33 Remove the camshafts following the procedure given above. Be sure to keep tension on the camshaft chain.

34 Make a holder with a separate section for each lifter and its valve adjusting shim (several egg cartons will work). Label the sections according to cylinder number (1, 2, 3 or 4), valve number (starting from the left end of the engine) and whether the lifter belongs with an intake or exhaust valve. The lifters form a wear pattern with their bores and must be returned to their original locations if reused.

35 Pull the lifter out of the bore with a magnet together with its valve adjusting shim (see Chapter 1). If the lifters are stuck, spray the area around them with carburetor cleaner and let it soak in. Place the lifters and shims in order in their holder.

Inspection

36 Check the lifters and their bores for wear, scuff marks, scratches or other damage. Yamaha doesn't provide specifications or wear tolerances for the lifters or their bores. If lifter wear or damage is found, replace the lifters as a set. Lifters are available in several oversizes for later FZR750 models. If the bores are worn or damaged, replace the camshaft case.

Installation

37 Coat the lifters and their bores with clean engine oil.

38 Installation is the reverse of the removal steps. Be sure to reinstall a valve adjusting shim between the each valve and its lifter.

---

10 Cylinder head - removal and installation

Caution: *The engine must be completely cool before beginning this procedure, or the cylinder head may become warped.*
Note: *This procedure can be performed with the engine in the frame. If the engine has been removed, ignore the steps which don't apply.*

Removal

Refer to illustrations 10.8a, 10.8b, 10.8c, 10.9 and 10.10

1 Support the bike securely so it can't be knocked over during this procedure.

2 Remove the carburetors and exhaust system (see Chapter 5).

3 Remove the valve cover (see Section 7).

4 Remove the cam chain tensioner (see Section 8).

5 Remove the camshafts (see Section 9).

6 Remove the coolant tube and thermostat housing from the rear of the engine (see Chapter 4).

10.8a Remove the cylinder head end nuts with a socket . . .

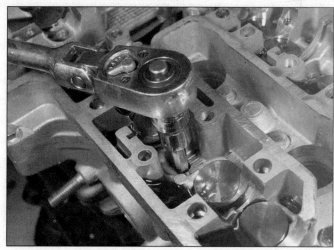

10.8b . . . and remove the center nuts with an Allen bolt bit

10.8c It isn't necessary to remove the camshaft case bolts
(arrows) in order to remove the cylinder head

10.9 Lift the cylinder head off the studs

7   Remove the external oil line from the rear of the engine (see Section 18).
8   Loosen the cylinder head nuts, 1/2 turn at a time, in the reverse of the tightening sequence **(see illustration 10.15b and the accompanying illustrations)**. Once all of the nuts are loose, remove the nuts and washers. **Caution:** *Don't remove the bolts that hold the camshaft case to the cylinder head* **(see illustration)**, *or you'll break the seal and the cylinder head halves will have to be completely separated to reseal it.*
9   Pull the cylinder head off the cylinder block studs, together with the lifters **(see illustration)**. If the head is stuck, tap upward with a rubber mallet to jar it loose, or use two wooden dowels inserted into the intake or exhaust ports to rock the head back and forth slightly (its movement will be limited by the studs). Don't attempt to pry the head off by inserting a screwdriver between the head and the cylinder block - you'll damage the sealing surfaces.
10   Lift the head gasket off the cylinder block and remove the dowel pins **(see illustration)**. Stuff a clean rag into the cam chain tunnel to prevent the entry of debris.
11   Check the cylinder head gasket and the mating surfaces on the cylinder head and block for leakage, which could indicate warpage. Refer to Section 12 and check the flatness of the cylinder head.
12   Clean all traces of old gasket material from the cylinder head and block. Be careful not to let any of the gasket material fall into the crankcase, the cylinder bores or the oil or coolant passages.

Installation

Refer to illustrations 10.13a, 10.13b, 10.14, 10.15a and 10.15b
13   Install the dowels on the cylinder head studs and lay the new gasket in place on the cylinder block **(see illustration)**. Make sure the UP cutout on the gasket is upright and toward the rear of the engine (if the word UP reads backwards, the gasket is upside down) **(see illustration)**. Never reuse the old gasket and don't use any type of gasket sealant.
14   Carefully lower the cylinder head over the studs. It's helpful to have an assistant support the camshaft chain with a piece of wire so it doesn't fall and become kinked or detached from the crankshaft. When the head is resting against the cylinder block, wire the cam chain to another component to keep tension on it. When the head is installed, the UP mark on the gasket should protrude and be upright **(see illustration)**.
15   Install the head washers and nuts. Push the washers down with a small screwdriver to make sure they've seated completely **(see illustration)**. Starting with the inner nuts and working outward, tighten the nuts to approximately half of the torque listed in this Chapter's Specifications **(see illustration)**.
16   Using the same sequence, tighten the nuts to the torque listed in this Chapter's Specifications.
17   Install the camshafts, timing chain tensioner and valve cover (see Sections 9, 8 and 7).
18   Change the engine oil (see Chapter 1).
19   The remainder of installation is the reverse of the removal steps.

10.10 Lift the gasket off

10.13a Make sure the dowels (arrows) are in position and place the new gasket over the studs

10.13b The UP cutout in the head gasket should be upright

10.14 The UP cutout in the gasket should be visible when the head is installed

10.15a Seat the cylinder head washers in their bores with a small screwdriver

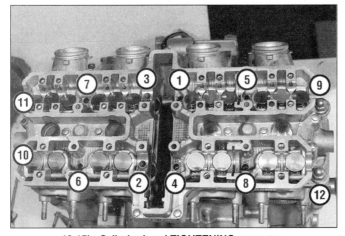

10.15b Cylinder head TIGHTENING sequence

11 Valves/valve seats/valve guides - servicing

1   Because of the complex nature of this job and the special tools and equipment required, servicing of the valves, the valve seats and the valve guides (commonly known as a valve job) is best left to a professional.

2   The home mechanic can, however, remove and disassemble the head, do the initial cleaning and inspection, then reassemble and deliver the head to a dealer service department or properly equipped motorcycle repair shop for the actual valve servicing. Refer to Section 12

for those procedures.

3   The dealer service department will remove the valves and springs, recondition or replace the valves and valve seats, replace the valve guides, check and replace the valve springs, spring retainers and keepers/collets (as necessary), replace the valve seals with new ones and reassemble the valve components.

4   After the valve job has been performed, the head will be in like-new condition. When the head is returned, be sure to clean it again very thoroughly before installation on the engine to remove any metal particles or abrasive grit that may still be present from the valve service operations. Use compressed air, if available, to blow out all the holes and passages.

12 Cylinder head and valves - disassembly, inspection and reassembly

1   As mentioned in the previous Section, valve servicing and valve guide replacement should be left to a dealer service department or motorcycle repair shop. However, disassembly, cleaning and inspection of the valves and related components can be done (if the necessary special tools are available) by the home mechanic. This way no expense is incurred if the inspection reveals that service work is not required at this time.

2   To properly disassemble the valve components without the risk of damaging them, a valve spring compressor is absolutely necessary. This special tool can usually be rented, but if it's not available, have a dealer service department or motorcycle repair shop handle the entire process of disassembly, inspection, service or repair (if required) and reassembly of the valves.

Disassembly

Refer to illustrations 12.7a, 12.7b and 12.7c

3   Remove the lifters and their shims if you haven't already done so (see Section 9). Store the components in such a way that they can be returned to their original locations without getting mixed up. Unbolt the camshaft case from the cylinder head so the valves can be removed **(see illustration 7.9b)**.

4   Before the valves are removed, scrape away any traces of gasket material from the head gasket sealing surface. Work slowly and do not nick or gouge the soft aluminum of the head. Gasket removing solvents, which work very well, are available at most motorcycle shops and auto parts stores.

5   Carefully scrape all carbon deposits out of the combustion chamber area. A hand held wire brush or a piece of fine emery cloth can be used once the majority of deposits have been scraped away. Do not use a wire brush mounted in a drill motor, or one with extremely stiff bristles, as the head material is soft and may be eroded away or scratched by the wire brush.

6   Before proceeding, arrange to label and store the valves along with their related components so they can be kept separate and reinstalled in the same valve guides they are removed from (labeled plastic bags work well for this).

7   Compress the valve spring on the first valve with a spring compressor, then remove the keepers/collets and the spring retainer from the valve assembly **(see illustration)**. Do not compress the springs any more than is absolutely necessary. Carefully release the valve spring compressor and remove the spring and the valve from the head **(see illustration)**. If the valve binds in the guide (won't pull through), push it back into the head and deburr the area around the keeper/collet groove with a very fine file or whetstone **(see illustration)**.

8   Repeat the procedure for the remaining valves. Remember to keep the parts for each valve together so they can be reinstalled in the same location.

9   Once the valves have been removed and labeled, pull off the valve stem seals with pliers and discard them (the old seals should never be reused), then remove the spring seats.

10   Next, clean the cylinder head with solvent and dry it thoroughly. Compressed air will speed the drying process and ensure that all holes and recessed areas are clean.

11   Clean all of the valve springs, keepers, retainers and spring seats with solvent and dry them thoroughly. Do the parts from one valve at a time so that no mixing of parts between valves occurs.

12   Scrape off any deposits that may have formed on the valve, then use a motorized wire brush to remove deposits from the valve heads and stems. Again, make sure the valves do not get mixed up.

Inspection

13   Inspection is the same as for FZR600 models. Refer to procedures in Chapter 2 and this Chapter's Specifications.

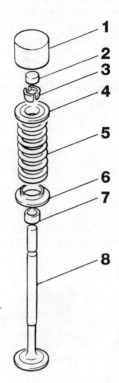

12.7a Valve components - exploded view

1	*Valve lifter*	5	*Valve spring*
2	*Adjusting shim*	6	*Spring seat*
3	*Valve keepers (collets)*	7	*Valve stem oil seal*
4	*Valve spring retainer*	8	*Valve*

Reassembly

Refer to illustration 12.15

14   Reassembly is the reverse of the disassembly procedure. Before installing the valves in the head, they should be lapped to ensure a positive seal between the valves and seats. Refer to Chapter 2 for details of the lapping procedure.

15   Once all of the valves have been installed in the head, check for proper valve sealing by pouring a small amount of solvent into each of the valve ports. If the solvent leaks past the valve(s) into the combustion chamber area **(see illustration)**, disassemble the valve(s) and repeat the lapping procedure, then reinstall the valve(s) and repeat the check. Repeat the procedure until a satisfactory seal is obtained.

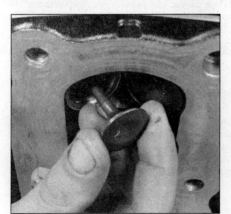

12.7b Take the valve out of the combustion chamber, but don't force it if it's stuck ...

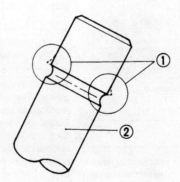

12.7c ... check the area around the keeper groove for burrs and remove any that you find

12.15 Check all around the edge of each valve (arrows) for solvent leakage

13 Cylinder block - removal, inspection and installation

Removal

Refer to illustrations 13.4a and 13.4b

1   Following the procedure given in Section 10, remove the cylinder head. Make sure the crankshaft is positioned at Top Dead Center (TDC) for cylinder no. 1.
2   Remove the external oil line from the rear of the engine (see Section 18).
3   Remove the coolant tube from the rear of the cylinder block (see Chapter 4).
4   Lift the cylinder block straight up to remove it **(see illustrations)**. If it's stuck, tap around its perimeter with a soft-faced hammer. Don't attempt to pry between the block and the crankcase, as you will ruin the sealing surfaces. As you lift, note the location of the dowel pins and oil jet nozzles. Be careful not to let these drop into the engine.
5   Stuff clean shop towels around the pistons and remove the gasket and all traces of old gasket material from the surfaces of the cylinder block, cylinder head and crankcase.

13.4a Lift the cylinder block straight off the studs

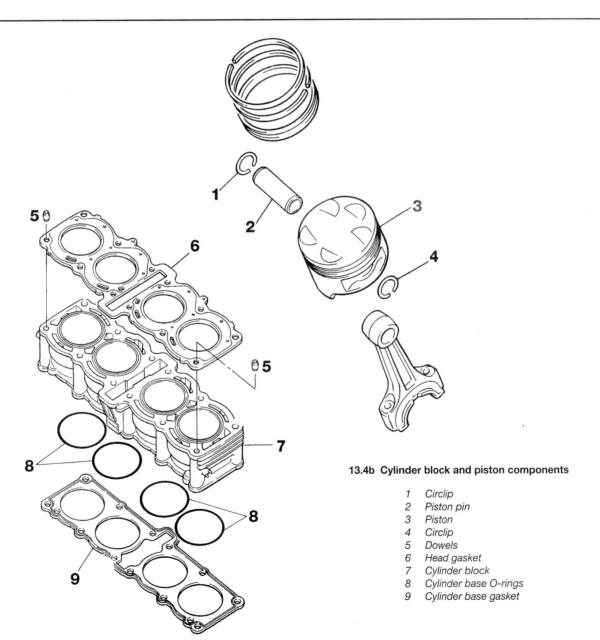

13.4b Cylinder block and piston components

1   Circlip
2   Piston pin
3   Piston
4   Circlip
5   Dowels
6   Head gasket
7   Cylinder block
8   Cylinder base O-rings
9   Cylinder base gasket

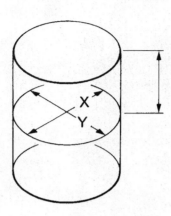

13.7 Measure across the bore in two directions, at the specified distance from the top of the bore

13.10 Move the hone quickly up-and-down and be careful not to remove too much material

Inspection

Refer to illustrations 13.7, 13.10 and 13.12

6   Check the cylinder walls carefully for scratches and score marks (don't attempt to separate the liners from the cylinder block).

7   Using the appropriate precision measuring tools, check each cylinder's diameter. Measure parallel to the crankshaft axis and across the crankshaft axis, at the depth from the top of the cylinder listed in this Chapter's Specifications **(see illustration)**. Average the two measurements and compare the results to this Chapter's Specifications. If the cylinder walls are tapered, out-of-round, worn beyond the specified limits, or badly scuffed or scored, have them rebored and honed by a dealer service department or a motorcycle repair shop. If a rebore is done, oversize pistons and rings will be required as well.

8   As an alternative, if the precision measuring tools are not available, a dealer service department or motorcycle repair shop will make the measurements and offer advice concerning servicing of the cylinders.

9   If they are in reasonably good condition and not worn to the outside of the limits, and if the piston-to-cylinder clearances can be maintained properly (see Section 14), then the cylinders do not have to be rebored; honing is all that is necessary.

10   To perform the honing operation you will need the proper size flexible hone with fine stones, or a "bottle brush" type hone, plenty of light oil or honing oil, some shop towels and an electric drill motor. Hold the cylinder block in a vise (cushioned with soft jaws or wood blocks) when performing the honing operation. Mount the hone in the drill motor, compress the stones and slip the hone into the cylinder. Lubricate the cylinder thoroughly, turn on the drill and move the hone up and down in the cylinder at a pace which will produce a fine crosshatch pattern on the cylinder wall with the crosshatch lines intersecting at approximately a 60-degree angle **(see illustration)**. Be sure to use plenty of lubricant and do not take off any more material than is absolutely necessary to produce the desired effect. Do not withdraw the hone from the cylinder while it is running. Instead, shut off the drill and continue moving the hone up and down in the cylinder until it comes to a complete stop, then compress the stones and withdraw the hone. Wipe the oil out of the cylinder and repeat the procedure on the remaining cylinder. Remember, do not remove too much material from the cylinder wall. If you do not have the tools, or do not desire to perform the honing operation, a dealer service department or motorcycle repair shop will generally do it for a reasonable fee.

11   Next, the cylinders must be thoroughly washed with warm soapy water to remove all traces of the abrasive grit produced during the honing operation. Be sure to run a brush through the bolt holes and flush them with running water. After rinsing, dry the cylinders thoroughly and apply a coat of light, rust-preventative oil to all machined surfaces.

12   Lift the oil jets out of their passages, replace the O-rings and reinstall the jets **(see illustration)**.

13.12 Lift out the oil jets (arrow) - there's one for each pair of cylinders - install new O-rings, then insert the oil jets firmly into their passages and be sure the spray nozzles on the oil jets point in the proper direction

Installation

Refer to illustrations 13.14a, 13.14b and 13.17

13   Lubricate the cylinder bores and pistons with plenty of clean engine oil.

14   Make sure the oil jets are installed correctly **(see illustration 13.12)**. Install the dowel pins and place a new cylinder base gasket on the crankcase **(see illustration)**. Make sure the UP mark on the gasket is upright and toward the front of the engine (if the UP cutout reads backwards, the gasket is upside down) **(see illustration)**. Install new O-rings on the base of each cylinder **(see illustration 13.4b)**.

15   Slowly rotate the crankshaft until two of the pistons are at the top of their travel and two are at the bottom.

16   Attach four piston ring compressors to the pistons and compress the piston rings. Large hose clamps can be used instead - just make sure they don't scratch the pistons, and don't tighten them too much.

17   Install the cylinder block over the pistons and carefully lower it down until the piston crowns fit into the cylinder liners **(see illustration)**. While doing this, pull the camshaft chain up, using a hooked tool or a piece of coat hanger. Also keep an eye on the cam chain guide to make sure it doesn't wedge against the block. Push down on the cylinder block, making sure the pistons don't get cocked sideways, until the bottoms of the cylinder liners slide down past the piston rings. A wood or plastic hammer handle can be used to gently tap the block down, but don't use too much force or the pistons will be damaged.

13.14a Make sure there's a dowel (arrow) at each front corner of the crankcase, then install the base gasket . . .

13.14b . . . make sure the UP mark on the cylinder base gasket is positioned correctly

18   Slide the cylinder block down over the remaining two pistons and guide the rings into the bores.
19   Remove the piston ring compressors or hose clamps, being careful not to scratch the pistons.
20   The remainder of installation is the reverse of removal.

14   Pistons - removal, inspection and installation

1   The pistons are attached to the connecting rods with piston pins that are a slip fit in the pistons and rods.
2   Before removing the pistons from the rods, stuff a clean shop towel into each crankcase hole, around the connecting rods. This will prevent the circlips from falling into the crankcase if they are inadvertently dropped.

Removal

Refer to illustrations 14.3a, 14.3b and 14.4

3   Using a sharp scribe, scratch the number of each piston into its crown (or use a felt pen if the piston is clean enough). Each piston should also have an arrow pointing toward the front of the engine **(see illustration)**. If not, scribe an arrow into the piston crown before removal. Support the first piston, grasp the circlip with a pointed tool or needle-nose pliers and remove it from the groove **(see illustration)**.
4   Push the piston pin out from the opposite end to free the piston from the rod **(see illustration)**. You may have to deburr the area around the groove to enable the pin to slide out (use a triangular file for

13.17 If you're experienced and very careful, you can install the cylinders over the rings using only a screwdriver, but it's a good idea to use ring compressors

this procedure). If the pin won't come out, remove the remaining circlip. Fabricate a piston pin removal tool from threaded stock, nuts, washers and a piece of pipe (see Chapter 2 for details).
5   Remove the remaining pistons in the same manner.

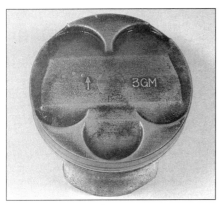

14.3a Mark the piston with its cylinder number; the arrow points to the front (exhaust) side of the engine when the piston is installed

14.3b Wear eye protection and pry out the clip with a pointed tool

14.4 Pull out the piston pin and lift the piston off the connecting rod

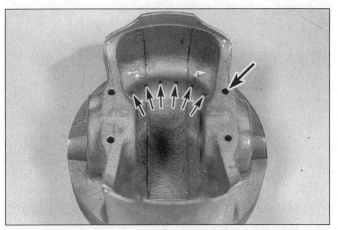

14.6 Check the piston pin bore and the piston skirt for wear, and make sure the internal holes are clear (arrows)

14.7 Make sure the piston pin clips are securely seated in the grooves (arrow)

16.7a Remove the oil pan bolts . . .

16.7b . . . and take the oil pan off

16.8 Remove the dowels and the oil pickup mounting bolts (arrows)

Inspection

Refer to illustration 14.6

6   Inspection is the same as for FZR600 models (see Chapter 2 and this Chapter's Specifications). The oil holes inside the pistons differ slightly **(see illustration)**.

Installation

Refer to illustration 14.7

7   Install the pistons in their original locations with the arrows pointing to the front of the engine. Lubricate the pins and the rod bores with clean engine oil. Install new circlips in the grooves in the inner sides of the pistons (don't reuse the old circlips). Push the pins into position from the opposite side and install new circlips. Compress the circlips only enough for them to fit in the piston. Make sure the clips are properly seated in the grooves **(see illustration)**.

---

15   Piston rings - installation

This procedure is the same as for FZR600 models (see Chapter 2 for details).

---

16   Oil pan and relief valve - removal, relief valve inspection and installation

Note: *The oil pan can be removed with the engine in the frame.*

Removal

Refer to illustrations 16.7a, 16.7b, 16.8, 16.10, 16.11a, 16.11b, 16.12, 16.13a and 16.13b

1   Support the bike securely so it can't be knocked over during this procedure.
2   Remove fairing panels as necessary for access (see Chapter 9).
3   Disconnect the wires for the oil level switch and neutral switch (see Chapter 10).
4   Remove the exhaust system (see Chapter 5).
5   Drain the engine oil and remove the oil filter (see Chapter 1).
6   Detach the oil cooler lines from the engine (see Section 32).
7   Remove the oil pan bolts and detach the pan from the crankcase **(see illustrations)**.

16.10 Pull the relief valve out of the case; it's a good idea to replace the O-ring whenever the relief valve is removed

16.11a Remove the large oil pipes from the crankcase; one can be pulled out and the other is secured by bolts (arrows) (FZR1000 shown)

16.11b Remove the remaining bolts (arrows) and take the small oil pipe out of the crankcase (FZR1000 shown)

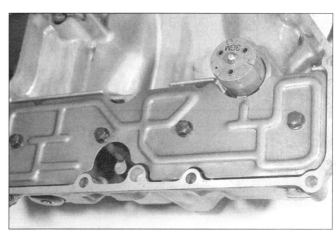

16.12 Remove the baffle from the oil pan

3

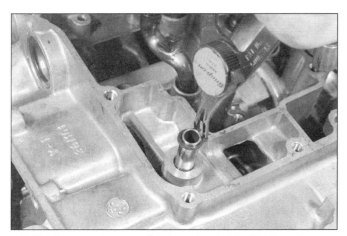

16.13a Remove the snap-ring from the clutch oil return pipe . . .

16.13b . . . and withdraw the pipe through the clutch housing (the clutch cover will have to be removed to do this)

8   Unbolt the pickup from the crankcase and lift it off **(see illustration)**.
9   Remove all traces of old gasket from the oil pan and crankcase.
10   Remove the relief valve from the crankcase **(see illustration)**. It should pull out with light hand pressure. If it's stuck, rock it back and forth slightly.
11   Remove the oil pipes from the crankcase **(see illustrations)**.
12   Unbolt the baffle from the oil pan **(see illustration)**.

13   If necessary, remove the clutch oil return pipe. Remove the snapring that holds the pipe against the crankcase **(see illustration)**. Remove the clutch cover (see Section 19) and withdraw the pipe into the clutch housing **(see illustration)**.

Relief valve inspection

14   This is the same as for FZR600 models (see Chapter 2 for details).

16.15 Make sure the oil pan dowels are in position (arrows)

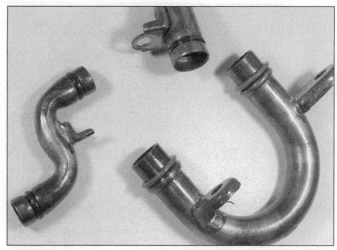

16.16 Inspect the O-rings on the pipes and pickup; it's a good idea to replace them whenever the pipes and pickup are removed

16.18 These two oil pan bolts secure a fairing bracket

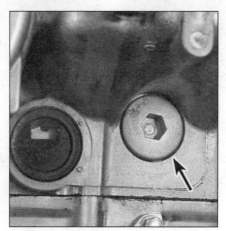

17.2 To check the oil pressure, remove the plug (arrow) and connect an oil pressure gauge using the proper adapter

17.8a Turn the pump gear to provide access to the mounting bolts

Installation

Refer to illustrations 16.15, 16.16 and 16.18

15   Install the oil pan dowels **(see illustration)**. Install the relief valve in the crankcase, using a new O-ring.

16   Install new O-rings on the oil pipes and pickup **(see illustration)**.

17   Install the oil pipes and pickup and tighten the bolts securely.

18   Position a new gasket on the oil pan. A thin film of RTV sealant can be used to hold the gasket in place. Install the oil pan and bolts, tightening the bolts to the torque listed in this Chapter's Specifications, using a criss-cross pattern. Two of the bolts secure a fairing bracket on later FZR1000 models **(see illustration)**.

19   The remainder of installation is the reverse of removal. Install a new filter and fill the crankcase with oil (see Chapter 1), then run the engine and check for leaks.

17   Oil pump - oil pressure check, removal, inspection and installation

Note: *The oil pump can be removed with the engine in the frame.*

Oil pressure check

Refer to illustration 17.2

Warning: *If the oil passage plug is removed when the engine is hot, hot oil will drain out - wait until the engine is cold before beginning this check.*

1   Remove fairing panels as necessary for access (see Chapter 9).

2   Remove the plug at the bottom of the crankcase on the right-hand side and install an oil pressure gauge **(see illustration)**.

3   Start the engine and watch the gauge while varying the engine rpm. The pressure should stay within the relief valve opening pressure listed in this Chapter's Specifications. If the pressure is too high, the relief valve is stuck closed. To remove and inspect it, see Section 16 and Chapter 2.

4   If the pressure is lower than the standard, either the relief valve is stuck open, the oil pump is faulty, or there is other engine damage. Begin diagnosis by checking the relief valve, then the oil pump. If those items check out okay, chances are the bearing oil clearances are excessive and the engine needs to be overhauled.

5   If the pressure reading is in the desired range, allow the engine to warm up to normal operating temperature and check the pressure again, at the specified engine rpm. Compare your findings with this Chapter's Specifications.

6   If the pressure is significantly lower than specified, check the relief valve and the oil pump.

Removal

Refer to illustrations 17.8a, 17.8b, 17.8c, 17.8d and 17.9

7   Remove the clutch (see Section 19).

8   Remove the oil pump mounting bolts and remove the pump **(see illustrations)**.

9   Remove the oil pump gasket and dowel **(see illustration)**.

17.8b Insert an Allen bolt bit (arrow)
through the holes in the oil pump gear
to remove the mounting bolts (viewed
from below with the oil pan removed
for clarity) . . .

17.8c . . . one of the bolts can be removed
completely through the access hole; the
others can't, but they can be loosened
far enough to permit pump
removal (arrow) . . .

17.8d . . . with all three bolts loose, take
the pump off

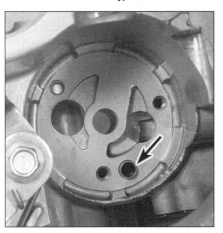

17.9 Remove the gasket and
dowel (arrow)

17.12a The pump drive tooth (arrow) must
align with the water pump impeller slot

17.12b Align the arrowhead mark on the
pump body with the arrow cast
in the crankcase

Inspection

10   This is the same as for FZR600 models (see Chapter 2 and this
Chapter's Specifications).

Installation

Refer to illustrations 17.12a and 17.12b

11   Before installing the pump, prime it by pouring oil into it while
turning the shaft by hand - this will ensure that it begins to pump oil
quickly. Align the drive tooth and drive slot with with the same mounting bolt hole so they will mesh when installed.

12   Installation is the reverse of removal, with the following additions:
  a) Engage the drive tooth on the pump with its corresponding notch
      in the water pump impeller **(see illustration).**
  b) Align the arrowhead mark on the pump body with the cast arrow
      on the crankcase **(see illustration).**

---

18   External oil lines - removal and installation

Refer to illustrations 18.4, 18.5 and 18.7

1   FZR1000 models use a single Y-shaped oil line with one fitting on
the crankcase and two fittings on the cylinder head. FZR750 models
use two oil lines that run from a single fitting on the crankcase to two
fittings in the cylinder head.

2   Remove the left and right fairings (see Chapter 9).

18.4 Remove the banjo bolts; on FZR1000 models remove
the bracket bolt (arrows)

3   Remove the fuel tank, air filter housing and carburetors (see
Chapter 5).

4   At the top of the oil lines, remove two banjo bolts; if you're working on an FZR1000, remove the bracket bolt **(see illustration).**

3

18.5 Remove the banjo bolt at the crankcase (FZR1000 shown)

18.7 Use a new sealing washer on both sides of each banjo fitting (FZR1000 shown)

19.3a Loosen the clutch cover bolts evenly . . .

19.3b . . . then take off the cover

5   At the bottom of the oil line, remove the banjo bolt **(see illustration)**.
6   Take off the oil lines and their sealing washers.
7   Installation is the reverse of the removal steps. Be sure to use a new sealing washer on each side of each banjo bolt and tighten them to the specified torque **(see illustration)**. On FZR750 models, position the oil lines so they don't touch any part of the engine except the cam chain tensioner.

---

19   Clutch - removal, inspection and installation

Note: *The clutch can be removed with the engine in the frame.*

Removal
Refer to illustrations 19.3a, 19.3b, 19.4a, 19.4b, 19.5, 19.6, 19.7a, 19.7b, 19.8a, 19.8b, 19.9a, 19.9b, 19.9c, 19.10a, 19.10b, 19.11, 19.12 and 19.13
1   Support the bike securely so it can't be knocked over during this procedure. Remove the right fairing (see Chapter 9).
2   Drain the engine oil (see Chapter 1).
3   Loosen the clutch cover bolts 1/4 turn at a time in a criss-cross pattern, then remove the cover, gasket and dowels **(see illustrations)**.
4   Loosen the pressure plate bolts evenly in a criss-cross pattern, then remove the bolts, springs and pressure plate **(see illustrations)**.
5   Remove the thrust washer and bearing from the short clutch

19.4a Loosen the pressure plate bolts evenly

pushrod **(see illustration)**.
6   On all except UK FZR750 models, remove the four outer friction plates, one center friction plate and the related steel plates **(see illustration)**. The outermost friction plate has a slot in one of its tabs which must be lined up with the marks on the clutch housing. The four outer

19.4b Clutch - exploded view

1 Pressure plate
2 Thrust washer
3 Bearing
4 Short pushrod and O-ring
5 Steel ball
6 Nut
7 Lockwasher
8 Friction plates (with red paint
   mark - outer plate has slot in tab)*
9 Cushion spring
10 Center friction plate (with
    blue paint mark)*
11 Steel plates
12 Clutch boss
13 Thrust washer (shown smooth; may
    have grooves)
14 Clutch housing
15 Bearing
16 Collar
17 Thrust washer (shown
    grooved; may be smooth)
18 Long pushrod
19 Oil seal
20 Release cylinder (except
    UK FZR750)
21 Release lever (UK FZR750)

*Friction plates interchangeable on
UK FZR750

ROUNDED END

**19.5 Remove the thrust washer
and bearing**

**19.6 The clutch plate with the slot (arrow)
is installed next to the pressure plate (all
except UK FZR750)**

**19.7a Remove the short pushrod
and steel ball**

and four inner friction plates have red paint marks and the center friction plate has a blue paint mark. Look for these marks as soon as you
remove the plates and make your own marks if they aren't visible. On
UK FZR750 models, the plates are interchangeable

7   Remove the short pushrod and the steel ball that fits behind it
(see illustration). There's another, longer pushrod behind the steel ball
which can be removed for inspection with a magnet. If it won't come
out easily, it can be removed from the other side of the engine if the

19.7b Remove the long pushrod; if necessary, it can be removed from the other side of the engine, as shown here

19.8a Remove the cushion spring . . .

19.8b . . . then remove the remaining steel plates and friction plates

19.9a Bend back the lockwasher tab . . .

19.9b . . . remove the clutch nut . . .

19.9c . . . and remove the lockwasher

19.10a Slide the clutch boss (arrow) off the transmission shaft . . .

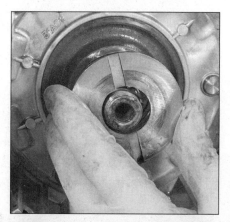

19.10b . . . and remove the thrust washer

19.11 Thread a bolt (or two bolts if necessary) into the collar, then pull on the bolts to remove the collar

clutch release cylinder or lever is removed **(see illustration)**.

8   Remove the cushion spring and the remaining steel plates and friction plates **(see illustrations)**.

9   Bend back the lockwasher on the clutch boss nut **(see illustration)**. Loosen the nut, using a special holding tool (Yamaha tool no. YM-91402, part no. 90890-04086 or equivalent) to prevent the clutch housing from turning (see Chapter 2 for details). An alternative to this tool can be fabricated from some steel strap, bent at the ends and bolted together in the middle. Once the nut is loose, remove the nut and lockwasher and discard the lockwasher **(see illustrations)**. Use a

new lockwasher during installation.

10   Remove the clutch boss and thrust washer **(see illustrations)**. **Note**: *The thrust washer may be grooved or smooth. Be sure to note which it is, because there's another washer which is not interchangeable.*

11   Thread a bolt into the collar and pull it out **(see illustration)**. Once the spacer is out, pull out the bearing.

12   Remove the clutch housing **(see illustration)**.

13   Remove the thrust washer from behind the clutch housing **(see illustration)**. Note whether it's grooved or smooth.

19.12 Remove the clutch housing

19.13 Remove the remaining thrust washer

19.16a Position the clutch boss on the transmission shaft and install the collar . . .

19.16b . . . then slide the bearing in between the collar and clutch housing

19.17 Install the lockwasher so its tabs fit into the clutch housing slots

19.19 Install the nut, tighten it to the specified torque and bend the lockwasher against the nut

3

Inspection

14   This is the same as for FZR600 models (see Chapter 2 and this Chapter's Specifications).

Installation

Refer to illustrations 19.16a, 19.16b, 19.17, 19.19, 19.24, 19.26a, 19.26b, 19.27a and 19.27b

15   Install the thrust washer **(see illustration 19.10b)** and clutch housing.

16   Coat the clutch housing bearing with engine oil, then install the bearing and collar **(see illustrations)**. Be sure the gear on the back of the clutch housing engages the oil pump gear.

17   Install the thrust washer, the clutch boss, a new lockwasher and the clutch boss nut **(see illustration)**.

18   Tighten the clutch boss nut to the torque listed in this Chapter's Specifications, using the technique described in Step 9 to prevent the hub from turning.

19   Bend the lockwasher against one of the flats on the nut with pliers **(see illustration)**.

20   On all except UK FZR750 models coat one of the red-painted friction plates with engine oil and install it in the clutch housing. Engage the tabs on the friction plate with the slots in the clutch housing.

21   Install a steel plate on top of the friction plate with its rounded side inward. Continue to install alternate friction and steel plates until you've installed four friction plates with steel plates next to them. Always install friction plates and steel plates next to each other; never install a steel plate next to a steel plate or a friction plate next to a friction plate.

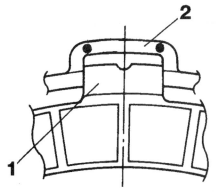

19.24 Align the slot in the outer friction plate with the marks on the clutch housing (except UK FZR750)

1   Slotted tab on outer friction plate
2   Clutch housing

22   Install the blue-painted friction plate and cushion spring **(see illustration 19.4b)**.

23   Install the remaining steel plates and red-painted friction plates.

24   Install the friction plate with the notch in one tab last. Align the notch with the marks on the clutch housing **(see illustration)**.

25   On UK FZR750 models, install a friction plate first, then alternate steel and friction plates.

19.26a Install the long pushrod with its rounded end away from the steel ball, then install the steel ball . . .

19.26b . . . then install the short pushrod and its O-ring

19.27a Align the marks on the clutch boss and pressure plate (arrows)

19.27b Fit the oil tube into its hole in the clutch cover (arrow)

20.2 Remove the union bolt from the clutch line (arrow); be careful not to spill fluid on painted or plastic surfaces

20.3a Remove the master cylinder clamp bolts (arrows)

26   Coat the pushrods and steel ball with multipurpose grease, then install the long pushrod, the steel ball and the short pushrod (see illustrations).

27   The remainder of installation is the reverse of the removal steps, with the following additions:

  a) Align the hole in the pressure plate with the mark on the clutch boss (see illustration).

  b) Tighten the pressure plate bolts in several stages in a criss-cross pattern to the torque listed in this Chapter's Specifications.

  c) Make sure the clutch cover dowels are in position and install a new gasket.

  d) Fit the oil tube into its hole in the cover as the cover is installed (see illustration).

  e) Tighten the clutch cover bolts in several stages to the torque listed in this Chapter's Specifications.

28   Fill the crankcase with the recommended type and amount of engine oil (see Chapter 1).

20   Clutch release mechanism

Master cylinder removal

Refer to illustrations 20.2, 20.3a and 20.3b

1   Disconnect the electrical connector from the clutch interlock switch beneath the master cylinder.

2   Place a towel under the master cylinder to catch any spilled fluid, then remove the union bolt from the master cylinder fluid line (see illustration). **Caution**: *Brake fluid will damage paint. Wipe up any spills*

immediately and wash the area with soap and water.

3   Remove the master cylinder clamp bolts and take the cylinder body off the handlebar (see illustrations).

Master cylinder overhaul

Refer to illustrations 20.4, 20.6, 20.7a, 20.7b, 20.13, 20.15

4   Remove the lever pivot bolt and nut and take off the lever (see illustration).

5   Remove the cap and rubber diaphragm from the reservoir (see illustration 20.3b).

6   Remove the rubber boot, pushrod and spring from the master cylinder (see illustration).

7   Remove the snap ring and retaining ring, then dump out the piston and primary cup, secondary cup and spring (see illustrations). If they won't come out, blow compressed air into the fluid line hole. **Warning**: *The piston may shoot out forcefully enough to cause injury. Point the piston at a block of wood or a pile of rags inside a box and apply air pressure gradually. Never point the end of the cylinder at yourself, including your fingers.*

8   Thoroughly clean all of the components in clean brake fluid (don't use any type of petroleum-based solvent).

9   Check the piston and cylinder bore for wear, scratches and rust. If the piston shows these conditions, replace it and both rubber cups as a set. If the cylinder bore has any defects, replace the entire master cylinder.

10   Install the spring in the cylinder bore, wide end first.

11   Coat a new cup with brake fluid and install it in the cylinder, wide side first.

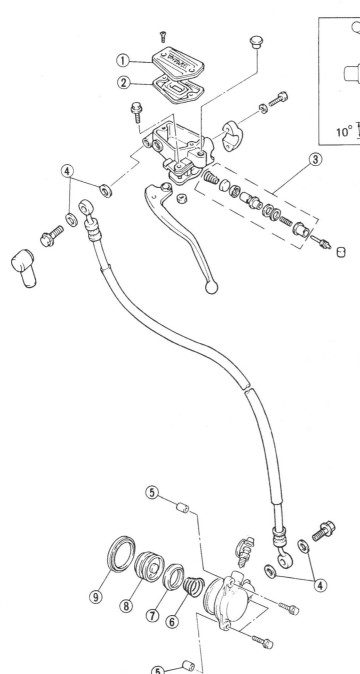

20.3b Clutch hydraulic system - exploded view

1 Reservoir cap
2 Diaphragm
3 Piston assembly
4 Sealing washers
5 Dowel
6 Release cylinder spring
7 Piston seal
8 Piston
9 Dust seal

3

20.4 Remove the pivot bolt and nut and separate the lever from the cylinder

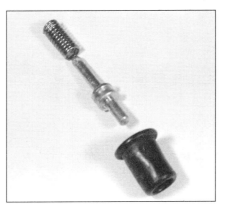

20.6 Remove the rubber boot, pushrod and spring

20.7a Remove the snap-ring from the bore . . .

20.7b . . . and take out the piston assembly, cup, spring seat and spring

20.13 Make sure the snap-ring seats in its groove

20.15 Align the lever bushing hole with the pushrod (arrows)

20.17 Disconnect the fluid line and remove the mounting bolts (arrows) and take the cylinder off - brake fluid will remove paint, so wipe up any spills right away and wash the area with soap and water

20.21 Take the spring off the piston

12   Coat the piston with brake fluid and install it in the cylinder.
13   Install the retaining ring. Press the piston into the bore and install the snap ring to hold it in place **(see illustration)**.
14   Install the rubber boot, pushrod and spring.
15   When you install the lever, align the hole in the lever bushing with the pushrod **(see illustration)**.

Master cylinder installation

16   Installation is the reverse of the removal steps, with the following additions:
   a) The arrow next to the UP mark on the clamp must point upward. Position the master cylinder at 10-degrees from horizontal **(see illustration 20.3b)**.
   b) Tighten the clamp bolts to the torque listed in this Chapter's Specifications.
   c) Fill and bleed the clutch hydraulic system.
   d) Operate the clutch lever and check for fluid leaks.

Release cylinder removal

Refer to illustration 20.17

17   Place rags and a container beneath the release cylinder to catch spilled fluid, then remove the union bolt and place the end of the hose in the container to let the fluid drain **(see illustration)**. **Caution**: *Brake fluid will damage paint. Wipe up any spills immediately and wash the area with soap and water.*
18   Remove the cylinder mounting bolts and take it off.

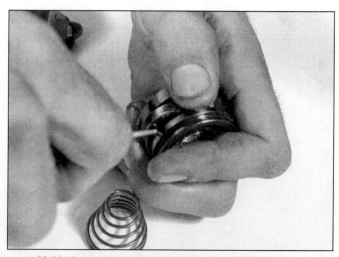

20.23 If you plan to reuse the piston, remove the seals and install new ones

Release cylinder overhaul

Refer to illustrations 20.21 and 20.23

19   Pull the dust seal off the cylinder **(see illustration 20.3b)**.
20   Remove the piston and spring. If they won't come out, blow compressed air into the fluid line hole. **Warning**: *The piston may shoot out forcefully enough to cause injury. Point the piston at a block of wood or*

20.27 Remove the rubber cap from the bleed valve (arrow)

21.2 The punch marks on the shift lever and shaft (arrows) should be aligned

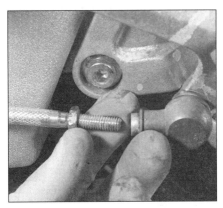

21.4 Loosen the locknut and rotate the linkage rod to detach it from the rear adjuster

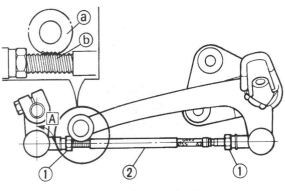

21.6 Shift linkage details

1	Adjusting nuts	a	Shift pedal
2	Linkage rod	b	Threads on linkage rod
A	90-degrees		

a pile of rags inside a box and apply air pressure gradually. Never point the end of the cylinder at yourself, including your fingers.

21   Separate the spring from the piston **(see illustration)**.

22   Thoroughly clean all of the components in clean brake fluid (don't use any type of petroleum-based solvent).

23   Check the piston and cylinder bore for wear, scratches and rust. If the piston shows these conditions, replace it and the seal as a set. If the cylinder bore has any defects, replace the entire release cylinder. If the piston and bore are good, carefully remove the seals from the piston and install new ones **(see illustration)**.

Release cylinder installation

24   Installation is the reverse of the removal procedure, with the following additions:

  a) Use new sealing washers on the fluid line.
  b) Tighten the cylinder mounting bolts and fluid line union bolt to the torques listed in this Chapter's Specifications.
  c) Bleed the clutch (see below).
  d) Operate the clutch and check for fluid leaks.

Clutch bleeding

Refer to illustration 20.27

25   Support the motorcycle upright and point the front wheel straight ahead.

26   Remove the master cylinder cap and diaphragm. Top up the master cylinder with fluid to the upper edge of the fluid level window, then set the diaphragm and cap on the reservoir (but don't install the screws yet).

27   Remove the cap from the bleed valve **(see illustration)**. Place a box wrench (ring spanner) over the bleed valve. Attach a rubber tube to

the valve fitting and put the other end of the tube in a container. Pour enough clean brake fluid into the container to cover the end of the tube.

28   Rapidly squeeze the clutch lever several times, then hold it in. With the clutch lever held in, open the bleed valve 1/4-turn with the wrench, let air and fluid escape, then tighten the valve.

29   Release the clutch lever.

30   Repeat Steps 28 and 29 until there aren't any more bubbles in the fluid flowing into the container. Top off the master cylinder with fluid, then reinstall the diaphragm and cap and tighten the screws to the specified torque.

Cable replacement (UK FZR750 models)

31   Loosen the cable adjusters at the handlebar and at the lower end of the cable near the release lever. Unbolt the release lever cover, straighten the lock tab and disconnect the cable from the release lever. Note how the cable is routed through the holder near the steering head, then disconnect it from the clutch lever and remove it.

32   Installation is the reverse of removal. Adjust the cable as described in Chapter 1.

---

21   External shift mechanism - removal, inspection and installation

---

Shift lever and pedal removal and installation

Refer to illustrations 21.2, 21.4 and 21.6

1   Support the bike securely so it can't be knocked over during this procedure.

2   Look for punch marks on the end of the shift shaft and lever **(see illustration)**. If you can't find them, make your own punch marks so the lever can be realigned correctly during installation.

3   Remove the lever pinch bolt. Pull the lever off the shaft, together with the linkage rod.

4   Loosen the locknut and unscrew the linkage rod from the rear adjuster **(see illustration)**.

5   Remove the shift pedal/footpeg bracket bolts and take the assembly off. If necessary, remove the Allen bolt and separate the footpeg and shift pedal from the bracket.

6   Installation is the reverse of removal. Position the linkage so the bottom of the shift pedal is even with the threads on the forward end of the linkage rod **(see illustration)**. The shift arm should be at 90-degrees to the linkage rod. Adjust the linkage as needed with the nuts on the linkage rod (see Chapter 1).

Shift mechanism removal

Refer to illustrations 21.8a, 21.8b, 21.8c, 21.10, 21.12a and 21.12b

7   Remove the shift lever and linkage (Steps 1 through 4) and the engine sprocket cover (see Chapter 7).

21.8a Slide the bushing off the shift shaft . . .

21.8b . . . pry the C-clip away from the shaft . . .

21.8c . . . and remove the washer

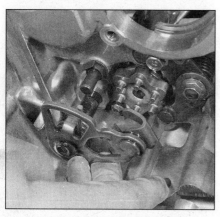

21.10 Pull the shift shaft out of the crankcase

21.12a Unbolt the stopper lever and the stopper plate (arrow) . . .

21.12b . . . and remove the stopper plate and return spring; check the guide bar (arrow) for looseness

21.17 Position the return spring like this

21.18 The end of the stopper lever (left arrow) should be in the neutral detent on the shift cam; the end of the return spring (right arrow) should be hooked over the stopper lever

21.21 The shift shaft looks like this when it's installed correctly

8   Remove the shift shaft bushing, C-clip and washer (see illustrations).
9   Remove the clutch (see Section 19).
10   Slide the shift shaft out of the crankcase (see illustration).
11   Remove the oil pump (see Section 17).
12   Unbolt the stopper lever and the stopper plate and the stopper plate that secures the shift fork guide bar, then remove the stopper lever return spring (see illustrations).

Shift mechanism inspection

13   Inspect the return spring guide bar (see illustration 21.12b). If it's worn or damaged, replace it. If it's loose, unscrew it, install a new lockwasher, reinstall the guide bar and tighten it securely. Bend the tab of the new lockwasher securely against one of the flats on the guide bar.
14   Check the shift shaft for bends and damage to the splines. If the shaft is bent, you can attempt to straighten it, but if the splines are damaged it will have to be replaced. Inspect the pawls and springs on the shift shaft and replace the shaft if they're worn or damaged.

22.6 Use a Torx bit to remove the bearing retainer screws (arrows)

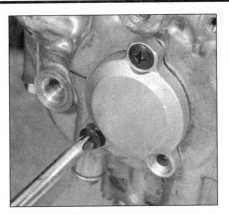

22.7a Remove the crankshaft end covers . . .

22.7b . . . there's one at each end of the crankshaft

15   Check the condition of the stopper lever and spring. Replace the stopper lever if it's worn where it contacts the shift cam. Replace the spring if it's distorted.
16   Inspect the pins on the end of the shift cam. If they're worn or damaged, you'll have to disassemble the crankcase to replace the shift cam.

Installation
Refer to illustrations 21.17, 21.18 and 21.21
17   Position the stopper lever return spring on the crankcase and engage its end with the stop **(see illustration)**.
18   Apply non-permanent thread locking agent to the threads of the shift fork guide bar retainer bolt, then install the retainer over the return spring. Apply the same thread locking agent to the stopper lever bolt, then install the stopper lever. Make sure the stopper lever engages the neutral detent in the shift cam and the spring is hooked over the lever **(see illustration)**. Tighten the bolts to the torque listed in this Chapter's Specifications.
19   Install the oil pump (see Section 17).
20   Apply high-temperature grease to the lip of the seal. Wrap the splines of the change lever shaft with electrical tape, so the splines won't damage the seal as the shaft is installed.
21   Slide the shaft into the crankcase. Engage the pawls evenly with the pins on the shift cam and position the return spring over the guide bar **(see illustration)**.
22   The remainder of installation is the reverse of the removal steps.
23   Check the engine oil level and add some, if necessary (see Chapter 1).

22   Crankcase - disassembly and reassembly

1   To examine and repair or replace the crankshaft, starter and camshaft chains, connecting rods, bearings, or transmission components, the crankcase must be split into two parts.

Disassembly
Refer to illustrations 22.6, 22.7a, 22.7b, 22.10, 22.11 and 22.12a through 22.12f
2   Remove the cylinder head, cylinder block and pistons (see Sections 10, 13 and 14). Remove the clutch (see Section 19).
3   Remove the water pump (see Chapter 4).
4   Remove the alternator and starter (see Chapter 10).
5   Remove the engine sprocket (see Chapter 7).
6   Remove the bearing retainers from behind the engine sprocket **(see illustration)** and from behind the clutch **(see illustration 19.13)**. **Caution:** *Use the correct size Torx bit to remove the screws. Don't use an Allen bit or the screw heads will be rounded out.*
7   Remove the cover from each end of the crankshaft **(see illustrations)**.
8   Remove the pickup coil (see Chapter 6).
9   Remove the oil pan (see Section 16).

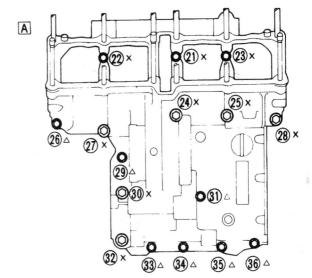
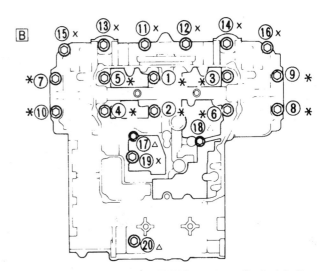

22.10 Crankcase bolt TIGHTENING sequence (typical; bolt numbers are cast in the crankcase)

A   Upper crankcase
B   Lower crankcase

10   Remove the upper crankcase bolts, then the lower crankcase bolts, starting with the highest-numbered bolt and working to the lowest (reverse of the tightening sequence **(see illustration)**.

11   Carefully separate the crankcase halves **(see illustration)**. If they won't come easily, make sure all fasteners have been removed. Don't pry against the crankcase mating surfaces or they will leak.

12   Look for the oil jet, O-rings and dowels **(see illustrations)**. If they're not in one of the crankcase halves, locate them.

13   Refer to Sections 23 through 31 for information on the internal components of the crankcase.

Reassembly

Refer to illustrations 22.15, 22.18, 22.20, 22.21a, 22.21b, 22.21c and 22.25

14   Make sure the crankshaft, starter clutch and transmission shafts are correctly positioned in the upper crankcase half (see Sections 25, 28 and 31).

15   Place the ends of the crankcase studs on a piece of 2-by-4 lumber or equivalent **(see illustration)**. This will prevent the connecting rods from pushing against the workbench and forcing the crankshaft out of its bearings.

16   Remove all traces of sealant from the crankcase mating surfaces. Be careful not to let any fall into the case as this is done. Check to make sure the oil jet (with a new O-ring) and the dowel pins are in place **(see illustrations 22.12a through 22.12f)**.

22.11 With the crankcase upside down, lift the bottom half off the top half

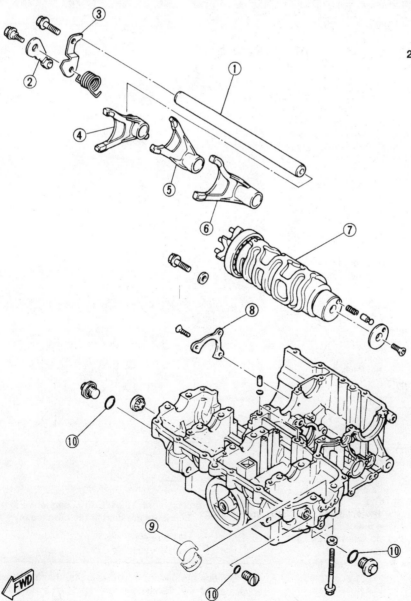

22.12a Lower crankcase components

1   *Shift fork guide bar*
2   *Stopper lever*
3   *Guide bar stopper plate*
4   *Right shift fork (labeled R)*
5   *Center shift fork (labeled C)*
6   *Left shift fork (labeled L)*
7   *Shift cam*
8   *Bearing retainer*
9   *Main bearings*
10   *O-rings*

FWD

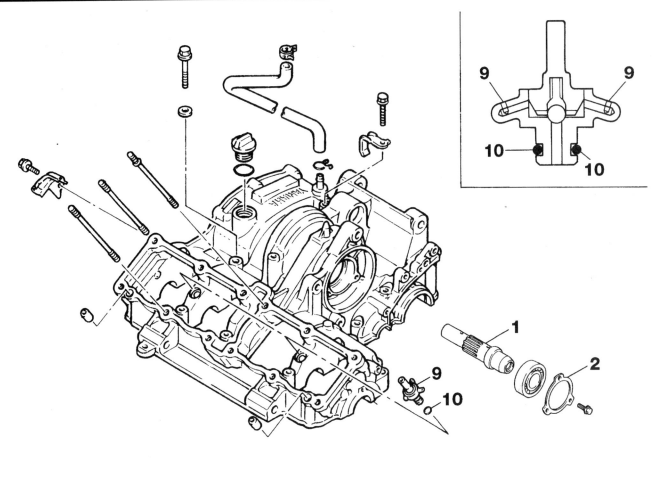

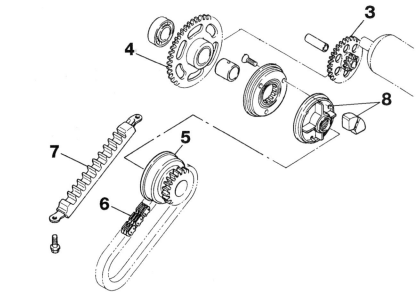

22.12b Upper crankcase components

1	Alternator drive shaft	6	Starter chain
2	Bearing retainer plate	7	Chain guide
3	Starter idle gear	8	Alternator damper
4	Starter clutch gear	9	Oil jet
5	Starter clutch	10	O-ring

22.12c Look for the inner dowels (arrow) . . .

22.12d . . . and their corresponding O-rings in the mating surface of the crankcase

22.12e Locate this dowel on the edge of the crankcase

22.12f There's an oil jet for each pair of cylinders

22.15 Rest the crankcase studs as shown

22.18 Apply sealant to the mating surfaces

22.20 The transmission and clutch pushrod seals should look this when the cases are assembled

22.21a The four end bolts have steel washers

22.21b Bolt 25 has a copper washer

17 Pour some engine oil over the transmission gears, the crankshaft main bearings and the shift cam. Don't get any oil on the crankcase mating surfaces.

18 Apply a thin, even bead of Yamaha Bond or Quick Gasket sealant (part no. ACC-11001-05-01) or equivalent to the crankcase mating surfaces **(see illustration)**. **Caution**: *Don't apply an excessive amount of sealant. Don't let it contact the oil jet. Don't apply it within 2 to 3 mm (0.8 to 1.2 inch) of the bearing inserts, as it will ooze out when the case halves are assembled and may obstruct oil passages and prevent the bearings from seating.*

19 Check the position of the shift cam, shift forks and transmission shafts - make sure they're in the neutral position (see Section 28). Make sure the locating pins in the transmission bearings are positioned correctly.

20 Carefully assemble the crankcase halves over the dowels. While doing this, make sure the shift forks fit into their gear grooves. Make sure the transmission seal and clutch pushrod seal are positioned correctly in the case **(see illustration)**. The seals should fit flush with the case surfaces when the case halves are assembled. **Caution**: *The crankcase halves should fit together completely without being forced. If*

22.21c Bolt 31 secures a ground wire

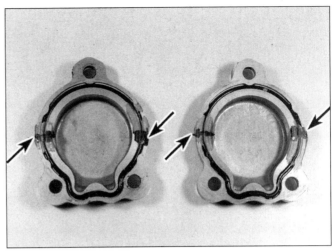

22.25 Install the O-rings in the end cover grooves and place a small dab of sealant on the points where the end covers meet the crankcase seam (arrows)

22   Tighten the bolts in numerical order, referring to the numbers cast in the crankcase. Tighten all bolts to the torque listed in this Chapter's Specifications. **Note:** *There are different torque settings for the 9 mm bolts, 8 mm bolts and the 6 mm bolts.*
23   Turn the mainshaft and the transmission driveshaft to make sure they turn freely. Also make sure the crankshaft turns freely.
24   Install the oil pan (see Section 16).
25   The remainder of assembly is the reverse of disassembly, with the following additions:
   a) Once the external shift linkage is installed, shift the transmission through all the gear positions and back to Neutral.
   b) Use new O-rings in the crankshaft end covers. Apply a small amount of sealant to the covers where they cross the crankcase seam (**see illustration**).
   b) Be sure to refill the engine oil.

23.2a This oil line is secured by bolts (arrows)

they're slightly apart, DO NOT force them together by tightening the crankcase bolts. The most likely reason they're apart is that the transmission bearing pins aren't positioned correctly. If the pins are forced against the crankcase halves, the cases will crack and have to be replaced.
21   Oil their threads and install the crankcase bolts in the correct holes (**see illustration 22.10**). Bolts 7 through 10 have steel washers (**see illustration**). Bolt 25 has a copper washer (**see illustration**). Bolt 31 secures a ground wire (**see illustration**).

23   Crankcase components - inspection and servicing

Refer to illustrations 23.2a, 23.2b. 23.2c, 23.2d and 23.3
1   After the crankcases have been separated and the crankshaft, starter clutch, shift cam and forks and transmission components removed, the crankcases should be cleaned thoroughly with new solvent and dried with compressed air.
2   All oil passages should be blown out with compressed air. Internal oil lines should be removed and flushed with solvent (**see illustrations**). Remove any oil passage plugs that haven't already been removed (**see illustration**).

23.2b Remove the securing bolt (arrow) . . .

23.2c . . . and slide the oil spray tube out of the crankcase

23.2d Remove any oil passage plugs not removed already

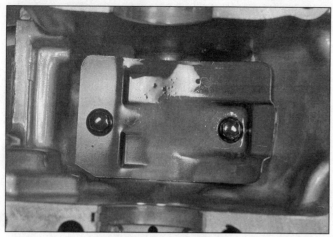

23.3 Unbolt the oil baffle plates

25.2a Lift the crankshaft out of the case

3   Remove the oil baffles **(see illustration)**.
4   Check the starter clutch and idle gears (see Section 31).
5   All traces of old gasket sealant should be removed from the mating surfaces. Minor damage to the surfaces can be cleaned up with a fine sharpening stone or grindstone. **Caution:** *Be very careful not to nick or gouge the crankcase mating surfaces or leaks will result. Check both crankcase halves very carefully for cracks and other damage.*
6   Check the starter chain guide and cam chain rear guide for wear. If they appear to be worn excessively, replace them.
7   If any damage is found that can't be repaired, replace the crankcase halves as a set.

24   Main and connecting rod bearings - general note

1   Even though main and connecting rod bearings are generally replaced with new ones during the engine overhaul, the old bearings should be retained for close examination as they may reveal valuable information about the condition of the engine.
2   Bearing failure occurs mainly because of lack of lubrication, the presence of dirt or other foreign particles, overloading the engine and/or corrosion. Regardless of the cause of bearing failure, it must be corrected before the engine is reassembled to prevent it from happening again.
3   When examining the bearings, remove the main bearings from the case halves and the rod bearings from the connecting rods and caps and lay them out on a clean surface in the same general position as their location on the crankshaft journals. This will enable you to match any noted bearing problems with the corresponding side of the crankshaft journal.
4   Dirt and other foreign particles get into the engine in a variety of ways. It may be left in the engine during assembly or it may pass through filters or breathers. It may get into the oil and from there into the bearings. Metal chips from machining operations and normal engine wear are often present. Abrasives are sometimes left in engine components after reconditioning operations such as cylinder honing, especially when parts are not thoroughly cleaned using the proper cleaning methods. Whatever the source, these foreign objects often end up imbedded in the soft bearing material and are easily recognized. Large particles will not imbed in the bearing and will score or gouge the bearing and journal. The best prevention for this cause of bearing failure is to clean all parts thoroughly and keep everything spotlessly clean during engine reassembly. Frequent and regular oil and filter changes are also recommended.
5   Lack of lubrication or lubrication breakdown has a number of inter-related causes. Excessive heat (which thins the oil), overloading (which squeezes the oil from the bearing face) and oil leakage or throw off (from excessive bearing clearances, worn oil pump or high engine speeds) all contribute to lubrication breakdown. Blocked oil passages will also starve a bearing and destroy it. When lack of lubrication is the cause of

bearing failure, the bearing material is wiped or extruded from the steel backing of the bearing. Temperatures may increase to the point where the steel backing and the journal turn blue from overheating.
6   Riding habits can have a definite effect on bearing life. Full throttle low speed operation, or lugging (labouring) the engine, puts very high loads on bearings, which tend to squeeze out the oil film. These loads cause the bearings to flex, which produces fine cracks in the bearing face (fatigue failure). Eventually the bearing material will loosen in pieces and tear away from the steel backing. Short trip riding leads to corrosion of bearings, as insufficient engine heat is produced to drive off the condensed water and corrosive gases produced. These products collect in the engine oil, forming acid and sludge. As the oil is carried to the engine bearings, the acid attacks and corrodes the bearing material.
7   Incorrect bearing installation during engine assembly will lead to bearing failure as well. Tight fitting bearings which leave insufficient bearing oil clearances result in oil starvation. Dirt or foreign particles trapped behind a bearing insert result in high spots on the bearing which lead to failure.
8   To avoid bearing problems, clean all parts thoroughly before reassembly, double check all bearing clearance measurements and lubricate the new bearings with engine assembly lube or moly-based grease during installation.

25   Crankshaft and main bearings - removal, inspection, main bearing selection and installation

Removal
Refer to illustrations 25.2a and 25.2b
1   Before removing the crankshaft check the endplay, using a dial indicator mounted in-line with the crankshaft. Yamaha doesn't provide endplay specifications, but if the endplay is excessive (more than a few thousandths of an inch), consider replacing the case halves.
2   Lift the crankshaft out, together with the connecting rods, starter chain and cam chain and set them on a clean surface **(see illustrations)**. Remove the oil seal from one end of the crankshaft and the blind plug from the other end.
3   The main bearing inserts can be removed from their saddles by pushing their centers to the side, then lifting them out. Keep the bearing inserts in order. The main bearing oil clearance should be checked, however, before removing the inserts (see Step 8).

Inspection
Refer to illustration 25.5
4   If you haven't already done so, mark and remove the connecting rods from the crankshaft (see Section 26).
5   Clean the crankshaft with solvent, using a rifle-cleaning brush to scrub out the oil passages. If available, blow the crank dry with

25.2b Set the crankshaft, connecting rods and chains
on a clean surface

25.5 Inspect the journals, gear and chain sprockets for wear,
damage, pitted surfaces or chipped teeth

25.8a These numbers on the crankshaft indicate journal
diameter; reading from left to right, the first five numbers
correspond with main bearing journals no. 1 through 5 -
the next four numbers correspond with connecting
rod journals no. 1 through 4

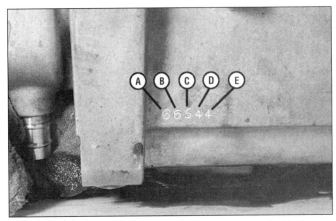

25.8b The numbers on the crankcase correspond with the
crankshaft main journals no. 1 through no. 5, reading from right to
left, with the numbers upright (and the crankcase upside down)

A	No. 5 journal	D	No. 2 journal
B	No. 4 journal	E	No. 1 journal
C	No. 3 journal		

Check the rest of the crankshaft for cracks and other damage. It should be magnafluxed to reveal hidden cracks - a dealer service department or motorcycle machine shop will handle the procedure.
7   Set the crankshaft on V-blocks and check the runout with a dial indicator touching each of the main journals, comparing your findings with this Chapter's Specifications. If the runout exceeds the limit, replace the crank.

Main bearing selection
Refer to illustrations 25.8a and 25.8b
8   Checking the main bearing clearance and selecting bearings is the same as for FZR600 models, except that the crankshaft has five main bearings instead of six, so the first five numbers on the crankshaft refer to the main journals **(see illustration)**. The corresponding numbers for the main bearing bores are stamped in the crankcase **(see illustration)**. Refer to this Chapter's Specifications.

Installation
Refer to illustrations 25.9
9   Clean the bearing saddles in the case halves, then install the bearing inserts in their webs in the case **(see illustration)**. When installing the bearings, use your hands only - don't tap them into place with a hammer.
10   Lubricate the bearing inserts with engine assembly lube or moly-based grease.

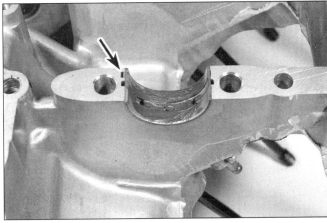

25.9 Make sure the tab on each bearing fits into the notch in the
case, then coat the bearings with assembly lube

compressed air. Check the main and connecting rod journals for uneven wear, scoring and pits **(see illustration)**. Rub a copper coin across the journal several times - if a journal picks up copper from the coin, it's too rough. Replace the crankshaft.
6   Check the primary gear and chain sprockets on the crankshaft for chipped teeth and other wear. If any undesirable conditions are found, replace the crankshaft. Check the chain as described in Section 27.

11   You can install the connecting rods on the crankshaft at this point if they were removed (see Section 26).
12   Loop the camshaft and starter chains over the crankshaft and engage them with their sprockets.
13   Carefully lower the crankshaft into place. If the connecting rods are on the crankshaft, guide them through their openings.
14   Assemble the case halves (see Section 22) and check to make sure the crankshaft and the transmission shafts turn freely.

---

26   Connecting rods and bearings - removal, inspection, bearing selection and installation

Removal and inspection

Refer to illustration 26.1
1   These procedures are the same as for FZR600 models (see Chapter 2). Pay special attention to the piston pin bore at the top of each rod **(see illustration)**. If it's scored or shows signs of seizure, the rod should be replaced.

Connecting rod bearing selection

Refer to illustration 26.2
2   Bearing selection is the same as for FZR600 models (see Chapter 2), except that the bearing selection number on the connecting rod may be 5 **(see illustration)**. Use this number together with the last four numbers on the crankshaft to select connecting rod bearings **(see illustration 25.8a)**. Refer to this Chapter's Specifications.

Installation

3   On all except 1989 and later (UK) FZR750 models, this is the same as for the FZR600 (see Chapter 2 and this Chapter's Specifications).
4   On UK FZR750 models, the connecting rod bolts must be discarded and replaced with new ones whenever they're removed. **Note:** *New connecting rod bolts may be tightened to measure bearing clearance with Plastigage, then installed and run in the engine.* Connecting rod bolt stretch must be measured during the tightening process. Measure and record the length of the bolts before tightening (measure at several points on the end of the bolt and calculate the average of the measurements). Tighten the bolts to the initial torque, then to the final torque. Measure the length of each bolt after tightening to calculate bolt stretch; if it has stretched more than the maximum listed in this Chapter's Specifications, replace the bolt. If it hasn't yet stretched the minimum amount listed in the Specifications, keep tightening until bolt stretch is within the specified range (each 10-degrees of tightening in-

creases bolt length by approximately 0.022 mm/0.00087 inch). Never loosen the bolts to bring bolt stretch within the specified range.

---

27   Camshaft and starter chains and guides - removal, inspection and installation

Warning: *Although the cam chain can be cut and reconnected, this should be done by a qualified Yamaha technician with the proper service tool. Chain separation while the engine is running may cause engine seizure, leading to loss of control of the motorcycle. Yamaha replacement cam chains may be equipped with a master (soft) link; if you're not experienced with this type of chain, have the master link connected by a qualified Yamaha technician.*

Removal

Refer to illustration 27.6 and 27.7
1   Remove the engine (see Section 5).
2   Separate the crankcase halves (see Section 22).
3   Remove the crankshaft (see Section 25).
4   Remove the chains from the crankshaft.
5   The cam chain front guide can be lifted from the cylinder head **(see illustration 9.8)**.
6   The cam chain rear guide is held in position by two Allen bolts **(see illustration)**. Separate the crankcase halves (see Section 22), then remove the Allen bolts and lift out the guide.
7   The starter chain guide is held in place by two hex-head bolts **(see illustration)**. Separate the crankcase halves (see Section 22), remove the starter clutch (see Section 31), then remove the Allen bolts and lift out the guide.

Inspection

8   Check the chains for binding and obvious damage. If these conditions are visible, or if the chains appear to be stretched, replace them.
9   Check the guides for deep grooves, cracking and other obvious damage, replacing them if necessary.

Installation

10   Installation of these components is the reverse of the removal procedure, with the following additions:
  a) When installing the rear cam chain guide or the starter chain guide, apply a non-hardening thread locking compound to the threads of the bolts. Tighten the bolts to the torque listed in this Chapter's Specifications.
  b) Apply engine oil to the faces of the guides and to the chain.

26.1 Carefully inspect the top end of each connecting rod; if the bore is scored like this one, the rod and piston pin should be replaced

26.2 The number on the connecting rod is used for bearing selection

27.6 The cam chain rear guide is held in place by two Allen bolts (arrows)

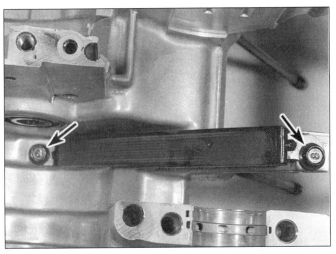

27.7 The starter chain guide is held in place by two hex bolts (arrows)

28.4 Lift out the mainshaft (upper arrow), then the driveshaft (lower arrow)

28 Transmission shafts - removal and installation

Removal

Refer to illustrations 28.4

1   If you plan to remove the engine sprocket, it will be easier to remove the sprocket nut while the engine is still in the frame (see Chapter 7).

2   Remove the engine and clutch, then separate the case halves (see Sections 5, 19 and 22).

3   If you haven't already done so, remove the long clutch pushrod from the mainshaft (see Section 19).

4   Lift out the mainshaft, then the driveshaft **(see illustration)**. If they are stuck, use a soft-face hammer and gently tap on the bearings on the ends of the shafts to free them. Lift out the half-circle retainer rings.

5   Refer to Section 29 for information pertaining to transmission shaft service and Section 30 for information pertaining to the shift cam and forks.

Installation

Refer to illustrations 28.6, 28.7a, 28.7b and 28.8

6   Install new half-circle retaining rings in their grooves in the crankcase **(see illustration)**.

7   Carefully lower each shaft into place. The pins in the bearing outer races must engage with the locating holes in the crankcase, and the grooves in the crankcase and the ball bearing outer races must engage with the retaining rings **(see illustrations)**. **Caution:** *If the pins are out of*

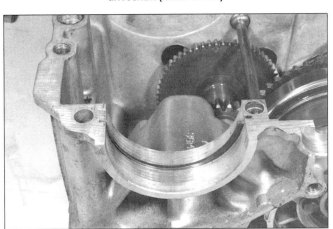

28.6 Install a new half-circle retaining ring in each of the grooves; center the rings in the grooves and seat them securely

position and you try to force the crankcase halves together by tightening the bolts, the crankcase halves will crack and will have to be replaced.

8   The remainder of installation is the reverse of removal. Make sure the clutch pushrod seal and driveshaft end seal are in position **(see illustration)**.

9   Make sure the gears are in the neutral position. When they are, it will be possible to rotate the transmission shafts independently of each other.

28.7a At the engine sprocket end of the transmission, the bearings have pins that lie flat against the case (arrows)

28.7b At the clutch end of the driveshaft, the small bearing has a pin that lies flat against the case

28.8 Install the transmission seal and clutch pushrod seal

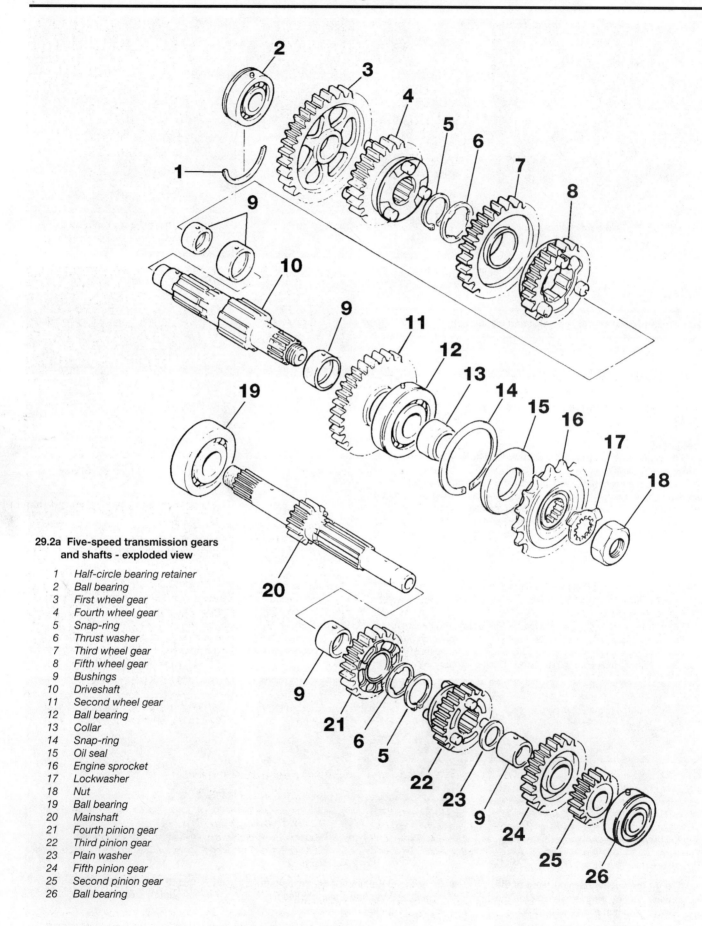

29.2a Five-speed transmission gears
and shafts - exploded view

1　Half-circle bearing retainer
2　Ball bearing
3　First wheel gear
4　Fourth wheel gear
5　Snap-ring
6　Thrust washer
7　Third wheel gear
8　Fifth wheel gear
9　Bushings
10　Driveshaft
11　Second wheel gear
12　Ball bearing
13　Collar
14　Snap-ring
15　Oil seal
16　Engine sprocket
17　Lockwasher
18　Nut
19　Ball bearing
20　Mainshaft
21　Fourth pinion gear
22　Third pinion gear
23　Plain washer
24　Fifth pinion gear
25　Second pinion gear
26　Ball bearing

29.2b Take the ball bearing off

29.3a Slide off the first wheel gear . . .

29.3b . . . the bushing will have to be pressed off if it's worn or damaged

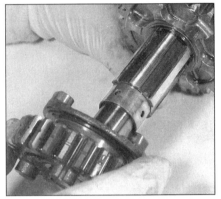

29.3c . . . slide off the fourth wheel gear

29.4a Remove the snap-ring . . .

29.4b . . . and thrust washer

29.5a Slide off the third wheel gear . . .

29.5b . . . and fifth wheel gear (this bushing is also a press fit)

29.6a If you haven't already done so, flatten the lockwasher tab (arrow) . . .

3

---

29 Transmission shafts - disassembly, inspection and reassembly

Note: *When disassembling the transmission shafts, place the parts on a long rod or thread a wire through them to keep them in order and facing the proper direction. Some of the steps require a press. If you don't have one, it may be more practical to have a Yamaha dealer disassemble and reassemble the shafts.*

1   FZR750 models have a six-speed transmission; FZR1000 models have a five-speed. The two designs are the same except that the six-speed has an additional gear on the driveshaft and a paired gear on the mainshaft where the five-speed has only a single gear. Remove the shafts from the case (see Section 28).

Five-speed transmission

Driveshaft disassembly

Refer to illustrations 29.2a, 29.2b, 29.3a, 29.3b, 29.3c, 29.4a, 29.4b, 29.5a, 29.5b, 29.6a, 29.6b, 29.7 and 29.8

2   Slide the bearing off the driveshaft **(see illustrations)**.

3   Slide off the first wheel gear and fourth wheel gear **(see illustrations)**.

4   Remove the snap-ring and thrust washer **(see illustrations)**.

5   Slide the third wheel gear and fifth wheel gear off the shaft **(see illustrations)**.

6   If you haven't already done so, remove the nut, lockwasher and engine sprocket from the other end of the shaft **(see illustrations)**.

29.6b ... and remove the nut

29.7 Remove the seal

29.8 Press off the collar, bearing and second wheel gear

29.12a Inspect the shift dogs, paying special attention to the corners (arrows); if they're worn, the transmission will jump out of gear ...

29.12b ... also check the edges of the gear slots (arrow); if they're visibly rounded off, replace the gear

29.15a Place the second wheel gear on the driveshaft, then press on the bearing and collar ...

29.15b ... the installed parts should look like this; make sure the gears spin freely

29.15c The assembled driveshaft should look like this

29.16a Take the bearing off the mainshaft

7   Remove the oil seal and bearing snap-ring (if equipped) from the shaft **(see illustration 29.2a and the accompanying illustration)**.
8   Press the collar, bearing and second wheel gear off the shaft **(see illustration)**.

Driveshaft inspection

Refer to illustrations 29.12a and 29.12b

9   Wash all of the components in clean solvent and dry them off. Rotate the ball bearing on the shaft, feeling for tightness, rough spots and excessive looseness and listening for noises. If any of these conditions are found, replace the bearing with a press.
10   Check the ball bearing that was removed from the other end of the shaft and replace it if it has any of the conditions described in

Step 6. The bearing seal should be replaced if oil has been leaking from it; it's a good idea to replace the seal whenever the engine is disassembled this far.
11   Check the gear teeth for cracking and other obvious damage. Check the gear bushings and the surface in the inner diameter of each gear for scoring or heat discoloration. If the gear or bushing is damaged, replace it.
12   Inspect the dogs and the dog holes in the gears for excessive wear **(see illustrations)**. Replace the paired gears as a set if necessary.
13   Place the shaft in V-blocks and check runout with a dial indicator. Replace the shaft if runout exceeds the value listed in this Chapter's Specifications.

29.16b Support the fifth pinion gear
and press the shaft out of
second pinion gear . . .

29.16c . . . then take off second
pinion gear . . .

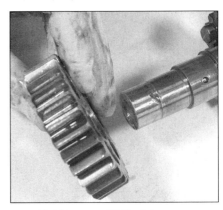

29.16d . . . and fifth pinion gear

29.16e Slide the bushing off . . .

29.16f . . . and remove the plain washer

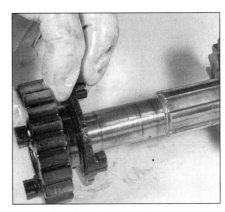

29.16g Slide off third pinion gear

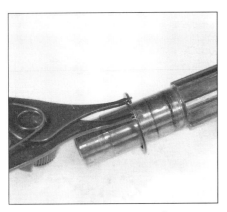

29.16h Remove the snap-ring . . .

29.16i . . . and thrust washer

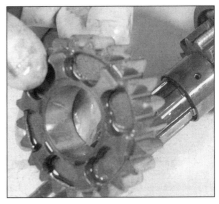

29.16j Slide off fourth pinion gear

Driveshaft reassembly

Refer to illustrations 29.15a, 29.15b and 29.15c

14   During reassembly, always use new snap-rings. Lubricate the components with engine oil before assembling them.

15   Assembly is the reverse of the disassembly procedure with the following additions:

a) The sharp side of the snap-ring faces away from the thrust washer; the rounded side faces toward the thrust washer.

b) Press the collar, bearing and second wheel gear onto the shaft together **(see illustrations)**.

c) Check the positions of the gears on the assembled shaft to make sure they are correct **(see illustration)**.

Mainshaft disassembly

Refer to illustrations 29.16a through 29.16j

16   To disassemble the mainshaft, refer to the accompanying **illustrations**.

Mainshaft inspection

Refer to illustration 29.17

17   Refer to Steps 9 through 13 above to inspect the mainshaft components. If the ball bearing and bushing need to be replaced, remove them with a press **(see illustration)**; otherwise, they can be left on the shaft.

29.17 If the bushing or ball bearing is worn, press it off the shaft; the gear is integral with the shaft, so the entire shaft must be replaced if the gear is worn or damaged

29.18a Press fifth pinion gear and second pinion gear onto the shaft and make sure they turn freely after they're installed

29.18b The assembled mainshaft should look like this

Mainshaft reassembly

Refer to illustrations 29.18a and 29.18b

18   Assembly is the reverse of the disassembly procedure, with the following additions:
  a) Use new snap-rings and lubricate the components with engine oil before assembling them.
  b) Press the second pinion gear and fifth pinion gear into the shaft together **(see illustration)**. Be sure the gears turn freely after installation; if they don't, they may have been pressed on too far.
  c) Check the assembled shaft to make sure the gears are in the correct positions **(see illustration)**.

Six-speed transmission

Driveshaft disassembly

Refer to illustration 29.19

19   Slide the bearing off the driveshaft **(see illustration)**.
20   Slide off the first wheel gear and fifth wheel gear.
21   Remove the snap ring and thrust washer.
22   Slide the fourth wheel gear, third wheel gear and sixth wheel gear off the shaft.
23   If you haven't already done so, remove the nut, lockwasher and engine sprocket from the other end of the shaft.
24   Remove the oil seal from the shaft.
25   Press the collar, bearing and second wheel gear off the shaft.

Driveshaft inspection

26   Refer to Steps 9 through 13 above to inspect the driveshaft and its components.

Driveshaft reassembly

27   Assembly is the reverse of the disassembly procedure, with the following additions:
  a) Use new snap-rings and lubricate the components with engine oil before assembling them. The sharp side of the snap-ring faces away from the thrust washer; the rounded side is toward the thrust washer.
  b) Press the collar, bearing and second wheel gear onto the shaft together **(see illustrations 29.15a and 29.15b)**.

Mainshaft disassembly

28   This is essentially the same as for five-speed models, except that the gear next to second pinion gear is the sixth pinion gear, and a combined third-fourth pinion gear is installed in the same location as the third pinion gear on five-speed models.

Mainshaft inspection

29   Perform Steps 9 through 13 above to inspect the mainshaft components.

Mainshaft reassembly

30   Assembly is the reverse of the disassembly procedure, with the following additions:
  a) Use new snap-rings and lubricate the components with engine oil before assembling them.
  b) Press the second pinion gear and sixth pinion gear into the shaft together. Be sure the gears turn freely after installation; if they don't, they may have been pressed on too far.
  c) Check the assembled shaft to make sure the gears are in the correct positions.

---

30   Shift cam and forks - removal, inspection and installation

---

Removal

Refer to illustrations 30.3, 30.4 and 30.5

1   Remove the engine and separate the crankcase halves (see Sections 5 and 22).
2   Remove the external shift mechanism (see Section 21).
3   Remove the shift cam retaining bolt **(see illustration)**.
4   Support the shift forks and pull the guide bar out **(see illustration)**.
5   Pull the shift cam out of the case **(see illustration)**.

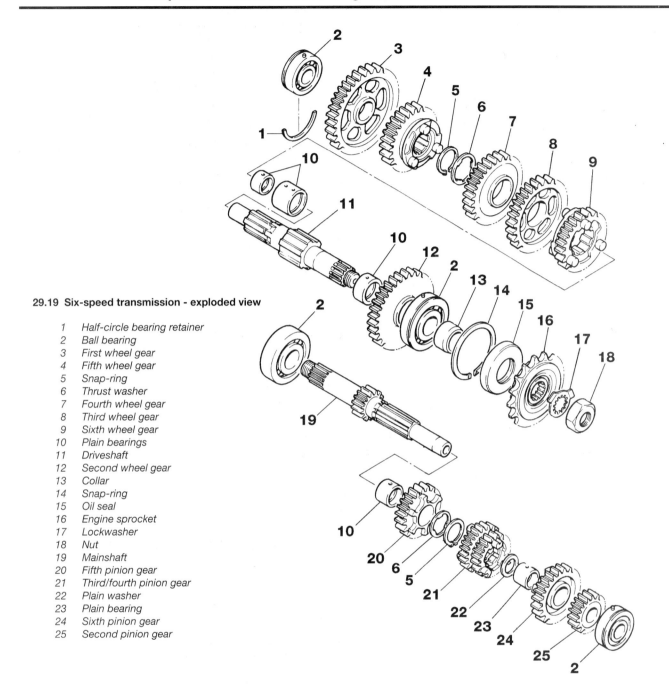

29.19 Six-speed transmission - exploded view

1 Half-circle bearing retainer
2 Ball bearing
3 First wheel gear
4 Fifth wheel gear
5 Snap-ring
6 Thrust washer
7 Fourth wheel gear
8 Third wheel gear
9 Sixth wheel gear
10 Plain bearings
11 Driveshaft
12 Second wheel gear
13 Collar
14 Snap-ring
15 Oil seal
16 Engine sprocket
17 Lockwasher
18 Nut
19 Mainshaft
20 Fifth pinion gear
21 Third/fourth pinion gear
22 Plain washer
23 Plain bearing
24 Sixth pinion gear
25 Second pinion gear

3

30.3 Remove the shift cam retaining bolt

30.4 Pull out the guide bar and remove the shift forks

30.5 Slide the shift cam out

30.7a The letters on the forks indicate left, center and right

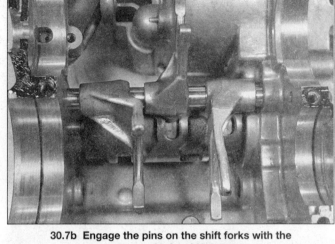

30.7b Engage the pins on the shift forks with the grooves in the shift cam

Inspection

6   This is the same as for FZR600 models (see Chapter 2 for details). Refer to **illustration 22.12a** in this Chapter.

Installation

Refer to illustrations 30.7a and 30.7b

7   Installation is the reverse of removal, noting the following points:
a) Lubricate all parts with engine oil before installing them.
b) Use the letters on the forks to position them correctly. The forks are lettered L, C and R, starting from the left side of the engine **(see illustration)**.
c) Engage the follower pin on each shift fork with the shift cam as you pass the guide bar through the fork. Position the shift cam and forks in the neutral position **(see illustrations)**.
d) Apply a non-permanent locking agent to the threads of the shift cam retaining bolt and tighten it to the torque listed in this Chapter's Specifications.

---

31   Starter clutch and idle gears - removal, disassembly, inspection and installation

---

1   The starter clutch on FZR750 models is removed and installed in the same manner as for FZR1000 models. Disassembly and inspection are the same as for the FZR600 (see Chapter 2 for details).

Removal

Refer to illustrations 31.4a, 31.4b, 31.4c, 31.5, 31.6a, 31.6b, 31.7, 31.8 and 31.9

2   Remove the engine, separate the crankcase halves and remove

31.4a Unbolt the oil plug plate . . .

the transmission shafts (see Sections 5, 22 and 28).
3   Remove the oil line above the starter clutch and idle gears **(see illustrations 23.2b and 23.2c)**.
4   Remove the plug plate and gasket, then pull the oil nozzle out of the case **(see illustrations)**.
5   Pull out the shaft and remove the starter idle gears **(see illustration)**.
6   Remove the bolts and take off the retainer that secures the alternator drive shaft bearing **(see illustrations)**.
7   Take the bearing out of its bore **(see illustration). Note:** *If the bearing is tight in its bore, it will be necessary to remove the alternator driveshaft and bearing together with a slide hammer* **(see illustration)**.
8   Support the starter clutch with one hand and pull out the alterna-

31.4b . . . take off the plate and gasket . . .

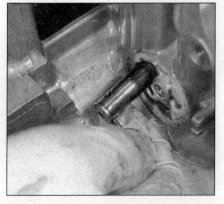

31.4c . . . and pull out the spray nozzle

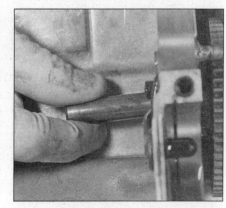

31.5 Remove the shaft and lift out the starter idle gears

31.6a Remove the bearing retainer bolts . . .

31.6b . . . and lift off the retainer

31.7 Take out the bearing; if it's tight, remove the bearing and alternator drive shaft together with a slide hammer

31.8 Pull out the alternator drive shaft

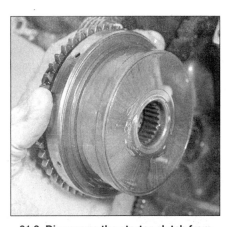

31.9 Disengage the starter clutch from the chain and lift it out

31.10a Lift the starter sprocket out of the starter clutch gear . . .

3

31.10b . . . and lift the starter clutch gear out of the starter clutch

31.12 Place the gear in the starter clutch and try to turn it in both directions; it should go one way only

31.14 If the bearing in the crankcase is worn or damaged, have it replaced by a Yamaha dealer

tor driveshaft with the other (see illustration).
9   Disengage the starter clutch from the chain and lift it out of the engine (see illustration).

Disassembly, inspection and reassembly (FZR1000 models)
Refer to illustrations 31.10a, 31.10b, 31.12 and 31.14
10   Lift the starter sprocket and starter clutch gear out of the starter clutch (see illustrations).
11   Check the sprocket and gears for chipped or worn teeth. Check

the idle gear shaft and its bearing surface inside the gear for wear or damage. If any defects are found, replace the affected parts.
12   Place the gear in the starter clutch and try to turn it in both directions (see illustration). The gear should turn in one direction only. If it goes both ways or neither way, replace the starter clutch.
13   Check the starter clutch rollers for wear or damage. Replace the starter clutch if defects are found.
14   Place the bearing on the alternator driveshaft. Rotate the bearing and check for roughness, looseness or noise. If it's defective, replace it. Also check the ball bearing in the case (see illustration). Have the bearing replaced by a Yamaha dealer if it's worn or damaged.

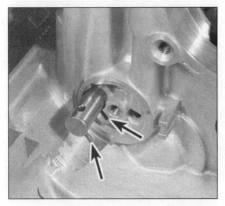

31.15a Align the pin on the oil spray
nozzle with the slot in the case (arrows),
then push the nozzle all the way in

31.15b Position the tab on the plug plate
in the crankcase slot (arrow)

31.15c The starter clutch and idle gears
should look like this when they're installed

32.2a Unbolt the oil line fittings from the sides of
the engine (FZR1000) . . .

32.2b . . . unbolt the retainer brackets from the engine . . .

Installation

Refer to illustrations 31.15a, 31.15b and 31.15c

15   Installation is the reverse of the removal steps, with the following additions:

a) Be sure the pin on the oil spray nozzle fits into the groove in the case and the tab on the plug plate fits into the slot in the case **(see illustrations)**.

b) Use non-permanent thread locking agent on the threads of the bearing retainer bolts for the alternator shaft.

c) Check to be sure the idle gear and starter clutch gear are correctly engaged after installation **(see illustration)**.

32   Oil cooler and lines - removal and installation

Refer to illustrations 32.2a, 32.2b and 32.2c

1   To replace the oil lines, drain the engine oil and remove fairing panels as needed for access.

2   If you're working on an FZR1000, remove the oil line fitting bolts at the engine, the retaining bracket bolts at the engine and the banjo bolts at the cooler **(see illustrations)**.

3   If you're working on an FZR750, remove the oil line banjo bolts from the front of the engine just below the oil filter.

4   Detach the cooler from its mountings and lift it out.

5   Installation is the reverse of the removal steps. Use new sealing washers at the banjo fittings and new O-rings at the oil line fittings on the engine. Tighten the banjo bolts to the Specified torque.

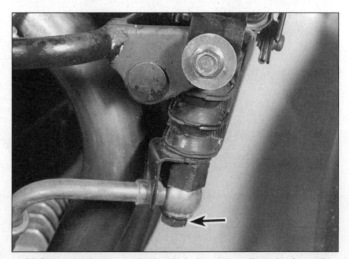

32.2c . . . and remove the banjo bolts at the oil cooler (arrow)

33   Initial start-up after overhaul

1   Make sure the engine oil level is correct and the cooling system is full, then remove the spark plugs from the engine. Place the engine kill switch in the Off position and unplug the primary (low tension) wires from the coils.

2   Turn on the key switch and crank the engine over with the starter several times to build up oil pressure. Reinstall the spark plugs, connect the wires and turn the switch to On.
3   Make sure there is fuel in the tank, then turn the fuel tap to the On position and operate the choke.
4   Start the engine and allow it to run at a moderately fast idle until it reaches operating temperature.
5   Check carefully for oil leaks and make sure the transmission and controls, especially the brakes, function properly before road testing the machine. Refer to Section 34 for the recommended break-in procedure.
6   Upon completion of the road test, and after the engine has cooled down completely, recheck the valve clearances (see Chapter 1).

34 Recommended break-in procedure

1   Any rebuilt engine needs time to break-in, even if parts have been installed in their original locations. For this reason, treat the machine gently for the first few miles to make sure oil has circulated throughout the engine and any new parts installed have started to seat.
2   Even greater care is necessary if the engine has been rebored or a new crankshaft has been installed. In the case of a rebore, the engine will have to be broken in as if the machine were new. This means greater use of the transmission and a restraining hand on the throttle until at least 500 miles (800 Km) have been covered. There's no point in keeping to any set speed limit - the main idea is to keep from lugging (labouring) the engine and to gradually increase performance until the 500 mile (800 Km) mark is reached. These recommendations can be lessened to an extent when only a new crankshaft is installed. Experience is the best guide, since it's easy to tell when an engine is running freely. The following recommendations, which Yamaha provides for new motorcycles, can be used as a guide:
   a) 0 to 90 miles (0 to 150 km): Keep engine speed below 5,000 rpm. Turn off the engine after each hour of operation and let it cool for 5 to 10 minutes. Vary the engine speed and don't use full throttle.
   b) 90 to 300 miles (150 to 500 km): Don't run the engine for long periods above 6,500 rpm. Rev the engine freely through the gears, but don't use full throttle.
   c) 300 to 600 miles (500 to 1000 km): Don't use full throttle for prolonged periods and don't cruise at speeds above 8,000 rpm.
   d) After 600 miles (1000 km): Full throttle can be used. Don't exceed maximum recommended engine speed (redline).
3   If a lubrication failure is suspected, stop the engine immediately and try to find the cause. If an engine is run without oil, even for a short period of time, severe damage will occur.

Notes

Chapter 4 Cooling system

Contents

Specifications

General

Coolant type	See Chapter 1
Mixture ratio	See Chapter 1
Cooling system capacity	See Chapter 1
Radiator cap pressure rating	
FZR600	
1989 models	0.69 to 0.96 Bar (10 to 14 psi)
1990-on models	0.93 to 1.24 Bar (13.5 to 18 psi)
FZR750/1000	
1987 and 1988 models	0.76 to 1.03 Bar (11 to 15 psi)
1989-on models	0.93 to 1.24 Bar (13.5 to 18 psi)
Thermostat rating	
Opening temperature	80 to 84-degrees C (176 to 183-degrees F)
Fully open at	95-degrees C (203-degrees F)
Valve travel (when fully open)	Not less than 8 mm (5/16 inch)
Fan thermoswitch continuity	
Heating up	
Below 98-degrees C (208.4-degrees F)	No continuity
Above 105 $\pm$ 3-degrees C (221 $\pm$ 5.4-degrees F)	Continuity
Cooling down	
105 to 98-degrees C (221 to 208.4-degrees F)	Continuity
Below 98-degrees C (208.4-degrees F)	No continuity

Torque specifications

Coolant tube bolts	10 Nm (7.2 ft-lbs)
Thermostat housing cover bolts	10 Nm (7.2 ft-lbs)
Water jacket joint bolts	10 Nm (7.2 ft-lbs)
Water pump bolts	10 Nm (7.2 ft-lbs)
Water pump cover bolts	10 Nm (7.2 ft-lbs)
Cooling fan thermoswitch	8 Nm (5.9 ft-lbs)
Temperature gauge sender unit	
1987 and 1988 FZR1000, US FZR750	14 Nm (10.3 ft-lbs)
All FZR600 models, UK FZR750, 1989-on FZR1000	15 Nm (11 ft-lbs)

4

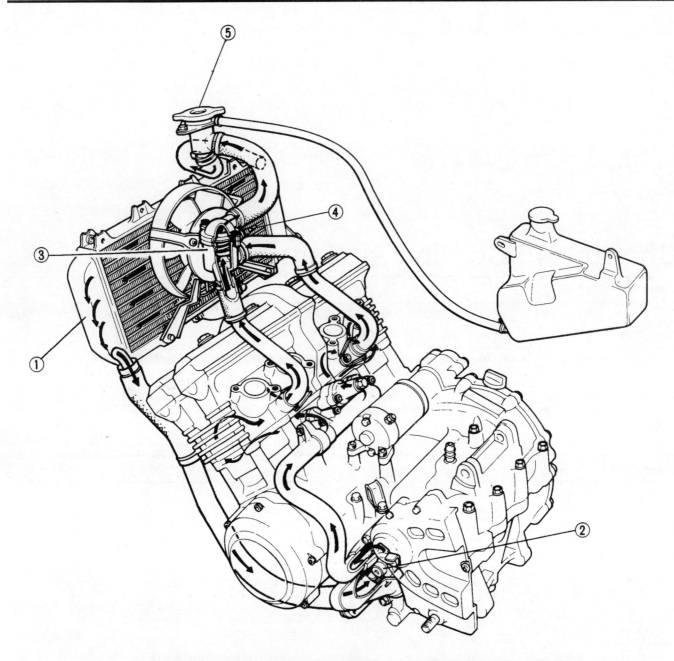

1.1a Cooling system details (1989 and 1990 FZR600 models shown; later models similar)

1   Radiator
2   Water pump
3   Thermostat housing

4   Thermostat valve
5   Pressure cap

1   General information

Refer to illustrations 1.1a, 1.1b, 1.1c and 1.1d

The models covered by this manual are equipped with a liquid cooling system which utilizes a water/antifreeze mixture to carry away excess heat produced during the combustion process **(see illustrations)**. The cylinders are surrounded by water jackets, through which the coolant is circulated by the water pump. The pump is mounted to the left side of the crankcase and driven by the oil pump shaft. The coolant passes through hoses and tubes, around the cylinders and to the thermostat. When the engine is warm, the thermostat opens and

allows coolant to flow down into the radiator (which is mounted on the frame downtubes to take advantage of maximum air flow), where it is cooled by the passing air, routed through another hose and back to the water pump, where the cycle is repeated.

An electric fan, mounted behind the radiator and automatically controlled by a thermostatic switch, provides a flow of cooling air through the radiator when the motorcycle is not moving.

The coolant temperature sender unit, threaded into the radiator, senses the temperature of the coolant and controls the coolant temperature gauge on the instrument cluster.

On all UK FZR750 models and all 1991-on FZR 600 and 1000 models, coolant is routed around the oil filter adapter on the front of

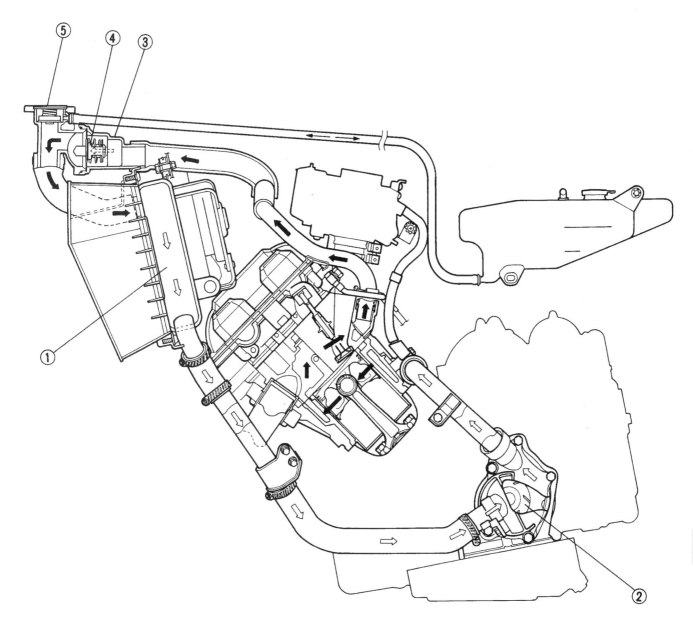

1.1b Cooling system details (US FZR750 and 1987 and 1988 FZR1000 models)

1 Radiator
2 Water pump
3 Thermostat housing

4 Thermostat
5 Pressure cap

the crankcase and then back into the cooling system.

The entire system is sealed and pressurized. The pressure is controlled by a valve which is part of the radiator cap. By pressurizing the coolant, the boiling point is raised, which prevents premature boiling of the coolant. An overflow hose, connected between the radiator and reservoir tank, directs coolant to the tank when the radiator cap valve is opened by excessive pressure. The coolant is automatically siphoned back to the radiator as the engine cools.

Many cooling system inspection and service procedures are considered part of routine maintenance and are included in Chapter 1.

Warning: *Do not allow antifreeze to come in contact with your skin or*

painted surfaces of the motorcycle. Rinse off spills immediately with plenty of water. Antifreeze is highly toxic if ingested. Never leave antifreeze lying around in an open container or in puddles on the floor; children and pets are attracted by its sweet smell and may drink it. Check with local authorities (councils) about disposing of used antifreeze. Many communities have collection centers which will see that antifreeze is disposed of safely.

Warning: *Do not remove the pressure cap from the thermostat housing when the engine and radiator are hot. Scalding hot coolant and steam may be blown out under pressure, which could cause serious injury. To open the pressure cap, remove the right side panel on the inside of the*

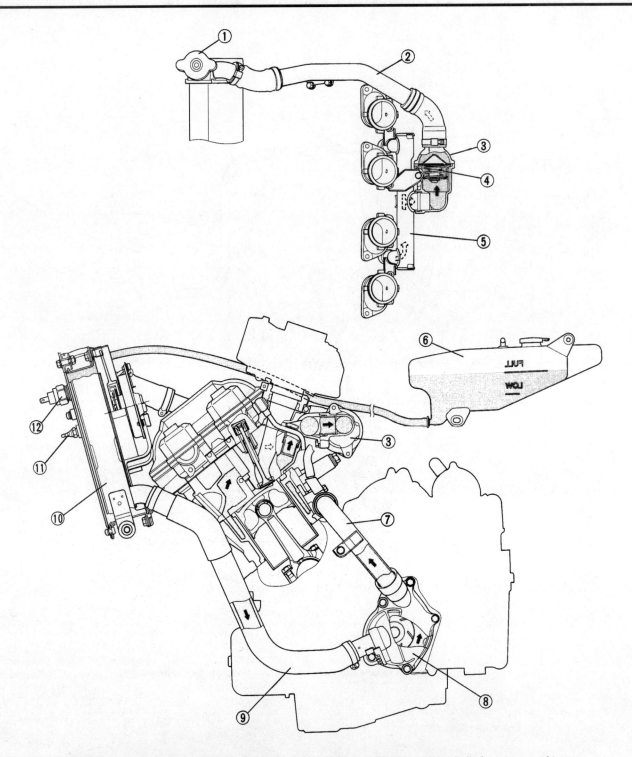

1.1c Cooling system details (1989-on FZR1000 models; 1989-on FZR750 models similar) - part one of two

1   Pressure cap
2   Engine-mounted coolant tube
3   Thermostat housing
4   Thermostat
5   Water jacket joint
6   Reservoir tank

7   Water pump outlet tube
8   Water pump
9   Water pump inlet hose
10 Radiator
11 Temperature sender
12 Thermoswitch (for cooling fan)

fairing. When the engine has cooled, lift up the panel and place a thick rag, like a towel, over the radiator cap; slowly rotate the cap counter-clockwise (anti-clockwise) to the first stop. This procedure allows any residual pressure to escape. When the steam has stopped escaping, press down on the cap while turning counterclockwise (anti-clockwise) and remove it.

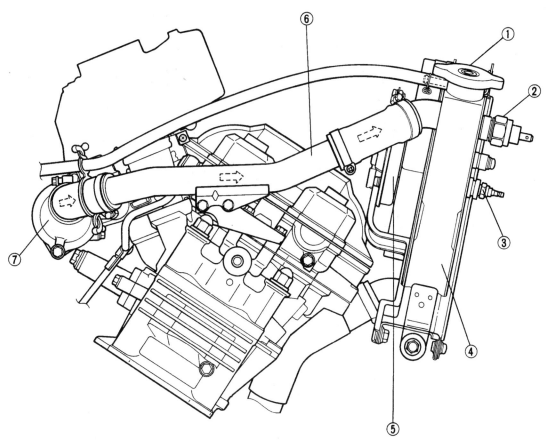

1.1d Cooling system details (1989-on FZR1000 models; 1989-on FZR750 models similar) - part two of two

1   Pressure cap
2   Thermoswitch (for cooling fan)
3   Temperature sender
4   Radiator

5   Fan
6   Water pump outlet tube
7   Water pump

2   Radiator cap - check

If problems such as overheating and loss of coolant occur, check the entire system as described in Chapter 1. The radiator cap opening pressure should be checked by a dealer service department or service station equipped with the special tester required to do the job. If the cap is defective, replace it with a new one.

3   Coolant reservoir - removal and installation

1   Remove the seat and the right side cover (left for UK FZR750) (see Chapter 9).
2   Disconnect the coolant hoses from the reservoir and catch any escaped coolant.
3   Remove the reservoir mounting screws and take it out.
4   Installation is the reverse of the removal steps.

4   Cooling fan and thermostatic switch - check and replacement

Check

Refer to illustrations 4.3, 4.5a, 4.5b and 4.6

1   If the engine is overheating and the cooling fan isn't coming on, first remove the seat or rear side cover (as applicable) and check the

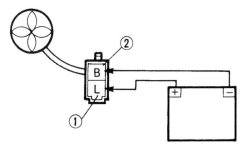

4.3 Connect a battery directly to the fan terminals

1   Blue wire terminal   *2   Black wire terminal*

fuses. If the fuse is blown, check the fan circuit for a short to ground/earth (see the *Wiring diagrams* at the end of this book). Check that the battery is fully charged.
2   If the fuses are all good, check for proper continuity at the red and brown wire terminals of the ignition main switch connector (see Chapter 10). Replace the switch if necessary and recheck the fan.
3   If the fuses and main switch are good, follow the wiring harness from the fan motor to the electrical connector and unplug the connector **(see illustration)**. Using two jumper wires, apply battery voltage to the terminals in the fan motor side of the electrical connector. If the fan doesn't work, replace the motor.

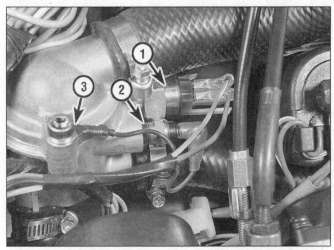

4.5a The fan thermoswitch and temperature gauge sender on 1987 and 1988 FZR750/1000 models and all FZR600 models are mounted on the thermostat housing (FZR600 shown)

1 Fan thermoswitch
2 Temperature sender
3 Ground (earth) wire

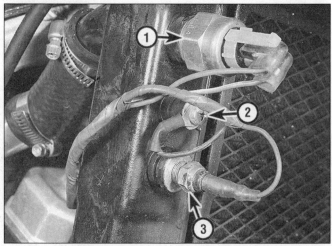

4.5b The fan thermoswitch and temperature gauge sender on 1989-on FZR750/1000 models are mounted on the radiator

1 Fan thermoswitch
2 Ground (earth) wire
3 Temperature sender

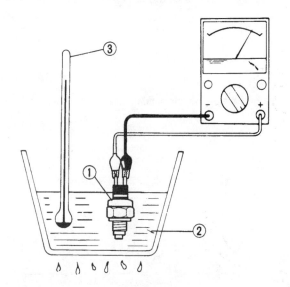

4.6 Place the thermoswitch in water, but don't get the terminals wet

1 Thermoswitch
2 Water
3 Thermometer

4   If the fan does come on, the problem lies in the fan thermoswitch or the wiring that connects the components. Remove the jumper wires and reconnect the electrical connector to the fan.

5   Unplug the electrical connector from the fan thermoswitch on the thermostat housing or radiator **(see illustrations)**. Connect the terminals in the wiring harness together with a jumper wire. If the fan comes on, the circuit to the motor is good and the switch is defective.

6   Before replacing the switch, test it. Unscrew the switch and immerse it in a pan of water (but keep the electrical terminals out of the water) **(see illustration)**. Connect an ohmmeter between the terminals, heat the water and compare the readings with those listed in this Chapter's Specifications. Let the water cool and note the ohmmeter readings as it cools If the readings aren't within the specified ranges, replace the switch.

Replacement

Fan motor

Refer to illustrations 4.8a, 4.8b, 4.8c and 4.8d

Warning: *The engine must be completely cool before beginning this procedure.*

7   Disconnect the cable from the negative terminal of the battery and remove the radiator (see Section 7).

8   Remove the three bolts or nuts securing the fan bracket to the radiator **(see illustrations)**. Separate the fan and bracket from the radiator.

9   If you're working on an FZR600, remove the bolt that retains the blades to the fan motor shaft **(see illustration 4.8a or 4.8b)** and remove the fan blade assembly from the motor.

10   If you're working on an FZR600, remove the screws that attach the fan motor to the bracket **(see illustration 4.8a or 4.8b)** and detach the motor from the bracket.

11   Installation is the reverse of the removal steps.

Thermoswitch

Warning: *The engine must be completely cool before beginning this procedure.*

12   Prepare the new switch by wrapping the new threads with Teflon tape or by coating the threads with RTV sealant.

13   Disconnect its electrical connector and unscrew the switch from the thermostat housing or radiator.

14   Quickly install the new switch, tightening it to the specified torque.

15   Connect the electrical connector to the switch. Check, and if necessary, add coolant to the system (see Chapter 1).

5   Coolant temperature gauge and sender unit - check and replacement

Check

1   If the engine has been overheating but the coolant temperature gauge hasn't been indicating a hotter than normal condition, begin with a check of the coolant level (see Chapter 1). If it's low, add the recommended type of coolant and be sure to locate the source of the leak.

2   Check the fuse and ignition switch (see Chapter 10) and replace them if necessary. Check that the battery is fully charged.

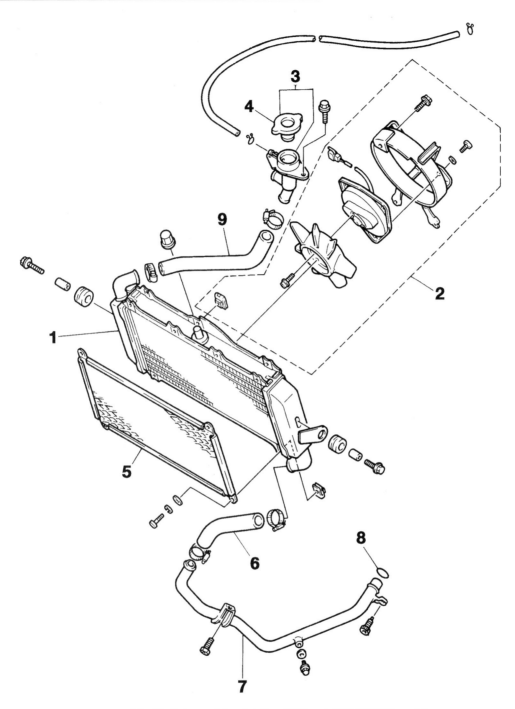

4.8a Radiator and fan details - 1989 and 1990 FZR600 models

1	Radiator	6	Radiator outlet hose
2	Fan assembly	7	Radiator outlet tube
3	Filler neck	8	O-ring (always replace)
4	Pressure cap	9	Radiator inlet hose
5	Stone shield		

1987 and 1988 models

3   Remove the upper and right fairings (see Chapter 9).
4   Remove the headlight assembly (see Chapter 10).
5   Locate the coolant temperature sender unit, which is screwed into the thermostat housing **(see illustration 4.5a)**. Disconnect the electrical connector from the sender unit, turn the ignition key to the On position (don't crank the engine over) and note the temperature gauge - it should read Cold.
6   Turn the key off and connect one end of a jumper wire to the sender unit wire and ground/earth the other end. Turn the key back on and watch the needle on the temperature gauge; it should swing over to the Hot mark. **Caution:** *Turn the key off as soon as the needle moves to the Hot mark or the gauge may be damaged.*

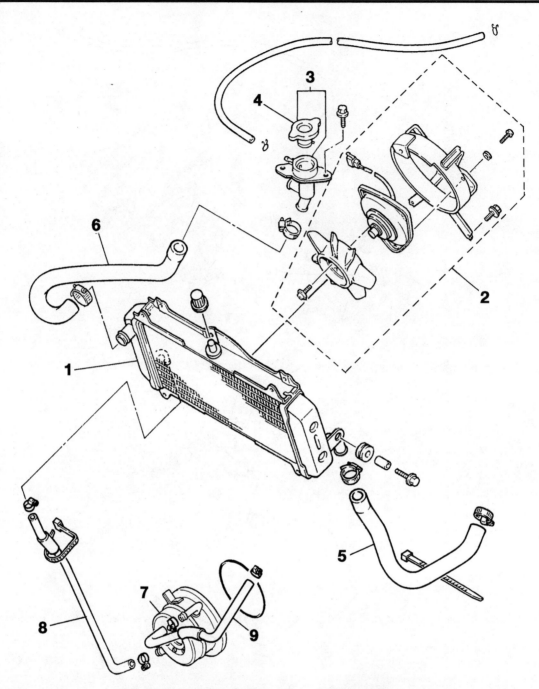

4.8b Radiator and fan details - 1991-on FZR600 models

1	Radiator	6	Radiator inlet hose
2	Fan assembly	7	Oil cooler (1991-on UK models)
3	Filler neck	8	Oil cooler outlet hose (1991-on UK models)
4	Pressure cap	9	Oil cooler inlet hose (1991-on UK models)
5	Radiator outlet hose		

7   If the gauge passes both of these tests, but doesn't operate correctly under normal riding conditions, the temperature sender unit is probably defective and must be replaced. Before replacing, test the sender in the same way as the fan thermoswitch (see Section 4) and compare the ohmmeter readings to those listed in this Chapter's Specifications.

8   If the gauge didn't respond to the tests properly, either the wire to the gauge is bad or the gauge itself is defective.

1989 and later models

9   Test the temperature sender in the same way as the fan thermoswitch (see Section 4) and compare the ohmmeter readings to those listed in this Chapter's Specifications. Replace the sender if it's defective.

10   Refer to the Wiring diagrams at the end of Chapter 10 and locate the brown wire and black wire for the temperature gauge in the instrument cluster connector.

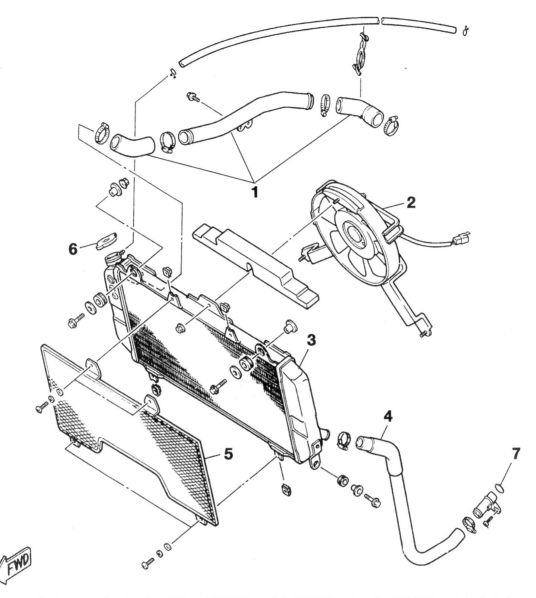

4.8c Radiator and fan details - 1989-on FZR1000 models (FZR750 and earlier FZR1000 models similar)

1	Radiator inlet hoses and tube	5	Stone shield
2	Fan and motor assembly	6	Pressure cap
3	Radiator	7	O-ring (always replace)
4	Radiator outlet hose		

11   Connect a DC voltmeter with a 0 to 20-volt range between the wires. On the harness side of the connector (positive meter lead to brown wire terminal, and negative to black) and turn the ignition switch to On. The voltmeter should indicate approximately 12 volts. If it does, the wiring to the gauge is good and the connections at the gauge or the gauge itself are probably bad. If there's a low reading or no voltage at all, there's a break or poor connection in the wiring to the gauge.

Replacement

Sender unit

Warning: *The engine must be completely cool before beginning this procedure.*

12   Prepare the new sender unit by wrapping the threads with Teflon tape or coating them with silicone sealant.

13   Disconnect its electrical connector and unscrew the sender unit from the thermostat housing or radiator and quickly install the new unit, tightening it to the specified torque.

14   Connect the electrical connector to the sender unit. Check, and if necessary, add coolant to the system (see Chapter 1).

Temperature gauge

15   Refer to Chapter 10 for the coolant temperature gauge replacement procedure.

---

6   Thermostat - removal, check and installation

Warning: *The engine must be completely cool before beginning this procedure.*

4.8d The fan bracket is secured by three nuts or screws - on FZR600 models, one screw is located inside the fan shroud (lower arrow)

Removal

1   If the thermostat is functioning properly, the coolant temperature gauge should rise to the normal operating temperature quickly and then stay there, only rising above the normal position occasionally when the engine gets abnormally hot. If the engine does not reach normal operating temperature quickly, or if it overheats, the thermostat should be removed and checked, or replaced with a new one.
2   Refer to Chapter 1 and drain the cooling system.

FZR600 models

Refer to illustrations 6.5a, 6.5b, 6.5c and 6.6

3   Remove the fuel tank cover and fairings (see Chapter 9).
4   Remove the fuel tank and air filter housing (see Chapter 5).
5   Remove the thermostat housing cover **(see illustrations)**. Note that the rearward bolt secures a ground/earth wire.
6   Note the position of the relief hole, then lift out the thermostat **(see illustration)**.

1987 and 1988 FZR750/1000 models

7   Remove the left and right fairings and the side covers (see Chapter 9).
8   Remove the fuel tank and air filter housing (see Chapter 5).

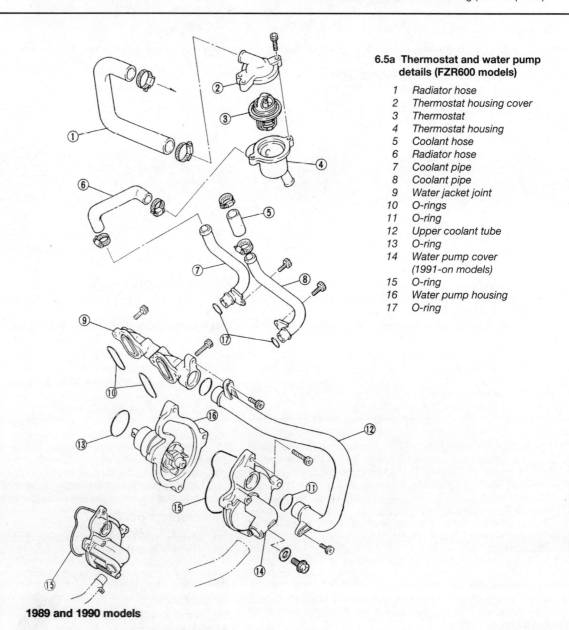

6.5a Thermostat and water pump details (FZR600 models)

1   Radiator hose
2   Thermostat housing cover
3   Thermostat
4   Thermostat housing
5   Coolant hose
6   Radiator hose
7   Coolant pipe
8   Coolant pipe
9   Water jacket joint
10 O-rings
11 O-ring
12 Upper coolant tube
13 O-ring
14 Water pump cover
    (1991-on models)
15 O-ring
16 Water pump housing
17 O-ring

1989 and 1990 models

6.5b There's a large wiring harness on top of the thermostat housing, so it may be easier to remove the housing mounting bolt and pull it out for access

6.5c Remove the thermostat housing cover bolts; the rearward bolt secures a ground (earth) wire (arrow)

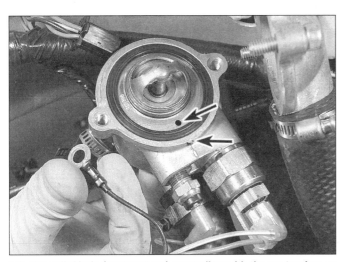

6.6 The relief hole (upper arrow) must align with the protrusion on the thermostat housing (lower arrow)

6.16a Remove the thermostat housing bolts (arrows)

9   Remove the filler neck/thermostat cover from the thermostat housing **(see illustration 1.1b)**.

10   Note the position of the relief hole (it should be upward), then lift out the thermostat.

11   If you're working on a model with a separate cover O-ring, check it and replace it if its condition is in doubt. It's a good idea to replace the O-ring as a matter of course.

1989 and later FZR750/1000 models

Refer to illustrations 6.16a, 6.16b, 6.17a and 6.17b

12   Remove the left, right and front fairings (see Chapter 9).

13   Remove the seat (see Chapter 9).

14   Remove the fuel tank. Remove the air filter housing (FZR750 models) or carburetors (FZR1000 models) (see Chapter 5).

15   If necessary for access, remove the outlet water jacket joint (see Section 10), together with the thermostat housing. On FZR750 models, disconnect the electrical connectors for the ignition coils, handlebar switches, clutch switch and ignition switch.

16   Unbolt the thermostat cover from the housing **(see illustrations)**.

17   Note the position of the relief hole, then lift out the thermostat **(see illustrations)**.

Check

18   Remove any coolant deposits, then visually check the thermostat for corrosion, cracks and other damage. If it was open when it was removed, the thermostat is defective.

19   To check the thermostat operation, submerge it in a container of water along with a thermometer. The thermostat should be suspended so it does not touch the sides of the container. **Warning**: *Antifreeze is poisonous. Do not use a cooking pan to test the thermostat.*

20   Gradually heat the water in the container with a hot plate or stove and check the temperature when the thermostat first starts to open.

21   Compare the opening temperature to the values listed in this Chapter's Specifications.

22   Continue heating the water until the valve is fully open.

23   Measure how far the thermostat valve has opened and compare to the value listed in this Chapter's Specifications.

24   If these specifications are not met, or if the thermostat doesn't open while the water is heated, replace it with a new one.

Installation

25   Install the thermostat into the housing, making sure the relief hole is positioned correctly.

4

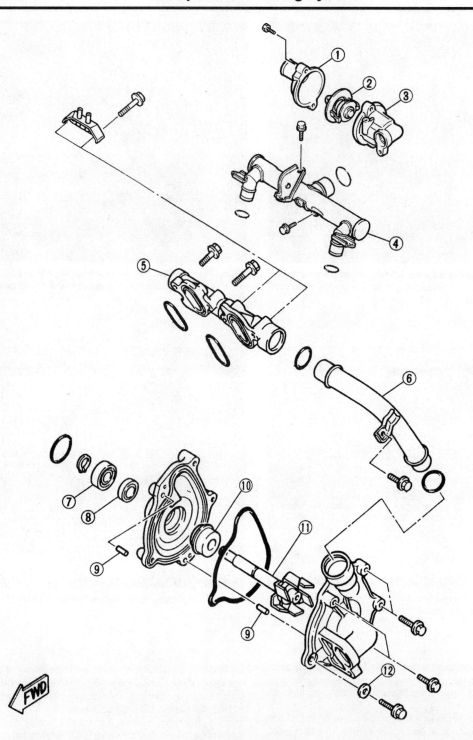

6.16b Thermostat and water pump details - 1989-on FZR1000 models (1989-on FZR750 models similar)

1	Thermostat housing cover	7	Bearing
2	Thermostat	8	Oil seal
3	Thermostat housing	9	Dowel
4	Outlet water jacket joint	10	Mechanical seal
5	Inlet water jacket joint	11	Impeller shaft
6	Water pump outlet tube	12	Sealing washer

26 If you're working on a model with a separate O-ring, install a new one in the groove.

27 Place the cover on the housing and install the bolts, tightening them securely.

28 The remainder of installation is the reverse of the removal steps. Fill the cooling system with the recommended coolant (see Chapter 1).

6.17a The relief hole in the thermostat (arrow) is upward . . .

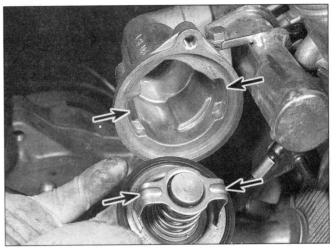

6.17b . . . when the thermostat is installed, its bridge (lower arrows) aligns with the slots in the thermostat housing (upper arrows)

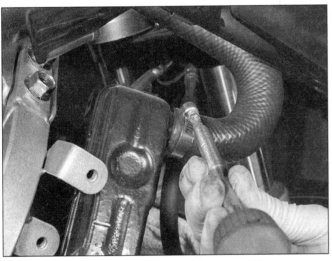

7.6a Loosen the hose clamp and disconnect the upper (inlet) hose . . .

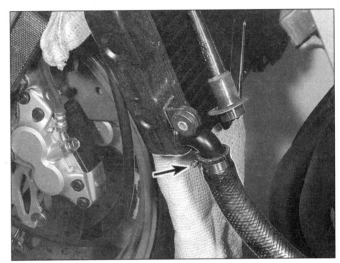

7.6b . . . and the lower (outlet) hose (arrow)

4

7 Radiator - removal and installation

Warning: *The engine must be completely cool before beginning this procedure.*

1   Support the bike securely so it can't be knocked over during this procedure.
2   Drain the cooling system (see Chapter 1).

FZR600 models

Refer to illustrations 7.6a, 7.6b and 7.7

3   Remove the fuel tank cover and fairings (see Chapter 9).
4   Remove the fuel tank and air filter housing (see Chapter 5).
5   Follow the wiring from the fan motor to the electrical connector and disconnect it.
6   Loosen the radiator hose clamps **(see illustrations)**. Work the hoses free from the fittings, taking care not to damage the fittings in the process. Disconnect the oil cooler hose on 1991-on models.
7   Remove the radiator mounting bolts **(see illustration)**. Take the radiator out.

7.7 Unbolt the radiator brace from the radiator and from the frame

7.17a Loosen the hose clamp (arrow) and disconnect the lower radiator hose . . .

7.17b . . . and the upper radiator hose

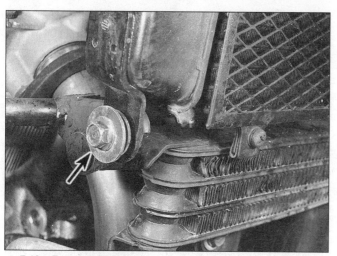

7.18a Remove the radiator lower mounting bolts (arrow) . . .

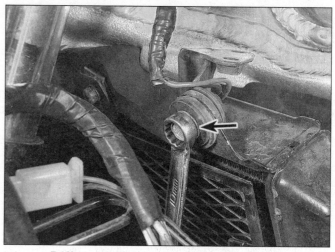

7.18b . . . and the upper mounting bolts (arrow)

US FZR750, 1987 and 1988 FZR1000 models

8   Remove the fairings, engine grille and side covers (see Chapter 9).
9   Remove the fuel tank and air filter housing (see Chapter 5).
10   Loosen the radiator hose clamps. Work the hoses free from the fittings, taking care not to damage the fittings in the process **(see illustration 1.1b)**.
11   Remove the mounting nut from the upper right corner of the radiator. Remove the upper and lower radiator mounting bolts and take the radiator out.

UK FZR750 and 1989-on FZR1000 models

Refer to illustrations 7.18a, 7.18b, 7.19a and 7.19b

12   Remove the left, right and front fairings (see Chapter 9).
13   Remove the seat (see Chapter 9).
14   Remove the fuel tank and air filter housing (see Chapter 5).
15   Disconnect the wiring connector for the fan thermoswitch and temperature sender, as well as the sender ground/earth wire **(see illustration 4.5b)**.
16   Disconnect the fan motor connector. Disconnect the ground/earth wire for the fan switch (if equipped).
17   Disconnect the radiator hoses **(see illustrations)**. Disconnect the oil cooler hose on all FZR750 models and 1991-on FZR1000 models.
18   Remove the radiator mounting bolts **(see illustrations)**. Take the radiator out.

All models

19   Inspect the radiator mounting bushings. Replace them if they're cracked or deteriorated.
20   Installation is the reverse of the removal steps, with the following additions:
   a) Don't forget to connect the fan switch ground/earth wire (if equipped).
   b) On all models, fill the cooling system with the recommended coolant (see Chapter 1).

---

8   Water pump - check, removal, disassembly, inspection and installation

---

Warning: *The engine must be completely cool before beginning this procedure.*

Check and removal

1   Visually check the area around the water pump for coolant leaks. Try to determine if the leak is simply the result of a loose hose clamp or deteriorated hose.
2   Support the bike securely so it can't be knocked over during this procedure.
3   Remove the left fairing panel (see Chapter 9) and the drive chain

8.5 On later FZR600 models, loosen the hose clamp and disconnect the hose; on early models, unbolt the lower coolant tube

8.6a On all FZR600 models, unbolt the upper coolant tube from the water pump . . .

8.6b . . . and from the water jacket joint

8.7a Remove the lower mounting bolt . . .

cover (see Chapter 7).

4   Drain the engine coolant following the procedure in Chapter 1.

FZR600 models

Refer to illustrations 8.5, 8.6a, 8.6b, 8.7a, 8.7b and 8.7c

5   Disconnect the lower hose or coolant tube from the water pump **(see illustration 6.5a and the accompanying illustration)**.

6   Unbolt the upper coolant tube from the water pump and pull its upper end out of the water jacket joint **(see illustration 6.5a and the accompanying illustrations)**.

7   Remove both mounting bolts and take the pump off **(see illustrations)**.

FZR750/1000 models

Refer to illustrations 8.8, 8.9, 8.10a, 8.10b and 8.10c

8   Disconnect the lower hose from the water pump **(see illustration)**.

9   Unbolt the coolant tube bracket from the engine **(see illustration)**.

10   Remove the water pump mounting bolts and pull the water pump away from the engine, separating the coolant tube from the cylinder block as you do so **(see illustration 6.16b and the accompanying illustrations)**.

8.7b . . . and the upper mounting bolt . . .

8.7c . . . and pull the water pump out of the engine

8.8 On FZR750/1000 models, disconnect the lower hose from the water pump (or unbolt the lower coolant tube if equipped) . . .

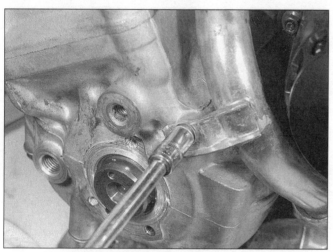

8.9 . . . unbolt the upper coolant tube bracket from the engine

8.10a Remove the pump mounting bolts (arrows) . . .

8.10b . . . and pull the pump off the engine, together with the coolant tube; the O-ring (arrow) should be replaced whenever the coolant tube is removed . . .

8.10c . . . the water pump O-ring (arrow) should also be replaced

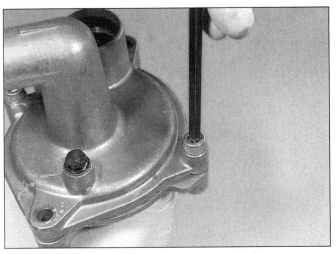

8.12a Remove the water pump cover bolts . . .

8.12b . . . and take the cover off

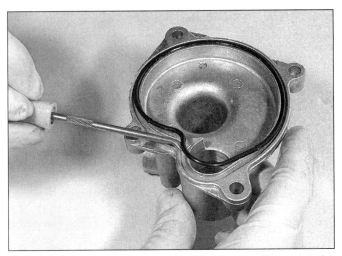

8.15 Remove the cover O-ring from the groove with a pointed tool and install a new one

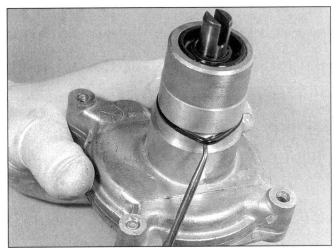

8.17a Remove the water pump O-ring with a pointed tool and install a new one (FZR600 shown; others similar)

4

Disassembly and inspection

Refer to illustrations 8.12a, 8.12b and 8.15

11   Check the shaft seal for leaks.
  a) If you're working on an FZR600, replace the water pump if the seal has been leaking.
  b) If you're working on an FZR750/1000, the water pump can be disassembled for seal replacement. However, the job requires a press and special tools and should be done by a Yamaha dealer.
12   Remove the pump cover bolts and take the cover off **(see illustrations)**.
13   Try to wiggle the pump impeller back-and-forth and in-and-out. Check the impeller blades for corrosion.
  a) If you're working on an FZR600 and you can feel movement or the impeller blades are heavily corroded, the water pump must be replaced.
  b) If you're working on an FZR750/1000 and you can feel movement or the impeller blades are heavily corroded, the water pump can be disassembled for bearing replacement. However, the job requires a press and special tools and should be done by a Yamaha dealer.

14   If the impeller blades are heavily corroded, flush the system thoroughly (it would also be a good idea to check the internal condition of the radiator).
15   Remove the O-ring from its groove with a pointed tool and install a new one **(see illustration)**.
16   Install the cover and tighten the bolts to the torque listed in this Chapter's Specifications.

Installation

Refer to illustrations 8.17a, 8.17b, 8.17c and 8.17d

17   Installation is the reverse of the removal steps with the following additions:
  a) Install new O-rings on the water pump and the coolant tube **(see illustrations)**.
  b) If you're working on an FZR750/1000, install the coolant tube on the water pump, then install the assembled water pump and coolant tube on the engine **(see illustration 8.10b)**.
  c) Align the slot in the water pump shaft with the drive tooth in the oil pump shaft **(see illustrations)**.
  d) Tighten the mounting bolts to the torque listed in this Chapter's Specifications.

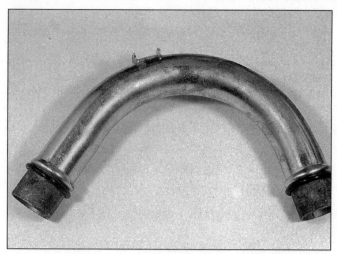

8.17b   There's an O-ring at each end of the coolant tube; these should be replaced each time the tube is removed

8.17c   Align the slot in the water pump (arrow) . . .

8.17d   . . . with the drive tooth on the oil pump shaft

9.5   Remove the mounting bolts (arrows) and take the inlet water jacket off; use new O-rings for reinstallation

10.6a   Remove the mounting bolts (arrows) . . .

10.6b   . . . and pull the outlet water jacket joint out of the cylinder block

10.7 Remove the mounting bolts (arrows) and take the inlet water
jacket joint off

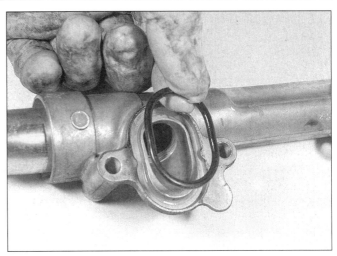

10.8a Use new O-rings . . .

9   Water jacket joint (FZR600 models) - removal and installation

Warning: *The engine must be completely cool for this procedure.
Refer to illustration 9.5*

1   Refer to Chapter 1 and drain the cooling system.
2   Remove the fuel tank cover and fairings (see Chapter 9).
3   Remove the fuel tank and air filter housing (see Chapter 5).
4   Remove the water pump upper tube **(see illustrations 8.6a
and 8.6b)**.
5   Remove the water jacket mounting bolts and take the water
jacket off the cylinder block **(see illustration 6.5a and the accompanying illustration)**.
6   Installation is the reverse of the removal steps, with the following
additions:
  a) Use new O-rings and lubricate them with multi-purpose grease.
  b) Tighten the mounting bolts to the torque listed in this Chapter's
     Specifications.

10   Water jacket joints (FZR750/1000 models) - removal and installation

1987 and 1988 models

1   Remove the left and right fairings and the side covers (see Chapter 9).
2   Refer to Chapter 1 and drain the cooling system. Remove the fuel
tank and air filter housing (see Chapter 5).

1989 and later models

Refer to illustrations 10.6a and 10.6b

3   Remove the left, right and front fairings (see Chapter 9).
4   Remove the seat (see Chapter 9).
5   Remove the fuel tank and carburetors (see Chapter 5). Refer to
Chapter 1 and drain the cooling system.

10.8b . . . and lubricate them with multi-purpose grease

6   Remove the mounting bolts and pull the outlet water jacket joint
out of the cylinder block **(see illustrations)**.

All models

Refer to illustrations 10.7, 10.8a and 10.8b

7   Remove the mounting bolts and take the inlet water jacket joint
off the cylinder block **(see illustration)**.
8   Installation is the reverse of the removal steps, with the following
additions:
  a) Use new O-rings and lubricate them with multi-purpose grease
     (see illustrations).
  b) Tighten the mounting bolts to the torque listed in this Chapter's
     Specifications.

4

Notes

Chapter 5 Fuel and exhaust systems

Contents

Specifications

Fuel tank capacity

FZR600
Main tank	18 liters (4.8 US gal, 4.0 Imperial gal)
Reserve	3.4 liters (0.9 US gal, 0.75 Imperial gal)

FZR750
1987 and 1988 - US
Main tank	20 liters (5.3 US gal, 4.4 Imperial gal)
Reserve	4.5 liters (1.19 US gal, 0.99 Imperial gal)

1989-on - UK
Main tank	19 liters (5.0 US gal, 4.2 Imperial gal)
Reserve	4.0 liters (1.06 US gal, 0.88 Imperial gal)

FZR1000
1987 and 1988
Main tank	20 liters (5.3 US gal, 4.4 Imperial gal)
Reserve	4.5 liters (1.19 US gal, 0.99 Imperial gal)

1989-on
Main tank	19 liters (5.0 US gal, 4.2 Imperial gal)
Reserve	3.5 liters, 0.92 US gal, 0.77 Imperial gal)

Fuel grade
All 1987 and 1988, 1989-on UK	Regular
1989-on US	Unleaded

Idle speed
FZR600	1150 to 1250 rpm
FZR750	
1987 and 1988 (US)	1000 to 1100 rpm
1989-on (UK)	1150 to 1250 rpm
FZR1000	950 to 1050 rpm

FZR600

Carburetor type ... Mikuni BDST32 (four)

Jet sizes
US models
Main jet	107.5
Main air jet	65
Jet needle/clip position	
1989 non-California	5CFZ4/2
California	5CFZ7/1

FZR600 (continued)

US models
Needle jet	Y-O
Pilot air jet	132.5
Pilot jet	32.5
Pilot screw	3.0 (preset)
Valve seat size	1.2
Starter jet	
Except California	52.5
California	50

UK models
Main jet	107.5
Main air jet	65
Jet needle/clip position	5CFZ4/2
Needle jet	Y-O
Pilot air jet	112.5
Pilot jet	30
Pilot screw	3 turns out
Valve seat size	1.2
Starter jet	52.5
Fuel level	3.8 to 4.8 mm (0.15 to 0.19 inch)

FZR750 (US)

Carburetor type	Mikuni BD34 (four)

Jet sizes

Main jet
Cylinders 1 and 4	107.5
Cylinders 2 and 3	105
Main air jet	65
Jet needle/clip position	
Cylinders 1 and 4	5CDZ/6
Cylinders 2 and 3	5CEZ/6
Needle jet	Y-O
Pilot air jet	125
Pilot jet	15
Pilot screw	2.0
Valve seat size	1.2
Starter jet	30
Fuel level	7.3 to 9.3 mm (0.287 to 0.366 inch)

FZR750 (UK)

Carburetor type	Mikuni BDST38 (four)

Jet sizes

Main jet
Cylinders 1 and 4	122.5
Cylinders 2 and 3	117.5
Main air jet	50
Jet needle	5CEW-11
Needle jet	Y-O
Pilot air jet	125
Pilot jet	42.5
Pilot screw	2-1/2 turns out
Valve seat size	1.6
Starter jet	57.5
Fuel level	7.8 to 8.8 mm (0.31 to 0.35 inch)

FZR1000 (1987 and 1988)

Carburetor type	Mikuni BDS37 (four)

Jet sizes

US models
Main jet (except California)	
Cylinders 1 and 4	110
Cylinders 2 and 3	107.5

Main jet (California)
Cylinders 1 and 4		107.5
Cylinders 2 and 3		105

Main air jet 65
Jet needle/clip position
    Except California 5CT/2
    California 5CZ/3
Needle jet .... Y-O
Pilot air jet 117.5
Pilot jet
    Except California 17.5
    California 20
Pilot screw
    Except California .... 3.0 (preset)
    California .... 2.0 (preset)
Valve seat size 1.5
Starter jet 30

UK models
Main jet
    Cylinders 1 and 4 110
    Cylinders 2 and 3 .... 107.5
Main jet (model 2LF00)
    Cylinders 1 and 4 .... 92.5
    Cylinders 2 and 3 90
Main air jet 65
Jet needle/clip position 5CFZ2/4
Needle jet .... Y-O
Pilot air jet 115
Pilot jet 20
Pilot screw .... 2-1/2 turns out
Valve seat size 1.5
Starter jet 30
Fuel level .... 7.3 to 9.3 mm (0.287 to 0.366 inch)

FZR1000 (1989-on)
Carburetor type .... Mikuni BDST38 (four)

Jet sizes
US models
Main jet
    Cylinders 1 and 4 125
    Cylinders 2 and 3 .... 122.5
Main air jet 85
Jet needle 5CEW9
Needle jet .... Y-O
Pilot air jet 125
Pilot jet 37.5
Pilot screw .... Preset
Valve seat size 1.7
Starter jet 60
UK models
Main jet
    Cylinders 1 and 4 125
    Cylinders 2 and 3 .... 122.5
Main air jet 85
Jet needle/clip position 5CEW8/3
Needle jet .... Y-O
Pilot air jet 115
Pilot jet 40
Pilot screw
    1989 .... 2-1/2 turns out
    1990-on .... 3 turns out
Valve seat size 1.7
Starter jet 60
Fuel level
    1989 .... 10.5 to 11.5 mm (0.41 to 0.45 inch)
    1990-on .... 10.6 to 11.6 mm (0.42 to 0.46 inch)

Tightening torques

FZR600

Carburetor connecting bolts/nuts
    Upper .... 3 Nm (26 in-lbs)
    Lower .... 5 Nm (43 in-lbs)
Exhaust pipe-to-cylinder head nuts .... 10 Nm (7.2 ft-lbs)
Muffler/silencer clamp bolt .... 20 Nm (14 ft-lbs)
Exhaust pipe support bolt .... 20 Nm (14 ft-lbs)
Muffler/silencer bracket bolt .... 20 Nm (14 ft-lbs)
EXUP pulley and cover bolts .... 10 Nm (7.2 ft-lbs)
Exhaust pipe blind plug (CO test) .... 10 Nm (7.2 ft-lbs)

FZR750/1000 models

Carburetor connecting screws (early models) or bolts/nuts (late models)
    Upper .... 3 Nm (26 in-lbs)
    Lower .... 5 Nm (43 in-lbs)
Exhaust pipe-to-cylinder head nuts
    (all except 1989-on FZR750R) .... 10 Nm (7.2 ft-lbs)
Exhaust flange-to-cylinder head bolts (1989-on FZR750R) .... 20 Nm (14 ft-lbs)
Exhaust pipe support bolt
    All except 1989-on FZR750R .... 25 Nm (18 ft-lbs)
    1989-on FZR750R .... 20 Nm (14 ft-lbs)
Muffler bracket bolt .... 20 Nm (14 ft-lbs)
EXUP pulley and cover bolts .... 10 Nm (7.2 ft-lbs)
Exhaust pipe and muffler stay (1989-on FZR750R) .... 10 Nm (7.2 ft-lbs)
Rear exhaust pipe to EXUP valve (1989-on FZR750R) .... 10 Nm (7.2 ft-lbs)

2.3 Use the key to unlock and remove the fuel tank cap

2.4 Remove the two Allen bolts (arrows) that secure the cover to the top of the fuel tank (they're identified by cast triangular marks)

2.5a Remove the cover screws at the rear ...

1 General information

The fuel system consists of the fuel tank, the fuel tap and filter, the carburetors and the connecting lines, hoses and control cables and an electric fuel pump.

The carburetors used on these motorcycles are four Mikunis with butterfly-type throttle valves. For cold starting, an enrichment circuit is actuated by a cable and the choke lever mounted on the left side of the frame.

The exhaust system is a four-into-one design. California and some UK models are equipped with Yamaha's Exhaust Ultimate Powervalve (EXUP). This valve, mounted in the exhaust system, regulates exhaust backpressure to increase performance and reduce exhaust emissions.

Many of the fuel system service procedures are considered routine maintenance items and for that reason are included in Chapter 1.

2 Fuel tank - removal and installation

Warning: *Gasoline (petrol) is extremely flammable, so take extra precautions when you work on any part of the fuel system. Don't smoke or allow open flames or bare light bulbs near the work area, and don't work in a garage where a natural gas-type appliance (such as a water heater or clothes dryer) is present. If you spill any fuel on your skin, rinse it off immediately with soap and water. When you perform any kind of work on the fuel system, wear safety glasses and have a fire extinguisher suitable for class B fires on hand.*

FZR600 models

Refer to illustrations 2.3, 2.4, 2.5a, 2.5b, 2.5c, 2.6, 2.7, 2.8, 2.9, 2.10a, 2.10b, 2.11a, 2.11b, 2.11c and 2.12

1   The fuel tank is mounted beneath a plastic cover and is held in

2.5b ... and at the front ...

2.5c ... and lift the cover off the mounts

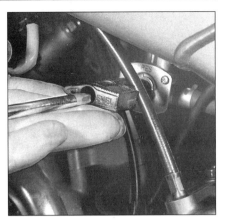

2.6 Remove the fuel tap knob

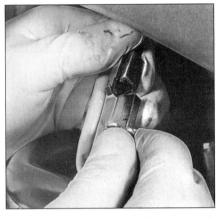

2.7 Locate and disconnect the electrical connectors for the fuel sender and fuel pump

2.8 Disconnect the vapor hose (California models)

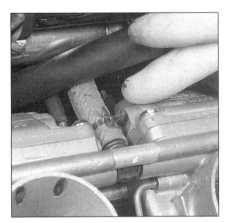

2.9 Disconnect the fuel line at the carburetors; clean up any spilled fuel immediately so it won't be a fire hazard

2.10a Unbolt the tank bracket at the rear ...

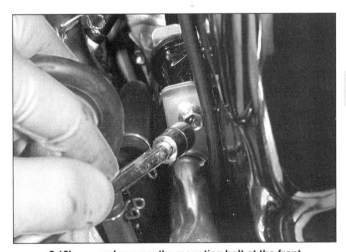

2.10b ... and remove the mounting bolt at the front

5

place at the forward end by a through-bolt which secures a mount on the tank to two brackets on the frame. The rear of the tank is fastened to a bracket, which also secures the tank cover.

2   Remove the seat and disconnect the cable from the negative terminal of the battery.

3   Remove the cap from the fuel tank **(see illustration)**.

4   Remove the two Allen bolts that secure the cap flange to the tank cover **(see illustration)**.

5   Remove the screws at the front and rear of the tank cover **(see illustrations)**. Lift the cover off the mount **(see illustration)**.

6   Turn the fuel tap off and remove the knob **(see illustration)**.

7   Disconnect the electrical connector for the fuel tank sender pump **(see illustration)**.

8   On California models, disconnect the vapor hose from the valve at the right side of the tank **(see illustration)**.

9   Disconnect the fuel line at the carburetors **(see illustration)**.

10   Remove the mounting bolts at the rear and front of the tank and lift the tank off **(see illustrations)**.

11   Before installing the tank, check the condition of the vapor hose (California models).

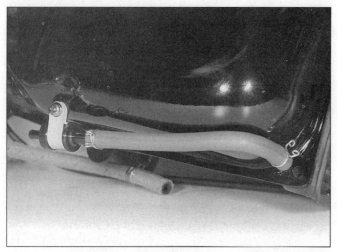

2.11a Inspect the vapor hose on the tank (California models). . .

2.11b . . . the mount on top of the tank (be sure to reinstall the reinforcing washers) . . .

2.11c . . . and the mount at the front of the tank

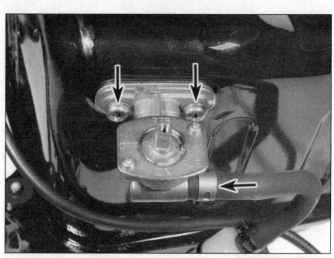

2.12 Disconnect the fuel line and remove the mounting screws (arrows) to remove the fuel tap

2.15 Turn the fuel tap knob to Off with pliers and disconnect the electrical connector for the fuel level sender (arrow)

2.17 Disconnect the hose from the fitting (left arrow) and remove the rear mounting bolt (right arrow)

2.18 Hold the nut with a wrench and remove the front mounting bolt

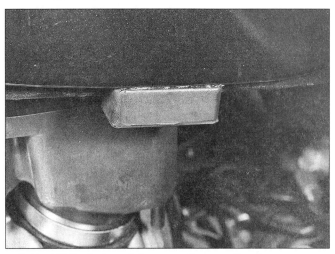

2.19a Lift the tank and disengage the mounting dampers . . .

2.19b . . . and disconnect the fuel line; wipe up any spilled fuel immediately so it doesn't become a fire hazard

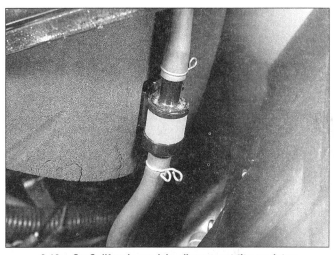

2.19c On California models, disconnect the canister hose from the valve

and rubber mounting dampers (see illustrations) - if they're hardened, cracked, or show any other signs of deterioration, replace them.

12   If necessary, pour the fuel from the tank, disconnect the hose and remove the mounting screws, then separate the fuel tap from the tank (see illustration).

13   When replacing the tank, reverse the above procedure. Make sure the tank seats properly and does not pinch any control cables or wires. If difficulty is encountered when trying to slide the tank cover onto the dampers, a small amount of light oil should be used to lubricate them.

1987 and 1988 FZR750 and all FZR1000 models

Refer to illustrations 2.15, 2.17, 2.18, 2.19a, 2.19b, 2.19c and 2.20

14   Remove the seat. If you're working on a 1987 or 1988 model, remove the side covers (see Chapter 9).

15   Turn the fuel tap knob to Off (see illustration). If you're working on a 1987 or 1988 model, remove the fuel tap screws.

16   Follow the wiring harness from the fuel level sender to the connector and disconnect the connector (see illustration 2.15).

17   Disconnect the hose from the breather fitting at the rear of the tank and remove the rear mounting bolt (see illustration).

18   Remove the mounting bolt from the front of the tank (see illustration).

19   Lift the tank off the mounts and disconnect the fuel line (see illustrations). On California models, disconnect the canister hose from the valve (see illustration).

2.20 Unbolt the tank mounting bracket and lift it off if necessary for access to other components

20   If necessary for access to other components, remove the tank mounting bracket (see illustration).

21   Perform Steps 11 through 13 above to inspect and reinstall the tank.

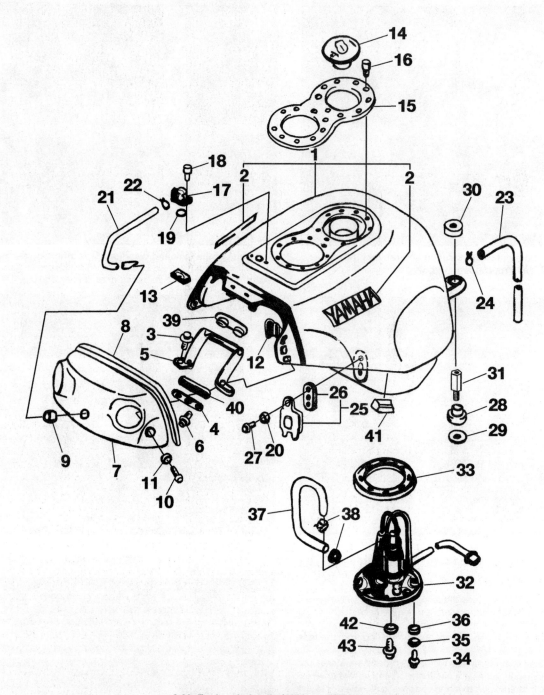

2.23 Fuel tank details (1989-on FZR750 models)

1	Fuel tank assembly	16	Allen bolt	30	Locating damper
2	Yamaha emblems	17	Rollover valve	31	Rear mounting bolt
3	Front mounting bolt	18	Allen bolt	32	Fuel pump
4	Special washer	19	O-ring	33	Seal
5	Fuel tank bracket	20	Plate washer	34	Pan head screw
6	Flange bolt	21	Breather hose	35	Spring washer
7	Tank front cover	22	Clip	36	Plate washer
8	Trim	23	Drain hose	37	Fuel line
9	Grommet	24	Clip	38	Clip
10	Quick-release fastener	25	Fuel tap	39	Locating damper
11	Special washer	26	Tap seal	40	Locating damper
12	Spring plate	27	Screw	41	Locating damper
13	Damper	28	Locating damper	42	Plate washer
14	Cap	29	Plate washer	43	Bolt
15	Filler cover				

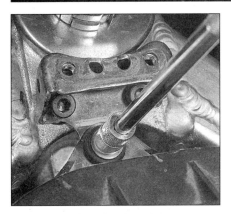

4.2a On FZR750/1000 models, remove the screw at the front of the air filter housing

4.2b Loosen the clamping band screw on each carburetor joint; this is an FZR600 . . .

4.2c . . . and this is an FZR1000

1989-on FZR750 models

Refer to illustration 2.23

22 Disconnect the breather hose from the rollover valve. Undo the two quick-release fasteners on either side of the tank front cover and release the air intake spring bands on the inside of the fairing. Remove the front cover, pulling the breather hose through the grommet. Unbolt and lift off the seat.

23 Remove the tank mounting bolts **(see illustration)**.

24 Carefully note how the drain hose is routed, then disconnect it from the rear of the tank.

25 Remove the locating dampers from the rear mountings.

26 Disconnect the fuel line and vacuum line from the fuel tap.

27 Disconnect the fuel pump electrical connector and lift the tank off.

28 Drain the tank if fuel tap or pump removal is required. Remove the tap mounting screws to free it. Always use a new tap seal on installation. Refer to Section 15 for pump removal.

29 Before installing the tank, check the condition of the locating dampers and hoses - if they're hardened, cracked or show other signs of deterioration, replace them.

30 Reverse the removal steps to install. Make sure the hoses are routed correctly, the tank is seated properly and no hoses or cables are pinched.

---

3 Fuel tank - cleaning and repair

1 All repairs to the fuel tank should be carried out by a professional who has experience in this critical and potentially dangerous work. Even after cleaning and flushing of the fuel system, explosive fumes can remain and ignite during repair of the tank.

2 If the fuel tank is removed from the vehicle, it should not be placed in an area where sparks or open flames could ignite the fumes coming out of the tank. Be especially careful inside garages where a natural gas-type appliance is located, because the pilot light could cause an explosion.

---

4 Air filter housing - removal and installation

Refer to illustrations 4.2a, 4.2b, 4.2c, 4.3a, 4.3b and 4.3c

1 Remove the seat (see Chapter 9) and the fuel tank (see Section 2).

2 If you're working on an FZR750/1000, remove the mounting screw at the front of the air cleaner housing **(see illustration)**. Loosen the clamps that secure the air box to the carburetors **(see illustrations)**. Pull the air box upward, away from the carburetors.

3 Lift the air box, disconnect the hoses and take the air box out **(see illustrations)**.

4 Installation is the reverse of the removal steps.

---

5 Idle fuel/air mixture adjustment - general information

1 Due to the increased emphasis on controlling motorcycle exhaust emissions, certain governmental regulations have been formulated which directly affect the carburetion of this machine. In order to comply with the regulations, the carburetors on some models have a metal sealing plug pressed into the hole over the pilot screw (which controls the idle fuel/air mixture) on each carburetor, so they can't be tampered with. These should only be removed in the event of a complete carburetor overhaul, and even then the screws should be returned to their

5

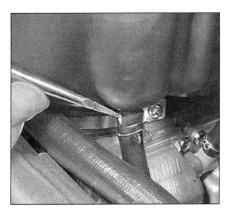

4.3a Disconnect the vapor hose . . .

4.3b . . . and the breather hose and air induction hose (if equipped) (this is an FZR600). . .

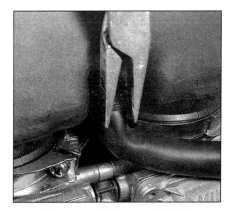

4.3c . . . and this is an FZR1000

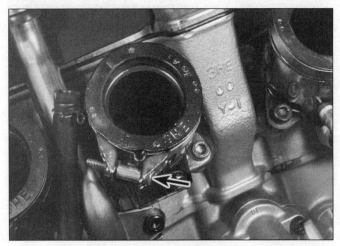

7.4 Loosen the clamping screw on the intake manifold (arrow) (carburetors removed for clarity)

7.6 Lift the carburetor assembly clear of the intake manifolds

original settings. The pilot screws on other models are accessible, but the use of an exhaust gas analyzer is the only accurate way to adjust the idle fuel/air mixture and be sure the machine doesn't exceed the emissions regulations.

2   If the engine runs extremely rough at idle or continually stalls, and if a carburetor overhaul does not cure the problem, take the motorcycle to a Yamaha dealer service department or other repair shop equipped with an exhaust gas analyzer. They will be able to properly adjust the idle fuel/air mixture to achieve a smooth idle and restore low speed performance.

6   Carburetor overhaul - general information

1   Poor engine performance, hesitation, hard starting, stalling, flooding and backfiring are all signs that major carburetor maintenance may be required.
2   Keep in mind that many so-called carburetor problems are really not carburetor problems at all, but mechanical problems within the engine or ignition system malfunctions. Try to establish for certain that the carburetors are in need of maintenance before beginning a major overhaul.
3   Check the fuel filter, the fuel lines, the fuel tank cap vent (if equipped), the intake manifold hose clamps, the vacuum hoses, the air filter element, the cylinder compression, the spark plugs, the carburetor synchronization and the fuel pump before assuming that a carburetor overhaul is required.
4   Most carburetor problems are caused by dirt particles, varnish and other deposits which build up in and block the fuel and air passages. Also, in time, gaskets and O-rings shrink or deteriorate and cause fuel and air leaks which lead to poor performance.
5   When the carburetor is overhauled, it is generally disassembled completely and the parts are cleaned thoroughly with a carburetor cleaning solvent and dried with filtered, unlubricated compressed air. The fuel and air passages are also blown through with compressed air to force out any dirt that may have been loosened but not removed by the solvent. Once the cleaning process is complete, the carburetor is reassembled using new gaskets, O-rings and, generally, a new inlet needle valve and seat.
6   Before disassembling the carburetors, make sure you have a carburetor rebuild kit (which will include all necessary O-rings and other parts), some carburetor cleaner, a supply of rags, some means of blowing out the carburetor passages and a clean place to work. It is recommended that only one carburetor be overhauled at a time to avoid mixing up parts.
7   Don't separate the carburetors from each other unless one of the joints between them is leaking. The carburetors can be overhauled completely without being separated, and reconnecting them properly can be difficult without special factory equipment.

7   Carburetors and intake manifolds - removal and installation

Warning: *Gasoline (petrol) is extremely flammable, so take extra precautions when you work on any part of the fuel system. Don't smoke or allow open flames or bare light bulbs near the work area, and don't work in a garage where a natural gas-type appliance (such as a water heater or clothes dryer) is present. If you spill any fuel on your skin, rinse it off immediately with soap and water. When you perform any kind of work on the fuel system, wear safety glasses and have a class B type fire extinguisher (flammable liquids) on hand.*

Removal
FZR600 models
Refer to illustrations 7.4, 7.6, 7.8a and 7.8b
1   Remove the seat and fairings (see Chapter 9).
2   Remove the fuel tank (see Section 2).
3   Remove the air filter housing (see Section 4).
4   Loosen the clamp screws on the intake manifolds (the rubber tubes that connect the carburetors to the engine) **(see illustration)**.
5   Disconnect the fuel line from the carburetor assembly and remove the inline strainer.
6   Lift the carburetor assembly clear of the intake manifold tubes **(see illustration)**. Raise the assembly up far enough to disconnect the throttle and choke cables (see Sections 11 and 12).
7   After the carburetors have been removed, stuff clean rags into the intake manifold tubes to prevent the entry of dirt or other objects.
8   Inspect the intake manifold tubes **(see illustrations)**. If they're cracked or brittle, replace them.

FZR750/1000 models
Refer to illustrations 7.13, 7.14a, 7.14b, 7.15, 7.18a and 7.18b
9   If you're working on a 1987 or 1988 model, remove the seat and side covers (see Chapter 9).
10   If you're working on a 1989 or later model, remove the left fairing (see Chapter 9).
11   Remove the fuel tank (see Section 2).
12   Remove the air filter housing (see Section 4).
13   Loosen the clamp screws on the intake manifolds (the rubber tubes that connect the carburetors to the engine) **(see illustration)**.
14   Disconnect the fuel line from the carburetor assembly and remove the inline strainer (if equipped) **(see illustrations)**.
15   Disconnect the breather hose from the carburetor assembly **(see illustration)**.
16   Lift the carburetor assembly clear of the intake manifold tubes. Raise the assembly up far enough to disconnect the throttle and choke cables (see Sections 11 and 12).
17   After the carburetors have been removed, stuff clean rags into the

7.8a Disconnect the vacuum line (if equipped) from the intake manifold . . .

7.8b . . . remove the mounting bolts (arrows) and take the manifold off the engine

7.13 Loosen the screw on each clamping band (arrow)

7.14a Disconnect the fuel line . . .

7.14b . . . and remove the inline strainer (if equipped) from the fitting

7.15 Disconnect the breather hose

7.18a Pull the rubber manifold off the aluminum manifold

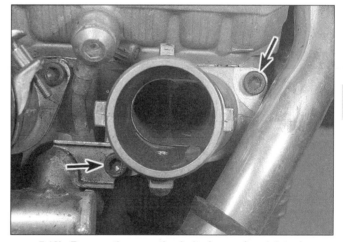

7.18b Remove the mounting bolts (arrows) and detach the aluminum manifold from the engine

5

intake manifold tubes to prevent the entry of dirt or other objects.

18   Inspect the intake manifold tubes **(see illustrations)**. If they're cracked or brittle, replace them.

Installation

19   Position the assembly over the intake manifold tubes. Lightly lubricate the ends of the throttle cables with multi-purpose grease and attach them to the throttle pulley. Make sure the accelerator and decelerator cables are in their proper positions.

20   Tilt the front of the assembly down and insert the fronts of the

carburetors into the intake manifold tubes. Push the assembly forward and tighten the clamps.

21   Install the air filter housing (see Section 4).

22   Make sure the ducts from the air filter housing are seated properly, then slide the spring bands into position.

23   Connect the choke cable to the assembly (see Section 12).

24   Adjust the throttle grip freeplay (see Chapter 1).

25   The remainder of installation is the reverse of the removal steps.

26   Check and, if necessary, adjust the idle speed and carburetor synchronization (see Chapter 1).

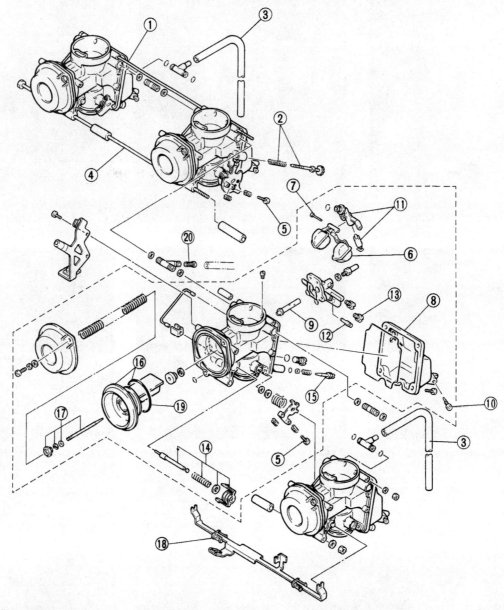

8.1 Carburetors (FZR600 models) - exploded view

1	Upper bracket bolt	11	Needle valve and seat
2	Throttle stop screw and spring	12	Pilot jet
3	Float chamber vent hose	13	Main jet
4	Lower bracket bolt	14	Choke plunger
5	Synchronizing screw	15	Pilot screw
6	Float	16	Throttle piston
7	Float pivot pin	17	Jet needle
8	Float chamber cover	18	Choke shaft
9	Needle jet	19	O-ring
10	Float chamber drain screw	20	Inline strainer

8   Carburetors - disassembly, cleaning and inspection

Warning: *Gasoline (petrol) is extremely flammable, so take extra precautions when you work on any part of the fuel system. Don't smoke or allow open flames or bare light bulbs near the work area, and don't work in a garage where a natural gas-type appliance (such as a water heater or clothes dryer) is present. If you spill any fuel on your skin, rinse it off immediately with soap and water. When you perform any* kind of work on the fuel system, wear safety glasses and have a fire extinguisher suitable for class B type fires (flammable liquids) on hand.

FZR600 models
Disassembly

Refer to illustrations 8.1, 8.2a, 8.2b, 8.3, 8.4a, 8.4b, 8.5a, 8.5b, 8.5c, 8.5d, 8.6a, 8.6b, 8.7, 8.8a, 8.8b, 8.8c, 8.9a, 8.9b, 8.10, 8.11a, 8.11b, 8.11c, 8.12, 8.13, 8.14a and 8.14b

1   Remove the carburetors from the machine as described in Sec-

8.2a Squeeze the spring clamps and slide them down the vent hoses . . .

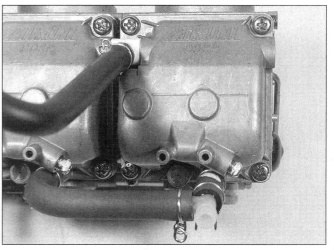

8.2b . . . and detach the hoses from the float chamber covers

8.3 Remove the bracket mounting screws and take off the throttle stop screw and bracket

8.4a Remove the float chamber cover screws (arrows) . . .

8.4b . . . and lift the float chamber covers off in pairs

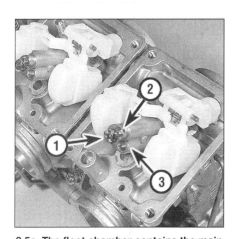

8.5a The float chamber contains the main jet (1), starter jet (2) and pilot jet (3)

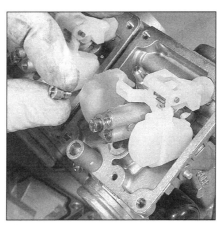

8.5b Unscrew the starter jet . . .

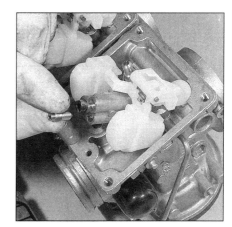

8.5c . . . the pilot jet . . .

tion 7. Set the assembly on a clean working surface. **Note:** *Unless the O-rings on the fuel and vent fittings between the carburetors are leaking, don't detach the carburetors from their mounting brackets. Also, work on one carburetor at a time to avoid getting parts mixed up. It's possible to overhaul the carburetors without removing them from the brackets* (see illustration).

2   Remove the vent hoses (see illustrations).

3   Remove the throttle stop screw and bracket (see illustration).

4   Remove the float chamber cover screws and lift off the float chamber covers (see illustrations).

5   Remove the starter jet, main jet and pilot jet (see illustrations).

6   The pilot (idle mixture) screw is located in the front of the carbure-

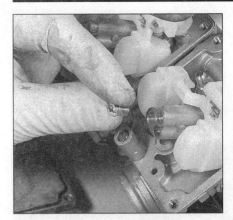

8.5d ... and the main jet

8.6a Remove the plug and turn the pilot screw (arrow) in until it bottoms lightly ...

8.6b ... then remove the screw, spring, washer and O-ring

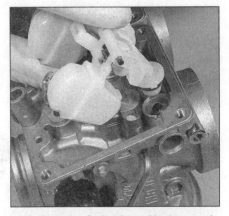

8.7 Work the O-ring free of its bore and lift the needle valve assembly out together with the floats

8.8a Unscrew the jet holder bolt with a box wrench (ring spanner) ...

8.8b ... lift out the bolt and washer; there's a projection on the jet holder (arrow) which aligns with a slot in the needle jet ...

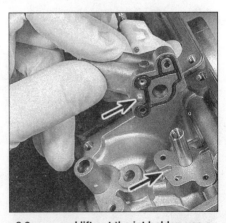

8.8c ... and lift out the jet holder; use a new O-ring during installation and be sure the locating pin aligns with the slot (arrows)

8.9a Unscrew the pilot air jet (arrow) ...

8.9b ... and lift it out of its bore

tor body. On US models, this screw is hidden behind a plug which will have to be removed if the screw is to be taken out. To do this, drill a hole in the plug, being careful not to drill into the screw, then pry the plug out or remove it with a small slide hammer. On all models, turn the pilot screw in, counting the number of turns until it bottoms lightly **(see illustration)**. Record that number for use when installing the screw. Now remove the pilot screw along with its spring, washer and O-ring **(see illustration)**.

7   Work the needle valve O-ring free of its bore and lift out the float and needle valve assembly **(see illustration)**.
8   Remove the jet holder bolt, washer and jet holder **(see illustrations)**.
9   Remove the pilot air jet **(see illustrations)**.
10   Turn the carburetor over and remove the vacuum chamber cover screws **(see illustration)**.
11   Lift off the cover, spring and throttle piston, then separate the pis-

8.10 Remove the vacuum chamber cover screws

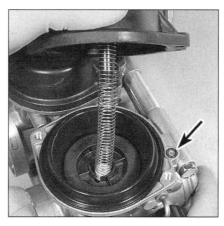

8.11a Lift off the cover and spring and note the location of the small O-ring (arrow) . . .

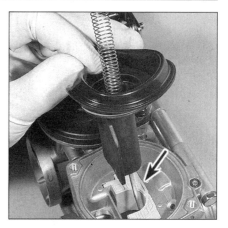

8.11b . . . lift out the throttle piston together with the diaphragm and jet needle and remove the throttle piston support (arrow)

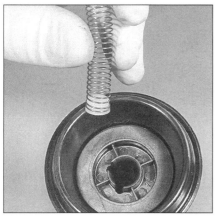

8.11c Separate the spring from the throttle piston

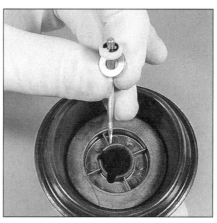

8.12 Lift the jet needle and washer out of the throttle piston

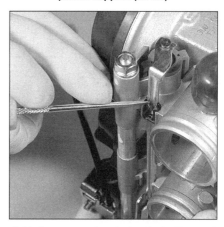

8.13 Compress the choke shaft clips and slide them out of their bores, then take off the choke shaft

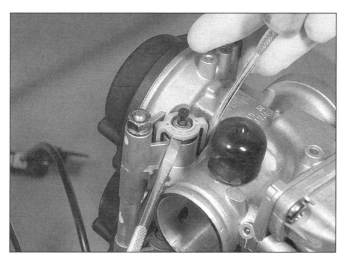

8.14a Squeeze the tab on one side of the choke plunger, then on the other, while applying light steady pressure with another screwdriver . . .

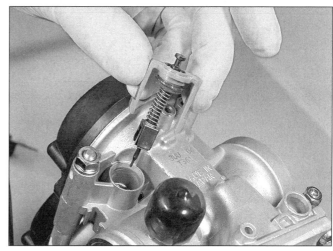

8.14b . . . until the choke plunger can be lifted out of its bore

ton spring from the throttle piston (see illustrations).
12   Take the jet needle and washer out of the throttle piston (see illustration).
13   Compress the choke shaft clips and take them out of their bores (see illustration). Remove the choke shaft from the carburetor

assembly.
14   Squeeze the retaining tangs on the choke plunger while applying gentle pressure on the retainer, then pull the choke plunger out of its bore (see illustrations).

8.15 The float chamber cover O-rings should be replaced whenever the carburetors are overhauled

8.16 If the fittings between the pairs of float chamber covers have been leaking, remove them and install new O-rings

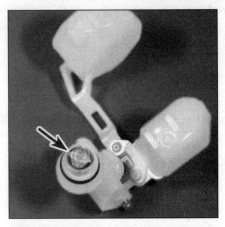

8.17 Make sure the fuel strainer (arrow) is clean; if it's torn or can't be cleaned, replace it

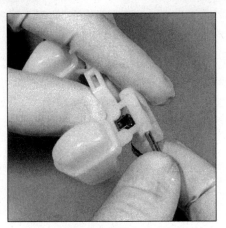

8.18a Pull the float pivot pin out . . .

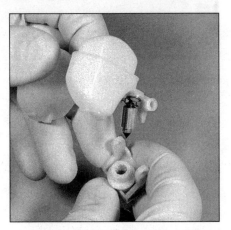

8.18b . . . separate the needle valve seat from the floats . . .

Inspection

Refer to illustrations 8.15, 8.16, 8.17, 8.18a, 8.18b, 8.18c and 8.18d

15   Remove the O-rings from the float chamber covers **(see illustration)**.

16   If fuel has been leaking from the fittings between the float chamber covers, pull them apart, install new O-rings and reassemble the covers **(see illustration)**.

17   Check the filter screen on the needle valve seat **(see illustration)** and replace it if it's torn or can't be cleaned.

18   Pull out the float pivot pin and separate the floats and needle valve from the needle valve seat **(see illustrations)**. Check the tip of the needle valve. If it has grooves or scratches in it, it must be replaced. Push in on the rod in the other end of the needle valve, then release it - if it doesn't spring back, replace the valve needle.

19   Check the operation of the choke plunger. If it doesn't move smoothly, replace it, along with the return spring. Inspect the needle on the end of the choke plunger and replace it if it's worn.

20   Check the tapered portion of the pilot screw for wear or damage. Replace the pilot screw if necessary.

21   Check the carburetor body, float chamber cover and vacuum chamber cover for cracks, distorted sealing surfaces and other damage. If any defects are found, replace the faulty component, although replacement of the entire carburetor will probably be necessary (check with your parts supplier for the availability of separate components).

22   Check the diaphragm for splits, holes and general deterioration. Holding it up to a light will help to reveal problems of this nature.

23   Insert the throttle piston in the carburetor body and see that it

moves up-and-down smoothly. Check the surface of the piston for wear. If it's worn excessively or doesn't move smoothly in the bore, replace the carburetor.

24   Check the jet needle for straightness by rolling it on a flat surface (such as a piece of glass). Replace it if it's bent or if the tip is worn.

25   Operate the throttle shaft to make sure the throttle butterfly valve opens and closes smoothly. If it doesn't, replace the carburetor.

26   Check the floats for damage. This will usually be apparent by the presence of fuel inside one of the floats. If the floats are damaged, they must be replaced.

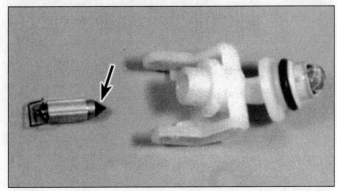

8.18c . . . replace the needle valve if it's worn at the tip (arrow) (install a new one in any case if it's included in the rebuild kit) . . .

Cleaning

Caution: *Use only a petroleum based solvent for carburetor cleaning. Don't use caustic cleaners.*

27   Submerge the metal components in the solvent for approximately thirty minutes (or longer, if the directions recommend it).

28   After the carburetor has soaked long enough for the cleaner to loosen and dissolve most of the varnish and other deposits, use a brush to remove the stubborn deposits. Rinse it again, then dry it with compressed air. Blow out all of the fuel and air passages in the main body. **Caution**: *Never clean the jets or passages with a piece of wire or a drill bit, as they will be enlarged, causing the fuel and air metering rates to be upset.*

1987 and 1988 FZR750/1000 models

Disassembly

Refer to illustration 8.29

29   Remove the choke shaft screws and take off the choke shaft **(see illustration)**. These screws have been secured with non-permanent thread locking agent, so you may need an impact driver.

30   Remove the choke plunger nut, spring and plunger.

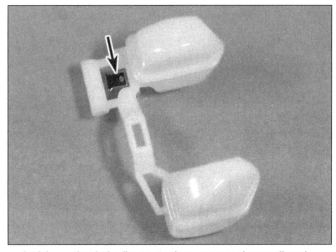

8.18d ... check the float tang that contacts the needle valve (arrow) and replace the floats if the tang is worn (bend this tang to change fuel level adjustment)

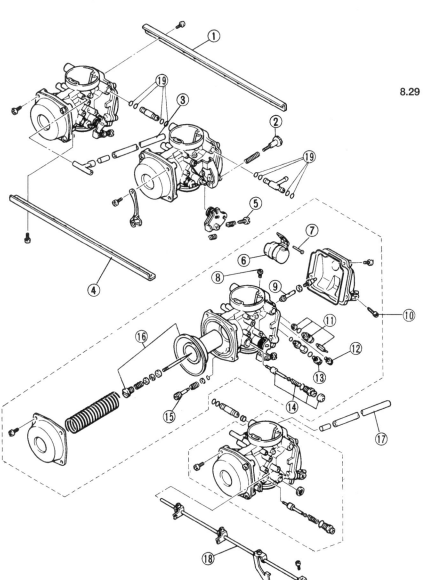

8.29 Carburetor (1987 and 1988 FZR750/ 1000 models) exploded view

1   Upper bracket
2   Throttle stop screw
3   Fuel overflow hose
4   Lower bracket
5   Synchronizing screw
6   Float
7   Float pivot pin
8   Pilot air jet
9   Needle jet
10   Fuel drain screw
11   Needle valve and seat
12   Pilot jet
13   Main jet
14   Choke plunger assembly
15   Pilot screw
16   Throttle piston
17   Fuel line
18   Choke shaft
19   O-ring

8.41 Carburetor (1989-on FZR750 models) exploded view

1   Carburetor set
2   Carburetor body
3   Carburetor components
4   Vacuum chamber cover
5   Vacuum chamber cover screw
6   Float chamber drain plug
7   Washer
8   Panhead screw
9   Screw
10 Bolt
11 O-ring
12 Float pivot pin
13 Floats
14 Choke plunger
15 Pilot screw set
16 O-ring
17 Vacuum chamber cover
18 Throttle piston
19 Piston valve support
20 Diaphragm spring
21 Jet needle
22 Needle jet holder
23 Main jet washer
24 Needle jet bolt
25 O-ring
26 O-ring
27 O-ring
28 Needle valve and seat
29 Washer
30 Lockwasher
31 Main jet
32 Needle jet
33 Pilot air jet
34 Pilot jet
35 Starter jet
36 Main air jet
37 Pipe clip
38 Plate washer
39 Nut
40 Throttle synchronizing screw
41 Rod
42 Choke shaft clip
43 Ring
44 Nipple
45 Pipe
46 Choke connecting tube
47 Seal
48 Strainer
49 O-ring
50 Pipe

51 Throttle stop screw
52 Plate washer
53 Nut
54 Choke connecting tube
55 Screw
56 Nipple
57 O-ring
58 Hose
59 Clamp

31   Remove four screws and take off the vacuum chamber cover. Remove the spring and throttle piston.
32   Unscrew the jet needle plug, then remove the spring, washer and jet needle.
33   Remove the float chamber cover screws, then lift off the cover and remove the gasket.
34   Pull out the float pivot pin and remove the float and needle valve.
35   Remove the needle valve seat screw and needle valve seat.
36   Remove the main jet, washer, main jet holder and its washer.
37   Remove the needle jet from its passage inside the float chamber.
38   Unscrew the pilot air jet from its bore in the intake passage of the carburetor.
39   The pilot (idle mixture) screw is located in the front of the carburetor body. On US models, this screw is hidden behind a plug which will have to be removed if the screw is to be taken out. To do this, drill a

hole in the plug, being careful not to drill into the screw, then pry the plug out or remove it with a small slide hammer. On all models, turn the pilot screw in, counting the number of turns until it bottoms lightly. Record that number for use when installing the screw. Now remove the pilot screw along with its spring, washer and O-ring.
Inspection and cleaning
40   Perform Steps 15 through 28 above to inspect and clean the carburetors.

1989-on FZR750 models

Refer to illustration 8.41

41   Remove the choke shaft clips and take off the choke shaft **(see illustration)**.
42   Squeeze the retaining tangs on the choke plunger while applying gentle pressure on the retainer, then lift the choke plunger out of

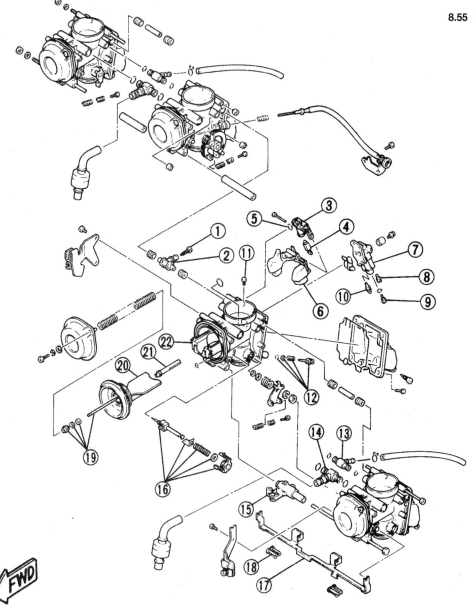

8.55 Carburetors (1989-on FZR1000 models) - exploded view

1   Fuel strainer
2   Fuel feed joint
3   Needle valve seat
4   Needle valve
5   O-ring
6   Floats
7   Jet holder
8   Starter jet
9   Main jet
10 Pilot jet
11 Pilot air jet
12 Pilot air screw
13 Overflow hose joint
14 Ventilation hose joint
15 Choke shaft joint
16 Choke plunger
17 Choke shaft
18 Choke shaft clip
19 Jet needle
20 Piston valve
21 Needle jet
22 Throttle piston support

5

its bore.

43   Remove two screws that secure the vacuum chamber cover. Hold the cover down and turn it about 45-degrees counterclockwise (anti-clockwise), then lift it off. Remove the spring, throttle piston, jet needle and O-ring.

44   Unscrew the jet needle plug, then remove the spring, washer and jet needle.

45   Remove the float chamber cover screws, then lift off the cover and remove the O-ring.

46   Pull out the float pivot pin and remove the float and needle valve.

47   Remove the needle valve seat.

48   Remove the main jet and its washer.

49   Remove the pilot jet and starter jet.

50   Unscrew the needle jet bolt and remove the needle jet holder and its O-ring from the carburetor body.

51   Remove the throttle piston support and the needle jet.

52   Turn the pilot air screw in until it bottoms lightly, then count the number of turns required to remove it and write this down. Remove the pilot air screw and its spring, washer and O-ring.

53   Remove the pilot air jet and main air jet from their bores in the intake passage.

54   Perform Steps 15 through 28 above to inspect and clean the carburetors.

1989-on FZR1000 models

Refer to illustrations 8.55, 8.56, 8.57a, 8.57b and 8.57c

55   Remove the choke shaft, throttle stop screw and bracket **(see illustration)**.

56   Remove the float chamber cover screws and lift off the float chamber cover **(see illustration)**.

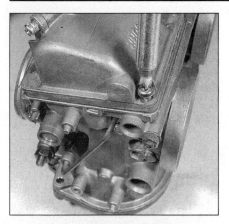

8.56 Remove the float chamber cover screws

8.57a Work the O-ring free of its bore and remove the needle valve and seat assembly

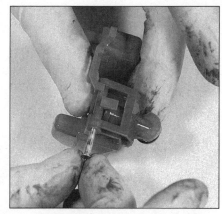

8.57b Pull out the float pivot pin

57   Work the needle valve O-ring free of its bore and lift out the float and needle valve assembly **(see illustration)**. Pull out the float pivot pin and unhook the needle valve from the float **(see illustrations)**.
58   Remove the starter jet, main jet and pilot jet.
59   Remove the needle jet bolt, needle jet holder, and O-ring.
60   Remove the pilot air jet **(see illustration 8.9a)**.
61   Turn the carburetor over and remove the vacuum chamber cover screws.
62   Lift off the cover, spring and throttle piston, then separate the spring from the throttle piston. Remove the needle jet and throttle valve support.
63   Take the jet needle and washer out of the throttle piston.
64   Compress the choke shaft clips and take them out of their bores **(see illustration 8.13)**. Remove the choke shaft from the carburetor assembly.
65   Squeeze the retaining tangs on the choke plunger while applying gentle pressure on the retainer, then lift the choke plunger out of its bore **(see illustrations 8.14a and 8.14b)**.

Cleaning and inspection
66   Perform Steps 15 through 28 above to clean and inspect the carburetor.

---

9   Carburetors - separation and reassembly

---

1   The carburetors needn't be separated for normal overhaul. If you need to separate them (to replace a carburetor body, for example), remove them (see Section 7) and refer to the following procedure.

FZR600 and all 1989-on FZR750/1000 models
2   Remove the choke shaft (see Section 8).
3   Remove the nuts from the two long bolts that hold the carburetors together (the upper bracket bolt and the lower bracket bolt) **(see illustration 8.1, 8.41 or 8.55)**.
4   Note how the synchronizing screws and springs are assembled (see Chapter 1). As you pull the carburetors apart, keep track of the synchronizer screw springs. They should stay with the adjusting screws, but if they don't, find them and install them as shown in Chapter 1 so they aren't lost.
5   Pull out the upper and lower bracket bolts and remove the spacers and fittings from between the carburetors.
6   Assembly is the reverse of the disassembly procedure. Before tightening the connecting bolts, place the carburetor assembly on a surface plate with the manifold side down. Use new O-rings on the fuel and vent line fittings. Tighten the connecting bolts and nuts to the torque listed in this Chapter's Specifications.

1987 and 1988 FZR750/1000 models
7   If you're going to separate the carburetors, remove eight screws each from the upper bracket and the lower bracket. These screws are

secured with thread locking agent, so you'll probably need an impact driver.
8   Note how the synchronizing screws and springs are assembled (see Chapter 1). As you pull the carburetors apart, keep track of the synchronizer screw springs. They should stay with the adjusting screws, but if they don't, find them and install them as shown in Chapter 1 so they aren't lost.
9   Assembly is the reverse of the disassembly procedure. Before tightening the connecting screws, make sure all four throttle valves are fully closed. Use new O-rings on the fuel and vent line fittings. Use non-permanent thread locking agent on the screw threads. Tighten the connecting bolts and nuts to the torque listed in this Chapter's Specifications.

---

10   Carburetors - reassembly and fuel level adjustment

Caution: *When installing the jets, be careful not to over-tighten them - they're made of soft material and can strip or shear easily.*
Note: *When reassembling the carburetors, be sure to use the new O-rings, gaskets and other parts supplied in the rebuild kit.*

Reassembly
1   Assembly is the reverse of the disassembly steps, with the following additions.

FZR600 models
Refer to illustrations 10.3 and 10.4
2   Install the pilot screw (if removed) along with its spring, washer and O-ring, turning it in until it seats lightly. Now, turn the screw out the number of turns that was previously recorded. On US models, install a new metal plug in the hole over the screw. Apply a little bonding agent around the circumference of the plug after it has been seated.
3   Be sure to install the small O-ring in its groove when installing the vacuum chamber cover **(see illustration)**.
4   Engage the choke shaft with the choke plunger **(see illustration)**.

1987 and 1988 FZR750/1000 models
5   When installing the diaphragm, be sure the tab on the edge of the diaphragm engages the notch in the carburetor body.

1989-on FZR750 models
6   If you removed the throttle piston support, align the tabs on its ends with the slots in the carburetor body.
7   Align the groove on the needle jet with the projection on the jet housing. Align the pin on the jet housing with the slot in the carburetor body.
8   Be sure to install the main jet and starter jet in the correct positions (the main jet has a larger orifice).
9   Align the projection on the needle valve seat with the slot in the carburetor body.

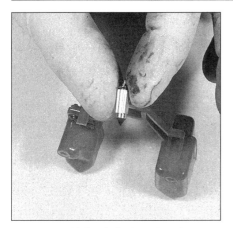

8.57c Unhook the needle valve from the float

10.3 Be sure to install this small O-ring in its groove (arrow)

10.4 The choke shaft should engage the choke plungers like this

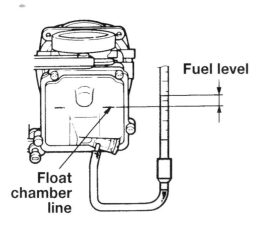

10.13 Fuel level adjustment details

10   If you've separated the cap from the vacuum chamber cover, apply a thin coating of grease to its O-ring. Align the three projections on the cap with the slots in the cover, insert the cap, push it down and turn it clockwise until it stops.

Fuel level adjustment

Refer to illustration 10.13

Warning: *Gasoline (petrol) is extremely flammable, so take extra precautions when you work on any part of the fuel system. Don't smoke or allow open flames or bare light bulbs near the work area, and don't work in a garage where a natural gas-type appliance (such as a water heater or clothes dryer) is present. If you spill any fuel on your skin, rinse it off immediately with soap and water. When you perform any kind of work on the fuel system, wear safety glasses and have a fire extinguisher suitable for class B type fires (flammable liquids) on hand.*

11   Support the bike securely so it can't be knocked over during this procedure.
12   Support the bike so the carburetors are upright.
13   Attach Yamaha service tool no. YM-01312 (part no. 90890-01312) to the drain fitting on the bottom of one of the carburetor float chamber covers (all four will be checked). This is a clear plastic tube graduated in millimeters **(see illustration)**. On 1987 and 1988 models, you'll also need an adapter (tool no. YM-01329/part no. 90890-01329). An alternative is to use a length of clear plastic tubing and an accurate ruler. Hold the graduated tube (or the free end of the clear plastic tube) vertically against the carburetor body.
14   Unscrew the drain screw at the bottom of the float chamber cover a couple of turns, then start the engine and let it idle - fuel will flow into

the tube. Wait for the fuel level to stabilize, then note how far the fuel level is above the float chamber line **(see illustration 10.13)**.
15   Measure the distance between the line on the float chamber/carburetor body and the top of the fuel level in the tube or gauge. This distance is the fuel level - write it down on a piece of paper, screw in the drain screw, then move on to the next carburetor and check it the same way.
16   Compare your fuel level readings to the value listed in this Chapter's Specifications. If the fuel level in any carburetor is incorrect, remove the carburetors (see Section 7), then remove the float chamber cover from the carburetor(s) with the incorrect fuel level. Make sure the needle valve and seat are in good condition, then bend the tang slightly up or down as necessary. Reinstall the float chamber cover(s) and carburetors, then recheck fuel level.

11   Throttle cables - removal, installation and adjustment

Refer to illustrations 11.4a, 11.4b, 11.4c, 11.5a and 11.5b

1   Remove the fuel tank (see Section 2).
2   Loosen the accelerator cables with the adjusters (see Throttle operation/grip freeplay - check and adjustment in Chapter 1).
3   Remove the handlebar switch mounting screws and separate the halves of the handlebar switch (see Chapter 10).
4   Detach the accelerator and decelerator cables from the throttle grip pulley and from the throttle pulley at the carburetors **(see illustrations)**. Remove the cables, noting how they are routed.

11.4a At the carburetors, loosen the cable locknut and adjusting nut (if equipped) and lift the cable out of the bracket . . .

5

11.4b ... if the decelerator cable doesn't have a locknut and adjusting nut, lift it out of the bracket and guide it through the slot (arrow)

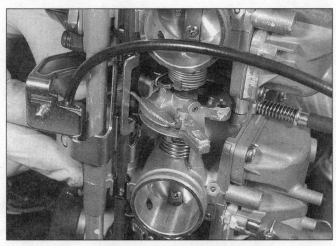

11.4c Lift the cable out of its groove in the throttle pulley and slide it sideways to disengage it

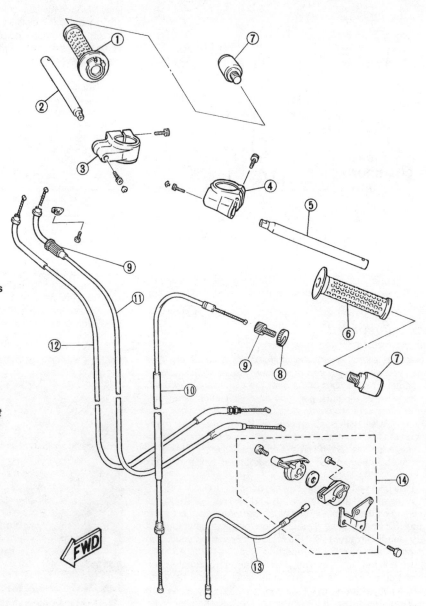

11.5a Throttle and choke cable details (FZR600 models)

1 Throttle grip
2 Right handlebar
3 Right handlebar boss
4 Left handlebar boss
5 Left handlebar
6 Left handlebar grip
7 Grip end weights
8 Clutch cable adjuster locknut
9 Clutch cable adjuster
10 Clutch cable
11 Accelerator cable
12 Decelerator cable
13 Choke cable
14 Choke lever assembly

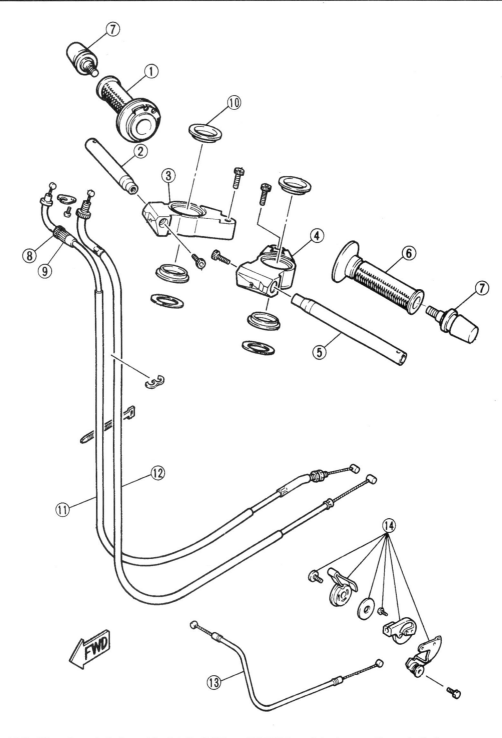

11.5b Throttle and choke cable details (1989-on FZR1000 models shown; others similar)

1	Throttle grip	8	Accelerator cable adjuster locknut
2	Right handlebar	9	Accelerator cable adjuster
3	Right handlebar boss	10	Rubber damper
4	Left handlebar boss	11	Accelerator cable
5	Left handlebar	12	Decelerator cable
6	Left handlebar grip	13	Choke cable
7	Grip end weights	14	Choke lever assembly

5   Unscrew the throttle grip weight and take the throttle grip off the handlebar **(see illustrations)**.

6   Clean the handlebar and apply a light coat of multi-purpose grease.

7   Route the cables into place. Make sure they don't interfere with any other components and aren't kinked or bent sharply.

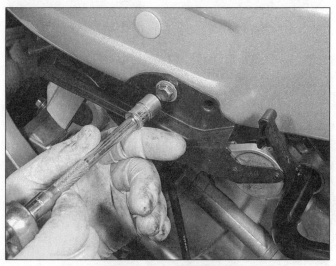

12.3a Unbolt the choke lever from the frame
(this is an FZR600) . . .

12.3b . . . and this is an FZR1000

12.4 Turn the lever around and disengage the
cable from the pulley

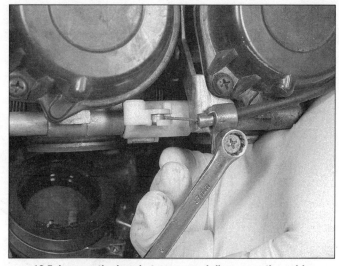

12.5 Loosen the bracket screw and disengage the cable
from the choke shaft

8   Lubricate the ends of the accelerator and decelerator cables with multi-purpose grease and connect them to the throttle pulleys at the carburetors and at the throttle grip.

9   Follow the procedure outlined in Chapter 1, Throttle operation/grip freeplay - check and adjustment, to adjust the cables.

10   Turn the handlebars back and forth to make sure the cables don't cause the steering to bind. With the engine idling, turn the handlebars back and forth and make sure idle speed doesn't change. If it does, find and fix the cause before riding the motorcycle.

11   Install the fuel tank.

12   Choke cable - removal and installation

Refer to illustrations 12.3a, 12.3b, 12.4 and 12.5

1   Remove the fuel tank (see Section 2).

2   Remove the left fairing panel (see Chapter 9).

3   Unbolt the choke lever from the frame **(see illustrations)**.

4   Turn the choke lever around, align the cable with the slot in the pulley and disengage the cable **(see illustration)**.

5   At the carburetor end of the cable, loosen the screw that secures

the outer housing in the bracket enough that you can separate the cable from the bracket. Align the inner cable with the slot in the choke shaft bracket, then separate the cable end from the bracket **(see illustration)**.

6   Installation is the reverse of the removal steps. Lubricate the pulley end of the choke cable with a film of multi-purpose grease.

13   Exhaust system - removal, EXUP inspection and installation

Removal

All except 1989-on FZR750 models

Refer to illustrations 13.2a, 13.2b, 13.2c, 13.3, 13.4a, 13.4b and 13.4c

1   Remove the left and right fairings (see Chapter 9).

2   Remove the exhaust pipe holder nuts at the cylinder head and slide the holders off the mounting studs **(see illustrations)**.

3   On EXUP-equipped models, disconnect the cables from the EXUP servo motor **(see illustration)**. This will eliminate the need to adjust the cables.

4   Remove the mounting bolt beneath the engine and detach the

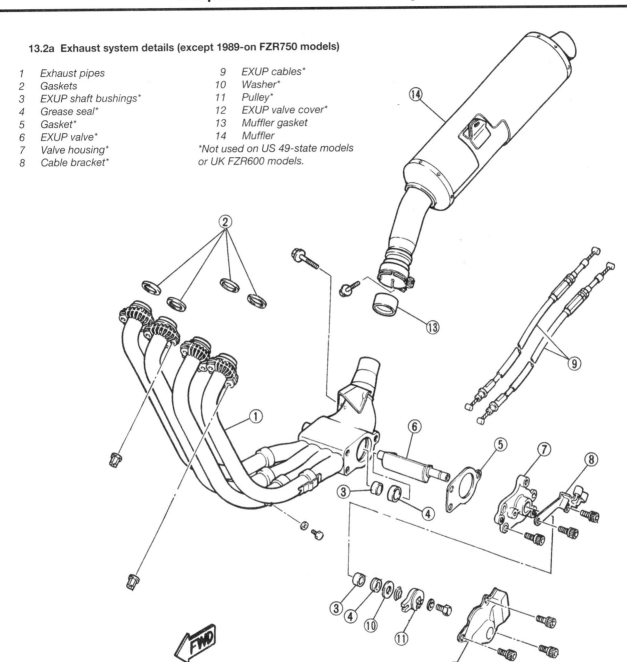

13.2a Exhaust system details (except 1989-on FZR750 models)

1 Exhaust pipes
2 Gaskets
3 EXUP shaft bushings*
4 Grease seal*
5 Gasket*
6 EXUP valve*
7 Valve housing*
8 Cable bracket*

9 EXUP cables*
10 Washer*
11 Pulley*
12 EXUP valve cover*
13 Muffler gasket
14 Muffler
*Not used on US 49-state models
or UK FZR600 models.

13.2b Remove the nuts . . .

13.2c . . . and slide the retainers off the studs

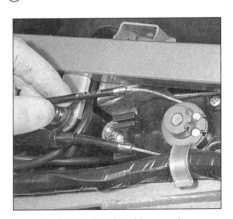

13.3 The EXUP cables can be disconnected from the servo motor without changing the adjustment

5

13.4a Remove the mounting bolt (this is an FZR600) . . .

13.4b . . . and this is an FZR1000

13.4c Unbolt the muffler bracket

13.7 Exhaust system (1989-on FZR750 models)

1	Muffler/silencer	9	Pulley
2	EXUP cable	10	Timing gear cover
3	EXUP cable	11	Timing gears
4	Muffler/silencer clamp	12	Valve shafts
5	Gasket	13	Bushings
6	EXUP valves	14	Valve case
7	Exhaust flanges	15	Spring
8	Pulley cover	16	Exhaust pipe

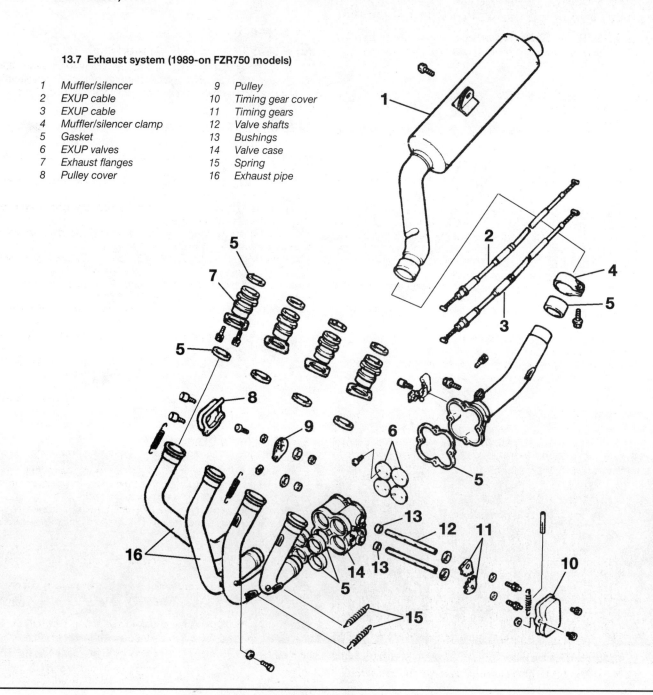

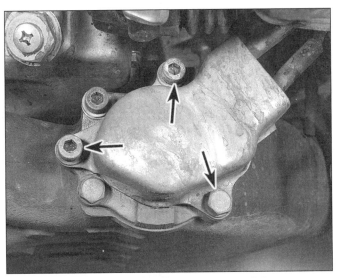

13.21 Remove the bolts (arrows) and take off the cover

13.23 The notch should be aligned with the hole (1)

muffler/silencer from the bracket near the right rear footpeg **(see illustrations)**. Lower the pipes and muffler/silencer away from the bike and take them out.

5   If necessary, loosen the clamp bolts and separate the muffler/silencer from the pipes.

1989-on FZR750 models

Refer to illustration 13.7

6   Remove the left and right fairings (see Chapter 9).

7   Loosen the locknuts on the EXUP cables all the way and turn the adjusters in as far as they will go. Remove the EXUP pulley cover and disconnect the cables, then remove the washer and the EXUP cable holder **(see illustration)**.

8   Unhook the springs that secure the exhaust pipes to the exhaust flanges at the cylinder head.

9   Remove the exhaust pipe gaskets, exhaust flanges and flange gaskets.

10   Unhook the springs that secure the exhaust pipes to the valve case. Label the pipes for reinstallation, then disconnect the pipes.

11   Remove the mounting bolts for the rear exhaust pipe and muffler/silencer. Take the exhaust system out.

12   If necessary, loosen the clamp and disconnect the muffler from the rear pipe. Detach the rear pipe and gasket from the EXUP valve case.

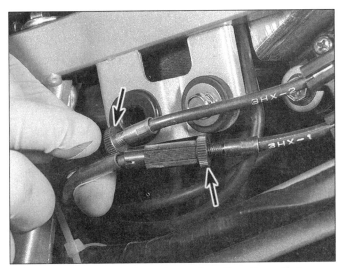

13.24 Loosen the locknuts (arrows) and turn the adjusters

EXUP inspection

All except 1989-on FZR750 models

13   Twist the shaft and check its movement **(see illustration 13.2a)**. If it sticks, remove the cover and lubricate the ends of the shaft and the bushings with molybdenum disulfide grease. If that doesn't help, replace the valve.

1989-on FZR750 models

14   Remove the timing gear cover from the valve. Note the position of the match marks on the timing gears; they should be aligned when both valves are closed.

15   Note which side of the shafts the valves are attached to, then remove the valves **(see illustration 13.7)**.

16   Remove the spring, then remove the circlip, washer, lower valve shaft and the remaining washer.

17   Remove the circlip from the upper valve shaft, then remove the washer, shaft and remaining washer.

18   If the shafts or timing gears are worn or damaged, remove the gears from the shafts.

19   Check the bushings in the valve and all removed parts for wear or damage and replace any parts with visible defects.

20   Assembly is the reverse of the disassembly steps, with the following additions:

a) Lubricate the bushings, shafts and washers with molybdenum disulfide grease.

b) If the timing gears were removed, install them with their toothed sides facing in the same direction as the valve attachment surfaces on the shafts.

c) Be sure the match marks on the timing gears are aligned when the valves are closed.

EXUP cable adjustment

Refer to illustrations 13.21, 13.23, 13.24 and 13.26

21   Remove the cover from the EXUP valve **(see illustration)**.

22   Turn the ignition switch to On. If the EXUP servo motor doesn't operate, refer further diagnosis to a Yamaha dealer.

23   Check the alignment marks **(see illustration)**. If they're aligned, no further adjustment is necessary. If they aren't aligned, adjust the cables (see below).

24   Loosen the cable adjuster locknuts and turn the adjuster in **(see illustration)**. Insert a 4 mm (0.16 inch) alignment pin through the pulley and into the hole.

25   Turn the adjusters counterclockwise (anti-clockwise) just enough to eliminate free-play in the cables, then turn them clockwise one half turn and tighten the locknuts.

26   Remove the alignment pin and turn off the ignition switch. Turn the pulley on the EXUP servo motor **(see illustration)** clockwise by hand until it stops, then turn on the ignition switch again. The EXUP pulley should move back to the aligned position. If it doesn't, try readjusting it. If that doesn't work, refer further service to a Yamaha dealer.

5

13.26 Turn the servo motor pulley clockwise until it stops

13.27 Use new gaskets at the cylinder head

Installation

Refer to illustration 13.27

27   Installation is the reverse of removal, with the following additions:
a) Use new gaskets at the cylinder head **(see illustration)**.
b) Tighten all fasteners to the torque settings listed in this Chapter's Specifications.

14   Fuel pump - circuit check and fuel pump test

1   With the engine kill switch in the On position, the fuel pump should start and run for approximately five seconds after the ignition is switched on. It should shut off once the carburetor float bowls are full, then run again once the engine is started.
2   The fuel pump circuit consists of the pump, the pump relay, the digital igniter unit (which controls the fuel pump as well as ignition timing), the engine kill switch, the ignition switch, the main and ignition fuses, the battery and related wiring.
3   If you're working on an FZR600, remove the seat, fuel tank cover and fuel tank (see Chapter 9 and Section 2).
4   If you're working on a 1987 or 1988 model, remove the seat, left side cover, fuel tank and air filter housing (see Chapter 9, Section 2 and Section 4).
5   If you're working on a 1989 or later FZR750R model, remove the upper and lower fairing panels, fresh air duct, inner panels, seat, fuel tank and air filter housing (see Chapter 9, Section 2 and Section 4).
6   If you're working on a 1989 or later FZR1000, remove the seat, fuel tank, left side cover and air filter housing (see Chapter 9, Section 2 and Section 4).

All models

7   Check the battery condition and charge (see Chapter 1).
8   Check the main and ignition fuses, the ignition switch and the engine kill switch (see Chapter 10). Replace them if they're defective, then try the fuel pump again.

1987 and 1988 models

Pump won't run

Refer to illustrations 14.9, 14.11 and 14.12

9   If the pump won't run while the engine is running, or if it won't run for five seconds with the ignition switch On and the kill switch in Run, check battery voltage to the pump. Disconnect the electrical connector at the relay and connect a 20-volt DC voltmeter between the red/white wire terminal in the harness and a good grounding/earthing point (bare metal on the motorcycle frame) **(see illustration)**.
10   Turn the ignition switch to On and the engine kill switch to Run. The voltmeter should indicate at least 12 volts.
a) If the reading is less than 12 volts, check the wiring in the fuel pump circuit for breaks or bad connections. Be sure to check the battery terminal connections and the battery ground/earth cable connection to the motorcycle.

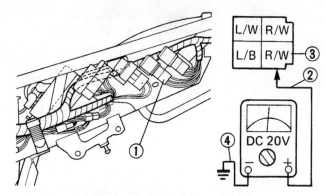

14.9 Connect a voltmeter to the relay connector

1   *Relay connector*
2   *Voltmeter positive lead*
3   *Red/white wire terminal*
4   *Voltmeter negative lead (to ground/earth)*

b) If the reading is at least 12 volts, the wiring is good. If the pump won't run with the engine running, go to Step 11. If the pump won't run for five seconds with the ignition switch On and the kill switch in Run, go to Step 12.
11   Connect a short length of wire between the blue/black wire terminal and the red/white wire terminal in the harness side of the relay connector **(see illustration)**. With the ignition switch On and the kill switch in Run, the fuel pump should run.
a) If the fuel pump won't run, test it (see below).
b) If the fuel pump now runs, check the wiring and connections in the fuel pump circuit. If they're good, the fuel pump relay is probably defective. Replace it.
12   Reconnect the connector to the fuel pump relay. Insert the voltmeter positive probe into the back of the blue/black wire connector and connect the voltmeter negative lead to ground/earth (bare metal on the motorcycle) **(see illustration)**. With the ignition switch On and the kill switch in Run, the voltmeter should indicate at least 11 volts.
a) If voltage is less than 11 volts, the fuel pump relay is probably defective. Replace it.
b) If voltage is 11 volts or more, check the wiring and connections in the fuel pump circuit. If they're good, the fuel pump is probably defective. Test it (see below).

Pump won't shut off after 30 seconds

13   Perform Steps 7 and 8 and Step 12 above.
a) If voltage is less than 11 volts in Step 12, the digital igniter is probably defective. Since it's an expensive part that can't be returned once purchased, consider having a Yamaha dealer verify your test results before replacing the igniter.

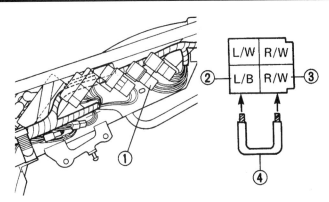

14.11 Connect a jumper wire between the blue/black and red/white wire terminals

1   Connector
2   Blue/black wire terminal
3   Red/white wire terminal
4   Jumper wire

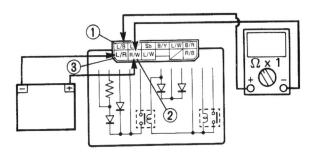

14.15a Connect a battery and ohmmeter to the relay connector

1   Blue/black terminal (ohmmeter positive lead)
2   Red/white terminal (ohmmeter negative lead and wire from battery positive terminal)
3   Blue/red terminal (wire from battery negative terminal)

15.3a The FZR600 fuel pump is mounted on the tank; slide the clamps (lower arrows) along the hoses, disconnect the hoses and remove the mounting nuts from the studs (upper arrows)

b) If voltage is 11 volts or more in Step 10, check the wiring and connections in the fuel pump circuit. If they're good, the fuel pump relay is probably defective. Replace it.

1989-on models

Refer to illustrations 14.15a and 14.15b

14   Perform Steps 8 and 9 above.

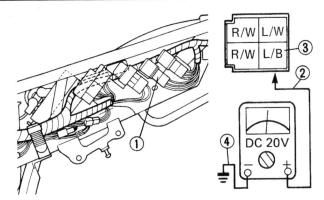

14.12 Connect a voltmeter to the relay connector

1   Relay connector
2   Voltmeter positive lead
3   Blue/black wire terminal
4   Voltmeter negative lead (to ground/earth)

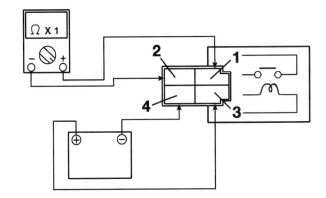

14.15b Connect a battery and ohmmeter to the relay connector

1   Ohmmeter positive lead (to red/white)
2   Ohmmeter negative lead (to blue/black)
3   Wire from battery positive terminal (to blue/white)
4   Wire from battery negative terminal (to blue/red)

15   Disconnect the wiring connector from the fuel pump relay **(see illustrations)**. Connect a 12-volt battery and an ohmmeter to the relay terminals shown. If the ohmmeter shows continuity, the relay is good. If not, replace the relay.
16   If the relay is good, test the fuel pump (see Step 17).

Fuel pump test (all models)

17   Disconnect the wiring connector from the fuel pump. Connect the pump directly to the battery with two lengths of wire (positive to blue/black; negative to black). If the pump doesn't run, replace it.

15   Fuel pump and relay - replacement

Fuel pump relay replacement

1   Disconnect the wiring connector from the relay.
2   Remove the relay from its mounting bracket, install a new one and reconnect the wiring connector.

Fuel pump replacement

All except 1989-on FZR750R models

Refer to illustrations 15.3a and 15.3b

3   Squeeze the fuel line clamps and push the ends of the fuel lines off the pump fittings **(see illustrations)**.

4   Disconnect the pump wiring connector. Remove the mounting
nuts or bolts and take the pump out.
5   Installation is the reverse of the removal steps. Connect the fuel
lines and wiring connector.

1989-on FZR750R models

6   Remove and drain the fuel tank (see Section 2).
7   Remove the pump mounting screws, then lower the pump and
gasket out of the tank (see illustration 2.23).
8   Installation is the reverse of the removal steps.

16   Air induction system (California FZR600 models) - inspection and component replacement

Refer to illustrations 16.1, 16.3a, 16.3b, 16.3c, 16.3d and 16.5

1   The air induction system uses exhaust gas pulses to suck fresh
air into the exhaust ports, where it mixes with hot combustion gases.
The additional oxygen provided by the fresh air allows combustion to
continue for a longer time, reducing unburned hydrocarbons in the exhaust (see illustration). Reed valves allow the flow of air into the ports
and prevent exhaust gas from flowing into the system. The air cut valve
shuts off the flow of air into the system during deceleration to prevent
backfiring.
2   Check the hoses for loose connections, damage and deterioration. Tighten or replace loose or damaged hoses.
3   To replace system components, unbolt the system mounting
plate from the frame (see illustration). Disconnect the air hose and the
metal tubes (see illustrations), then take the assembly off the motorcycle (see illustration).

**15.3b The FZR1000 fuel pump is mounted on the frame; slide the
clamps (lower arrow) along the hose, then disconnect the
lower hose and the upper hose (upper arrow)**

4   To replace the air cut valve, remove the retaining clip screw and
disconnect the hoses.
5   To replace reed valves, remove the mounting bolts and disconnect the hoses (see illustration).
6   Installation is the reverse of the removal steps.

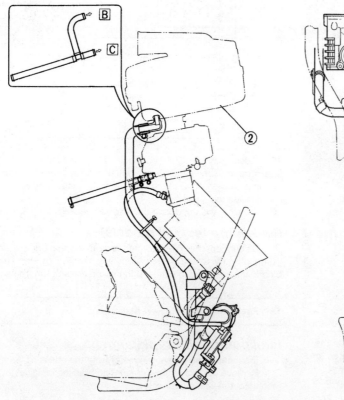

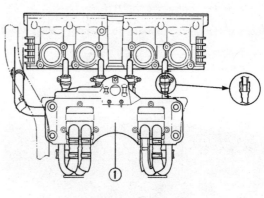

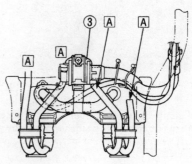

16.1 Air induction system details

1 *Reed valve assembly*	3 *Air cut valve*	B *To no. 3 cylinder*
2 *Air filter housing*	A *To cylinders*	C *To no. 4 cylinder*

16.3a Unbolt the reed valve assembly . . .

16.3b . . . disconnect the air intake hose . . .

16.3c . . . and the air induction tubes . . .

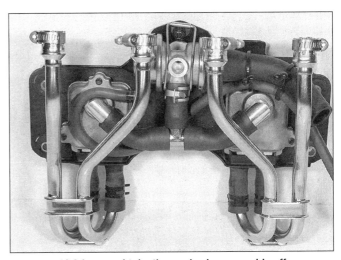

16.3d . . . and take the reed valve assembly off

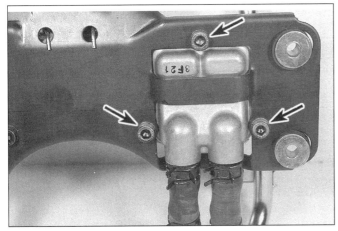

16.5 To remove a reed valve from the assembly, disconnect the hoses and remove the Allen bolts (arrows)

17 Evaporation control system (California models) - inspection and canister replacement

Refer to illustrations 17.1a, 17.1b, 17.3a and 17.3b

1 The evaporation control system used on California models prevents fuel vapor from escaping into the atmosphere. When the engine isn't running, the vapor is stored in a canister, then routed into the combustion chambers for burning when the engine starts **(see illustrations)**.

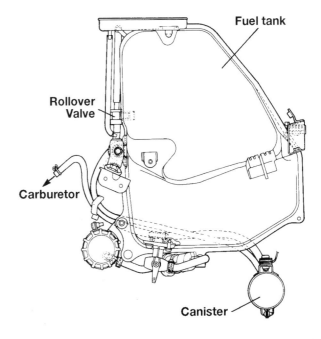

17.1a Evaporation control system details (FZR600 models)

5

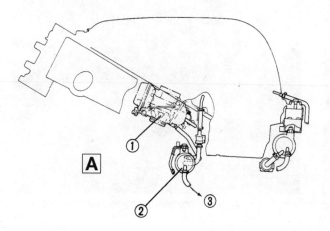

**17.1b Evaporation control system details
(FZR1000 models)**

1   Carburetor
2   Canister
3   To atmosphere
4   To carburetor
A   Side view
B   Bottom view

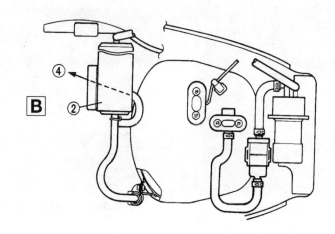

17.3a To remove the canister, disconnect the hoses and remove
the mounting bolts (this is an FZR600) . . .

17.3b . . . and this is an FZR1000

2   The hoses should be checked periodically for loose connections, damage and deterioration. Tighten or replace the hoses as needed.
3   To remove the canister, remove the seat and fuel tank (see Chapter 9 and Section 2). Disconnect the hoses and remove the mounting

bolts (see illustrations).
4   Inspect the rubber mounting bushings and replace them if they're cracked or deteriorated. Bolt the canister to its bracket and reconnect the hoses.

Chapter 6   Ignition system

Contents

Specifications

Ignition coil primary resistance	1.8 to 2.2 ohms at 20-degrees C (68-degrees F)
Ignition coil secondary resistance	
All except 1987 and 1988 UK FZR1000	9,600 to 14,400 ohms at 20-degrees C (68-degrees F)
1987 and 1988 UK FZR1000	10,800 to 13,200 ohms at 20-degrees C (68-degrees F)
Spark plug cap resistance	9,000 to 11,000 ohms at 20-degrees C (68-degrees F)
Arcing distance	6 mm (1/4 inch)
Pickup coil resistance	135 to 165 ohms at 20-degrees C (68-degrees F)
Ignition timing	Not adjustable
Spark plugs	See Chapter 1

1   General information

This motorcycle is equipped with a battery operated, fully transistorized, breakerless ignition system. The system consists of the following components:

Pickup coil
Igniter unit
Battery and fuse
Ignition coils
Spark plugs
Ignition (main) and engine kill (stop) switches
Primary and secondary circuit wiring

The transistorized ignition system functions on the same principle as a breaker point DC ignition system with the pickup unit and igniter performing the tasks previously associated with the breaker points and mechanical advance system. As a result, adjustment and maintenance of ignition components is eliminated (with the exception of spark plug replacement).

All models use a digital microprocessor and a single pickup coil. The digital microprocessor system also increases ignition coil primary current during starting, prevents excessive engine speed and controls the electric fuel pump.

Because of their nature, the individual ignition system components can be checked but not repaired. If ignition system troubles occur, and the faulty component can be isolated, the only cure for the problem is to replace the part with a new one. Keep in mind that most electrical parts, once purchased, can't be returned. To avoid unnecessary expense, make very sure the faulty component has been positively identified before buying a replacement part.

2   Ignition system - check

Refer to illustration 2.14
Warning: *Because of the very high voltage generated by the ignition system, extreme care should be taken when these checks are performed.*
1   If the ignition system is the suspected cause of poor engine performance or failure to start, a number of checks can be made to isolate the problem.
2   Make sure the engine kill switch is in the Run position.

Engine will not start

3   Disconnect one of the spark plug wires, connect the wire to a spare spark plug and lay the plug on the engine with the threads contacting the engine. If necessary, hold the spark plug with an insulated tool. Crank the engine over and make sure a well-defined, blue spark occurs between the spark plug electrodes. **Warning**: *Don't remove one of the spark plugs from the engine to perform this check - atomized fuel being pumped out of the open spark plug hole could ignite, causing severe injury!*
4   If no spark occurs, the following checks should be made:
5   Unscrew a spark plug cap from a plug wire and check the cap resistance with an ohmmeter. If the resistance exceeds Specifications, replace it with a new one. Repeat this check on the remaining plug caps.
6   Make sure all electrical connectors are clean and tight. Check all wires for shorts, opens and correct installation.
7   Check the battery voltage with a voltmeter and - on models equipped with batteries having removable filler caps - check the spe-

6

2.14 A simple spark gap testing fixture can be made from a block of wood, a large alligator clip, two nails, a screw and a piece of wire

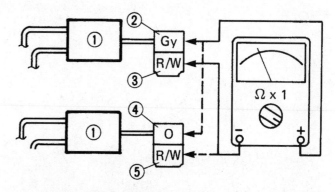

3.4 To test the coil primary resistance, connect the ohmmeter leads between the primary terminals in the coil connector

1   Coils
2   Gray wire terminal (cylinders 2 and 3)
3   Red/white wire terminal (cylinders 2 and 3)
4   Orange wire terminal (cylinders 1 and 4)
5   Red/white wire terminal (cylinders 1 and 4)

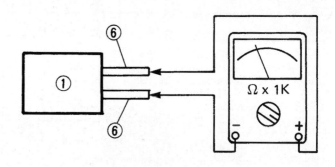

3.6 To test the coil secondary resistance, connect the ohmmeter between the spark plug wires

1   Coil
2   Spark plug wires

cific gravity with a hydrometer (see Chapter 1). If the voltage is less than 12-volts or if the specific gravity is low, recharge the battery.

8   Check the ignition fuse and the fuse connections. If the fuse is blown, replace it with a new one; if the connections are loose or corroded, clean or repair them.

9   Refer to Chapter 10 and check the ignition switch, engine kill switch, neutral switch and sidestand switch.

10   Refer to Section 3 and check the ignition coil primary and secondary resistance.

11   Refer to Section 4 and check the pickup coil resistance.

12   On 1989 and later models, disconnect the electrical connector from the relay assembly behind the left side cover (FZR600 and 1000) or under the seat (FZR750). Connect an ohmmeter as follows:
   a) Positive lead to relay assembly terminal pin that connects to blue-yellow wire;
   b) Negative lead to relay assembly terminal pin that connects to sky blue wire.

The ohmmeter should indicate continuity (little or no resistance). Switch the ohmmeter leads; it should now indicate very high or infinite resistance. If the readings aren't as described, the diode is bad and the relay assembly will have to be replaced. Before you buy this non-returnable part, have the ignition system tested by a Yamaha dealer or other qualified technician. **Note:** *If the preceding checks produce positive results but there is still no spark at the plug, the igniter may be at fault. Have the ignition system tested by a Yamaha dealer or other qualified technician.*

Engine starts but misfires

13   If the engine starts but misfires, make the following checks before deciding that the ignition system is at fault.

14   The ignition system must be able to produce a spark across a six millimeter (1/4-inch) gap (minimum). A simple test fixture **(see illustration)** can be constructed to make sure the minimum spark gap can be jumped. Make sure the fixture electrodes are positioned six millimeters apart.

15   Connect one of the spark plug wires to the protruding test fixture electrode, then attach the fixture's alligator clip to a good engine ground/earth.

16   Crank the engine over (it will probably start and run on the remaining cylinders) and see if well-defined, blue sparks occur between the test fixture electrodes. If the minimum spark gap test is positive, the ignition coil for that cylinder (and its companion cylinder) is functioning properly. Repeat the check on one of the spark plug wires that is connected to the other coil. If the spark will not jump the gap during either test, or if it is weak (orange colored), refer to steps 5 through 11 of this Section and perform the component checks described.

3   Ignition coils - check, removal and installation

Check

Refer to illustrations 3.4 and 3.6

1   In order to determine conclusively that the ignition coils are defective, they should be tested by an authorized Yamaha dealer service department which is equipped with the special electrical tester required for this check.

2   However, the coils can be checked visually (for cracks and other damage) and the primary and secondary coil resistances can be measured with an ohmmeter. If the coils are undamaged, and if the resistances are as specified, they are probably capable of proper operation.

3   To check the coils for physical damage, they must be removed (see Step 9). To check the resistances, simply remove the fuel tank (see Chapter 5), unplug the primary circuit electrical connectors from the coil(s) and remove the spark plug wires from the plugs that are connected to the coil being checked. Mark the locations of all wires before disconnecting them.

4   To check the coil primary resistance, attach one ohmmeter lead to one of the primary terminals and the other ohmmeter lead to the other primary terminal in the connector **(see illustration)**.

5   Place the ohmmeter selector switch in the Rx1 position and

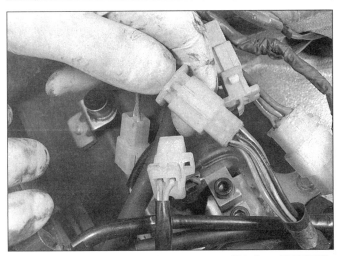

3.9 Disconnect the coil primary connectors (this is an FZR1000)

3.11 On FZR600 models with bracket-mounted coils, remove the bracket bolt (upper arrow); remove the coil mounting bolt (lower arrow) to separate the coils from the bracket

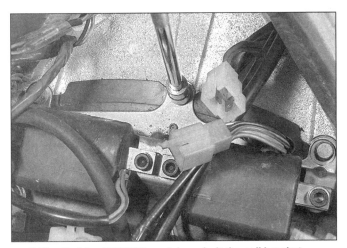

3.12a On later FZR1000 models, unbolt the coil bracket . . .

3.12b . . . lift the bracket out of the frame together with the coils . . .

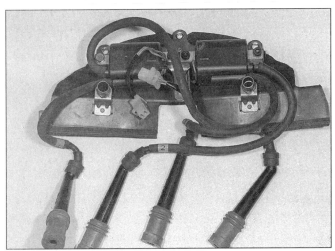

3.12c . . . and detach the coil(s) from the bracket

compare the measured resistance to the value listed in this Chapter's Specifications.

6   If the coil primary resistance is as specified, check the coil secondary resistance. Remove the spark plug caps, disconnect the meter leads from the primary terminals and attach them to the spark plug wire terminals (see illustration).

7   Place the ohmmeter selector switch in the Rx100 position and compare the measured resistance to the values listed in this Chapter's Specifications.

8   If the resistances are not as specified, the coil is probably defective and should be replaced with a new one.

Removal and installation

Refer to illustrations 3.9, 3.11, 3.12a, 3.12b and 3.12c

9   To remove the coils, refer to Chapter 5 and remove the fuel tank, then disconnect the spark plug wires from the plugs. Remove the coil cover (if equipped). After labeling them with tape to aid in reinstallation, unplug the coil primary circuit electrical connectors (see illustration).

10   If you're working on a model with separately mounted coils, remove the coil mounting bolt and take the coil out.

11   If you're working on an FZR600 with bracket-mounted coils, unbolt the bracket and remove it from the frame (see illustration). Remove the coil mounting bolt and take the coil(s) off the bracket.

12   If the coils are bracket-mounted, support the coils with one hand and remove the coil bracket mounting bolt, then withdraw the coil bracket (see illustrations). Unbolt the individual coil(s) from the bracket (see illustration).

13   Installation is the reverse of removal. Make sure the primary circuit electrical connectors are attached to the proper terminals and the plug wires to the correct plugs.

6

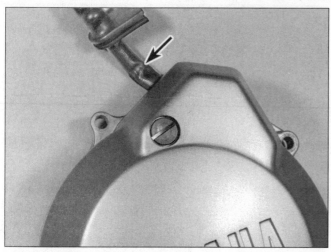

4.1a Follow the wiring harness (arrow) from behind the alternator cover to the connector, then disconnect the connector cover

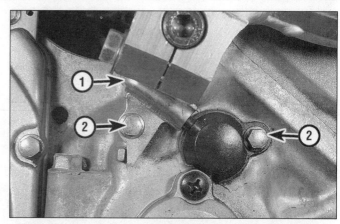

4.1b The wiring harness on FZR750/1000 models is protected by a metal cover

  1   Harness cover
  2   Pickup coil mounting bolts

---

4   Pickup coil - check, removal and installation

Check

Refer to illustrations 4.1a and 4.1b

1   Follow the wiring harness from the pickup coil to the connector, then unplug the connector **(see illustrations)**.
2   Probe the terminals in the pickup coil connector with an ohmmeter and compare the resistance reading with the value listed in this Chapter's Specifications.
3   Set the ohmmeter on the highest resistance range. Measure the resistance between a good ground and each terminal in the electrical connector. The meter should read infinity.
4   If the pickup coil fails either of the above tests, it must be replaced.

Removal

FZR600 models

Refer to illustration 4.6

5   Remove the alternator cover from the left side of the engine (see Chapter 10).
6   Unscrew the pickup coil mounting screws and remove the pickup coil **(see illustration)**.

FZR750/1000 models

7   Remove the pickup coil mounting bolts and remove the pickup coil from the right side of the engine **(see illustration 4.1b)**.

Installation

8   Installation is the reverse of the removal steps.

---

5   Igniter - check, removal and installation

Check

1   The igniter is checked by process of elimination (when all other possible causes have been checked and eliminated, the igniter is at fault). Because the igniter is expensive and can't be returned once purchased, consider having a Yamaha dealer test the ignition system before you buy a new igniter.

Removal and installation

Refer to illustrations 5.3a and 5.3b

2   Remove the seat (see Chapter 9).
3   Unplug the electrical connectors. Remove the mounting screws and take the igniter out **(see illustrations)**.
4   Installation is the reverse of the removal steps.

4.6 On FZR600 models, remove the mounting screws (arrows) and take the pickup coil out of the alternator cover

5.3a The digital igniter is mounted under the seat (this is an FZR600) . . .

5.3b . . . and this is an FZR1000 (FZR750 models similar)

Chapter 7 Frame, suspension and final drive

Contents

Specifications

7

General specifications

FZR600

Fork spring length	
Standard	415 mm (16.3 inches)
Minimum	410 mm (16.1 inches)
Fork oil capacity	435 cc (14.9 US fl oz, 15.3 Imp fl oz)
Fork oil level (fully compressed)	101 mm (3.98 inches) below top of inner fork tube
Rear spring free length	
Standard	180.5 mm (7.11 inches)
Minimum	170.5 mm (6.71 inches)
Rear spring installed length	170.0 mm (6.69 inches)
Swingarm end play and side play limits	1 mm (0.004 inch)
Suspension settings (rear spring preload)	
Hard	7
Standard	3
Soft	1

FZR750 (1987 and 1988)

Fork spring length	
Standard	529 mm (20.84 inches)
Minimum	524 mm (20.63 inches)
Fork oil capacity	434 cc (14.7 US fl oz, 15.31 Imp fl oz)
Fork oil level (fully compressed)	138 mm (5.43 inches) below top of inner fork tube
Swingarm end play and side play limits	1 mm (0.004 inch)
Front fork spring preload adjustment	
Minimum	Full counterclockwise (anti-clockwise)
Standard	Position 6
Maximum	Full clockwise
Front fork damping adjustment	
Minimum	Setting 1
Standard	Setting 2
Maximum	Setting 4
Rear spring preload adjustment	
Minimum	157 mm (6.2 inches)
Standard	175 mm (6.9 inches)
Maximum	180 mm (7.1 inches)
Rear shock damping adjustment	
Maximum (slower)	Zero
Standard	5 clicks out
Minimum (faster)	10 clicks out

FZR750 (1989-on)

Fork spring length	
Standard	367 mm (5.12 inches)
Minimum	363 mm (14.3 inches)
Fork oil capacity	437 cc (14.8 US fl oz, 15.4 Imp fl oz)
Fork oil level (fully compressed)	131 mm (5.16 inches) below top of inner fork tube
Swingarm end play and side play limits	1 mm (0.004 inch)
Front fork preload adjustment	
Maximum	Groove 1
Standard	Groove 6
Minimum	Groove 9
Front fork rebound damping adjustment	
Maximum	Fully turned in
Standard	8 clicks out from full-in
Minimum	10 clicks out from full-in
Front fork compression damping adjustment	
Maximum	Fully turned in
Standard	8 clicks out from full-in
Minimum	10 clicks out from full-in
Front fork height adjustment	
Highest	Groove 1
Lowest	Groove 5
Rear spring preload adjustment	
Maximum	15 mm (0.6 inch) on scale
Standard (and minimum)	Zero mm (zero inch) on scale
Rear shock rebound damping adjustment	
Maximum	Fully turned in
Standard	12 clicks out
Minimum (faster)	23 clicks out
Rear shock compression damping adjustment	
Maximum	Fully turned in
Standard	15 clicks out
Minimum (faster)	23 clicks out

FZR1000 (1987 and 1988)

Fork spring length	
Standard	533 mm (20.98 inches)
Minimum	528 mm (20.79 inches)
Fork oil capacity	425 cc (14.4 US fl oz, 15.0 Imp fl oz)
Fork oil level (fully compressed)	143 mm (5.63 inches) below top of inner fork tube
Swingarm end play and side play limits	1 mm (0.004 inch)
Front fork preload adjustment	
Maximum	Groove 1
Standard	Groove 5
Minimum	Groove 7

Rear spring preload adjustment length	
Maximum...	20.5 mm (0.81 inch)
Standard...	14.5 mm (0.57 inch)
Minimum...	12.5 mm (0.49 inch)
Recommended suspension settings	
With rider only	
Front...	Groove 4 to 7
Rear	12.5 to 16.5 mm (0.49 to 0.65 inch)
With passenger OR accessories and equipment	
Front...	Groove 2 to 5
Rear	14.5 to 18.5 mm (0.57 to 0.73 inch)
With passenger AND accessories and equipment	
Front...	Groove 1 to 4
Rear	16.5 to 20.5 mm (0.65 to 0.81 inch)

FZR1000 (1989)

Fork spring length	
Standard...	321.3 mm (12.6 inches)
Minimum...	318 mm (12.5 inches)
Fork oil capacity (fully compressed)	535 cc (18.1 US fl oz, 18.9 Imp fl oz)
Fork oil level (fully compressed)	116 mm (4.57 inches) below top of inner fork tube
Swingarm end play and side play limits	1 mm (0.004 inch)
Front fork preload adjustment	
Maximum...	4 (fully turned in)
Standard...	2
Minimum...	1
Rear spring preload adjustment length	
Maximum...	47.5 mm (1.87 inch)
Standard...	40.5 mm (1.59 inch)
Minimum...	37.5 mm (1.87 inch)
Rear shock damping adjustment	
Maximum...	Zero (fully turned in)
Standard...	7 clicks out
Minimum...	9 clicks out
Recommended suspension settings	
With rider only	
Front...	1 or 2
Rear preload	37.5 to 42.5 mm (1.48 to 1.67 inch)
Rear damping	5 to 9 clicks out
With passenger OR accessories and equipment	
Front...	2 or 3
Rear preload	40 to 45 mm (1.57 to 1.77 inch)
Rear damping	4 to 7 clicks out
With passenger AND accessories and equipment	
Front...	3 or 4
Rear preload	42.5 to 47.5 mm (1.57 to 1.77 inch)
Rear damping	3 to 6 clicks out

FZR1000 (1990-on)

Fork spring length	
1990	
Standard...	321.3 mm (12.6 inches)
Minimum...	318 mm (12.5 inches)
1991-on	
Standard...	331.5 mm (13.1 inches)
Minimum...	328 mm (12.9 inches)
Fork oil capacity	
1990	535 cc (18.1 US fl oz, 18.9 Imp fl oz)
1991-on...	462 cc (15.6 US fl oz, 16.3 Imp fl oz.
Fork oil level (fully compressed)	
1990	116 mm (4.57 inches) below top of inner fork tube
1991-on...	124 mm (4.88 inches) below top of inner fork tube
Swingarm end play and side play limits	1 mm (0.004 inch)
Front fork preload adjustment	
Maximum (hardest)...................................	Groove 1
Standard...	Groove 5
Minimum (softest)...................................	Groove 7
Rear spring preload adjustment length	
Maximum...	47.5 mm (1.87 inch)
Standard...	40.5 mm (1.59 inch)
Minimum...	37.5 mm (1.87 inch)

7

FZR1000 (1990-on) continued

Rear shock damping adjustment

Maximum..	Zero (full in)
Standard...	7 clicks out
Minimum...	9 clicks out

Recommended suspension settings

With rider only

Front..	Groove 4 to 7
Rear preload	37.5 to 42.5 mm (1.48 to 1.67 inch)
Rear damping	5 to 9 clicks out

With passenger OR accessories and equipment

Front..	Groove 2 to 5
Rear preload	40 to 45 mm (1.57 to 1.77 inch)
Rear damping	4 to 7 clicks out

With passenger AND accessories and equipment

Front..	Groove 1 to 4
Rear preload	42.5 to 47.5 mm (1.57 to 1.77 inch)
Rear damping	3 to 6 clicks out

Torque specifications

FZR600

Footpegs to bracket	55 Nm (40 ft-lbs)
Footpeg bracket to frame	22 Nm (16 ft-lbs)

Frame downtubes to frame

Front	60 Nm (43 ft-lbs)
Rear	33 Nm (24 ft-lbs)

Rear frame section to frame

Upper bolts (M10)	64 Nm (46 ft-lbs)
Lower bolts (M12)	88 Nm (64 ft-lbs)

Front forks

Cap bolt to fork	Not specified
Damper rod bolt	40 Nm (29 ft-lbs)*

Handlebars and steering stem

Handlebar to boss Allen bolts	23 Nm (17 ft-lbs)
Handlebar boss to fork tube pinch bolts	13 Nm 9.5 ft-lbs)
Lower triple clamp bolts	22 Nm (16 ft-lbs)
Upper triple clamp bolts	26 Nm (19 ft-lbs)
Steering stem nut	110 Nm (80 ft-lbs)
Grip weight to handlebar	25 Nm (18 ft-lbs)
Rear shock absorber pivot bolts/nuts	40 Nm (29 ft-lbs)

Rear suspension linkage

Relay arm to frame	40 Nm (29 ft-lbs)
Tie rods to relay arm	40 Nm (29 ft-lbs)
Tie rods to frame	40 Nm (29 ft-lbs)
Swingarm pivot shaft nut..	90 Nm (65 ft-lbs)
Drive chain front sprocket	60 Nm (43 ft-lbs)
Drive chain rear sprocket..	32 Nm (23 ft-lbs)
Engine sprocket cover bolts	10 Nm (7.2 ft-lbs)

FZR750 (1987 and 1988)

Footpegs to bracket	55 Nm (40 ft-lbs)
Front footpeg bracket to frame	28 Nm (20 ft-lbs)

Frame downtubes to frame

Front	63 Nm (46 ft-lbs)
Rear	28 Nm (20 ft-lbs)
Rear frame section to frame (M10)	55Nm (40 ft-lbs)

Front forks

Cap bolt to fork	23 Nm (17 ft-lbs)
Damper rod bolt	62 Nm (45 ft-lbs)*

Handlebars and steering stem

Handlebar to upper triple clamp Allen bolts	9 Nm (6.5 ft-lbs)
Handlebar to fork tube pinch bolts	20 Nm (14 ft-lbs)
Lower triple clamp bolts	20 Nm (14 ft-lbs)
Upper triple clamp bolts	20 Nm (14 ft-lbs)
Steering stem nut	110 Nm (80 ft-lbs)
Grip weight to handlebar	26 Nm (19 ft-lbs)

Rear shock absorber pivot bolts/nuts

Upper	42 Nm (30 ft-lbs)
Lower	40 Nm (28 ft-lbs)

Rear suspension linkage
    Relay arm to frame .... 48 Nm (35 ft-lbs)
    Tie rods to relay arm .... 74 Nm (54 ft-lbs)
    Tie rods to frame .... 74 Nm (54 ft-lbs)
Swingarm pivot shaft nut .... 90 Nm (65 ft-lbs)
Drive chain front sprocket nut .... 60 Nm (43 ft-lbs)
Drive chain rear sprocket nuts .... 55 Nm (40 ft-lbs)
Engine sprocket cover bolts .... Not specified

FZR750 (1989-on)

Front footpegs to bracket .... 55 Nm (40 ft-lbs)
Front footpeg bracket to frame .... 28 Nm (20 ft-lbs)
Rear frame section to frame (M8) .... 30 Nm (22 ft-lbs)
Front forks
    Cap bolt to fork .... 23 Nm (17 ft-lbs)
    Preload adjuster locknut .... 15 Nm (11 ft-lbs)
    Damper rod bolt .... 40 Nm (29 ft-lbs)*
Handlebars and steering stem
    Handlebar to spacer through-bolt .... 8 Nm (5.8 ft-lbs)
    Handlebar to fork tube clamp bolts .... 8 Nm (5.8 ft-lbs)
    Lower triple clamp bolts .... 23 Nm (17 ft-lbs)
    Upper triple clamp bolts .... 20 Nm (14 ft-lbs)
    Steering stem bolt .... 55 Nm (40 ft-lbs)
    Grip weight to handlebar .... 26 Nm (19 ft-lbs)
Rear shock absorber pivot bolts/nuts
    Upper .... 42 Nm (30 ft-lbs)
    Lower .... 40 Nm (28 ft-lbs)
Rear suspension linkage
    Relay arm to frame .... 45 Nm (32 ft-lbs)
    Tie rods to relay arm .... 70 Nm (50 ft-lbs)
    Tie rods to frame .... 70 Nm (50 ft-lbs)
Swingarm pivot shaft nut .... 130 Nm (94 ft-lbs)
Drive chain front sprocket nut .... 70 Nm (50 ft-lbs)
Drive chain rear sprocket nuts .... 55 Nm (40 ft-lbs)
Engine sprocket cover bolts .... 10 Nm (7.2 ft-lbs)

FZR1000 (1987 and 1988)

Footpegs to bracket .... 55 Nm (40 ft-lbs)
Front footpeg bracket to frame .... 28 Nm (20 ft-lbs)
Frame downtubes to frame
    Front .... 63 Nm (46 ft-lbs)
    Rear .... 28 Nm (20 ft-lbs)
Rear frame section to frame (M10) .... 55 Nm (40 ft-lbs)
Front forks
    Cap bolt to fork .... 23 Nm (17 ft-lbs)
    Damper rod bolt .... 62 Nm (45 ft-lbs)*
Handlebars and steering stem
    Handlebar to upper triple clamp Allen bolts .... 9 Nm (6.5 ft-lbs)
    Handlebar to fork tube pinch bolts .... 20 Nm (14 ft-lbs)
    Lower triple clamp bolts .... 20 Nm (14 ft-lbs)
    Upper triple clamp bolts .... 20 Nm (14 ft-lbs)
    Steering stem nut .... 110 Nm (80 ft-lbs)
    Grip weight to handlebar .... 26 Nm (19 ft-lbs)
Rear shock absorber pivot bolts/nuts
    Upper .... 42 Nm (30 ft-lbs)
    Lower .... 40 Nm (28 ft-lbs)
Rear suspension linkage
    Relay arm to frame .... 48 Nm (35 ft-lbs)
    Tie rods to relay arm .... 74 Nm (54 ft-lbs)
    Tie rods to frame .... 74 Nm (54 ft-lbs)
Swingarm pivot shaft nut .... 90 Nm (65 ft-lbs)
Drive chain front sprocket nut .... 70 Nm (50 ft-lbs)
Drive chain rear sprocket nuts .... 55 Nm (40 ft-lbs)
Engine sprocket cover bolts .... 10 Nm (7.2 ft-lbs)

FZR1000 (1989-on)

Footpegs to bracket .... 55 Nm (40 ft-lbs)
Footpeg brackets to frame .... 28 Nm (20 ft-lbs)
Rear frame section to frame (M10) .... 55 Nm (40 ft-lbs)

7

FZR1000 (1989-on) continued

Front forks	
Cap bolt to fork	
1989 and 1990	Not specified
1991-on	23 Nm (17 ft-lbs)
Adjuster bolt locknut (1991-on)	15 Nm (11 ft-lbs)
Damper rod bolt	
1989 and 1990	62 Nm (45 ft-lbs)*
1991-on	40 Nm 29 ft-lbs)
Handlebars and steering stem	
Handlebar boss to upper triple clamp Allen bolts	
1989 and 1990	20 Nm (14 ft-lbs)
1991-on	19 Nm (13 ft-lbs)
Handlebar to boss Allen bolts	28 Nm (20 ft-lbs)
Lower triple clamp bolts	23 Nm (17 ft-lbs)
Upper triple clamp bolts	23 Nm (17 ft-lbs)
Steering stem nut	110 Nm (80 ft-lbs)
Grip weight to handlebar	25 Nm (18 ft-lbs)
Rear shock absorber pivot bolts/nuts	
Upper	42 Nm (30 ft-lbs)
Lower	40 Nm (28 ft-lbs)
Rear suspension linkage	
Relay arm to frame	48 Nm (35 ft-lbs)
Tie rods to relay arm	74 Nm (54 ft-lbs)
Tie rods to frame	74 Nm (54 ft-lbs)
Swingarm pivot shaft nut..	130 Nm (94 ft-lbs)
Drive chain front sprocket nut	70 Nm (50 ft-lbs)
Drive chain rear sprocket nuts...	60 Nm (43 ft-lbs)
Engine sprocket cover bolts	10 Nm (7.2 ft-lbs)

Apply non-permanent thread locking agent to the damper rod bolt threads.

1   General information

FZR600 models and 1987 and 1988 FZR750/1000 models use a frame with detachable downtubes. The rear section of the frame on all models is detachable.

The front forks on FZR600 models, 1987 and 1988 FZR750R models and 1987 through 1990 FZR1000 models are of the conventional coil spring, hydraulically-damped telescopic type. The 1989 and later FZR750R and the 1991 and later FZR1000 use cartridge forks. The front forks on FZR750/1000 models include adjustments for fork spring preload; 750 models also include damping adjustments.

The rear suspension is Yamaha's Monocross design, which consists of a single shock absorber, a linkage which provides progressive damping and spring rate, and a swingarm. The shock absorber preload is adjustable on all models. The damping settings are adjustable on 750 and later 1000 models.

The final drive uses an endless chain (which means it doesn't have a master link). A rubber damper (often called a "cush drive") is installed between the rear wheel coupling and the wheel.

2   Frame - inspection and repair

1   The frame should not require attention unless accident damage has occurred. In most cases, frame replacement is the only satisfactory remedy for such damage. A few frame specialists have the jigs and other equipment necessary for straightening the frame to the required standard of accuracy, but even then there is no simple way of assessing to what extent the frame may have been overstressed.

2   After the machine has accumulated a lot of miles, the frame should be examined closely for signs of cracking or splitting at the welded joints. Corrosion can also cause weakness at these joints. Loose engine mount bolts can cause ovaling or fracturing of the mounting tabs. Minor damage can often be repaired by welding, depending on the extent and nature of the damage.

3   Remember that a frame which is out of alignment will cause handling problems. If misalignment is suspected as the result of an accident, it will be necessary to strip the machine completely so the frame can be thoroughly checked.

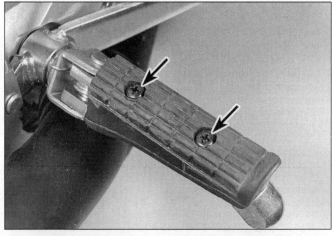

3.1 The footpeg pads are secured by screws (arrows)

3   Footpegs and pads - removal and installation

Refer to illustrations 3.1, 3.2, 3.4a and 3.4b

All except 1989-on FZR750 models

1   To replace a rubber pad, remove the screws and lift it off **(see illustration)**. Position the new pad and install the screws.

2   To remove a front footpeg, detach the brake master cylinder pushrod, brake pedal spring and stoplight switch spring (right side) or gearshift linkage (left side). Unbolt the footpeg bracket from the frame **(see illustration)**.

3   Remove the Allen bolt that secures the footpeg to the bracket and remove the footpeg and brake pedal.

4   To remove a rear footpeg from its bracket, remove the cotter pin and pivot pin (or pivot bolt and nut) and take the footpeg off **(see illustrations)**. To remove the bracket, unbolt the muffler/silencer bracket from it (right side only). Unbolt the footpeg bracket from the frame.

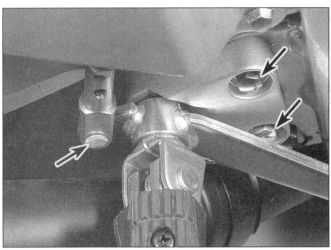

3.2 The right footpeg includes a brake pedal pivot; to remove the assembly, remove the brake master cylinder clevis pin (left arrow) and remove the bracket bolts (right arrows) (FZR600 shown)

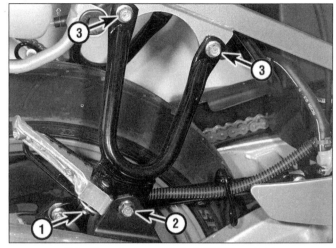

3.4a Rear footpeg details (FZR600 models)

1 Footpeg pivot pin   3 Footpeg bracket bolts
2 Muffler/silencer mounting
   bolt (right side only)

3.4b Rear footpeg details (FZR1000 models)

1 Footpeg pivot bolt   3 Footpeg bracket bolts
2 Muffler/silencer mounting
   bracket (right side only)

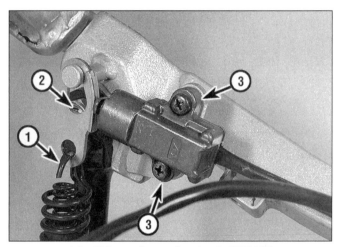

4.1a Sidestand mounting details (FZR600)

1 Retracting springs   3 Switch mounting screws
2 Pivot nut

1989-on FZR750 models

5 Remove the bolt from underneath the footpeg and withdraw the footpeg from its bracket.

All models

6 Installation is the reverse of removal. Lubricate the footpeg pivot as well as the bearing surfaces of the brake pedal and gearshift linkage arm (if removed). Tighten the bracket-to-frame and footpeg-to-bracket bolts to the torque listed in this Chapter's Specifications. Use new cotter pins. Adjust the gearshift linkage (see Chapter 1).

---

4 Sidestand - maintenance

Refer to illustrations 4.1a and 4.1b

1 The sidestand is attached to a bracket on the frame. An extension spring(s) anchored to the bracket ensures that the stand is held in the retracted position **(see illustrations)**.

2 Make sure the pivot bolt is tight and the extension spring is in good condition and not overstretched. An accident is almost certain to occur if the stand extends while the machine is in motion.

4.1b Sidestand mounting details (1989-on FZR1000)

1 Switch bracket bolts   3 Sidestand pivot bolt
2 Sidestand bracket bolts

7

5.2 The handlebar is secured to the boss by an Allen bolt behind this plastic plug (arrow)

5.3a The handlebar boss is secured by pinch bolts (arrows) . . .

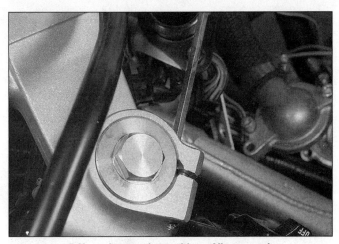

5.3b . . . loosen them with an Allen wrench

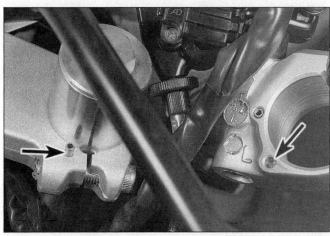

5.5 Align the pin with the hole (arrows)

5   Handlebars - removal and installation

1   The handlebars on all except 1989 and later FZR750 models are individual assemblies that slip over the tops of the fork tubes, each being retained by pinch bolts. The handlebars on 1989 and later FZR750 models are individual assemblies which are secured to the fork tubes by integral clamps.

FZR600 models
Refer to illustrations 5.2, 5.3a, 5.3b and 5.5

2   If you're going to remove the handlebar from the handlebar boss, remove the rubber plug and remove the Allen bolt that secures the bar **(see illustration)**.

3   If the handlebars must be removed for access to other components, such as the forks or the steering head, simply remove the bolts and slip the handlebar(s) off the fork tubes **(see illustrations)**. It's not necessary to disconnect the cables, wires or hoses, but it is a good idea to support the assembly with a piece of wire or rope, to avoid unnecessary strain on the cables, wires and the brake or clutch hose.

4   If the handlebars are to be removed completely, refer to Chapter 2 for clutch cable removal procedures, Chapter 8 for the brake master cylinder removal procedures, Chapter 5 for the throttle cable removal procedure and Chapter 10 for the switch removal procedure.

5   Check the handlebars for cracks and distortion and replace them if any undesirable conditions are found. When installing the handlebars, align the pin in the upper triple clamp with the hole in the handlebar boss **(see illustration)**. Tighten the bolts to the torque listed in this Chapter's Specifications.

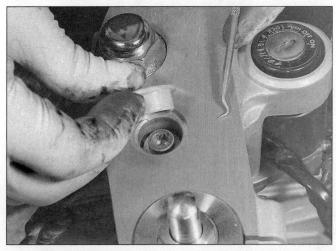

5.6a Pry out the plastic plugs with a pointed tool . . .

FZR750/1000 models (except 1989-on FZR750R)
Refer to illustrations 5.6a, 5.6b, 5.7, 5.8, 5.9a and 5.9b

6   Pry the plastic plugs out of the upper triple clamp, then remove the Allen bolts that secure the triple clamp to the handlebars **(see illustrations)**.

7   Remove the steering stem nut. Loosen the pinch bolts that secure the upper triple clamp to the forks and lift the triple clamp off **(see illustration)**.

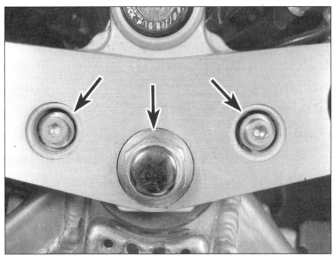

5.6b . . . and remove the Allen bolts that locate the handlebar bosses, then remove the steering stem nut (arrows)

5.7 Loosen the pinch bolts with an Allen wrench

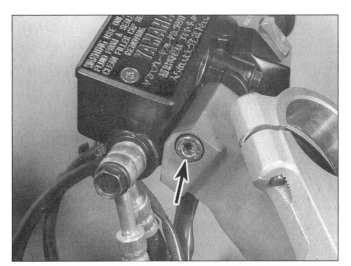

5.8 Remove the Allen bolt (arrow) to separate the handlebar from the boss

5.9a Note the location of the rubber dampers (1989-on FZR1000; the upper one fits on top of the handlebar boss (arrow) . . .

8   To remove the handlebar from the handlebar boss on 1989 and later FZR1000 models, remove the Allen bolt that secures the handlebar (see illustration).

9   If the handlebars must be removed for access to other components, such as the forks or the steering head, simply slip the handlebar(s) off the fork tubes (see illustrations). It's not necessary to disconnect the cables, wires or hoses, but it is a good idea to support the assembly with a piece of wire or rope, to avoid unnecessary strain on the cables, wires and the brake or clutch hose.

10   If the handlebars are to be removed completely, refer to Chapter 3 for clutch master cylinder removal procedures, Chapter 8 for the brake master cylinder removal procedures, Chapter 5 for the throttle cable removal procedure and Chapter 10 for the switch removal procedure.

11   Check the handlebars for cracks and distortion and replace them if any undesirable conditions are found. Be sure to reinstall the handlebar dampers (1989 and later FZR1000 models). Tighten the bolts to the torque listed in this Chapter's Specifications.

1989-on FZR750

Refer to illustration 5.15

12   Remove the clutch lever bracket from the left handlebar.

13   Remove the master cylinder and its reservoir from the right handlebar.

5.9b . . . while the lower damper fits over the fork tube

14   Disconnect the brake light switch electrical connectors and remove the handlebar switches (see Chapter 10).

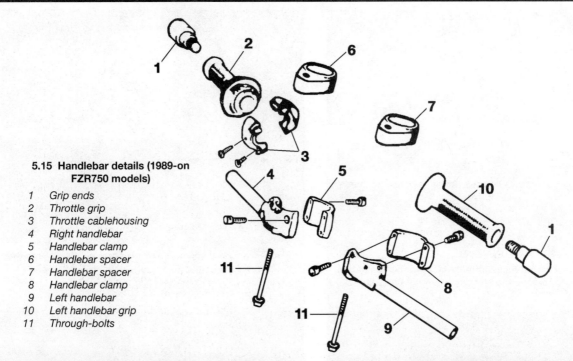

5.15 Handlebar details (1989-on FZR750 models)

1   Grip ends
2   Throttle grip
3   Throttle cablehousing
4   Right handlebar
5   Handlebar clamp
6   Handlebar spacer
7   Handlebar spacer
8   Handlebar clamp
9   Left handlebar
10   Left handlebar grip
11   Through-bolts

6.3a Unscrew the fork cap (this is an FZR600) . . .

6.3b . . . and this is an FZR1000 equipped with spring preload adjusters

15   Unscrew the grip ends and take off the left handlebar grip **(see illustration)**.

16   Pull back the rubber cover and separate the halves of the throttle cable housing.

17   Disconnect the throttle cables and remove the throttle grip.

18   Remove the handlebar clamp bolts, followed by the long through-bolt and remove the handlebar.

19   Installation is the reverse of the removal steps. Slide the spacer up against its triple clamp and install the handlebar and its clamp. Insert the long through-bolt through the hole in the spacer and thread it into the triple clamp. Tighten the clamp bolts to the torque listed in this Chapter's specification (tighten the inner bolts fully before tightening the outer bolts).

6   Fork oil change

Conventional forks

Refer to illustrations 6.3a, 6.3b, 6.3c, 6.3d, 6.4, 6.6, 6.7 and 6.9

1   Support the bike securely so it can't be knocked over during this procedure. Remove the fairing and position a jack with a block of wood on the jack head under the engine to support the motorcycle when the fork cap bolts are removed.

6.3c On FZR750/1000 models, lift out the spring washer (arrow) . .

2   Loosen the handlebar pinch bolts (FZR600) or the upper triple clamp pinch bolts (FZR750/1000).

3   Unscrew the fork cap and lift it out **(see illustrations)**. If you're working on an FZR750/1000, lift out the spring washer **(see illustra-**

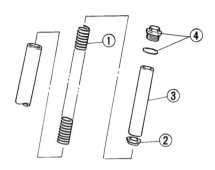

6.3d . . . and on all models remove the spacer, spring seat
and spring

1 Spring 3 Spacer
2 Spring seat 4 Fork cap and O-ring

6.4 Remove the fork drain screw (arrow) and its gasket

6.6 Replace the O-ring on the fork cap if it's damaged
or deteriorated

6.7 Pour the specified amount of fork oil into the top of the fork

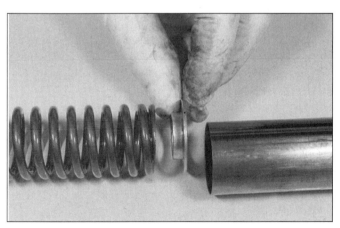

6.9 The spring seat fits on the spring like this

the drain screw with solvent and let it dry, then install the screw and gasket, tightening it securely.
7 Pour the type and amount of fork oil, listed in this Chapter's Specifications, into the fork tube through the opening at the top (see illustration).
8 Remove the jack from under the engine and slowly pump the forks a few times to purge the air. Measure the level of the oil in the fork with the fork fully compressed and without the spring in position. Compare it to the value listed in this Chapter's Specifications. Add or remove oil as necessary.
9 Install the spring, spring seat and spacer (see illustration). If you're working on an FZR750/1000, install the spring washer.
10 Coat the O-ring on the cap bolt with a thin layer of multi-purpose grease.
11 Install the O-ring and the cap bolt. Tighten the cap bolt securely.
12 The remainder of installation is the reverse of the removal steps. Tighten all fasteners to the torque listed in this Chapter's Specifications.

Cartridge forks

13 Changing the oil in cartridge forks requires removal and partial disassembly of the forks (see Section 9).

7 Forks - removal and installation

Removal

1 Support the bike securely so it can't be knocked over during this procedure.
2 Place a jack under the engine and raise it slightly to lift the front tire off the ground.

tion). On all models, remove the spacer, spring seat and spring (see illustration).
4 Place a drain pan under the fork leg and remove the drain screw (see illustration). Warning: Do not allow fork oil to contact the brake discs, pads or tire. If it does, clean the discs with brake system cleaner, replace the pads with new ones or wash the tire clean before riding the motorcycle.
5 After most of the oil has drained, slowly compress and release the forks to pump out the remaining oil. An assistant will most likely be required to do this.
6 Check the drain screw gasket and fork cap O-ring for damage and replace them if necessary (see illustration). Clean the threads of

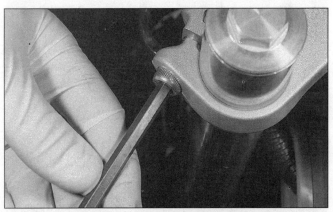

7.9a Loosen the upper triple clamp bolt . . .

7.9b . . . and the lower triple clamp bolt

7.14 The forks are held in the lower triple clamps by a pair
of clamp bolts

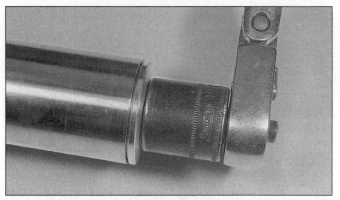

8.2a Remove the fork cap with a socket or box wrench
(ring spanner)

3   Remove the brake calipers and front wheel (see Chapter 8).
4   Remove the front fender (see Chapter 9).

FZR600 models

Refer to illustrations 7.9a and 7.9b

5   Loosen the clamp bolts in the handlebar bosses, then lift the handlebars off the forks and support them from
above (see Section 5).
6   Remove any wiring harness clamps or straps from the fork tubes.
7   If the fork will be disassembled after removal, read through the disassembly procedure (see Section 8), paying special attention to the damper rod bolt removal steps. If you don't have the necessary special tool or a substitute for it, you can remove the damper rod bolt before the fork is disassembled, while the spring tension will keep the damper rod from spinning inside the fork tube.
8   If the forks will be disassembled after removal, refer to Section 6 and loosen the fork caps.
9   Loosen the fork upper and lower triple clamp bolts **(see illustrations)**, then slide the fork tubes down and remove the forks from the motorcycle.

1987 and 1988 FZR750; all FZR1000 models

Refer to illustration 7.14

10   Remove the left, right and front fairing panels and the seat (see Chapter 9).
11   Remove the fuel tank and the air cleaner housing (see Chapter 5).
12   Disconnect the electrical connector for the ignition switch. On 1991 and later models, remove the tie wrap that secures the horn wiring connector.
13   Remove the upper triple clamp and the handlebars (see Section 5).
14   Loosen the lower triple clamp bolts **(see illustration)**, then slide the fork tubes down and remove the forks from the motorcycle.

1989-on FZR750 models

15   Remove the lower fairing (see Chapter 9).
16   Remove the handlebars (see Section 5).
17   Loosen the upper and lower triple clamp bolts, then slide the fork tubes down and remove the forks and handlebar spacers from the motorcycle.

Installation

18   Slide each fork leg into the lower triple clamp.
19   Slide the fork legs up, installing the tops of the tubes into the upper triple clamp. Position the top of the fork tube the distance above the upper triple clamp listed in this Chapter's Specifications.
20   The remainder of installation is the reverse of the removal procedure. Tighten all fasteners to the torques listed in this Chapter's Specifications and the Chapter 8 Specifications.
21   Pump the front brake lever several times to bring the pads into contact with the discs.

***

8   Conventional forks - disassembly, inspection and reassembly

FZR600 models

Disassembly

Refer to illustrations 8.2a, 8.2b, 8.3, 8.4, 8.5, 8.6a, 8.6b, 8.8, 8.9 and 8.10

1   Remove the forks following the procedure in Section 6. Work on one fork leg at a time to avoid mixing up the parts.
2   Remove the fork cap and O-ring (it should have been loosened before the forks were removed) **(see illustrations)**. Remove the spacer, spring seat and spring.
3   Invert the fork assembly over a container and allow the oil to drain

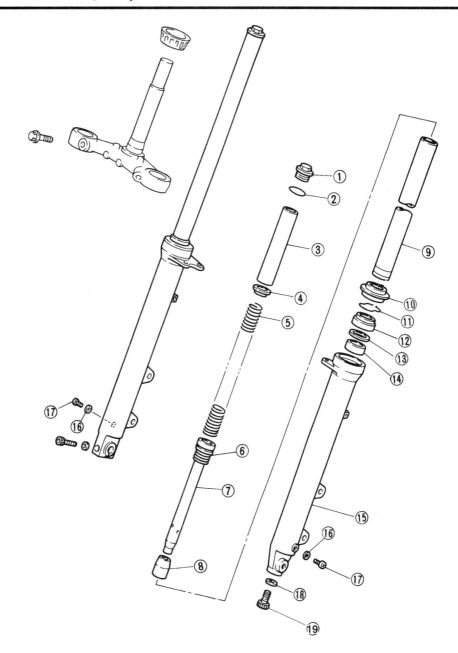

8.2b Front fork (FZR600 models) - exploded view

1 Fork cap
2 O-ring
3 Spacer
4 Spring seat
5 Spring
6 Rebound spring
7 Damper rod
8 Oil lock piece
9 Inner fork tube
10 Dust seal
11 Retainer
12 Oil seal
13 Seal spacer
14 Guide bushing
15 Outer fork tube
16 Gasket
17 Drain screw
18 Copper washer
19 Damper rod bolt

out **(see illustration)**.

4 Pry the dust seal from the outer tube **(see illustration)**.

5 Pry the retaining ring from its groove in the outer tube **(see illustration)**. Remove the ring and the washer that's present underneath it.

6 Prevent the damper rod from turning using a holding handle (Yamaha tool no. YM-01326, part no. 90890-01326) and adapter (Yamaha tool no. YM-01300-01, part no. 90890-01294) **(see illustration)**. Unscrew the Allen bolt at the bottom of the outer tube and remove the copper washer **(see illustration)**.

7 Pull the damper rod and the rebound spring from the top of the fork tube. Don't remove the Teflon ring from the damper rod unless a new one will be installed.

8 Hold the outer tube and yank the inner tube away from it, repeatedly (like a slide hammer), until the seal and outer tube guide bushing pop loose **(see illustration)**.

9 Remove the oil lock piece **(see illustration)**.

10 Slide the oil seal, spacer and guide bushing from the inner tube **(see illustration)**.

8.3 Pour the oil into a pan

8.4 Pry the dust seal out of the outer fork tube

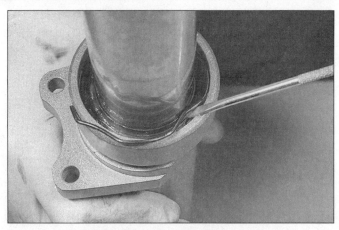

8.5 Pry the retainer out of its groove

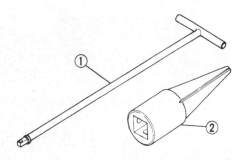

8.6a This special tool is inserted from the top of the fork to hold the damper rod from turning while the damper rod bolt is loosened or tightened

1 Handle   2 Adapter

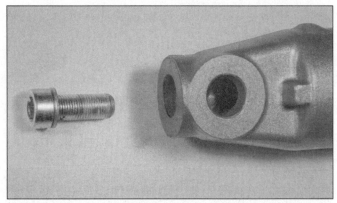

8.6b Remove the damper rod bolt and copper washer

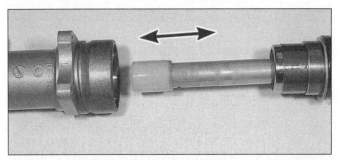

8.8 Use a slide-hammer motion to separate the outer tube guide bushing from the outer tube

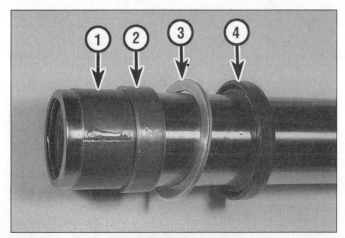

8.10 Once the fork tubes are separated, slide the oil seal, spacer and guide bushing off the inner fork tube

1 Slide bushing   3 Seal spacer
2 Guide bushing   4 Oil seal

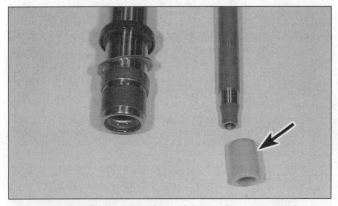

8.9 The oil lock piece (arrow) fits on the narrow end of the damper rod

Inspection

11 Clean all parts in solvent and blow them dry with compressed air, if available. Check the inner and outer fork tubes, the guide bushings and the damper rod for score marks, scratches, flaking of the chrome and excessive or abnormal wear. Look for dents in the tubes and replace them if any are found. Check the fork seal seat for nicks, gouges and scratches. If damage is evident, leaks will occur around the seal-to-outer tube junction. Replace worn or defective parts with new ones.

8.16a Let the damper rod protrude from the inner fork tube and install the oil lock piece . . .

8.16b . . . the damper rod and oil lock piece should look like this when they're assembled

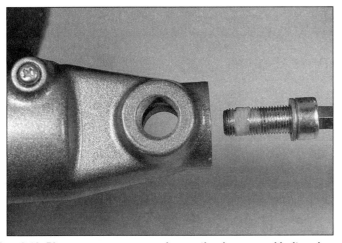

8.18 Place a new copper washer on the damper rod bolt and apply non-permanent thread locking agent to the threads, then install the bolt

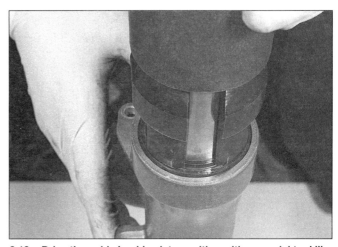

8.19a Drive the guide bushing into position with a special tool like this one . . .

12 Have the inner fork tube checked for runout at a dealer service department or other repair shop. **Warning:** *If it is bent, it should not be straightened; replace it with a new one.*

13 Measure the overall length of the long spring and check it for cracks and other damage. Compare the length to the minimum length listed in this Chapter's Specifications. If it's defective or sagged, re-place both fork springs with new ones. Never replace only one spring.

Reassembly

Refer to illustrations 8.16a, 8.16b, 8.18, 8.19a, 8.19b, 8.21, 8.22 and 8.23

14 Always replace the slide bushing (the one that won't come off that's on the bottom of the inner tube) (see illustration 8.10). Pry it apart at the slit and slide it off. Make sure the new one seats properly.

15 Install the rebound spring on the damper rod. Install the damper rod in the inner fork tube, then let it slide slowly down until it protrudes from the bottom of the inner fork tube.

16 Install the oil lock piece over the end of the damper rod that pro-trudes from the fork tube **(see illustrations)**.

17 Install the inner fork tube in the outer fork tube.

18 Apply non-permanent thread locking agent to the damper rod bolt, then install the bolt and tighten it to the torque listed in this Chap-ter's Specifications **(see illustration)**. Hold the damper rod from turn-ing with the tool used in Step 6. **Note:** *If you didn't use the tool, tighten the damper rod bolt after the fork spring and cap bolt are installed.*

19 Slide the outer guide bushing down the inner tube. Using a spe-cial bushing driver (Yamaha tool no. YM-33963 and 01372, part nos. 90890-01367 and 90890-01372 or equivalent) and a used guide bush-

8.19b . . . if you don't have the proper tool, a section of pipe can be used the same way the special tool would be used - as a slide hammer (be sure to tape the ends of the pipe so it doesn't scratch the fork tube)

ing placed on top of the guide bushing being installed, drive the bush-ing into place until it is fully seated. If you don't have access to one of these tools, it is highly recommended that you take the assembly to a Yamaha dealer service department or other motorcycle repair shop to have this done. It is possible, however, to drive the bushing into place

7

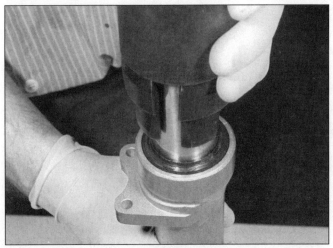

8.21 Tap the new oil seal into its bore with the same tool used for the guide bushing

8.22 Make sure the retainer is seated securely in its groove

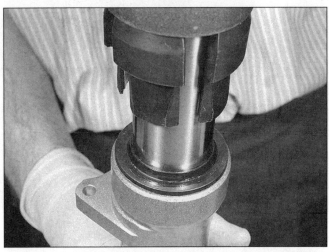

8.23 Tap the dust seal into its bore with the same tool used for the guide bushing

8.30a Remove the spring seat and spring

using a section of pipe and an old guide bushing **(see illustrations)**. Wrap tape around the ends of the pipe to prevent it from scratching the fork tube.

20   Slide the oil seal spacer down the inner tube, into position over the guide bushing.

21   Lubricate the lips and the outer diameter of the oil seal with the recommended fork oil (see Chapter 1) and slide it down the inner tube, with the seal lip facing up. Drive the seal into place with the same tools used to drive in the guide bushing **(see illustration)**. If you don't have access to these, it is recommended that you take the assembly to a Yamaha dealer service department or other motorcycle repair shop to have the seal driven in. If you are very careful, the seal can be driven in with a hammer and a drift punch. Work around the circumference of the seal, tapping gently on the outer edge of the seal until it's seated. Be careful - if you distort the seal, you'll have to disassemble the fork again and end up taking it to a dealer anyway!

22   Install the retainer, making sure the ring is completely seated in its groove **(see illustration)**.

23   Install the dust seal, making sure it seats completely **(see illustration)**. The same tool used to drive in the oil seal can be used for the dust seal.

24   Install the drain screw and a new gasket, if it was removed.

25   Add the recommended type and amount of fork oil (see Section 6).

26   Install the fork spring, with the closer-wound coils at the top. In-

stall the spring seat and spacer.

27   Install the O-ring and fork cap.

28   Install the fork by following the procedure outlined in Section 7. If you won't be installing the fork right away, store it in an upright position.

1987 and 1988 FZR750 models and 1987 through 1990 FZR1000 models

Disassembly

Refer to illustrations 8.30a, 8.30b, 8.31, 8.32, 8.33, 8.34a, 8.34b, 8.35, 8.36, 8.37 and 8.38

29   Remove the forks following the procedure in Section 7. Work on one fork leg at a time to avoid mixing up the parts.

30   Remove the fork cap and O-ring (it should have been loosened before the forks were removed). Remove the spring washer **(see illustration 6.3c)**, spacer, spring seat and spring **(see illustrations)**.

31   Invert the fork assembly over a container and allow the oil to drain out **(see illustration)**.

32   Pry the dust seal from the outer tube **(see illustration)**.

33   Pry the retaining ring from its groove in the outer tube **(see illustration)**.

34   Prevent the damper rod from turning using a holding handle (Yamaha tool no. YM-01326, part no. 90890-01326) and adapter **(see illustration)**.

8.30b Front fork details (1987 and 1988 FZR750R and 1987 through 1990 FZR1000 models)

1 Fork cap
2 O-ring
3 Spring washer
4 Spacer
5 Spring seat
6 Fork spring
7 Rebound spring
8 Damper rod
9 Inner fork tube
10 Slide bushing
11 Oil lock piece
12 Dust seal
13 Retainer
14 Oil seal
15 Seal spacer
16 Guide bushing
17 Outer fork tube
18 Drain screw
19 Gasket
20 Copper washer
21 Damper rod bolt

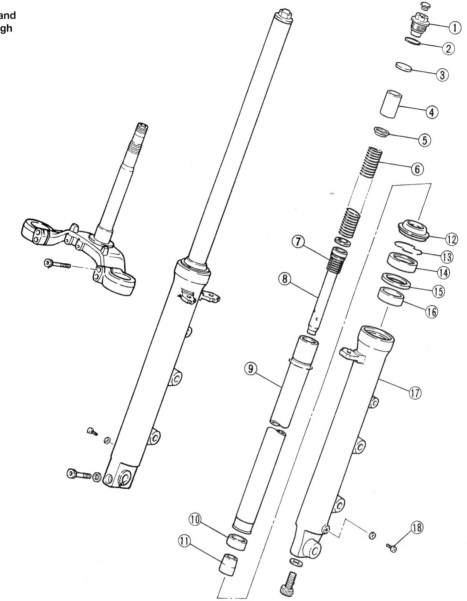

a) For FZR750 models, the adapter is Yamaha tool no. YM-33298. The hex size is 27 mm.
b) For FZR1000 models, the adapter is YM-01327 (part no. 90890-01327). The hex size is 30 mm.
Unscrew the Allen bolt at the bottom of the outer tube and remove the copper washer **(see illustration)**.
35   Pull out the damper rod and the rebound spring **(see illustration)**. Don't remove the Teflon ring from the damper rod unless a new one will be installed.
36   Hold the outer tube and yank the inner tube away from it, repeatedly (like a slide hammer), until the seal and outer tube guide bushing pop loose **(see illustration)**.
37   Remove the oil lock piece **(see illustration)**.
38   Slide the oil seal, spacer and guide bushing from the inner tube **(see illustration)**.

Inspection

39   Perform Steps 11 through 13 above to inspect the fork components.

8.31 Let the oil drain into a container

8.32 Pry the dust seal out of its bore, taking care not to scratch the fork tube

8.33 Pry the retainer out of its groove

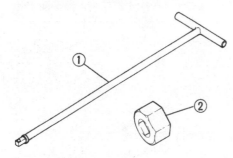

8.34a These are the Yamaha special tools used to hold the damper rod from turning

1   Handle   2   Adapter

8.34b Unscrew the damper rod bolt with an Allen bolt bit

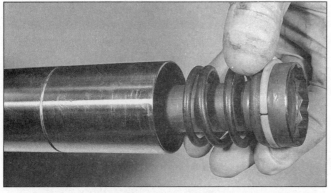

8.35 Remove the damper rod and rebound spring from the fork tube

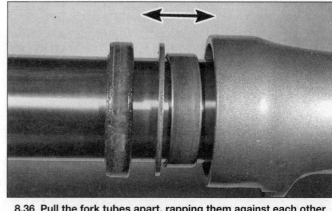

8.36 Pull the fork tubes apart, rapping them against each other like a slide hammer, until the tubes separate and the oil seal and guide bushing emerge

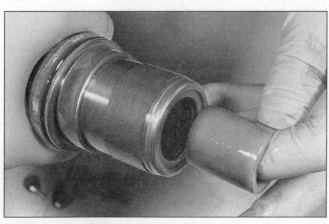

8.37 Remove the oil lock piece

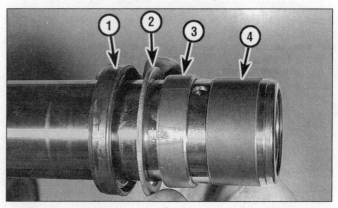

8.38 Slide the oil seal, spacer and guide bushing off the inner fork tube

1   Oil seal   3   Guide bushing
2   Spacer   4   Slide bushing

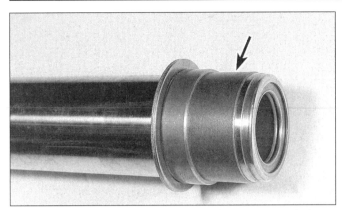

8.40 Replace the slide bushing (arrow) whenever the fork is overhauled

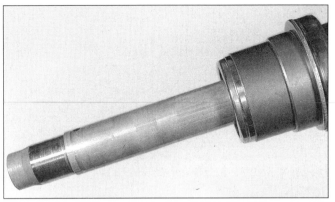

8.41 Install the damper rod in the inner fork tube and let it slide down until it emerges from the bottom end like this

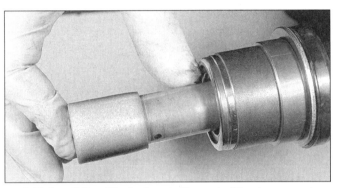

8.42 Install the oil lock piece on the end of the damper rod

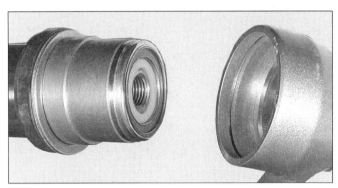

8.43 Assemble the inner and outer fork tubes

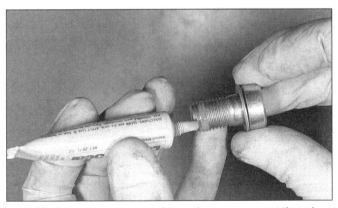

8.44 Use a new copper washer and non-permanent thread locking agent on the damper rod bolt

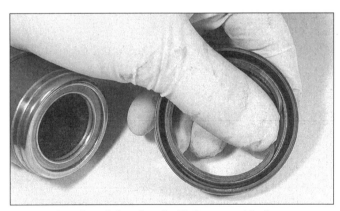

8.47 Install the oil seal with the open side down

Reassembly

Refer to illustrations 8.40, 8.41, 8.42, 8.43, 8.44 and 8.47

40   Always replace the slide bushing (the one that won't come off that's on the bottom of the inner tube) **(see illustration)**. Pry it apart at the slit and slide it off. Make sure the new one seats properly.

41   Install the rebound spring on the damper rod. Install the damper rod in the inner fork tube, then let it slide slowly down until it protrudes from the bottom of the inner fork tube **(see illustration)**.

42   Install the oil lock piece over the end of the damper rod that protrudes from the fork tube **(see illustration)**.

43   Install the inner fork tube in the outer fork tube **(see illustration)**.

44   Apply non-permanent thread locking agent to the damper rod bolt, then install the bolt and tighten it to the torque listed in this Chapter's Specifications **(see illustration)**. Hold the damper rod from turning with the tool used in Step 34. **Note:** *If you didn't use the tool, tighten the damper rod bolt after the fork spring and cap bolt are installed.*

45   Install the outer guide bushing (see Step 19 above).

46   Slide the oil seal spacer down the inner tube, into position over the guide bushing.

47   Lubricate the lips and the outer diameter of the oil seal with the recommended fork oil (see Chapter 1) and slide it down the inner tube, with the open side of the seal lip facing the spacer **(see illustration)**. Drive the seal into place with the same tools used to drive in the guide bushing (see illustration 8.21). If you don't have access to these, it is recommended that you take the assembly to a Yamaha dealer service department or other motorcycle repair shop to have the seal driven in. If you are very careful, the seal can be driven in with a hammer and a drift punch. Work around the circumference of the seal, tapping gently on the outer edge of the seal until it's seated. Be careful - if you distort the seal, you'll have to disassemble the fork again and end up taking it to a dealer anyway!

48   Install the retainer, making sure the ring is completely seated in its groove (see illustration 8.33).

49   Install the dust seal, making sure it seats completely (see illustration 8.23).

7

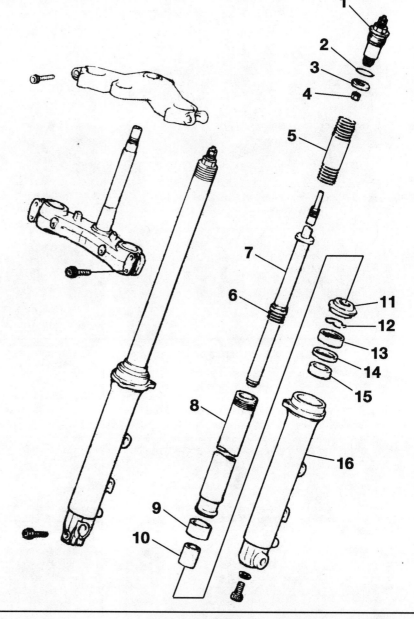

9.1 Front fork details (1989-on FZR750 models)

1 Cap bolt
2 O-ring
3 Spring seat
4 Preload adjuster locknut
5 Fork spring
6 Rebound spring
7 Damper rod (cartridge)
8 Inner fork tube
9 Slide bushing
10 Oil lock piece
11 Dust seal
12 Retainer
13 Oil seal
14 Seal spacer
15 Guide bushing
16 Outer fork tube

50   Install the drain screw and a new gasket, if it was removed.
51   Add the recommended type and amount of fork oil (see Chapter 1).
52   Install the fork spring, with the closer-wound coils at the top. Install the spring seat and spacer.
53   Refer to Section 6 and install the spring washer, O-ring and fork cap.
54   Install the fork by following the procedure outlined in Section 7. If you won't be installing the fork right away, store it in an upright position.

9 Cartridge forks - disassembly, inspection and reassembly

1989-on FZR750R models

Disassembly

Refer to illustration 9.1

1   Unscrew the cap bolt and pour the fork oil into a container **(see illustration)**.
2   Compress the fork spring and remove the spring seat (it's slotted so it can be slid off the damping adjusting rod).

3   Slip an open-end wrench over the preload adjuster locknut and place another wrench on the preload adjuster hex on the cap bolt. Loosen the cap bolt, then unscrew the adjuster from the damping adjusting rod and unscrew the locknut.
4   Pull out the thin damping force adjusting rod and the fork spring.
5   Prevent the damper rod from turning using a holder (Yamaha tool no. YM-01425, part no. 90890-01425). Unscrew the Allen bolt at the bottom of the outer tube and remove the copper washer.
6   Remove the damper rod and the oil lock piece from the inner fork tube.
7   Pry the dust seal out of the outer fork tube and slide it up the inner fork tube. **Caution:** *Don't scratch the inner fork tube while you pry the dust seal out.*
8   If necessary, pry the retainer out of its groove and remove the front fender stay, ball and spring. **Note:** *The ball and spring are very small. Take care not to lose them.*
9   Hold the outer tube and yank the inner tube away from it, repeatedly (like a slide hammer), until the seal and outer tube guide bushing pop loose.
10   Slide the oil seal, spacer and guide bushing off the fork tube, then remove the slide bushing.
11   Carefully note the position of the preload adjuster in the cap bolt, then remove the preload adjuster if necessary.

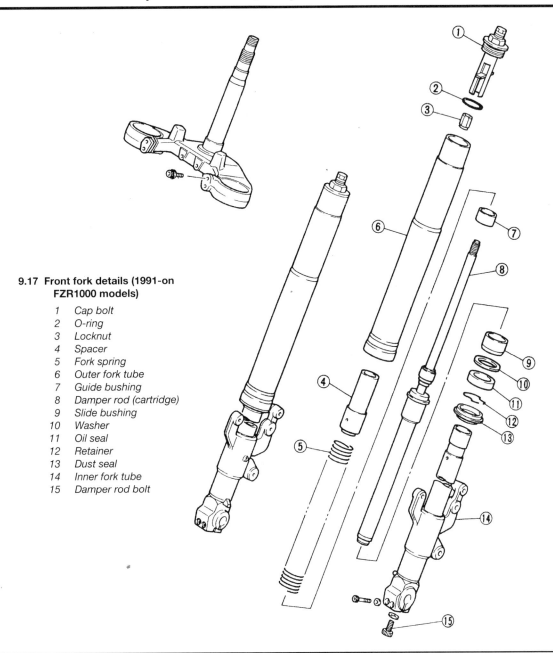

9.17 Front fork details (1991-on FZR1000 models)

1 Cap bolt
2 O-ring
3 Locknut
4 Spacer
5 Fork spring
6 Outer fork tube
7 Guide bushing
8 Damper rod (cartridge)
9 Slide bushing
10 Washer
11 Oil seal
12 Retainer
13 Dust seal
14 Inner fork tube
15 Damper rod bolt

Inspection

12 Clean all parts in solvent and blow them dry with compressed air, if available. Blow out the passages in the damper rod, but don't try to disassemble it. Check the inner and outer fork tubes, the guide bushings and the damper rod for score marks, scratches, flaking of the chrome and excessive or abnormal wear. Look for dents in the tubes and replace them if any are found. Check the fork seal seat for nicks, gouges and scratches. If damage is evident, leaks will occur around the seal-to-outer tube junction. Replace worn or defective parts with new ones.

13 Have the inner fork tube checked for runout at a dealer service department or other repair shop. **Warning:** *If it is bent, it should not be straightened; replace it with a new one.*

14 Measure the overall length of the fork spring and check it for cracks and other damage. Compare the length to the minimum length listed in this Chapter's Specifications. If it's defective or sagged, replace both fork springs with new ones. Never replace only one spring.

15 Check the damping force adjuster rod for bending and replace it if it's bent at all.

Assembly

16 Assembly is the reverse of the disassembly steps. Whenever the forks are overhauled, replace the bushings, oil seal, dust seal and the copper washer that goes on the damper rod bolt. Install the oil seal with its numbered side upward. Lubricate the outer surface of the inner fork tube with fork oil before assembly. Fill the oil to the level listed in this Chapter's Specifications (with the fork fully compressed).

1991-on FZR1000 models

Disassembly

Refer to illustrations 9.17, 9.19a, 9.19b and 9.27

17 Unscrew the fork cap bolt from the outer tube **(see illustration)**.
18 Lift up the fork cap bolt, spacer and fork spring.
19 Install a fork spring compressor (Yamaha tool no. YM-01441) on the spacer and compress the fork spring **(see illustration)**. Slip a rod holder (Yamaha tool no. YM-01434) between the spacer and the locknut **(see illustration)**.
20 Turn the locknut away from the fork cap bolt, then unscrew the cap bolt from the damper rod.
21 Carefully remove the rod holder and spring compressor from the

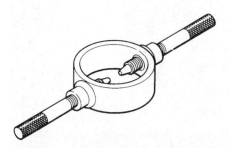

9.19a This tool is used to compress the fork spring . . .

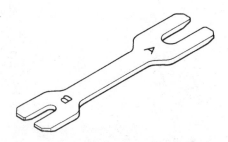

9.19b . . . and this tool is used to hold the spring down while the locknut is loosened

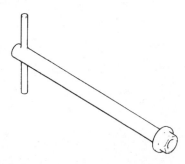

9.27 This tool is used to hold the damper rod from turning while the damper rod bolt is loosened or tightened (the hex size is 24 mm)

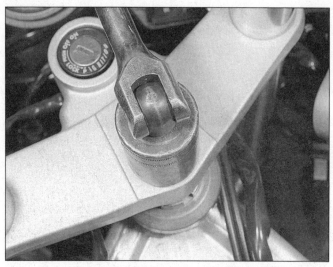

10.3a Loosen the steering stem nut with a socket . . .

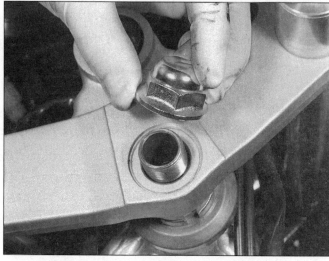

10.3b . . . unscrew the nut from the steering stem . . .

damper rod and spacer. **Warning:** *The spring is compressed. Keep your fingers clear of it to prevent injury.*

22   Remove the spacer and spring from the fork tube.

23   Thread the cap bolt back onto the damper rod, then turn the fork upside down over a container. Grasp the cap bolt and use it to pump the damper rod several times to drain the fork oil.

24   Carefully pry the dust seal and retainer out of the outer fork tube with a small standard screwdriver.

25   Hold the outer tube and yank the inner tube away from it, repeatedly (like a slide hammer), until the seal and outer tube guide bushing pop loose.

26   Remove the dust seal, retainer, oil seal, spacer, slide bushing and piston bushing from the inner fork tube.

27   Hold the damper rod from turning with Yamaha tool no. YM-01445, part no. 90890-01445 **(see illustration)** and remove the damper rod bolt. The tool has a 24 mm hex size.

28   Remove the damper rod from the fork tube. **Caution:** *Keep the damper rod clean. Its internal valves and passages can be contaminated by small bits of foreign material.*

Inspection

29   Perform Steps 12 through 15 above to inspect the fork.

30   Install the damper rod and let it slide slowly into the inner fork tube without scratching the inner fork tube surface.

31   Apply non-permanent thread locking agent to the threads of the damper rod bolt. Hold the damper rod from turning with the tool used in Step 27, install the damper rod bolt and tighten it to the torque listed in this Chapter's Specifications.

32   Coat the outer surface of the inner fork tube with fork oil. Wrap the end of the inner fork tube with plastic wrap to protect the oil seal.

Install the new dust seal, retainer, new oil seal (with its numbered or marked side toward the axle holder), washer, slide bushing and guide bushing on the inner fork tube.

33   Assemble the outer tube and inner tube, then press the oil seal into the outer tube with the tool used in Step 21.

34   Install the oil seal retainer securely in its groove.

35   Install the dust seal in the outer fork tube with the tool used in Step 33.

36   Fill the fork with the amount of oil listed in this Chapter's Specifications (before installing the spring and with the damper rod fully compressed). The oil must rise to the top surface of the outer fork tube or it will be impossible to adjust fork oil level correctly. After filling, pump the damper rod slowly up and down at least ten times to distribute the oil. **Note:** *Don't pump rapidly or oil will spray out.*

37   Pump the outer fork tube slowly through a stroke of about 120 mm (4.7 inches) to complete distribution of the fork oil. Don't use too long a stroke or air will be drawn into the oil. If this happens, pump the damper rod and outer tube again as described in Steps e and f.

38   Wait ten minutes for the oil to settle and air bubbles to leave the fork oil, then check fork oil level, measuring down from the top of the inner fork tube with the damper rod fully compressed and the spring not yet installed. **Warning:** *Oil level must be correct and even between the two forks or unstable handling may occur.*

39   Thread the locknut onto the damper rod the distance listed in this Chapter's Specifications.

40   Tighten the spring preload adjuster until there's no play in the stopper inside the adjuster.

41   Thread an internally threaded rod onto the end of the damper rod and pull it up. Install the fork spring (with its small diameter end upward) and the spring spacer.

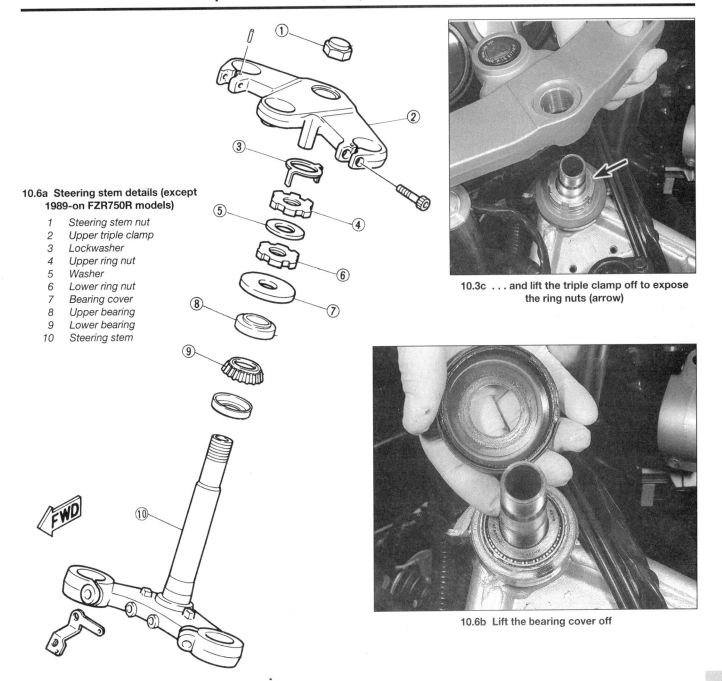

10.6a Steering stem details (except 1989-on FZR750R models)

1   Steering stem nut
2   Upper triple clamp
3   Lockwasher
4   Upper ring nut
5   Washer
6   Lower ring nut
7   Bearing cover
8   Upper bearing
9   Lower bearing
10 Steering stem

10.3c . . . and lift the triple clamp off to expose the ring nuts (arrow)

10.6b Lift the bearing cover off

7

42   Press down the spacer and fork spring with the fork spring compressor **(see illustration 9.19a)**. Pull the damper rod upward and slip the rod holder between the locknut and spring spacer **(see illustration 9.19b)**.
43   Unscrew the rod puller. Thread the cap bolt onto the rod and tighten it slightly with fingers. Hold the cap bolt from turning and tighten the locknut to the torque listed in this Chapter's Specifications.
44   Carefully remove the rod holder and fork spring compressor. **Warning**: *The spring is under pressure.*
45   Thread the cap bolt into the outer fork tube.
46   After installation, adjust the fork spring preload (see Section 19).

10   Steering head bearings - replacement

1   If the steering head bearing check/adjustment (see Chapter 1) does not remedy excessive play or roughness in the steering head

bearings, the entire front end must be disassembled and the bearings and races replaced with new ones.
2   Refer to Chapter 5 and remove the fuel tank. Refer to Section 7 and remove the front forks.

All except 1989-on FZR750 models

Refer to illustrations 10.3a, 10.3b, 10.3c, 10.6a, 10.6b, 10.7a, 10.7b, 10.10, 10.13 and 10.16

3   If you're working on an FZR600, remove the handlebars (see Section 5) and steering stem nut, then lift off the upper triple clamp (sometimes called the fork bridge or crown) **(see illustrations)**.
4   If you're working on an FZR750/1000, remove the upper triple clamp and handlebars (see Section 5).
5   Unbolt the brake hose junction from the steering head (see Chapter 8).
6   Remove the lockwasher and upper ring nut from the steering stem (see Chapter 1). Remove the lower ring nut and

10.7a Lift the upper bearing out of its race

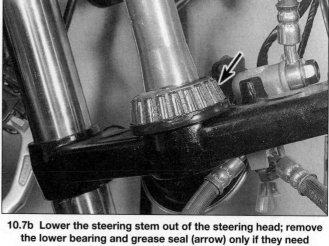

10.7b Lower the steering stem out of the steering head; remove the lower bearing and grease seal (arrow) only if they need to be replaced

10.10 Drive the races out with a hammer and long rod

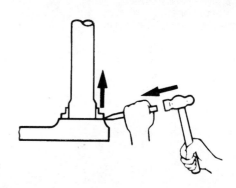

10.13 Gently tap between the lower bearing and triple clamp with a hammer and cold chisel to separate the bearing from the steering stem

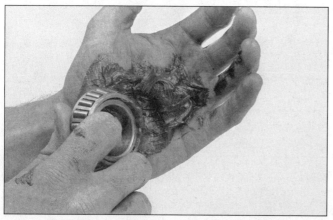

10.16 Work the grease completely into the rollers

bearing cover **(see illustrations)**.

7   Remove the upper bearing and lower the steering stem and lower triple clamp assembly out of the steering head **(see illustrations)**. If it's stuck, gently tap on the top of the steering stem with a plastic mallet or a hammer and a wood block.

8   Clean all the parts with solvent and dry them thoroughly, using compressed air, if available. If you do use compressed air, don't let the bearings spin as they're dried - it could ruin them. Wipe the old grease out of the frame steering head and bearing races.

9   Examine the races in the steering head for cracks, dents, and pits. If even the slightest amount of wear or damage is evident, the races

should be replaced with new ones.

10   To remove the bearing races, drive them out of the steering head with a hammer and long rod **(see illustration)**. A slide hammer with the proper internal-jaw puller will also work.

11   Since the races are an interference fit in the frame, installation will be easier if the new races are left overnight in a refrigerator. This will cause them to contract and slip into place in the frame with very little effort. When installing the races, tap them gently into place with a hammer and punch or a large socket. Do not strike the bearing surface or the race will be damaged.

12   Check the bearings for wear. Look for cracks, dents, and pits in the races and flat spots on the bearings. Replace any defective parts with new ones. If a new bearing is required, replace both of them as a set.

13   Don't remove the lower bearing unless it, or the grease seal underneath, must be replaced **(see illustration 10.7b)**. To remove the bearing from the steering stem, carefully tap between the bearing and steering stem with a hammer and cold chisel **(see illustration)**. You can also use a bearing splitter and puller setup (these can be rented). Tap the lower bearing on with a hammer and piece of pipe the same diameter as the bearing inner race. Don't tap against the rollers or outer race or the bearing will be ruined. As an alternative, take the steering stem to a Yamaha dealer or motorcycle repair shop and have the old bearing pressed off and a new one pressed on.

14   Check the grease seal under the lower bearing and replace it with a new one if necessary.

15   Inspect the steering stem/lower triple clamp for cracks and other damage. Do not attempt to repair any steering components. Replace them with new parts if defects are found.

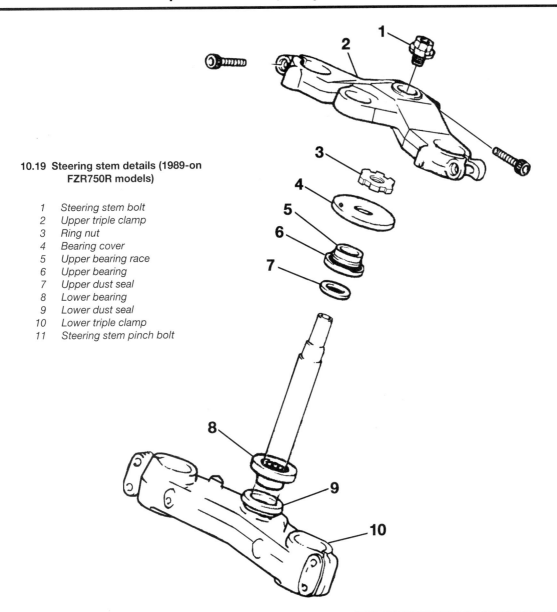

10.19 Steering stem details (1989-on FZR750R models)

1 Steering stem bolt
2 Upper triple clamp
3 Ring nut
4 Bearing cover
5 Upper bearing race
6 Upper bearing
7 Upper dust seal
8 Lower bearing
9 Lower dust seal
10 Lower triple clamp
11 Steering stem pinch bolt

16 Pack the bearings with high-quality grease (preferably a moly-based grease) **(see illustration)**. Coat the outer races with grease also.
17 Insert the steering stem/lower triple clamp into the steering head. Install the upper bearing and lower ring nut. refer to Chapter 1 and adjust the bearings.
18 The remainder of installation is the reverse of removal.

1989-on FZR750R models

Removal

Refer to illustration 10.19

19 Loosen the steering stem pinch bolt and remove the steering stem bolt **(see illustration)**.
20 Lift the upper triple clamp off the steering head.
21 Remove the brake hose brackets and disconnect the horn wires.
22 Remove the bearing adjuster ring nut. Remove the bearing cover, the upper bearing race and the upper bearing out of the steering head.
23 Slide the upper dust seal, lower bearing and lower dust seal off the steering stem.

Inspection

24 Check the bearings for wear. Look for cracks, dents, and pits in the races and flat spots, pitting or galling on the bearing balls. Replace any defective parts with new ones. If a new bearing is required, replace both bearings, their races and both dust seals as a set.
25 To remove the bearing races, drive them out of the steering head with a hammer and long rod **(see illustration 10.10)**. A slide hammer with the proper internal-jaw puller will also work.
26 Since the races are an interference fit in the frame, installation will be easier if the new races are left overnight in a refrigerator. This will cause them to contract and slip into place in the frame with very little effort. When installing the races, tap them gently into place with a hammer and punch or a large socket. Do not strike the bearing surface or the race will be damaged.
27 Inspect the steering stem/lower triple clamp for cracks and other damage. Do not attempt to repair any steering components. Replace them with new parts if defects are found.
28 Pack the bearings with high-quality bearing grease (preferably a moly-based grease). Coat the outer races with grease also.

Installation

29 Install the lower dust seal, lower bearing and upper dust seal on the steering stem.
30 Install the steering stem in the steering head. Install the upper bearing and race, the bearing cover and the ring nut (the tapered side of the ring nut must be up).
31 Refer to Chapter 1 and adjust the bearings.
32 The remainder of installation is the reverse of the removal steps.

7

11.3 Remove the nut and take out the suspension linkage lower pivot bolt (arrow)

11   Rear shock absorber - removal, inspection and installation

Removal

1   Support the bike securely so it can't be knocked over during this procedure. Place a jack beneath the frame to lift the rear tire off the ground. Remove the rear wheel (see Chapter 8).

FZR600 models

Refer to illustrations 11.3, 11.4, 11.5a, 11.5b and 11.5c

2   Remove the left and right fairings, the seat and the side covers (see Chapter 9).
3   Support the swingarm so it can't drop. Remove the lower pivot bolt from the relay arm and move the linkage aside **(see illustration)**.
4   Remove the shock absorber lower bolt and nut, washers, collars and grease seals **(see illustration 11.3** and the accompanying illustration).
5   Remove the shock absorber upper nut, washer and bolt **(see illustrations)**.
6   Take the shock absorber out.

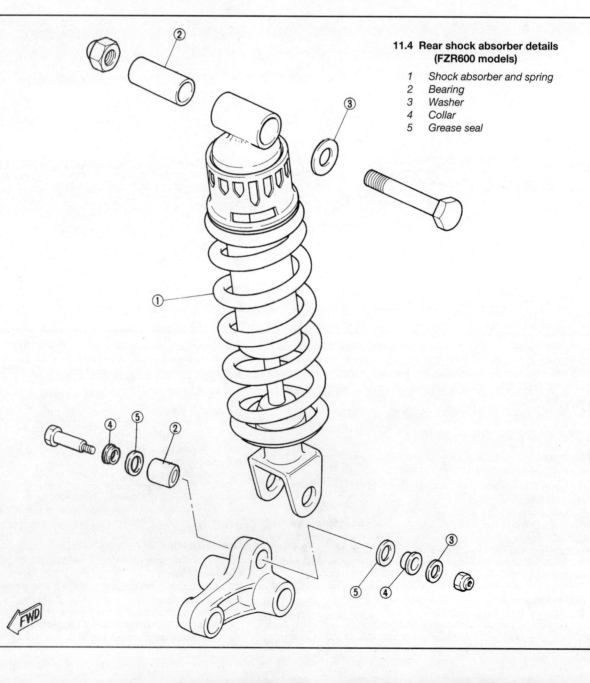

11.4 Rear shock absorber details (FZR600 models)

1   *Shock absorber and spring*
2   *Bearing*
3   *Washer*
4   *Collar*
5   *Grease seal*

11.5a Remove the nut from the upper pivot bolt (arrow) . . .

11.5b . . . then slide out the bolt and remove the shock absorber

11.5c . . . and remove the collar

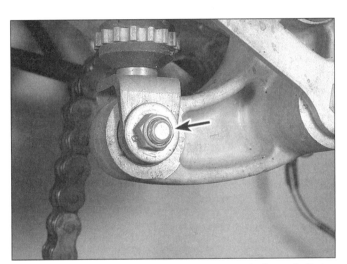

11.12a Loosen the nut (arrow) and remove the lower bolt

FZR750/1000 models (except 1989-on FZR750R)

Refer to illustrations 11.12a, 11.12b, 11.12c and 11.12d

7   Remove the left, right and lower front fairings, the seat and the side covers (see Chapter 9).

8   Remove the fuel tank (see Chapter 5).

9   Support the swingarm so it can't drop.

10   If you're working on a 1987 or 1988 model, remove the suspension linkage tie rods (see Section 12).

11   If you're working on a 1989 or later model, unbolt the upper ends of the suspension linkage tie rods from the frame and move the linkage aside (see Section 12).

12   Remove the shock absorber lower bolt and nut, spacers and collar **(see illustrations)**. Detach the reservoir (if equipped).

13   Remove the shock absorber upper nut, washer and bolt.

14   Take the shock absorber out.

1989-on FZR750R models

Refer to illustration 11.16

15   Remove the lower fairing (see Chapter 9).

16   Unbolt the spring preload adjuster and remove the retaining bands for the compression damping adjuster **(see illustration)**.

17   Support the swingarm so it can't drop

18   Remove the upper shock absorber bolt.

19   Remove the lower fairing stay.

20   Remove the suspension linkage tie rods (see Section 12).

21   Remove the shock absorber lower bolt. Guide the preload and

damping adjusters down through the frame and take the shock absorber out.

Inspection

Refer to illustration 11.22

22   Check the shock for signs of oil or gas leaks and replace it if you find any. Yamaha specifies releasing the nitrogen gas pressure before throwing away the shock absorber. **Warning:** *Wear eye protection while drilling to prevent injury from flying metal chips. To release the gas pressure, drill a hole through the cylinder wall. The hole should be 2 to 3 mm (0.08 to 0.12 inch) in diameter.*

   a) On all except 1989 and later FZR750R models, the hole should be located 25 to 30 mm (one inch to 1-3/16 inch) beneath the spring seat **(see illustration)**.

   b) On 1989 and later FZR750R models, the hole should be 30 to 35 mm (1.2 to 1.4 inch) from the end of the gas-containing portion of the shock absorber.

23   Inspect the pivot hardware at the top and bottom of the shock and replace any worn or damaged parts.

Installation

24   Installation is the reverse of the removal procedure, with the following additions:

   a) Lubricate the collars at the top and bottom of the shock absorber with multi-purpose grease. Also grease the washers and seals at the bottom of the shock absorber.

7

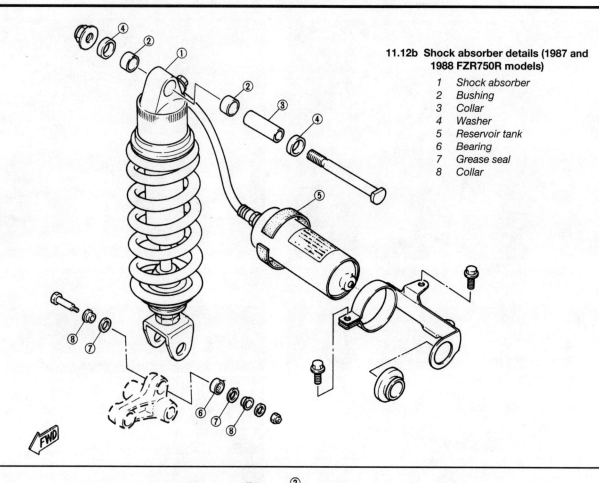

**11.12b Shock absorber details (1987 and
            1988 FZR750R models)**

1   Shock absorber
2   Bushing
3   Collar
4   Washer
5   Reservoir tank
6   Bearing
7   Grease seal
8   Collar

**11.12c Shock absorber details (1987 and
            1988 FZR1000 models)**

1   Shock absorber
2   Bushing
3   Collar
4   Bearing
5   Grease seal
6   Collar

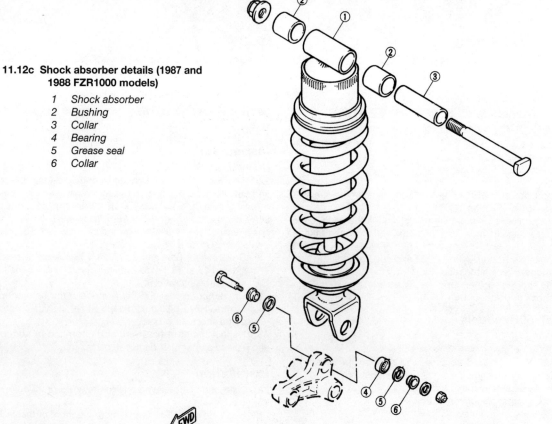

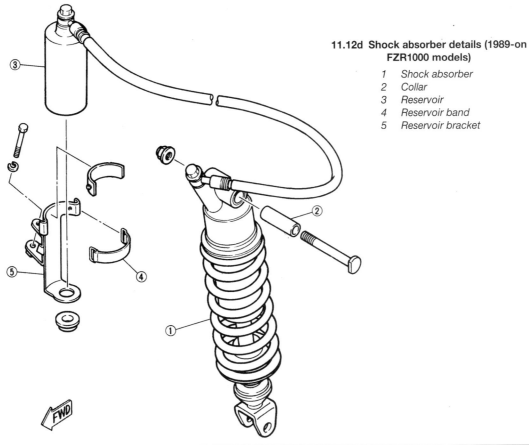

11.12d Shock absorber details (1989-on FZR1000 models)

1   Shock absorber
2   Collar
3   Reservoir
4   Reservoir band
5   Reservoir bracket

11.16 Shock absorber details (1989-on FZR750R models)

1   Shock absorber
2   Seat height adjuster
3   Compression damping force adjuster
4   Band
5   Stay
6   Spring preload adjuster

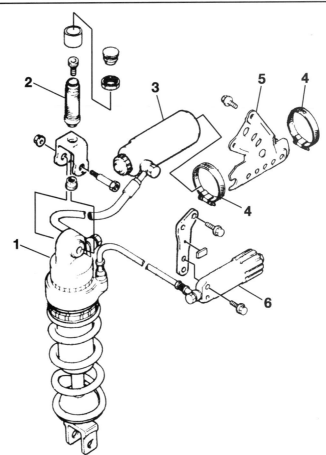

7

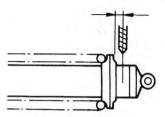

11.22 Drill a 2 to 3 mm hole at the specified location (it varies depending on model)

12.4a Loosen the nut and remove the bolt at the upper end of the tie rods . . .

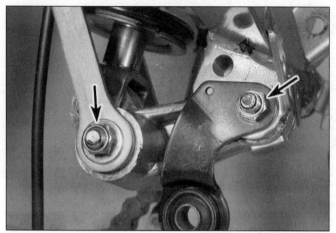

12.4b . . . and at the lower end (left arrow); the relay arm bolt and nut (right arrow) also secure the muffler/silencer support bracket

12.4c Remove the relay arm nut and slide the bolt (arrow) out of the relay arm and frame

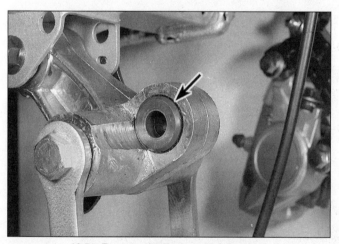

12.5a Remove the dust cover (arrow) . . .

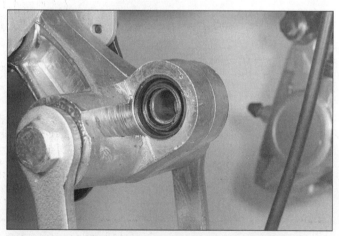

12.5b . . . and the grease seal to expose the bearing

b) Install the upper and lower shock absorber bolts and nuts and the linkage bolts and nuts, then tighten them to the torque values listed in this Chapter's Specifications.

12 Rear suspension linkage - removal, check and installation

1   Support the bike securely so it can't be knocked over during this procedure.
2   Perform the first few steps of the shock absorber procedure to provide access for removal (see Section 11).
3   Disconnect the lower end of the rear shock absorber (see Section 11).

FZR600 models

Refer to illustrations 12.4a, 12.4b, 12.4c, 12.5a, 12.5b and 12.5c
4   Remove the nuts and bolts that secure the tie-rods to the swingarm and remove the tie-rods (see illustrations). Remove the pivot bolt from the front of the relay arm and remove the relay arm (see illustration).
5   Push the sleeves out of the relay arm (see illustration). Check the sleeves and the bearings in the relay arm for wear (see illustrations).
6   Apply moly-based grease to the bearings and sleeves and install the sleeves in the bearings.

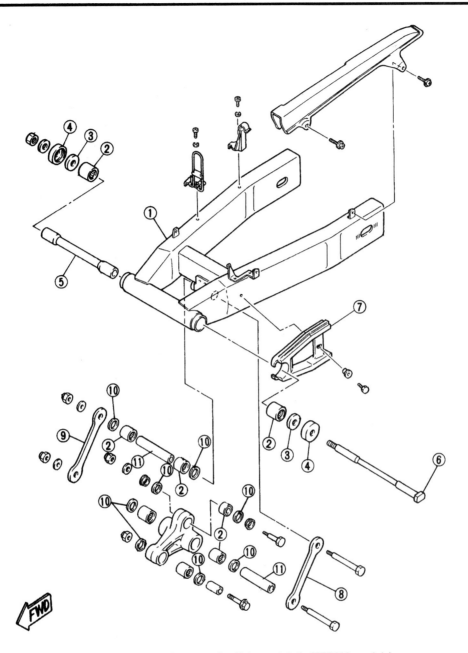

12.5c Swingarm and suspension linkage details (FZR600 models)

1	Swingarm	5	Pivot shaft bushing	9	Right tie rod
2	Bearing	6	Pivot shaft	10	Grease seal
3	Thrust washer	7	Chain guard seal	11	Collar
4	Thrust cover	8	Left tie rod	12	Relay arm

7   Installation is the reverse of removal. Tighten the bolts and nuts to the torque listed in this Chapter's Specifications.

FZR750/1000 models

Refer to illustrations 12.8a, 12.8b, 12.9a and 12.9b

8   Remove the nuts and bolts that secure the tie-rods to the swingarm and remove the tie-rods **(see illustrations)**. Remove the pivot bolt from the front of the relay arm and remove the relay arm.

9   Push the collars out of the relay arm **(see illustrations)**. Check the collars and the bearings in the relay arm for wear **(see illustrations 12.5b and 12.5c)**. Have them replaced if they're worn.

10   Apply moly-based grease to the bearings and collars and install them in the bearings. Install any grease seals and dust covers.

11   Installation is the reverse of removal. Tighten the bolts and nuts to the torque listed in this Chapter's Specifications.

13   Swingarm bearings - check

1   Refer to Chapter 8 and remove the rear wheel, then refer to Section 11 and remove the rear shock absorber.

2   Grasp the rear of the swingarm with one hand and place your other hand at the junction of the swingarm and the frame. Try to move the rear of the swingarm from side-to-side. Any wear (play) in the bearings should be felt as movement between the swingarm and the frame at the front. The swingarm will actually be felt to move forward and

12.8a Remove the nuts from the linkage bolts and the shock absorber lower pivot bolt (arrows) . . .

12.8b . . . and slide the bolts out

12.9a Swingarm and suspension linkage details (1987 and 1988 models)

1 Swingarm
2 Bearing
3 Thrust washer
4 Thrust cover
5 Collar
6 Left tie rod
7 Right tie rod
8 Grease seal
9 Dust cover

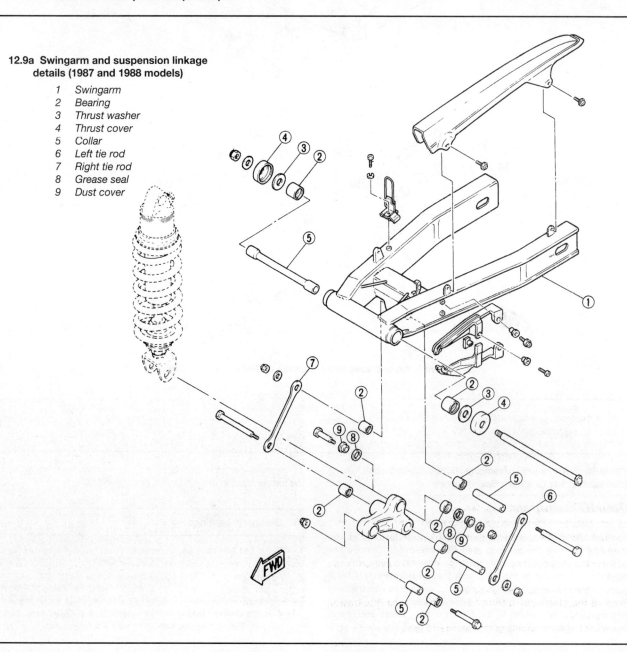

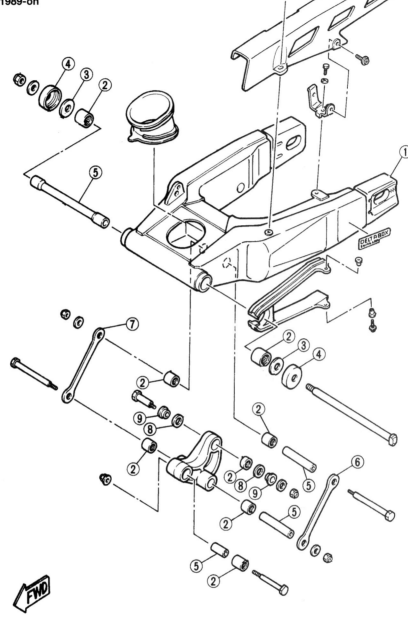

12.9b Swingarm and suspension linkage details (1989-on FZR1000 models; 1989-on FZR750R similar))

1 Swingarm
2 Bearing
3 Thrust washer
4 Thrust cover
5 Collar
6 Left tie rod
7 Right tie rod
8 Grease seal
9 Dust cover

7

backward at the front (not from side-to-side). If any play is noted, the bearings should be replaced with new ones (see Section 15).
3   Next, move the swingarm up and down through its full travel. It should move freely, without any binding or rough spots. If it does not move freely, refer to Section 16 for servicing procedures.

14 Swingarm - removal and installation

Refer to illustrations 14.4, 14.7a, 14.7b, 14.8, 14.9a, 14.9b, 14.10a, 14.10b and 14.12

1   Support the bike securely so it can't be knocked over during this procedure.
2   Remove the rear wheel (see Chapter 8).
3   Remove the chain guard from the swingarm **(see illustration 12.5a, 12.9a or 12.9b)**.
4   Detach the torque link from the swingarm **(see illustration)**. If

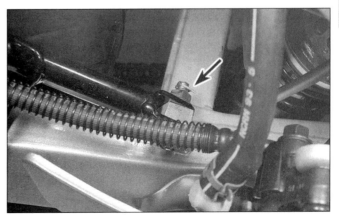

14.4 Remove the cotter pin, nut and bolt and detach the torque link from the swingarm (FZR600 shown)

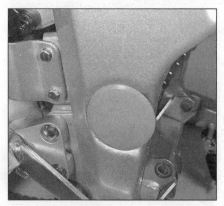

14.7a Pry the plastic plug out of the recess . . .

14.7b . . . to expose the pivot shaft nut

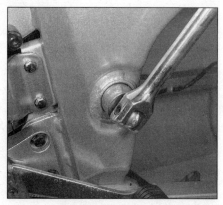

14.8 Remove the nut

14.9a Support the swingarm; pull out the pivot shaft . . .

14.9b . . . and pull the swingarm back away from the motorcycle

14.10a The chain buffer is attached at the front . . .

14.10b . . . and at the rear on the inside of the swingarm (FZR600 shown)

you're working on a model with an underslung rear caliper, remove the caliper bracket. Support the rear brake caliper and torque link with a piece of rope or wire - don't let them hang by the brake hose.

5   Detach the rear brake hose bracket(s) from the swingarm (if equipped).

6   Detach the shock absorber and rear suspension linkage from the swingarm (see Sections 11 and 12).

7   Pry the plastic cover from the swingarm pivot nut **(see illustrations)**.

8   Remove the swingarm pivot nut and washer **(see illustration)**.

9   Support the swingarm and pull the pivot shaft out **(see illustration)**. Remove the swingarm **(see illustration)**.

10 If necessary, detach the chain buffer from the swingarm (see il-

lustrations 12.4a, 12.9a 12.9b and the accompanying illustrations).

11 Check the pivot bearings in the swingarm for dryness or deterioration and lubricate or replace them as necessary (see Section 15).

12 Installation is the reverse of the removal procedure, with the following additions:

a) Be sure the bearing thrust covers and washers are in position before installing the pivot shaft.

b) Be sure the pivot shaft head is seated in its slot before tightening the nut **(see illustration)**.

c) Tighten the pivot shaft nut and the shock absorber and tie-rod lower mounting bolts/nuts to the torque values listed in this Chapter's Specifications.

d) Adjust the chain as described in Chapter 1.

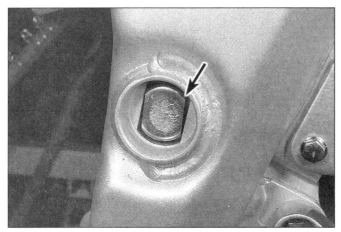

14.12 Be sure the head of the pivot shaft fits into its slot (arrow)

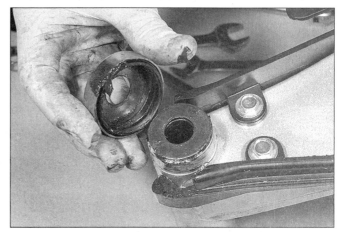

15.2a Lift off the thrust cover . . .

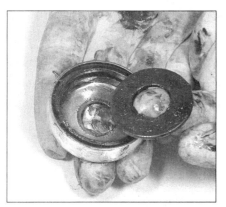

15.2b . . . and the thrust washer

15.3 Pull out the pivot shaft collar

15.4 Inspect the bearing in each side of the swingarm

15 Swingarm bearings - inspection and replacement

Refer to illustrations 15.2a, 15.2b, 15.3 and 15.4
1   Remove the swingarm (see Section 14).
2   Pry off the thrust cover and remove the thrust washer from each side of the swingarm **(see illustrations)**.
3   Slide the collar out **(see illustration)**.
4   Inspect the bearings **(see illustration)**. If they're dry, lubricate them with lithium-based waterproof wheel bearing grease. If they're worn or damaged, take the swingarm to a Yamaha dealer or motorcycle repair shop for bearing replacement.

16 Drive chain - removal, cleaning and installation

Removal
Refer to illustrations 16.3a, 16.3b, 16.3c, 16.3d, 16.4 and 16.5
1   Disconnect the shift arm from its shaft in the engine (see Chapter 2 or Chapter 3).
2   If the motorcycle is equipped with a hydraulic clutch, remove the clutch release cylinder (see Chapter 3).
3   Remove the bolts securing the engine sprocket cover to the engine case. Take the sprocket cover off and inspect its seals **(see illustrations)**. Replace them if they're worn.
4   Disengage the chain **(see illustration)** and remove the rear wheel (see Chapter 8).
5   Lift the chain off the engine sprocket **(see illustration)**.
6   Detach the swingarm from the frame by following the first few Steps of Section 12. Pull the swingarm back far enough to allow the chain to slip between the frame and the front of the swingarm.

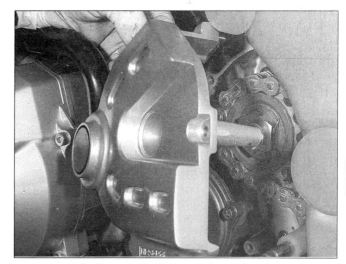

16.3a Remove the bolt and take off the cover (this is an FZR600) . . .

Cleaning
7   Soak the chain in kerosene (paraffin) for approximately five or six minutes. **Caution:** *Don't use gasoline (petrol), solvent or other cleaning fluids. Don't use high-pressure water. Remove the chain, wipe it off, then blow it dry with compressed air immediately. The entire process shouldn't take longer than ten minutes - if it does, the O-rings in the chain rollers could be damaged.*

7

16.3b . . . and this is an FZR1000

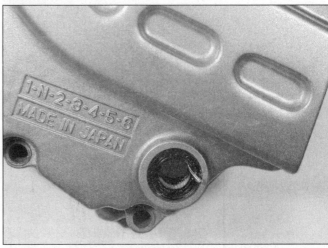

16.3c Inspect the shift shaft seal in the outside of the cover . . .

16.3d . . . and the one in the inside

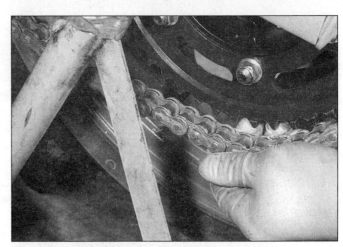

16.4 Slip the chain off the rear sprocket

16.5 With slack in the chain, lift it off the engine sprocket

16.8 Be sure the cover dowel (arrow) is in position

Installation

Refer to illustration 16.8

8   Installation is the reverse of the removal procedure. Make sure the cover dowel is in position **(see illustration)**. Tighten the suspension fasteners and the engine sprocket cover bolts to the torque values listed in this Chapter's Specifications. Adjust the chain (see Chapter 1).

Tighten the rear axle nut to the torque listed in the Chapter 8 Specifications.

9   Connect the shift arm to the shift shaft. Be sure to align the punch marks on arm and shaft.

10   Lubricate the chain following the procedure described in Chapter 1. **Caution:** Use *only the recommended engine oil.*

17.4 Replace the sprocket if the rubber coating is worn
or damaged (arrow)

17.5a Bend back the lockwasher (arrow) . . .

17.5b . . . and remove the nut

17.6 If the transmission seal has been leaking (arrow), replace it

17 Sprockets - check and replacement

Refer to illustrations 17.4, 17.5a, 17.5b and 17.6
1   Support the bike securely so it can't be knocked over during this procedure.
2   Whenever the drive chain is inspected, the sprockets should be inspected also. If you are replacing the chain, replace the sprockets as well. Likewise, if the sprockets are in need of replacement, install a new chain also.
3   Remove the engine sprocket cover following the procedure outlined in the previous Section.
4   Check the wear pattern on the sprockets (see Chapter 1). If the sprocket teeth or rubber coating are worn excessively, replace the chain and sprockets **(see illustration)**.
5   To replace the engine sprocket, engage a low transmission gear and have an assistant apply the rear brake. Bend back the lockwasher and remove the nut **(see illustrations)**.
6   With the engine sprocket removed, inspect the transmission output shaft seal **(see illustration)**. If it has been leaking oil, replace it.
7   To remove the rear sprocket, remove the rear wheel (see Chapter 8). Unscrew the nuts holding the sprocket to the wheel coupling and lift it off. Check the condition of the rubber damper under the rear wheel coupling (see Section 18).
8   When installing the rear sprocket, either use new self-locking nuts

(models so equipped), or apply a non-hardening thread locking compound to the threads of the studs (standard nuts). Tighten the nuts to the torque listed in this Chapter's Specifications.
9   When installing the engine sprocket, engage it with the chain. Install a new lockwasher, tighten the nut to the torque listed in this Chapter's Specifications and bend a lockwasher tab against the nut.
10   Install the engine sprocket cover (see Section 16) and the shift arm (see Chapter 2 or Chapter 3).

18 Rear wheel coupling/rubber damper - check and replacement

Refer to illustrations 18.2 and 18.3
1   Remove the rear wheel (see Chapter 8).
2   Lift the collar and rear sprocket/rear wheel coupling from the wheel **(see illustration)**.
3   Lift the rubber damper segments from the wheel **(see illustration)** and check them for cracks, hardening and general deterioration. Replace the rubber damper with a new one if necessary.
4   Checking and replacement procedures for the coupling bearing are similar to those described for the wheel bearings. Refer to Chapter 8.
5   Installation is the reverse of the removal procedure.

7

18.2 Lift the sprocket out of the wheel

18.3 Lift the damper segments out of the wheel

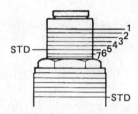

19.4 Turn the adjuster with a wrench to change spring preload;
the upper grooves indicate the preload setting and the lower
grooves indicate the fork height setting

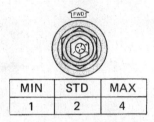

MIN	STD	MAX
1	2	4

19.5 Turn the damping adjuster on top of the fork cap to increase
or decrease damping

19 Suspension adjustments

1   The front suspension (FZR750/1000 models only) and rear suspension can be made firmer or softer for different riding conditions. **Warning:** *If you're working on an FZR750/1000, always set both front forks to the same preload setting. Uneven settings can cause unstable handling.* **Caution:** *Turn the adjusters in progressive steps through all of the settings without skipping any of the intermediate settings (for example, don't skip from setting 1 to setting 3).*
2   Find the proper settings for your riding conditions in this Chapter's Specifications.

Front forks (1987 and 1988 FZR750R)

Refer to illustrations 19.4 and 19.5
3   Spring preload and fork damping can be increased or decreased by turning an adjuster on the top of each fork. Fork top height can be adjusted by moving the fork up or down in the triple clamps.
4   Adjust spring preload by turning the preload adjuster at the top of the fork **(see illustration)**. The grooves on the adjuster indicate the setting.
5   Adjust fork damping force by turning the damping adjuster at the top of the fork **(see illustration)**. Turning the adjuster toward the no. 4 setting stiffens the fork; turning toward no. 1 setting softens it.
6   To adjust fork top height, remove the side fairings (see Chapter 9). Support the bike securely so it can't be knocked over during this procedure, then raise the front tire off the ground with a jack placed under the engine.
7   Loosen the pinch bolts for the handlebars, upper triple clamp and lower triple clamp (see Sections 5 and 7). Raise or lower the forks, using the grooves as a guide (see illustration 19.4). Be sure the settings are even, then tighten the bolts to the torques listed in this Chapter's Specifications.

Front forks (1989-on FZR750)

8   Spring preload, fork compression damping and fork rebound

19.13a Place an open-end wrench on the flat at the top of the
adjuster (arrow) and turn the adjuster . . .

damping can be increased or decreased by turning an adjuster on the top or bottom of each fork. Fork top height can be adjusted by moving the fork up or down in the triple clamps.
9   Perform Steps 4, 6 and 7 above to adjust spring preload and fork height.
10   To set rebound damping, turn the adjuster at the top of the fork all the way in, then back it out the number of clicks necessary to reach the desired setting. **Caution:** *Don't try to turn the adjuster beyond its minimum or maximum settings.*
11   To set compression damping, turn the adjuster at the bottom of the fork all the way in, then back it out the number of clicks necessary to reach the desired setting. **Caution:** *Don't try to turn the adjuster beyond its minimum or maximum settings.*

Front forks (FZR1000)

Refer to illustrations 19.13a, 19.13b and 19.14
12   Spring preload is adjustable. Turning the adjuster clockwise makes the suspension firmer and turning it counterclockwise (anticlockwise) makes it softer.
13   If you're working on a 1987, 1988 or 1990 and later model, turn

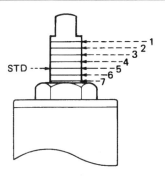

19.13b . . . the grooves indicate the settings

19.14 Turn the preload adjuster (1) clockwise to stiffen the suspension and counterclockwise (anti-clockwise) to soften it (1989 FZR1000)

19.17a The rear spring preload adjuster on FZR600 models is located at the top of the shock absorber (the numbers indicate settings) . . .

19.17b . . . turn it with the special wrench provided in the bike's tool kit

the adjuster with an open-end wrench **(see illustrations)**.
14   If you're working on a 1989 model, remove the cap from the top of the fork and turn the adjuster with a screwdriver **(see illustration)**.

Rear shock and spring (all models)

15   Adjustments include spring preload (all models) and shock damping (1989 and later FZR750/1000 only).
16   Support the bike securely so it can't be knocked over during this procedure.

FZR600 models

Refer to illustrations 19.17a and 19.17b

17   Turn the spring adjuster at the top of the shock clockwise to increase spring preload and counterclockwise (anti-clockwise) to decrease it **(see illustration)**. Use the special wrench included in the motorcycle's tool kit or equivalent **(see illustration)**.

1987 and 1988 FZR750R models

Refer to illustration 19.18

18   Loosen the locknut at the bottom of the shock absorber and turn the preload adjuster with the special wrench from the bike's tool kit **(see illustration)**. Measure the length of the spring and compare it with the recommended settings listed in this Chapter's Specifications.
19   Set rebound damping force by turning the adjuster all the way in, then turning it out and counting the clicks. Compare the setting to the values listed in this Chapter's Specifications.

1989-on FZR750 models

20   Set spring preload by turning the adjuster in or out. Compare the reading on the adjuster scale to the values listed in this Chapter's

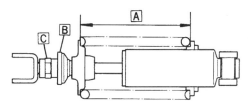

19.18 Loosen the locknut and turn the adjuster to change spring length (and spring preload)

A   Spring length   C   Locknut
B   Adjuster

Specifications. **Caution:** *Don't turn any of the adjusters past the specified range.*
21   Set rebound damping force by turning the adjuster all the way in, then turning it out and counting the clicks. Compare the setting to the values listed in this Chapter's Specifications.
22   Set compression damping force by turning the adjuster all the way in, then turning it out and counting the clicks. Compare the setting to the values listed in this Chapter's Specifications.

FZR1000 models

Refer to illustrations 19.23a and 19.23b

23   Loosen the locknut and turn the adjusting nut at the bottom of the shock to set spring preload **(see illustration)**. Measure the distance from the line between the adjusting nut and locknut to the top of the lower mounting bracket **(see illustration)** and compare it with the

7

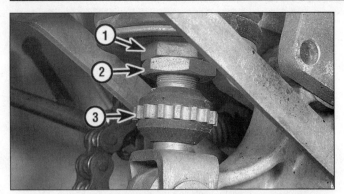

19.23a Loosen the locknut and turn the adjusting nut to change spring preload

1   *Preload adjusting nut*   3   *Damping adjuster*
2   *Locknut*

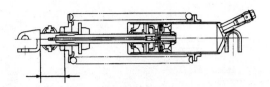

19.23b Measure from between the locknut and adjusting nut to the top of the lower bracket

range listed in this Chapter's Specifications. Spring length changes 1 mm (0.040 inch) for each turn of the adjuster. **Caution:** *Don't adjust the spring to a length outside the specified range.*

24   If you're working on a 1989 or later FZR1000, turn the adjuster at the bottom of the shock to set damping force (see illustration 19.23a). **Caution:** *Don't turn the adjuster out more than nine clicks from the fully-in position.*

Chapter 8 Brakes, wheels and tires

Contents

Specifications

Brakes

Brake lever free-play and pedal position see Chapter 1

FZR600/600R

Brake fluid type	See Chapter 1
Front brake disc thickness	
Standard	4.0 mm (0.16 inch)
Minimum*	3.5 mm (0.14 inch)
Rear brake disc thickness	
Standard	5.0 mm (0.20 inch)
Minimum*	4.5 mm (0.18 inch)
*Refer to marks stamped into the disc (they supersede information printed here)	
Disc runout limit	0.5 mm (0.02 inch)
Pad thickness (front and rear)	
Standard	5 mm (0.2 inch)
Minimum	0.5 mm (0.02 inch)

FZR750R

Brake fluid type	See Chapter 1
Front brake disc thickness (1987 and 1988)	
Standard	Not specified
Minimum*	4.5 mm (0.18 inch)
Front brake disc thickness (1989-on)	
Standard	5 mm (0.20 inch)
Minimum*	3 mm (0.12 inch)
Rear brake disc thickness (1987 and 1988)	
Standard	Not specified
Minimum*	5.5 mm (0.22 inch)
Rear brake disc thickness (1989-on)	
Standard	7 mm (0.28 inch)
Minimum*	4 mm (0.16 inch)
*Refer to marks stamped into the disc (they supersede information printed here)	
Disc runout limit	0.15 mm (0.006 inch)
Pad thickness (front)	
US models	
Standard	5.0 mm (0.20 inch)
Minimum	0.5 mm (0.02 inch)
UK models	
Standard	5.3 mm (0.21 inch)
Minimum	1.0 mm (0.04 inch)
Pad thickness (rear)	
All except 1989-on FZR750 models	
Standard	5.5 mm (0.22 inch)
Minimum	0.5 mm (0.02 inch)
1989-on FZR750 models	
Standard	5.5 mm (0.22 inch)
Minimum	1.0 mm (0.04 inch)

FZR1000

Brake fluid type	See Chapter 1
Front brake disc thickness	
1987 and 1988 models	
Standard	Not specified
Minimum*	3.5 mm (0.14 inch)

FZR1000 (continued)

1989-on

    Standard .... 4.0 mm (0.16 inch)

    Minimum* .... 3.0 mm (0.12 inch)

Rear brake disc thickness

1987 and 1988

    Standard .... Not specified

    Minimum* .... 4.5 mm (0.18 inch)

1989-on

    Standard .... 5.0 mm (0.20 inch)

    Minimum* .... 4.0 mm (0.16 inch)

Refer to marks stamped into the disc (they supersede information printed here)

Disc runout limit.. 0.15 mm (0.006 inch)

Pad thickness (front and rear)

    Standard.. 5.5 mm (0.22 inch)

    Minimum.. 0.5 mm (0.02 inch)

Wheels and tires

Wheel runout

FZR600

    Radial (up-and-down) .... 2.0 mm (0.05 inch)

    Axial (side-to-side) .... 2.0 mm (0.05 inch)

FZR750 (US)

    Radial (up-and-down) .... 1.0 mm (0.04 inch)

    Axial (side-to-side) .... 0.5 mm (0.02 inch)

FZR750 (UK)

    Radial (up-and-down) .... 2.0 mm (0.05 inch)

    Axial (side-to-side) .... 2.0 mm (0.05 inch)

FZR1000 (1987 and 1988)

    Radial (up-and-down) .... 1.0 mm (0.04 inch)

    Axial (side-to-side) .... 0.5 mm (0.02 inch)

FZR1000 (1989-on)

    Radial (up-and-down) .... 2.0 mm (0.05 inch)

    Axial (side-to-side) .... 2.0 mm (0.05 inch)

Tire pressures .... See Chapter 1

Tire sizes

FZR600 (1989 US, 1989 and 1990 UK)

    Front.. 110/70 V17-V240

    Rear 130/70 V18-V240

FZR600 (1990 US)

    Front.. 110/70 ZR17

    Rear 140/60 ZR18

FZR600 (1991-on)

    Front.. 110/70 ZR17 or 110/70 VR-17/V240

    Rear .... 140/60 ZR18 or 140/60 VR18-V240

FZR750

    1987 (US)

        Front 120/70 VR17/V270

        Rear.. 160/60 VR18/V270

    1988 (US)

        Front 120/70 ZR17

        Rear.. 160/60 ZR18

    1989-on (UK)

        Front .... 120/70 ZR17 or 120/70 VR17/V260 or 120/70 VR17/V270

        Rear.. 170/60 ZR17 or 170/70 VR17/V260 or 170/60 VR17/V270

FZR1000

    1987 (US)

        Front 120/70 VR17/V270

        Rear.. 160/60 VR18/V270

    1988 (US)

        Front .... 120/70 ZR17 or 120/70 VR17/V270

        Rear.. 160/60 ZR18 or 160/60 VR18/V270

    1987 and 1988 (UK) .... as 1988 US

    1989 and 1990 (US)

        Front.. 130/60 ZR-17

        Rear.. 170/60 ZR-17

    1989-on (UK)

        Front.. 130/60 ZR-17 or 130/60 VR17/V280

        Rear.. 170/60 ZR-17 or 170/60 VR17/V280

    1991-on (US)

        Front.. 130/60 ZR-17 or 130/60 VR17/V280

        Rear .... 170/60 ZR-17 or 170/60 VR-17/V280

Torque specifications

Caliper mounting bolts	35 Nm (25 ft-lbs)
Front caliper pad retaining bolt (1989-on FZR750)	18 Nm (13 ft-lbs)
Caliper bleed valve(s)	6 Nm (53 in-lbs)
Front axle	
All except 1989-on FZR750/1000 models	58 Nm (42 ft-lbs)
1989-on FZR750/1000 models	75 Nm (54 ft-lbs)
Front axle clamp bolt	
All except 1989-on FZR750 models	20 Nm (14 ft-lbs)
1989-on FZR750 models	35 Nm (25 ft-lbs)
Brake disc mounting bolts	20 Nm (14 ft-lbs)*
Union (banjo fitting) bolts	
FZR600 models	26 Nm (19 ft-lbs)
FZR750/1000 models	25 Nm (18 ft-lbs)
Master cylinder mounting bolts	
Front	
All except 1989-on FZR750 models	9 Nm (6.5 ft-lbs)
1989-on FZR750 models	8 Nm (5.8 ft-lbs)
Rear	20 Nm (14 ft-lbs)
Rear axle nut	
FZR600 models	107 Nm (77 ft-lbs)
1987 and 1988 FZR750/1000 models	110 Nm (80 ft-lbs)
1989-on FZR750 models	75 Nm (54 ft-lbs)
1989-on FZR1000 models	150 Nm (110 ft-lbs)

Apply non-permanent thread locking agent to the threads.

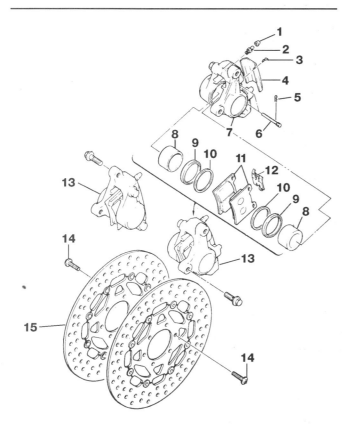

2.3a Dual-piston front calipers - exploded view

1	Bleed valve cap	9	Piston seals
2	Bleed valve	10	Dust seals
3	Pad pin retaining clip	11	Pads
4	Pad cover	12	Pad spring
5	Pad pin retaining clip	13	Caliper assemblies
6	Pad pin	14	Brake disc mounting
7	Caliper body		bolts
8	Pistons	15	Brake discs

1 General information

The models covered by this manual are equipped with hydraulic disc brakes on the front and rear. 1989 FZR600 models use a pair of dual-piston calipers at the front. All other models use a pair of four-piston calipers at the front. All models use one dual-piston caliper at the rear. The rear caliper on 1988 and later FZR750 models is mounted beneath the disc; on all others it's mounted above the disc.

All models are equipped with cast aluminum wheels, which require very little maintenance and allow tubeless tires to be used.

Caution: *Disc brake components rarely require disassembly. Do not disassemble components unless absolutely necessary. If any hydraulic brake line connection in the system is loosened, the entire system should be disassembled, drained, cleaned and then properly filled and bled upon reassembly. Do not use solvents on internal brake components. Solvents will cause seals to swell and distort. Use only clean brake fluid, brake cleaner or alcohol for cleaning. Use care when working with brake fluid as it can injure your eyes and it will damage painted surfaces and plastic parts.*

2 Brake pads - replacement

Front calipers

Warning: *When replacing the front brake pads always replace the pads in BOTH calipers - never just on one side. Replace the anti-squeal shims and pad spring whenever the pads are replaced. Also, the dust created by the brake system may contain asbestos, which is harmful to your health. Never blow it out with compressed air and don't inhale any of it. An approved filtering mask should be worn when working on the brakes.*

1   Support the bike securely so it can't be knocked over during this procedure.

All except 1989-on FZR750 models

Refer to illustrations 2.3a, 2.3b, 2.3c, 2.4, 2.5 and 2.6

2   Remove the brake pad cover from each caliper (see Chapter 1).

3   Pull the retaining clips out of the pad pins **(see illustrations)**.

8

**2.3b Pull out the pad pin retaining clips (all except
1989 and later FZR750 models)**

4   Pull out one of the pad pins **(see illustration)**.
5   Remove the pad spring **(see illustration)**. Note that the longer
end of the spring faces forward (in the rotating direction of the brake
discs).
6   Pull out the remaining pad pin and lift the pads out of the caliper
(see illustration).

1989-on FZR750 models

Refer to illustration 2.7

7   Unscrew the pad retaining bolt and take off the pad spring **(see illustration)**. Pull the pads out of their slots.

All models

Refer to illustrations 2.10a and 2.10b

8   Check the condition of the brake discs (see Section 4). If they are
in need of machining or replacement, follow the procedure in that Section to remove them. If they are okay, deglaze them with sandpaper or
emery cloth, using a swirling motion.
9   Remove the cap from the master cylinder reservoir and siphon
out some fluid. Push the pistons into the caliper as far as possible,

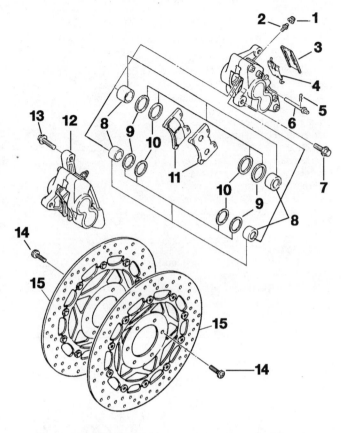

**2.3c Four-piston front calipers - exploded view (600 and late
1000 model shown; US 750 and early 1000 models similar)**

1	Bleed valve cap	9	Piston seals
2	Bleed valve	10	Dust seals
3	Pad cover	11	Pads
4	Pad spring	12	Caliper assembly
5	Pad pin retaining clip	13	Caliper mounting bolt
6	Pad pin	14	Brake disc mounting
7	Caliper mounting bolt		bolt
8	Pistons	15	Brake discs

**2.4 Pull out one of the pad pins (1989 and
later FZR750 models use a single pad
retaining bolt)**

**2.5 Remove the pad spring and pull out
the remaining pad pin**

2.6 Pull the pads out of their slots

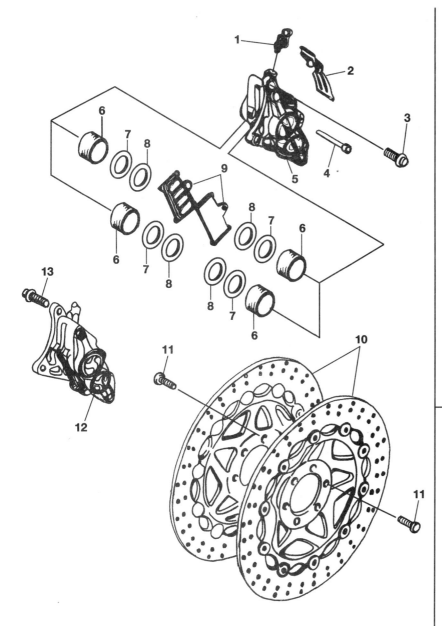

2.7 Front calipers (1989-on FZR750 models) - exploded view

1	Bleed valve and cap	8	Dust seals
2	Pad spring	9	Brake pads
3	Caliper mounting bolt	10	Brake discs
4	Pad retaining bolt	11	Brake disc mounting bolt
5	Caliper body	12	Caliper assembly
6	Pistons	13	Caliper mounting bolt
7	Piston seals		

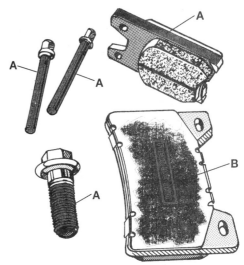

2.10a Special lubricants are required in the UK (and recommended anywhere salt is used on the roads) to prevent corrosion

A   *Apply Duckhams Copper 10 or equivalent to the shaded areas*
B   *Apply Shin-Etsu G-40M or equivalent silicone grease to the shaded areas*

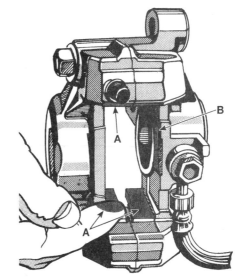

2.10b Apply the recommended lubricants to the pad friction areas inside the caliper and to the exposed portion of the caliper pistons

A   *Duckhams Copper 10*
B   *Shin-Etsu G-40M silicone grease*

8

while checking the master cylinder reservoir to make sure it doesn't overflow. If you can't depress the pistons with thumb pressure, try using a C-clamp (G-clamp). If the piston sticks, remove the caliper and overhaul it as described in Section 3.

10 **Warning**: *This step is necessary to ensure that the pads move freely in the calipers. Because a large amount of salt is used on roads in the UK, special lubrication of the pads and calipers is required.* Before installing the pads on UK models, apply a thin film of Duckhams Copper 10 or equivalent to the following areas **(see illustrations)**:

a) To the edges of the metal backing on the brake pads

b) To the pad retaining pins or bolt shaft
c) To the areas of the caliper where the pads rub
d) To the threads of the caliper mounting bolts.

Apply a thin film of Shin-Etsu G-40M or equivalent silicone grease to the following:

e) Exposed areas of the caliper pistons
f) The areas of the pad backing plates that contact the pistons.

Caution: *Don't use too much Copper 10 and don't apply it to the pad pin retaining clips or the anti-squeal shim(s). Make sure no Copper 10 contacts the brake discs or the pad friction surfaces.*

All except 1989-on FZR750 models

Refer to illustration 2.11

11   If you're working on an FZR600 with four-piston calipers, assemble the pads, shims and shim retainers **(see illustration)**.

12   Install the pads in the caliper.

13   Position the pad spring on the pads with its longer end facing forward. Slide the pad pins into their holes, making sure they pass over the fingers on the pad spring.

14   Install the retaining clips in the pad pins.

1989-on FZR750 models

15   Slide the pads into their slots and install the pad spring with its longer tangs forward. Install the pad retaining bolt over the spring and tighten it to the torque listed in this Chapter's Specifications.

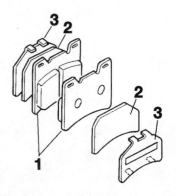

2.11 Pads and shims (FZR600 models with four-piston calipers)

1   *Brake pads*
2   *Pad shims*
3   *Shim retainers*

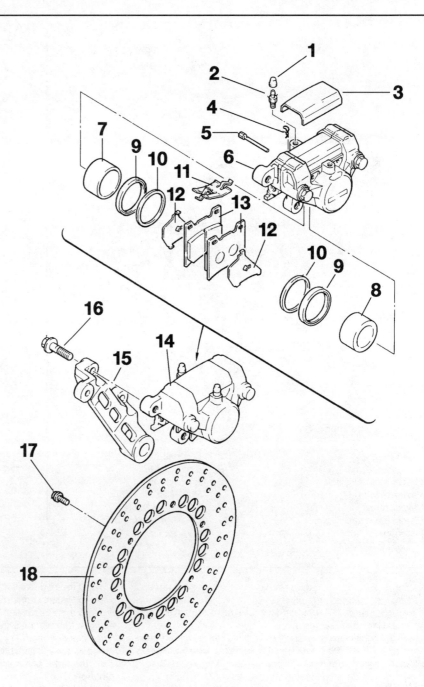

2.20a High-mount rear caliper - exploded view

1   *Bleed valve cap*
2   *Bleed valve*
3   *Pad cover*
4   *Pad pin retaining clip*
5   *Pad pin*
6   *Caliper body*
7   *Piston*
8   *Piston*
9   *Piston seals*
10   *Dust seals*
11   *Pad spring*
12   *Pad shims*
13   *Pads*
14   *Caliper assembly*
15   *Torque arm*
16   *Caliper mounting bolt*
17   *Brake disc mounting bolt*
18   *Brake disc*

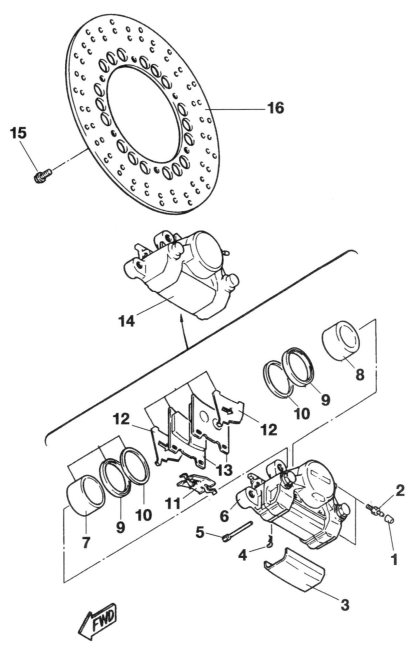

2.20b Low-mount (underslung) rear caliper - exploded view

1	Bleed valve cap	7	Piston	12	Pad shims
2	Bleed valve	8	Piston	13	Pads
3	Pad cover	9	Piston seals	14	Caliper assembly
4	Pad pin retaining clip	10	Dust seals	15	Brake disc mounting bolt
5	Pad pin	11	Pad spring	16	Brake disc
6	Caliper body				

All models

16   Refill the master cylinder reservoir (see Chapter 1) and install the diaphragm and cap.

17   Operate the brake lever several times to bring the pads into contact with the disc. Check the operation of the brakes carefully before riding the motorcycle.

Rear calipers

Refer to illustrations 2.20a, 2.20b, 2.21a, 2.21b, 2.22 and 2.24

Warning: *The dust created by the brake system may contain asbestos, which is harmful to your health. Never blow it out with compressed air and don't inhale any of it. An approved filtering mask should be worn when working on the brakes. Replace the anti-squeal shims and pad spring whenever the pads are replaced.*

18   Support the bike securely so it can't be knocked over during this procedure.

19   Remove the pad cover (see Chapter 1).

20   Pull the retaining clips out of the pad pins **(see illustrations)**.

8

2.21a Pull out the pad pin . . .

2.21b . . . and remove the pad spring

2.22 Pull the pads out of their slots

2.24 Be sure the arrows on the pad shims point in the forward rotating direction of the wheel

21   Pull one of the pad pins out of the caliper, then lift the pad spring off of the other pad pin and pull it out **(see illustrations)**.

22   Lift the pads out of the caliper (see illustration).

23   Perform Steps 7, 8 and 9 above to inspect the disc and prepare the caliper for pad installation.

24   Note the arrow on each pad shim **(see illustration)**. Be sure it points forward (in the direction of disc rotation) when the pad is installed.

25   Installation is the reverse of the removal steps, with the following additions:

　a) Install the pad spring with its longer tangs pointing in the forward rotating direction of the wheel and secure it with the pad pins.

　b) Refill the master cylinder reservoir (see Chapter 1).

　c) Operate the brake pedal to bring the pads back into contact with the disc. Check the operation of the brakes carefully before riding the motorcycle.

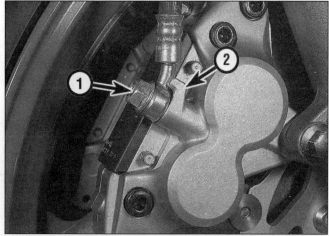

3.2a Remove the union bolt and two sealing washers - this is a front caliper . . .

1   Union bolt and sealing   2   Brake hose fitting locating
    washers   tab

3   Brake caliper - removal, overhaul and installation

Warning: *If a front caliper indicates the need for an overhaul (usually due to leaking fluid or sticky operation), BOTH front calipers should be overhauled and all old brake fluid flushed from the system. Also, the*

3.2b . . . and this is a rear caliper; be sure to use a new sealing
washer on each side of the union bolt

1 Caliper mounting bolts   3 Brake hose fitting locating
2 Union bolt and sealing   tab
   washers

3.3a Remove the lower mounting bolt . . .

dust created by the brake system may contain asbestos, which is
harmful to your health. Never blow it out with compressed air and don't
inhale any of it. An approved filtering mask should be worn when working on the brakes. Do not, under any circumstances, use petroleum-
based solvents to clean brake parts. Use brake cleaner or denatured alcohol only!

Removal

Refer to illustrations 3.2a, 3.2b, 3.3a, 3.3b and 3.3c
1   Support the bike securely so it can't be knocked over during this
procedure.
2   With a clean rag handy to catch spills, remove the brake hose
banjo fitting bolt and separate the hose from the caliper (see illustrations). Discard the sealing washers. Place the end of the hose in a
container and operate the brake lever to pump out the fluid. Once this
is done, wrap a clean shop rag tightly around the hose fitting to soak
up any drips and prevent contamination.
3   Unscrew the caliper mounting bolts (refer to illustrations 2.3a,
2.3c, 2.7, 2.20a, 2.20b and the accompanying illustrations). Caution: Don't remove the bolts that hold the caliper halves together.
4   Lift off the caliper and remove the brake pads (see Section 2).

Overhaul

Refer to illustrations 3.6a, 3.6b, 3.8a, 3.8b, 3.8c and 3.9
5   Clean the exterior of the caliper with denatured alcohol or brake

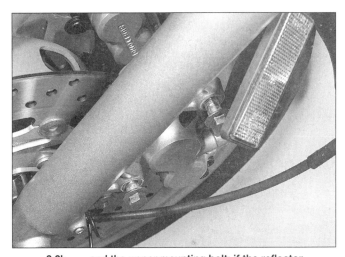

3.3b . . . and the upper mounting bolt; if the reflector
is in the way . . .

system cleaner.
6   Place a few rags between the piston(s) and the caliper frame to
act as a cushion, then use compressed air, directed into the fluid inlet,
to remove the piston(s) (see illustrations). Use only enough air pressure to ease the piston(s) out of the bore. If a piston is blown out, even
with the cushion in place, it may be damaged. Warning: Never place

3.3c . . . remove its mounting nut (arrow)

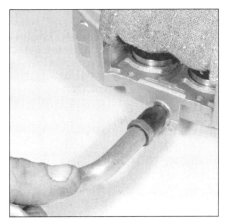

3.6a Blow air into the fluid inlet hole to
force the pistons out, but DO NOT get
your fingers in the way; this is a
front caliper . . .

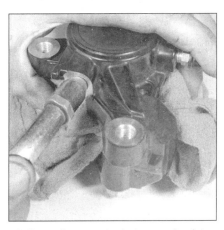

3.6b . . . the same technique and safety
precautions apply to the rear caliper

8

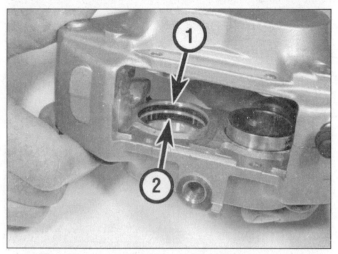

3.8a Each caliper bore contains a dust seal and a piston seal (this is a four-piston front caliper) . . .

1   *Dust seal*   2   *Piston seal*

3.8b . . . and this is a rear caliper

1   *Dust seal*   2   *Piston seal*

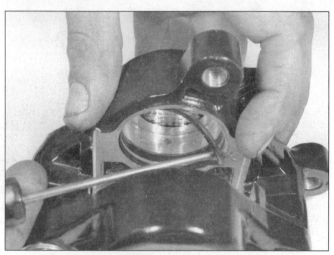

3.8c Remove the dust seal from its groove . . .

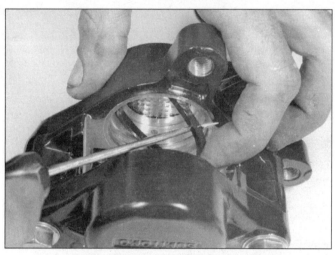

3.9 . . . then remove the piston seal

your fingers in front of the piston in an attempt to catch or protect it when applying compressed air, as serious injury could occur.

7   If compressed air isn't available, reconnect the caliper to the brake hose and pump the brake lever or pedal until the pistons are free.

8   Using a wood or plastic tool, remove the dust seal(s) **(see illustrations)**. Metal tools may cause bore damage.

9   Using a wood or plastic tool, remove the piston seal(s) from the groove in the caliper bore **(see illustration)**.

10   Clean the piston(s) and the bore(s) with denatured alcohol, clean brake fluid or brake system cleaner and blow dry them with filtered, unlubricated compressed air. Inspect the surfaces of the piston(s) for nicks and burrs and loss of plating. Check the caliper bore(s), too. If surface defects are present, the caliper must be replaced. If the caliper is in bad shape, the master cylinder should also be checked.

11   Lubricate new piston seal(s) with clean brake fluid and install it in its groove in the caliper bore. Make sure it isn't twisted and seats completely.

12   Lubricate new dust seal(s) with clean brake fluid and install it in its groove, making sure it seats correctly.

13   Lubricate the piston(s) with clean brake fluid and install it into the caliper bore. Using your thumbs, push the piston all the way in, making sure it doesn't get cocked in the bore.

Installation

14   Install the caliper, tightening the mounting bolts to the torque listed in this Chapter's Specifications. Install the brake pads.

15   Connect the brake hose to the caliper, using new sealing washers on each side of the fitting. Align the banjo fitting with its tab and tighten the bolt to the torque listed in this Chapter's Specifications.

16   Fill the master cylinder with the recommended brake fluid (see Chapter 1) and bleed the system (see Section 8). Check for leaks.

17   Check the operation of the brakes carefully before riding the motorcycle.

---

4   Brake disc(s) - inspection, removal and installation

Inspection

Refer to illustration 4.3

1   Support the bike securely so it can't be knocked over during this procedure, with the wheel to be checked off the ground.

2   Visually inspect the surface of the disc(s) for score marks and other damage. Light scratches are normal after use and won't affect brake operation, but deep grooves and heavy score marks will reduce braking efficiency and accelerate pad wear. If the discs are badly

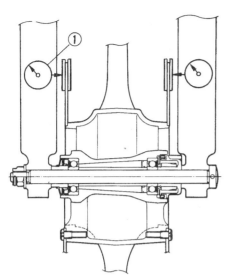

4.3 Set up a dial indicator (1) to contact each brake disc, then rotate the wheel to check for runout

4.6a Brake discs are secured by Allen bolts (arrows) . . .

4.6b . . . loosen the bolts evenly with an Allen bolt bit . . .

4.6c . . . and lift the disc off the hub

grooved they must be machined or replaced.

3   To check disc runout, mount a dial indicator to a fork leg or the swing-arm, with the plunger on the indicator touching the surface of the disc about 1/2-inch from the outer edge **(see illustration)**. Slowly turn the wheel and watch the indicator needle, comparing your reading with the limit listed in this Chapter's Specifications. If the runout is greater than allowed, check the hub bearings for play (see Section 9). If the bearings are worn, replace them and repeat this check. If the disc runout is still excessive, it will have to be replaced.

4   The disc must not be machined or allowed to wear down to a thickness less than the minimum allowable thickness, stamped on the disc and listed in this Chapter's Specifications. The thickness of the disc can be checked with a micrometer. If the thickness of the disc is less than the minimum allowable, it must be replaced.

Removal

Refer to illustrations 4.6a, 4.6b and 4.6c

5   Remove the wheel (see Section 11 for front wheel removal or Section 12 for rear wheel removal). **Caution:** *Don't lay the wheel down and allow it to rest on one of the discs - the disc could become warped. Set the wheel on wood blocks so the disc doesn't support the weight of the wheel.*

6   Mark the relationship of the disc to the wheel, so it can be in-

stalled in the same position. Remove the Allen head bolts that retain the disc to the wheel **(see illustrations)**. Loosen the bolts a little at a time, in a criss-cross pattern, to avoid distorting the disc. Once all the bolts are loose, take the disc off **(see illustration)**.

7   Take note of any paper shims that may be present where the disc mates to the wheel. If there are any, mark their position and be sure to include them when installing the disc.

Installation

Refer to illustrations 4.9a and 4.9b

8   Position the disc on the wheel, aligning the previously applied matchmarks (if you're reinstalling the original disc). Make sure the arrow (stamped on the disc) marking the direction of rotation is pointing in the proper direction.

9   Apply a non-permanent thread locking compound to the threads of the bolts **(see illustration)**. Install the bolts, tightening them a little at a time, in a criss-cross pattern, until the torque listed in this Chapter's Specifications is reached **(see illustration)**. Thoroughly clean off all grease from the brake disc(s) using acetone or brake system cleaner.

10   Install the wheel.

11   Operate the brake lever or pedal several times to bring the pads into contact with the disc. Check the operation of the brakes carefully before riding the motorcycle.

8

4.9a Apply non-permanent thread locking agent to the threads of the disc mounting bolts . . .

4.9b . . . and tighten the bolts evenly to the torque listed in this Chapter's Specifications

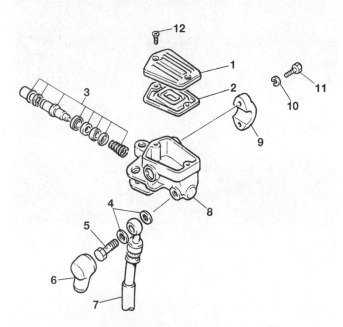

5.3a Front master cylinder (all except 1989-on FZR750 models) - exploded view

1	Reservoir cap	7	Brake hose
2	Diaphragm	8	Master cylinder body
3	Piston assembly and spring	9	Clamp
4	Brake hose sealing washers	10	Lockwasher
5	Union bolt	11	Allen bolt
6	Rubber cap	12	Cover screw

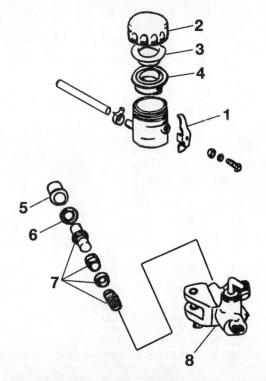

5.3b Front master cylinder (1989-on FZR750 models) - exploded view

1	Reservoir cover retainer	6	Snap-ring
2	Reservoir cover	7	Master cylinder kit
3	Diaphragm support		(replace as a set)
4	Diaphragm	8	Master cylinder body
5	Dust boot		

5 Front brake master cylinder - removal, overhaul and installation

1 If the master cylinder is leaking fluid, or if the lever does not produce a firm feel when the brake is applied, and bleeding the brakes does not help, master cylinder overhaul is recommended. Before disassembling the master cylinder, read through the entire procedure and make sure that you have the correct rebuild kit. Also, you will need some new, clean brake fluid of the recommended type, some clean rags and internal snap-ring pliers. **Note**: *To prevent damage to the paint from spilled brake fluid, always cover the fuel tank when working on the master cylinder.*

2 **Caution**: *Disassembly, overhaul and reassembly of the brake master cylinder must be done in a spotlessly clean work area to avoid contamination and possible failure of the brake hydraulic system components.*

Removal

Refer to illustrations 5.3a, 5.3b, 5.5a, 5.5b, 5.6, 5.7a and 5.7b

3 On all except UK FZR750 models, loosen but do not remove the screws holding the reservoir cover in place **(see illustration)**. On UK

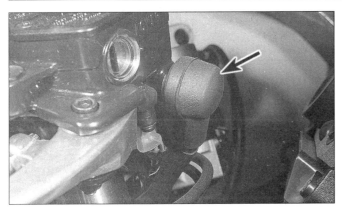

5.5a If there's a rubber boot over the union bolt (arrow), pull it back (this is an FZR600)

5.5b Remove the union bolt (arrow) and sealing washers; on later FZR750/1000 models, the union bolt secures two brake hoses

5.6 Remove the locknut (arrow) and pivot bolt

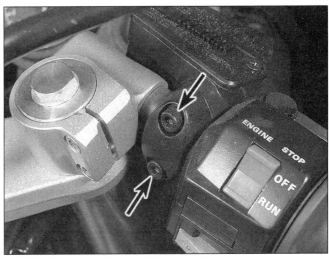

5.7a The master cylinder is secured by Allen bolts (arrows) . . .

5.7b . . . or hex bolts (arrows), depending on model; be sure the UP mark on the clamp is upright during installation

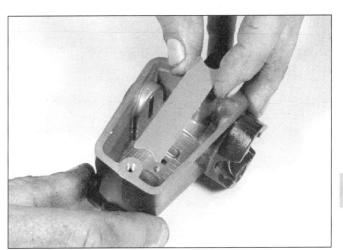

5.8 Lift the splash plate out of the cylinder body so you can clean the fluid ports in the bottom

FZR750 models, disconnect the feed hose from the master cylinder body and drain the fluid into a container (see illustration).

4   Disconnect the electrical connectors from the brake light switch (see Chapter 10).

5   Pull back the rubber boot (if equipped), loosen the banjo fitting bolt (see illustrations) and separate the brake hose(s) from the master cylinder. Wrap the end of the hose in a clean rag and suspend the hose in an upright position or bend it down carefully and place the open end in a clean container. The objective is to prevent excessive loss of brake fluid, fluid spills and system contamination.

6   Remove the locknut from the underside of the lever pivot bolt, then unscrew the bolt (see illustration).

7   Remove the master cylinder mounting bolts (see illustrations) and separate the master cylinder from the handlebar. On 1989 and later FZR750 models, remove the fluid reservoir if necessary.

Overhaul

Refer to illustrations 5.8, 5.9, 5.10a, 5.10b, 5.10c, 5.11a and 5.11b

8   Detach the cover and the rubber diaphragm, then drain the brake fluid into a suitable container. Remove the splash plate from the bottom of the reservoir (if equipped) (see illustration), then wipe any remaining fluid out of the reservoir with a clean rag.

8

5.9 Remove the rubber boot

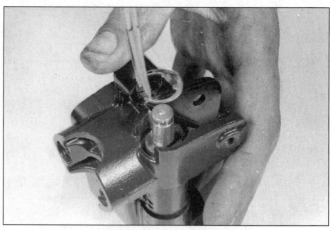

5.10a Remove the snap-ring from the cylinder bore . . .

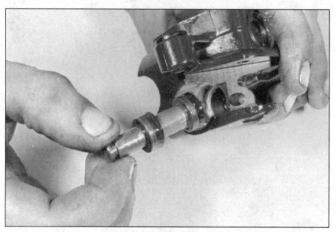

5.10b . . . then pull out the piston assembly . . .

5.10c . . . and spring

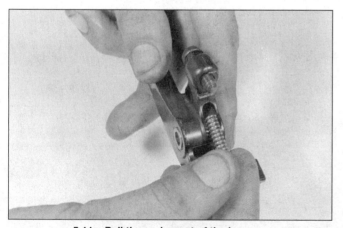

5.11a Pull the spring out of the lever . . .

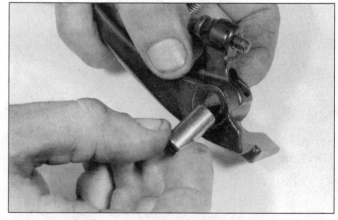

5.11b . . . and remove the pivot bushing

9   Carefully remove the rubber dust boot from the end of the piston **(see illustration)**.
10   Using snap-ring pliers, remove the snap-ring **(see illustration)** and slide out the piston assembly and the spring **(see illustrations)**. Lay the parts out in the proper order to prevent confusion during reassembly.
11   Remove the spring and pivot bushing from the lever **(see illustrations)**.
12   Clean all of the parts with brake system cleaner (available at auto parts stores), isopropyl alcohol or clean brake fluid. **Caution:** *Do not,*

under any circumstances, use a petroleum-based solvent to clean brake parts. If compressed air is available, use it to dry the parts thoroughly (make sure it's filtered and unlubricated). Check the master cylinder bore for corrosion, scratches, nicks and score marks. If damage is evident, the master cylinder must be replaced with a new one. If the master cylinder is in poor condition, then the calipers should be checked as well.
13   The piston assembly and spring are included in the rebuild kit. Use all of the new parts, regardless of the apparent condition of the old ones.

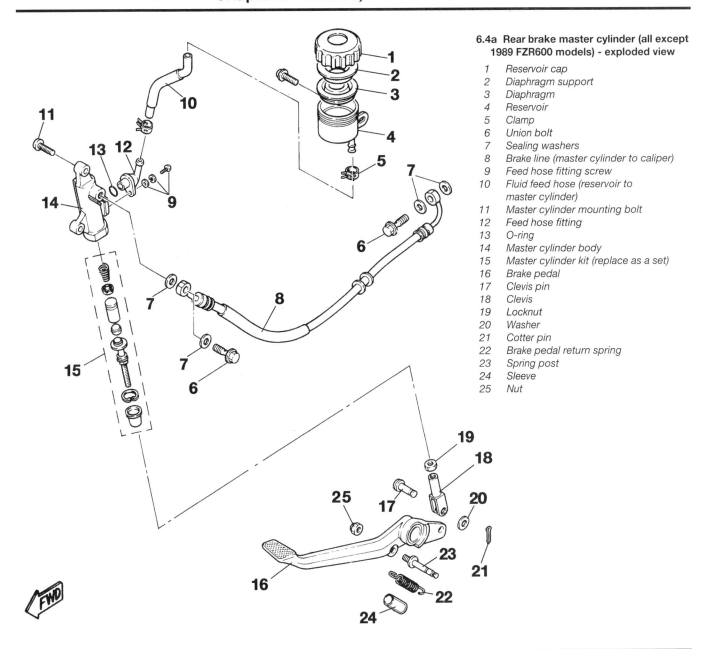

6.4a Rear brake master cylinder (all except 1989 FZR600 models) - exploded view

1   Reservoir cap
2   Diaphragm support
3   Diaphragm
4   Reservoir
5   Clamp
6   Union bolt
7   Sealing washers
8   Brake line (master cylinder to caliper)
9   Feed hose fitting screw
10 Fluid feed hose (reservoir to master cylinder)
11 Master cylinder mounting bolt
12 Feed hose fitting
13 O-ring
14 Master cylinder body
15 Master cylinder kit (replace as a set)
16 Brake pedal
17 Clevis pin
18 Clevis
19 Locknut
20 Washer
21 Cotter pin
22 Brake pedal return spring
23 Spring post
24 Sleeve
25 Nut

14   Before reassembling the master cylinder, soak the piston and the rubber cup seals in clean brake fluid for ten or fifteen minutes. Lubricate the master cylinder bore with clean brake fluid, then carefully insert the piston and related parts in the reverse order of disassembly. Make sure the lips on the cup seals do not turn inside out when they are slipped into the bore.

15   Depress the piston, then install the snap-ring (make sure the snap-ring is properly seated in the groove). Install the rubber dust boot (make sure the lip is seated properly in the piston groove).

Installation

16   Attach the master cylinder to the handlebar and tighten the bolts to the torque listed in this Chapter's Specifications. **Caution**: *If you're working on a model with a hydraulic clutch, don't mix up the clutch master cylinder clamp and the brake master cylinder clamp. The clamps or cylinders may be damaged if the clamps are installed on the wrong cylinders.*

17   Connect the brake hose to the master cylinder, using new sealing washers. Tighten the banjo fitting bolt to the torque listed in this Chapter's Specifications. Refer to Section 8 and bleed the air from the system.

6 Rear brake master cylinder - removal, overhaul and installation

1   If the master cylinder is leaking fluid, or if the pedal does not produce a firm feel when the brake is applied, and bleeding the brakes does not help, master cylinder overhaul is recommended. Before disassembling the master cylinder, read through the entire procedure and make sure that you have the correct rebuild kit. Also, you will need some new, clean brake fluid of the recommended type, some clean rags and internal snap-ring pliers.

2   **Caution**: *Disassembly, overhaul and reassembly of the brake master cylinder must be done in a spotlessly clean work area to avoid contamination and possible failure of the brake hydraulic system components.*

Removal

Refer to illustrations 6.4a, 6.4b and 6.5

3   Support the bike securely so it can't be knocked over during this procedure. Remove the protective aluminum cover for access to the mounting bolts.

4   Remove the cotter pin from the clevis pin on the master cylinder

8

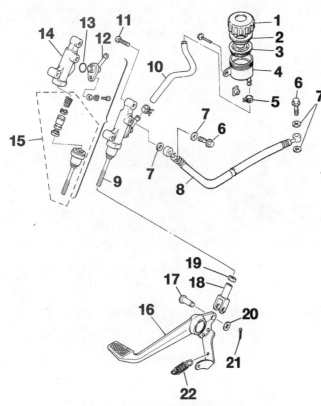

6.5 Remove the clamp (left arrow) and disconnect the feed hose from the master cylinder; the cylinder body is secured by two Allen bolts (right arrows)

6.4b Rear brake master cylinder (1989 FZR600 models) - exploded view

1	*Reservoir cap*	*12*	*Feed hose fitting*
2	*Gasket*	*13*	*O-ring*
3	*Diaphragm*	*14*	*Master cylinder*
4	*Reservoir*		*body*
5	*Clamp*	*15*	*Master cylinder kit*
6	*Union bolt*		*(replace as a set)*
7	*Sealing washers*	*16*	*Brake pedal*
8	*Brake line (master*	*17*	*Clevis pin*
	cylinder to caliper)	*18*	*Clevis*
9	*Master cylinder as-*	*19*	*Locknut*
	sembly	*20*	*Washer*
10	*Fluid feed hose*	*21*	*Cotter pin*
	(reservoir to mas-	*22*	*Brake pedal return*
	ter cylinder)		*spring*
11	*Master cylinder*		
	mounting bolt		

pushrod **(see illustrations)**. Remove the clevis pin.

5   Have a container and some rags ready to catch spilling brake fluid. Using a pair of pliers, slide the clamp up the fluid feed hose and detach the hose from the master cylinder **(see illustration)**. Direct the end of the hose into the container, unscrew the cap on the master cylinder reservoir and allow the fluid to drain.

6   Using a six-point box-end wrench (ring spanner), unscrew the fluid line union bolt from the master cylinder **(see illustration 6.4a or 6.4b)**. Discard the sealing washers on either side of the fitting.

7   Remove the mounting bolts **(see illustration 6.5)** and take the master cylinder off the frame. Remove the reservoir if necessary.

Overhaul

8   Remove the screw, lockwasher and washer and detach the fluid inlet fitting from the master cylinder. Remove the O-ring from the bore.

9   Hold the clevis with a pair of pliers and loosen the locknut. Unscrew the clevis and locknut from the pushrod and carefully remove the rubber dust boot from the pushrod.

10   Depress the pushrod and, using snap-ring pliers, remove the

snap-ring. Slide out the piston assembly and spring. Lay the parts out in the proper order to prevent confusion during reassembly.

11   Clean all of the parts with brake system cleaner (available at auto parts stores), isopropyl alcohol or clean brake fluid. **Caution**: *Do not, under any circumstances, use a petroleum-based solvent to clean brake parts. If compressed air is available, use it to dry the parts thoroughly (make sure it's filtered and unlubricated). Check the master cylinder bore for corrosion, scratches, nicks and score marks. If damage is evident, the master cylinder must be replaced with a new one. If the master cylinder is in poor condition, then the caliper should be checked as well.*

12   A new piston and spring are included in the rebuild kit. Use them regardless of the condition of the old ones.

13   Before reassembling the master cylinder, soak the piston and the rubber cup seals in clean brake fluid for ten or fifteen minutes. Lubricate the master cylinder bore with clean brake fluid, then carefully insert the parts in the reverse order of disassembly. Make sure the lips on the cup seals do not turn inside out when they are slipped into the bore.

14   Depress the pushrod, then install the snap-ring (make sure the snap-ring is properly seated in the groove). Install the rubber dust boot (make sure the lip is seated properly in the groove).

15   Install the clevis to the end of the pushrod, then tighten the locknut.

16   Install the feed hose fitting, using a new O-ring.

Installation

17   Install the reservoir (if removed) and engage it with the stay. Connect the banjo fitting to the top of the master cylinder, using a new sealing washer on each side of the fitting. Tighten the union bolt to the torque listed in this Chapter's Specifications.

18   Connect the fluid feed hose to the inlet fitting and install the hose clamp.

19   Connect the clevis to the brake pedal and secure the clevis pin with a new cotter pin.

20   Fill the fluid reservoir with the specified fluid (see Chapter 1) and bleed the system following the procedure in Section 8. Install the aluminum protective cover.

21   Check the position of the brake pedal (see Chapter 1) and adjust it if necessary. Check the operation of the brakes carefully before riding the motorcycle.

---

7   Brake hoses - inspection and replacement

Inspection

Refer to illustrations 7.2a, 7.2b and 7.2c

1   Once a week, or if the motorcycle is used less frequently, before every ride, check the condition of the brake hoses and, on early mod-

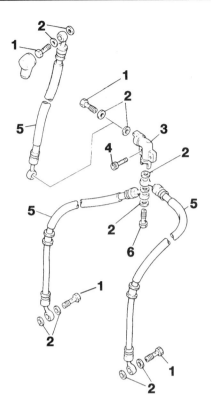

7.2a Front brake hose details (FZR600; US FZR750; 1987 and 1988 FZR1000 models)

1	Union bolts	4	Junction mounting bolt
2	Sealing washers	5	Brake hoses
3	Brake hose junction		

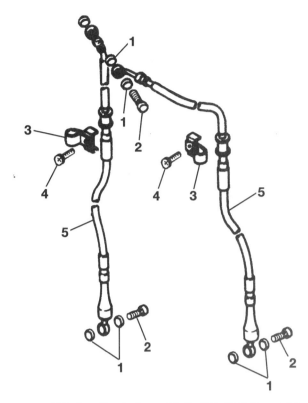

7.2b Front brake hose details (UK FZR750 models)

1	Sealing washers	4	Retainer bolts
2	Union bolts	5	Brake hoses
3	Retainers		

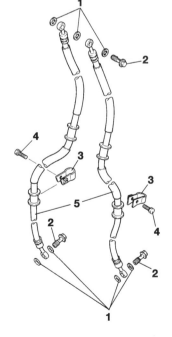

7.2c Front brake hose details (1989-on FZR1000 models)

1	Sealing washers	4	Retainer bolts
2	Union bolts	5	Brake hoses
3	Retainers		

els, the hoses that feed brake fluid to the anti-dive units on the front forks.

2   Twist and flex the rubber hoses **(see illustrations 6.4a, 6.4b and the accompanying illustrations)** while looking for cracks, bulges and seeping fluid. Check extra carefully around the areas where the hoses connect with the banjo fittings, as these are common areas for hose failure.

3   Inspect the metal banjo fittings connected to brake hoses. If the fittings are rusted, scratched or cracked, replace them.

Replacement

Refer to illustration 7.4

4   Most brake hoses have banjo fittings on each end of the hose.

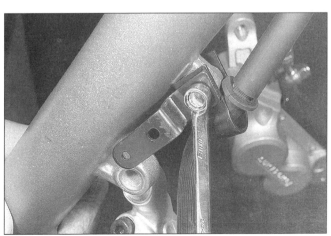

7.4 There's a hose retainer attached to each front fork

8

8.5a Each front caliper has a single bleed valve (arrow) . . .

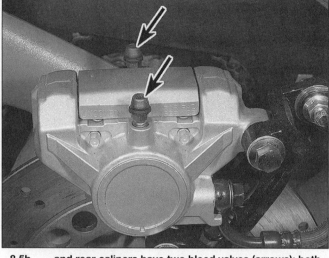

8.5b . . . and rear calipers have two bleed valves (arrows); both valves must be bled whenever the rear caliper is bled

Cover the surrounding area with plenty of rags and unscrew the union bolts on either end of the hose. Detach the hose from any clips that may be present **(see illustration)** and remove the hose.

5   Position the new hose, making sure it isn't twisted or otherwise strained, between the two components. Make sure the metal tube portion of the banjo fitting is located next to the tab on the component it's connected to, if equipped **(see illustrations 3.2a and 3.2b)**. Install the union bolts, using new sealing washers on both sides of the fittings, and tighten them to the torque listed in this Chapter's Specifications.

6   Flush the old brake fluid from the system, refill the system with the recommended fluid (see Chapter 1) and bleed the air from the system (see Section 8). Check the operation of the brakes carefully before riding the motorcycle.

8   Brake system bleeding

Refer to illustrations 8.5a and 8.5b

1   Bleeding the brake is simply the process of removing all the air bubbles from the brake fluid reservoirs, the lines and the brake calipers. Bleeding is necessary whenever a brake system hydraulic connection is loosened, when a component or hose is replaced, or when the master cylinder or caliper is overhauled. Leaks in the system may also allow air to enter, but leaking brake fluid will reveal their presence and warn you of the need for repair.

2   To bleed the brakes, you will need some new, clean brake fluid of the recommended type (see Chapter 1), a length of clear vinyl or plastic tubing, a small container partially filled with clean brake fluid, some rags and a wrench to fit the brake caliper bleeder valves.

3   Cover the fuel tank and other painted components to prevent damage in the event that brake fluid is spilled.

4   Remove the reservoir cap or cover and slowly pump the brake lever or pedal a few times, until no air bubbles can be seen floating up from the holes at the bottom of the reservoir. Doing this bleeds the air from the master cylinder end of the line. Reinstall the reservoir cap or cover.

5   Slip a box wrench over the caliper bleed valve **(see illustrations)**. Attach one end of the clear vinyl or plastic tubing to the bleeder valve and submerge the other end in the brake fluid in the container.

6   Remove the reservoir cap or cover and check the fluid level. Do not allow the fluid level to drop below the lower mark during the bleeding process.

7   Carefully pump the brake lever or pedal three or four times and hold it while opening the caliper bleeder valve. When the valve is opened, brake fluid will flow out of the caliper into the clear tubing and

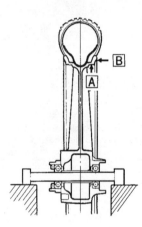

9.2 Use a dial indicator to measure wheel runout

A   Radial runout   *B   Axial runout*

the lever will move toward the handlebar or the pedal will move down.

8   Retighten the bleeder valve, then release the brake lever or pedal gradually. Repeat the process until no air bubbles are visible in the brake fluid leaving the caliper and the lever or pedal is firm when applied. **Note**: *On rear calipers with two bleeder valves, air must be bled from both, one after the other. Remember to add fluid to the reservoir as the level drops. Use only new, clean brake fluid of the recommended type. Never reuse the fluid lost during bleeding.*

9   Replace the reservoir cover, wipe up any spilled brake fluid and check the entire system for leaks. **Note**: *If bleeding is difficult, it may be necessary to let the brake fluid in the system stabilize for a few hours (it may be aerated). Repeat the bleeding procedure when the tiny bubbles in the system have settled out.*

9   Wheels - inspection and repair

Refer to illustration 9.2

1   Support the motorcycle securely upright, then clean the wheels thoroughly to remove mud and dirt that may interfere with the inspection procedure or mask defects. Make a general check of the wheels and tires as described in Chapter 1.

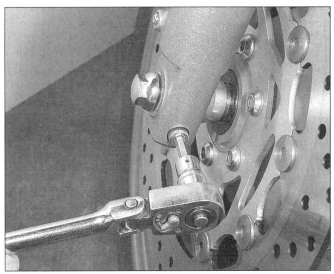

11.5a Loosen the pinch bolt . . .

11.5b . . . and unscrew the axle

2   Raise the wheel to be checked off the ground, then attach a dial indicator to the fork slider or the swingarm and position the stem against the side of the rim. Spin the wheel slowly and check the side-to-side (axial) runout of the rim, then compare your readings with the value listed in this Chapter's Specifications **(see illustration)**. In order to accurately check radial runout with the dial indicator, the wheel would have to be removed from the machine and the tire removed from the wheel. With the axle clamped in a vise, the wheel can be rotated to check the runout.
3   An easier, though slightly less accurate, method is to attach a stiff wire pointer to the fork or the swingarm and position the end a fraction of an inch from the wheel (where the wheel and tire join). If the wheel is true, the distance from the pointer to the rim will be constant as the wheel is rotated. **Note:** *If wheel runout is excessive, refer to the appropriate Section in this Chapter and check the wheel bearings very carefully before replacing the wheel.*
4   The wheels should also be visually inspected for cracks, flat spots on the rim and other damage. Since tubeless tires are involved, look very closely for dents in the area where the tire bead contacts the rim. Dents in this area may prevent complete sealing of the tire against the rim, which leads to deflation of the tire over a period of time.
5   If damage is evident, or if runout in either direction is excessive, the wheel will have to be replaced with a new one. Never attempt to repair a damaged cast aluminum wheel.

10   Wheels - alignment check

1   Misalignment of the wheels, which may be due to a cocked rear wheel or a bent frame or triple clamps, can cause strange and possibly serious handling problems. If the frame or triple clamps are at fault, repair by a frame specialist or replacement with new parts are the only alternatives.
2   To check the alignment you will need an assistant, a length of string or a perfectly straight piece of wood and a ruler graduated in 1/64 inch increments. A plumb bob or other suitable weight will also be required.
3   Support the motorcycle in a level position, then measure the width of both tires at their widest points. Subtract the smaller measurement from the larger measurement, then divide the difference by two. The result is the amount of offset that should exist between the front and rear tires on both sides.
4   If a string is used, have your assistant hold one end of it about half way between the floor and the rear axle, touching the rear sidewall of the tire.

5   Run the other end of the string forward and pull it tight so that it is roughly parallel to the floor. Slowly bring the string into contact with the front sidewall of the rear tire, then turn the front wheel until it is parallel with the string. Measure the distance from the front tire sidewall to the string.
6   Repeat the procedure on the other side of the motorcycle. The distance from the front tire sidewall to the string should be equal on both sides.
7   As was previously pointed out, a perfectly straight length of wood may be substituted for the string. The procedure is the same.
8   If the distance between the string and tire is greater on one side, or if the rear wheel appears to be cocked, refer to Chapter 7, Swingarm bearings - check, and make sure the swingarm is tight.
9   If the front-to-back alignment is correct, the wheels still may be out of alignment vertically.
10   Using the plumb bob, or other suitable weight, and a length of string, check the rear wheel to make sure it is vertical. To do this, hold the string against the tire upper sidewall and allow the weight to settle just off the floor. When the string touches both the upper and lower tire sidewalls and is perfectly straight, the wheel is vertical. If it is not, place thin spacers under one leg of the centerstand.
11   Once the rear wheel is vertical, check the front wheel in the same manner. If both wheels are not perfectly vertical, the frame and/or major suspension components are bent.

11   Front wheel - removal, inspection and installation

Removal
1   Support the bike securely so it can't be knocked over during this procedure. Raise the front wheel off the ground by placing a floor jack, with a wood block on the jack head, under the engine.
2   Disconnect the speedometer cable from the drive unit (see Chapter 10).

All except 1989-on FZR750 models
Refer to illustrations 11.5a, 11.5b, 11.5c, 11.6, 11.7a and 11.7b
3   If you're working on an FZR600 or a 1989-on FZR1000, remove the left and right fairings (see Chapter 9).
4   Remove the left brake caliper (FZR600) or both brake calipers (all others) and support the caliper(s) with a piece of wire. Don't disconnect the brake hose from the caliper(s).
5   Loosen the axle pinch bolt and unscrew the axle **(see illustrations)**.

8

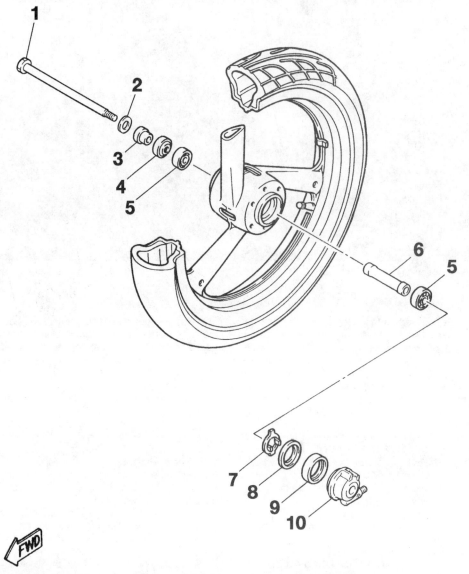

11.5c   Front wheel details (all except 1989-on FZR750 models)

1	Axle	6	Spacer
2	Washer (1987 and 1988 models only)	7	Speedometer clutch
3	Collar	8	Speedometer clutch retainer
4	Seal	9	Seal
5	Wheel bearing	10	Speedometer drive unit

11.6   Pull the axle out of the forks and wheel

11.7a   This collar goes between the fork and the right side of the wheel; don't forget to reinstall it

11.7b   Pull the speedometer drive out of the wheel; the notch (arrow) aligns with a protrusion on the fork

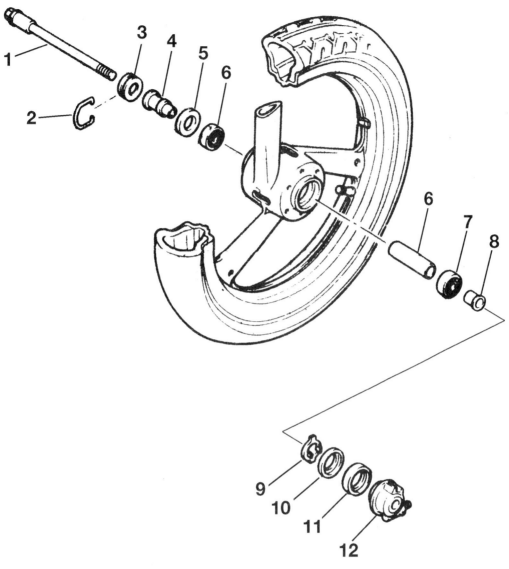

11.11 Front wheel details - 1989-on FZR750 models

1	Axle	7	Spacer
2	Clip	8	Collar
3	Flange	9	Speedometer clutch
4	Collar	10	Speedometer clutch retainer
5	Seal	11	Seal
6	Wheel bearings	12	Speedometer drive unit

8

6   Support the wheel, then pull out the axle **(see illustration)** and carefully lower the wheel away from the forks.

7   Remove the collar from the right side and the speedometer drive assembly from the left side **(see illustrations)**. Set the wheel aside. **Caution**: *Don't lay the wheel down and allow it to rest on one of the discs - the disc could become warped. Set the wheel on wood blocks so the disc doesn't support the weight of the wheel.* **Note**: *Don't operate the front brake lever with the wheel removed.*

1989-on FZR750 models

Refer to illustration 11.11

8   Remove the lower fairing (see Chapter 9).

9   Disconnect the speedometer cable from the drive unit at the left

fork (see Chapter 10).

10   Unbolt the brake calipers without disconnecting the brake hoses and support them with pieces of wire.

11   Loosen the axle pinch bolt and unscrew the axle **(see illustration)**.

12   Support the wheel, then pull out the axle and carefully lower the wheel away from the forks.

13   Remove the collar from the right side and the speedometer drive assembly and collar from the left side. Set the wheel aside. **Caution**: *Don't lay the wheel down and allow it to rest on one of the discs - the disc could become warped. Set the wheel on wood blocks so the disc doesn't support the weight of the wheel.* **Note**: *Don't operate the front brake lever with the wheel removed.*

11.16 Be sure the tabs on the speedometer clutch (upper arrows) align with the notches in the speedometer drive unit (lower arrows) when the unit is installed

Inspection

14   Roll the axle on a flat surface such as a piece of plate glass. If it's bent at all, replace it. If the axle is corroded, remove the corrosion with fine emery cloth.

15   Check the condition of the wheel bearings (see Section 13).

Installation

Refer to illustration 11.16

16   Installation is the reverse of removal. Apply a thin coat of grease to the seal lip, then slide the axle into the hub. Slide the wheel into place. Make sure the lugs in the speedometer drive clutch line up with the notches in the speedometer drive gear **(see illustration)**. Make sure the protrusion on the inner side of the left fork fits into the notch in the speedometer gear housing **(see illustration 11.7b)**.

17   Slip the axle into place, then tighten the axle to the torque listed in this Chapter's Specifications. Tighten the axle pinch bolt to the torque listed in this Chapter's Specifications.

18   Apply the front brake, pump the forks up and down several times and check for binding and proper brake operation.

**12.3a Rear wheel details
(FZR600 models)**

1   Axle
2   Washer
3   Cotter pin
4   Nut
5   Bolt
6   Torque link
7   Chain adjuster
8   Adjuster plate
9   Washer
10   Adjusting nut
11   Locknut
12   Caliper bracket
13   Collar
14   Grease seal
15   Wheel bearing
16   Spacer
17   Damper segments (cush drive)
18   Wheel bearings
19   Coupling
20   Sprocket stud
21   Nut
22   Collar
23   Coupling bearing
24   Grease seal
25   Collar
26   Washer
27   Axle nut
28   Cotter pin

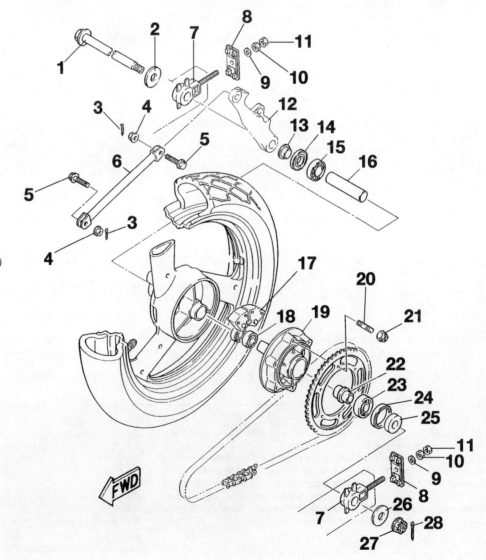

12.3b Rear wheel details (1987 and 1988 FZR750 and 1000 models)

1   Axle
2   Cotter pin
3   Washer
4   Brake hose clip
5   Lockwasher
6   Bolt
7   Chain adjuster bolt
8   Chain adjuster block
9   Nut
10 Chain adjuster plate
11 Washer
12 Nut
13 Locknut
14 Torque link bolt
15 Torque link
16 Caliper bracket (high-mount design shown; low-mount design similar)
17 Collar
18 Seal
19 Wheel bearing
20 Spacer
21 Damper segments (cush drive)
22 Wheel bearing
23 Coupling
24 Sprocket stud
25 Nut
26 Sprocket
27 Collar
28 Coupling bearing
29 Seal
30 Collar
31 Chain
32 Washer
33 Axle nut

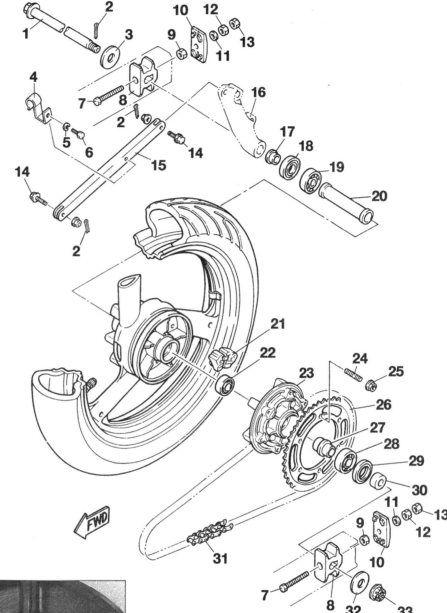

12.3c Bend back the cotter pin (arrow) and pull it out, then loosen the axle nut (but don't remove it yet)

12   Rear wheel - removal, inspection and installation

Refer to illustrations 12.3a through 12.3e, 12.4a, 12.4b, 12.6, 12.7a, 12.7b, 12.7c and 12.7d

Removal

1   Support the bike securely so it can't be knocked over during this procedure.

2   If you're working on a model with a low-mount (underslung) rear brake caliper, remove the rear brake caliper (see Section 3). If you're working on a model with a high-mount rear caliper, the caliper can be left in place.

3   Remove the cotter pin from the axle nut and loosen the nut **(see illustrations)**.

8

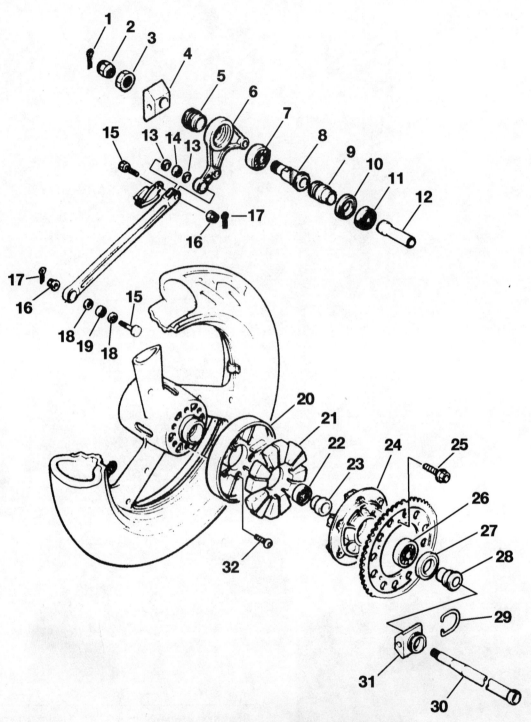

12.3d Rear wheel details (1989-on FZR750 models)

1	Cotter pin	12	Spacer	23	Collar
2	Axle nut	13	Seal	24	Coupling clutch
3	Locknut	14	Bearing	25	Sprocket bolt
4	Chain adjuster block	15	Torque link bolt	26	Coupling bearing
5	Collar	16	Nut	27	Seal
6	Caliper bracket	17	Cotter pin	28	Collar
7	Wheel bearing	18	Seal	29	Retaining ring
8	Collar	19	Bearing	30	Axle
9	Collar	20	Damper hub	31	Chain adjuster block
10	Seal	21	Coupling segments	32	Bolt
11	Wheel bearing	22	Wheel bearing		

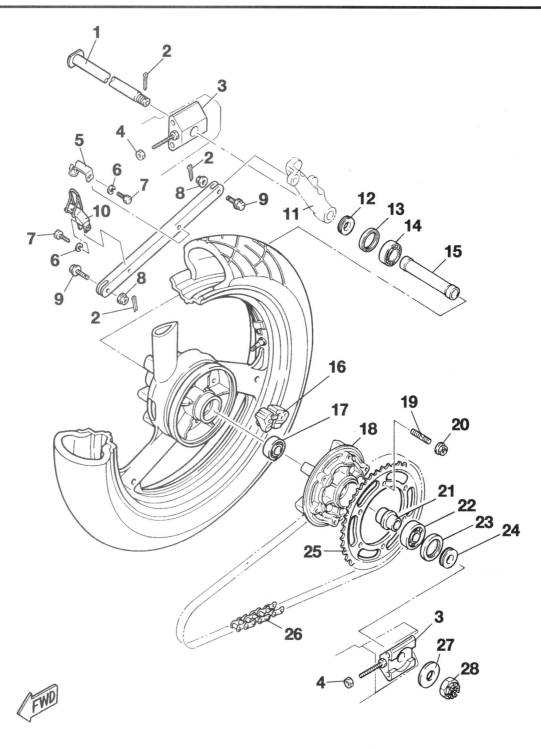

12.3e Rear wheel details (1989-on FZR1000 models)

1	Axle	11	Caliper bracket
2	Cotter pin	12	Collar
3	Chain adjuster	13	Seal
4	Nut	14	Wheel bearing
5	Brake hose bracket	15	Spacer
6	Lockwasher	16	Damper segments (cush drive)
7	Bolt	17	Wheel bearing
8	Nut	18	Coupling
9	Torque link bolt	19	Sprocket stud
10	Brake hose bracket		

20	Nut
21	Collar
22	Coupling bearing
23	Seal
24	Collar
25	Sprocket
26	Chain
27	Washer
28	Axle nut

8

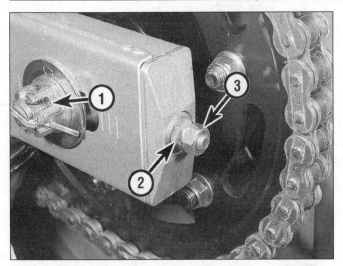

12.4a Loosen the chain adjuster locknut (this is an FZR600; early 750/1000 models similar) . . .

1	Axle nut (remove cotter pin and loosen first)
2	Adjuster nut
3	Locknut

12.4b . . . then loosen the chain adjuster nut or bolt to create as much slack in the chain as possible (this is a 1989-on FZR1000; later 750 models similar)

1	Locknut
2	Adjuster bolt

12.6 Remove the axle nut (this is an FZR1000)

12.7a Pull out the axle (this is an FZR600) . . .

12.7b . . . and this is an FZR1000 (750 models similar)

12.7c Remove the collar from the brake disc side of the wheel . . .

12.7d . . . and from the sprocket side

12.12a Position the wheel between the sides of the swingarm with the brake disc on the right . . .

12.12b . . . and lift it into position; on models with high-mount calipers, slip the brake disc between the pads

13.5a Pry out the grease seal . . .

13.5b . . . then lift out the speedometer clutch retainer and the speedometer clutch

4   Loosen the chain adjusting bolt locknuts and fully loosen both adjusters **(see illustrations)**.
5   Push the rear wheel as far forward as possible. Lift the top of the chain up off the rear sprocket and pull it to the left while rotating the wheel backwards. This will disengage the chain from the sprocket. **Warning**: *Don't let your fingers slip between the chain and the sprocket.*
6   Unscrew the axle nut **(see illustration)**.
7   Support the wheel and slide the axle and washer out **(see illustrations)**. Lower the wheel and remove it from the swingarm, being careful not to lose the collars on either side of the hub **(see illustrations)**. **Caution**: *Don't lay the wheel down and allow it to rest on the disc or the sprocket - they could become warped. Set the wheel on wood blocks so the disc or the sprocket doesn't support the weight of the wheel. Do not operate the brake pedal with the wheel removed.*

Inspection

8   Before installing the wheel, check the axle for straightness by rolling it on a flat surface such as a piece of plate glass (if the axle is corroded, first remove the corrosion with fine emery cloth). If the axle is bent at all, replace it.
9   Check the condition of the wheel bearings (see Section 13).

Installation

Refer to illustrations 12.12a and 12.12b
10   Apply a thin coat of grease to the seal lips.
11   Slide the spacers into their proper positions on the sides of the hub **(see illustrations 12.7c and 12.7d)**.
12   Slide the wheel into place **(see illustration)**. If you're working on a model with a high-mount rear brake caliper, slide the brake disc between the pads **(see illustration)**.
13   Lift the chain over the sprocket, raise the wheel, install the axle (pass it through the caliper bracket and all collars) and finger-tighten the axle nut.
14   Adjust the chain slack (see Chapter 1) and tighten the adjuster locknuts.
15   Tighten the axle nut to the torque listed in this Chapter's Specifications. Install a new cotter pin, tightening the axle nut an additional amount, if necessary, to align the hole in the axle with the castellations on the nut. Be sure to bend the cotter pin correctly (see Drive chain and sprockets - check, adjustment and lubrication in Chapter 1).
16   If you're working on a model with a low-mount (underslung) rear brake caliper, install the caliper (see Section 3).
17   Check the operation of the brakes carefully before riding the motorcycle.

13   Wheel bearings - replacement

1   Support the bike securely so it can't be knocked over during this procedure and remove the wheel (see Section 11 (front wheel) or 12 (rear wheel).
2   Set the wheel on blocks so as not to allow the weight of the wheel rest on the brake disc or sprocket.

Front wheel bearings

Refer to illustrations 13.5a, 13.5b, 13.6a, 13.6b, 13.10a, 13.10b, 13.11, 13.12a and 13.12b
3   From the right side of the wheel, lift out the collar (if you haven't already done so - **see illustration 11.7a**) and pry out the grease seal **(see illustration 11.5c or 11.11)**.
4   From the left side of the wheel, lift out the speedometer drive unit (if you haven't already done so - **see illustration 11.7b**).
5   From the left side of the wheel, pry out the grease seal, then lift out the speedometer clutch retainer and speedometer clutch **(see illustrations)**.
6   Using a metal rod (preferably a brass drift punch) inserted through the center of the hub bearing, tap evenly around the inner race of the

8

13.6a Insert a drift punch through one bearing and tap out the opposite bearing . . .

13.6b Then turn the wheel over and lift out the bearing and spacer

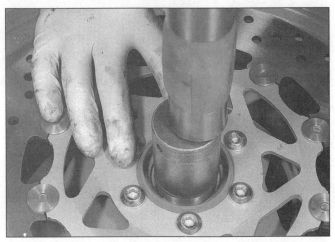

13.10a Install the bearing with a socket the same diameter as the bearing outer race (shown) or with a bearing driver

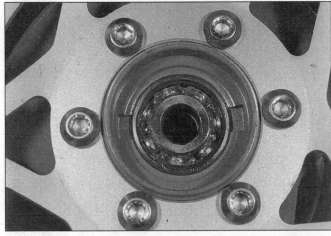

13.10b The bearing should look like this when it's installed

opposite bearing to drive it from the hub **(see illustration)**. The bearing spacer will also come out **(see illustration)**.

7   Lay the wheel on its other side and remove the remaining bearing using the same technique.

8   Clean the bearings with a high flash-point solvent (one which won't leave any residue) and blow them dry with compressed air (don't let the bearing spin as you dry them). Apply a few drops of oil to the bearing. Hold the outer race of the bearing and rotate the inner race - if the bearing doesn't turn smoothly, has rough spots or is noisy, replace it with a new one.

9   If the bearing checks out okay and will be reused, wash it in solvent once again and dry it, then pack the bearing with medium-weight multi-purpose lithium-based grease.

10   Thoroughly clean the hub area of the wheel. Install the bearing into the recess in the hub, with the marked or shielded side facing out. Using a bearing driver or a socket large enough to contact the outer race of the bearing, drive it in **(see illustration)** until it's completely seated **(see illustration)**.

11   Turn the wheel over and install the bearing spacer and bearing, driving the bearing into place as described in Step 10. Install the speedometer clutch and retainer on the left side of the wheel **(see illustration)**.

12   Coat new grease seals with grease **(see illustration)**, then install them. It should be possible to push the seals in with even finger pressure **(see illustration)**, but if necessary use a seal driver, large socket or a flat piece of wood to drive the seals into place.

13   Install the speedometer drive unit, making sure the lugs in the

13.11 Install the speedometer clutch and retainer

speedometer clutch align with the notches in the gear **(see illustration 11.16)**.

14   Clean off all grease from the brake disc(s) using acetone or brake system cleaner.

15   Make sure the collar is in place **(see illustration 11.7a)** and install the wheel.

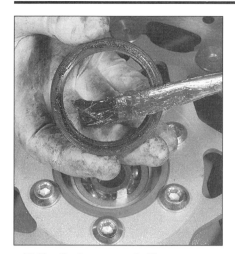

13.12a Coat a new seal with grease . . .

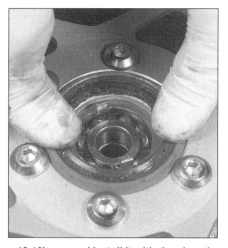

13.12b . . . and install it with the closed side outward; evenly-applied pressure with thumbs should be enough, but you can use a bearing driver or block of wood if it isn't

13.17a Lift out the collar if it's loose enough . . .

13.17b . . . or tap it out with a socket if it's tight

13.19 Don't forget to install the coupling collar or the bearings will be damaged

Rear coupling bearing

Refer to illustrations 13.17a, 13.17b and 13.19

16   Lift the collar from the coupling on the sprocket side of the wheel **(see illustrations 12.3a, 12.3b, 12.3d and 12.3e)**. Pry out the grease seal.

17   Lift the sprocket out of the damper assembly (see Chapter 7). Lift the collar out of the bearing **(see illustration)**. If it's tight, drive it out from the other side with a socket **(see illustration)**. Drive out the coupling bearing with a bearing driver or socket **(see illustrations 12.3a, 12.3b, 12.3d and 12.3e)**.

18   Hold the coupling bearing by the inner race and spin the outer race. If it's rough, loose or noisy, replace the bearing and collar.

19   Drive the bearing and grease seal into the coupling with a bearing driver or socket. Be certain to reinstall the collar **(see illustration)**; if it's left out, the rear wheel bearings will be damaged when the axle nut is tightened.

Rear wheel bearings

Refer to illustrations 13.20, 13.21, 13.22a, 13.22b, 13.25a, 13.25b, 13.25c, 13.26a, 13.26b and 13.26c

20   Lift out the sprocket and damper (see Chapter 7). On the brake disc side of the wheel, lift out the collar **(see illustration)**.

13.20 Lift the collar out of the brake disc side of the wheel

8

13.21 Pry loose the grease seal

13.22a Insert a drift punch through one bearing and tap loose the opposite bearing . . .

13.22b . . . then turn the wheel over and take out the bearing and the spacer

13.25a Tap in the bearing with a socket the same diameter as the outer race (shown) or with a bearing driver

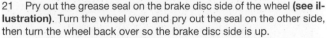

13.25b On FZR600 models, there are two wheel bearings next to each other on the coupling side of the wheel; the first bearing should be installed to this depth . . .

13.25c . . . and the second bearing should be installed next to it like this

21   Pry out the grease seal on the brake disc side of the wheel **(see illustration)**. Turn the wheel over and pry out the seal on the other side, then turn the wheel back over so the brake disc side is up.

22   Using a metal rod (preferably a brass drift punch) inserted through the center of the hub bearing on the brake disc side, tap evenly around the inner race of the opposite bearing to drive it from the hub **(see illustration)**. Turn the wheel over and remove the bearing and spacer

(see illustration).

23   From the sprocket side of the wheel, drive out the remaining bearing in the same manner.

24   Perform Steps 8 and 9 above to inspect the bearings.

25   Install the bearings with their sealed sides facing out. Drive them in with a bearing driver or a socket the same diameter as the bearing outer race. FZR600 models use two wheel bearings on the sprocket side of the wheel **(see illustrations)**.

TIRE CHANGING SEQUENCE - TUBELESS TIRES

Deflate tire. After releasing beads, push tire bead into well of rim at point opposite valve. Insert lever next to valve and work bead over edge of rim.

Use two levers to work bead over edge of rim. Note use of rim protectors.

When first bead is clear, remove tire as shown.

Before installing, ensure that tire is suitable for wheel. Take note of any sidewall markings such as direction of rotation arrows.

Work first bead over the rim flange.

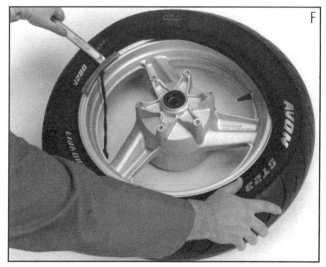

Use a tire lever to work the second bead over rim flange.

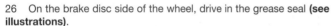

13.26a Position the grease seal in its bore . . .

13.26b . . . then tap it into position with a socket, block of wood or bearing driver . . .

26   On the brake disc side of the wheel, drive in the grease seal **(see illustrations)**.

27   Install the coupling to the wheel, making sure the coupling collar is in position **(see illustration 13.19)**.

---

14   Tubeless tires - general information

---

1   Tubeless tires are used as standard equipment on this motorcycle. They are generally safer than tube-type tires but if problems do occur they require special repair techniques.

2   The force required to break the seal between the rim and the bead of the tire is substantial, and is usually beyond the capabilities of an individual working with normal tire irons.

3   Also, repair of the punctured tire and replacement on the wheel rim requires special tools, skills and experience that the average do-it-yourselfer lacks.

4   For these reasons, if a puncture or flat occurs with a tubeless tire, the wheel should be removed from the motorcycle and taken to a dealer service department or a motorcycle repair shop for repair or replacement of the tire. The accompanying illustrations can be used to replace a tubeless tire in an emergency.

13.26c . . . the seal should be flush with the wheel when installed

Chapter 9   Fairing and bodywork

9

Contents

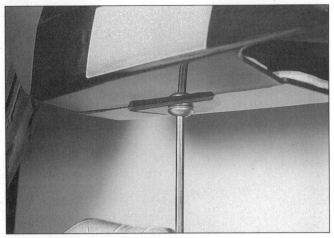

2.2a Remove the Allen bolts beneath the fairing halves at the front . . .

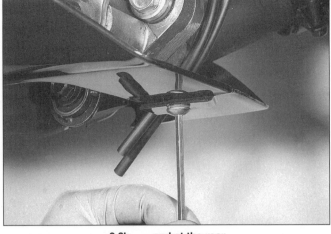

2.2b . . . and at the rear

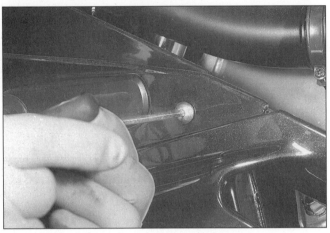

2.2c Remove the bolts on each side that attach the front fairing to the left and right fairing halves . . .

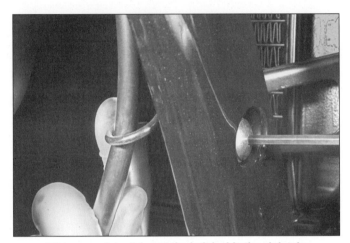

2.2d . . . and don't forget the bolt inside the air intake

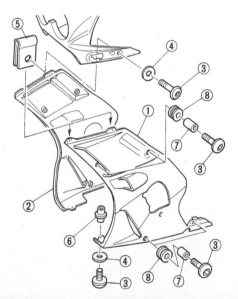

2.2e Left and right fairing details (FZR600 dual-headlight models)

1	Left fairing	5	Spring nut
2	Right fairing	6	Special nut
3	Allen bolt	7	Collar
4	Plastic washer	8	Damper

1   General information

This Chapter covers the procedures necessary to remove and install the fairings and other body parts. Since many service and repair operations on these motorcycles require removal of the fairings and/or other body parts, the procedures are grouped here and referred to from other Chapters.

In the event of damage to the fairings or other body part, it is usually necessary to remove the broken component and replace it with a new (or used) one. The material that the fairings are composed of doesn't lend itself to conventional repair techniques. There are, however, some shops that specialize in "plastic welding," so it would be advantageous to check around first before throwing the damaged part away.

2   Fairing - removal and installation

1   Support the bike securely so it can't be knocked over during this procedure.

FZR600 models

Refer to illustrations 2.2a through 2.2f, 2.3, 2.5a, 2.5b and 2.6a through 2.6e

2   Support the left and right fairings and remove the mounting bolts **(see illustrations)**.

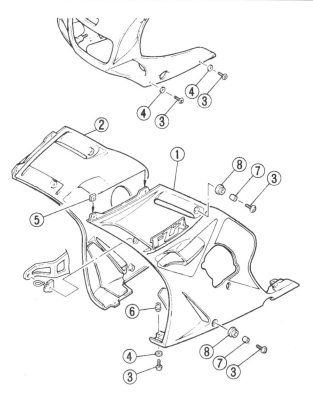

**2.2f Left and right fairing details
(FZR600 single-headlight models)**

1 Left fairing   5 Spring nut
2 Right fairing   6 Special nut
3 Allen bolt   7 Collar
4 Plastic washer   8 Damper

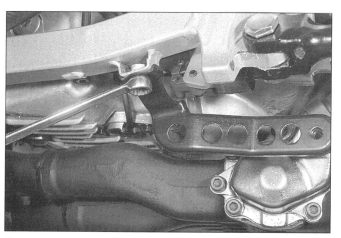

**2.3 Unbolt the left lower fairing stay for access to the EXUP valve
(if equipped)**

3   Carefully maneuver the fairings away from the bike. If necessary (for access to the EXUP valve, for example), remove the fairing bracket on the left side **(see illustration)**.
4   Disconnect the turn signal wiring connectors and remove the turn signal assemblies (see Chapter 10).
5   Remove the rearview mirrors **(see illustrations)**.
6   Remove the air intake duct covers (if equipped) and air intake ducts, then remove the fasteners and lift off the front fairing **(see illustrations)**.
7   Installation is the reverse of removal. Tighten all fasteners securely, but don't overtighten them and crack the fairing.

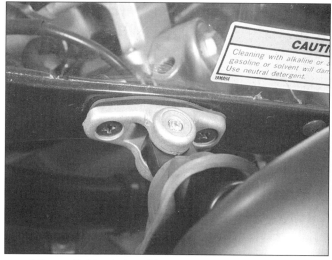

**2.5a . . . Pull back the rubber cover to expose the mirror
mounting screws . . .**

**2.5b . . . hold the mirror mounting nuts with a wrench and remove
the mounting screws to detach the mirror**

2.6a Loosen the clamp screw at each end of the air duct (left arrow), then remove the front fairing mounting nuts (right arrow; lower right nut shown)

9

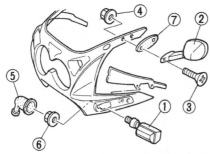

2.6b Front fairing details (FZR600 dual-headlight models)

1	Turn signal	5	Rubber cap
2	Mirror	6	Turn signal mounting nut
3	Screw	7	Damper
4	Mirror mounting nut		

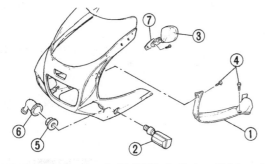

2.6d Front fairing details (FZR600 single-headlight models)

1	Air duct cover	5	Turn signal mounting nut
2	Turn signal	6	Rubber cap
3	Mirror	7	Damper
4	Screws		

2.8 Fairing details (1987 and 1988 FZR750/1000 models)

1	Allen bolt	6	Collar
2	Plain washer	7	Grommet
3	Spring nut	8	Nut
4	Front fairing panel	9	Stay
5	Side fairing panel		

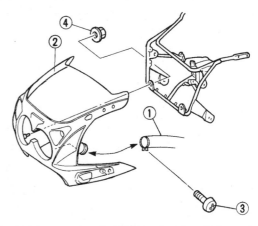

2.6c Fairing stay details (FZR600 dual-headlight models)

1	Air duct	3	Screw
2	Front fairing	4	Nut

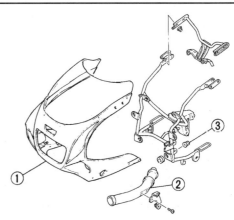

2.6e Fairing stay details (FZR600 single-headlight models)

1	Front fairing	3	Nut
2	Air duct		

1987 and 1988 FZR750/1000 models

Refer to illustration 2.8

8   Support the left and right fairings and remove the mounting bolts **(see illustration)**. Carefully maneuver the fairings away from the bike.

9   Disconnect the turn signal wiring connectors and remove the turn signal assemblies (see Chapter 10).

10   Remove the rearview mirrors (see illustrations 2.5a and 2.5b). Disconnect the electrical connectors for the headlights and front position light (if equipped).

11   Remove the air intake ducts.

12   Remove the four mounting nuts and lift off the front fairing together with the headlight assembly. **Caution:** *Don't drop the headlight assembly as the fairing is removed.*

13   Installation is the reverse of removal. Tighten all fasteners securely, but don't overtighten them and crack the fairing.

1989-on FZR750R models

14   Reach through the access hole in each side of the fairing at the rear lower corner and remove the mounting bolt.

15   Turn three quick-release fasteners on each side of the lower fairing counterclockwise, then lower the fairing away from the machine.

16   Disconnect the fuel tank breather pipe from the rollover valve on the tank's top surface.

17   Turn two quick-release fasteners on each side of the small upper fairing panel (over front of fuel tank) counterclockwise. Release the air duct spring bands and remove the fresh air intake.

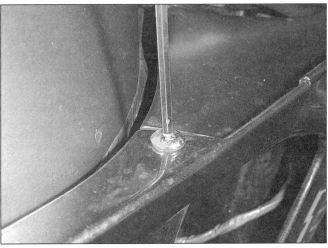

2.25a The fairing panels on 1989 and later FZR1000 models are
secured by Allen bolts

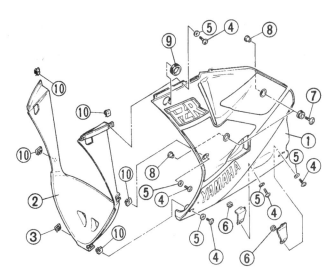

2.25b Fairing details (1989 and 1990 FZR1000; 1991 and later
models similar)

1	Fairing panel	6	Nut
2	Lower front fairing panel	7	Large bolt
3	Spring nut	8	Collar
4	Bolt	9	Grommet
5	Plastic washer	10	Spring nut

2.28a Remove the air duct bolts . . .

2.28b . . . and disengage the duct from the fitting

18 Remove the inner fairing panel on each side of the motorcycle.
19 Disconnect the fuel reserve switch electrical connector on the left side of the motorcycle.
20 Remove the turn signals (see Chapter 10).
21 Remove the rearview mirrors.
22 Disconnect the speedometer cable, remove the upper fairing bolts (one at each rear edge of the upper fairing and another just under the headlights) and take the upper fairing off.
23 Installation is the reverse of removal. Tighten all fasteners securely, but don't overtighten them and crack the fairing.

1989-on FZR1000 models

Refer to illustrations 2.25a, 2.25b, 2.28a, 2.28b, 2.29a, 2.29b, 2.29c and 2.31

24 Remove the turn signals (see Chapter 10).
25 Support the left, right and lower front fairings and remove the mounting bolts **(see illustrations)**.
26 Carefully maneuver the fairings away from the bike.
27 Remove the rearview mirrors **(see illustrations 2.5a and 2.5b)**.
28 Remove the air intake ducts **(see illustration)**.
29 Remove the inner fairing panels on both sides and disconnect the electrical connector for the fuel reserve switch **(see illustrations)**.
30 Remove the rubber covers from the rear of the headlights and disconnect the headlight electrical connectors (see Chapter 10).
31 Remove the mounting nuts and lift the front fairing off the stay together with the headlight assembly **(see illustration)**. **Caution:** *Don't let the headlight assembly fall as the fairing is removed. Disconnect the*

9

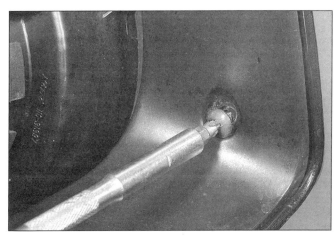

2.29a Remove the upper panel screws . . .

2.29b . . . and on the left side, remove two screws above the fuel reserve switch . . .

2.29c . . . and disconnect the switch electrical connector

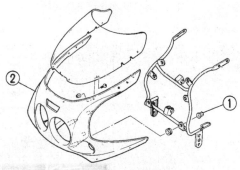

2.31 Front fairing and stay (FZR1000 models)

1   Mounting nut   *2   Fairing panel*

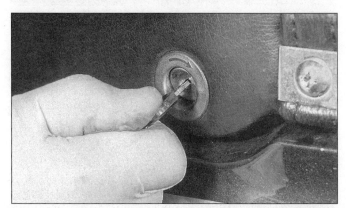

3.1 Insert the key and turn it clockwise to release the seat

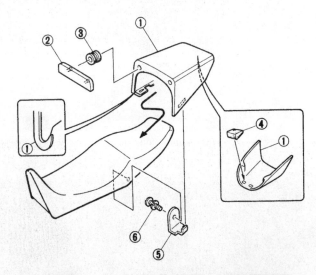
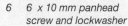

3.2 Pillion seat cover details (1987 and 1988 FZR750)

1   Cover   *5   Bracket*
2   Backrest   *6   6 x 10 mm panhead*
3   Grommet   *screw and lockwasher*
4   Damper

electrical connector for the front position light (if equipped) and take the fairing off the motorcycle.
32 Installation is the reverse of removal. Tighten all fasteners securely, but don't overtighten them and crack the fairing.

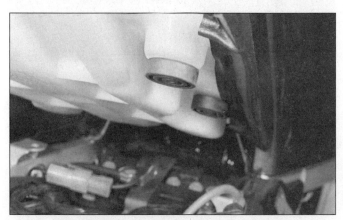

3.3 Lift the seat and remove it toward the rear

3   Seat - removal and installation

All except 1989-on FZR750 models

Refer to illustrations 3.1, 3.2 and 3.3
1   Release the seat lock with the ignition key **(see illustration)**.
2   If you're working on a 1987 or 1988 FZR750, remove the pillion seat cover **(see illustration)**.
3   Lift the rear of the seat and pull it out toward the rear **(see illustration)**.
4   If the motorcycle has a separate passenger seat, lift it off.
5   Installation is the reverse of removal. Be sure the retaining tabs at the front of the seat engage their slots.

4.3a Remove the screw along the top of the side cover
(this is an FZR600) . . .

4.3b . . . and this is an FZR1000

4.3c The lower edge of the side cover is secured by a series of
rubber grommets (arrow) . . .

4.3d . . . and molded pins (upper arrow); the rear is secured by
molded hooks that fit into slots (lower arrows) . . .

1989-on FZR750 models

6   To remove the seat, unscrew its mounting bolts and lift off (two
bolts at front of seat pad and two bolts on each side of tailpiece). The
seat pad is held to the tailpiece by four nuts and tow bolts accessed
from the underside.
7   Installation is the reverse of removal.

---

4   Side covers - removal and installation

Refer to illustrations 4.3a through 4.3e
1   Remove the seat (see Section 3).
2   The side covers are attached by a single screw along the top,
molded pins that fit into rubber grommets, as well as molded hooks at
the rear that fit into the tailpiece.
3   To detach a side cover, remove the screw, gently pull the cover
away from the bike to separate the molded pins from the grommets,
then detach the hooks from the tailpiece **(see illustrations)**. **Caution:**
Do not use force. The pins and hooks can easily be broken.
4   Installation is the reverse of removal.

---

5   Rear view mirrors - removal and installation

Mirror removal and installation are part of the fairing removal and
installation procedures (see Section 2).

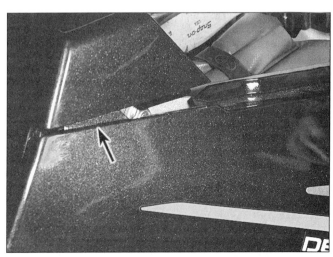

4.3e . . . there's also a hook and slot at the upper rear of the side
cover (arrow)

9

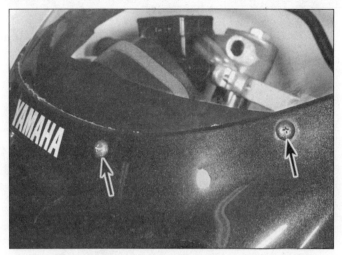

6.1 The windshield is secured a row of screws along the bottom (arrows)

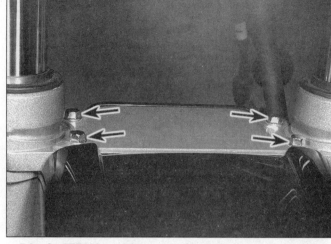

7.6a On FZR600 models, remove four bolts (arrows), the fork brace and the fender

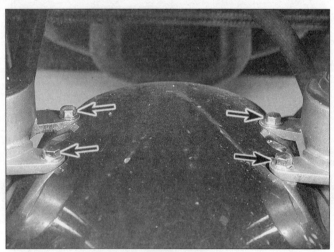

7.6b On 1989 and 1990 FZR1000 models, remove four fender mounting bolts (arrows)

7.8 Fender (mudguard) mounting details
(1991 and later FZR1000 models)

1   Bolt   2   Collar

6   Windshield - removal and installation

Refer to illustration 6.1
1   Remove the screws securing the windshield to the fairing **(see il-lustration)**.
2   Carefully separate the windshield from the fairing. If it sticks, don't attempt to pry it off - just keep applying steady pressure with your fingers.
3   Installation is the reverse of the removal procedure. Be sure each screw has a plastic washer under its head. Tighten the screws securely, but be careful not to overtighten them, as the windshield might crack.

7   Front fender (mudguard) - removal and installation

1   Support the bike securely so it can't be knocked over during this procedure.

1987 and 1988 models
2   Disconnect the speedometer cable and pull it through the loop attached to the fender.
3   Remove the bolts that hold the front and rear halves of the fender together.

4   Between the forks, remove four bolts and the fork brace. Separate the halves of the fender and remove them from the motorcycle.
5   Installation is the reverse of the removal steps.

All FZR600 and 1989/1990 FZR1000 models
Refer to illustrations 7.6a and 7.6b
6   Between the forks, remove the bolts that secure the fork brace (if equipped) and fender **(see illustrations)**. Carefully lift the fender out, taking care not to scratch it.
7   Installation is the reverse of the removal steps.

1991-on FZR1000 models
Refer to illustrations 7.8 and 7.9
8   Remove the fasteners and take the fender off the motorcycle **(see illustration)**.
9   If necessary, remove the over fenders from the fender **(see illustration)**.

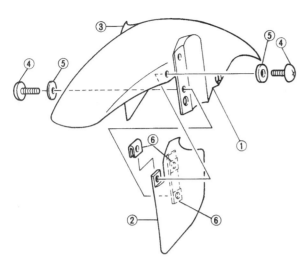

7.9 Fender components (1991 and later FZR1000 models)

1	Fender	4	Screw
2	Over fender	5	Plain washer
3	Over fender (installed)	6	Spring nut

8.2 Tailpiece mounting screws (arrows); some models use only the lower screws

8   Tailpiece - removal and installation

Refer to illustration 8.2

1   Remove the seat (and separate pillion seat on models so equipped).

2   Remove the tailpiece screws and take the tailpiece off **(see illustration)**.

3   Installation is the reverse of removal.

9

Notes

Chapter 10 Electrical system

Contents

Specifications

Battery

Capacity/type	
FZR600..	12V 12Ah, GM12AZ
FZR750..	12V 8Ah, MF9 (maintenance-free)
FZR1000 - 1987 through 1990 models	12V 14Ah, YB14L
FZR1000 - 1991-on..	12V 12Ah, YTX14-BS (maintenance-free)
Specific gravity	See Chapter 1
Battery open circuit voltage (1991-on FZR1000 with maintenance-free battery)	
12.8 volts or more	No charge needed
11.5 to 12.7 volts	Charge for 5 to 10 hours
Less than 11.5 volts	Charge for 15 to 20 hours

Fuse specifications

Main	30 amps
Headlight	
1987 and 1988	15 amps
1989 on	20 amps
Signal, ignition, fan	10 amps

Charging system

Output	
FZR600..	12V, 21A at 5000 rpm
FZR750 and 1000...	12V, 28A at 5000 rpm
No-load voltage	
FZR600..	14.3 to 15.3V at 3000 rpm
FZR750 and 1000...	14.2 to 14.8V at 3000 rpm
Stator coil resistance (FZR600)	0.31 to 0.37 ohms
Stator coil resistance (FZR750/1000)	0.16 to 0.18 ohms
Field coil resistance (FZR750/1000)	3.8 to 4.2 ohms
Brush minimum length (FZR750/1000).....................................	4.7 mm (0.19 inch)

Starter motor

Commutator diameter
    Standard... 28 mm (1.1 inch)
    Minimum... 27 mm (1.06 inch)
Brush length
    FZR600
        Standard .... 12.5 mm (0.49 inch)
        Minimum .... 4.0 mm (0.16 inch)
    FZR750/1000
        Standard .... 12.0 mm (0.47 inch)
        Minimum .... 5.0 mm (0.20 inch)

Torque specifications

Oil level sender bolts
    FZR600 .... 7 Nm (5.1 ft-lbs)
    FZR750/1000 .... 10 Nm (7.2 ft-lbs)
Alternator rotor bolt (FZR600)... 80 Nm (58 ft-lbs)
Alternator mounting bolts (FZR750/1000) .... 20 Nm (14 ft-lbs)
Stator coil bolts (FZR600)... 10 Nm (7.2 ft-lbs)*
    All except UK FZR750... 20 Nm (14 ft-lbs)
    UK FZR750.. 25 Nm (18 ft-lbs)
Starter mounting bolts... 10 Nm (7.2 ft-lbs)

Apply non-permanent thread locking agent to the threads.

1   General information

The machines covered by this manual are equipped with a 12-volt electrical system.

The charging system on FZR600 models uses a rotor with permanent magnets that rotates around a stator coil of copper wire. This produces alternating current, which is converted to direct current by the rectifier. The regulator controls the charging system output.

All other models use a three-phase alternator with an integrated circuit regulator built in. The regulator maintains the charging system output within the specified range to prevent overcharging. The alternator diodes (rectifier) convert the AC (alternating current) output of the alternator to DC (direct current) to power the lights and other components and to charge the battery. The alternator is similar to an automotive alternator, with the field current being produced electromagnetically, rather than by permanent magnets.

An electric starter mounted to the engine case behind the cylinders is standard equipment. The starter on early models has four brushes; the starter on later models has two brushes. The starting system includes the motor, the battery, the relay and the various wires and switches. On models equipped with a sidestand switch and clutch switch, if the engine kill switch and the ignition (main key) switch are both in the On position, the circuit relay allows the starter motor to operate only if the transmission is in Neutral (Neutral switch on) or the clutch lever is pulled to the handlebar (clutch switch on) and the sidestand is up (sidestand switch on).

Note: *Keep in mind that electrical parts, once purchased, can't be returned. To avoid unnecessary expense, make very sure the faulty component has been positively identified before buying a replacement part.*

2   Electrical troubleshooting

A typical electrical circuit consists of an electrical component, the switches, relays, etc. related to that component and the wiring and connectors that hook the component to both the battery and the frame. To aid in locating a problem in any electrical circuit, refer to the wiring diagrams at the end of this Chapter.

Before tackling any troublesome electrical circuit, first study the appropriate diagrams thoroughly to get a complete picture of what makes up that individual circuit. Trouble spots, for instance, can often be narrowed down by noting if other components related to that circuit are operating properly or not. If several components or circuits fail at one time, chances are the fault lies in the fuse or ground/earth connection, as several circuits often are routed through the same fuse and ground/earth connections.

Electrical problems often stem from simple causes, such as loose or corroded connections or a blown fuse. Prior to any electrical troubleshooting, always visually check the condition of the fuse, wires and connections in the problem circuit. Intermittent failures can be especially frustrating, since you can't always duplicate the failure when it's convenient to test. In such situations, a good practice is to clean all connections in the affected circuit, whether or not they appear to be good. All of the connections and wires should also be wiggled to check for looseness which can cause intermittent failure.

If testing instruments are going to be utilized, use the diagrams to plan where you will make the necessary connections in order to accurately pinpoint the trouble spot.

The basic tools needed for electrical troubleshooting include a test light or voltmeter, a continuity tester (which includes a bulb, battery and set of test leads) and a jumper wire, preferably with a circuit breaker incorporated, which can be used to bypass electrical components. Specific checks described later in this Chapter may also require an ohmmeter.

Voltage checks should be performed if a circuit is not functioning properly. Connect one lead of a test light or voltmeter to either the negative battery terminal or a known good ground/earth. Connect the other lead to a connector in the circuit being tested, preferably nearest to the battery or fuse. If the bulb lights, voltage is reaching that point, which means the part of the circuit between that connector and the battery is problem-free. Continue checking the remainder of the circuit in the same manner. When you reach a point where no voltage is present, the problem lies between there and the last good test point. Most of the time the problem is due to a loose connection. Keep in mind that some circuits only receive voltage when the ignition key is in the On position.

One method of finding short circuits is to remove the fuse and connect a test light or voltmeter in its place to the fuse terminals. There should be no load in the circuit (it should be switched off). Move the wiring harness from side-to-side while watching the test light. If the bulb lights, there is a short to ground/earth somewhere in that area, probably where insulation has rubbed off a wire. The same test can be performed on other components in the circuit, including the switch.

A ground/earth check should be done to see if a component is grounded properly. Disconnect the battery and connect one lead of a self-powered test light (continuity tester) to a known good

3.4 Always disconnect the negative battery cable first and reconnect it last to prevent sparks which could cause the battery to explode

ground/earth. Connect the other lead to the wire or ground/earth connection being tested. If the bulb lights, the ground/earth is good. If the bulb does not light, the ground/earth is not good.

A continuity check is performed to see if a circuit, section of circuit or individual component is capable of passing electricity through it. Disconnect the battery and connect one lead of a self-powered test light (continuity tester) to one end of the circuit being tested and the other lead to the other end of the circuit. If the bulb lights, there is continuity, which means the circuit is passing electricity through it properly. Switches can be checked in the same way.

Remember that all electrical circuits are designed to conduct electricity from the battery, through the wires, switches, relays, etc. to the electrical component (light bulb, motor, etc.). From there it is directed to the frame (ground/earth) where it is passed back to the battery. Electrical problems are basically an interruption in the flow of electricity from the battery or back to it.

---

3 Battery - inspection and maintenance

Refer to illustration 3.4

1   Most battery damage is caused by heat, vibration, and/or low electrolyte levels, so keep the battery securely mounted, check the electrolyte level frequently and make sure the charging system is functioning properly.
2   Refer to Chapter 1 for electrolyte level and specific gravity checking procedures.
3   Check around the base inside of the battery for sediment, which is the result of sulfation caused by low electrolyte levels. These deposits will cause internal short circuits, which can quickly discharge the battery. Look for cracks in the case and replace the battery if either of these conditions is found.
4   Check the battery terminals and cable ends for tightness and corrosion. If corrosion is evident, remove the cables from the battery **(see illustration)** and clean the terminals and cable ends with a wire brush or knife and emery paper. Reconnect the cables and apply a thin coat of petroleum jelly to the connections to slow further corrosion.
5   The battery case should be kept clean to prevent current leakage, which can discharge the battery over a period of time (especially when it sits unused). Wash the outside of the case with a solution of baking soda and water. Do not get any baking soda solution in the battery cells. Rinse the battery thoroughly, then dry it.
6   If acid has been spilled on the frame or battery box, neutralize it with the baking soda and water solution, dry it thoroughly, then touch

up any damaged paint. Make sure the battery vent tube (if equipped) is directed away from the frame and is not kinked or pinched.
7   If the motorcycle sits unused for long periods of time, disconnect the cables from the battery terminals. Refer to Section 4 and charge the battery approximately once every month.

---

4   Battery - charging

Refer to illustration 4.12

1   If the machine sits idle for extended periods or if the charging system malfunctions, the battery can be charged from an external source.

Batteries with removable filler caps

2   To properly charge the battery, you will need a charger of the correct rating, a hydrometer, a clean rag and a syringe for adding distilled water to the battery cells.
3   The maximum charging rate for any battery is 1/10 of the rated amp/hour capacity. As an example, the maximum charging rate for a 12 amp/hour battery would be 1.2 amps and the maximum charging rate for a 14 amp/hour battery would be 1.4 amps. If the battery is charged at a higher rate, it could be damaged.
4   Do not allow the battery to be subjected to a so-called quick charge (high rate of charge over a short period of time) unless you are prepared to buy a new battery.
5   When charging the battery, always remove it from the machine and be sure to check the electrolyte level before hooking up the charger. Add distilled water to any cells that are low.
6   Loosen the cell caps, hook up the battery charger leads (red to positive, black to negative), cover the top of the battery with a clean rag, then, and only then, plug in the battery charger. **Warning:** *Remember, the gas escaping from a charging battery is explosive, so keep open flames and sparks well away from the area. Also, the electrolyte is extremely corrosive and will damage anything it comes in contact with.*
7   Allow the battery to charge until the specific gravity is as specified (refer to Chapter 1 for specific gravity checking procedures). The charger must be unplugged and disconnected from the battery when making specific gravity checks. If the battery overheats or gases excessively, the charging rate is too high. Either disconnect the charger or lower the charging rate to prevent damage to the battery.
8   It's time for a new battery if:
a)   One or more of the cells is significantly lower in specific gravity than the others after a long slow charge;
b)   The battery as a whole doesn't seem to want to take a charge;
c)   Battery voltage won't increase;
d)   The electrolyte doesn't bubble;
e)   The plates are white (indicating sulfation) or debris has accumulated in the bottom of a cell;
f)   The plates or insulators are warped or buckled.
9   When the battery is fully charged, unplug the charger first, then disconnect the leads from the battery. Install the cell caps and wipe any electrolyte off the outside of the battery case.

Maintenance free (sealed) batteries

10   Yamaha recommends different charging techniques, depending on the type of battery charger. Since a hydrometer can't be used to check battery condition (there's no way to insert it into the cells), a voltmeter is used instead to measure the voltage between the positive and negative terminals (open circuit voltage). Before taking the measurement, wait at least 30 minutes after any charging has taken place (including running the engine).
11   To check open circuit voltage, disconnect the negative cable from the battery, then the positive cable. Make sure the battery terminals are clean, then connect the positive terminal of the voltmeter to the battery positive terminal and the negative terminal of the voltmeter to the negative battery terminal. Compare the voltage readings with those listed in this Chapter's Specifications to determine whether, and for how long, the battery needs to be charged.

10

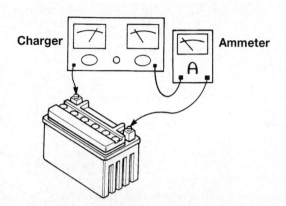

4.12 If the charger doesn't have an ammeter built in, connect one in series with the charger like this; DO NOT connect the ammeter between the battery terminals or it will be ruined

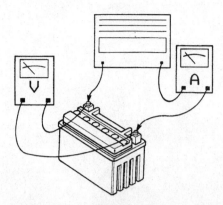

4.21 Connect the charger, ammeter and voltmeter to the battery like this; DO NOT connect the ammeter between the battery terminals or it will be ruined

Variable current (adjustable voltage) charger

12   Connect the charger to the battery. If the charger doesn't have an ammeter built in, connect one in series with the charger **(see illustration)**.

13   Plug in the charger, set the voltage at 16 to 17 volts and note the charging current. If it's less than the standard charging current printed on the battery, go to Step 14. If it's more than the standard charging current, skip to Step 15.

14   Set the charging voltage at 20 to 25 volts, then watch the charging current for 3 to 5 minutes. If it reaches one amp or more, reset the voltage at 16 to 17 volts and continue charging. If the current isn't higher than the standard charging current after five minutes, replace the battery.

15   Adjust the voltage so the charging current is at the standard charging level. Set the timer on the charger according to the charging time determined in Step 11.

16   If the required charging time is more than five hours, recheck the charging current after five hours. If necessary, readjust the charging voltage to set the charging current at the standard charging current.

17   After the battery has charged, unplug the charger and disconnect it from the battery. Wait 30 minutes, then connect a voltmeter between the battery terminals and measure open-circuit voltage (the battery needs this time to stabilize).
   a) If the reading is 12.8 volts or more, the battery is charged.
   b) If the reading is 12.0 to 12.7 volts, continue charging the battery.
   c) If the reading is less than 12.0 volts, replace the battery.

Constant current charger

18   Connect the charger and an ammeter to the battery **(see illustration 4.12)**.

19   Plug in the charger. After one hour, make sure that the charger's rated current is flowing.
   a) If the current flow is less than the charger's rated current, replace the battery.
   b) If the current flow is at the charger's rated current, set charging time according to the charger manufacturer's instructions and go to Step 20.

20   After the battery has charged, unplug the charger and disconnect it from the battery. Refer to Step 17 and check open circuit voltage.

Constant voltage charger

Refer to illustration 4.21

21   Connect the charger, an ammeter and a voltmeter to the battery **(see illustration)**.

22   Plug in the charger and check the ammeter reading.
   a) If it's less than the standard charging current printed on the battery, the charger won't work with a maintenance free battery. Use a variable voltage or constant current charger instead.
   b) If the current flow is at the standard charging current, set charging time to a maximum of 20 hours and continue charging until charging voltage reaches 16 volts or higher.

23   Once charging voltage has reached 16 volts, unplug the charger. Disconnect the charger from the battery and refer to Step 17 to check open circuit voltage.

---

5   Fuses - check and replacement

Refer to illustrations 5.1a, 5.1b, 5.1c, 5.3a and 5.3b

1   FZR600 models have two fuse blocks, one containing a 30-amp

5.1a The FZR600 accessory fuses are located in a block on the right side of the motorcycle . . .

5.1b . . . lift the cover for access

5.1c The main fuse and a spare are located in this fuse block on the left side of the motorcycle

5.3a On FZR1000 models, the accessory fuse block is on the left side of the motorcycle . . .

5.3b . . . and the main fuse is in this block, also on the left side

main fuse and a spare and the other containing accessory fuses and spares **(see illustrations)**. The main fuse is located on the left side of the motorcycle and the accessory fuses are on the right side. Fuse functions and ratings are listed in this Chapter's Specifications.

2   The fuses on FZR750 and 1987 and 1988 FZR1000 models are located beneath the seat.

3   All FZR1000 models have two fuse blocks on the left side of the motorcycle **(see illustrations)**. Fuse functions and ratings are listed in this Chapter's Specifications.

4   If you have a test light, all of the fuses can be checked without removing them. Turn the ignition key to the On position, connect one end of the test light to a good ground (earth), then probe each terminal on top of the fuse. If the fuse is good, there will be voltage available at both terminals. If the fuse is blown, there will only be voltage present at one of the terminals.

5   The fuses can also be tested with an ohmmeter or self-powered test light. Remove the fuse and connect the tester to the ends of the fuse. If the ohmmeter shows continuity or the test lamp lights, the fuse is good. If the ohmmeter shows infinite resistance or the test lamp stays out, the fuse is blown.

6   The fuses can be removed and checked visually. If you can't pull the fuse out with your fingertips, use a pair of needle-nose pliers. A blown fuse is easily identified by a break in the element.

7   If a fuse blows, be sure to check the wiring harnesses very carefully for evidence of a short circuit. Look for bare wires and chafed, melted or burned insulation. If a fuse is replaced before the cause is located, the new fuse will blow immediately.

8   Never, under any circumstances, use a higher rated fuse or bridge the fuse block terminals, as damage to the electrical system could result.

9   Occasionally a fuse will blow or cause an open circuit for no obvious reason. Corrosion of the fuse ends and fuse block terminals may occur and cause poor fuse contact. If this happens, remove the corrosion with a wire brush or emery paper, then spray the fuse end and terminals with electrical contact cleaner.

6   Lighting system - check

1   The battery provides power for operation of the headlight, taillight, brake light, license plate light and instrument cluster lights. If none of the lights operate, always check battery voltage before proceeding. Low battery voltage indicates either a faulty battery, low battery electrolyte level or a defective charging system. Refer to Chapter 1 for battery checks and Sections 28 and 29 for charging system tests. Also, check the condition of the fuses and replace any blown fuses with new ones.

Headlight

2   If the headlight is out when the engine is running (US models) or it won't switch on (UK models), check the fuse first with the key On (see Section 5), then unplug the electrical connector for the headlight and use jumper wires to connect the bulb directly to the battery terminals. If the light comes on, the problem lies in the wiring or one of the switches in the circuit. Refer to Section 18 for the switch testing procedures, and also the wiring diagrams at the end of this Chapter.

Taillight/license plate light

3   If the taillight fails to work, check the bulbs and the bulb terminals first, then check for battery voltage at the taillight electrical connector. If voltage is present, check the ground/earth circuit for an open or poor connection.

4   If no voltage is indicated, check the wiring between the taillight and the ignition switch, then check the switch. On UK models, check the lighting switch as well.

Brake light

5   See Section 11 for the brake light switch checking procedure.

Neutral indicator light

6   If the neutral light fails to operate when the transmission is in Neutral, check the fuses and the bulb (see Section 15 for bulb removal procedures). If the bulb and fuses are in good condition, check for battery voltage at the connector attached to the neutral switch on the left side of the engine. If battery voltage is present, refer to Section 20 for the neutral switch check and replacement procedures.

7   If no voltage is indicated, check the wiring between the switch and the bulb for open circuits and poor connections.

Oil level warning light

8   See Section 16 for the oil level sender check.

7   Headlight bulb - replacement

Refer to illustrations 7.3a, 7.3b, 7.3c, 7.4a and 7.4b
Warning: *If the bulb has just burned out, allow it to cool. It will be hot enough to burn your fingers.*

1   If you're working on an FZR600, remove the left air duct (see Chapter 9). On 1994 FZR600 models, remove the outer cover from the headlight assembly.

2   If you're working on a 1987 or 1988 FZR750 model, remove the left and right fairings, the air ducts and the front fairing together with the headlight assembly (see Chapter 9).

10

7.3a Lift the cover off to expose the electrical connector (on some models, the connector is disconnected first, then the cover is removed) . . .

7.3b . . . disconnect the electrical connector . . .

7.3c . . . and remove the dust cover

7.4a Unscrew the retainer or lift the wire ring . . .

7.4b . . . and lift the bulb out; don't touch the glass on the new bulb

3   Unplug the electrical connector from the headlight. Note the position of any Top, L or R markings for reinstallation and remove the dust cover **(see illustrations)**.
4   Turn the bulb retainer counterclockwise (anti-clockwise) or lift up the retaining clip and swing it out of the way **(see illustration)**. Remove the bulb **(see illustration)**.
5   When installing the new bulb, reverse the removal procedure. Be sure not to touch the bulb with your fingers - oil from your skin will cause the bulb to overheat and fail prematurely. If you do touch the bulb, wipe it off with a clean rag dampened with rubbing alcohol.

8   Headlight aim - check and adjustment

Refer to illustrations 8.3a and 8.3b

1   An improperly adjusted headlight may cause problems for on-coming traffic or provide poor, unsafe illumination of the road ahead. Before adjusting the headlight, be sure to consult with local traffic laws and regulations.
2   The headlight beam can be adjusted both vertically and horizontally. Before performing the adjustment, make sure the fuel tank is at least half full, and have an assistant sit on the seat.
3   On dual-headlight models, the horizontal adjusting screws are at the lower center of the headlight assembly **(see illustration)**. The vertical adjusting screws are located at the upper outer corners of the headlight assembly **(see illustration)**.

8.3a The horizontal adjusters on dual-headlight models are at the lower center (arrows) . . .

4   On single-headlight models, the adjusting screws are at the back of the headlight assembly. Models with separate bulbs for high and low beam have two sets of horizontal and vertical screws; models with a single bulb have one set of horizontal and vertical screws.

8.3b . . . and the vertical adjusters are at the upper corners

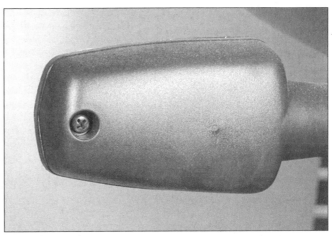

9.1 Remove the screw from the back of the turn signal housing

9.4 The turn signal housing is secured by a nut (arrow)

9.6a Turn the bulb socket (arrow) counterclockwise (anti-clockwise) and take it out of the housing . . .

necessary. Line up the pins on the new bulb with the slots in the socket, push in and turn the bulb clockwise until it locks in place. **Note:** *The pins on some bulbs are offset so it can only be installed one way. It is a good idea to use a paper towel or dry cloth when handling the new bulb to prevent injury if the bulb should break and to increase bulb life.*

3   Position the lens on the reflector and install the screw. Be careful not to overtighten it.

Turn signal housings

Refer to illustration 9.4

4   The turn signal housings are secured to the inside of the fairing (front) or fender/mudguard (rear) by a single nut. To replace a housing, disconnect its electrical connector. Pull back the rubber cap and remove the nut **(see illustration)**. Guide the wiring harness through the nut and the cap and take the housing off the motorcycle. Installation is the reverse of removal.

Taillight bulbs

Refer to illustrations 9.6a and 9.6b

5   To remove the taillight bulbs, remove the seat (see Chapter 9).
6   Turn the bulb holders counterclockwise (anti-clockwise) **(see illustration)** until they stop, then pull straight out to remove them from the taillight housing **(see illustration)**. The bulbs can be removed from the holders by turning them counterclockwise (anti-clockwise) and pulling straight out.
7   Check the socket terminals for corrosion and clean them if necessary. Line up the pins on the new bulb with the slots in the socket, push in and turn the bulb clockwise until it locks in place. **Note:** *The pins on the bulb are offset so it can only be installed one way. It is a*

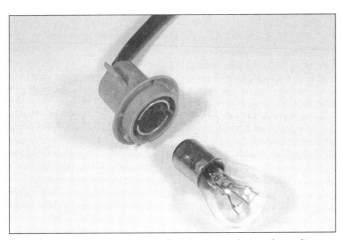

9.6b . . . then press the bulb into the socket and turn it counterclockwise (anti-clockwise) to remove

9   Turn signals and taillight bulbs - replacement

Turn signal bulbs

Refer to illustration 9.1

1   To replace a turn signal bulb, remove the screw that holds the lens to the turn signal housing **(see illustration)**. Pull out the lens.
2   Push the bulb in and turn it counterclockwise (anti-clockwise) to remove it. Check the socket terminals for corrosion and clean them if

10

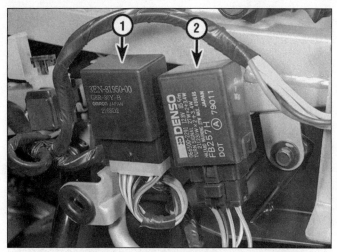

10.3a The FZR600 turn signal relay is on the left side of the motorcycle

1   *Relay assembly*   2   *Turn signal relay*

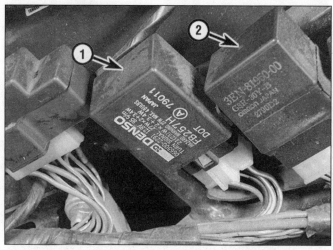

10.3b The FZR1000 turn signal relay is on the left side of the motorcycle on 1989-on models

1   *Turn signal relay*   2   *Relay assembly*

good idea to use a paper towel or dry cloth when handling the new bulb to prevent injury if the bulb should break and to increase bulb life.
8   Make sure the rubber gaskets are in place and in good condition, then line up the tabs on the holder with the slots in the housing and push the holder into the mounting hole. Turn it clockwise until it stops to lock it in place.
9   Reinstall the seat.

10   Turn signal circuit - check

Refer to illustrations 10.3a and 10.3b

1   The battery provides power for operation of the signal lights, so if they do not operate, always check the battery voltage and specific gravity first. Low battery voltage indicates either a faulty battery, low electrolyte level or a defective charging system. Refer to Chapter 1 for battery checks and Sections 28 and 29 for charging system tests. Also, check the fuses (see Section 5).
2   Most turn signal problems are the result of a burned out bulb or corroded socket. This is especially true when the turn signals function properly in one direction, but fail to flash in the other direction. Check the bulbs and the sockets (see Section 9).
3   If the bulbs and sockets check out okay, check for power at the turn signal relay with the ignition On. On FZR600 and 1989-on FZR1000 models the relay is located on the left side of the frame at the rear **(see illustrations)**. On 1987 and 1988 FZR1000 and FZR750 models it is under the seat, just forward of the battery. On UK FZR750 models, it is under the seat next to the starting cut-off relay. Refer to wiring diagrams at the end of the book to identify the power source terminal.
4   If the relay is okay, check the wiring between the turn signal relay and the turn signal lights (see the wiring diagrams at the end of this Chapter).
5   If the wiring checks out okay, replace the turn signal relay.

11   Brake light switches - check and replacement

Refer to illustrations 11.5, 11.6 and 11.9

Circuit check

1   Before checking any electrical circuit, check the fuses (see Section 5).
2   Using a test light connected to a good ground (earth), check for voltage at the brake light switch. If there's no voltage present, check

11.5 To remove this type of brake light switch, disconnect the electrical connectors and remove the switch mounting screw from below

the wire between the switch and the fuse box (see the wiring diagrams at the end of this Chapter).
3   If voltage is available, touch the probe of the test light to the other terminal of the switch, then pull the brake lever or depress the brake pedal - if the test light doesn't light up, replace the switch.
4   If the test light does light, check the wiring between the switch and the brake lights (see the wiring diagrams at the end of this Chapter).

Switch replacement

Front brake lever switch

5   The switch on some models is secured by a single mounting screw. If you're working on this type, remove the mounting screw and unplug the electrical connectors from the switch **(see illustration)**.
6   The switch on other models slides into the handle pivot and is secured by a prong **(see illustration)**. If you're working on this type, disconnect the electrical connector. Insert a small screwdriver or probe into the release hole on the underside of the lever bracket, press up on the retaining prong and pull out the switch.
7   Installation is the reverse of the removal procedure. The brake lever switch isn't adjustable.

11.6 To remove this type of brake light switch, insert a tool into the hole under the bracket (arrow) and release the retainer

11.9 Disconnect the brake light switch spring (arrow)

12.2a Unscrew the speedometer cable from the speedometer . . .

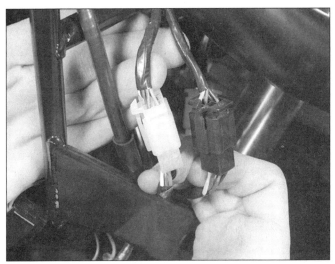

12.2b . . . and disconnect the cluster electrical connectors (this is an FZR600)

Rear brake pedal switch

8   Unplug the electrical connector in the switch harness.
9   Unhook the switch spring **(see illustration)**.
10   Refer to the switch adjustment procedure in Chapter 1 and re-move the switch from its bracket.
11   Install the switch by reversing the removal procedure, then adjust the switch by following the procedure described in Chapter 1.

---

12   **Instrument cluster and speedometer cable - removal and installation**

Cluster removal

Refer to illustrations 12.2a, 12.2b, 12.3a, 12.3b, 12.5 and 12.6
1   Remove the front fairing (see Chapter 9).
2   Detach the speedometer cable from the speedometer and unplug the electrical connectors from the cluster harness **(see illustrations)**.
3   Remove the instrument cluster mounting nuts **(see illustrations)** and detach the cluster from the front fairing stay.

12.3a Remove the cluster mounting nuts . . .

10

12.3b . . . and slide the cluster mounting studs out
of their brackets

12.5 Disconnect the lower end of the speedometer cable

12.6 Be sure the squared-off ends of the speedometer cable
(arrow) fit into their sockets

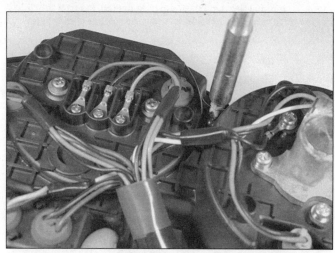

14.2a Remove the case screw between the tachometer
and speedometer . . .

Speedometer cable removal

4   Disconnect the speedometer cable from the cluster **(see illustration 12.2a)**.
5   Note how it's routed, then disconnect the speedometer cable
from the drive gear at the left front fork **(see illustration)**.

Installation

6   Installation is the reverse of the removal procedure. Be sure the
speedometer cable is routed so it doesn't cause the steering to bind or
interfere with other components. Be sure the squared-off ends of the
cable fit into their spindles in the cluster and drive gear **(see illustration)**.

---

13   Meters and gauges - check

Coolant temperature gauge

1   Refer to Chapter 4 for coolant temperature gauge checking procedures.

Tachometer and speedometer

2   Special instruments are required to properly check the operation
of these meters. Take the instrument cluster to a Yamaha dealer service department or other qualified repair shop for diagnosis.

14.2b and those around the edge of the case

---

14   Instrument cluster - disassembly and reassembly

Refer to illustrations 14.2a through 14.2j
1   Remove the cluster (see Section 12).
2   The accompanying photos show the disassembly of a US 1994
FZR600R instrument cluster. Other models are similar. To disassemble
the cluster and replace individual gauges, refer to the photos **(see illustrations)**.
3   Reassembly is the reverse of the disassembly procedure.

14.2c Lift the lenses off the case

14.2d Remove the tachometer screws . . .

14.2e . . . and disconnect the wires . . .

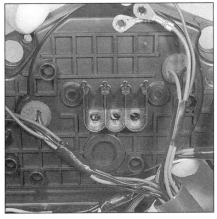

14.2f . . . the wire colors should be molded into the case, but label the wires if the marks aren't clearly visible

14.2g Lift the tachometer out of the case

14.2h Remove the speedometer gear screws and wires to take the speedometer out

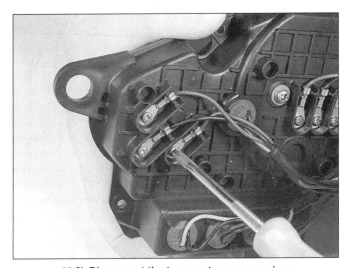

14.2i Disconnect the temperature gauge wires

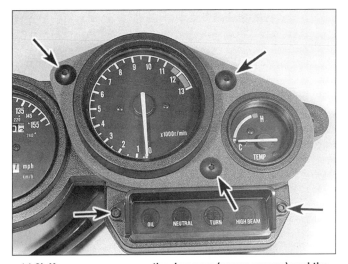

14.2j If necessary, remove the dampers (upper arrows) and the screws that secure the warning light lens (lower arrows)

10

15 Instrument and warning light bulbs - replacement

Refer to illustrations 15.2a and 15.2b

1   Remove the front fairing if necessary for access (see Chapter 9).
2   To replace a bulb, pull the appropriate rubber socket out of the

back of the instrument cluster housing **(see illustration)**, then pull the bulb out of the socket **(see illustration)**. If the socket contacts are dirty or corroded, they should be scraped clean and sprayed with electrical contact cleaner before new bulbs are installed.
3   Carefully push the new bulb into position, then push the socket into the cluster housing.

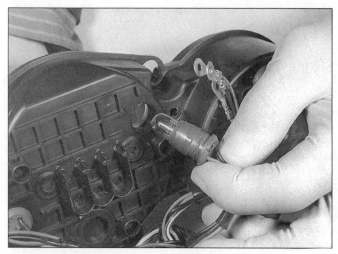

15.2a Work the bulb socket free of the cluster . . .

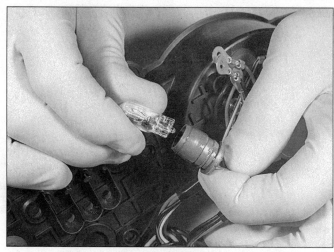

15.2b . . . and pull the bulb out of the socket

16.3a Remove the sender mounting bolts . . .

16.3b . . . and take the sender out of the oil pan; replace the O-ring whenever the sender is removed

16 Oil level sender - removal, check and installation

Refer to illustrations 16.3a and 16.3b

Removal

1   Drain the engine oil (see Chapter 1).
2   The oil level sender is mounted in the bottom of the oil pan. Note how its wiring harness is routed, then unplug the electrical connector.
3   Remove the sender mounting bolts and remove the sender **(see illustrations)**.

Check

4   Connect an ohmmeter between the terminals of the sender harness. With the sender in its normal installed position (flange and wiring harness at the bottom), the ohmmeter should indicate infinite resistance.
5   Turn the sender upside down. The ohmmeter should now read zero ohms.
6   If the ohmmeter doesn't give the correct indication in Step 4 or 5, replace the sender.

Installation

7   Installation is the reverse of the removal steps. Use a new O-ring and tighten the sender mounting bolts to the torque listed in this Chapter's Specifications.

Switch	Wire Color		
Position	R	Br	L
ON	o———	———o———	———o
OFF			
P	o———		———o

17.2 Continuity table for the ignition switch

17 Ignition main (key) switch - check and replacement

Check

Refer to illustrations 17.2 and 17.6

1   Remove the front fairing (see Chapter 9). This isn't absolutely necessary, but it makes access to the switch electrical connector easier. Disconnect the electrical connector.
2   Using an ohmmeter, check the continuity of the terminal pairs indicated in the accompanying table **(see illustration)**. Continuity should exist between the terminals connected by a solid line when the switch is in the indicated position.
3   If the switch fails any of the tests, replace it.

17.6 Remove the switch mounting screws or bolts

Replacement

4   Remove the front fairing, if you haven't already done so (see Chapter 9).

5   Unplug the switch electrical connector.

6   The switch is held to the upper triple clamp with two bolts or Torx screws **(see illustration)**. Unlock the switch with the ignition key and remove the bolts. If necessary, remove the fairing mount for better access to the bolts. Detach the switch from the upper triple clamp.

7   If necessary, remove the Phillips screws and separate the switch from the bracket.

8   Attach the new switch to the bracket with the Phillips screws (if it was removed). Tighten the screws securely. Hold the new switch in position and install the bolts.

9   The remainder of installation is the reverse of the removal procedure.

18   Handlebar switches - check

Refer to illustration 18.4

1   Generally speaking, the switches are reliable and trouble-free. Most troubles, when they do occur, are caused by dirty or corroded contacts, but wear and breakage of internal parts is a possibility that should not be overlooked. If breakage does occur, the entire switch and related wiring harness will have to be replaced with a new one, since individual parts are not usually available.

2   The switches can be checked for continuity with an ohmmeter or a continuity test light. Always disconnect the battery negative cable, which will prevent the possibility of a short circuit, before making the checks.

3   Trace the wiring harness of the switch in question and unplug the electrical connectors.

4   Using the ohmmeter or test light, check for continuity between the terminals of the switch harness with the switch in the various positions **(see illustration)**. Continuity should exist between the terminals connected by a solid line when the switch is in the indicated position.

5   If the continuity check indicates a problem exists, refer to Sec-

"LIGHTING" Switch (UK only)

Switch Position	Wire Color		
	R/Y	L	L/B
OFF			
PO	o—o		
ON	o—o—o		

"ENGINE KILL" Switch

Switch Position	Wire Color	
	R/W	R/W
OFF		
ON	o——o	

"START" Switch

Button Position	Wire Color			
	L/W	B	R/Y *	L/B *
OFF			o——o	
PUSH	o——o			

* US models only

"DIMMER" Switch

Switch Position	Wire Color		
	Y	L/B	G
HI	o—o		
LO		o——o	

"TURN" Switch

Switch Position	Wire Color				
	Ch	Br/W	Dg	Y/R	B
L	o——o			o——o	
L → N	o——o				
N → Push					
R → N		o——o			
R		o——o		o——o	

"HORN" Switch

Button Position	Wire Color	
	P	B
PUSH	o——o	
OFF		

"CLUTCH" Switch

Clutch lever Position	Wire Color	
	B/Y	L/Y
FREE		
DEPRESS	o——o	

"BRAKE" Switch (Front)

Brake lever Position	Wire Color	
	Br	G/Y
FREE		
DEPRESS	o——o	

18.4 Continuity table for the handlebar switches

10

19.1a On the throttle side, remove one screw that secures the throttle cable (all except 1989 and later FZR750 models) and two screws that hold the switch housing halves together

19.1b On the clutch side, remove the screws (arrows) and separate the switch housing

tion 11, 19, or 22, remove the switch and spray the switch contacts with electrical contact cleaner. If they are accessible, the contacts can be scraped clean with a knife or polished with crocus cloth. If switch components are damaged or broken, it will be obvious when the switch is disassembled.

19 Handlebar switches - removal and installation

Refer to illustrations 19.1a and 19.1b

1   The handlebar switches are composed of two halves that clamp around the bars. They are easily removed for cleaning or inspection by taking out the clamp screws and pulling the switch halves away from the handlebars **(see illustrations)**.
2   To completely remove the switches, the electrical connectors in the wiring harness should be unplugged.
3   When installing the switches, make sure the wiring harnesses are properly routed to avoid pinching or stretching the wires.

20 Neutral switch - check and replacement

Refer to illustrations 20.6a and 20.6b

Check

1   Make sure the transmission is in neutral.
2   Remove the left side of the fairing (lower fairing on 1989 and later FZR750 models) (see Chapter 9). Follow the switch harness (it comes from behind the engine sprocket cover on the left side of the engine) to its connector, then unplug the connector.
3   Locate the sky blue wire's terminal in the harness side of the connector (not the side of the connector that goes to the neutral switch). Connect the terminal to ground/earth (bare metal on the motorcycle frame) with a short length of wire.
   a) If the light stays out, check the bulb and the wiring between the ignition switch and neutral switch.
   b) If the neutral indicator light comes on, the neutral switch may be bad. Connect an ohmmeter between the sky blue terminal in the switch side of the connector and ground/earth. Shift through the gears. The ohmmeter should indicate continuity in neutral and infinite resistance in all other gears. If not, replace the neutral switch.

Replacement

4   Remove the engine sprocket cover (see Chapter 7).
5   Unplug the electrical connector (if you haven't already done so). Detach any wiring harness retainers.

20.6a Remove the neutral switch screws . . .

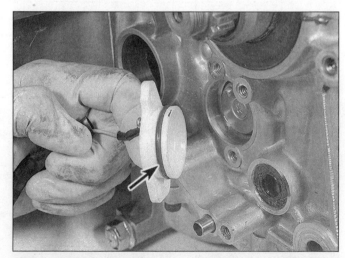

20.6b . . . and take the switch out of the engine; replace the O-ring (arrow) with a new one

6   Remove the switch mounting screws **(see illustration)** and detach the switch from the crankcase **(see illustration)**. Remove the O-ring and install a new one.
7   Installation is the reverse of the removal steps. Tighten the switch screws securely.

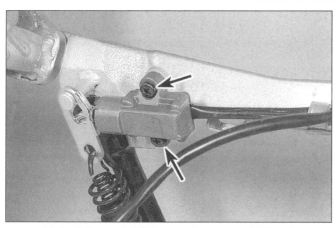

21.4a Sidestand switch mounting screws (FZR600)

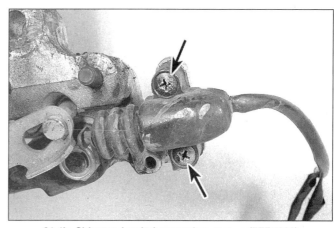

21.4b Sidestand switch mounting screws (FZR1000)

21 Sidestand switch - check and replacement

Refer to illustrations 21.4a and 21.4b

Check

1 Follow the wiring harness from the switch to the connector, then unplug the connector. Connect the leads of an ohmmeter to the wire terminals on the switch side of the connector. With the sidestand in the up position, there should be continuity through the switch (0 ohms).

2 With the sidestand in the down position, the meter should indicate infinite resistance.

3 If the switch fails either of these tests, replace it.

Replacement

4 With the sidestand in the up position, unscrew the two screws and remove the switch **(see illustrations)**. Disconnect the switch electrical connector.

5 Installation is the reverse of the removal procedure.

22 Clutch switch - check and replacement

Refer to illustration 22.1

Check

1 Disconnect the electrical connector from the clutch switch **(see illustration)**.

2 Connect an ohmmeter between the terminals in the clutch switch. With the clutch lever pulled in, the ohmmeter should show continuity (little or no resistance). With the lever out, the ohmmeter should show infinite resistance.

3 If the switch doesn't check out as described, replace it.

Replacement

4 If you haven't already done so, unplug the wiring connector. Remove the mounting screw and take the switch off **(see illustration 22.1)**.

5 Installation is the reverse of removal.

23 Horn - check and replacement

Check

Refer to illustration 23.1

1 Unplug the electrical connectors from the horn **(see illustration)**. Using two jumper wires, apply battery voltage directly to the terminals on the horn. If the horn sounds, check the switch (see Section 18) and the wiring between the switch and the horn (see the wiring diagrams at

22.1 Unplug the electrical connector (left arrow) and remove the mounting screw (right arrow)

23.1 Disconnect the electrical connectors and remove the bracket bolt (arrow) (FZR600 shown; others similar)

the end of this Chapter).

2 If the horn doesn't sound, replace it.

Replacement

3 Unbolt the horn bracket from the frame **(see illustration 23.1)** and detach the electrical connectors.

10

24.3a If necessary for access, lift the relay off its mounting tabs . . .

24.3c . . . and this is an FZR1000

24.3b . . . and disconnect the thin wire and ground/earth it to the frame (this is an FZR600) . . .

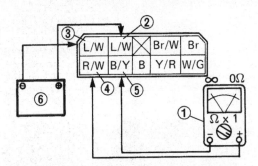

25.2 Starting circuit cut-off relay test (1987 and 1988 models)

1	Ohmmeter	4	Red-white terminal
2	Blue-white terminal	5	Black-yellow terminal
3	Blue-white terminal	6	12-volt battery

4   Unbolt the horn from the bracket and transfer the bracket to the new horn.
5   Installation is the reverse of removal.

24 Starter relay - check and replacement

Refer to illustrations 24.3a, 24.3b and 24.3c

Check

1   Remove the seat (see Chapter 9).
2   Make sure the battery is fully charged and the relay wiring connections are clean and tight.
3   Disconnect the thin wire from the starter relay and connect it to ground/earth (bare metal on the frame) **(see illustrations)**. The relay should click as the wire is connected and disconnected. If it doesn't, replace the relay.

Replacement

4   Disconnect the cable from the negative terminal of the battery.
5   Detach the battery positive cable, the starter cable and electrical connector from the relay **(see illustrations 24.3a, 24.3b and 24.3c)**.
6   Slide the relay off its mounting tabs.
7   Installation is the reverse of removal. Reconnect the negative battery cable after all the other electrical connections are made.

25 Starting circuit cut-off relay - check and replacement

Refer to illustrations 25.2 and 25.5

Check

1   The cut-off relay is part of the relay assembly unit. On 1987 and 1988 FZR1000 models and UK FZR750 models the unit is located under the seat. On FZR600 and 1989-on FZR1000 models it is situated next to the turn signal relay **(see illustrations 10.3a and 10.3b)** and can be accessed after the left side cover has been removed (see Chapter 9). Use the unit's wire colors as a guide to identification (see the wiring diagrams at the end of this book). Having located the relay, disconnect its wire connector and make the tests directly on the relay terminals as described below.

1987 and 1988 models

2   Connect an ohmmeter between the terminals in the relay that connect to the red-white and black-yellow wires in the wiring harness **(see illustration)**. The ohmmeter should show infinite resistance.
3   Connect a 12-volt battery between the terminals for the black-white wires in the relay **(see illustration 25.2)** (the motorcycle's battery will work if it's charged). The ohmmeter should now show continuity (little or no resistance).
4   Disconnect and reconnect the battery. The ohmmeter should show continuity whenever the battery is connected and no continuity whenever it's disconnected. If not, replace the relay assembly.

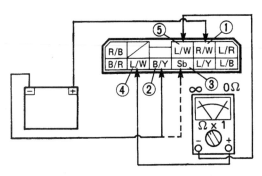

25.5 Starting circuit cut-off relay test (1989 and later models)

1 Red-white wire terminal	4 Blue-white terminal
2 Black-yellow terminal	5 Blue-white terminal
3 Sky blue terminal	

26.3 Remove the nut (arrow) and disconnect the cable

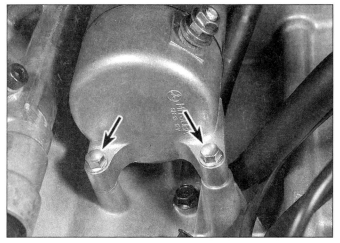

26.4a Remove the mounting bolts (arrows) (this is an FZR600) . . .

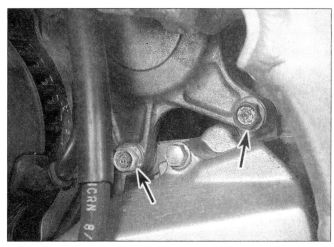

26.4b . . . and this is an FZR1000 (FZR750 similar)

1989-on models

5   Connect an ohmmeter between the terminals in the relay that connect to the blue-white wires in the wiring harness **(see illustration)**. The ohmmeter should show infinite resistance.

6   Connect the positive terminal of a 12-volt battery (the motorcycle's battery will work if it's charged) to the terminal for the red-white wire in the relay **(see illustration 25.5)**. Connect the battery negative terminal to the relay terminal that connects to the black yellow wire. The ohmmeter should now show continuity (little or no resistance).

7   Move the battery negative terminal's jumper wire from the black-yellow terminal to the sky blue terminal. Again, the ohmmeter should show continuity.

8   If the ohmmeter shows continuity when it should, the cut-off relay is good. If not, replace the relay assembly.

Replacement

9   Remove the seat or left side cover (see Chapter 9).

10   Disconnect the relay assembly's wiring connector. Slip the relay assembly off its mounting tab.

11   Installation is the reverse of the removal steps.

---

26   Starter motor - removal and installation

Refer to illustrations 26.3, 26.4a, 26.4b, 26.5 and 26.6

Removal

1   Remove the seat and side covers (see Chapter 9). Remove the

fuel tank (see Chapter 5).

2   Disconnect the cable from the negative terminal of the battery.

3   Pull back the rubber cover, remove the nut retaining the starter cable to the starter and disconnect the cable **(see illustration)**.

4   Remove the starter mounting bolts **(see illustrations)**.

5   Lift the outer end of the starter up a little bit and slide the starter out of the engine case **(see illustration)**.

6   Check the condition of the O-ring on the end of the starter and re-

26.5 Slide the starter out; inspect the O-ring and gear teeth . . .

26.6 . . . as well as the teeth on the gear inside the engine (arrow)

place it if necessary. Also check the starter pinion gear and the driven gear inside the engine for chipped or worn teeth **(see illustration)**.

Installation

7   Apply a little engine oil to the O-ring and install the starter by reversing the removal procedure.

---

27   Starter motor - disassembly, inspection and reassembly

Refer to illustrations 27.2a, 27.2b, 27.2c, 27.3, 27.4 ,27.5, 27.6a, 27.6b, 27.6c, 27.6d, 27.7a, 27.7b, 27.9, 27.10, 27.11a, 27.11b, 27.12 , 27.13 27.16, 27.17a, 27.17b 27.16, 27.17a, 27.17b 27.19, 27.20a and 27.20b

1   Remove the starter motor (see Section 26).

Disassembly
Four-brush starter

2   Mark the position of the housing to each end cover. Remove the

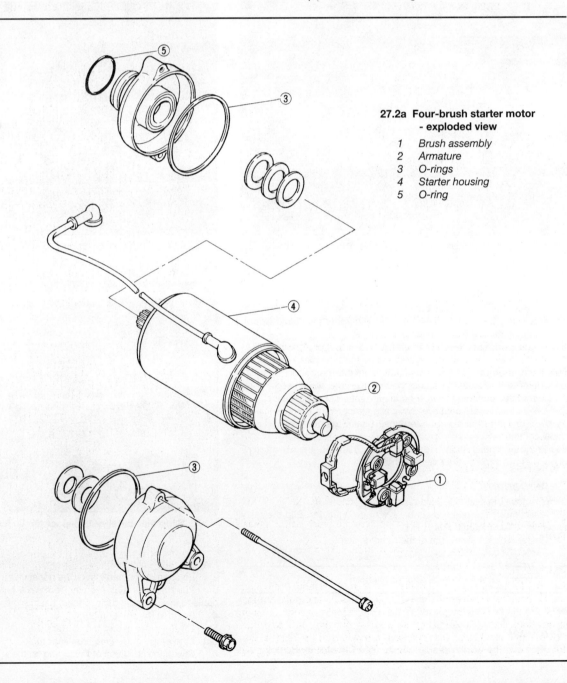

27.2a Four-brush starter motor - exploded view

1   Brush assembly
2   Armature
3   O-rings
4   Starter housing
5   O-ring

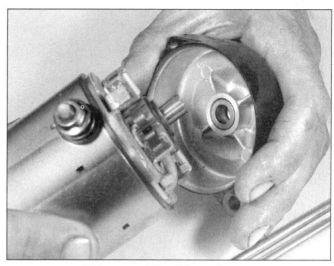

27.2b Remove the two long screws . . .

27.2c . . . and lift off the end covers

27.3 Lower the armature (arrow) out of the brush plate
and starter housing

27.4 Remove the brush plate from the housing

two long screws and detach both end covers **(see illustrations)**.

3   Pull the armature out of the housing (toward the pinion gear side) **(see illustration)**.

4   Remove the brush plate from the housing **(see illustration)**.

5   Carefully note how the washers are arranged on the terminal bolt. Remove the nut and push the terminal bolt through the starter housing, then reinstall the washers and nut on the bolt so you don't forget how they go. Remove the two brushes with the plastic holder from the housing **(see illustration)**.

Two-brush starter

6   Mark the position of the housing to each end cover if not already marked. Remove the two long screws and detach both end covers **(see illustrations)**.

7   Remove the shims and brush plate from the brush housing **(see illustrations)**.

8   Pull the armature out of the housing (toward the pinion gear side).

Inspection

9   The parts of the starter motor that most likely will require attention are the brushes. Measure the length of the brushes and compare the results to the brush length listed in this Chapter's Specifications **(see illustration)**. If any of the brushes are worn beyond the specified limits, replace the brush holder assembly with a new one. If the brushes are not worn excessively, cracked, chipped, or otherwise damaged, they

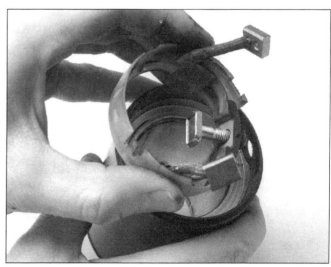

27.5 Push the terminal bolt through the housing and remove the
brush holder

10

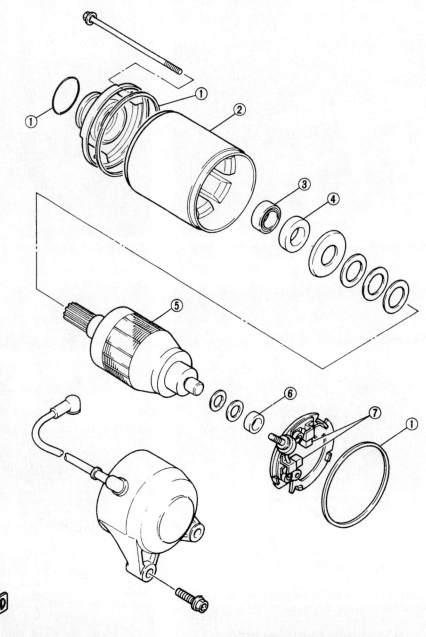

27.6a Two-brush starter
       - exploded view

1   O-rings
2   Starter housing
3   Bearing
4   Oil seal
5   Armature
6   Bushing
7   Brushes

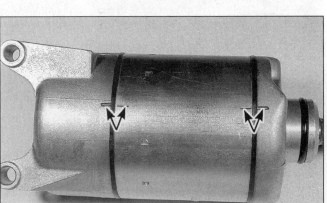

27.6b Note the alignment marks on the end covers and housing
(arrows) - these must be aligned when the starter is reassembled

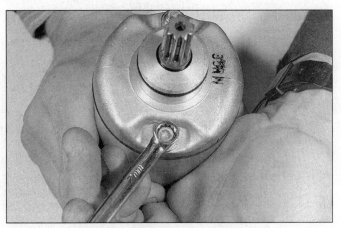

27.6c Remove the two long screws

27.6d Lift off the brush end cover together with the brushes and shims

27.7a Remove the washers and shims, noting carefully their number and order

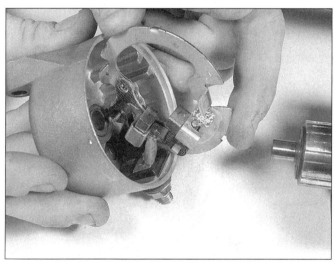

27.7b Lift the brush assembly out of the housing so the brushes can be inspected

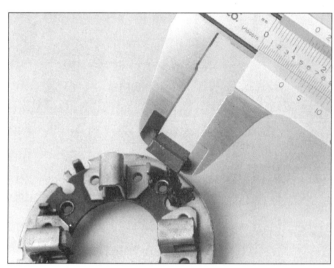

27.9 Measure the length of the brushes and compare the length of the shortest brush with the length listed in this Chapter's Specifications (four-brush starter shown; two-brush model similar)

27.10 Check the commutator for cracks and discoloring, then measure the diameter and compare it with the minimum diameter listed in this Chapter's Specifications

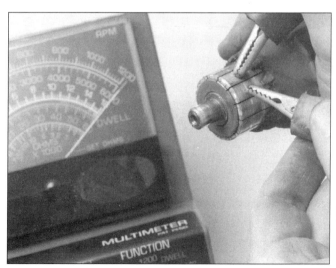

27.11a Continuity should exist between the commutator bars

10

27.11b There should be no continuity between the commutator bars and the armature shaft

27.12 There should be almost no resistance (0 ohms) between the brushes and the brush plate

27.13 There should be no continuity between the brush plate and the brush holders (the resistance reading should be infinite)

27.16 When installing the brush plate, make sure the brush leads fit into the notches in the plate (arrow) - also, make sure the tongue on the plate fits into the notch in the housing (arrows)

27.17a Install each brush spring on the post in this position . . .

27.17b . . . then pull the end of the spring 1/2 turn counterclockwise (anti-clockwise) and seat the end of it in the groove in the end of the brush

may be re-used.

10   Inspect the commutator **(see illustration)** for scoring, scratches and discoloration. The commutator can be cleaned and polished with crocus cloth, but do not use sandpaper or emery paper. After cleaning, wipe away any residue with a cloth soaked in an electrical system cleaner or denatured alcohol. Measure the commutator diameter and compare it to the diameter listed in this Chapter's Specifications. If it is less than the service limit, the motor must be replaced with a new one.

11   Using an ohmmeter or a continuity test light, check for continuity between the commutator bars **(see illustration)**. Continuity should exist between each bar and all of the others. Also, check for continuity between the commutator bars and the armature shaft **(see illustration)**. There should be no continuity between the commutator and the shaft. If the checks indicate otherwise, the armature is defective.

12   Check for continuity between the brush plate and the brushes **(see illustration)**. The meter should read close to 0 ohms. If it doesn't, the brush plate has an open and must be replaced.

13   Using the highest range on the ohmmeter, measure the resistance between the brush holders and the brush plate **(see illustration)**. The reading should be infinite. If there is any reading at all, replace the brush plate.

14   Check the starter pinion gear for worn, cracked, chipped and broken teeth. If the gear is damaged or worn, replace the starter motor.

27.19 Be sure the shims and washers are in place on both ends of the armature shaft

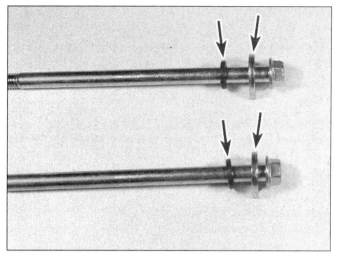

27.20a Install the washers and O-rings on the long screws (if they were removed)

27.20b Install the screws and be sure to line up the alignment marks on the starter housing and end covers

Reassembly

Four-brush starter

15   Install the plastic brush holder into the housing. Make sure the terminal bolt and washers are assembled in their original order. Tighten the terminal nut securely.

16   Detach the brush springs from the brush plate (this will make armature installation much easier). Install the brush plate into the housing, routing the brush leads into the notches in the plate **(see illustration)**. Make sure the tongue on the brush plate fits into the notch in the housing.

17   Install the brushes into their holders and slide the armature into place. Install the brush springs **(see illustrations)**.

Two-brush starter

18   Reinstall the brush plate in the end housing **(see illustrations 27.7b and 27.6d)**.

All models

19   Install any washers that were present on the end of the armature shaft **(see illustration)**.

20   Install the end covers, aligning the previously applied matchmarks (be sure to install the large O-rings between the starter housing and end covers). Install the O-rings and washers on the two long screws, then install the screws and tighten them securely **(see illustrations)**.

28   Charging system testing - general information and precautions

1   If the performance of the charging system is suspect, the system as a whole should be checked first, followed by testing of the individual components (the alternator and the voltage regulator/rectifier). **Note:** *Before beginning the checks, make sure the battery is fully charged and that all system connections are clean and tight.*

2   Checking the output of the charging system and the performance of the various components within the charging system requires the use of special electrical test equipment. A voltmeter or a multimeter are the absolute minimum tools required. In addition, an ohmmeter is generally required for checking the remainder of the system.

3   When making the checks, follow the procedures carefully to prevent incorrect connections or short circuits, as irreparable damage to electrical system components may result if short circuits occur. Because of the special tools and expertise required, it is recommended that the job of checking the charging system be left to a dealer service department or a reputable motorcycle repair shop.

29   Charging system - output test

Refer to illustration 29.7

Caution: *Never disconnect the battery cables from the battery while the engine is running. If the battery is disconnected, the alternator and regulator/rectifier will be damaged.*

1   To check the charging system output, you will need a voltmeter or a multimeter with a voltmeter function.

2   The battery must be fully charged (charge it from an external source if necessary) and the engine must be at normal operating temperature to obtain an accurate reading.

3   Attach the positive (red) voltmeter lead to the positive (+) battery terminal and the negative (black) lead to the battery negative (-) terminal. The voltmeter selector switch (if equipped) must be in a DC volt range greater than 15 volts.

4   Start the engine.

5   The charging system no-load voltage should be within the range listed in this Chapter's Specifications. If it's not, refer to the appropriate sub-heading below.

FZR600 models

6   Follow the wiring harness from the upper side of the alternator cover (on the left side of the engine) to the electrical connector and unplug the connector.

10

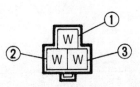

29.7 Connect the positive lead of an ohmmeter to terminal 1, then connect the negative lead in turn to terminals 2 and 3 (FZR600)

30.2 Remove the Allen bolt (arrows) to detach the stator

30.5a Loosen the rotor bolt . . .

7   Connect the positive lead of an ohmmeter to the single terminal of the connector (the side that runs back to the alternator, not the wiring harness side) **(see illustration)**. Connect the negative lead to each of the other terminals in turn and note the reading.

8   If the reading is not within the stator coil resistance range listed in this Chapter's Specifications, replace the stator (see Section 30).

9   If the reading is within the Specifications, refer to the wiring diagrams at the end of the book and check the charging circuit for breaks or poor connections. If the wiring is good, replace the regulator/rectifier unit (see Section 30).

FZR750/1000 models

10   If the no-load voltage is as specified, the alternator is functioning properly. If the voltage is too high, the regulator is at fault and should be replaced. The regulator is located under the cover and is retained by three screws.

11   If the voltage is too low, there may be a fault in the alternator stator or field coils or the brushes may be worn.

12   To check the stator coils, remove the alternator end cover and us-

ing an ohmmeter set on the ohms x 1 range, connect one probe to the left white wire terminal and the other first to the center white wire terminal and then to the right wire terminal; in each test the resistance should be as shown in this Chapter's Specifications. If outside of specification, replace the stator coil.

13   Check the brush length as described in Section 32, and replace as a set if worn or damaged.

14   To check the field coil, remove the alternator end cover and using an ohmmeter set on the ohms x 1 range, connect its probes between the field coil terminals. If the resistance is outside of that specified (see Specifications) the alternator field coil should be replaced.

---

30   Alternator stator, rotor and regulator/rectifier (FZR600 models) - removal and installation

Stator

Refer to illustrations 30.2, 30.5a, 30.5b, 30.6a, 30.6b, 30.6c, 30.7a, 30.7b and 30.9

1   Remove the alternator cover (see Chapter 5).

2   Remove the stator Allen bolts and take the stator out **(see illustration)**.

3   Installation is the reverse of the removal steps. Tighten the Allen bolts securely.

Rotor

4   Remove the alternator cover (see Chapter 5).

5   Shift the transmission into gear and have an assistant apply the rear brake. Remove the rotor bolt and washer **(see illustrations)**.

6   Thread a rotor puller such as Yamaha tool no. YM-01080 (part no. 90890-01080) into the rotor **(see illustration)**. Remove the rotor from

30.5b . . . unscrew the bolt and remove the washer

30.6a Use a tool like this one to separate the rotor from the crankshaft . . .

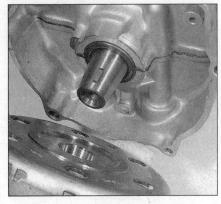

30.6b . . . then take the rotor off . . .

30.6c . . . and lift the Woodruff key out of its slot

30.7a Be sure there aren't any small metal objects stuck to the rotor magnets; an inconspicuous item like this Woodruff key (arrow) can ruin the rotor and stator if the engine is run

30.7b Seat the Woodruff key securely in its slot

30.9 The regulator/rectifier is mounted on this bracket on the left side of the motorcycle

the end of the crankshaft and take the Woodruff key out of its slot **(see illustrations)**.

7   Installation is the reverse of the removal steps. Be sure to reinstall the Woodruff key and make sure no metal objects have stuck to the magnets inside the rotor **(see illustrations)**. Align the slot in the rotor with the Woodruff key and install the rotor. Tighten the rotor bolt to the specified torque.

Regulator/rectifier

8   Remove the seat and left side cover (see Chapter 9).
9   Disconnect the electrical connector and remove the unit's mounting screws **(see illustration)**.
10   Installation is the reverse of the removal steps.

---

31   Alternator (FZR750/1000) - removal and installation

Refer to illustrations 31.4a, 31.4b, 31.4c and 31.5
1   Disconnect the cable from the negative terminal of the battery.
2   Remove the seat, side covers and fuel tank (see Chapters 9 and 5).
3   Unplug the alternator electrical connector.
4   Remove the alternator mounting bolts and lift the alternator off the engine **(see illustrations)**. Inspect the alternator O-ring and replace if it's damaged or brittle. If oil has been leaking past the alternator drive shaft seal, refer to Chapter 2 and replace it.

10

31.4a Remove the mounting bolt under the alternator . . .

31.4b ... and the two on top ...

31.4c ... and take the alternator off the engine

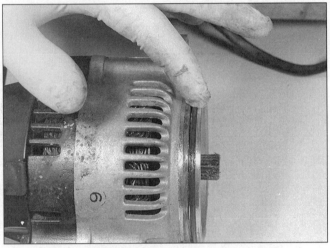

31.5 Coat the O-ring with multi-purpose grease

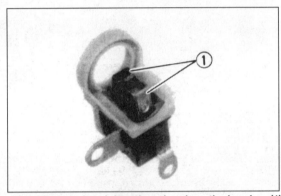

**32.5 Measure brush length and replace the brushes (1)
if they're worn**

are worn, replace them.
6   Reverse Steps 2 through 4 to reassemble and install the alternator.

5   Installation is the reverse of the removal steps with the following additions:
   a) Coat the O-ring with multi-purpose grease **(see illustration)**.
   b) Tighten the alternator mounting bolts to the torque listed in this Chapter's Specifications.

32   Alternator brushes (FZR750/1000) - inspection and replacement

Refer to illustration 32.5
1   This check, combined with the charging system output test described in Section 29, should diagnose most charging system problems on 750/1000 models. If the brushes are good and alternator output is low, take the alternator to a dealer service department or other repair shop for further checks, or substitute a known good unit and recheck the charging system output.
2   Remove the alternator (see Section 31).
3   Remove the screws and take the end cover off the alternator.
4   Remove two screws and lift out the brush assembly.
5   Measure the length of the brushes and compare it to the value listed in this Chapter's Specifications **(see illustration)**. If the brushes

33   Fuel reserve system

Some models are equipped with an electric fuel reserve system activated by a switch on the top left side of the fairing. If the fuel tank won't switch over to Reserve, check the wiring for breaks and bad connections, referring to the Wiring diagrams at the end of the book. To test the switch, disconnect its wiring connector and connect an ohmmeter between the terminals in the switch side of the connector, then turn the switch on and off. The ohmmeter should switch back and forth from infinite resistance to little or no resistance as the switch is operated. If not, replace the switch.

34   Wiring diagrams

Prior to troubleshooting a circuit, check the fuses to make sure they're in good condition. Make sure the battery is fully charged and check the cable connections.
When checking a circuit, make sure all connectors are clean, with no broken or loose terminals or wires. When unplugging a connector, don't pull on the wires - pull only on the connector housings themselves.

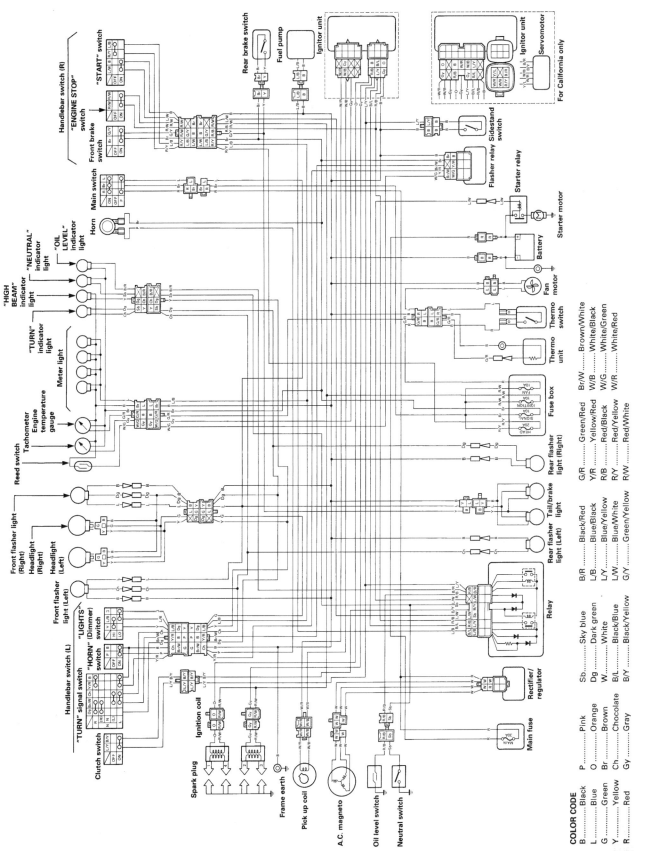

Wiring diagram - US FZR600/600R (dual-headlight model shown; single-headlight model similar)

COLOR CODE

B	Black	Sb	Sky blue	Br/W	Brown/White
L	Blue	Dg	Dark green	W/B	White/Black
G	Green	W	White	W/G	White/Green
Y	Yellow	B/L	Black/Blue	W/R	White/Red
R	Red	B/Y	Black/Yellow		
P	Pink	B/R	Black/Red	G/R	Green/Red
O	Orange	L/B	Blue/Black	Y/R	Yellow/Red
Br	Brown	L/Y	Blue/Yellow	R/B	Red/Black
Ch	Chocolate	L/W	Blue/White	R/Y	Red/Yellow
Gy	Gray	G/Y	Green/Yellow	R/W	Red/White

10

1. Clutch switch
2. "TURN" switch
3. "HORN" switch
4. "LIGHTS" (Dimmer) switch
5. Headlight (Left)
6. Front flasher light (Left)
7. Tempmeter
8. Tachometer
9. Reed switch
10. "TURN" indicator light
11. Meter illumination
12. "HIGH BEAM" indicator light
13. "NEUTRAL" indicator light
14. "OIL" level indicator light
15. Front flasher light (Right)
16. Headlight (Right)
17. Horn
18. Thermo unit
19. Thermo switch
20. Main switch
21. "ENGINE STOP" switch
22. "START" switch
23. Front brake switch
24. Relay assembly
25. Digital ignitor unit
26. Fuse
27. Rear brake switch
28. Starter relay
29. Starter motor
30. Battery
31. Main fuse
32. Tail/Brake light
33. Rear flasher light
34. Sidestand switch
35. Sidestand relay
36. Diode block
37. Fuel pump
38. Fuel pump relay
39. Fan motor
40. Neutral switch
41. Oil level switch
42. A.C. generator
43. Rectifier/Regulator
44. Pickup coil
45. Spark plug
46. Ignition coil

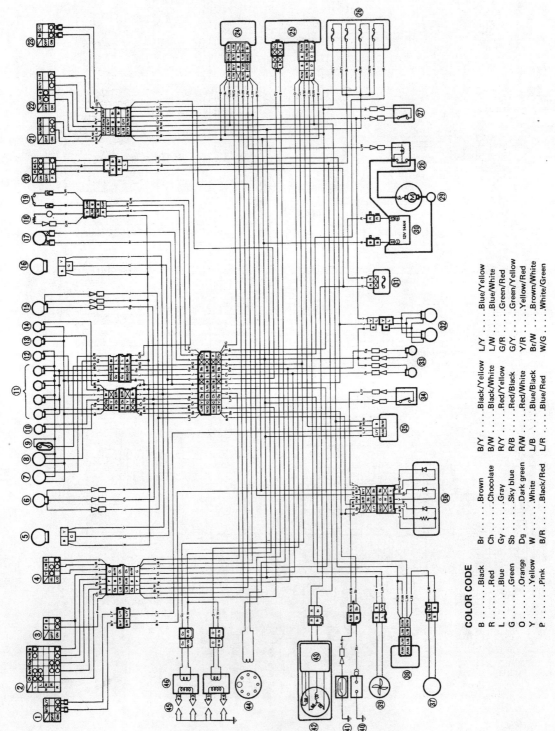

Wiring diagram – 1987 and 1988 (US) FZR750 models

COLOR CODE

B ...... Black	Br ...... Brown	B/Y ...... Black/Yellow	L/Y ...... Blue/Yellow
R ...... Red	Ch ...... Chocolate	B/W ...... Black/White	L/W ...... Blue/White
L ...... Blue	Gy ...... Gray	R/Y ...... Red/Yellow	G/R ...... Green/Red
G ...... Green	Sb ...... Sky blue	R/B ...... Red/Black	G/Y ...... Green/Yellow
O ...... Orange	Dg ...... Dark green	R/W ...... Red/White	Y/R ...... Yellow/Red
Y ...... Yellow	W ...... White	L/B ...... Blue/Black	Br/R ...... Brown/White
P ...... Pink	B/R ...... Black/Red	L/R ...... Blue/Red	W/G ...... White/Green

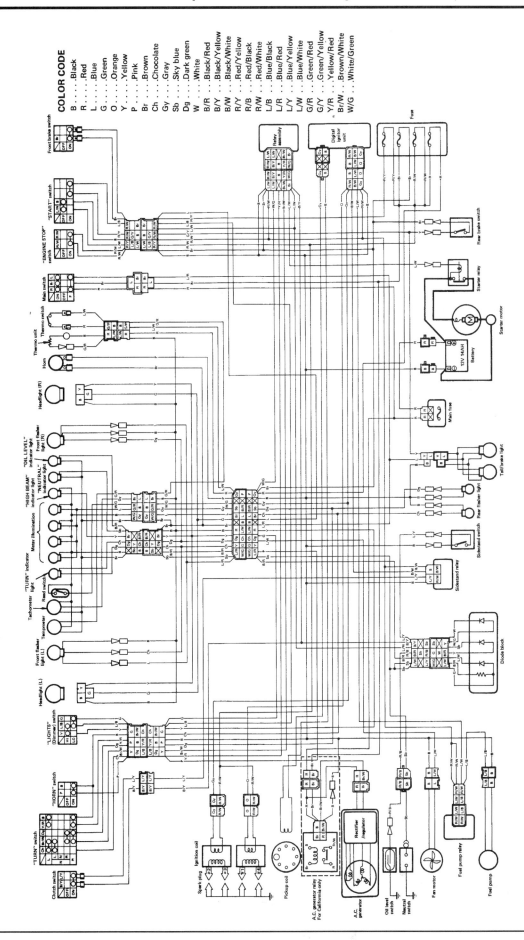

Wiring diagram - 1987 and 1988 (US) FZR1000 models

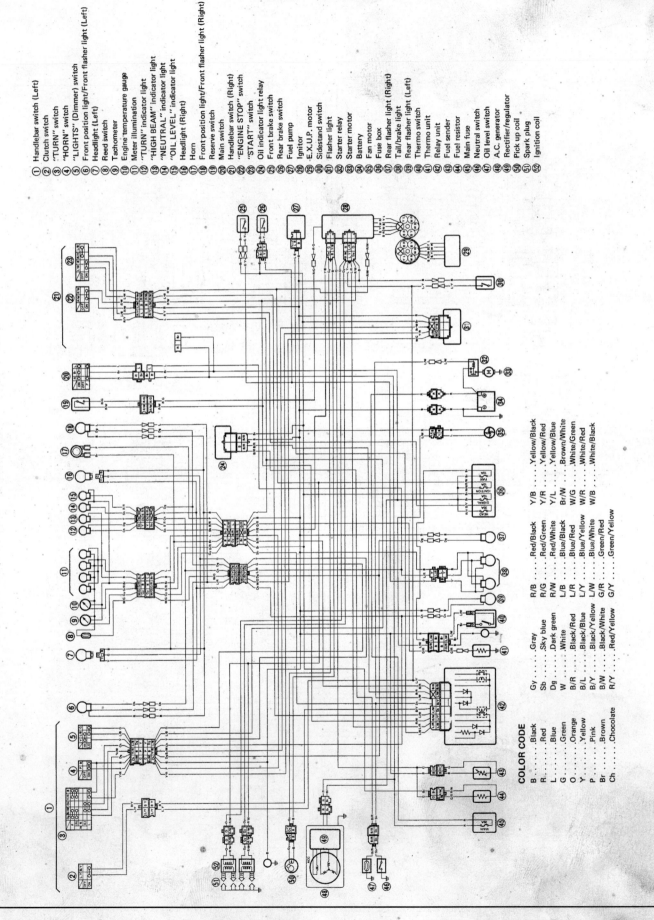

① Handlebar switch (Left)
② Clutch switch
③ "TURN" switch
④ "HORN" switch
⑤ "LIGHTS" (Dimmer) switch
⑥ Front position light/Front flasher light (Left)
⑦ Headlight (Left)
⑧ Reed switch
⑨ Tachometer
⑩ Engine temperature gauge
⑪ Meter illumination
⑫ "TURN" indicator light
⑬ "HIGH BEAM" indicator light
⑭ "NEUTRAL" indicator light
⑮ "OIL LEVEL" indicator light
⑯ Headlight (Right)
⑰ Horn
⑱ Front position light/Front flasher light (Right)
⑲ Reserve switch
⑳ Main switch
㉑ Handlebar switch (Right)
㉒ "ENGINE STOP" switch
㉓ "START" switch
㉔ Oil indicator light relay
㉕ Front brake switch
㉖ Rear brake switch
㉗ Fuel pump
㉘ Ignitor
㉙ E.X.U.P. motor
㉚ Sidestand switch
㉛ Flasher light
㉜ Starter relay
㉝ Starter motor
㉞ Battery
㉟ Fan motor
㊱ Fuse box
㊲ Rear flasher light (Right)
㊳ Tail/brake light
㊴ Rear flasher light (Left)
㊵ Thermo unit
㊶ Thermo unit
㊷ Relay unit
㊸ Fuel sender
㊹ Fuel resistor
㊺ Main fuse
㊻ Neutral switch
㊼ Oil level switch
㊽ A.C. generator
㊾ Rectifier/regulator
㊿ Pick up coil
51 Spark plug
52 Ignition coil

Wiring diagram – 1989 and 1990 US FZR1000 models (UK models similar)

COLOR CODE

B . . . . . . Black	Gy . . . . . Gray	R/B . . . . . Red/Black	Y/B . . . . . Yellow/Black
R . . . . . . Red	Sb . . . . . Sky blue	R/G . . . . . Red/Green	Y/R . . . . . Yellow/Red
L . . . . . . Blue	Dg . . . . . Dark green	R/W . . . . . Red/White	Y/L . . . . . Yellow/Blue
G . . . . . . Green	W . . . . . White	L/B . . . . . Blue/Black	Br/W . . . . . Brown/White
O . . . . . . Orange	B/R . . . . . Black/Red	L/R . . . . . Blue/Red	W/G . . . . . White/Green
Y . . . . . . Yellow	B/L . . . . . Black/Blue	L/Y . . . . . Blue/Yellow	W/R . . . . . White/Red
P . . . . . . Pink	B/Y . . . . . Black/Yellow	L/W . . . . . Blue/White	W/B . . . . . White/Black
Br . . . . . Brown	B/W . . . . . Black/White	G/R . . . . . Green/Red	
Ch . . . . . Chocolate	R/Y . . . . . Red/Yellow	G/Y . . . . . Green/Yellow	

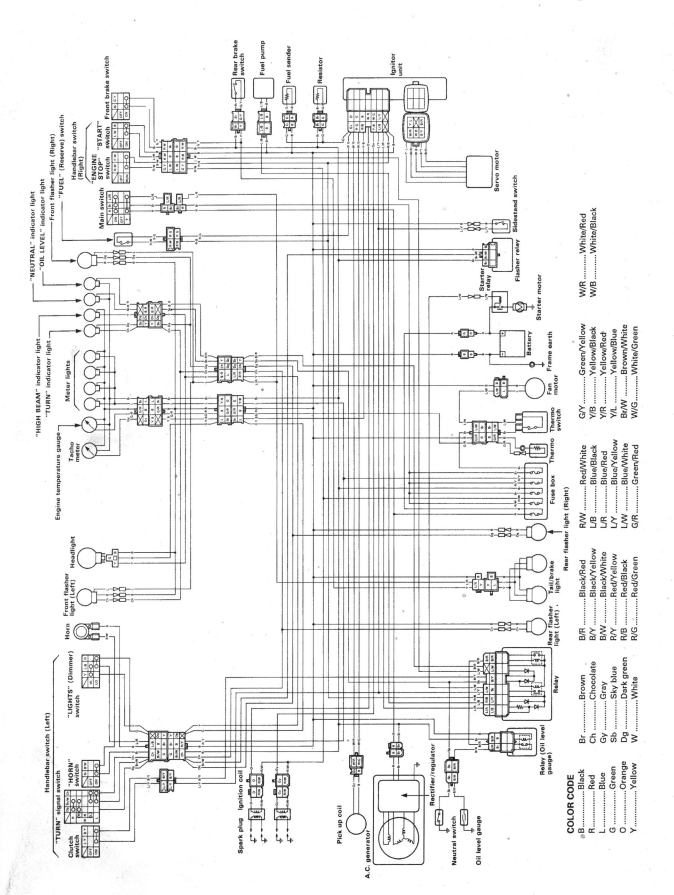

Wiring diagram – 1991 and later US FZR1000 models

COLOR CODE

B	Black	R/W	Red/White
R	Red	B/R	Black/Red
L	Blue	B/Y	Black/Yellow
G	Green	B/W	Black/White
O	Orange	R/Y	Red/Yellow
Y	Yellow	R/B	Red/Black
		R/G	Red/Green

Br	Brown	G/Y	Green/Yellow
Ch	Chocolate	Y/B	Yellow/Black
Gy	Gray	Y/R	Yellow/Red
Sb	Sky blue	Y/L	Yellow/Blue
Dg	Dark green	L/W	Blue/White
W	White	Br/W	Brown/White
		W/G	White/Green
		W/R	White/Red
		W/B	White/Black

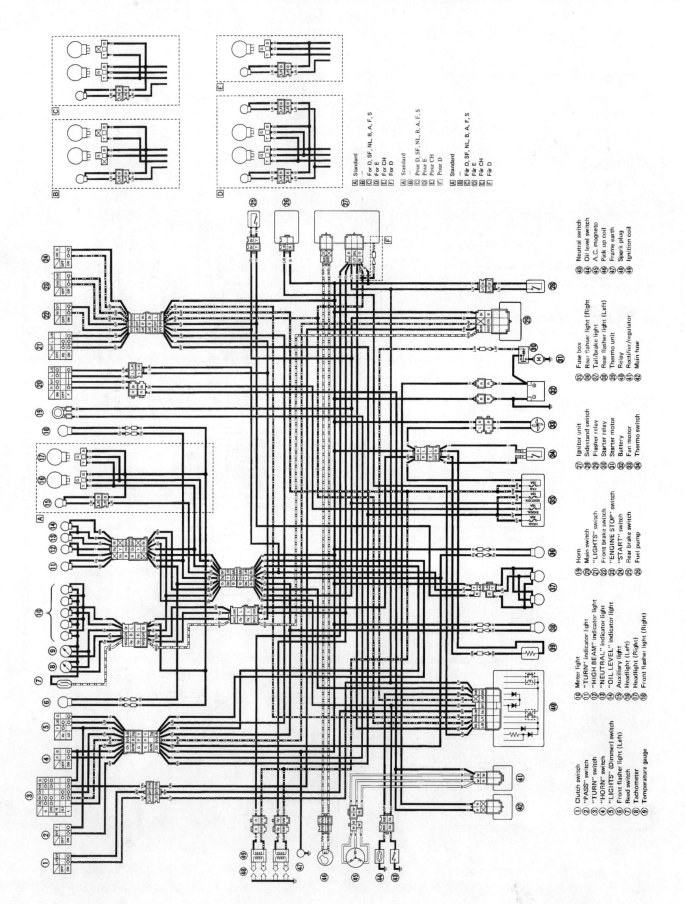

Wiring diagram - 1989 and 1990 FZR600 models (UK and other markets except US)

A Standard
B –
C For D, SF, NL, B, A, F, S
D For E
E For CH
F For D

A Standard
B –
C Pour D, SF, NL, B, A, F, S
D Pour E
E Pour CH
F Pour D

A Standard
B –
C Für D, SF, NL, B, A, F, S
D Für E
E Für CH
F Für D

1 Clutch switch
2 "PASS" switch
3 "TURN" switch
4 "HORN" switch
5 "LIGHTS" (Dimmer) switch
6 Front flasher light (Left)
7 Tachometer
8 Reed switch
9 Temperature gauge
10 Meter light
11 "TURN" indicator light
12 "HIGH BEAM" indicator light
13 "NEUTRAL" indicator light
14 "OIL LEVEL" indicator light
15 Auxiliary light
16 Headlight (Right)
17 Headlight (Left)
18 Front flasher light (Right)
19 Horn
20 Main switch
21 "LIGHTS" switch
22 Front brake switch
23 "ENGINE STOP" switch
24 Rear brake switch
25 "START" switch
26 Fuel pump
27 Ignitor unit
28 Sidestand switch
29 Flasher relay
30 Starter relay
31 Starter motor
32 Battery
33 Thermo switch
34 Thermo switch
35 Fuse box
36 Rear flasher light (Right
37 Tail/brake light
38 Rear flasher light (Left)
39 Thermo unit
40 Relay
41 Rectifier/regulator
42 Main fuse
43 Neutral switch
44 Oil level switch
45 A.C. magneto
46 Pick up coil
47 Frame earth
48 Spark plug
49 Ignition coil

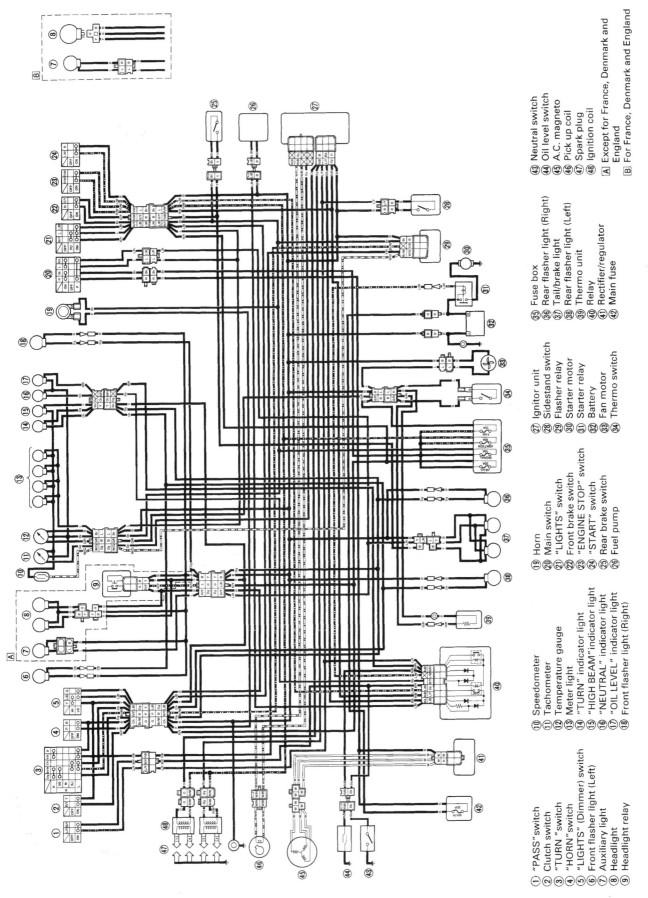

Wiring diagram - 1991 and later FZR600 models (UK and other markets except US)

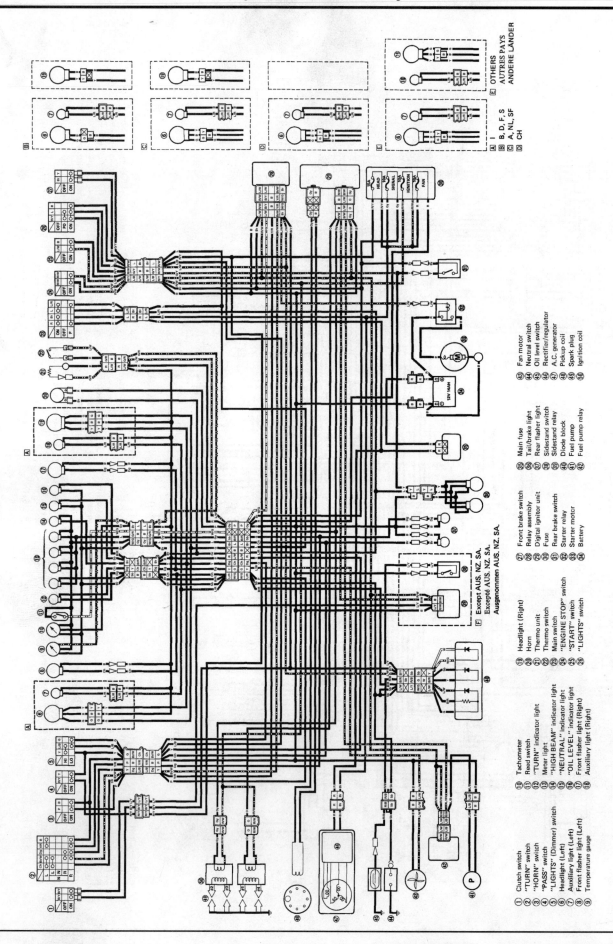

Wiring diagram – FZR1000 models (1987 and 1988 UK and other markets except US)

Wiring diagram – 1991 and later FZR1000 models (UK and other markets except US)

1 Handlebar switch (Left)
2 Clutch switch
3 "TURN" signal switch
4 "HORN" switch
5 "LIGHTS" switch
6 "PASS" switch
7 "LIGHTS" (Dimmer) switch
8 Horn
9 Front flasher light (Left)

10 Headlight
11 Auxiliary light
12 Diode
13 Tachometer
14 Engine temperature gauge
15 Meter light
16 "TURN" indicator light
17 "HIGH BEAM" indicator light
18 "NEUTRAL" indicator light

19 "OIL LEVEL" indicator light
20 Front flasher light (Right)
21 "FUEL" (Reserve) switch
22 Main switch
23 Handlebar switch (Right)
24 "ENGINE STOP" switch
25 "START" switch
26 Front brake switch
27 Rear brake switch

28 Fuel pump
29 Fuel sender
30 Resistor
31 Ignitor unit
32 Servo motor
33 Sidestand switch
34 Flasher relay
35 Starter relay
36 Starter motor

37 Battery
38 Frame earth
39 Fan motor
40 Thermo switch
41 Thermo unit
42 Fuse box
43 Rear flasher light (Right)
44 Tail/brake light
45 Rear flasher light (Left)

46 Relay
47 Relay (Oil level gauge)
48 Oil level gauge
49 Neutral switch
50 A.C. generator
51 Rectifier/regulator
52 Pick up coil
53 Spark plug
54 Ignition coil

A For F, DK, GB, AUS, NZ

10

Conversion factors

Length (distance)

Inches (in)	25.4	= Millimetres (mm)	X 0.0394	= Inches (in)
Feet (ft)	0.305	= Metres (m)	X 3.281	= Feet (ft)
Miles	1.609	= Kilometres (km)	X 0.621	= Miles

Volume (capacity)

Cubic inches (cu in; in³)	X 16.387	= Cubic centimetres (cc; cm³)	X 0.061	= Cubic inches (cu in; in³)
Imperial pints (Imp pt)	X 0.568	= Litres (l)	X 1.76	= Imperial pints (Imp pt)
Imperial quarts (Imp qt)	X 1.137	= Litres (l)	X 0.88	= Imperial quarts (Imp qt)
Imperial quarts (Imp qt)	X 1.201	= US quarts (US qt)	X 0.833	= Imperial quarts (Imp qt)
US quarts (US qt)	X 0.946	= Litres (l)	X 1.057	= US quarts (US qt)
Imperial gallons (Imp gal)	X 4.546	= Litres (l)	X 0.22	= Imperial gallons (Imp gal)
Imperial gallons (Imp gal)	X 1.201	= US gallons (US gal)	X 0.833	= Imperial gallons (Imp gal)
US gallons (US gal)	X 3.785	= Litres (l)	X 0.264	= US gallons (US gal)

Mass (weight)

Ounces (oz)	X 28.35	= Grams (g)	X 0.035	= Ounces (oz)
Pounds (lb)	X 0.454	= Kilograms (kg)	X 2.205	= Pounds (lb)

Force

Ounces-force (ozf; oz)	X 0.278	= Newtons (N)	X 3.6	= Ounces-force (ozf; oz)
Pounds-force (lbf; lb)	X 4.448	= Newtons (N)	X 0.225	= Pounds-force (lbf; lb)
Newtons (N)	X 0.1	= Kilograms-force (kgf; kg)	X 9.81	= Newtons (N)

Pressure

Pounds-force per square inch (psi; lbf/in²; lb/in²)	X 0.070	= Kilograms-force per square centimetre (kgf/cm²; kg/cm²)	X 14.223	= Pounds-force per square inch (psi; lbf/in²; lb/in²)
Pounds-force per square inch (psi; lbf/in²; lb/in²)	X 0.068	= Atmospheres (atm)	X 14.696	= Pounds-force per square inch (psi; lbf/in²; lb/in²)
Pounds-force per square inch (psi; lbf/in²; lb/in²)	X 0.069	= Bars	X 14.5	= Pounds-force per square inch (psi; lbf/in²; lb/in²)
Pounds-force per square inch (psi; lbf/in²; lb/in²)	X 6.895	= Kilopascals (kPa)	X 0.145	= Pounds-force per square inch (psi; lbf/in²; lb/in²)
Kilopascals (kPa)	X 0.01	= Kilograms-force per square centimetre (kgf/cm²; kg/cm²)	X 98.1	= Kilopascals (kPa)
Millibar (mbar)	X 100	= Pascals (Pa)	X 0.01	= Millibar (mbar)
Millibar (mbar)	X 0.0145	= Pounds-force per square inch (psi; lbf/in²; lb/in²)	X 68.947	= Millibar (mbar)
Millibar (mbar)	X 0.75	= Millimetres of mercury (mmHg)	X 1.333	= Millibar (mbar)
Millibar (mbar)	X 0.401	= Inches of water (inH₂O)	X 2.491	= Millibar (mbar)
Millimetres of mercury (mmHg)	X 0.535	= Inches of water (inH₂O)	X 1.868	= Millimetres of mercury (mmHg)
Inches of water (inH₂O)	X 0.036	= Pounds-force per square inch (psi; lbf/in²; lb/in²)	X 27.68	= Inches of water (inH₂O)

Torque (moment of force)

Pounds-force inches (lbf in; lb in)	X 1.152	= Kilograms-force centimetre (kgf cm; kg cm)	X 0.868	= Pounds-force inches (lbf in; lb in)
Pounds-force inches (lbf in; lb in)	X 0.113	= Newton metres (Nm)	X 8.85	= Pounds-force inches (lbf in; lb in)
Pounds-force inches (lbf in; lb in)	X 0.083	= Pounds-force feet (lbf ft; lb ft)	X 12	= Pounds-force inches (lbf in; lb in)
Pounds-force feet (lbf ft; lb ft)	X 0.138	= Kilograms-force metres (kgf m; kg m)	X 7.233	= Pounds-force feet (lbf ft; lb ft)
Pounds-force feet (lbf ft; lb ft)	X 1.356	= Newton metres (Nm)	X 0.738	= Pounds-force feet (lbf ft; lb ft)
Newton metres (Nm)	X 0.102	= Kilograms-force metres (kgf m; kg m)	X 9.804	= Newton metres (Nm)

Power

Horsepower (hp)	X 745.7	= Watts (W)	X 0.0013	= Horsepower (hp)

Velocity (speed)

Miles per hour (miles/hr; mph)	X 1.609	= Kilometres per hour (km/hr; kph)	X 0.621	= Miles per hour (miles/hr; mph)

Fuel consumption*

Miles per gallon, Imperial (mpg)	X 0.354	= Kilometres per litre (km/l)	X 2.825	= Miles per gallon, Imperial (mpg)
Miles per gallon, US (mpg)	X 0.425	= Kilometres per litre (km/l)	X 2.352	= Miles per gallon, US (mpg)

Temperature

Degrees Fahrenheit = (°C x 1.8) + 32   Degrees Celsius (Degrees Centigrade; °C) = (°F - 32) x 0.56

It is common practice to convert from miles per gallon (mpg) to litres/100 kilometres (l/100km), where mpg (Imperial) x l/100 km = 282 and mpg (US) x l/100 km = 235

Index